# Child Protection Proceedings: Care and Adoption Orders

Simon Johnson

Joanne Porter

LexisNexis

Published by Family Law
a publishing imprint of LexisNexis

LexisNexis
Regus
Terrace Floor
Castlemead
Lower Castle Street
Bristol BS1 3AG

Whilst the publishers and the author have taken every care in preparing the material included in this work, any statements made as to the legal or other implications of particular transactions are made in good faith purely for general guidance and cannot be regarded as a substitute for professional advice. Consequently, no liability can be accepted for loss or expense incurred as a result of relying in particular circumstances on statements made in this work.

© RELX (UK) Limited, trading as LexisNexis 2017

All rights reserved. No part of this publication may be reproduced, stored in a retrieval system, or transmitted in any way or by any means, including photocopying or recording, without the written permission of the copyright holder, application for which should be addressed to the publisher.

Crown Copyright material is reproduced with kind permission of the Controller of Her Majesty's Stationery Office.

**British Library Cataloguing-in-Publication Data**

A catalogue record for this book is available from the British Library.

ISBN 978 1 78473 337 7

Typeset by Letterpart Limited, Caterham on the Hill, Surrey CR3 5XL

Printed in Great Britain by Hobbs the Printers Limited, Totton, Hampshire SO40 3WX

# Child Protection Proceedings:
# Care and Adoption Orders

# FOREWORD

I welcome publication of *Child Protection Proceedings: Care and Adoption Orders*.

At a time when, rightly, issues relating to child protection are a matter of public debate this book will make a very valuable contribution. It has the enormous benefit of having been written by two specialist family practitioners, each of whom have considerable expertise in this important area of the law. Both Simon Johnson and Joanne Porter practised as family solicitors before coming to the specialist family bar. Their depth of knowledge of the relevant law and procedure, along with their own experience in representing both parents and children, shines out from each page.

This comprehensive and well-structured book sets out with commendable clarity the obligations and duties imposed on the Local Authority to protect and safeguard children, irrespective of whether any legal proceedings have been issued. It continues with an analysis of the issues that arise as any care and/or placement application makes its way towards a final hearing, pausing at each stage to provide excellent practical advice, thereby allowing the reader to benefit from the long experience of each of the authors.

Having the relevant legal provisions and guidance to hand, along with a detailed analysis of the myriad of issues that arise in these difficult cases will mean no practitioner advising in this area will want to do so without reference to this book.

The Hon Mrs Justice Theis

*November 2017*

# ACKNOWLEDGMENTS

We are grateful for all of the help from Greg Woodgate, Katherine Hather, Tracy Robinson and all of the team at Jordan Publishing for their assistance and support throughout the time we have been working on this book.

Simon Johnson would like to thank the members and clerks at Stour Chambers for their support and help during his work on this book. He would also like to thank all the colleagues (within chambers and beyond) and friends who have assisted in that work by their comments and encouragement.

Joanne Porter would like to thank 4PB for all of their support and in particular would like to give a very special thank you to Charlotte Baker for her hard work and her enthusiasm for the task at hand.

We are both enormously grateful to the Honourable Mrs Justice Theis DBE for finding time in her very busy schedule to provide a Foreword, and for her kind comments.

Finally, we would both like to thank our families for their support throughout the writing of this book.

The law is stated as at 1 November 2017.

# CONTENTS

Foreword v
Acknowledgments vii
Table of Cases xxiii
Table of Statutes xxxi
Table of Statutory Instruments xxxix
Table of International Material xliii

## Part 1
## Introduction, Background and General Principles

### Chapter 1
### Child Protection in England and Wales: An Overview 3
Children, families and the state 3
   The importance of the autonomy of the family 3
   Child protection or 'social engineering': judicial comment and the
      approach of the court 4
   Public perception 6
The child protection system in action: statistics on children needing
   protection and related issues 7
   Children in need and the child protection process 7
   Court proceedings 9
   The other side of the story: parents and families in care proceedings 9
Responsibility for child protection: local authorities and the courts 11
   Statutory duties of local authorities 11
   The role of the courts 12
   A final word from Sir James Munby P 13

### Chapter 2
### Fundamentals of the Children Act 1989 15
Welfare and delay 15
The welfare principle 15
   The child's welfare shall be the court's paramount consideration 15
      Yardstick of welfare 16
      What standard, or yardstick, is welfare to be assessed by? 17
Welfare checklist 18
No delay principle 20
   26 weeks rule 21
Parental responsibility 21
   What is parental responsibility? 21

| | |
|---|---|
| Who has parental responsibility? | 22 |
| Acquiring and losing parental responsibility | 23 |
| Alternative families | 23 |
| Losing parental responsibility | 24 |
| Available orders under the Children Act 1989 | 24 |
| No order principle | 24 |
| Care and supervision orders | 25 |
| Care orders | 26 |
| Supervision order | 27 |
| Special guardianship order | 28 |
| Family assistance order | 29 |
| Section 8 orders | 30 |

## Chapter 3
## Jurisdiction 33

| | |
|---|---|
| With which children and families are the England and Wales system concerned? | 33 |
| The practicalities of considering jurisdiction at an early stage | 35 |
| Pre-proceedings: sharing information | 36 |
| At the commencement of proceedings | 37 |
| Section 20 accommodation | 37 |
| When does the court have jurisdiction? | 38 |
| Habitual residence | 39 |
| When the child is not present in the jurisdiction at the time of issue | 42 |
| Transfer to another jurisdiction | 43 |

## Chapter 4
## Human Rights Considerations 49

| | |
|---|---|
| Human Rights Act 1998 | 49 |
| Right to liberty and security | 50 |
| Right to a fair trial | 53 |
| Fair and public hearing and the press | 53 |
| Within a reasonable time | 55 |
| Independent and impartial tribunal | 57 |
| Right to respect of private and family life | 59 |
| Infringement of rights and remedies | 61 |
| Section 20 and human rights claims | 64 |
| Procedure for applications under Human Rights Act 1998 | 66 |

## Part 2
## Child Protection Measures Short of Care Proceedings

## Chapter 5
| | |
|---|---|
| **Local Authority Support, Investigation and Intervention** | **73** |
| Local authority support for children and their families | 73 |
| Children in need | 74 |
| Local authority investigation | 75 |
| Section 47 investigations | 76 |

| | |
|---|---:|
| Section 37 Children Act 1989 | 76 |
| Child assessment orders | 78 |
| Local authority intervention | 80 |
|     Children protection plans | 80 |
|         Child protection conference | 81 |
|     Section 20 accommodation | 82 |
|         Parental consent | 83 |
|         Capacity to provide parental consent | 84 |
|         Ensuring parental consent is freely given | 85 |
|         Information given to parents as to the meaning of s 20 | 85 |
|         Ability of a parent to withdraw their consent to s 20 accommodation | 86 |
|         Proper use of s 20 accommodation | 86 |

## Chapter 6
### The Pre-proceedings Process

| | |
|---|---:|
| | 91 |
| Introduction | 91 |
|     Parents who may have learning difficulties or mental health issues | 92 |
|     Wider family | 92 |
|         Family group conference | 93 |
|     Pre-proceedings meeting | 94 |
|         Legal planning meeting | 94 |
|         Letter before proceedings and pre-proceedings meetings | 94 |
| Decision to commence proceedings | 96 |
|     Preparation in readiness for proceedings | 96 |
|     Preparation prior to proceedings involving new-borns | 97 |

## Chapter 7
### Threshold Criteria

| | |
|---|---:|
| | 99 |
| Introduction | 99 |
| The first limb: what is 'significant harm'? | 100 |
| Suffering or likely to suffer | 102 |
| The second limb: attributable to the care provided | 103 |
|     A reasonable parent | 104 |
| Beyond parental control | 105 |
|     Difference between interim and final threshold | 105 |

## Part 3
### Emergency Intervention

### Chapter 8
### Police Protection: Section 46 of the Children Act 1989

| | |
|---|---:|
| | 109 |
| The role of the police in child protection | 109 |
| Police powers to remove children | 109 |
|     A unique, emergency, power | 110 |
|     Police protection and voluntary accommodation | 111 |
|     The power and the decision to exercise it | 112 |
|     The consequences of a child being taken into police protection | 113 |
|         Accommodating the child | 113 |

| | |
|---|---|
| Duration of, and discharge from, police protection | 114 |
| Parental responsibility | 115 |
| Communication with parents and contact with a child in police protection | 115 |
| What follows police protection of a child? | 116 |
| Involvement of the local authority | 116 |
| Applications by the police | 117 |
| Evidence in subsequent proceedings | 117 |

## Chapter 9
## Emergency Protection Orders

| | |
|---|---|
| Emergency Protection Orders | 119 |
| The nature of an emergency protection order | 119 |
| 'A terrible and drastic remedy' | 119 |
| The effect of an emergency protection order | 121 |
| The application for an emergency protection order | 122 |
| Applicants and applications | 122 |
| Without notice applications | 123 |
| Evidence | 124 |
| The X Council v B (Emergency Protection Orders) factors | 125 |
| The decision to make an emergency protection order | 126 |
| The grounds for making an order | 126 |
| Alternatives to making an order: cooperation and voluntary arrangements | 127 |
| Alternatives to making an order: family assessment orders | 128 |
| Alternatives to removal of children: exclusion requirements and undertakings | 129 |
| The consequences of making an emergency protection order | 130 |
| Parental responsibility | 130 |
| Removal of the child | 131 |
| Contact with children who are subject to emergency protection orders | 132 |
| Duration, extension and discharge of emergency protection orders | 133 |
| Duration and extension of order | 133 |
| Applications to discharge an emergency protection order | 134 |
| Consequences of the expiry of an emergency protection order | 135 |

## Part 4
## Care Proceedings: From Issue to Final Hearing

### Chapter 10

| | |
|---|---|
| Procedural Stages of an Application for a Care Order: An Overview | 139 |
| Public Law Outline | 139 |
| Revised Public Law Outline 2014 | 139 |
| FPR 2010: Part 12, Chapter 3 | 142 |
| Timetable for the proceedings | 143 |
| 26 weeks rule | 143 |
| Timetable for the child | 145 |
| PD12A | 146 |
| Pre-proceedings checklist | 146 |

| | |
|---|---|
| Day 1: issue and allocation | 147 |
| Days 12–18: case management hearing | 148 |
| Further case management hearing | 148 |
| Issues resolution hearing | 149 |
| Evidence to be gathered in care proceedings | 149 |
| What constitutes evidence? | 150 |
| Documentation from previous proceedings | 151 |
| Parenting assessments | 152 |
| Independent expert evidence | 152 |
| Guardian's reports | 153 |
| Application for the withdrawal of care proceedings | 154 |

## Chapter 11
### Application for a Care or Supervision Order and Case Management

| | |
|---|---|
| | 155 |
| Local authority's application | 155 |
| Threshold document | 155 |
| Initial social work evidence | 156 |
| Issuing an application for a care or supervision order | 157 |
| Gatekeeping | 157 |
| Allocation to appropriate level of judge | 158 |
| Directions and case management at gatekeeping | 158 |
| Jurisdiction | 159 |
| Documents required for the CMH | 159 |
| Local authority case summary | 159 |
| Case analysis from the children's guardian | 160 |
| Parents' response document | 160 |
| Disclosure | 161 |
| Documentation from previous proceedings | 161 |
| Police disclosure | 162 |
| Medical disclosure | 163 |
| Appointing an expert | 163 |
| Advocates meeting | 164 |
| Decision to list an application for an interim care order | 165 |

## Chapter 12
### Representation of the Respondents in Care Proceedings

| | |
|---|---|
| | 167 |
| Who is party to public law proceedings? | 167 |
| Joinder | 168 |
| An application by a father who does not hold parental responsibility | 169 |
| An application by a grandparent | 169 |
| Leave for a person to intervene in the proceedings for a specific purpose | 170 |
| Representation of parents and people with parental responsibility | 171 |
| Parents with parental responsibility | 171 |
| Fathers without parental responsibility | 171 |
| Holders of parental responsibility by virtue of a child arrangements order | 171 |

| | |
|---|---|
| Holder of parental responsibility by virtue of a special guardianship order | 172 |
| Other carers without parental responsibility | 172 |
| Representation of intervenors | 172 |
| Litigation capacity of an adult party or intervener | 173 |
| Assessing capacity to conduct proceedings | 174 |
| Ability of a party to contest their assessment as to capacity | 179 |
| Litigation friend | 179 |
| Ability to give written and oral evidence | 180 |
| Intermediary assessment | 180 |
| Representation of children | 181 |
| Powers and duties of a children's guardian | 181 |
| Separate representation of a child | 183 |

## Chapter 13
### Interim Care Orders (Part 1): General Principles of Interim Orders and Interim Threshold

| | |
|---|---|
| | 185 |
| Introduction: The need for an interim orders regime | 185 |
| The basis for applying for a care order: protection from significant harm | 185 |
| The timescale of proceedings and possible duration of interim orders | 186 |
| The circumstances in which the court can make an interim order | 187 |
| The statutory provision for making interim orders | 187 |
| Orders made when a s 31 application is before the court | 188 |
| A special case: interim orders and appeals | 189 |
| Cases where a direction under s 37(1) has been made | 190 |
| Interim threshold | 193 |
| The court's enquiry as to threshold at the interim stage: 'reasonable grounds for believing' | 193 |
| On what basis can 'reasonable grounds' be found to exist? | 194 |
| Looking at all the 'circumstances' | 199 |
| Likelihood of harm as the basis for interim threshold | 200 |
| A reminder: 'interim threshold' is still 'threshold' | 201 |
| The limitations of the court's investigation of interim threshold | 203 |
| The nature and conduct of an interim hearing: 'a line beyond which it is impermissible for the court to go'? | 203 |
| The problem of oral evidence | 205 |

## Chapter 14
### Interim Care Orders (Part 2): Welfare Decisions at the Interim Order Stage

| | |
|---|---|
| | 207 |
| Introduction | 207 |
| The court's dilemma when considering an interim order | 207 |
| The court's approach to the making of an order | 210 |
| The welfare principle | 210 |
| The nature of an interim care order | 210 |
| Decisions to authorise removal of children at the interim order stage: the requirement for interim protection | 212 |

| | |
|---|---|
| Welfare considerations and sibling groups | 214 |
| 'Safety' or 'welfare': a distinction without a difference? Or all a question of proportion? | 215 |
| Re L (Care Proceedings: Removal of Child): 'safety' and 'imminent risk of really serious harm' | 215 |
| Chronic neglect: risk, safety and welfare | 217 |
| Interim protection of the child's psychological welfare | 218 |
| Threshold, welfare and the burden of proof | 219 |
| Black LJ reviews the authorities: The court's paramount consideration and the need to determine if removal is proportionate | 221 |
| The other side of the equation: The consequences of removal and interim care plans | 222 |
| Some conclusions on the test for removal | 224 |

## Chapter 15
### Interim Care Orders (Part 3): Case Management of Interim Care Order Applications

| | |
|---|---|
| | 227 |
| Case management for an interim care order hearing | 227 |
| Directions and case management | 229 |
| Jurisdiction and ICO applications | 230 |
| Evidence available at an ICO hearing | 230 |
| At the beginning of proceedings | 230 |
| During proceedings | 231 |
| The ICO hearing | 232 |
| Documents to be made available to the court | 232 |
| Live evidence or submissions | 233 |
| Section 38(6) of the CA 1989 | 235 |
| Part 25 of the FPR 2010 | 237 |

## Chapter 16
### Interim Care Orders (Part 4): The Interim Care Order

| | |
|---|---|
| | 239 |
| Purpose of an interim care order | 239 |
| Parental responsibility under a care order | 240 |
| Exclusion requirement | 240 |
| Local authority duties under an interim care order | 242 |
| Interim care plans | 242 |
| Placement of the child | 244 |
| Placement of the child with local authority foster carers | 244 |
| Placement with friends or family members | 245 |
| Placement with parents | 246 |
| Contact | 249 |
| No contact | 251 |
| Section 38(6) assessments | 251 |

## Chapter 17
### Interim Orders Alternatives

| | |
|---|---|
| | 255 |
| Introduction | 255 |

xvi    *Child Protection Proceedings: Care and Adoption Orders*

| | |
|---|---|
| Interim care order without removal to foster care | 256 |
|    The roles of the local authority and the court | 256 |
|    Alternatives to separation from the parents | 256 |
|    Placement with a 'connected person' | 257 |
|    Changes to the local authority's plan | 258 |
|    The need to refer to the court | 258 |
|    Challenging a decision to remove | 261 |
|    The nature of the court's decision | 262 |
|    Injunctions under Human Rights Act 1998 | 263 |
|    Judicial review | 265 |
| Voluntary accommodation | 266 |
| Interim supervision orders | 267 |
| Child arrangements orders | 268 |

## Chapter 18
## Contact with Children in Care                                                    271

| | |
|---|---|
| Contact with children in care: basic principles | 271 |
|    The importance of contact for children and the need for planning | 271 |
|    The statutory framework: the local authority's duties in relation to contact and the supervisory role of the court | 271 |
|    A note on terminology: 'contact at the discretion of the local authority' | 274 |
| The role of the court | 275 |
|    Section 34 Children Act 1989: available orders | 275 |
|    Orders for contact: types of contact and conditions | 276 |
|    Orders authorising the refusal of contact: powers of the local authority | 277 |
| The court's decision making process | 278 |
|    The decision to make an order as to contact: welfare and the balancing exercise | 278 |
|    The balancing exercise: relevant considerations and the welfare of the individual child | 278 |
| The circumstances in which orders under s 34 may be made | 280 |
|    When can orders under s 34 may be made? | 280 |
|    Applications and orders made of the court's own motion | 281 |
|    Leave to apply for contact | 282 |
|    Variation of contact arrangements without reference to the court | 286 |

## Part 5
## Care Proceedings: Final Hearings and Final Orders

## Chapter 19
## Preparation for Final Hearings                                                    291

| | |
|---|---|
| Separate fact finding or threshold hearing | 291 |
|    Decision to undertake a split hearing | 291 |
|       Preparation for a split hearing | 293 |
|       Parties in a split hearing | 294 |
| Case management for a final hearing | 294 |
|    Issue resolutions hearing | 294 |

| | |
|---|---|
| Final decisions for the child | 296 |
| Filing evidence | 296 |
| Preparation of evidence | 296 |
| Local authority evidence | 298 |
| Evidence of the guardian | 299 |
| Bundles | 300 |
| Practice Direction 27A | 300 |

**Chapter 20**
**The Final Hearing: Practical Considerations**

| | |
|---|---|
| The Final Hearing: Practical Considerations | 303 |
| The court's considerations: threshold and welfare | 303 |
| Threshold and the burden of proof | 304 |
| Jurisdiction | 306 |
| Witness attendance | 306 |
| Hearsay evidence | 307 |
| Parents' evidence | 308 |
| Children giving evidence | 308 |
| Assessment of the child | 309 |
| The court's decision | 310 |
| Quality of the ABE interview | 310 |
| Witnesses requiring special measures | 311 |
| Ground rules hearing | 312 |
| Cross-examination of experts | 313 |
| Oral evidence | 314 |
| Submissions | 314 |
| Judgment | 315 |

**Chapter 21**
**Welfare Test for Making a Final Care Order**

| | |
|---|---|
| Welfare Test for Making a Final Care Order | 317 |
| What do we mean by welfare? | 318 |
| What standard, or yardstick, is welfare to be assessed by? | 318 |
| Welfare checklist | 319 |
| Ascertainable wishes and feelings of the child | 320 |
| Seeing the judge | 321 |
| Local authority's care plan | 322 |
| No order | 322 |
| Care plan for adoption | 323 |
| Realistic options | 324 |
| Holistic approach | 325 |
| Proportionality and the 'least interventionist' approach | 326 |
| Balance of welfare considerations | 327 |

**Chapter 22**
**Final Care Plans**

| | |
|---|---|
| Final Care Plans | 329 |
| Introduction | 329 |
| Formal requirements | 329 |
| Parental responsibility under a care order | 331 |

| | |
|---|---|
| Placement | 332 |
|    Placement of the child with local authority foster carers | 332 |
|    Placement with friends or family members | 333 |
|    Placement with parents | 333 |
| Contact with children in care | 336 |
|    No contact | 338 |
| Independent reviewing officer | 338 |
| Care plan for adoption | 339 |

## Chapter 23
### The Effect of a Final Care Order — 341

| | |
|---|---|
| Preliminary: The roles of the family court and of the local authority | 341 |
|    'A cardinal principle' | 341 |
|    The care plan | 342 |
| The duties of the local authority | 345 |
|    Receiving the child into care | 345 |
|    Designation of local authority: 'these undoubtedly difficult subsections' | 346 |
|    The duty to provide accommodation for a child in care | 348 |
|    Duration of care orders and the problem of the 17 year old 'child' | 351 |
|    Applications to discharge care orders | 352 |
|    Duties to children leaving care | 353 |
| Parental responsibility for children in care | 353 |
|    The core statutory concepts | 354 |
|    The limits of a local authority's parental responsibility | 355 |
|    The local authority's power to determine the extent to which others may meet their parental responsibility | 356 |
|    Remedies: local authority powers in respect of parental responsibility and human rights issues | 357 |
| Contact with children in care | 360 |
| The relationship between care orders and other orders | 360 |
|    The effect of care orders on other orders | 360 |
|    The effect of other orders on care orders | 360 |
|    Care orders and the inherent jurisdiction of the court | 361 |

## Chapter 24
### Applications to Discharge a Care Order — 367

| | |
|---|---|
| Discharge of a care order | 367 |
|    Procedure | 367 |
|    Local authority as applicant | 368 |
|    Parent as applicant | 368 |
|       Removal from a parent | 369 |
|       Return to a parent | 371 |
|    Child as applicant | 372 |
|    Another person as applicant | 372 |
|    Substitution of a care order for a supervision order | 373 |
| Variation or discharge of a supervision order | 374 |

## Part 6
## Alternatives to the Making of a Final Care Order

### Chapter 25
### Supervision Orders — 377
Introduction — 377
  The significance of holding parental responsibility — 377
Supervision orders — 378
  Supervision orders and proportionality in a post *Re B-S* world — 378
  The nature of a supervision order — 379
  The consequences of failure to co-operate with a supervision order — 381
  When can a supervision order be made? — 383
  The responsibility of the court to determine the appropriate order — 384
  Threshold and supervision orders — 387
  The welfare decision: 'proportionality ... is the key' — 388
  Supervision order or care order? — 388
  Supervision order or no order? — 392
  The terms and effect of the supervision order: directions, obligations and requirements and the extent of the court's powers — 398
  Duration, extension and discharge of supervision orders — 401

### Chapter 26
### Private Law Orders in the Context of Care Proceedings (Part 1) — 407
General principles and s 8 orders: introduction — 407
  Alternative orders in public law proceedings — 407
Two fundamental distinctions — 408
  Jurisdiction — 408
  Effect of orders — 409
Section 8 orders — 410
  The court's power to make s 8 orders within care proceedings — 410
  Who can apply for s 8 orders within care proceedings? — 411
Applications for leave to apply — 411
The orders available under s 8 — 412
Parental responsibility and s 8 orders — 414
  Making and duration of s 8 orders: considerations as to the age of the child — 416
  Variation and discharge of s 8 orders — 417

### Chapter 27
### Private Law Orders in the Context of Care Proceedings (Part 2): Special Guardianship Orders in Care Proceedings — 419
Introduction — 419
  The 2000 White Paper: Adoption: a new approach — 419
  The Adoption and Children Act 2002 and its amendments to the Children Act 1989 — 420
  Special guardianship: basic points — 421
  Special guardianship orders in public law proceedings: some statistics — 422

| | |
|---|---|
| Special guardianship orders: nature and effect | 422 |
|   The key concept: special guardianship and parental responsibility | 422 |
|   The position of birth parents | 424 |
|   Applications in relation to children who are the subject of special guardianship orders | 425 |
| Making special guardianship orders within care proceedings | 427 |
|   The power to make orders: the statutory basics | 427 |
|   Case management when the issue of the making of a special guardianship order arises within care proceedings | 429 |
|   Case management guidance from Ryder LJ | 431 |
|   The court's duty to consider ancillary matters | 433 |
| The decision to make a special guardianship order: welfare considerations | 434 |
|   The statutory provisions | 434 |
|   Special guardianship order or placement for adoption? 'The core, long-term welfare decision' | 434 |
|   A presumption in favour of special guardianship order as, 'the least interventionist option'? | 435 |

## Chapter 28
## Adoption: General Considerations

| | |
|---|---|
| Adoption: General Considerations | 439 |
| The process of adoption | 439 |
|   What is adoption? | 439 |
|   Adoption with an international element | 440 |
| The Adoption and Children Act 2002 | 440 |
|     The welfare checklist under the ACA 2002 | 441 |
|   Requirements for making an adoption order | 443 |
|   Opposing an adoption order | 443 |
|     'Change of circumstances' and the considerations for granting leave to oppose an adoption application | 444 |
| Contact with a child pursuant to an adoption order | 447 |

## Chapter 29
## Adoption: Parental Consent and Placement Orders

| | |
|---|---|
| Placement order | 449 |
|   Adoption and Children Act 2002 | 450 |
|     Welfare checklist under the ACA 2002 | 451 |
| Effect of a placement order | 453 |
|   Parental responsibility under a placement order | 453 |
|   Contact to a child subject to a placement order | 453 |
|   Effect on any other orders in place at the point at which a placement order is made | 455 |
| Process of application | 455 |
|   When an application can be made | 455 |
|   Case management | 456 |
| Welfare test | 457 |
| Parental consent | 458 |
|   Dispensing with the consent of a parent | 458 |

**Chapter 30**
**Appeals**     **461**
General principles     461
  Which court?     461
Procedure     464
  Clarification     465
  Permission to appeal     465
  Time limitation     466
  Application     467
    Grounds of appeal     467
  Appellants notice     468
    Skeleton argument     470
  Respondent's notice     471
  Orders pending an appeal     473

**Appendix 1**
**Children Act 1989**     475

**Appendix 2**
**Adoption and Children Act 2002**     559

**Appendix 3**
**Family Procedure Rules 2010, SI 2010/2955, Part 12**     595

**Appendix 4**
**Family Procedure Rules 2010, SI 2010/2955, Part 14**     671

**Appendix 5**
**Care Planning, Placement and Case Review (England)**
**Regulations 2010, SI 2010/959**     719

**Appendix 6**
**Special Guardianship Regulations 2005, SI 2005/1109**     763

**Appendix 7**
**Emergency Protection Order: the X *Council* Guidance**     781

**Index**     785

# TABLE OF CASES

References are to paragraph numbers.

A (A Child) (No 2), Re [2011] EWCA Civ 12         10.49, 19.30, 19.34, 20.12, 20.16
A (A Child) v Chief Constable of Dorset Police [2011] 1 FLR 11         8.14
A (A Child), Re [2013] EWCA Civ 543         16.47
A (A Child), Re [2015] EWFC 11, [2016] 1 FLR 1, [2015] Fam Law 367   1.9, 7.17, 7.30, 10.47,
    10.48, 19.13, 19.27, 19.28, 20.10, 20.27, 21.52
A (Area of Freedom, Security and Justice), Re (C-523/2007) [2010] Fam 42,
    [2009] ECR I-2805, [2009] 2 FLR 1, [2009] Fam Law 568         3.35
A (Care Plan), Re [2008] 2 FLR 1183         16.23, 22.6
A (Care: Discharge Application by Child), Re [1995] 1 FLR 599         23.36
A (Fact-Finding: Disputed Findings), Re [2011] EWCA Civ 12, [2011] 1 FLR
    1817         13.41–13.45
A (Supervision Order: Extension), Re [1995] 1 WLR 482, [1995] 3 All ER
    401, [1995] 1 FLR 335, CA         25.83
A and D (Local Authority: Religious Upbringing), Re [2011] 1 FLR 615         23.48
A and L (Fact-finding Hearing Extempore Judgment), Re [2012] 1 FLR
    1243, CA         30.8, 30.9, 30.13
A Local Authority v D & Ors [2016] 1 WLR 1160         4.11
A Local Authority v SB, AB & MB [2010] 2 FLR 1203         23.68
A v A and Another (Children: Habitual Residence) (Reunite International
    Child Abduction Centre and Others Intervening) [2013] UKSC 60,
    [2014] AC 1, [2013] 3 WLR 761, *sub nom* Re A (Jurisdiction: Return
    of Child) [2014] 1 FLR 111, [2014] 1 All ER 827, SC         3.23, 3.27, 3.29
A v B and C (Lesbian co-parents: Role of Father) [2012] 2 FLR 607         2.40
A v East Sussex County Council and Chief Constable of Sussex Police [2010]
    EWCA Civ 743, [2011] 1 FCR 116, [2010] 2 FLR 1596, [2010] Fam
    Law 924         8.12, 9.32
A v Liverpool City Council (1981) 2 FLR 222         1.35, 23.65
A, B, C and D (Welfare of Children: Immunisation), Re [2011] EWHC 4033
    (Fam), (unreported) 26 May 2011, FD         23.68
AB (Care Proceedings: Service on Husband Ignorant of Child's Existence), Re
    [2004] 1 FLR 527         12.5
AB v JLB (Brussels II Revised: Article 15) [2008] EWHC 2965 (Fam), [2009]
    1 FLR 517, FD         3.43, 3.44, 3.46, 3.48, 3.49
Anufrijeva v Southwark London Borough Council [2003] EWCA Civ 1406,
    [2004] QB 1124         4.71
AS (Unlawful Removal of a Child), Re [2015] EWFC B150         5.56

B (A Child) (Care Proceedings: Threshold Criteria), Re [2013] UKSC 33,
    [2013] 1 WLR 1911, *sub nom* Re B (Care Proceedings: Appeal)
    [2013] 2 FLR 1075, [2013] 3 All ER 929, SC         7.28
B (A Child) (Habitual Residence: Inherent Jurisdiction), Re [2016] UKSC 4,
    [2016] AC 606, [2017] 1 All ER 899, [2016] 2 WLR 557, [2016] 1
    FLR 561         3.5, 3.25, 3.30
B (A Child), Re [2013] UKSC 33, [2013] 1 WLR 1911, *sub nom* Re B (Care
    Proceedings: Appeal) [2013] 2 FLR 1075, [2013] 3 All ER 929, SC   1.9, 4.58, 4.59, 7.12,
    7.13, 7.26, 7.27, 19.45, 21.34, 21.35, 28.34, 29.42, 29.43
B (A Local Authority) v RM, MM AND AM [2011] 1 FLR 1635         23.32

B (A Minor) (Wardship: Sterilisation), Re [1988] AC 199                2.12, 21.7
B (Care Proceedings: Appeal), Re [2013] UKSC 33, [2013] 3 All ER 929,
   [2013] 1 WLR 1911, [2013] 2 FLR 1075         1.7, 9.26, 14.4, 25.5, 27.2
B (Care Proceedings: Interim Care Order), Re [2009] EWCA Civ 1254,
   [2010] 1 FLR 1211         13.29, 14.18, 14.21, 14.27, 14.32, 14.37, 14.39, 14.40
B (Care Proceedings: Standard of Proof), Re [2008] UKHL 35, [2009] 1 AC
   11, [2008] 3 WLR 1, [2008] 2 FLR 141                                   13.57
B (Children) (Care Order: Threshold for making Order), Re [2012] EWCA
   Civ 1275, [2013] 2 FLR 153                                  14.21
B (Children) (Residence: Interim Care Order), Re [2002] EWCA Civ 1225,
   [2002] 3 FCR 562, CA                             13.18
B (Interim Care Order), Re [2010] EWCA Civ 324, [2010] 2 FLR 283     14.18, 14.36, 14.40
B (Interim Care Order: Directions), Re [2002] 1 FLR 545         15.44, 16.59
B (Interim Care Orders: Renewal), Re [2001] 2 FLR 1217, [2001] Fam Law
   802, [2001] TLR 418, FD                       13.63
B (Minors) (Care: Contact: Local Authority's Plans), Re [1993] 1 FLR 543    18.27
B (Minors) (Contact), Re [1994] 2 FLR 1                 13.64
B (Paternal Grandmother: Joinder as Party), Re [2012] EWCA Civ 737,
   [2012] 2 FLR 1358, CA                        12.17, 26.17
B (Supervision Order: Parental Undertaking), Re [1996] 1 WLR 716, [1996]
   1 FLR 676, 94 LGR 244, CA                         25.70
B v B (Interim Contact with Grandparents), Re [1993] Fam Law 393       15.5, 15.34, 16.1
B v B (Residence Order: Reasons for decision) [1997] 2 FLR 602     2.25, 21.18, 28.19, 29.20
B, Re [1996] 2 FLR 693                              25.39
B-C (A Child), Re [2016] EWCA Civ 970                   9.29
B-S (Children) (Adoption Order: Leave to Oppose), Re [2013] EWCA Civ
   1146, [2014] 1 WLR 563, *sub nom* Re B-S (Adoption: Application of
   s 47(5)) [2014] 1 FLR 1035, CA     4.58–4.60, 10.16, 14.4, 19.44–19.46, 21.34–21.36,
                        21.39, 21.42, 21.44, 21.48, 23.10, 25.5, 26.7, 27.2, 28.31, 28.34,
                                                             29.42–29.44
BC (A Minor) (Care Order: Appropriate Local Authority), Re [1995] 3 FCR
   598                                         23.18, 23.19
Berkshire County Council v B [1997] 1 FLR 171                18.26, 18.28
Birmingham City Council v H (No 3) [1994] 1 FLR 224            18.26
Birmingham City Council v R [2007] 1 FLR 564                 27.15
BR (Proof of facts), Re [2015] EWFC 41                    20.9
Bridgend County Borough Council v GM & Anor [2012] EWHC 3118
   (Fam)                                     3.35
Bush v Bush [2008] 2 FLR 1437                           3.40

C (A Child) v Plymouth City Council [2000] 1 FLR 875            23.19
C (A Child), Re [2014] EWCA Civ 128, [2014] 1 WLR 2495, [2014] 3 FCR
   627, [2015] 1 FLR 521                           10.16
C (Appeal from Care and Placement Orders), Re [2014] 2 FLR 131        27.47, 27.48
C (Care Order or Supervision Order), Re [2001] 2 FLR 466, [2001] Fam
   Law 580, FD                                  25.49
C (Care Order: Appropriate Local Authority), Re [1997] 1 FLR 544       23.19
C (Care: Consultation with Parents not in Child's Best Interests), Re [2006]
   2 FLR 787                                    12.16
C (Children), Re [2016] EWCA Civ 374, [2016] 3 WLR 1557, [2017] 1 FLR
   487                                        23.70
C (Contact), Re [2008] 1 FLR 1151                      28.41, 29.29
C (Interim Care Order), Re [2012] 2 FLR 251                  14.6
C (Welfare of Child: Immunisation), Re [2003] 2 FLR 1095          23.68
C and B (Care Order: Future Harm), Re [2000] EWCA Civ 3040, [2001] 1
   FLR 611, [2001] Fam Law 253         7.14, 7.23, 9.4, 21.53, 25.45
C v Bury MBC [2002] EWHC 1438 (Fam), [2002] 2 FLR 868         4.82
C v Soulihull MBC [1993] 1 FLR 290                      10.14
Cheshire County Council v M [1993] 1 FLR 463                 18.44
Coventry City Council v C, B, CA and CH [2013] 2 FLR 987      4.75, 4.77, 5.61, 5.63, 5.65,
                                                                5.69, 5.76
Croydon London Borough Council v A (No 2) [1992] 2 FLR 348         13.23, 30.55

## Table of Cases                                                          xxv

| | |
|---|---|
| Croydon London Borough Council v A (No 3) [1992] 2 FLR 350 | 25.13 |
| Cumbria County Council v M & Others [2016] EWFC 27 | 11.44 |

| | |
|---|---|
| D (A child), Re [2017] EWCA Civ 1695 | 4.18 |
| D (Local Authority Responsibility), Re [2013] 2 FLR 673 | 23.18 |
| D (Withdrawal of Parental Responsibility), Re [2014] EWCA Civ 315, [2015] 1 FLR 166 | 2.33, 2.45, 21.29 |
| D, L and LA (Care: Change of Forename), Re [2003] 1 FLR 339 | 23.72 |
| D, Re [1993] 2 FLR 423 | 25.39 |
| D, Re [2000] Fam Law 600 | 25.39 |
| Dawson v Wearmouth [1999] 1 FLR 1167 | 23.51 |
| DE (A Child), Re [2014] EWFC 6, [2015] 1 FLR 1001 | 4.69, 17.12–17.14, 17.26, 22.27, 23.56, 23.59, 23.71, 24.18, 24.19, 24.21, 25.44 |
| Down Lisburn Health and Social Services Trust v H [2007] 1 FLR 121 | 18.29 |

| | |
|---|---|
| E (A Child) [2014] EWCA Civ 1754 | 13.56 |
| E (A Child), Re [2013] EWHC 2400 (Fam), [2014] 1 FCR 429 | 8.8 |
| E (A Child), Re [2014] EWHC 6 (Fam), [2014] 2 FCR 264, [2014] 2 FLR 151 | 3.11–3.13, 3.38, 3.49 |
| E (A Child), Re; E v Chief Constable of the Royal Ulster Constabulary (Northern Ireland Human Rights Commission intervening) [2008] UKHL 66, [2009] AC 536, [2008] 3 WLR 1208, [2009] NI 141, [2009] 1 All ER 467, HL | 20.34, 20.38, 20.39, 20.45 |
| E (A Minor) (Care Order: Contact), Re [1994] 1 FLR 146 | 18.27 |
| E (Adoption Order: Proportionality of Outcome to Circumstances), Re [2014] 2 FLR 514 | 2.23, 20.73, 21.16, 28.17, 29.18 |
| EC (Disclosure of Material), Re [1997] Fam 76, [1997] 2 WLR 322, [1996] 2 FLR 725, CA | 20.30 |
| El Al Israeli Airlines Ltd v Danielowitz [1992] Isrl LR 478 | 1.6 |

| | |
|---|---|
| F (A Child), Re [2014] EWCA Civ 789 | 3.14, 3.38 |
| F (Contact: Child in Care), Re [1995] 1 FLR 510 | 18.26 |
| F (Special Guardianship Order: Contact with birth family), Re [2015] EWFC 25, [2016] 1 FLR 593 | 27.16, 27.41 |
| F, Re: F v Lambeth London Borough Council [2002] 1 FLR 217 | 23.13 |

| | |
|---|---|
| G (A Child) (Special Guardianship Order), Re [2010] 2 FLR 696, CA | 27.26 |
| G (A Child), Re [2013] EWCA Civ 965 | 4.60, 19.46, 21.36, 21.44, 29.44 |
| G (A Minor) (Care Proceedings), Re [1994] 2 FLR 69 | 25.56 |
| G (Adoption: Contact) [2003] 1 FLR 270 | 18.29 |
| G (Care Proceedings: Welfare Evaluation), Re [2014] 1 FLR 670 | 27.48 |
| G (Care: Challenge to Local Authority Decision), Re [2003] EWHC 551 (Fam), [2003] 2 FLR 42 | 4.69, 4.82, 17.29, 23.28, 24.21 |
| G (Interim Care Order: Residential Assessment), Re [2005] UKHL 68, [2006] 1 FLR 601, HL; [2004] EWCA Civ 24, [2004] 1 FLR 876, [2004] Fam Law 325, [2004] TLR 60, CA | 15.45, 16.61, 17.7 |
| G (Minors) (Interim Care Order), Re [1993] 2 FLR 839, CA | 13.6, 14.13, 14.18, 14.25 |
| G (Shared Residence Order: Biological Mother of Donor Egg), Re [2014] 2 FLR 897 | 2.40 |
| G and B (Fact-Finding Hearing), Re [2009] 1 FLR 1145 | 19.15 |
| G v N County Council [2009] 1 FLR 774 | 17.27 |
| G v Nottingham City Council and Nottingham University Hospital, Re [2008] EWHC 400 (Admin) | 5.65 |
| G, Re [2012] EWCA Civ 1233, [2013] 1 FLR 677, [2012] 3 FCR 524 | 2.9–2.17, 2.22, 20.4–20.7, 21.6–21.12, 21.15, 28.34 |
| Gateshead Metropolitan Borough Council v L and another [1996] 2 FLR 179 | 23.18 |
| Gloucestershire County Council v M and C [2015] EWFC B147 | 5.56 |
| Gloucestershire County Council v S [2015] EWFC B149 | 5.56 |
| GR (Care Order), Re [2010] EWCA Civ 871, [2011] 1 FLR 669 | 13.15, 14.11, 14.18, 14.39, 14.41 |

H (A Child) (Analysis of Realistic Options and SGOS), Re [2016] 1 FLR 286    27.30, 27.36, 27.37
H (A Child) (Interim Care Order), Re [2002] EWCA Civ 1932, [2002] 1
    FCR 350    14.8, 14.14, 14.18, 14.25, 14.37, 15.5, 15.34, 16.1
H (A Child), Re [2014] EWCA Civ 271    21.19
H (A Minor) v Northamptonshire County Council & Anor, Re [2017]
    EWHC 282 (Fam)    4.83, 4.86
H (Care Order: Appropriate Local Authority), Re [2003] EWCA Civ 1629,
    [2004] 1 FLR 534    23.19
H (Care Proceedings: Intervener), Re [2000] 1 FLR 775    12.22, 19.17
H (Children) (Application to Extend Time: Merits of Proposed Appeal), Re
    [2016] 1 FLR 952    30.22
H (Children) (Care Proceedings: Sexual Abuse), Re [2000] 2 FCR 499    12.21
H (Minors) (Sexual Abuse: Standard of Proof), Re [1996] AC 563, [1996] 2
    WLR 8, [1996] 1 All ER 1; *sub nom* H and R (Child Sexual Abuse:
    Standard of Proof), Re [1996] 1 FLR 80, HL    7.22, 13.53, 13.57
H (Supervision Order), Re [1994] 2 FLR 979, *sub nom* H (Minors) (Terms
    of Supervision Order), Re [1994] Fam Law 486, FD    25.69, 25.71
H v H (Residence Order: leave to remove from the jurisdiction) [1995] 1
    FLR 529    2.24, 21.17, 28.18, 29.19
H, Re [2014] EWCA Civ 1011    3.27
H-B, Re [2015] EWCA Civ 389    2.33
Hampshire County Council v S [1993] Fam 158, [1993] 2 WLR 216, [1993]
    1 FLR 559, [1993] 1 All ER 944, FD    13.60, 13.63, 13.66, 15.5, 15.34, 16.1

I (A Child), Re [2009] UKSC 10, [2010] 1 All ER 445, [2010] 1 FCR 200,
    [2010] 1 FLR 361    3.50, 3.53
I County Council v TD and Others [2017] EWHC 379 (Fam)    25.39
(Interim Care Order: Prison Mother and Baby Unit), Re [2014] 1 FLR 807    14.40

J (A Child) (Private Law Proceedings: Fact Finding), Re [2014] EWCA Civ
    875, [2014] 3 FCR 534, [2015] 1 FLR 1152,    20.56
J (A Child), Re [2015] EWCA Civ 222    1.9
J (A Child: Brussels II Revised: Art 15 – Practice Procedure), Re [2014]
    EWFC 41, [2015] Fam Law 129    3.1, 3.14, 3.39, 3.40, 3.42
J (Care Proceedings: Possible Perpetrators), Re [2013] UKSC 9, [2013] 1
    FLR 1373    13.57, 13.58, 26.9
J (Leave to Issue Applications for Residence Order), Re [2002] EWCA Civ
    1364, [2003] 1 FLR 114    18.44–18.46, 26.17
J (Specific Issue Orders: Child's Religious Upbringing and Circumcision), Re
    [2000] 1 FLR 571    23.68
J and E (Children: Brussels II Revised: Article 15), Re [2014] EWFC 45    3.44
Jake (A Child) (Withholding of Medical Treatment), Re [2015] EWHC 2442
    (Fam)    23.68
Johansen v Norway (No 17383/90) (1996) 23 EHRR 33, (1996) III RJD
    1008, ECtHR    14.5

K (Children), Re [2015] 1 FLR 95    26.21
K (Supervision Order), Re [1999] 2 FLR 303    25.54, 25.55, 25.61, 25.64
K and H, Re [2006] EWCA Civ 1898, [2007] 1 FLR 2043    14.17, 14.18
K, A Local Authority v N and Others, Re [2005] EWHC 2956 (Fam),
    [2007] 1 FLR 399    7.31, 25.61–25.64
KD (A Minor) (Ward: Termination of Access), Re [1988] AC 806, [1988] 2
    WLR 398, [1988] 2 FLR 139    1.7
Kelly v British Broadcasting Corporation [2001] Fam 59, [2001] 2 WLR
    253, [2001] 1 All ER 323, [2001] 1 FLR 197, [2001] 1 All ER 323,
    FD    9.17
Kent County Council v C & Others [2014] EWHC 604 (Fam)    3.28
Kent County Council v C [1993] 1 FLR 308    18.19
Kent County Council v M and K (Section 20: Declaration and Damages)
    [2016] EWFC 28    4.72, 4.79, 17.36

| | |
|---|---|
| KP (Abduction: Child's Objections), Re [2014] 2 FLR 660 | 21.23 |
| KS v Neath Port Talbot Borough Council [2014] EWCA Civ 941 | 26.17, 26.18 |
| | |
| L (A Child: Custody: Habitual Residence), Re [2013] UKSC 75 | 3.27 |
| L (Care Proceedings: Human Rights Claims), Re [2003] EWHC 665 (Fam), [2003] 2 FLR 160 | 4.82, 4.83 |
| L (Care Proceedings: Removal of Child), Re [2008] 1 FLR 575, FD | 14.24, 14.31, 14.36, 14.47 |
| L (Care Proceedings: Risk Assessment), Re [2010] 1 FLR 790 | 19.12 |
| L (Care: Assessment: Fair Trial), Re [2002] EWHC 1379 (Fam), [2002] 2 FLR 730 | 4.32, 4.82, 24.21 |
| L (Care: Threshold Criteria), Re [2007] 1 FLR 2050 | 7.15, 7.16, 7.19, 13.31, 21.54 |
| L (Children) (Care Proceedings: Significant Harm), Re [2006] EWCA Civ 1282 | 1.7 |
| L (Children), Re [2016] EWCA Civ 1110 | 13.15, 14.43–14.46 |
| L (Interim Care Order: Extended Family), Re [2013] 2 FLR 302, CA | 13.28, 13.29 |
| L (Interim Care Order: Prison Mother and Baby Unit), Re [2013] EWCA Civ 489, [2014] 1 FLR 807, CA | 13.15, 14.18–14.20 |
| L (Interim Care Order: Prison Mother and Baby Unit), Re [2014] 1 FLR 807 | 14.3 |
| L (Sexual Abuse: Standard of Proof), Re [1996] 1 FLR 116 | 18.9 |
| L v London Borough of Bromley [1998] 1 FLR 709, [1998] Fam Law 251, FD | 18.12, 18.18 |
| L-R (Children), Re [2013] EWCA Civ 1129 | 20.31 |
| LA (Care; Chronic Neglect), Re [2009] EWCA Civ 822, [2010] 1 FLR 80 | 13.29, 14.11, 14.17, 14.18, 14.29–14.34, 14.37, 14.39, 14.40, 17.21 |
| Lancashire County Council and Another v Barlow and Another [2000] UKHL 16 | 7.36 |
| Lancashire County Council v B [2000] 2 AC 147, [2000] 2 WLR 590, [2000] 1 FLR 583 | 13.57 |
| Langley v Liverpool City Council [2006] 1 FLR 342, CA | 8.11 |
| LC (Reunite: International Child Abduction Centre Intervening), Re [2014] UKSC 1, [2014] 1 FLR 1486 | 3.26, 3.27 |
| Leicester City Council v S [2014] EWHC 1575 | 3.15 |
| Lesage v Mauritius Commercial Bank Ltd [2012] UKPC 41 | 4.44 |
| Liversedge v Anderson [1943] UKHL 1 | 13.44 |
| London Borough of Brent, and Medway Council v M and T (By Her Children's Guardian) [2015] EWFC B164 | 5.56 |
| London Borough of Camden v RZ and Others [2017] 1 FLR 873 | 13.47 |
| London Borough of Hackney v Williams & Anor [2017] EWCA Civ 26 | 4.77 |
| London Borough of Redbridge v Newport City Council [2004] 2 FLR 226 | 23.19 |
| | |
| M (A Minor) (Care Order: Threshold Conditions), Re [1994] 2 AC 424, [1994] 3 WLR 558, [1994] 2 FLR 577 | 13.57 |
| M (Brussels II Revised: Art 15), Re [2014] EWCA Civ 152, [2014] 2 FLR 1372 | 3.17, 3.44, 3.48, 3.50–3.52 |
| M (Care Order: Parental Responsibility), Re [1996] 2 FLR 84, FD | 23.43 |
| M (Care: Challenging Decisions by Local Authority), Re [2001] 2 FLR 1300 | 4.82 |
| M (Care: Contact: Grandmother's Application for Leave), Re [1995] 2 FLR 86, [1995] Fam Law 540, [1995] TLR 228, CA | 18.42–18.44, 18.46 |
| M (Children), Re [2010] 1 FLR 1355 | 12.5 |
| M (Children), Re [2016] EWCA Civ 937 | 23.31 |
| M (Interim Care Order: Removal), Re [2005] EWCA Civ 1954, [2006] 1 FLR 1043 | 13.35–13.41, 13.43, 13.44, 14.7, 14.18 |
| M (Intractable Contact Dispute: Interim Care Order), Re [2003] 2 FLR 636 | 5.24 |
| M (Minors) (Sexual Abuse: Evidence) [1993] 1 FLR 822 | 18.48 |
| M (Residence), Re [2002] EWCA Civ 1052, [2002] 2 FLR 1059, [2002] Fam Law 807, (2002) *The Times*, 24 July, CA | 25.37 |
| M v Warwickshire County Council [1994] 2 FLR 593 | 2.60, 25.77, 25.78 |
| M v Warwickshire County Council [2007] EWCA Civ 1084, [2008] 1 WLR 991, [2008] 1 FLR 1093, CA | 27.26 |
| M, T, P, K and B (Care: Change of Name), Re [2000] 2 FLR 645, [2000] Fam Law 601, FD | 23.51 |
| M-F (Children), Re [2014] EWCA Civ 991 | 4.33, 10.15, 10.17 |

| | |
|---|---|
| M-J (Adoption Order or Special Guardianship Order), Re [2007] 1 FLR 691 | 27.52 |
| MA (Care Threshold), Re [2010] 1 FLR 431 | 7.18 |
| McMichael v UK (1995) Series A No 308, (1995) 20 EHRR 205, [1995] Fam Law 478, ECtHR | 4.54 |
| MD and TD (Minors) (No 2) [1994] Fam Law 489, FD | 23.37 |
| Medway Council v A and ors (Learning Disability: Foster Placement) [2015] EWFC B66 | 5.56 |
| Medway Council v JL, AJ and X [2016] EWFC 78 (Fam) | 27.2 |
| Medway Council v M & T [2015] EWFC B164 | 4.79 |
| Medway Council v M, F and G (By Her Children's Guardian) [2014] 2 FLR 982 | 9.33, 17.36 |
| Monroe v Hopkins [2017] EWHC 645 (QB) | 30.14 |
| | |
| N (Adoption: Jurisdiction), Re [2015] EWCA Civ 1112, [2016] 1 FLR 621 | 3.14, 3.38, 3.44, 3.49, 4.37, 4.38, 4.79, 5.56, 5.72–5.75, 5.77, 6.37, 8.7, 9.33, 17.37 |
| N (Care Proceedings: Adoption), Re [2013] 1 FLR 1244 | 13.60, 13.64, 15.40 |
| N (Children), Re [2015] EWFC 37 | 5.56 |
| N (Children: Adoption: Jurisdiction), Re [2015] EWCA Civ 1112 | 3.7 |
| Newcastle City Council v WM & Others [2015] EWFC 42 | 4.79, 5.62, 5.63 |
| NL (A child) (Appeal: Interim Care Order: Facts and Reasons), Re [2014] EWHC 270 (Fam), [2014] 1 FLR 1384 | 4.33, 10.15, 14.17 |
| North East Lincolnshire Council v G & L [2014] EWCC B77 (Fam) | 7.17 |
| North Yorkshire County Council v G [1993] 2 FLR 732 | 12.15, 18.48 |
| Northamptonshire County Council v AS and Others [2015] EWHC 199 | 4.79 |
| Northamptonshire County Council v Islington London Borough Council [1999] 2 FLR 881 | 23.15, 23.18, 23.19 |
| | |
| O (A Minor) (Custody: Adoption), Re [1992] 1 FLR 77 | 1.7 |
| O (Care or Supervision Order), Re [1996] 2 FLR 755 | 21.48 |
| O (Care Proceedings: Evidence), Re [2004] 1 FLR 161 | 20.28 |
| O (Contact: Imposition of Conditions), Re [1995] 2 FLR 124 | 2.13, 20.4, 21.8, 28.34 |
| O (Supervision Order), Re [2001] EWCA Civ 16, [2001] 1 FLR 923, [2001] Fam Law 326, CA | 25.16, 25.39, 25.41, 25.44, 25.46 |
| O and N, Re; Re B [2003] UKHL 18, [2003] 1 FLR 1169 | 13.57 |
| Oxfordshire County Council v L (Care or Supervision Order) [1998] 1 FLR 70, [1998] Fam Law 22, FD | 25.31, 25.39, 25.54 |
| | |
| P (A Child) (Adoption: Parental Consent), Re [2008] EWCA Civ 535, [2008] 2 FLR 625 | 29.50 |
| P (A Child) [2016] EWCA Civ 3, [2016] Fam Law 282 | 2.23, 2.24, 20.73, 21.16, 21.17, 28.18, 29.18, 29.19 |
| P (A child: Use of section 20), Re [2014] EWFC 775 | 4.79, 5.56 |
| P (Adoption: Leave Provisions) [2007] EWCA Civ 616 | 28.30, 28.33, 28.34 |
| P (Care Proceedings: Father's Application to be Joined as Party), Re [2001] 1 FLR 781 | 12.15 |
| P (Children), Re [2015] EWCA Civ 466 | 2.71 |
| P (Minors) (Contact with Children in Care), Re [1993] 2 FLR 156, [1993] Fam Law 394, FD | 18.7, 18.11 |
| P (Placement Orders: Parental Consent), Re [2008] EWCA Civ 535 | 28.41, 29.29 |
| P (Step-Parent Adoption), Re [2014] EWCA Civ 1174 | 27.2 |
| Porter v Magill, Weeks v Magill [2001] UKHL 67, [2002] AC 357, [2002] 2 WLR 37, [2002] 1 All ER 465, [2002] LGR 51, HL | 4.42 |
| Prospective Adopters v IA and Croyden LBC [2014] 2 FLR 1158 | 28.35 |
| | |
| Q (Children), Re [2014] EWCA Civ 918 | 4.47–4.49 |
| | |
| R (A) v Croydon London Borough Council; R (M) v Lambeth London Borough Council [2010] 1 FLR 959 | 25.54 |
| R (Care Order: Jurisdiction), Re [1995] 1 FLR 711 | 23.18 |
| R (Care Proceedings: Appeal), Re [2013] 1 FLR 467, CA | 30.11 |
| R (Children), Re [2013] EWCA Civ 1018 | 21.39, 21.42 |

| | |
|---|---|
| R (G) v Nottingham City Council [2008] 1 FLR 1660 | 8.4, 8.7 |
| R (H) v Kingston Upon Hull City Council [2014] 1 FLR 1094 | 17.4, 17.17, 17.30–17.33 |
| R (LH and MH) v London Borough of Lambeth [2006] 2 FLR 1275 | 5.9 |
| R (TT) v London Borough of Merton [2010] EWHC 2055 (Admin) | 27.34 |
| R (Williamson) v Secretary of State for Education and Employment [2005] 2 FLR 374 | 1.6 |
| R v Barnet London Borough Council, ex p Shah [1983] 2 AC 309, HL | 3.23 |
| R v Cornwall County Council ex parte G [1992] 1 FLR 270 | 12.68 |
| R v Lucas [1981] QB 720, [1981] 3 WLR 120, [1981] 2 All ER 1008, [1981] Crim LR 624, 73 Cr App Rep 159, CA | 20.70 |
| R, Re [2015] 1 FLR 715 | 25.5 |
| Redbridge LBC v B and C and A (through his Children's Guardian) [2011] 2 FLR 117 | 10.79 |
| Regina v Secretary of State for the Home Department (Respondent) ex parte Greenfield [2005] UKHL 14, [2005] 1 WLR 673 | 4.72 |
| RP v Nottingham City Council and the Official Solicitor (Mental Capacity of Parent) [2008] EWCA Civ 462, [2008] 2 FLR 1516, CA | 6.9 |
| | |
| S (A Child), Re [2014] EWCA Civ 25, [2014] 1 FLR 1421, [2014] Fam Law 429 | 10.16, 19.7–19.11 |
| S (A Child), Re [2014] EWCC B44 (Fam) | 4.33, 10.16 |
| S (Adoption Order or Special Guardianship Order (No 2), Re [2007] 1 FLR 855 | 27.30, 27.46 |
| S (Adoption Order or Special Guardianship Order), Re [2007] 1 FLR 819 | 27.2, 27.5, 27.7, 27.15, 27.18, 27.52 |
| S (Adult Patient: Sterilisation), Re [2001] Fam 15, [2000] 3 WLR 1288, [2000] 2 FLR 389, CA | 2.17, 20.8, 21.12 |
| S (Authorising Children's Immediate Removal), Re [2010] 2 FLR 873 | 17.18–17.21, 17.26 |
| S (Care or Supervision Order), Re [1996] 1 FLR 753 | 25.47, 25.48 |
| S (Discharge of Care Order) [1995] 2 FLR 639, CA | 23.37 |
| S (Ex Parte Orders), Re [2001] 1 WLR 211, [2001] 1 FLR 308, [2001] 1 All ER 362, FD | 9.17 |
| S (Minors) (Care Order: Implementation of Care Plan); Re W (Minors) (Care Order: Adequacy of Care Plan) [2002] UKHL 10, [2002] 2 AC 291, [2002] 2 WLR 720, [2002] 1 FLR 815, HL | 1.35, 17.13, 17.29, 18.15, 23.2, 23.28, 23.57, 23.59, 25.44 |
| S and W (Care Proceedings), Re [2007] EWCA Civ 232, [2007] 2 FLR 275 | 1.35 |
| S(J) (A Minor) (Care or Supervision Order), Re [1993] 2 FLR 919 | 25.3 |
| S-B (Children) (Care Proceedings: Standard of Proof), Re [2009] UKSC 17, [2010] 1 AC 678, [2010] 2 WLR 238, [2010] 1 FLR 1161 | 13.57 |
| S-W (Care Proceedings: Case Management Hearing), Re [2015] 2 FLR 136 | 23.8 |
| Sheffield City Council v Bradford City Council [2013] 1 FLR 1027 | 23.18, 23.20 |
| Singh v Entry Clearance Officer, New Delhi [2005] 1 FLR 308, CA | 4.53 |
| SL (Permission to Vaccinate), Re [2017] EWHC 125 (Fam) | 23.68 |
| Stockport Metropolitan Borough Council v D [1995] 1 FLR 873 | 25.56 |
| Storck v Germany (Application No 61603/00) [2005] ECHR 406 (2006) 43 EHRR 6, ECHR | 4.13 |
| Suffolk County Council v Nottinghamshire County Council [2013] 2 FLR 106 | 27.35 |
| Surrey County Council v P and Others, Cheshire West and Chester Council v P and Another [2014] UKSC 19, [2014] COPLR 313 | 4.16 |
| Surrey County Council v S [2014] EWCA Civ 601 | 21.48 |
| SW & TW (Human Rights Claim: Procedure) (No 1) [2017] EWHC 450 (Fam) | 4.82, 4.83 |
| | |
| T (A Child) v Wakefield Metropolitan District Council [2008] EWCA Civ 199 | 25.50, 25.77, 25.80 |
| T (A Minor) (Care or Supervision Order), Re [1994] 1 FLR 103, CA | 25.13 |
| T (Brussels II Revised, Article 15), Re sub nom Re K (A Child) [2013] EWCA Civ 895, [2014] 2 FCR 369, [2014] 1 FLR 749 | 3.40, 3.42, 3.48–3.50 |
| T (Care Order), Re [2009] 2 FLR 574 | 25.14, 25.25, 25.31, 25.32 |

T (Interim Care Order: Removal of Children Where No Immediate
    Emergency), Re [2016] 1 FLR 347                                      30.56
T (Termination of Contact: Discharge of Order), Re [1997] 1 WLR 393,
    [1997] 1 FLR 517, [1997] 1 All ER 65, CA                             18.38
TB (Care Proceedings: Criminal Trial), Re [1995] 2 FLR 801               10.20

V (Care or Supervision Order), Re [1996] 1 FLR 776, [1996] Fam Law 269,
    CA                                              25.3, 25.18, 25.23, 25.47
V (Care Proceedings: Human Rights Claims), Re [2004] 1 FLR 944            4.83

W (A Child) v Neath Port Talbot County Borough Council [2013] EWCA
    Civ 1227                                                             21.49
W (A Child), Re [2016] EWCA Civ 793, [2017] 1 WLR 889, [2017] 2 FLR
    31                                         4.61, 21.37, 25.5, 26.7, 29.45
W (A Minor) (Interim Care Order), Re [1994] 2 FLR 892, [1994] Fam Law
    612, (1994) 158 JPN 636, CA                         13.61, 17.2, 17.11
W (Assessment of Child), Re [1998] 2 FLR 130, [1998] Fam Law 318, CA     10.65
W (Care Proceedings: Functions of Court and Local Authority), Re [2013]
    EWCA Civ 1227, [2014] 2 FLR 431                              1.35, 23.10
W (Care Proceedings: Leave to Apply), Re [2005] 2 FLR 468           18.46, 18.48
W (Children) (Abuse: Oral Evidence), Re [2010] UKSC 12, [2010] 1 FLR
    1485, [2010] Fam Law 449                                     20.34, 20.35
W (Children), Re [2014] EWCA Civ 1065                                     5.66
W (Direct Contact), Re [2012] EWCA Civ 999                           2.46, 21.30
W (Ex Parte Orders), Re [2000] 2 FLR 927, [2000] Fam Law 811, FD          9.17
W (Interim Care Order), Re [2012] EWCA Civ 106, [2012] 2 FLR 240  13.52–13.54, 13.68,
                                                                   15.38, 15.39
W (Removal into Care), Re [2005] EWCA Civ 642, [2005] 2 FLR 1022,
    [2005] TLR 292; *sub nom* W (Children) (Care: Interference with
    Family Life) [2005] All ER (D) 36 (May) (CA)                 17.16, 24.21
W (Section 34(2) Orders), Re [1993] 2 FLR 156                 18.8, 18.9, 18.16
W and X (Wardship: Relatives Rejected as Foster Carers), Re [2004] 1 FLR
    415                                                                   17.9
W v Ealing London Borough Council [1993] 2 FLR 788                       18.44
Wiltshire County Council v F [2014] 2 FLR 336                            25.59

X (A Child) (No 3) [2017] EWHC 2036 (Fam)                                 1.36
X (Emergency Protection Orders), Re [2006] EWHC 510 (Fam), [2006] 2
    FLR 701                                               8.8, 9.6, 9.18, 9.24
X Council v B (Emergency Protection Orders) [2004] EWHC 2015 (Fam),
    [2005] 1 FLR 341, [2005] Fam Law 13, FD   9.1, 9.5, 9.16, 9.21, 9.23, 9.24, 9.28, 9.35,
                                                                           9.45
X, Re; Barnet London Borough Council v Y and X [2006] 2 FLR 998          23.10

Y (A Child), Re [2013] EWCA Civ 1337                  10.52, 19.34, 20.16, 21.45
YC v United Kingdom (Application No 4547/10) [2012] ECHR 433, (2012)
    55 EHRR 33, [2012] 2 FLR 332, ECHR                           28.14, 29.15

# TABLE OF STATUTES

References are to paragraph numbers.

| | | | |
|---|---|---|---|
| Administration of Justice Act 1960 | 1.11 | Adoption and Children Act 2002—*continued* | |
| s 12 | 1.11 | s 27(4) | 28.36, 29.25 |
| Adoption Act 1976 | 28.7, 29.7 | s 29 | 29.32 |
| Adoption and Children Act 2002 | 1.29, 1.31, | s 29(1) | 23.63 |
| | 1.34, 2.3, 2.18, 2.19, 2.21, 2.43, | s 29(5) | 27.29 |
| | 2.55, 2.63, 3.21, 4.69, 7.9, 12.3, | s 29(6) | 27.29 |
| | 13.2, 18.29, 21.4, 21.13, 23.4, | s 46(1) | 28.2 |
| | 23.6, 23.25, 23.47, 23.63, 26.1, | s 46(1)(a) | 27.15 |
| | 27.1, 27.4, 27.15, 27.17, 27.21, | s 46(2) | 28.3 |
| | 27.26, 27.29, 27.47, 27.49, | s 46(2)(b) | 23.63 |
| | 28.1–28.3, 28.6–28.13, 28.15, | s 46(6) | 18.29 |
| | 28.20–28.22, 28.24–28.29, 28.36, | s 47 | 28.20 |
| | 28.38, 28.43, 29.1–29.5, 29.7, | s 47(1) | 28.20 |
| | 29.8, 29.10, 29.12, 29.13, 29.16, | s 47(2) | 28.20, 28.24 |
| | 29.21, 29.23, 29.25, 29.26, 29.31, | s 47(2)(c) | 28.27 |
| | 29.32, 29.34, 29.35, 29.40, 29.47, | s 47(3) | 28.28 |
| | 29.49, 29.51, 30.3 | s 47(4) | 28.22, 28.24 |
| s 1 | 27.2, 27.49, 28.28, 28.30, 28.43, | s 47(4)(b)(i) | 28.25 |
| | 29.31 | s 47(5) | 27.2, 28.26, 28.28, 28.34 |
| s 1(1) | 28.8, 28.9, 29.8 | s 47(7) | 28.24, 28.30, 28.33 |
| s 1(2) | 2.3, 21.4, 28.9, 28.29, 29.9, 29.10, | s 50 | 28.2 |
| | 29.50 | s 51 | 28.2 |
| s 1(3) | 28.10, 29.9, 29.10 | s 51A | 18.29 |
| s 1(4) | 2.18, 2.21, 27.47, 28.8, 28.13, | s 52 | 28.20, 28.21, 29.5, 29.47 |
| | 28.29, 29.13, 29.14, 29.40, | s 52(1)(b) | 29.50 |
| | 29.49–29.51 | s 67 | 28.6 |
| s 1(4)(c) | 28.15, 29.16, 29.50 | s 67(1) | 27.17 |
| s 1(4)(f) | 27.2, 29.50 | s 84 | 23.47 |
| s 1(6) | 21.48, 29.11, 29.41 | s 87 | 28.6 |
| s 1(7) | 28.12, 29.12 | s 115(1) | 27.5 |
| s 1(7)(a) | 27.47 | s 120 | 7.9 |
| s 1(7)(b) | 28.28 | | |
| s 2(1) | 1.31, 23.47, 29.2, 29.21 | Care Standards Act 2000 | 23.24 |
| s 3 | 1.31 | Child Abduction and Custody Act | |
| s 8 | 28.44 | 1985 | 25.75, 25.76 |
| s 10 | 28.44 | s 25(1) | 25.76 |
| s 19 | 29.1, 29.23, 29.34 | s 25(1)(a) | 25.75 |
| s 20 | 28.20 | Children Act 1989 | 1.8, 1.11, 1.14, 1.17, |
| s 21 | 1.34, 2.55, 27.47, 29.1 | | 1.29, 1.30, 1.34, 1.35, 2.1, 2.2, |
| s 21(1) | 29.3 | | 2.6, 2.8, 2.10, 2.17–2.21, 2.26, |
| s 21(2) | 29.4 | | 2.28, 2.32, 2.34–2.37, 2.39, |
| s 21(3) | 29.5, 29.47 | | 2.42–2.44, 2.48–2.51, 2.54–2.56, |
| s 21(4) | 29.22 | | 2.58, 2.60, 2.61, 2.63–2.67, |
| s 22(1) | 29.35 | | 2.69–2.71, 2.73, 2.75, 2.77, 3.15, |
| s 24 | 27.26, 29.22 | | 3.16, 3.21, 4.2, 4.12, 4.31, 4.36, |
| s 24(2) | 27.26 | | 4.82, 4.83, 5.2–5.5, 5.7–5.9, 5.15, |
| s 24(3) | 27.26 | | 5.18–5.20, 5.22, 5.23, 5.25, 5.28, |
| s 25 | 29.23 | | 5.29, 5.31–5.37, 5.54–5.56, 5.58, |
| s 26 | 28.38, 28.43, 29.12, 29.26, 29.31 | | 6.17, 7.3, 7.4, 7.9, 7.10, 7.13, |
| s 26(2) | 28.39, 29.27 | | 7.19, 7.20, 7.38, 8.1, 8.3, 8.4, |
| s 26(3) | 28.40, 29.28 | | |

## Children Act 1989—continued

| | |
|---|---|
| | 9.1, 9.6, 9.32, 9.35, 9.57, 10.2, 10.10–10.13, 10.16, 10.18, 10.22, 10.74, 10.79, 11.62, 12.11, 12.17, 12.25, 12.65, 12.68, 12.70, 13.1, 13.4, 13.5, 13.8, 13.10, 13.11, 13.13, 13.18, 13.20, 13.23, 13.24, 13.28, 13.32, 13.33, 13.43, 13.45, 13.47, 13.60–13.62, 14.1, 14.3, 14.4, 14.25, 14.39, 14.47, 15.1, 15.3, 15.4, 15.28, 15.34, 15.42, 15.43, 15.48, 15.49, 16.2, 16.3, 16.5, 16.7–16.11, 16.13, 16.15, 16.16, 16.21, 16.23, 16.26, 16.43, 16.44, 16.46, 16.54, 16.58, 16.64, 17.12, 18.1, 18.13, 18.26, 19.49, 20.2, 20.3, 20.8, 20.29, 20.30, 20.33, 20.60, 20.72, 20.73, 21.3, 21.6, 21.12–21.14, 21.28, 22.6, 22.9–22.12, 22.28–22.30, 22.38, 23.1, 23.2, 23.4–23.6, 23.8, 23.10, 23.12, 23.13, 23.19, 23.21, 23.39, 23.41, 23.57–23.59, 23.62, 23.63, 23.66, 23.68, 23.71, 23.72, 24.4, 24.16, 24.17, 24.28, 24.30, 24.31, 24.33–24.35, 24.37, 24.38, 24.40, 25.1, 25.2, 25.4–25.6, 25.9, 25.11, 25.16, 25.24, 25.29, 25.30, 25.45, 25.83, 25.85, 25.87, 25.88, 26.10, 26.17, 26.20, 27.38, 28.7, 28.10, 28.13, 28.38, 29.7, 29.9, 29.11, 29.14, 29.26, 29.32, 29.41, 30.3 |
| Pt II | 26.1 |
| Pt III | 25.53 |
| Pt IV | 1.35, 9.49, 23.65, 24.7, 24.39, 26.1, 26.12 |
| Pt V | 9.49 |
| s 1 | 2.2, 9.56, 14.22, 14.39, 14.48, 18.10, 21.3, 23.43, 25.60, 26.5, 26.34 |
| s 1(1 | 25.41 |
| s 1(1) | 9.27, 14.4, 14.10, 14.22, 24.35, 25.60, 27.8, 29.50 |
| s 1(1)(a) | 27.44 |
| s 1(2) | 2.26, 12.67, 14.10, 27.32 |
| s 1(2A) | 2.6 |
| s 1(2B) | 2.6, 2.7 |
| s 1(3) | 2.18, 2.20, 9.27, 13.43, 14.10, 14.37, 18.26, 20.3, 20.73, 21.13, 21.14, 23.37, 23.51, 25.41, 25.60, 26.34, 27.8, 27.44, 27.47, 29.50 |
| s 1(3)(a)–(f) | 12.67 |
| s 1(3)(c) | 18.33 |
| s 1(3)(e) | 14.22 |
| s 1(3)(g) | 17.2, 21.48, 25.42 |
| s 1(4) | 9.27, 25.87, 26.34 |
| s 1(4)(b) | 14.10, 18.26, 23.37, 25.41, 27.8, 27.44, 27.49 |
| s 1(5) | 2.44, 9.27, 10.79, 14.11, 14.37, 17.2, 18.31, 21.28, 21.48, 25.41, 25.51, 26.34, 27.52 |
| s 2 | 25.4, 26.2 |
| s 2(1) | 2.34 |
| s 2(2) | 2.35 |

## Children Act 1989—continued

| | |
|---|---|
| s 2(2A) | 2.39 |
| s 2(6) | 2.36 |
| s 2(8) | 25.11, 26.27 |
| s 2(9) | 2.36 |
| s 3 | 2.32, 26.2 |
| s 3(1) | 26.26 |
| s 3(5) | 8.4, 8.22, 26.26 |
| s 3(6) | 26.27 |
| s 3(7) | 26.27 |
| s 4 | 2.37, 25.4, 26.2, 26.26 |
| s 4(1) | 2.42 |
| s 4(1)(b) | 2.37 |
| s 4(1)(c) | 2.37 |
| s 4(1A) | 2.37, 12.25 |
| s 4(2A) | 26.26 |
| s 4(7) | 9.22 |
| s 4A | 2.52, 16.7, 16.43, 18.4, 22.10, 22.28, 23.44, 23.45, 24.17, 25.4, 26.2, 27.25 |
| s 4ZA | 2.39, 25.4, 26.2, 26.26 |
| s 4ZA(5) | 26.26 |
| s 5 | 23.47, 25.4, 26.2, 26.26 |
| s 7 | 2.73, 5.25, 6.35, 10.25 |
| s 8 | 2.69, 6.35, 12.18, 13.10, 13.24, 16.10, 16.24, 17.43, 18.42, 22.7, 22.12, 23.36, 23.62, 23.63, 26.1, 26.3, 26.5–26.7, 26.9–26.14, 26.16, 26.17, 26.20, 26.22–26.24, 26.28–26.33, 26.35, 27.5, 27.10, 27.17–27.19, 27.22, 27.23, 27.29, 27.42, 28.42, 29.30 |
| s 8(1) | 2.75, 18.14, 26.20, 26.21, 26.33 |
| s 8(1)(a) | 18.44 |
| s 8(2) | 26.1, 26.33 |
| s 8(3) | 13.24, 17.47 |
| s 8(3)(b) | 26.12 |
| s 8(4) | 17.44 |
| s 9 | 26.23, 26.29 |
| s 9(1) | 18.14, 23.2, 23.56, 23.63, 23.68 |
| s 9(3) | 27.29 |
| s 9(6) | 26.30–26.32 |
| s 9(6A) | 26.31 |
| s 9(6B) | 26.31 |
| s 9(7) | 26.32 |
| s 9(10) | 26.16 |
| s 10 | 24.33, 26.11, 26.14, 26.15, 26.23, 27.23, 27.29 |
| s 10(1) | 26.11 |
| s 10(1)(b) | 17.44, 17.47, 18.40 |
| s 10(2) | 24.33 |
| s 10(4)(a) | 27.17 |
| s 10(4)(b) | 27.17 |
| s 10(5) | 24.31 |
| s 10(5A) | 24.32 |
| s 10(5B) | 24.32 |
| s 10(6)(a) | 26.33 |
| s 10(6)(b) | 26.33 |
| s 10(7A) | 27.16, 27.21 |
| s 10(7B) | 27.16, 27.21 |
| s 10(8) | 23.36, 27.22 |
| s 10(9) | 12.17–12.19, 18.42, 18.44, 18.46, 26.17, 26.18, 27.22, 27.27, 27.38 |

## Children Act 1989—continued

| | |
|---|---|
| s 10(9)(c) | 18.46 |
| s 10(9)(d) | 18.42 |
| s 11 | 26.23 |
| s 11(7) | 26.23, 26.35, 27.10 |
| s 11(7)(c) | 26.24, 26.28, 27.10 |
| s 11A | 23.62 |
| s 12 | 25.4, 26.21, 26.23, 26.26 |
| s 12(1) | 26.26 |
| s 12(1A) | 26.26 |
| s 12(2) | 2.77, 13.18, 23.44, 26.26 |
| s 12(2A) | 23.44, 24.31, 26.26 |
| s 12(4) | 26.26 |
| s 13 | 26.23 |
| s 13(1) | 26.27 |
| s 14(8)(c) | 27.33 |
| s 14A | 26.1, 27.28, 27.29 |
| ss 14A–14F | 26.1 |
| ss 14A–14G | 27.5 |
| s 14A(1) | 2.63, 27.6 |
| s 14A(2) | 2.63, 27.6 |
| s 14A(2)(b) | 26.27 |
| s 14A(3) | 27.30 |
| s 14A(6)(b) | 27.30, 27.38 |
| s 14A(7) | 27.30 |
| s 14A(8) | 2.65, 27.30, 27.33, 27.38 |
| s 14A(10) | 2.65 |
| s 14A(11) | 27.38 |
| s 14B(1) | 27.40 |
| s 14B(1)(a) | 27.40 |
| s 14B(2) | 27.43 |
| s 14C | 25.4, 27.16 |
| s 14C(1) | 27.14, 27.38 |
| s 14C(1)(b) | 2.64 |
| s 14C(2)(a) | 27.16 |
| s 14C(2)(b) | 27.16 |
| s 14C(3)(a) | 27.16 |
| s 14C(4) | 27.16 |
| s 14D | 27.9, 27.16, 27.27 |
| s 14D(1) | 27.24 |
| s 14D(3) | 2.67, 27.25 |
| s 14D(3)(b) | 27.26 |
| s 14D(3)(c) | 27.26 |
| s 14D(3)(d) | 27.26 |
| s 14D(4) | 27.26 |
| s 14D(5) | 27.26 |
| s 14E(1) | 27.31 |
| s 14E(4) | 27.10 |
| s 14E(5) | 27.10 |
| s 14F | 2.66, 26.10, 27.34, 27.35 |
| s 14G | 27.5 |
| s 16 | 2.69, 17.47, 18.26, 25.5, 26.10 |
| s 16(1) | 2.69 |
| s 16(2) | 2.70 |
| s 16(3) | 2.70 |
| s 16(4A) | 2.73 |
| s 16(5) | 2.73 |
| s 16(7) | 2.71 |
| s 17 | 1.14, 23.41, 25.60, 26.10 |
| s 17(1) | 5.3–5.5, 25.53 |
| s 17(1)(b) | 5.10 |
| s 17(2) | 5.4 |
| s 17(3) | 5.5 |
| s 17(4A) | 5.11 |

## Children Act 1989—continued

| | |
|---|---|
| s 17(10) | 5.6 |
| s 17(11) | 5.7, 5.8 |
| s 20 | 3.15, 4.35–4.39, 4.73–4.80, 5.52, 5.56–5.60, 5.65–5.68, 5.70, 5.72–5.79, 6.17, 6.37, 8.7, 8.8, 8.20, 8.26, 9.33, 9.68, 11.62, 11.63, 12.39, 15.1, 15.2, 17.35, 17.36 |
| s 20(1) | 5.52, 8.7 |
| s 20(1)(a)–(c) | 5.58 |
| s 20(2) | 5.54 |
| s 20(4) | 4.75, 5.53, 5.76 |
| s 20(7) | 5.58, 8.7 |
| s 20(7)(b)(ii) | 4.78 |
| s 20(8) | 5.71, 5.72, 5.75, 17.37 |
| s 20(9) | 8.7, 17.37 |
| s 21 | 5.55 |
| s 22 | 23.21, 23.24 |
| s 22(1) | 10.22, 27.35 |
| s 22(1)(a) | 23.21, 23.39 |
| s 22(1)(b) | 23.23 |
| s 22(3)(a) | 16.43, 18.4, 22.28, 23.21 |
| s 22(6)(a) | 23.25 |
| s 22(9A) | 23.25 |
| s 22(9B) | 23.25 |
| s 22(9C) | 23.25 |
| s 22A | 23.14, 23.22 |
| ss 22A–22G | 23.21 |
| s 22C | 23.14, 23.20, 23.23, 23.24, 25.33 |
| s 22C(2) | 17.6 |
| s 22C(3) | 17.6, 23.20, 23.50 |
| s 22C(5) | 17.4 |
| s 22C(6) | 23.50 |
| s 22C(6)(a) | 17.8, 23.20 |
| s 22D | 23.24 |
| s 23(2) | 27.35 |
| s 23(6) | 27.35 |
| s 23A | 23.40 |
| ss 23A–23D | 23.39 |
| s 23C | 23.40 |
| s 25 | 4.12, 4.19 |
| s 25A | 23.10 |
| s 25B | 23.10 |
| s 25C | 23.10 |
| s 31 | 2.48, 2.50, 4.36, 4.47, 7.26, 10.48, 13.30, 14.37, 17.39, 19.29, 20.11, 23.7, 23.19, 23.43, 24.35, 25.54, 25.82–25.84, 26.8, 26.10, 27.49 |
| s 31(1) | 9.62, 13.1, 23.15, 25.6, 25.24 |
| s 31(1)(a) | 23.15 |
| s 31(1)(b) | 23.15, 25.2 |
| s 31(2) | 1.8, 7.3, 7.4, 7.20, 7.22, 7.38, 7.39, 10.79, 13.14, 13.29, 13.32, 13.33, 13.43, 13.45, 13.46, 13.53, 13.55, 13.65, 14.3, 15.3, 15.4, 16.2, 16.3, 17.2, 20.2, 26.4, 26.5, 29.4, 29.35 |
| s 31(2)(a) | 13.1, 16.11 |
| s 31(2)(b) | 7.36, 13.1, 13.57 |
| s 31(2)(b)(ii) | 7.33 |
| s 31(3) | 13.13, 23.30, 23.31, 25.30 |
| s 31(3A) | 23.6 |
| s 31(3A)(b) | 18.32 |

Children Act 1989—*continued*

| | |
|---|---|
| s 31(3B) | 18.32 |
| s 31(5) | 17.38, 25.35, 25.36, 25.84 |
| s 31(5)(a) | 25.25, 25.27 |
| s 31(5)(b) | 25.25 |
| s 31(8) | 23.16, 23.19, 25.9 |
| s 31(8)(b) | 23.19 |
| s 31(9) | 2.49, 7.9, 9.12, 25.24 |
| s 31(10) | 7.10 |
| s 31(11) | 13.13, 17.39, 18.30, 23.26 |
| s 31(11)(b) | 25.30 |
| s 31A | 1.34, 14.44, 16.21, 23.4, 23.6, 23.10, 25.60 |
| s 31A(1) | 16.22, 22.4, 23.4 |
| s 31A(2) | 16.23, 22.6 |
| s 31A(3) | 23.5 |
| s 31A(5) | 14.44, 14.46 |
| s 32 | 2.28, 10.10, 10.18, 13.8 |
| s 32(1) | 10.11 |
| s 32(1)(a)(ii) | 13.8, 27.32 |
| s 32(5) | 10.12, 10.16, 13.9 |
| s 32(6) | 10.13, 13.9 |
| s 32(7) | 10.16, 13.9 |
| s 32(8) | 10.18, 13.9 |
| s 33 | 23.2, 23.13, 23.42, 23.44, 23.46, 24.15, 26.9 |
| s 33(1) | 2.51, 17.3, 23.12 |
| s 33(2) | 2.50, 27.20 |
| s 33(3) | 1.34, 2.52, 16.7, 16.8, 22.10, 23.13, 23.42, 23.68, 23.73, 24.17, 25.1 |
| s 33(3)(a) | 17.3 |
| s 33(3)(b) | 17.3, 23.54, 23.56, 23.70–23.72 |
| s 33(3)(b)(i) | 27.24 |
| s 33(4) | 2.54, 16.8, 17.12, 22.9, 23.54, 23.59, 24.16 |
| s 33(6) | 16.9, 17.3, 22.11, 23.47 |
| s 33(6)(a) | 23.48 |
| s 33(7) | 23.49 |
| s 33(8)(a) | 23.52 |
| s 33(8)(b) | 23.53 |
| s 33(9) | 23.55, 23.59 |
| s 34 | 1.35, 5.37, 9.51, 9.52, 13.62, 16.24, 16.43, 18.8–18.10, 18.14, 18.16, 18.20, 18.25, 18.26, 18.30, 18.31, 18.33, 18.36, 18.37, 18.39, 18.41, 18.44, 18.45, 18.49, 18.50, 22.7, 22.28, 23.2, 23.14, 23.58, 23.62 |
| s 34(1) | 9.52, 16.44, 16.46, 18.4, 18.7, 18.12, 18.18, 18.22, 18.50, 22.29, 22.30 |
| s 34(1)(a) | 18.25, 18.35 |
| s 34(1)(a)–(d) | 18.21, 18.41 |
| s 34(2) | 16.46, 18.8–18.10, 18.12, 18.14, 18.16, 18.18, 18.34, 18.35, 18.50, 22.30 |
| s 34(3) | 16.46, 18.12, 18.14, 18.22, 18.35, 18.42, 18.44, 18.46, 22.30 |
| s 34(3)(b) | 18.41 |
| s 34(4) | 16.54, 18.13, 18.14, 18.21, 18.22, 18.38, 18.40, 18.50, 22.38 |
| s 34(5) | 18.17, 18.39 |
| s 34(6) | 16.55, 18.23–18.25, 22.39 |

Children Act 1989—*continued*

| | |
|---|---|
| s 34(6A) | 18.14, 18.25 |
| s 34(6B) | 18.14, 18.25 |
| s 34(7) | 18.14, 18.20 |
| s 34(9) | 18.14, 18.34, 18.36 |
| s 34(10) | 18.30 |
| s 34(11) | 18.31, 23.6, 23.8 |
| s 35 | 2.58, 25.57 |
| s 35(1(c) | 25.86 |
| s 35(1) | 25.6, 25.65 |
| s 36 | 25.2 |
| s 36(3) | 25.2 |
| s 37 | 2.76, 5.19, 5.21, 5.24–5.29, 10.25, 13.24, 13.28–13.30 |
| s 37(1) | 2.56, 5.27, 13.11, 13.12, 13.23–13.25, 13.28, 13.29, 15.3, 16.3 |
| s 37(2) | 5.21, 5.22, 13.25 |
| s 37(3) | 5.22, 13.27 |
| s 37(4) | 5.23, 13.27 |
| s 37(5) | 5.20, 13.26 |
| s 37(6) | 5.23 |
| s 38 | 4.36, 7.38, 8.4, 9.60, 9.68, 13.4, 13.13, 13.19, 13.23, 13.53, 13.62, 13.67, 14.1–14.3, 14.17, 14.25, 14.34, 14.37, 14.40, 15.3, 15.34, 16.2, 16.3, 17.46, 25.30 |
| s 38(1) | 2.56, 2.61, 5.29, 13.11, 13.28, 13.59, 17.38, 25.29, 30.19 |
| s 38(1)(a) | 13.15 |
| s 38(2) | 7.38, 13.19, 13.28, 13.29, 13.33, 13.34, 13.47, 13.49, 13.51, 13.55, 13.56, 13.58, 14.3, 14.48, 17.46 |
| s 38(3) | 13.10, 13.17, 13.19, 17.46, 25.29 |
| s 38(3A) | 13.17 |
| s 38(4) | 16.5, 23.29 |
| s 38(4)(a) | 13.6 |
| s 38(4)(b) | 13.6, 13.10, 17.12 |
| s 38(5) | 13.6 |
| s 38(6) | 10.65, 14.2, 14.26, 15.42–15.44, 15.46–15.49, 16.26–16.28, 16.58–16.64, 17.4, 17.7, 17.24 |
| s 38(7A) | 15.47, 16.63 |
| s 38(7B) | 15.47, 16.63 |
| s 38(9) | 17.39 |
| s 38A | 9.38, 16.11, 17.6 |
| s 38A(3) | 16.13 |
| s 38A(5) | 16.15 |
| s 38A(10) | 16.16 |
| s 38B | 9.38, 16.17, 17.6 |
| s 39 | 1.35, 2.55, 4.82, 17.16, 23.2, 23.33, 23.36 |
| s 39(1) | 23.33, 24.4, 24.30 |
| s 39(1)(a) | 27.20 |
| s 39(2) | 24.37, 24.38, 24.40, 25.85 |
| s 39(3) | 24.38, 25.87 |
| s 39(4) | 23.34, 24.34, 25.28 |
| s 40 | 13.22, 13.23, 30.53 |
| s 40(1) | 13.20 |
| s 40(2) | 13.20, 25.29 |
| s 40(3) | 13.20, 25.29 |
| s 40(4) | 13.21, 30.54 |
| s 40(6) | 13.21, 30.54 |
| s 41 | 9.14, 24.8, 24.28, 24.39, 29.36 |

Children Act 1989—*continued*

| | |
|---|---|
| s 41(1) | 18.34, 23.35 |
| s 41(2)(b) | 12.68 |
| s 41(6)(a) | 12.65 |
| s 41(6)(b) | 5.28 |
| s 41(6)(c) | 23.35, 24.8 |
| s 41(6)(f) | 18.34 |
| s 41(6)(g) | 9.14 |
| s 42 | 10.74, 12.70, 19.49 |
| s 43 | 9.34, 9.35 |
| s 43(1) | 5.31 |
| s 43(3) | 5.33, 9.36 |
| s 43(4) | 9.36 |
| s 43(5) | 5.34 |
| s 43(6) | 5.32, 9.34 |
| s 43(8) | 5.36 |
| s 43(9) | 5.35 |
| s 43(10) | 5.35 |
| s 43(11) | 5.37 |
| s 44 | 8.4, 8.12, 9.1, 9.3, 9.27, 15.28 |
| s 44(1) | 9.4, 9.12, 9.25, 9.39, 9.58 |
| s 44(1)(a) | 9.39 |
| s 44(1)(a)(i) | 9.39 |
| s 44(1)(a)(ii) | 9.39 |
| s 44(2)(a) | 9.12 |
| s 44(4) | 9.9 |
| s 44(4)(b) | 9.1, 9.45 |
| s 44(4)(b)(i) | 9.38 |
| s 44(4)(c) | 9.1, 9.43 |
| s 44(5) | 9.6, 9.10 |
| s 44(5)(b) | 9.43 |
| s 44(6) | 9.1 |
| s 44(6)(a) | 9.53 |
| s 44(6)(b) | 9.44 |
| s 44(9) | 9.55 |
| s 44(10) | 9.46 |
| s 44(11)(b)(iii) | 9.48 |
| s 44(12) | 9.47 |
| s 44(13) | 9.1, 9.51, 9.53 |
| s 44(15) | 9.1, 9.11 |
| s 44(16) | 9.1 |
| s 44(b)(ii) | 9.34 |
| s 44(b)(iii) | 9.34 |
| s 44A(2) | 9.39 |
| s 44A(2)(b) | 9.41 |
| s 44A(5) | 9.40 |
| s 44B(2) | 9.40 |
| s 45 | 9.57 |
| s 45(2) | 9.59 |
| s 45(3) | 9.61 |
| s 45(4) | 9.62 |
| s 45(5) | 9.62 |
| s 45(7) | 9.63 |
| s 45(8) | 9.64 |
| s 45(8A) | 9.42 |
| s 45(8B) | 9.42 |
| s 45(10) | 9.2, 9.64 |
| s 45(11) | 9.65 |
| s 46 | 8.1, 8.3, 8.4, 8.11, 8.12, 8.14, 8.16, 8.17, 8.21, 8.31, 9.61 |
| s 46(1) | 8.10 |
| s 46(2) | 8.6 |
| s 46(3)(a) | 8.25 |
| s 46(3)(b) | 8.25 |

Children Act 1989—*continued*

| | |
|---|---|
| s 46(3)(c) | 8.23 |
| s 46(3)(e) | 8.17 |
| s 46(3)(f) | 8.16 |
| s 46(4) | 8.23 |
| s 46(5) | 8.20 |
| s 46(6) | 8.18 |
| s 46(7) | 8.29, 9.12, 9.61 |
| s 46(8) | 8.29, 9.61 |
| s 46(9) | 8.21 |
| s 46(9)(b) | 8.22 |
| s 46(10) | 8.24 |
| s 47 | 1.17, 5.15–5.18, 5.44 |
| s 47(1) | 5.15, 8.25 |
| s 47(1)(b) | 9.25 |
| s 47(5) | 27.50 |
| s 47(6) | 5.17 |
| s 48 | 9.50 |
| s 48(1) | 9.50 |
| s 48(4) | 9.50 |
| s 48(9) | 9.50 |
| s 49(2)(b) | 9.50 |
| s 50(2) | 9.50 |
| s 51 | 8.16, 9.13 |
| s 91 | 23.62, 25.75 |
| s 91(1) | 23.63, 24.31 |
| s 91(1A) | 23.63 |
| s 91(2) | 23.44, 23.62 |
| s 91(2A) | 23.62 |
| s 91(3) | 23.62, 25.76, 25.89 |
| s 91(4) | 23.62 |
| s 91(5) | 23.62 |
| s 91(5A) | 23.63, 27.24 |
| s 91(6) | 23.63 |
| s 91(12) | 23.29 |
| s 91(13) | 25.76, 27.9 |
| s 91(14) | 23.38, 27.19 |
| s 91(15) | 23.38, 25.88, 27.20 |
| s 91(16) | 27.20 |
| s 91(17) | 18.37, 18.38 |
| s 92(7) | 13.23 |
| s 96 | 20.33, 20.60 |
| s 97(2) | 1.11 |
| s 98 | 20.29 |
| s 98(2) | 20.29, 20.30 |
| s 100 | 8.4, 23.31, 23.66 |
| s 100(2) | 23.31, 23.68 |
| s 100(2)(c) | 23.2, 23.62 |
| s 100(4) | 23.68 |
| s 101(4) | 23.64 |
| s 105(1) | 26.28, 27.35 |
| s 105(6) | 23.17, 23.19 |
| s 105(6)(c) | 23.19 |
| Sch 2 | |
| para 7 | 5.10 |
| para 8 | 5.10 |
| para 15 | 18.5, 18.18 |
| para 16 | 18.5 |
| para 19 | 23.53 |
| paras 19A–19C | 23.39 |
| Pt I | 5.4 |
| Sch 3 | 25.10, 25.12, 25.13, 25.21, 25.38, 25.47, 25.57, 25.65 |
| para 2 | 25.66, 25.67 |

Children Act 1989—*continued*
  Sch 3—*continued*
    para 3                                   25.68–25.70
    para 4                17.39, 25.65, 25.71
    para 4(1)                                25.72
    para 4(2)(c)                          25.73
    para 4(3)                                25.73
    para 5        17.39, 25.65, 25.71, 25.74
    para 5(1)                                25.74
    para 5(2)(c)                        25.74
    para 5(3)                                25.74
    para 5(4)(c)                        25.74
    para 5(5)(a)                        25.74
    para 6                       25.75, 25.77
    para 6(3)             1.35, 2.60, 24.40
    para 6(4)                      1.35, 2.60
    para 9                                     25.7
    para 15(3)                             25.82
Children Act 2004                          5.1
Children (Leaving Care) Act 2000     23.39
Children (Scotland) Act 1995            28.3
Children and Families Act 2014      2.6, 6.2,
             10.5, 17.4, 17.6, 23.6, 25.33,
             26.20, 26.21, 26.31, 27.5, 27.21
  s 14                 2.28, 10.10, 13.8
  s 14(4)                      13.6, 17.12
Children and Social Work Act 2017
  s 8                                         23.7
Children and Young Persons Act 1969    1.35,
                                     8.3, 25.5
  s 28(2)                                  8.3
  s 28(5)                                  8.3
  s 35                                      25.5
Children and Young Persons Act 2008    17.4,
               17.6, 23.20, 23.21, 25.33
Civil Evidence Act 1995                20.26
  s 4                                     20.26
County Courts Act 1984          4.68, 23.59
  s 38                          4.68, 23.59
Crime and Courts Act 2013
  Sch 10                     4.68, 23.59
Criminal Justice Act 1988               20.61
  s 33A                              20.61
Criminal Justice and Immigration Act
  2008
  Pt 1                                    23.17

Education Act 1996                1.6, 23.62
  s 437                               23.62
  s 548(1)                                1.6

Family Law Act 1986                    3.16
  s 3                                     3.16
Family Law Act 1996     9.38, 13.47, 13.49
  s 63A                               13.47
  s 63B                               13.47
  s 63R                               13.47
Family Law Reform Act 1969     23.66, 26.28
  s 7                                    23.66
  s 9(1)                                 26.28
Family Law Reform Act 1987              2.39
  s 1(3)                                  2.39

Guardianship of Infants Act 1925
  s 1                                        2.5

Health and Social Care (Community
  Health and Standards) Act 2003    27.5
Human Fertilisation and Embryology
  Act 2008
  s 33                                     2.38
  s 35                                     2.38
  s 36                                     2.39
  s 37                                     2.39
  s 42                                     2.38
  s 43                                     2.39
  ss 43–47                               26.26
Human Rights Act 1998    1.4, 2.45, 4.1, 4.2,
              4.6, 4.7, 4.65–4.67, 4.81–4.83,
             5.59, 8.13, 9.68, 17.12, 17.13,
           17.15, 17.25, 17.26, 20.72, 23.11,
           23.28, 23.57–23.59, 24.20, 24.21,
                         25.14, 25.44, 25.45
  s 2(1)                                    4.3
  s 6(1)      4.5, 4.6, 4.65, 4.66, 23.59, 24.20
  s 7                            8.13, 23.57, 23.58
  s 7(1)                                4.6, 23.59
  s 7(1)(a)                                4.82
  s 7(1)(b)                          4.66, 4.82
  s 8    4.67, 4.83, 9.68, 17.12, 17.15, 23.28,
                            23.59, 24.20, 24.21
  s 8(1)                              17.27, 23.59
  Sch 1         4.4, 4.9, 4.21, 4.52, 21.29

Legal Aid, Sentencing and Punishment
  of Offenders Act 2012               4.12
  s 4                                     4.26
  s 25                                     4.85
Local Authority Social Services Act
  1970                                  1.33
  s 1                                       1.30
  s 7                                       1.33
  Sch 1                                 1.30

Matrimonial and Family Proceedings
  Act 1984                      4.68, 23.59
  s 31E                          4.68, 23.59
Mental Capacity Act 2005     12.37, 12.43,
                       12.45, 12.49, 23.32
  s 1                                    12.43
  s 2(1)                                 12.43
  s 2(5)                                 23.32
  s 3                        4.75, 5.61, 5.76
  s 3(1)                                 12.45
Mental Health Act 1983                  4.12
  Pt III                                 25.74

Police and Criminal Evidence Act 1984    8.32
Power of Criminal Courts (Sentencing)
  Act 2000                              4.12
Prevention of Cruelty to, and
  Protection of, Children Act
  1889
  s 4(1)                                    8.3
  s 5(2)                                 23.48

| | | | |
|---|---|---|---|
| Senior Courts Act 1981 | | Social Services and Well-being (Wales) Act 2014—*continued* | |
| s 9(1) | 30.4 | s 124 | 23.53 |
| s 9(4) | 30.4 | s 143 | 1.32 |
| s 37(1) | 4.68, 23.59 | Sch 2 | 1.32 |
| s 102 | 30.4 | | |
| Social Security Contributions and Benefits Act 1992 | | Youth Justice and Criminal Evidence Act 1999 | |
| s 141 | 26.25 | s 16 | 20.49 |
| s 143(1)(a) | 26.25 | s 17 | 20.49 |
| Social Services and Well-being (Wales) Act 2014 | 1.21 | | |
| s 78(1)(a) | 18.4 | | |

# TABLE OF STATUTORY INSTRUMENTS

References are to paragraph numbers.

Adoption Agency Regulations 2005,
SI 2005/389
  reg 3    28.37
  reg 46    28.37, 29.25
Allocation and Transfer of Proceedings
Order 2008, SI 2008/2836
  art 5(2)    9.2

Care Planning, Placement and Case
Review and Fostering Services
(Miscellaneous Amendments)
Regulations 2013, SI 2013/984    16.33, 22.18
Care Planning, Placement and Case
Review (England) Regulations
2010, SI 2010/959
  Pt 2    14.46
  Pt 3    23.27
  Pt 4    16.37, 17.6, 17.9, 22.22, 23.27, 25.33
  Pt 8    23.10
  reg 8    16.56, 18.24, 18.49, 22.40
  reg 8(2)    18.24
  reg 8(3)    18.24, 18.49
  reg 8(4)    18.50
  reg 8(5)    18.50
  reg 8ZA    16.44, 22.29
  reg 14    16.24, 22.7
  reg 17    16.39, 16.41, 22.23, 22.25
  reg 18    16.41, 22.25
  reg 19    16.41, 22.25
  reg 22    16.31, 16.32, 22.16, 22.17
  reg 24    16.35, 16.36, 22.20
  reg 24(1)    17.31
  reg 24(3)    16.34, 22.19
  reg 26    17.9
  reg 27    17.9
  reg 28(5)(b)    16.32, 22.17
  reg 31    16.24, 22.7
  reg 36    23.10
  Sch 1    23.5
  Sch 2    16.24, 22.7
  Sch 3    16.40, 16.41, 22.24
Children (Admissibility of Hearsay
Evidence) Order 1993,
SI 1993/623    20.26
Children and Social Work Act 2017
(Commencement No 1)
Regulations 2017, SI 2017/918    23.7

Children (Prescribed Orders –
Northern Ireland, Guernsey and
Isle of Man) Amendment
Regulations 2006, SI 2006/837    23.64
Children (Prescribed Orders –
Northern Ireland, Guernsey and
Isle of Man) Regulations 1991,
SI 1991/2032    23.64
Civil Procedure Rules 1998,
SI 1998/3132
  r 21.10    4.86
  r 23.7(b)    11.64, 15.9, 15.28
  r 52.10(2)(a)    17.25
  r 52.21    30.1, 30.24

Family Court (Composition and
Distribution of Business) Rules
2014, SI 2014/840
  art 16(3)    9.2, 9.15
Family Procedure Rules 2010,
SI 2010/2955    2.27, 3.42, 9.2, 9.13, 9.15, 9.16, 9.20, 10.8, 10.10, 10.22, 10.35, 10.78, 11.51, 12.1, 12.17, 12.49, 12.53, 12.55, 12.56, 13.24, 13.28, 13.61, 15.50, 19.7, 19.20, 20.57, 30.7, 30.12, 30.15, 30.18, 30.24, 30.26, 30.27, 30.52
  Pt 1    2.29, 10.8
  r 1    19.7
  r 1.1    2.28, 12.11, 12.22, 19.17
  r 1.1(1)    4.45
  r 1.2    26.17
  r 1.4(1)    4.45
  r 1.4(2)    4.45
  r 1.4(a)    27.31
  r 2.3(1)    12.37
  r 2.6(1)(a)    9.2
  Pt 4    10.8
  r 4.1(3)(a)    30.21
  r 4.1(3)(h), (i), (g)    26.13
  Pt 5    26.13
  PD5A    26.13, 30.28
  Pt 12    2.28, 6.34, 10.5, 10.8, 10.24, 18.34, 23.35, 26.13
  r 12.2    18.34, 23.35
  r 12.2(c)    9.15
  r 12.3    9.13, 12.1, 18.34, 23.35
  r 12.5    9.2
  r 12.6    12.66

| Family Procedure Rules 2010, SI 2010/2955—continued | | Family Procedure Rules 2010, SI 2010/2955—continued | |
|---|---|---|---|
| r 12.16 | 9.16 | PD22A | 10.57, 11.7, 11.29, 19.38 |
| r 12.16(4) | 9.20 | Pt 24 | 10.8 |
| r 12.16(5) | 9.20 | Pt 25 | 10.8, 10.65, 10.67, 10.70, 10.72, 11.19, 11.49, 11.50, 11.53, 11.55, 12.46, 12.75, 15.11, 15.49, 15.52, 20.62 |
| r 12.17 | 13.24 | | |
| r 12.21 | 13.61, 13.64, 20.65 | | |
| r 12.21(2) | 20.66 | | |
| r 12.22 | 10.10 | r 25.4(2) | 10.68, 11.51, 15.50 |
| r 12.24 | 2.27 | r 25.4(3) | 10.68, 11.51, 15.50 |
| r 12.25(3) | 19.20 | PD25C | |
| r 12.28 | 16.11 | para 2.1 | 10.70, 11.53, 15.52 |
| r 12.73 | 4.26 | para 2.4 | 10.70, 11.53, 15.52 |
| r 12.75 | 4.26 | para 3 | 10.70 |
| PD12A | 10.8, 10.24, 19.21, 24.7, 24.13, 24.39, 26.13 | Pt 27 | 10.8 |
| | | r 27.10 | 1.11 |
| para 2.4 | 10.35 | r 27.11 | 4.28 |
| para 5.3 | 2.31, 10.21 | r 27.11(2) | 4.27 |
| para 5.4 | 10.21 | r 27.11(3) | 4.28 |
| para 5.5 | 10.22 | PD27A | 10.8 |
| para 5.7 | 10.21 | para 4.1 | 15.29, 19.53 |
| para 7.1 | 27.32 | para 4.2 | 15.31, 19.55 |
| para 8 | 12.42 | para 4.3 | 15.32, 19.56 |
| PD12C, para 3.1 | 9.13 | para 5.1 | 19.58 |
| PD12E | 9.16 | para 6.1 | 19.59 |
| PD12G | 4.26 | para 6.3 | 19.59 |
| PD12J | 19.4 | r 29.4 | 10.78 |
| para 17 | 19.5 | r 29.4(3) | 10.78 |
| PD12K | 16.11 | r 29.17 | 9.15, 29.38 |
| para 19 | 19.13 | r 29.18 | 9.15 |
| PD12M | 2.71 | r 29.19 | 9.15 |
| para 1.2 | 2.71 | Pt 30 | 10.8, 30.1 |
| Pt 14 | 29.33 | r 30.3(3) | 30.12 |
| r 14.3 | 29.33, 29.38 | r 30.4(2) | 13.21, 30.18 |
| r 14.6 | 29.37 | r 30.4(3) | 30.19 |
| r 14.7 | 29.37 | r 30.5(2) | 30.41 |
| Pt 15 | 10.8, 12.37 | r 30.5(4) | 30.42 |
| r 15.2 | 12.49, 12.53 | r 30.5(5) | 30.42 |
| r 15.3 | 12.53, 12.54 | r 30.7 | 30.21 |
| r 15.3(2) | 12.42 | r 30.7(1) | 13.21 |
| r 15.3(3) | 12.42 | r 30.8 | 30.7, 30.52 |
| r 15.6 | 12.56 | r 30.12 | 30.1, 30.30 |
| r 15.9 | 12.55 | r 30.12(2) | 30.26 |
| PD15B | 10.8 | r 30.12(3) | 30.24 |
| Pt 16 | 12.65 | r 30.12(3)(a) | 30.29 |
| r 16.3 | 12.65 | r 30.12(3)(b) | 30.29 |
| r 16.20 | 12.67 | r 30.12(5) | 30.26 |
| PD16A | | PD30A | 10.8, 30.3, 30.4, 30.21 |
| para 6.2 | 12.66 | para 3.2 | 30.29 |
| para 6.3 | 12.75 | para 4.6 | 30.10 |
| para 6.5 | 10.76, 12.72 | para 4.7 | 30.13 |
| para 6.6 | 10.75, 12.71, 19.50 | para 4.8 | 30.13 |
| para 6.8 | 10.76, 12.72 | para 4.9 | 30.13 |
| para 7.7 | 21.21 | para 5,4 | 30.23 |
| Pt 18 | 10.8 | para 5.5 | 30.23 |
| rr 18.1–18.13 | 12.10 | para 5.6 | 30.23 |
| PD18A | 12.10 | para 5.8 | 30.31 |
| Pt 22 | 10.8, 10.54, 19.36 | para 5.9 | 30.32 |
| r 22.1 | 10.55, 19.36 | para 5.10 | 30.33 |
| r 22.2 | 10.56, 15.37, 19.37, 20.22 | para 5.10A | 30.34 |
| r 22.2(2)(b) | 20.22 | para 5.13 | 30.36 |
| r 22.4 | 11.7, 11.29 | para 5.14 | 30.36 |
| r 22.6 | 20.24 | para 5.14A | 30.36 |
| r 22.7 | 15.37 | para 5.15 | 30.40 |

Family Procedure Rules 2010,
SI 2010/2955—*continued*
PD30A—*continued*
| | |
|---|---|
| paras 5.16–5.20 | 30.37 |
| paras 5.16–5.22 | 30.47 |
| para 5.21 | 30.38 |
| para 5.22 | 30.39 |
| para 5.37 | 30.20 |
| para 5.39 | 30.48 |
| para 7.2 | 30.41 |
| para 7.6 | 30.43 |
| para 7.7 | 30.44 |
| para 7.8 | 30.49 |
| para 7.9A | 30.45 |
| para 7.12 | 30.47 |
| para 7.14 | 30.48 |
| para 7.15 | 30.49 |
| para 7.16 | 30.50 |
| para 7.19 | 30.51 |
| r 39.3(7) | 30.15 |

Fostering Services (England)
Regulations 2011, SI 2011/581    16.33, 22.18

Fostering Services Regulations 2002,
SI 2002/57    16.34, 22.19

Mental Capacity Act 2005 (Transfer of Proceedings) Order 2007
| | |
|---|---|
| SI 2007/1899 | 10.8 |
| art 2 | 23.32 |
| art 3 | 23.32 |

Special Guardianship Regulations 2005, SI 2005/1109
| | |
|---|---|
| reg 6 | 27.34 |
| reg 6(2)(a) | 27.34 |
| Schedule | 27.33 |

# TABLE OF INTERNATIONAL MATERIAL

References are to paragraph numbers.

Convention of 19 October 1996 on Jurisdiction, Applicable Law, Recognition,
    Enforcement and Co-operation in Respect of Parental Responsibility and Measures
    for the Protection of Children     3.3, 3.5, 3.6, 3.10, 3.16, 3.23, 10.8
    Art 5     3.17, 3.20
    Art 6     3.30
    Art 8     3.18
    Art 11     3.31, 15.17
    Art 34     3.9
Convention of 25 October 1980 on the Civil Aspects of International Child Abduction     3.28, 25.76
Convention of 29 May 1993 on Protection of Children and Co-operation in Respect of
    Intercountry Adoption     28.6

European Convention for the Protection of Human Rights and Fundamental Freedoms
    1950     4.1, 9.32, 14.37, 23.58
    Art 5     4.4, 4.9
    Art 6     4.4, 4.21, 4.73, 13.64, 14.24, 17.20
    Art 8     1.4, 4.4, 4.51, 4.52, 4.54, 4.73, 4.82, 13.2, 13.64, 17.12, 17.20, 21.29, 23.23, 23.57, 23.73, 24.19–24.22, 25.43, 25.45, 27.46
    Art 8(2)     1.5
    Art 26     4.3
    Art 27(2)     4.3
    Art 31     4.3
    Art 46     4.3
European Council Regulation No 2201/2003 concerning jurisdiction and the recognition
    and enforcement of judgments in matrimonial matters and the matters of parental
    responsibility (BIIR)     3.3, 3.5, 3.10, 3.16, 3.23, 10.8
    Art 1(1)(b)     3.6
    Art 1(3)(b)     3.6
    Art 8     3.17, 3.19
    Art 10     3.19
    Art 12     3.30
    Art 13     3.30
    Art 15     3.12, 3.18, 3.41–3.44, 3.56
    Art 15(1)     3.41
    Art 15(1)(a)     3.46
    Art 15(1)(b)     3.46
    Art 15(3)     3.47, 3.50, 3.53
    Art 15(4)     3.55
    Art 15(5)     3.55
    Art 17     3.56
    Art 20     3.31, 15.17
    Art 55     3.9, 3.11
    Art 55(a)     3.9
    Art 56(1)     3.54
    Art 56(2)     3.54

United Nations Convention of the Rights of the Child 1989                14.37, 28.4
   Art 5                                                                         1.3
Universal Declaration of Human Rights 1948
   Art 16                                                                        1.2

# Part 1

# INTRODUCTION, BACKGROUND AND GENERAL PRINCIPLES

# CHAPTER 1

# CHILD PROTECTION IN ENGLAND AND WALES: AN OVERVIEW

## CHILDREN, FAMILIES AND THE STATE

**1.1** This book is concerned with state interference in family life. Specifically, it is concerned with the law of England and Wales as to when such interference can and should take place, and the form that this interference can take, when state intervention may be needed to protect the welfare of children.

### The importance of the autonomy of the family

**1.2** The United Nations General Assembly's 1948 Universal Declaration of Human Rights gives a very clear statement of the role of the family within society and the role of the state in relation to the family:[1]

> 'The family is the natural and fundamental group unit of society and is entitled to protection by society and the State.'

**1.3** The 1989 United Nations Convention of the Rights of the Child expanded on this principle in its statement as to both the role of families in relation to their children, and the duty of the state to respect that role:[2]

> 'States Parties shall respect the responsibilities, rights and duties of parents or, where applicable, the members of the extended family or community as provided for by local custom, legal guardians or other persons legally responsible for the child, to provide, in a manner consistent with the evolving capacities of the child, appropriate direction and guidance in the exercise by the child of the rights recognized in the present Convention.'

**1.4** Nearer home, in Europe, Art 8 of the 1950 Convention for the Protection of Human Rights and Fundamental Freedoms[3] is explicit in its protection of the family from state interference:

> '1. Everyone has the right to respect for his private and family life, his home and his correspondence.
>
> 2. There shall be no interference by a public authority with the exercise of this right except such as is in accordance with the law and is necessary in a democratic society in the interests of national security, public safety or the economic

---

[1] Article 16.3.
[2] Article 5.
[3] Incorporated in the law of England and Wales by operation of the Human Rights Act 1998.

well-being of the country, for the prevention of disorder or crime, for the protection of health or morals, or for the protection of the rights and freedoms of others.'

**1.5** The final words of Art 8(2) lead directly to the central question that all the legislation and case law discussed in the following chapters can be said to be directed to answering, that of when the state is justified in interfering in family life to protect the health, morals, rights and freedoms of children, and when it is not.

**1.6** In discussing the subject of child protection law, it is important never to lose sight of the fact that every act of child protection is also an act of interference by the state in family life, the justification for which must be rigorously examined. Baroness Hale of Richmond[4] has this to say about the importance of the scrupulous observance of the responsibilities and rights of parents towards their children in a free society:

> 'Children have the right to be properly cared for and brought up so that they can fulfil their potential and play their part in society. Their parents have both the primary responsibility and the primary right to do this. The state steps in to regulate the exercise of that responsibility in the interests of children and society as a whole. But "the child is not the child of the state" and it is important in a free society that parents should be allowed a large measure of autonomy in the way in which they discharge their parental responsibilities. A free society is premised on the fact that people are different from one another. A free society respects individual differences. "Only the worst dictatorships try to eradicate those differences": see *El Al Israeli Airlines Ltd v Danielowitz* [1992] Isrl LR 478, para 14, Barak J. Often they try to do this by intervening between parent and child.'

## Child protection or 'social engineering': judicial comment and the approach of the court

**1.7** As numerous reported cases[5] remind us, a clear distinction must be drawn between necessary regulation of the exercise of responsibility by parents, in the interests of children, and impermissible, 'social engineering'. As Baroness Hale of Richmond JSC puts it in the case of *Re B (Care Proceedings: Appeal)*:[6]

> '[179] Since well before the Children Act came into force, the courts have recognised that there is a line to be drawn between parents whose personal characteristics mean that they may be less than perfect parents and parents who

---

[4] In her speech in the House of Lords case of *R (Williamson) v Secretary of State for Education and Employment* [2005] 2 FLR 374 at para [72]. The case was concerned with the issue of whether the prohibition of corporal punishment in schools set out in s 548(1) of the Education Act 1996 amounted to an unjustified interference with the religious freedom (guaranteed by Art 9 of the European Convention) of parents who believed that the availability of such punishment was mandated by scripture as part of the proper upbringing of their children.

[5] A search for the phrase, 'social engineering' in the *Family Law Reports* on *Family Law Online* identified 41 cases in which it appears: search conducted 6 October 2017.

[6] [2013] 2 FLR 1075.

may cause harm to their children. Lord Templeman put the point this way in his well-known words in *Re KD (A Minor) (Ward: Termination of Access)* [1988] AC 806, [1988] 2 WLR 398, [1988] 2 FLR 139, at 812, 400 and 141 respectively:

> "The best person to bring up a child is the natural parent. It matters not whether the parent is wise or foolish, rich or poor, educated or illiterate, provided the child's moral and physical health are not endangered. Public authorities cannot improve on nature."

If, by that last sentence, Lord Templeman was making a factual statement, then some might disagree: if local authorities remove children from unsatisfactory parents at birth and swiftly place them with highly satisfactory adoptive parents they can undoubtedly improve on nature. But in my view Lord Templeman was making a normative statement: public authorities have no right to improve on nature.

[180] That thought has been followed through in numerous cases since. As Wall LJ pointed out in *Re L (Children) (Care Proceedings: Significant Harm)*, at 1084, 'There are, of course, many statements in the law reports warning of the dangers of social engineering', citing in particular Butler-Sloss LJ in *Re O (A Minor) (Custody: Adoption)* [1992] 1 FLR 77 at 79:

> "If it were a choice of balancing the known defects of every parent with some added problems that this father has, against idealised perfect adopters, in a very large number of cases, children would immediately move out of the family circle and towards adopters. That would be social engineering ..."

...

[182] But clearly we do remove *some*[7] of those children. The difficulty is to identify what it is that tips the case over the threshold.'

**1.8** The identification of the point at which this 'line' or 'threshold'[8] is crossed is one of the most difficult, but necessary, tasks for all involved in child care law.

**1.9** More recently, Aikens LJ made the same point[9] but did so in terms that set it within the framework of the approach to deciding when state intervention[10] is justified that is set out in current legislation and case law:

> 'It is vital that local authorities, and, even more importantly, judges, bear in mind that nearly all parents will be imperfect in some way or other. The State will not take away the children of "those who commit crimes, abuse alcohol or drugs or suffer from physical or mental illness or disability, or who espouse

---

[7] Emphasis in original.
[8] 'Threshold' has, of course, a technical meaning, discussed in detail elsewhere in this book, in child care law as shorthand for the test for the existence of circumstances in which a court can make a care or supervision order: see s 31(2) of the Children Act 1989.
[9] In *Re J (A Child)* [2015] EWCA Civ 222.
[10] His Lordship is referring specifically to the most extreme form of such intervention, that of the child being removed from their birth family and placed with adoptive parents.

antisocial, political or religious beliefs"[11] simply because those facts are established. It must be demonstrated by the local authority, in the first place, that by reason of one or more of those facts, the child has suffered or is at risk of suffering significant harm. Even if that is demonstrated, adoption will not be ordered unless it is demonstrated by the local authority that "nothing else will do" when having regard to the overriding requirements of the child's welfare. The court must guard against "social engineering".'[12]

**1.10** This two stage process by which the court decides, first, if a child has suffered or is at risk of suffering significant harm and, secondly, if this means that the child's welfare requires state intervention in the family, by way of temporary or permanent removal of the child or otherwise, is central to the legal process of child protection in England and Wales.

## Public perception

**1.11** The issues that arise from drawing the line identified by Baroness Hale of Richmond JSC and the wider issues of whether state authorities were right to intervene, or not intervene, in a particular family or type of family often attract wide public interest and media comment.[13] Such comment is of widely varying quality in terms of its accuracy and its understanding of the issues concerned. This interest and comment is, once again, an essential feature of a free society, despite the concerns sometimes felt by lawyers and other professionals working within the child care system as to the effect that it has on both general public understanding and the perceptions of parents and others who become involved in the child care system. This is not helped by the fact that, for valid and important reasons, proceedings about children are required to take place in private and reporting is subject to strict limitations.[14] As Lord Justice McFarlane commented in March 2017:[15]

> 'Unfortunately, the vacuum created by the lack of sound and accurate information about the system provides a space into which ill-informed and, at times deliberately incorrect commentary and advice can be introduced. Regular ill-informed and deliberately partial press commentary must have an impact upon the perception of the public in general.'

---

[11] This quotation is from the judgment of Baroness Hale of Richmond JSC in *Re B* [2013] 2 FLR 1075 at para [143] and is cited by Sir James Munby P in *Re A* [2015] EWFC 11 at para [15]. The passage set out in the text is part of Aikens LJ's discussion of the learned President's judgment in *Re A*.
[12] Paragraph [56].
[13] A cursory glance at the internet will show an abundance of comment ranging from scholarly legal, sociological and psychological studies through journalistic reportage, comment and polemic to discussion of soap opera story lines.
[14] See Administration of Justice Act 1960, s 12, Children Act 1989, s 97(2) and Family Procedure Rules 2010, r 27.10.
[15] Giving the *Bridget Lindley Memorial Lecture* 2017, available on the *Family Justice Council* website.

**1.12** The current President on the Family Division, Sir James Munby, has been forthright in advocating greater transparency in, and hence understanding of, the whole family law system.

## THE CHILD PROTECTION SYSTEM IN ACTION: STATISTICS ON CHILDREN NEEDING PROTECTION AND RELATED ISSUES

**1.13** Published statistics provide important insights, from various perspectives, into the issues that arise in relation to child protection in England and Wales.

### Children in need and the child protection process

**1.14** It is relatively unusual for an application for a care order to be made in relation to a child who has not previously been known to its local social services department. An example of such a case would be where a child, about whom there had previously been no recorded concerns, is presented to medical professionals with unexplained, and possibly non-accidental, injuries. More typical is the case of a child whose parenting has given cause for concern over a period of time but where that concern has now reached a level that leads to proceedings being taken. Such a child will have been classified as being, 'in need'[16] prior to the issue of proceedings.

**1.15** The Department for Education publishes comprehensive statistics[17] as to the number of children in England who are or may be, 'in need', the reasons for this and the action being taken. These statistics are of great interest in themselves. However, they also define a pool of children whose circumstances mean that they require some degree of state involvement in their lives and a significant proportion of whom will become the subject of care (or other public law) proceedings.[18]

**1.16** From these statistics, it appears that 394,400 children were identified as being, 'in need' as at 31 March 2016 (a rate of 337.7 per 10,000 children aged under 18 years).[19] This figure has been stable since 2010.

**1.17** During the year ending 31 March 2016 172,290 children[20] were the subject of enquiries under s 47 of the Children Act 1989 ('CA 1989'),[21] 73,050

---

[16] See s 17 of the Children Act 1989.
[17] The most recent such statistics appear in *Characteristics of Children in Need: 2015 to 2016 (SFR 52/2016, 3 November 2016)*, available online.
[18] It should be emphasised that the identification of a child as being, 'in need' does not necessarily imply any failing on the part of its parents. For example, for 9.6 per cent of children identified as, 'in need' as at 31 March 2016 the primary need that led to the child being assessed was its disability or illness and in a further 2.9 per cent of cases the primary need was parent's disability or illness: Table B3.
[19] Figure C.
[20] Figure K.
[21] This section imposes a duty on local authorities to investigate the circumstances of a child in

children were the subject of an initial child protection case conference[22] and 63,310 (a rate of 54.2 per 10,000 children aged under 18 years) were made the subject of a child protection plan.[23] These are the three stages that will mark an increasing level of concern, and hence of local authority intervention, in relation to a child. In most cases where court proceedings are taken, they were the way-markers that were passed on the road to the decision to take court proceedings. All these figures have shown a steady increase since 2010.

**1.18** Unsurprisingly, perhaps, the, most common 'primary need' identified at the first assessment stage in 2016 was, 'abuse or neglect' (50.6 per cent of children in need) followed by, 'family dysfunction' (17.4 per cent of children in need).[24]

**1.19** Figure J and Table C3 set out factors leading to the child being in need that were identified at the conclusion of assessment.[25] From these it is notable that domestic violence was a factor for 49.6 per cent children in need, mental health for 36.6 per cent, drug misuse for 19.3 per cent, emotional abuse also for 19.3 per cent, alcohol abuse for 17.5 per cent and neglect for 17.5 per cent. Although they feature in the most widely publicised child protection cases, and are the factors that the general public tends to think of when the subject of, 'child protection' is raised, physical abuse and sexual abuse are factors in relatively small percentages of cases of children classified as, 'in need': 14 per cent and 6.4 per cent respectively.

**1.20** The, 'multi-disciplinary' nature of child protection is illustrated by the source of, 'referrals'[26] to social services. By far the commonest source of referrals in England is the police (27.6 per cent of children referred) followed by schools (16.7 per cent), health services (14.3 per cent) and local authority services (13.4 per cent).

**1.21** Provision for children in need in Wales is now the subject of devolved legislation[27] and statistics are published separately. The Wales Children in Need

---

their area who may be suffering or at risk of significant harm and to decide whether they should take action to safeguard or promote that child's welfare.
[22] Figure K.
[23] Table D1.
[24] Both figures from Table B3.
[25] Where more than one factor is present, all are enumerated. An example would be the, 'toxic triad' of domestic abuse, mental illness and substance misuse with which all practitioners will be familiar.
[26] Figure H. A, 'referral' is defined a request for provision of services for a child not previously recognised as being, 'in need'. Note that about one in four referrals require no further action after initial assessment and one in ten referrals require no formal action at all.
[27] See Social Services and Well-being Act (Wales) 2014.

Census 2016[28] shows that 18,990 children in Wales (a rate of 302 per 10,000 persons under 18 years of age) were identified as being, in need' as at 31 March 2016.[29]

## Court proceedings

**1.22** The extent to which recognition as being, 'in need' or being subject to local authority child protection procedures does not serve to protect a child and the court becomes involved can be seen from the Ministry of Justice's published statistics.[30] For the calendar year 2016, the figures in respect of the principle court orders discussed in this book were as follows (all figures are for the number of children affected):

|  | Applications Made[31] | Orders Made[32] |
| --- | --- | --- |
| Care orders | 25,691 | 13,953 |
| Supervision orders | 2,149 | 7,676 |
| Emergency protection orders | 1,758 | 1,287 |
| Adoption orders | 5,871 | 5,829 |
| Special guardianship orders (in Public Law proceedings) | 160 | 5,631 |

**1.23** An interesting feature of these figures is that they illustrate the extent to which applications for care orders ultimately lead instead to the making of supervision orders and special guardianship orders. Both of these orders represent a substantially less severe intrusion into the family life of the child and their birth family than would the making of a care order.

## The other side of the story: parents and families in care proceedings

**1.24** Whilst the welfare of the children involved in care proceedings must always be the overriding concern of the courts and all who work within the system, it is wrong to ignore the human cost of care proceedings for parents,

---

[28] Welsh Government: 8 March 2017 SFR 24/2017.
[29] Section 1 and notes to Map 1 (which shows the percentage of children in need in each local government area in Wales).
[30] The following statistics are all taken from: Family Court Statistics Quarterly England and Wales: April to June 2017: Ministry of Justice.
[31] All figures from Table 3, save in respect of adoption, which are from Table 18.
[32] All figures from Table 4, save in respect of adoption, which are from Table 19.

grandparents and other family members. It is also wrong to ignore the fact that the adults involved in care proceedings, whatever their own shortcomings, almost always love the children concerned and want to do their best for them. Much court time is taken up with an anxious consideration of whether that, 'best' is in fact, 'good enough' for the children in the particular case being considered.

**1.25** One of the saddest and most troubling features of care proceedings is the extent to which the parents whose ability to care for their children is being questioned are often themselves troubled and damaged individuals who suffer severe disadvantage in many forms. Often, the difficulties that parents labour under are a result of their own upbringing, which has left them devoid of the skills they need to meet the needs of their own children.

**1.26** A 2012 article in *Family Law* magazine[33] drew together research from various sources that starkly illustrated these points. Amongst the statistics about parents involved in care proceedings that are given by the authors, the following are particularly striking:

- 90% are below the poverty line;
- 60% have been abused as a child;
- 45% experience mental health problems;
- 25% suffer from drug and alcohol addictions;
- 30% went through the care system when they were children;
- 35% have been through care proceedings with a previous child;
- 20% have a learning disability.

**1.27** More recently, a study by the Centre for Child and Family Justice at Lancaster University of a sample of mothers involved in repeated care proceedings found that 66 per cent had experienced neglect in their childhood, 67 per cent had experienced emotional abuse, 52 per cent physical abuse and 53 per cent sexual abuse.[34]

**1.28** These findings inevitably raise questions of whether, and if so how, the overlapping issues of parents who are incapable of meeting their children's needs as a result of their own problems and of inadequately parented children becoming in turn inadequate parents can be resolved. Attempts to answer these questions are far beyond the scope of this book. These questions must, however, be ones of real and immediate concern to a society in which, on the basis of the statistics set out above, one child in every 30 is regarded as being, 'in need' and about one child in every 320 is the subject of an application in which the court is asked to sanction state intervention in their lives.

---

[33] Charlotte Rachel Proudman and Frances Trevena: 'Setting Parents up to Fail: Punishing Hopeless Parents is Integral to Care Proceedings' [2012] Fam Law 987. The statistics cited, and their sources, appear at pp 987–988.
[34] Reported on familylawweek.co.uk, 9 October 2017.

# RESPONSIBILITY FOR CHILD PROTECTION: LOCAL AUTHORITIES AND THE COURTS

**1.29** Although this chapter makes numerous references to, 'the state' intervening in family life when the welfare of children is at stake, national government has no direct role in carrying out such intervention. Direct work with families is carried out by social workers who are employed by local authorities, although in carrying out that work they will act in collaboration with other agencies and professionals. The vital role of the court lies in deciding when the most extreme forms of intervention in family life provided for in the CA 1989 and the Adoption and Children Act 2002 ('ACA 2002') should be sanctioned.

## Statutory duties of local authorities

**1.30** The Local Authority Social Services Act 1970, as amended, provides that, 'local authorities'[35] are to have, 'social services functions' as set out in Sch 1 of that Act and these functions include all the functions derived from the CA 1989 that are relevant to the subject matter of this book. The 1970 Act, and subsequent legislation, make detailed provision for manner in which these functions are performed.

**1.31** In relation to adoption, the local authority acts as an, 'adoption agency' as defined by s 2(1) of the ACA 2002 and local authorities have a duty under s 3 of that Act to maintain an, 'adoption service'.

**1.32** In Wales, local authorities now have the functions under both the 1989 and the 2002 Acts by operation of s 143 of, and Sch 2 to, the Social Services and Well-being (Wales) Act 2014.

**1.33** In carrying out their functions, local authorities are obliged[36] to act in accordance with the guidance set out in *Working together to safeguard children: A guide to inter-agency working to safeguard and promote the welfare of children.*[37] This document also sets out[38] the responsibilities of other agencies that may become concerned in child protection issues, notable examples being schools, the police and the National Health Service.

---

[35] Defined for the purpose of this Act as '. . . the councils of the non-metropolitan counties and metropolitan districts in England, the councils of London Boroughs and the Common Council of the City of London' (s 1). (During the year ending 31 March 2016 43 children in the City of London were identified as being, 'in need' and 6 become the subject of child protection plans: *Characteristics of Children in Need: 2015 to 2016 (SFR 52/2016, 3 November 2016)* Tables B1 and D1 respectively.)
[36] See s 7 of the Local Authority Social Services Act 1970.
[37] March 2015, updated February 2017.
[38] Chapter 2 of the Guide.

## The role of the courts

**1.34** It is a fundamental principle of child protection law that it is for a court to decide if an order should be made but that it is then for the local authority to decide how to give effect to that order. This is particularly clearly the case when a care order is made and the local authority accordingly obtains, 'overriding' parental responsibility in accordance with s 33(3) of the CA 1989[39] and will be expected to proceed to implement its care plan[40] for the child. That care plan may provide for the child to be placed for adoption, in which case a placement order under s 21 of the ACA 2002 will invariably be sought. The making of care and placement orders and the issues of local authority parental responsibility and care plans are all considered in detail within this work.

**1.35** This fundamental principle has been endorsed in numerous cases both before[41] and after the enactment of the CA 1989.[42] In the case of *Re W (Care Proceedings: Functions of Court and Local Authority)*[43] Ryder LJ carried out a comprehensive review of the authorities on the respective roles of the court and the local authority. He summarised the effect of these authorities, whilst also drawing attention to the areas in which the court continued to have a role, in the following passage:

> '[30] The analysis of this case begins where their Lordships' House finished in *Re S (Minors) (Care Order: Implementation of Care Plan); Re W (Minors) (Care Order: Adequacy of Care Plan)* [2002] UKHL 10, [2002] 2 AC 291, [2002] 2 WLR 720, [2002] 1 FLR 815. There has been (and could be) no attempt before this court to re-open the issues of principle decided by it. The purpose of this hearing has been to find practical solutions to the problem that arises when a judge concludes that a care plan is inadequate or wrong but that a care order may be necessary. To do so, it is helpful to recollect the statutory scheme of the CA 1989 and some of the principles which are established in the authorities including *Re S and W (Care Proceedings)* [2007] EWCA Civ 232, [2007] 2 FLR 275.
>
> [31] The statutory scheme includes, inter alia, the following division of functions as between local authorities and the courts:

---

[39] A concept discussed in detail in chapter 23 of this work.
[40] See s 31A of the 1989 Act.
[41] See for example, *A v Liverpool City Council* (1981) 2 FLR 222, House of Lords. In this case, the House of Lords rejected an attempt to use the court's wardship jurisdiction as a vehicle to challenge a local authority's decision to reduce the level of contact between a mother and her child, who was in care in accordance with an order made under the Children and Young Persons Act 1969.
[42] The most important post *Children Act* decision remains that of the House of Lords in *Re S (Minors) (Care Order: Implementation of Care Plan); Re W (Minors) (Care Order: Adequacy of Care Plan)* [2002] UKHL 10, [2002] 2 AC 291, [2002] 2 WLR 720, [2002] 1 FLR 815. In this case, their Lordships' House rejected arguments that the court could retain a role in monitoring the implementation of a care plan either by the device of a continuing series of interim care orders or, more radically, by identifying, 'starred milestones' for progress in implementing the plan, with the proviso that failure to reach such a milestone would result in the case being returned to court.
[43] [2013] EWCA Civ 1227.

(i) the decision to apply for a care or supervision order under Part IV of the CA 1989 is that of the local authority (or an authorised person) and not the court;
(ii) decisions about the conduct of proceedings are exclusively those of the court;
(iii) the decision whether to make an order and if so, what order is exclusively that of the court;
(iv) decisions about the implementation and review of arrangements for looking after a child including, inter alia, the care plan and any full care order that the court may make are governed by subordinate legislation administered by the local authority not the court and decisions about the steps which are reasonably necessary to give effect to a supervision order are matters for the supervisor not the court.

[32] Before considering the statutory scheme and the functions of the court and the local authority, it is worthwhile noting that the court's jurisdiction is not entirely at an end when a care order is made. Although the family court retains no supervisory jurisdiction over the local authority's implementation of the order made, there remains the jurisdiction in the family court to make decisions about contact with a child in care under s 34 of the CA 1989, to consider an application for the discharge of a care order under s 39 of the CA 1989 and to extend the duration of a supervision order for up to a maximum period of 3 years under paras 6(3) and (4) of Sch 3 to the CA 1989, in appropriate circumstances. The High Court retains a supervisory jurisdiction to restrain unlawful acts and to exercise its supervisory jurisdiction to remedy illegalities either in classic public law terms or for breach of a person's Convention rights, including by injunctive relief.'

These observations were strongly endorsed Sir James Munby P.[44]

## A final word from Sir James Munby P

**1.36** Above and beyond the technical issues of the ambit of the court's role in protecting children from inadequate parenting, or indeed from unjustified state interference in their family life, there lies to fundamental principle that the court's first duty is to advance the welfare of children. In a recent, and widely publicised, case Sir James Munby P had this to say:[45]

'My judicial duty, as with every judge in this country, is "to do right to all manner of people after the laws and usages of this realm." There are occasions, and this is one, where doing "right" includes speaking truth to power. The entrance to the Old Bailey, the Central Criminal Court, admonishes those who enter to "Defend the Children of the Poor." Is less required of the Family Court or of the Family Division of the High Court? I think not.'

**1.37** The way in which judges, at all levels in the court system, have striven to apply these sentiments within the framework established by Parliament and by judicial precedent is the real subject of this book.

---

[44] See para 115.
[45] *X (A Child) (No 3)* [2017] EWHC 2036 (Fam) at para [40].

# CHAPTER 2

# FUNDAMENTALS OF THE CHILDREN ACT 1989

## WELFARE AND DELAY

**2.1** Two principles underpin all proceedings under the Children Act 1989 ('CA 1989'): the paramountcy of the child's welfare and the positive duty on all professionals involved in such proceedings to avoid delay.

## THE WELFARE PRINCIPLE

### The child's welfare shall be the court's paramount consideration[1]

**2.2** The term 'welfare' will be familiar to family practitioners and pervades all children law proceedings. Section 1 of the CA 1989 stipulates that:

> 'When a court determines any question with respect to –
> 
> (a) the upbringing of a child; or
> (b) the administration of a child's property or the application of income arising from it,
> 
> the child's welfare shall be the court's paramount consideration.'

**2.3** This is echoed in the Adoption and Children Act 2002 ('ACA 2002') which specifies in s 1(2) that when considering an application for a placement or adoption order:

> 'The paramount consideration of the court or adoption agency must be the child's welfare, throughout his life.'

**2.4** It is clear from the legislation then, that the court's primary concern when making decisions about a child's future must be the 'welfare' of that child. However, what 'welfare' means on a practical level; and how the 'welfare' of a child can be quantified, are just two of the difficult questions that the family court has grappled with over the years. Defining 'welfare' is of particular importance when considering the gravity of the decisions that courts are required to make within care and adoption proceedings. Promoting and

---

[1] CA 1989, s 1.

prioritising a child's welfare goes to the heart of all decisions made which will affect children not just in their minority, but into adulthood and throughout the rest of their lives.

**2.5** The principle of the paramountcy of a child's welfare in the family court can be traced as far back as the late nineteenth century, and has been enshrined in statute since 1925.[2] The move away from the father's absolute parental authority at the close of the nineteenth century ushered in a new welfare-based structure which saw both parents being seen on equal footing for the first time.

**2.6** The equal footing of both parents was further emphasised by the insertion of subs 2A and 2B into s 1 of the CA 1989 by the Children and Families Act 2014 ('CFA 2014'). Section 1(2A) provides:

> 'A court, in the circumstances mentioned in subsection (4)(a) or (7), is as respects each parent within subsection (6)(a) to presume, unless the contrary is shown, that involvement of that parent in the life of the child concerned will further the child's welfare.'

**2.7** Section 1(2B) continues:

> 'In subsection (2A) "involvement" means involvement of some kind, either direct or indirect, but not any particular division of the child's time.'

**2.8** Whilst the CA 1989 does not go so far as to require face-to-face contact, or an equal division of time, it does recognise that promoting a child's welfare will normally require some interaction with *both* of their parents. Since a child's parents will often be the first building blocks in the construction of their identity, it makes sense that some knowledge and involvement with both of them is important for a child's welfare in both the short and long-term.

## Yardstick of welfare

**2.9** Governing both private law (with whom a child lives and spends time with, and the exercise of parental responsibility) and public law (care, supervision and adoption orders) is the 'standard or yardstick'[3] of welfare, a particularly important feature of all children law proceedings.

**2.10** In the Court of Appeal case of *Re G*,[4] Lord Justice Munby, as he then was, considered what the term 'welfare' meant in the context of the CA 1989. Although this case concerned the specific matters of the education and religious upbringing of Orthodox Jewish children after their parents' separation, it still provides a very helpful, general discussion as to the meaning of 'welfare' in both public and private law proceedings.

---

[2] Guardianship of Infants Act 1925, s 1.
[3] *Re G* [2012] EWCA Civ 1233 at [25].
[4] [2012] EWCA Civ 1233.

**2.11** In his judgment, Munby LJ considered the importance of the developments of the welfare principle in the late nineteenth and early twentieth centuries and examined the current understanding of 'welfare'. Accepting that the paramountcy of welfare is undeniably enshrined in statue, he considered two crucial questions:[5]

> 'First, what do we mean by welfare; and, second, by reference to what standard or yardstick is welfare to be assessed?'

**2.12** Munby LJ addressed the first question by reiterating the understanding of welfare as articulated by Lord Hailsham LC in *Re B (A Minor) (Wardship: Sterilisation)* and commenting:[6]

> '"Welfare", which in this context is synonymous with "well-being" and "interests" (see Lord Hailsham LC in *Re B (A Minor) (Wardship: Sterilisation)* [1988] AC 199, 202), extends to and embraces everything that relates to the child's development as a human being and to the child's present and future life as a human being.'

**2.13** Munby LJ emphasised Sir Thomas Bingham MR's comments in *Re O (Contact: Imposition of Conditions)*,[7] that is that a child's welfare is to be considered throughout the child's minority and 'into and through adulthood'.[8] *Re O* was again, a private law matter, but Munby LJ considered it held a 'wider resonance', and added that how far one is required to look into the future will depend on the question before the court. For example, a change in school may require less of a 'forward-looking' approach versus that required in the context of the far-reaching ramifications of making a placement or adoption order.

## What standard, or yardstick, is welfare to be assessed by?

**2.14** In answer to the second question posed, Munby placed the standards to be applied squarely in the context of the here and now, that is:[9]

> '[...] the standards of reasonable men and women in 2012, not by the standards of their parents in 1970, and having regard to the ever changing nature of our world: changes in our understanding of the natural world, technological changes, changes in social standards and, perhaps most important of all, changes in social attitudes.'

**2.15** Moreover, he held that the court must take a holistic approach to the evaluation of a child's welfare:[10]

> 'Evaluating a child's best interests involves a welfare appraisal in the widest sense, taking into account, where appropriate, a wide range of ethical, social, moral,

---

[5] *Re G* [2012] EWCA Civ 1233 at [25].
[6] *Re G* [2012] EWCA Civ 1233 at [26].
[7] *Re O (Contact: Imposition of Conditions)* [1995] 2 FLR 124 at 129.
[8] *Re G* [2012] EWCA Civ 1233 at [26].
[9] *Re G* [2012] EWCA Civ 1233 at [33].
[10] *Re G* [2012] EWCA Civ 1233 at [27].

religious, cultural, emotional and welfare considerations. Everything that conduces to a child's welfare and happiness or relates to the child's development and present and future life as a human being, including the child's familial, educational and social environment, and the child's social, cultural, ethnic and religious community, is potentially relevant and has, where appropriate, to be taken into account.'

**2.16** By extension then, he held that it is important to recognise that a child's welfare cannot be assessed in isolation:[11]

'It is only by considering the child's network of relationships that their well-being can be properly considered. So a child's relationships, both within and without the family, are always relevant to the child's interests; often they will be determinative.'

**2.17** It is upon this basis that the CA 1989 operates. However, the 'yardstick of welfare' does not set a restrictive framework in which children law proceedings must be resolved, nor does it prescribe in any detail what factors or situations should be viewed as 'good' or 'bad' in the context of a child's welfare. As Thorpe LJ remarked in *Re S (Adult Patient: Sterilisation)*, 'it would be undesirable and probably impossible to set bounds to what is relevant to a welfare determination'.[12] The court must and will always consider every case on its own facts, however, the ever-evolving concept of 'welfare' has been bought into the present day by *Re G* and has remained strong and clear ever since.

## WELFARE CHECKLIST

**2.18** When considering making an order under the CA 1989 and the ACA 2002, the court shall have regard to particular matters set out in s 1(3) of the CA 1989 (when looking at private law or care and supervision orders) and s 1(4) of the ACA 2002 (when looking at placement or adoption orders). The list of welfare considerations set out in the two acts have come to be known as 'the welfare checklists' and assist the court in applying the welfare principle.

**2.19** Both the CA 1989 and the ACA 2002 contain similar provisions although necessarily differ slightly because the orders governed by the ACA 2002 impact significantly on the exercise of parental responsibility (discussed below), and can result in a child ceasing to be a member of their birth family. The court must consider the checklists when looking at what order it intends to make.

**2.20** Section 1(3) of the CA 1989 provides:

'In circumstances mentioned in subsection (4) [whether to make an order or not], a court shall have regard in particular to –

    (a)    the ascertainable wishes and feelings of the child concerned (considered in the light of his age and understanding);

---

[11] *Re G* [2012] EWCA Civ 1233 at [30].
[12] *Re S (Adult Patient: Sterilisation* [2001] Fam 15.

(b) his physical, emotional and educational needs;
(c) the likely effect on his of any change in his circumstances;
(d) his age, sex, background and any characteristics of his which the court considers relevant;
(e) any harm which he has suffered or is at risk of suffering;
(f) how capable each of his parents, and any other person in relation to who the court considers the question to be relevant, is of meeting his needs;
(g) the range of powers available to the court under this Act in the proceedings in question.'

**2.21** Section 1(4) of the ACA 2002 provides:

'The court or adoption agency must have regard to the following matters (among others) –

(a) the child's ascertainable wishes and feelings regarding the decision (considered in the light of the child's age and understanding);
(b) the child's particular needs;
(c) the likely effect on the child (throughout his life) of having ceased to be a member of the original family and become an adopted person;
(d) the child's age, sex, background and any of the child's characteristics which the court or agency considers relevant;
(e) any harm (within the meaning of the Children Act 1989 (c. 41)) which the child has suffered or is at risk of suffering;
(f) the relationship which the child has with relatives, and with any other person in relation to whom the court or agency considers the relationship to be relevant, including—
  (i) the likelihood of any such relationship continuing and the value to the child of its doing so;
  (ii) the ability and willingness of any of the child's relatives, or of any such person, to provide the child with a secure environment in which the child can develop, and otherwise to meet the child's needs;
  (iii) the wishes and feelings of any of the child's relatives, or of any such person, regarding the child.'

**2.22** Evidently, both checklists encompass the meaning and standard of 'welfare' set out by Munby LJ in *Re G*.[13] The paramountcy of welfare is clear and must be specifically considered when determining what orders (if any) the court should make in relation to the arrangements for the children it is concerned with.

**2.23** The court must demonstrate that the elements of the checklist are at the forefront of its mind when making final orders. The judge does not need to address each element of the checklist in the judgment provided, but they must make it clear that they have considered the elements,[14] and that the court's approach is compatible with the law.[15]

---

[13] *Re G* [2012] EWCA Civ 1233.
[14] *P (A Child)* [2016] EWCA Civ 3.
[15] *Re E (Adoption Order: Proportionality of Outcome to Circumstances)* [2014] 2 FLR 514.

**2.24** The Senior President of the Tribunals, Lord Justice Vos, addressed the issue of how thoroughly a judge is required to address the welfare checklist in judgments in the matter of *P (A Child)*:[16]

> 'We are entitled to assume that a judge of the experience of Judge Ansell knew how to perform the welfare review, and knew which matters he should take into account, unless he has demonstrated the contrary. There was no need for him laboriously to rehearse each item of the checklist as if a pilot conducting his pre-flight checks (see Staughton LJ in *H v H (Residence Order: leave to remove from the jurisdiction)* [1995] 1 FLR 529), even if, in a difficult or finely balanced case, it is a great help to address each of the factors in the list, along with any others which may be relevant, so as to ensure that no particular feature of the case is given more weight than it should properly bear.'

**2.25** The checklist serves as a balancing exercise for the court when considering the range of potential outcomes available, and whether any order should be made.[17] However, the court is not bound to solely consider the issues raised by the parties and may highlight other issues it considers relevant. Importantly, no one element of the checklist is more important than another. For a full discussion of the welfare decisions to be made by the court, see chapter 14, in relation to interim orders, and chapter 21 in relation to final orders.

## NO DELAY PRINCIPLE

**2.26** Having considered the paramountcy of the welfare principle in children law proceedings, what constitutes 'welfare' within the meaning CA 1989, and the welfare checklists, the second general principle enshrined in the CA 1989 is that there should be no delay in determining a question with respect to the upbringing of a child. This is for the simple reason that any delay is likely to be detrimental to the child's welfare.[18] Considering the rate of the development of a child and their own concept of time, it is obvious that any period of uncertainty or instability in the provision of basic and emotional parenting of a child must be kept to a minimum. However, the removal of a child from a parent and/or any lack of clarity as to their long term future will in itself necessarily create uncertainty and instability.

**2.27** The concept that the process of protecting a child's welfare can, in itself, be detrimental is a sobering one. To protect against this detriment, the courts and all practitioners, be it judges, lawyers, social workers or children's guardians, have a duty to avoid delay.[19] The duty is a positive one, and the court's attention must be drawn to any failure to comply with its directions.

---

[16] *P (A Child)* [2016] EWCA Civ 3 at [48].
[17] *B v B (Residence Order: Reasons for decision)* [1997] 2 FLR 602.
[18] CA 1989, s 1(2).
[19] FPR 2010, r 12.24.

## 26 weeks rule

**2.28** It is now a statutory requirement that any application for a care or supervision order shall be concluded within 26 weeks from the date of the application.[20] The CA 1989 was amended by the CFA 2014 to provide that applications for care or supervision orders must be completed without delay and on a default timetable in 26 weeks.[21] This new timetable is encapsulated in Part 12, Chapter 3 the Family Procedure Rules 2010 ('FPR 2010') and expands on the overriding objective contained in r 1.1 of the FPR 2010, that is: '[with the] overriding objective of enabling the court to deal with cases justly, having regard to the welfare issues involved'.

**2.29** Part 1 of the FPR 2010 includes reference to factors such as fairness and expedition, proportionality, saving expense and ensuring that the parties are on an equal footing. The overriding objective should be the focus of all of the parties to proceedings, and the court must ensure that it is adhered to throughout.

**2.30** In the interests of the no delay principle, it is essential that matters are dealt with fully and fairly without any unnecessary delay, whilst at the same time ensuring that the court is in possession of all of the information necessary to conclude the matter in the best interests of the children, fairly and justly.

**2.31** In order for the court to further its objective of avoiding delay, the court will set the timetable for the proceedings taking into account the 'timetable for the child', that is all dates which are important to the child's welfare and development.[22] If the court is considering more than one child, it will set a timetable for each child individually. The timetable for the proceedings will be regularly reviewed in light of any changes to the timetable for the child throughout the proceedings, again to ensure that each child's needs are considered whilst ensuring that the matter is concluded fairly and as expeditiously as possible. The timetable for proceedings and 26 week rule are considered fully in chapter 10 of this book.

## PARENTAL RESPONSIBILITY

### What is parental responsibility?

**2.32** The term 'parental responsibility' is used frequently in relation to child protection proceedings and within legislation but, much like the 'welfare' principle discussed above, is often difficult to pin down. Section 3 of the CA 1989 provides that 'parental responsibility' comprises:

---

[20] CA 1989, s 32.
[21] CFA 2014, s 14.
[22] FPR 2010, PD12A, para 5.3.

'All the rights, duties, powers, responsibilities and authority which by law a parent of a child has in relation to the child and his property.'

**2.33** The concept of parental responsibility is relevant insofar as it relates to the promotion of the welfare of the parent's child, and not just merely the existence of parenthood.[23] In the matter of *Re H-B*, the court considered what is expected of parents in their exercise of parental responsibility.[24] The President, Munby P, commented:[25]

> 'I wish to emphasise this, parental responsibility is more, much more, than a mere lawyer's concept or a principle of law. It is a fundamentally important reflection of the realities of the human condition, of the very essence of the relationship of parent and child. Parental responsibility exists outside and anterior to the law. Parental responsibility involves duties owed by the parent not just to the court. First and foremost, and even more importantly, parental responsibility involves duties owed by each parent to the child.'

## Who has parental responsibility?

**2.34** There are a number of scenarios in which a person can acquire parental responsibility. All birth mothers immediately have parental responsibility upon the birth of the child. Section 2(1) of the CA 1989 establishes that:

> 'Where a child's father and mother were married to each other at the time of his birth, they shall each have parental responsibility for the child.'

**2.35** Further, s 2(2) of the CA 1989 provides:

> 'Where a child's father and mother were not married to each other at the time of this birth –
> 
> (a) the mother shall have parental responsibility for the child;
> (b) the father shall have parental responsibility for the child if he has acquired it (and has not ceased to have it) in accordance with the provisions of this Act.'

**2.36** More than one person can have parental responsibility for a child at one time, and a person does not lose parental responsibility as a result of another person acquiring it.[26] Moreover, a holder of parental responsibility cannot surrender or transfer their parental responsibility to another person, but may arrange for some or all of it to be met by one or more persons acting on their behalf.[27]

---

[23] *Re D (Withdrawal of parental responsibility)* [2015] 1 FLR 166.
[24] *Re H-B* [2015] EWCA Civ 389.
[25] *Re H-B* [2015] EWCA Civ 389 at para 72.
[26] CA 1989, s 2(6).
[27] CA 1989, s 2(9).

## Acquiring and losing parental responsibility

**2.37** Section 4 of the CA 1989 confirms that where a child's father was not married to the mother at the time of the child's birth, he shall acquire parental responsibility if he becomes registered on the child's birth certificate.[28] It is also possible for a father to acquire parental responsibility by entering into a 'parental responsibility agreement' with the mother,[29] or by virtue of a court order.[30]

## Alternative families

**2.38** Not all children are brought into the world by traditional means, and new legislation has tried to cater for situations in which children are conceived via surrogacy and artificial insemination. Under s 33 of the Human Fertilisation and Embryology Act 2008 ('HFEA 2008') the mother who gives birth to a child will automatically have parental responsibility for that child, regardless of any biological connection. Moreover, the married or civil partner of the birth mother will be treated as a father / parent of the child pursuant to ss 35 and 42 of the HFEA 2008 respectively, unless they are shown to have not consented to the pregnancy.

**2.39** If the birth mother is unmarried (or her partner has not consented to the pregnancy) then there is scope for another man to be treated as the father of the child under s 36 (and complying with the conditions in s 37) of the HFEA 2008. Section 4ZA of the CA 1989 governs the acquisition of parental responsibility by a second female parent, and should be considered alongside s 43 of HFEA 2008. Section 2(2A) of the CA 1989 provides:

> 'Where a child has a parent by virtue of section 43 of the Human Fertilisation and Embryology Act 2008 and is not a person to whom section 1(3) of the Family Law Reform Act 1987 applies –
>
> (a) the mother shall have parental responsibility for the child;
> (b) the other parent shall have parental responsibility for the child if she has acquired it (and has not ceased to have it) in accordance with the provisions of this Act.'

**2.40** In relation to same sex couples, there is no generalised guidance as to when parental responsibility will be conferred. Since the child's welfare will be the paramount consideration, each case will be considered on its facts and in accordance with the welfare checklist discussed above.[31]

**2.41** A person can also acquire parental responsibility by virtue of a child arrangements or special guardianship order made by the court (see below) as a matter of practicality.

---

[28] CA 1989, s 4(1A), if the child was born after December 2003.
[29] CA 1989, s 4(1)(b).
[30] CA 1989, s 4(1)(c).
[31] *A v B and C (Lesbian co-parents: Role of Father)* [2012] 2 FLR 607, see also *Re G (Shared Residence Order: Biological Mother of Donor Egg)* [2014] 2 FLR 897.

## Losing parental responsibility

**2.42** A person who has acquired parental responsibility by virtue of a child arrangements or special guardianship order will lose it when that order is discharged. A *parent* however, cannot lose parental responsibility unless an adoption order is made in respect of the child, or, in the case of unmarried fathers who have acquired parental responsibility under s 4(1) of the CA 1989, if a court removes it by way of an order. Beyond adoption, orders removing parental responsibility are extremely rare.

# AVAILABLE ORDERS UNDER THE CHILDREN ACT 1989[32]

**2.43** Under the CA 1989 the court has the ability to make a number of different orders in relation to the future care of children. Each order will have an impact upon a parent's ability to exercise their parental responsibility over their child and consideration must be given by the court to making the least interventionist order possible, if it deems an order is necessary at all. The court will consider the raft of orders it can make when deciding which order, or combination of orders, are in the child's best interests.

## No order principle

**2.44** Section 1(5) of the CA 1989 provides:

> 'Where a court is considering whether or not to make one or more orders under this Act with respect to a child, it shall not make the order or any of the orders unless is considers that doing so would be better for the child than making no order at all.'

**2.45** There is an expectation that parents should and will exercise their parental responsibility to promote the welfare of their children and this remains at the heart of the 'no order' principle.[33] Furthermore, Art 8 of the European Convention on Human Rights (as per Sch 1 of the Human Rights Act 1998) provides that:

> 'Right to respect for private and family life
>
> 1 Everyone has the right to respect for his private and family life, his home and his correspondence.
>
> 2 There shall be no interference by a public authority with the exercise of this right except such as is in accordance with the law and is necessary in a democratic society in the interests of national security, public safety or the economic well-being of the country, for the prevention of disorder or crime, for the protection of health or morals, or for the protection of the rights and freedoms of others.'

---

[32] The orders available under the ACA 2002 are considered separately in this book.
[33] *Re D (Withdrawal of parental responsibility)* [2015] 1 FLR 166.

**2.46** McFarlane LJ in the matter of *Re W (Direct Contact)* expanded on this further:[34]

> 'It is the parents, rather than the court or more generally the State, who are the primary decision makers and actors for determining and delivering the upbringing that the welfare of their child requires [...] the courts are entitled to look to each parent to use their best endeavours to deliver what their child needs, hard or burdensome or downright tough though that may be. The statute places the primary responsibility for delivering a good outcome for a child upon each of his or her parents, rather than upon the courts or some other agency.'

**2.47** In the event that the court is called upon to interfere in arrangements for children, this interference must be no more than is necessary to safeguard the child and promote their welfare and should be proportionate. The balance to be struck terms of the need for an order is considered further in chapter 14, in relation to interim orders, and chapter 21 in relation to final orders.

## Care and supervision orders

**2.48** Section 31 of the CA 1989 enables a care or supervision order to be made in favour of the local authority who applies for it:

> '(1) On the application of any local authority or authorised person, the court may make an order –
>
> (a) placing the child with respect to whom the application is made in the care of a designated local authority; or
> (b) putting him under the supervision of a designated local authority.
>
> (2) A court may only make a care order or supervision order if it is satisfied –
>
> (a) that the child concerned is suffering, or is likely to suffer, significant harm; and
> (b) that the harm, or likelihood of harm, is attributable to –
> (i) the care given to the child, or likely to be given to him if the order were not made, not being what it would be reasonable to expect a parent to give to him; or
> (ii) the child's being beyond parental control.
>
> (3) No care order or supervision order may be made with respect to a child who has reached the age of seventeen (or sixteen, in the case of a child who is married).'

**2.49** An application for a care order or supervision order can only be made by a local authority or authorised person, identified in s 31(9) of the CA 1989 as the NSPCC or any other person authorised by order of the Secretary of State.

**2.50** In practice, it is rare for any authorised person other than a local authority to issue proceedings under s 31. In the event that an authorised person does make an application, the order will designate a local authority to take the child into their care, as long as the local authority had notice of the

---

[34] *Re W (Direct Contact)* [2012] EWCA Civ 999 at [74], [76].

application.[35] See chapter 14 for a full discussion of interim care orders. The CA 1989 also sets out the duties of a local authority in relation to children residing in their area, including duties to assess families,[36] which is dealt with fully in chapter 5.

## Care orders

**2.51** Section 33(1) of the CA 1989 provides:

> 'Where a care order is made with respect to a child it shall be the duty of the local authority designated by the order to receive the child into their care and to keep him in their care while the order remains in force.'

**2.52** A care order confers parental responsibility for the child to the local authority in whose favour it is made. Section 33(3) provides:

> 'While a care order is in force with respect to a child, the local authority designated by the order shall –
> 
> (a) have parental responsibility for the child; and
> (b) have the power (subject to the following provisions of this section) to determine the extent to which –
>   (i) a parent, guardian or special guardian of the child; or
>   (ii) a person who by virtue of section 4A has parental responsibility for the child, may meet his parental responsibility for him.'

**2.53** Under a care order, the local authority shares parental responsibility with the parents, but can exercise its parental responsibility unilaterally and without the agreement of the parents. It is under this order that the local authority is able to remove children from the care of their parents without parental consent.[37] In all other circumstances, a child cannot be removed from the care of their parents without parental consent or by virtue of an order of the court.

**2.54** The local authority can only exercise its parental responsibility if they are satisfied that it is necessary in order to safeguard the child or to promote the child's welfare.[38]

**2.55** When a care order is made, it will last until the child reaches the age of 18 unless it is discharged earlier by another order of the court,[39] or as a result of a placement order being made.[40]

---

[35] CA 1989, s 33(2).
[36] *CA 1989, Part III: Support for Children and Families Provided by Local Authorities in England.*
[37] A local authority is also able to remove a child under an emergency protection order considered in chapter 9.
[38] CA 1989, s 33(4).
[39] CA 1989, s 39.
[40] ACA 2002, s 21.

**2.56** During the course of the care proceedings, the court is able to make an interim care order to deal with the interim position of the child. Section 38(1) of the CA 1989 provides:

'Where –

(a) in any proceedings on an application for a care order or supervision order, the proceedings are adjourned; or

(b) the court gives a direction under section 37(1),

the court may make an interim care order or an interim supervision order with respect to the child concerned.'

**2.57** The grounds that must be established before the court can make a care order or interim care order are considered later in this book at chapter 14, in relation to interim orders, and chapter 21, in relation to final orders.

## Supervision order

**2.58** Section 35 of the CA 1989 provides:

'While a supervision order is in force it shall be the duty of the supervisor –

(a) to advise, assist and befriend the supervised child;

(b) to take such steps as are reasonably necessary to give effect to the order;

(c) where –

   (i) the order is not wholly complied with; or

   (ii) the supervisor considers that the order may no longer be necessary

to consider whether or not to apply to the court for its variation or discharge.'

**2.59** Unlike a care order, a supervision order does not confer parental responsibility on the local authority. It does however impose a duty upon the local authority to 'advise, assist and befriend' the child who is the subject of the order.

**2.60** When a court makes a supervision order it will cease one year after the making of the order[41] although the court can also set a term of less than one year.[42] Whilst an application can be made to extend a supervision order prior to the end of the original order,[43] it cannot be extended for a period exceeding three years from the date on which the first order was made.[44] In the event that the local authority wishes to extend a supervision order beyond three years from the original order, a fresh application must be made.

**2.61** Like a care order, the court is able to make an interim supervision order during proceedings prior to making a final determination.[45]

---

[41] CA 1989, Sch 3, para 6(1).
[42] M v Warwickshire County Council [1994] 2 FLR 593.
[43] CA 1989, Sch 3, para 6(3).
[44] CA 1989, Sch 3, para 6(4).
[45] CA 1989, s 38(1).

**2.62** The basis upon which the court is able to make a supervision order or interim supervision order is further explored later at chapter 14.

## Special guardianship order

**2.63** The CA 1989 was amended by the ACA 2002 to introduce special guardianship orders, appointing one or more individuals to act as a 'special guardian' for a child.[46] Any person may apply to be a special guardian as long as they are over 18 years of age and not a parent of the child.[47] Certain people will need to leave from the court before they can apply for a special guardianship order, which is considered further at chapter 27.

**2.64** In the event that an individual is appointed a special guardian for a child, they acquire parental responsibility for that child. A special guardian shares parental responsibility with the other holders, but, as per s 14C(1)(b) of the CA 1989:

> 'Subject to any other order in force with respect to the child under this Act, a special guardian is entitled to exercise parental responsibility to the exclusion of any other person with parental responsibility for the child (apart from another special guardian).'

**2.65** The local authority must be provided with 3 months' notice of any application before a special guardianship order can be made.[48] Upon being put on notice, they must then undertake an assessment of the applicants and file a report with the court.[49] Without a special guardianship report as set out in s 14A(8) of the CA 1989 a special guardianship order cannot be made.

**2.66** Once made, a special guardianship order attracts support services from the local authority to assist the special guardians with the care of the child. The need for support services, including financial services, must be assessed in the report.[50]

**2.67** A special guardianship order is a permanent order, which will last until a child reaches the age of 18 unless discharged sooner. Unlike the other orders discussed in this section, in the event that a parent wishes to discharge a special guardianship order, they must first apply for permission from the court to do so.[51]

**2.68** The impact of the order upon the parental responsibility of a parent, and the fact that a parent must obtain permission before applying to discharge a special guardianship order, demonstrates its strength. The intention of the

---

[46] CA 1989, s 14A(1).
[47] CA 1989, s 14A(2).
[48] CA 1989, s 14A(8).
[49] A local authority may also commission a report to be undertaken on their behalf under CA 1989, s 14A(10).
[50] CA 1989, s 14F.
[51] CA 1989, s 14D(3).

legislators when drafting this order was to provide a middle ground between adoption and a residence order. It has been designed to enable more children to have permanent placements arranged to promote their welfare whilst they transition into adulthood, and so should be viewed as a permanent solution for the child. Full discussion in relation to special guardianship orders can be found at chapter 27.

## Family assistance order

**2.69** Section 16 of the CA 1989 provides the court to make a family assistance order, appointing a Cafcass officer or the local authority to 'advise, assist and (where appropriate) befriend any person named in the order'.[52] A family assistance order can only be made in conjunction with another order, usually a s 8 order (discussed below). Section 16(1) of the CA 1989 provides:

> 'Where, in any family proceedings, the court has power to make an order under this Part with respect to any child, it may (whether or not it makes such an order) make an order requiring –
> 
> (a) an officer of the Service or a Welsh family proceedings officer to be made available, or
> (b) a local authority to make an officer of the authority available,
> 
> to advise, assist and (where appropriate) befriend any person named in the order.'

**2.70** The wording used to describe the requirements of the local authority or Cafcass officer under a family assistance order is similar to that of a supervision order discussed above. However, it is not necessary to establish that there is any 'harm' envisaged in relation to the child as per a supervision order. Instead, the consent of all of the parties named in the order (which will normally include all parties with parental responsibility), other than the child, is required.[53] Whilst under a supervision order it is only the child that can be named as a person to be assisted, under a family assistance order it is possible to name the child's parent, guardian, special guardian, a person with whom the child lives or spends time with as well as the child themselves.[54]

**2.71** This is an underused order, not least because neither the FPR 2010[55] nor statute make provision for an application for a family assistance order to be made, so the court is usually left to make an order of its own motion as and when it sees fit. A local authority can only be nominated in the order if they agree, and if the child lives or will live in their area.[56] Moreover, PD12M

---

[52] CA 1989, s 16(1).
[53] CA 1989, s 16(3).
[54] CA 1989, s 16(2).
[55] FPR 2010, PD12M.
[56] CA 1989, s 16(7).

requires the opinion of the appropriate officer as to whether such an order would be in the interests of the child,[57] although their opinion is not always determinative.[58]

**2.72** In the event that any person to be named in the order, save for the child, does not provide their consent, the order cannot be made.

**2.73** Section 7 reports (completed by Cafcass or the local authority within private law proceedings) may recommend a family assistance order be made alongside a child arrangements order to enable the family to be supported for a specified period of time. Provision for this can be found in s 16(4A) of the CA 1989:

> 'If the court makes a family assistance order with respect to a child and the order is to be in force at the same time as a contact provision contained in a child arrangement order made with respect to the child, the family assistance order may direct the officer concerned to give advice and assistance as regards establishing, improving and maintaining contact to such of the person named in the order as may be specified in the order.'

A family assistance order is a short term order that lasts for no more than 12 months.[59]

## Section 8 orders

**2.74** When relationships break down and parents separate, the court is often asked to intervene in any disputes concerning with whom the child shall live, with whom the child shall otherwise spend time with and specific issues such as their schooling, holidays outside the jurisdiction and a raft of other decisions that are central to raising a child.

**2.75** Section 8(1) of the CA 1989 provides for a variety of orders to be made under the new, child arrangements programme:

> 'In this Act –
>
> > "child arrangements order" means an order regulating arrangements relating to any of the following;
> > (a) with whom a child is to live, spend time or otherwise have contact, and
> > (b) when a child is to live, spend time or otherwise have contact with any person;
> >
> > "a prohibited steps order" means an order that no step which could be taken by a parent in meeting his parental responsibility for a child, and which is of a kind specified in the order, shall be taken by any person without the consent of the court;

---

[57] FPR 2010, PD12M, para 1.2.
[58] *Re P (Children)* [2015] EWCA Civ 466.
[59] CA 1989, s 16(5).

"a specific issue order" means an order giving directions for the purpose of determining a specific question which has arisen, or which may arise, in connection with any aspect of parental responsibility for a child.'

**2.76** As the making of a child arrangements order concerns private disputes between parents, it does not normally require the involvement of the local authority. The local authority may continue to assist in the background under its usual statutory duties, but will not be a party to the order. In the event a family assistance order is recommended, the local authority may be contacted as the 'appropriate officer' and would have to consent to being nominated before the family assistance order can be made. A court may order a s 37 report if, within the private law proceedings, it begins to have concerns about the child's welfare.

**2.77** The court can specify where a child is to live and what time a child will spend with the other holders of parental responsibility. In the event that a child arrangements order is made specifying that the child should live with a person who does not have parental responsibility for the child, they shall acquire parental responsibility for as long as the child resides with them.[60]

**2.78** A prohibited steps order enables the court to prevent a holder of parental responsibility from exercising it in relation to a specific matter, whereas a specific issue order ensures that a holder of parental reasonability acts in a certain way. These orders are commonly required following disputes relating to religious, educational and medical decisions and can also be utilised when there is a dispute as to where a child should reside with one parent, especially when considering the removal of a child from the jurisdiction.

---

[60] CA 1989, s 12(2).

# CHAPTER 3

# JURISDICTION

## WITH WHICH CHILDREN AND FAMILIES ARE THE ENGLAND AND WALES SYSTEM CONCERNED?

**3.1** Consideration must be given at the earliest opportunity as to whether the English and Welsh court system has jurisdiction to deal with families from another country.[1] This is a very fast moving area requiring careful consideration from local authorities, even pre-proceedings, as to whether to issue proceedings to resolve any potential jurisdictional matters arising.

**3.2** The first step is understanding the international regulations and conventions in play when determining issues relating to jurisdiction.

**3.3** The European Council Regulation Brussels II Revised ('BIIR')[2] applies when the court is considering any orders relating to parental responsibility regarding families from EU countries, as listed in fig 1 below.[3] The UK is also a contracting state of the 1996 Hague Convention on Parental Responsibility (the '1996 Convention')[4] which reflects the provisions in BIIR and aims to improve the protection of children in international situations by avoiding conflict between different legal systems (fig 2).

**3.4** As is clear from the tables below, a number of countries are party to both treaties.

*Fig 1: members of the EU[5]*

| Austria | Bulgaria |
|---------|----------|
| Belgium | Croatia  |

---

[1] *Re J (A Child: Brussels II Revised: Art 15 – Practice Procedure)* [2014] EWFC 41.
[2] European Council Regulation No 2201/2003 concerning jurisdiction and the recognition and enforcement of judgments in matrimonial matters and the matters of parental responsibility.
[3] For the avoidance of doubt, the UK will remain in the European Union until the UK's exit has been negotiated. This is unlikely to happen before December 2018.
[4] Convention of 19 October 1996 on Jurisdiction, Applicable Law, Recognition, Enforcement and Co-operation in Respect of Parental Responsibility and Measures for the Protection of Children.
[5] List of member states correct as at August 2016.

| | |
|---|---|
| Cyprus | Luxemburg |
| Czech Republic | Malta |
| Denmark | Netherlands |
| Estonia | Poland |
| Finland | Portugal |
| France | Romania |
| Germany | Slovakia |
| Greece | Slovenia |
| Hungary | Spain |
| Ireland | Sweden |
| Lithuania | United Kingdom |

Fig 2: contracting countries to the 1996 Convention[6]

| | |
|---|---|
| Albania | France |
| Argentina | Georgia |
| Armenia | Germany |
| Australia | Hungary |
| Austria | Ireland |
| Belgium | Italy |
| Croatia | Latvia |
| Cyprus | Lithuania |
| Czech Republic | Luxembourg |
| Denmark | Malta |
| Ecuador | Monaco |
| Estonia | Montenegro |
| Finland | Morocco |

---

[6] List of contracting countries correct as at August 2016.

| | |
|---|---|
| Netherlands | Spain |
| Norway | Sweden |
| Poland | Switzerland |
| Portugal | Ukraine |
| Romania | United Kingdom and Northern Ireland |
| Russian Federation | United States of America |
| Serbia | Uruguay |
| Slovakia | |
| Slovenia | |

**3.5** As long as the UK is still an EU Member State, the court system is bound by the provisions in BIIR when considering its jurisdiction in matters relating to parental responsibility. In the event the family is connected to a country which is not an EU Member State, but is a signatory to the 1996 Convention, the 1996 Convention that will apply. In the event that the family is connected to a country which is neither a member of the EU nor a signatory to the 1996 Convention, BIIR will still apply.[7]

**3.6** Care proceedings fall within the scope of Art 1(1)(b) BIIR and placement order proceedings fall within the scope of Art 1(3)(b) BIIR. An application for an adoption order does not fall within the scope of BIIR.

## The practicalities of considering jurisdiction at an early stage

**3.7** Jurisdiction should be at the forefront of the minds of all professionals when working with a family from another country, or with a child who has a link to another country. As a matter of practicality, it should become second nature to consider the cultural and linguistic implications of working with such families. Interpreters should be used when communicating with the family and important documents should be translated as soon as possible to ensure that the family are able to fully engage with the allocated social worker and the process as a whole.[8]

**3.8** Consideration should also be given as to whether contact should be made with the authorities of the other countries involved at an early stage. Such contact serves two functions: both to put the other country on notice that there are concerns regarding a family with a connection there; and to gather information relating to the family which can often be invaluable. The UK

---

[7] Reiterated in *B (A Child), Re* [2016] UKSC 4.
[8] *Re N (Children: Adoption: Jurisdiction)* [2015] EWCA Civ 1112.

government has issued departmental guidance for local authorities on BIIR and the 1996 Convention in order to assist cross-border working.[9]

## Pre-proceedings: sharing information

**3.9** Article 55 of BIIR provides for the cooperation between Member States on cases concerning parental responsibility by way of sharing information. There is a similar provision contained in Art 34 of the 1996 Convention. Article 55(a) of BIIR provides:

> 'The central authorities shall, upon request from a central authority of another Member State or from a holder of parental responsibility, cooperate on specific cases to achieve the purpose of this Regulation. To this end, they shall, acting directly or through public authorities or other bodies, take all appropriate steps in accordance with the law of that member State in matters of personal data protection to:
>
> (a) collect and exchange information:
> (i) in the situation of the child;
> (ii) on any procedures under way; or
> (iii) on decisions taken concerning the child.'

**3.10** The central authority in the UK is the International Child Abduction and Contact Unit ('ICACU').[10] ICACU is a small administrative office that can assist with the liaison with other central authorities and in particular, with the sharing and exchange of information. They can only assist with EU and 1996 Convention countries. In the event that the family is from a country that does not come under BIIR or the 1996 Convention, the embassy of the relevant country should be contacted.

**3.11** This obligation to share information works both ways and UK authorities and the courts must be prepared to be open and exchange information when requested to do so. This was emphasised by the President in *Re E (A Child)*:[11]

> 'As I have observed, the process envisaged by Article 55 works both ways. The English courts must be assiduous in providing, speedily and without reservation, information sought by the Central Authority of another Member State. At the same time judges will wish to make appropriate use of this channel of communication to obtain information from the other Member State wherever this may assist them in deciding a care case with a European dimension.'

This 'good practice' guidance applies to the local authority as well as the court.

---

[9] *Cross-border child protection cases: the 1996 Hague Convention* (October 2012, Department of Education); *Working with foreign authorities: child protection and court orders* (September 2014, Department of Education); for Wales: *Handling cross-border child protection cases*, published by the Welsh Government.
[10] Contact details for the ICACU are: Official Solicitor, Victory House, 30–34 Kingsway, London, WC2B 6EX, Tel: (International Child Abduction Unit) 020 3681 2608, DX: 141423 Bloomsbury 7, Fax: 020 3681 2762.
[11] *Re E (A Child)* [2014] EWHC 6 (Fam) at [37].

## At the commencement of proceedings

**3.12** When care proceedings are issued, the court must consider jurisdiction at the first available opportunity. In the matter of *Re E (A Child)* the President set out the following requirements for any judgments and orders dealing with cases with a European dimension:[12]

> 'It is highly desirable, and from now on good practice will require, that in any care or other public law case with a European dimension the court should set out quite explicitly, both in its judgment and in its order:
>
> i) the basis upon which, in accordance with the relevant provisions of BIIR, it is, as the case may be, either accepting or rejecting jurisdiction;
> ii) the basis upon which, in accordance with Article 15, it either has or, as the case may be, has not decided to exercise its powers under Article 15.'

**3.13** The different articles of BIIR are considered below, but *Re E* sets out very helpfully what considerations the court must have at the first opportunity in order to decide whether it has jurisdiction or whether the case should be transferred to another jurisdiction. The UK is one of very few jurisdictions that allows children to be adopted without parental consent which has concerned central authorities from other jurisdictions and generated a great deal of debate as to whether the UK court should have jurisdiction in proceedings which could result in adoption without parental consent.[13]

**3.14** The necessity to address the issue of jurisdiction head on was further reiterated by Pauffley J in *Re J (A Child: Brussels II Revised: Art 15 – Practice and Procedure)*. Pauffley J warned that:[14]

> 'They should be regarded as urgent and requiring of decisions within a matter of days, not weeks. By no stretch of the imagination could it be regarded as acceptable practice to leave the jurisdiction question in 'cold storage' until the final hearing.'

Even if jurisdiction has not been raised by the parties, there is still an expectation that judges should consider jurisdictional issues if they consider them to be relevant.[15]

## Section 20 accommodation

**3.15** The arrangements and enquires that should be made before a child is accommodated under s 20 of the Children Act 1989 (the 'CA 1989') are discussed further at chapter 5, however, where there are jurisdictional issues, local authorities should commence proceedings expeditiously in line with the comments in *Leicester City Council v S*. This case concerned a child from

---

[12] *Re E (A Child)* [2014] EWHC 6 (Fam) at [35].
[13] See chapter 29 for further discussion.
[14] *Re J (A Child: Brussels II Revised: Art 15 – Practice and Procedure)* [2014] EWFC 41 at [45].
[15] *Re F (A Child)* [2014] EWCA Civ 789; *Re N (Adoption: Jurisdiction* [2016] 1 FLR 621.

Hungary who had been subject to a s 20 accommodation order for 6 months after being abandoned in the UK by his mother. When proceedings were finally issued, after the mother had returned to Hungary and after a further delay in considering the jurisdiction issues, Moylan J held:[16]

> 'Where is appears that jurisdiction (including under Article 15) is likely to be a substantive issue in relation to care proceedings, the local authority, absent very good reasons, should commence proceedings expeditiously so that a forum is available for such issues to be determined as early as possible in the child's life.'

## When does the court have jurisdiction?

**3.16** Section 3 of the Family Law Act 1986 provides for when the court can assume jurisdiction of a matter, but there is no reciprocal provision in the CA 1989. Instead, the courts must rely on the provisions contained in BIIR and the 1996 Convention for care and adoption proceedings.

**3.17** In accordance with both BIIR[17] and the 1996 Convention,[18] the starting point is that it is a child's place of habitual residence (and not their nationality) which determines which court has jurisdiction. This is echoed by the President in *Re M (Brussels II Revised: Art 15)*:[19]

> 'Jurisdiction is vested in the courts of the Member State where the child is habitually resident (Art 8), *not* the courts of the Member State of which the child is a national.'

**3.18** However, even if it is established that the child is habitually resident in the UK, it is still possible for a matter to be transferred to another jurisdiction if it is considered to be in the child's best interests to do so (see below for further discussion on transfer).[20]

**3.19** The BIIR regulations do not make specific reference to the law of Member States when considering the meaning of habitual residence under Arts 8 and 10. Art 8 of BIIR provides:

> '(1) The court of a Member State shall have jurisdiction in matters of parental responsibility over a child who is habitually residence in that Member State at the time the court is seised.
>
> (2) Paragraph 1 shall be subject to the provisions of Articles 9, 10 and 12.'

**3.20** Article 5 of the 1996 Convention provides:

> '(1) The judicial or administrative authorities of the Contracting State of the habitual residence of the child have jurisdiction to take measures directed to the protection of the child's person or property.

---

[16] *Leicester City Council v S* [2014] EWHC 1575 at [9].
[17] BIIR, Art 8.
[18] The 1996 Convention, Art 5.
[19] *Re M (Brussels II Revised: Art 15)* [2014] EWCA Civ 152, [2014] 2 FLR 1372 at [54].
[20] BIIR, Art 15; the 1996 Convention, Art 8.

(2) Subject to Article 7, in case of a change of the child's habitual residence to another Contracting State, the authorities of the State of the new habitual residence have jurisdiction.'

**3.21** It is clear therefore, that establishing a child's habitual residence is the key to unlocking the jurisdiction of the court for the purposes of any application under the CA 1989 and the ACA 2002.

## Habitual residence

**3.22** There is no statutory definition of habitual residence, instead it has fallen to the courts to establish its parameters through case law. The body of case law that has developed on habitual residence is invaluable when determining such an issue in care and adoption proceedings.

**3.23** The question of a child's habitual residence was considered extensively by Lady Hale in *A v A (Children: Habitual Residence)* which remains clear guidance on the matter:[21]

> 'i) All are agreed that habitual residence is a question of fact and not a legal concept such as domicile. There is no legal rule akin to that whereby a child automatically takes the domicile of his parents.
>
> ii) It was the purpose of the 1986 Act to adopt a concept which was the same as that adopted in The Hague and European Conventions. The Regulation must also be interpreted consistently with those Conventions.
>
> iii) The test adopted by the European Court is "the place which reflects some degree of integration by the child in a social and family environment" in the country concerned. This depends upon numerous factors, including the reasons for the family's stay in the country in question.
>
> iv) It is now unlikely that that test would produce any different results from that hitherto adopted in the English courts under the 1986 Act and The Hague Child Abduction Convention.
>
> v) In my view, the test adopted by the European Court is preferable to that earlier adopted by the English courts, being focused on the situation of the child, with the purposes and intentions of the parents being merely one of the relevant factors. The test derived from *R v Barnet London Borough Council, ex p Shah* should be abandoned when deciding the habitual residence of a child.
>
> vi) The social and family environment of an infant or young child is shared with those (whether parents or others) upon whom he is dependent. Hence it is necessary to assess the integration of that person or persons in the social and family environment of the country concerned.

---

[21] *A v A (Children: Habitual Residence)* [2013] UKSC 60 at [54].

vii) The essentially factual and individual nature of the inquiry should not be glossed with legal concepts which would produce a different result from that which the factual inquiry would produce.

viii) As the Advocate General pointed out in para AG45 and the court confirmed in para 43 of Proceedings brought by A, it is possible that a child may have no country of habitual residence at a particular point in time.'

**3.24** As is clear from Lady Hale's guidance: habitual residence is a question of fact and reflects some degree of integration by the child in a social and family environment (including the reasons for the family's stay in the country). It does not rest on the purposes and intentions of the parents, although they may be a factor and it may be necessary to assess the integration of parents when the child is young. There should be no gloss on the factual nature of the enquiry, and it may be the case that a child has no country of habitual residence at a particular point in time.

**3.25** Lady Hale's guidance was developed further by Lord Wilson (for the majority) in the Supreme Court in *Re B (A Child)*, who introduced three 'expectations' on the gain and loss of habitual residence:[22]

'The identification of a child's habitual residence is overarchingly a question of fact. In making the following three suggestions about the point at which habitual residence might be lost and gained, I offer not sub-rules but expectations which the fact-finder may well find to be unfulfilled in the case before him:

(a) the deeper the child's integration in the old state, probably the less fast his achievement of the requisite degree of integration in the new state;
(b) the greater the amount of adult pre-planning of the move, including pre-arrangements for the child's day-to-day life in the new state, probably the faster his achievement of that requisite degree; and
(c) were all the central members of the child's life in the old state to have moved with him, probably the faster his achievement of it and, conversely, were any of them to have remained behind and thus to represent for him a continuing link with the old state, probably the less fast his achievement of it.'

**3.26** A child's habitual residence is not necessarily tied to that of their parents, although it does require a degree of stability beyond merely their 'intention or decision' regarding their residence. This was emphasised by Lady Hale in the matter of *Re LC (Reunite: International Child Abduction Centre Intervening)* who was keen to emphasise that habitual residence is a question of the 'quality' of a child's residence:[23]

'In the case of these three children, as of others, the question is the quality of their residence, in which all sorts of factors may be relevant. Some of these are objective: how long were they there, what were their living conditions while there, were they

---

[22] *Re B (A Child)* [2016] UKSC 4 at [46].
[23] *Re LC (Reunite: International Child Abduction Centre Intervening)* [2014] UKSC 1, [2014] 1 FLR 1486 at [60].

at school or at work, and so on? But subjective factors are also relevant: what was the reason for their being there, and what were their perceptions about being there? I agree with Lord Wilson (para 37) that "wishes", "views", "intentions" and "decisions" are not the right words, whether we are considering the habitual residence of a child or indeed an adult. It is better to think in terms of the reasons why a person is in a particular place and his or her perception of the situation while there – their state of mind. All of these factors feed into the essential question, which is whether the child has achieved a sufficient degree of integration into a social and family environment in the country in question for his or her residence there to be termed "habitual".'

**3.27** There is no 'rule' that where one parent has unilaterally relocated a child without the consent of the other, then the child remains habitually resident at the first country, as confirmed by Black LJ in *Re H*, considering Supreme Court jurisprudence on the matter:[24]

'Given the Supreme Court's clear emphasis that habitual residence is essentially a factual question and its distaste for subsidiary rules about it, and given that the parties' purpose and intention in any event play a part in the factual enquiry, I would now consign the "rule", whether it was truly a binding rule or whether it was just a well-established method of approaching cases, to history in favour of a factual enquiry tailored to the circumstances of the individual case.'

**3.28** In the event that an application is made by a parent for the return of a child, wrongfully removed under the Hague Convention 1980[25] this matter will need to be dealt with prior to the court's jurisdiction determination within care proceedings.[26]

**3.29** As is clear from the case law discussed above, whether the child is habitually resident in the UK is a question of fact, 'not a legal concept'.[27] The integration of the child into the family and social environment needs to be assessed in light of the stability of the child's circumstances and the reasons for the change of residence. The focus should be on the habitual residence of the child alone, which will not necessarily follow a parent's change of residence. There must be careful analysis of all of the child's circumstances before a deciding that a child is habitually resident in the UK. Evidently all cases will hinge on their own, unique facts and circumstances.

**3.30** Once all of the facts have been considered, it is possible that a child is no longer habitually resident in their country of origin *but* have not acquired habitual residence in another jurisdiction. In light of the comments of

---

[24] *Re H* [2014] EWCA Civ 1011 [34], considering *A v A* [2013] UKSC 60, *Re L (A Child: Custody: Habitual Residence)* [2013] UKSC 75 and *Re LC (Children)* [2014] UKSC 1.
[25] Convention of 25 October 1980 on the Civil Aspects of International Child Abduction.
[26] *Kent County Council v C & Others* [2014] EWHC 604 (Fam).
[27] *A v A (Children: Habitual Residence)* [2013] UKSC 60 at [54].

Lord Wilson in *Re B (A Child) [2016]*, the potential for this is slim, but nevertheless possible. In such situations, Art 13 of BIIR[28] provides:[29]

> '(1) Where a child's habitual residence cannot be established and jurisdiction cannot be determined on the basis of Article 12, the courts of the Member State where the child is present shall have jurisdiction.
>
> (2) Paragraph 1 shall also apply to refugee children or children internationally displaced because of disturbances occurring in their country.'

**3.31** In the event that urgent action is necessary and the child is in the country (although not within the jurisdiction of the court), Art 20 of BIIR stipulates:[30]

> 'In urgent cases, the provisions of this Regulation shall not prevent the court of a Member State from taking such provisional, including protective, measures in respect of persons or assets in that State as may be available under the law of that Member State, even if, under this Regulation, the court of another Member State has jurisdiction as to the substance of the matter.'

**3.32** This provision enables the court to assume jurisdiction of the matter to ensure that protective measures can be taken to safeguard a child. The substantive questions as to jurisdiction and habitual residence must then be dealt with as soon as possible thereafter.

## When the child is not present in the jurisdiction at the time of issue

**3.33** In the event that a child has been removed from the UK prior to the application for a care or supervision order, the court will only have jurisdiction if it can be established that the child was habitually resident at the point when the court was first seised with the application.

**3.34** If there is any uncertainty as to the child's habitual residence, this must be dealt with first and prior to the making of any order. Without both parents taking part in this element of the hearing and providing instructions as to their positions on habitual residence, the court cannot consider it.

**3.35** This issue was considered in *Bridgend County Borough Council v GM & Anor*[31] which considered the situation where a child had been born in Spain after its parents had fled the UK upon learning that the local authority intended to issue proceedings upon the baby's birth. Consideration was given as to whether the UK had jurisdiction to make any orders following the removal of the child from Spain back to the UK as a result of collaboration between the relevant authorities. Although the child had never been resident here, the Spanish court had transferred the case to the UK under Art 15 at the request of

---

[28] The equivalent provision in the 1996 Convention can be found in Art 6. Applications under this provision must be made in the High Court.
[29] Article 12 of BIIR applies when the holders of parental responsibility expressly and unequivocally accept the jurisdiction of the court seised.
[30] There is a similar provision in Art 11 of the 1996 Convention.
[31] *Bridgend County Borough Council v GM & Anor* [2012] EWHC 3118 (Fam).

Hedley J at an earlier stage. When determining the issue of habitual residence upon the local authority's subsequent application for a care order, Moore J considered the case of *Re A (Area of Freedom, Security and Justice)* (C-523 of 2007) in which the European Court of Justice held that:[32]

> '(38) **In addition to the physical presence of the child in a Member State** other factors must be chosen which are capable of showing that that presence is not in any way temporary or intermittent and that the residence of the child reflects some degree of integration in a social and family environment.'

**3.36** Moore J was clear that the parents' initial move to Spain was not unlawful, but that the mother (the father did not hold parental responsibility at this time) was not habitually resident in Spain and neither was the child. However, he declined to make a finding that the mother was habitually resident in the UK either and concluded that the child was not habitually resident in either jurisdiction. He concluded:[33]

> 'Having said all that, I accept Mr. Tillyard's submission that to establish jurisdiction the child must be present at the time the proceedings were issued. In this case the proceedings were issued one day before SA arrived here. It follows that I find the current proceedings are flawed. The local authority must issue fresh proceedings.'

## *Transfer to another jurisdiction*

**3.37** In the event it is established that the UK court does have jurisdiction, it is still possible for the case, or part of the case, to be transferred to another jurisdiction the child has a connection with under Art 15 of BIIR or Art 8 of the 1996 Convention.

**3.38** This is another matter that the court must consider even if not raised by the parties.[34] In accordance with President's observations in *Re E*,[35] in every case where there is a jurisdictional dimension, consideration must be given as to whether the matter would be better heard in the other jurisdiction. Article 15 of BIIR applies to care proceedings (even if the local authority care plan is for adoption), but not to proceedings for a placement order.[36]

**3.39** In the matter of *Re J (A Child: Brussels II Revised: Art 15 – Practice and Procedure)*, Pauffley J stated:[37]

---

[32] Ibid at [26], emphasis added.
[33] Ibid at [45].
[34] *Re F (A Child)* [2014] EWCA Civ 789; *Re N (Adoption: Jurisdiction)* [2016] 1 FLR 621.
[35] *Re E (A Child)* [2014] EWHC 6 (Fam).
[36] *N (Children) (Adoption: Jurisdiction)* [2015] EWCA Civ 1112 at [66]–[73].
[37] *Re J (A Child: Brussels II Revised: Art 15 – Practice and Procedure)* [2014] EWFC 41 at [19].

'It is not permissible for this court to abrogate its decision making responsibility under Article 15 to the courts or Central Authority of another Member State. Irrespective of the answers to the questions posed, it was and is for the English court to grasp the Article 15 nettle.'

**3.40** She also emphasised that:[38]

'Although an Article 15 request may be made at any stage in the proceedings (see *Bush v Bush* [2008] 2 FLR 1437; and *Re T (Brussels II Revised, Article 15)* [2014] 1 FLR 749) it must be overwhelmingly more efficient and accord with the welfare interests of children, for jurisdictional decision making to occur, as a matter of priority, during the initial stages of the proceedings.'

**3.41** Article 15 requires the court to conduct a straightforward evaluation of the circumstances of the case. It is not an investigation into the merits of the case but sets out the provisions for when and how a matter can transfer to another jurisdiction. Article 15(1) provides:

'1. By way of exception, the courts of a Member State having jurisdiction as to the substance of the matter may, if they consider that a court of another Member State, with which the child has a particular connection, would be better placed to hear the case, or a specific part therefore, and where this is in the best interests of the child;

(a) stay the case or the part thereof in question and invite the parties to introduce a request before the court of that other Member State in accordance with paragraph 4; or
(b) request a court of another Member State to assume jurisdiction in accordance with paragraph 5.'

**3.42** Decisions on transfer under Art 15 must be dealt with prior to the substantive issue being determined,[39] along with consideration as to which tier of court that should deal with the matter. District judges may decide that the matter should be transferred to a circuit judge or to the High Court. The designated family judge will assist with this decision and any transfer to another tier of the court will need to be considered within the usual provisions in the Family Procedure Rules.[40]

**3.43** Munby J, as he then was, in *AB v JLB (Brussels II Revised: Article 15)*[41] identified three questions to be answered when making a decision under Art 15:

'(1) Does the child have, within the meaning of Article 15(3), 'a particular connection' with another Member State?
(2) Would the court of that other Member State 'be better placed to hear the case, or a specific part thereof'?
(3) Will a transfer to the other court be 'in the best interests of the child?'

---

[38] *Re J (A Child: Brussels II Revised: Art 15 – Practice and Procedure)* [2014] EWFC 41 at [36].
[39] *Re T (A Child: Article 15 of Brussels II Revised)* [2014] 1 FLR 749.
[40] *Re J (A Child: Brussels II Revised: Art 15 – Practice and Procedure)* [2014] EWFC 41.
[41] *AB v JLB (Brussels II Revised: Article 15)* [2009] 1 FLR 517.

**3.44** In a subsequent judgment, he confirmed that all three must be answered in the affirmative in order for the matter to be transferred to another jurisdiction[42] and emphasised what was said in *Re J and E (Children: Brussels II Revised: Article 15)*[43] that:[44]

> 'In framing these questions I have deliberately tracked the language of Article 15. The language of Article 15 is clear and simple. It requires no gloss. It is to be read without preconceptions or assumptions imported from our domestic law. In particular, and as this case demonstrates, it is unnecessary and potentially confusing to refer to the paramountcy of the child's interests. Judges should focus on the language of Article 15: will a transfer be "in the best interests of the child"? That is the relevant question, and that is the question which the judge should ask himself.'

**3.45** It is interesting to note that Munby J found it to be unnecessary and 'potentially confusing' to refer to the paramountcy of the child's interests in the context of an Art 15 decision. Instead the court should consider whether a transfer is in the best interests of the child as a separate and express question.

**3.46** Even if all questions are answered in the affirmative there remains a residual discretion in the English court on whether or not to make the transfer, as per Art 15(1)(a) or (b).[45] However, as per Munby J's comments, decisions not to make the transfer at this stage will be rare:[46]

> '[…] since the discretion is exercisable only if the court has satisfied itself both that the other court is 'better placed' to deal with the case … and that it is in the best interests of the child to transfer the case, it is not easy to envisage circumstances where, those two conditions having been met, it would nonetheless be appropriate not to transfer the case.'

**3.47** Munby's first question is one of fact: whether the child has a particular connection to another jurisdiction. Article 15(3) of BIIR provides:

> 'The child shall be considered to have a particular connection to a Member State as mentioned in paragraph 1, if that Member State:
>
> (a) has become the habitual residence of the child after the court referred to in paragraph 1 was seised; or
> (b) is the former habitual residence of the child; or
> (c) is the place of the child's nationality; or
> (d) is the habitual residence of a holder of parental responsibility; or
> (e) is the place where property of the child is located and the case concerns measures for the protection of the child relating to the administration, conservation or disposal of this property.'

---

[42] *AB v JLB (Brussels II Revised: Article 15)* [2009] 1 FLR 517 at [37], confirmed in *N (Children) (Adoption: Jurisdiction)* [2015] EWCA Civ 1112 at [191].
[43] [2014] EWFC 45.
[44] *Re M (Brussels II Revised: Art 15)* [2014] EWCA Civ 152 at [54].
[45] *AB v JLB (Brussels II Revised: Article 15)* [2009] 1 FLR 517 at [36].
[46] *AB v JLB (Brussels II Revised: Article 15)* [2009] 1 FLR 517 at [36].

**3.48** Once a 'particular connection' has been established, the court will then consider whether the court in the connected jurisdiction would be better placed to consider the case, or part thereof. This is 'an exercise in evaluation, to be undertaken in the light of all the circumstances of the particular case'.[47] In conducting this evaluation, the starting point for the inquiry is the principle of comity. The judicial and social care arrangements in other Member States are to be treated by the courts in England and Wales as being equally competent. Ryder LJ neatly summarises the considerations in *Re M (Brussels II Revised: Art 15)*:[48]

> 'The question of whether a court of another relevant Member State would be better placed to hear the case (or a specific part of the case) is an evaluation to be performed on all the circumstances of the case. It is intimately connected with the question of the best interests of the child, given the construction of the regulation and the logical connection between the questions. That said, the starting point for the enquiry into the second question is the principle of comity and co-operation between Member States of the European Union enshrined in the European Union Treaty which the provisions of B2R were designed to reflect and implement (see, for example [2], [21] and [23] of the preamble to B2R). In particular, the judicial and social care arrangements in Member States are to be treated by the courts in England and Wales as being equally competent: *Re K (A Child)* [2013] EWCA Civ 895 at [24] per Thorpe LJ.'

**3.49** This approach was confirmed by the President in *Re N (Adoption: Jurisdiction)*, reiterating Ryder LJ's comments and emphasising what was held in *AB v JLB (Brussels II Revised: Article 15)*[49] (approved in *Re K (A Child)*[50]), and his own comments in *Re E*[51] that:[52]

> 'In relation to the second and third questions there is one point to be added. In determining whether the other court is "better placed to hear the case" and whether, if it is, a transfer will be "in the best interests of the child", it is not permissible for the court to enter into a comparison of such matters as the competence, diligence, resources or efficacy of either the child protection services or the courts of the other State.'

**3.50** The question must be limited to whether the court is better placed to deal with the case, or part thereof, and the President was clear that:[53]

> 'The question of whether the other court will have available to it the full list of options available to the English court – for example, the ability to order a non-consensual adoption – is simply not relevant to either the second or the third question. As Ryder LJ has explained, by reference to the decisions of the Supreme Court in *Re I* and of this court in *Re K*, the question asked by Article 15 is whether

---

[47] *AB v JLB (Brussels II Revised: Article 15)* [2009] 1 FLR 517 at [35].
[48] *Re M (Brussels II Revised: Art 15)* [2014] EWCA Civ 152 at [19].
[49] [2008] EWHC 2965 (Fam) [2009].
[50] [2013] EWCA Civ 895.
[51] [2014] EWHC 6 (Fam).
[52] *Re N (Adoption: Jurisdiction)* [2016] 1 FLR 621 at [22] and [113].
[53] *Re M (Brussels II Revised: Art 15)* [2014] EWCA Civ 152 at [54].

it is in the child's best interests for the case to be determined in another jurisdiction, and that is quite different from the substantive question in the proceedings, "what outcome to these proceedings will be in the best interests of the child?".'

**3.51** Ryder LJ set out a non-exhaustive list of some of the relevant considerations when looking at whether a matter might be better dealt with in another, connected jurisdiction:[54]

> 'It is entirely proper to enquire into questions of fact that might inform the court's evaluation of whether a court is better placed to hear a case. Without wishing to prescribe an exhaustive list, those facts might include the availability of witnesses of fact, whether assessments can be conducted and if so by whom (i.e. not a comparative analysis of welfare perceptions and principles but, for example, whether an assessor will have to travel to another jurisdiction to undertake an assessment and whether that is a lawful and/or professionally appropriate course), and whether one court's knowledge of the case provides an advantage, for example by judicial continuity between fact finding and evaluation and so on.'

**3.52** As discussed above, the third question as to whether it is in the child's best interest for the case to be dealt with in a connected jurisdiction, is closely linked to the question of whether the courts in that jurisdiction is better placed to hear the matter. Bearing in mind that reference does not need to be given to the paramountcy principal, the court must, as a separate question, consider whether transferring the matter to the connected jurisdiction is in the child's best interests. Ryder LJ states that:[55]

> 'In my judgment, there is no utility in trying to improve on the plain language of the Regulation. The autonomous meaning should not be limited or enlarged upon by the domestic concept of paramountcy or any other reference to national law unless that is express or implied in the language of the Regulation.'

**3.53** Answering the 'best interests' question should not include any consideration of the differences (if any) in the child protection services, procedures or possible orders available in the other jurisdiction. Nor should there be a full investigation as to the merits of the case at this stage since Art 15 transfer is a question of venue only and not the substantive issues in the case, as per Lady Hale in *I (A Child)*:[56]

> 'This question is quite different from the substantive question in the proceedings, which is "what outcome to these proceedings will be in the best interests of the child?" It will not depend upon a profound investigation of the child's situation and upbringing but upon the sort of considerations which come into play when deciding upon the most appropriate forum.'

---

[54] *Re M (Brussels II Revised: Art 15)* [2014] EWCA Civ 152 at [20].
[55] *Re M (Brussels II Revised: Art 15)* [2014] EWCA Civ 152 at [24].
[56] *I (A Child)* [2009] UKSC 10 at [36].

**3.54** In the event that the court decides to transfer the case, a request should be made promptly through the International Judicial Network and in accordance with Art 56(1) of BIIR if necessary. Article 56(1) provides:

> 'Where a court having jurisdiction under Articles 8 to 15 contemplates the placement of a child in institutional care or with a foster family and where such a placement is to take place in another Member State, it shall first consult the central authority or other authority having jurisdiction in the latter State where public authority intervention in that Member State is required for domestic cases of child placement.'

Article 56(2) states that a placement can only be made if the authority in the Member State consents to the placement.

**3.55** Article 15(4) and (5) provide:

> '(4) The Court of a Member State having jurisdiction as to the substance of the matter shall set a time limit by which the courts of that other Member State shall be seised in accordance with paragraph 1. If the courts are not seised by that time, the court which has been seised shall continue to exercise jurisdiction in accordance with Articles 8 to 14.
>
> (5) The courts of that other Member State may, where due to the specific circumstances of the case, this is in the best interests of the child, accept jurisdiction within 6 weeks of their seizure in accordance with paragraph 1(a) or 1(b). In this case, the court first seised shall decline jurisdiction. Otherwise, the court first seised shall continue to exercise jurisdiction in accordance with Articles 8 to 14.'

**3.56** Where a transfer request has been made under Art 15, a Member State can decline jurisdiction despite the determination of the UK court, or declare that it does not have jurisdiction under Art 17 of BIIR. This can only be done after a proper judicial process.

**3.57** A Member State court should not accept jurisdiction following a request unless it is satisfied that it is in the child's best interests for the matter to be determined there.

**3.58** In the event that the Member State that has received the request for transfer for the matter declines jurisdiction, the case will remain to be determined by the UK court.

# CHAPTER 4

# HUMAN RIGHTS CONSIDERATIONS

## HUMAN RIGHTS ACT 1998

**4.1** In these uncertain and changing times relating to the UK's membership of the EU, it is not surprising that questions are being raised as to whether the Human Rights Act 1998 ('HRA 1998') remains relevant. The HRA 1998 was enacted to reflect the rights protected by the European Convention for the Protection of Human Rights and Fundamental Freedoms ('ECHR' or 'the Convention') in UK law and has remained a key consideration throughout court proceedings relating to children. The HRA 1998 remains in force and will continue to be a prominent feature in proceedings relating to children until the law is repealed or changed in any way.

**4.2** HRA 1998 came into force on 2nd October 2000. This Act gave further effect to rights and freedoms guaranteed under the ECHR which, until the introduction of the HRA 1998, were not directly actionable in the UK. Prior to the enactment of the HRA 1998 courts would consider any tension between the Children Act 1989 ('CA 1989') and Convention rights.

**4.3** Section 2(1) provides:

'(1) A court or tribunal determining a question which has arisen in connection with a Convention right must take into account any –

(a) judgment, decision, declaration or advisory opinion of the European Court of Human Rights,
(b) opinion of the Commission given in a report adopted under Article 31 of the Convention,
(c) decision of the Commission in connection with Article 26 or 27(2) of the Convention, or
(d) decision of the Committee of Ministers taken under Article 46 of the Convention,

whenever made or given, so far as, in the opinion of the court or tribunal, it is relevant to the proceedings in which that question has arisen.'

**4.4** In the context of proceedings relating to children, the most relevant provisions in HRA 1998 are a right to liberty and security,[1] a right to a fair trial,[2] and a right to the respect for private and family life.[3] These provisions will be considered below.

**4.5** In accordance with s 6(1) of the HRA 1998:

'It is unlawful for a public authority to act in a way which is incompatible with a Convention right.'

**4.6** If it is believed that a right has been infringed by a public authority s 7(1) HRA 1998 provides:

'A person who claims that a public authority has acted (or proposes to act) in a way which is made unlawful by section 6(1) may –

(a) bring proceedings against the authority under this Act in the appropriate court or tribunal, or
(b) rely on the Convention right or rights concerned in any legal proceedings,

but only if he is (or would be) a victim of the unlawful act.'

**4.7** This chapter will concentrate of the issues relevant to proceedings relating to children, the court's consideration of the HRA 1998, and when and how proceedings can be issued regarding steps taken by the local authority.

## Right to liberty and security

**4.8** An action started in relation to the contravention of this right within family proceedings is commonly as a result of perceived deprivation of a child's liberty.

**4.9** HRA 1998, Sch 1 recites Art 5 of the ECHR and provides:

'1 Everyone has the right to liberty and security of person. No one shall be deprived of his liberty save in the following cases and in accordance with a procedure prescribed by law:

(a) the lawful detention of a person after conviction by a competent court;
(b) the lawful arrest or detention of a person for non-compliance with the lawful order of a court or in order to secure the fulfilment of any obligation prescribed by law;
(c) the lawful arrest or detention of a person effected for the purpose of bringing him before the competent legal authority on reasonable suspicion of having committed an offence or when it is reasonably considered necessary to prevent his committing an offence or fleeing after having done so;

---

[1] HRA 1998, Sch 1, Art 5.
[2] HRA 1998, Sch 1, Art 6.
[3] HRA 1998, Sch 1, Art 8.

(d) the detention of a minor by lawful order for the purpose of educational supervision or his lawful detention for the purpose of bringing him before the competent legal authority;

(e) the lawful detention of persons for the prevention of the spreading of infectious diseases, of persons of unsound mind, alcoholics or drug addicts or vagrants;

(f) the lawful arrest or detention of a person to prevent his effecting an unauthorised entry into the country or of a person against whom action is being taken with a view to deportation or extradition.'

**4.10** Actions taken in relation to matters relating to the deprivation of liberty are often issued in the Court of Protection relating to children and young people with disabilities. Consideration of the Court of Protection is outside the scope of this book, however, the question as to whether an action amounts to the deprivation of liberty has wider issues across family proceedings.

**4.11** The detention of a child or young person is only lawful if in accordance with statute. Local authorities are under a duty to consider whether any child in need, or looked-after child, is subject to restrictions amounting to a deprivation of liberty. This is especially relevant in relation to those in foster care or in a residential placement.[4]

**4.12** A deprivation of liberty will be lawful if provided for under statute, for example, under:

- section 25 of the Children Act 1989, which provides for the placement of looked-after children in secure accommodation;
- the Mental Health Act 1983;
- the youth remand provisions of the Legal Aid, Sentencing and Punishment of Offenders Act 2012; or
- the custodial sentencing provisions of the Power of Criminal Courts (Sentencing) Act 2000.

**4.13** The question as to whether there is a deprivation of liberty has three elements:[5]

(1) the objective element of a person's confinement to a certain limited place for a not negligible length of time;
(2) the additional subjective element that they had not validly consented to the confinement in question; and
(3) the confinement had to be imputable to the state.

**4.14** The case law considers situations where children and young people with disabilities are deprived of their liberty without lawful authority in foster homes, children's homes, care homes, residential special schools, boarding

---

[4] *A Local Authority v D & Ors* [2016] 1 WLR 1160.
[5] *Storck v Germany* (2006) 43 EHRR 6, ECtHR.

schools, further education colleges with residential accommodation, hospitals and elsewhere. The ramifications of the case law are relevant to matters relating to children placed in local authority care.

**4.15** In light of the three elements, it is not enough for a child to simply be placed in foster care or a children's home, the situation for the child within the placement is relevant. If the child is living a normal life in the placement, they are not confined. However, in a situation where it is considered that the circumstances for a child in a placement in which he lives amounts to a deprivation of his liberty as opposed to merely a restriction upon it are relevant.

**4.16** Following the decision in *Surrey County Council v P and Others, Cheshire West and Chester Council v P and Another*[6] the number of such applications rose. In this case the justices of the Supreme Court clarified the 'acid test' for determining whether the arrangements in place to safeguard a child amounted to a deprivation of liberty. This case has become known as the Cheshire West case and provides a two stage test:

(1) Is the person subject to continuous supervision and control?
(2) Is the person free to leave?

**4.17** For the test to be satisfied there must be all elements found. In relation to whether a person is free to leave a placement, the focus is not on the person's ability to express a desire to leave, but on what those with control over their care arrangements would do if they sought to leave.

**4.18** Furthermore, parental responsibility is important in terms of consent. A child can be accommodated with the consent of a holder of parental responsibility. The parent's consent renders the deprivation of liberty not imputable to the State. There has been a great deal of discussion in relation to this point in *Re D (A child)*.[7] In this case, the President clearly analysis the current case law in relation to the placement of children and deprivation of liberty.

**4.19** If a placement is identified as depriving a child or young person of their liberty, an application should be made to the court to sanction the deprivation of liberty of a child or young person. As mentioned above, deprivation of liberty will be lawful if enabled by statutory provision and the most common statutory provision in the family court is s 25 CA 1989, a secure accommodation order. If the placement is not under a secure accommodation order, an application must be made to the court to consider the deprivation of liberty and whether it is necessary to safeguard the child.

---

[6] *Surrey County Council v P and Others, Cheshire West and Chester Council v P and Another* [2014] UKSC 19, [2014] COPLR 313.
[7] [2017] EWCA Civ 1695.

## Right to a fair trial

**4.20** A Convention right that must, and is, considered by the court when dealing with family matters is the absolute right to a fair trial. In judgments handed down the court must confirm that it has had consideration to the preservation of this right when determining the matter before it.

**4.21** HRA 1998, Sch 1 recites Art 6 of the Convention and provides:

> 'In the determination of his civil rights and obligations or of any criminal charge against him, everyone is entitled to a fair and public hearing within a reasonable time by an independent and impartial tribunal established by law. Judgment shall be pronounced publicly but the press and public may be excluded from all or part of the trial in the interest of morals, public order or national security in a democratic society, where the interests of juveniles or the protection of the private life of the parties so require, or to the extent strictly necessary in the opinion of the court in special circumstances where publicity would prejudice the interests of justice.'

The core of this Convention right is the entitlement to 'a fair and public hearing within a reasonable time by an independent and impartial tribunal established by law'.

**4.22** The right to a fair trial is an absolute right, however, what is deemed to be 'fair' is open to consideration. This right is not defined by rigid rules of interpretation of what is 'fair' but rather something that is subject to the analysis of the facts themselves.

## *Fair and public hearing and the press*

**4.23** Taking the elements of the Convention one by one, the first entitlement is a fair and public hearing. The issue as to whether hearings within family proceedings should be open to the public and press has been much debated recently. The suggestion of 'secret' courts and the need for the family courts to become accountable to public scrutiny has been widely discussed attracting some very unpleasant press.

**4.24** The right to a public hearing is limited in the Convention with the wording providing for the press and public being excluded from all or part of the trial 'where the interests of juveniles or the protection of the private life of the parties so requires'. The need for the information that is heard within family proceedings to be kept confidential is a closely held view by some family practitioners in order to limit the impact upon the children involved in the proceedings.

**4.25** The question must be asked as to whether it is essential for family proceedings to be heard in public to ensure transparency and scrutiny of the decisions made. It is arguable that the decision that a child should be adopted without the consent of their parents is one of, if not the most, severe order that

54    *Child Protection Proceedings: Care and Adoption Orders*

can be made. Should the public be aware of the evidence before the court and the way in which the decision is reached? The full debate is outside the scope of this book, but the current situation so far as the rules of disclosure and communication of information are concerned is set out below.

**4.26** The rules governing the communication of information to a non-party to the proceedings is set out by r 12.73 of the Family Procedure Rules 2010 ('FPR 2010'). This rule provides:

> '**Communication of information: general**
>
> (1) For the purposes of the law relating to contempt of court, information relating to proceedings held in private (whether or not contained in a document filed with the court) may be communicated –
>
> > (a) where the communication is to –
> > (i) a party;
> > (ii) the legal representative of a party;
> > (iii) a professional legal adviser;
> > (iv) an officer of the service or a Welsh family proceedings officer;
> > (v) the welfare officer;
> > (vi) the Director of Legal Aid Casework (within the meaning of section 4 of the Legal Aid, Sentencing and Punishment of Offenders Act 2012);
> > (vii) an expert whose instruction by a party has been authorised by the court for the purposes of the proceedings;
> > (viii) a professional acting in furtherance of the protection of children;
> > (ix) an independent reviewing officer appointed in respect of a child who is, or has been, subject to proceedings to which this rule applies;
> > (b) where the court gives permission; or
> > (c) subject to any direction of the court, in accordance with rule 12.75 and Practice Direction 12G.
>
> (2) Nothing in this Chapter permits the communication to the public at large, or any section of the public, of any information relating to the proceedings.
>
> (3) Nothing in rule 12.75 and Practice Direction 12G permits the disclosure of an unapproved draft judgment handed down by any court.'

**4.27** The only people allowed into a hearing in a family matter is provided for in FPR 2010, r 27.11(2):

> '(2) When this rule applies, no person shall be present during any hearing other than –
>
> > (a) an officer of the court;
> > (b) a party to the proceedings;
> > (c) a litigation friend for any party, or legal representative instructed to act on that party's behalf;
> > (d) an officer of the service or Welsh family proceedings officer;
> > (e) a witness;
> > (f) duly accredited representatives of news gathering and reporting organisations; and

(g) any other person whom the court permits to be present.'

**4.28** FPR 2010, r 27.11 now allows for the attendance, during specified family proceedings, of accredited media representatives (and any other person whom the court permits to be present, but not the general public). At any stage of the proceedings the court may exclude a person from the proceedings if:[8]

'(a) this is necessary –
   (i) in the interests of any child concerned in, or connected with, the proceedings;
   (ii) for the safety or protection of a party, a witness in the proceedings, or a person connected with such a party or witness; or
   (iii) for the orderly conduct of the proceedings; or
(b) justice will otherwise be impeded or prejudiced.'

**4.29** In order for a judgment to be pronounced publically, it does not need to be delivered in public, it is enough for the judgment to be available. To this end, the President issued guidance on 16 January 2014 'Transparency in the family courts publications of judgments'. The President was clear that:

'there is a need for greater transparency in order to improve public understanding of the court process and confidence in the court system. At present too few judgments are made available to the public, which has a legitimate interest in being able to read what is being done by the judges in its name. The Guidance will have the effect of increasing the number of judgments available for publication (even if they will often need to be published in appropriately anonymised form).'

**4.30** Judgments are now frequently published in anonymised form so as to enable the decisions made by the family courts to be considered whilst maintaining the confidentiality of the details of the children and the family themselves.

## Within a reasonable time

**4.31** The CA 1989 has as one of its key provisions the 'no delay principle'. It is enshrined in the CA 1989 that there should be no delay in determining a question with respect to the upbringing of a child. Any delay by the local authority may attract an application on the basis of a fair trial. Within care proceedings being issued it is not possible for a court to have oversight of a situation and to determine the matter without delay.

**4.32** How parties behave once proceedings have been issued may also raise concerns as to whether there has been a fair trial. Failure to provide full and frank disclosure as well as failing to ensure that parties can adequately participate in proceedings also have an impact. In *Re L (Care: Assessment: Fair Trial)*[9] Munby J, as he then was, noted that the positive duty of disclosure

---

[8] FPR 2010, r 27.11(3).
[9] *Re L (Care: Assessment: Fair Trial)* [2002] 2 FLR 730.

imposed a wide obligation on the local authority under Art 8.[10] This duty applies at all stages of the proceedings and must be adhered to in order to ensure procedural fairness.

**4.33** It is essential in the interests of justice that a matter is fully heard on full evidence with all parties having the opportunity of seeing the evidence and considering it as well as providing their own evidence on an informed basis. For discussion of the use of special measures for vulnerable witnesses and intermediaries see chapter 12. The 26-week rule for the conclusion of care proceedings emphasises the need for everything to be concluded in an expeditious fashion. But as discussed in chapter 10 of this book, the President, Sir James Munby, in his judgment in *M-F (Children)* made clear that the 26 week rule should not be applied at the expense of justice:[11]

> 'my observation [in *In Re S*] that the 26 weeks rule "is not, and must never be allowed to become, a straightjacket, least of all if rigorous adherence to an inflexible timetable risks putting justice in jeopardy", and my endorsement ... of Pauffley J's warning in *Re NL (A child) (Appeal: Interim Care Order: Facts and Reasons)* [2014] EWHC 270 (Fam), [2014] 1 FLR 1384, that "Justice must never be sacrificed upon the altar of speed".'

**4.34** There is a clear balance to be had between the matter being dealt with within reasonable time, but not rushed so as to risk the matter not being fairly heard.

**4.35** Section 20 accommodation is an area that has seen a number of applications made due to the failure of the local authority to seek consent to a placement but also delays in the local authority referring the matter to court thus preventing the usual safeguards to be considered when a child is away from their birth family. The arguments in relation to the contravention of the right to family life is discussed below, but in situations where an application has not been made to a court and children have remained outside of their birth family for considerable periods of time, it is arguable that the right to a fair trial has also been infringed.

**4.36** Agreement to accommodation under s 20 of the Children Act 1989, even if it is properly obtained, is not intended for use over a long period of time. It is a short term measure and is not an alternative to acting in accordance with the law relating to the accommodation and care planning for children as provided under ss 31 and 38 of the CA 1989.

**4.37** In *Re N (Adoption: Jurisdiction)*, the President made clear that:[12]

> 'Accommodation of a child under a section 20 agreement deprives the child of the benefit of having an independent children's guardian to represent and safeguard his

---

[10] *Re L (Care: Assessment: Fair Trial)* [2002] 2 FLR 730.
[11] *M-F (Children)* [2014] EWCA Civ 991 at [26].
[12] *Re N (Adoption: Jurisdiction)* [2016] 1 FLR 621 at [158].

interests and deprives the court of the ability to control the planning for the child and prevent or reduce unnecessary and avoidable delay.'

**4.38** He continued:[13]

'The misuse and abuse of section 20 in this context is not just a matter of bad practice. It is wrong; it is a denial of the fundamental rights of both the parent and the child; it will no longer be tolerated; and it must stop. Judges will and must be alert to the problem and pro-active in putting an end to it. From now on, local authorities which use section 20 as a prelude to care proceedings for lengthy periods or which fail to follow the good practice I have identified, can expect to be subjected to probing questioning by the court. If the answers are not satisfactory, the local authority can expect stringent criticism and possible exposure to successful claims for damages.'

**4.39** Section 20 does not provide the child with any stability or permanency. Their parents remain the only holders of parental responsibility and there will have been no judicial scrutiny of their removal from the family. A children's guardian can only be appointed within care proceedings, and it is only then that the child's position will be considered separately from the local authority's position and the position of the parents. This is discussed further in chapter 12 of this book, and below.

## *Independent and impartial tribunal*

**4.40** In the age of the 26 week timetable and robust judicial case management it is sometimes difficult for lay clients and child protection professionals alike to understand why a judge is expressing particular views or refusing assessments. It is a difficult path for a judge to tread. On the one hand the judge is to be an impartial tribunal and on the other the judge has to carefully manage proceedings.

**4.41** In the event that it is believed that a judge has manifested apparent bias, an application can be made for that judge to recuse themselves from the case and for the matter to be heard by a different tribunal. The key principle is that justice must be seen to be done.

**4.42** In *Porter v Magill*,[14] the House of Lords approved the test to be applied in such cases in the following terms:[15]

'The court must first ascertain all the circumstances which have a bearing on the suggestion that the judge was biased. It must then ask whether those circumstances would lead a fair-minded and informed observer to conclude that there was a real possibility ... that the tribunal was biased.'

---

[13] *Re N (Adoption: Jurisdiction)* [2016] 1 FLR 621 at [171].
[14] *Porter v Magill* [2002] AC 357.
[15] *Porter v Magill* [2002] AC 357 at [102] and [103].

**4.43** This reflected the importance of justice 'being seen to be done' and rejected the previous tests of 'reasonable likelihood' and 'real danger' of apparent bias which tended to concentrate on the court's actual assessment of the facts as opposed to the perception of 'a fair-minded and informed observer'.

**4.44** In *Lesage v Mauritius Commercial Bank Ltd*,[16] a matter considered by the Privy Council, the importance of looking at the proceedings as a whole and questioning whether, overall, the proceedings would have created at least the impression of bias and unfairness is highlighted. Lord Kerr said:[17]

> 'Whether, in the mind of the informed observer, the failure to consider the propriety of their continuing to hear the case creates a possibility of bias is to be judged both prospectively and retrospectively. The actual conduct of the judges during the trial is to be examined therefore to see whether it supports or detracts from the suggestion that there was the appearance of possible prejudice.'

**4.45** A duty is conferred to a judge to further the overriding objective of dealing with cases justly in family proceedings, having regard to any welfare issues. This duty requires active case management as set out in FPR 2010, rr 1.1(1) and 1.4(1). Active case management involves a range of matters set out at FPR 2010, r 1.4(2) which include identifying the issues at an early stage and deciding promptly which issues need full investigation and which do not.

**4.46** This can be frustrating for the parties to the proceedings in the event that there is a disagreement as to what issues should be fully investigated and what issues should not. In terms of a fair trial, as set out above, it is essential in the interests of justice that a matter is fully heard on full evidence with all parties having the opportunity of seeing the evidence and considering it as well as providing their own evidence on an informed basis. If in proceedings a matter is disputed but the local authority does not seek to prove it as a fact, that matter must be treated as unproven and therefore not a fact to consider in the court's final determination. The judge must play a role in determining whether a fact should be investigated and either proved or disproved. This determination will consider the proportionality of investigation an issue and whether it is relevant to the question before the court.

**4.47** When considering whether an issue should be heard or not, the judge must be wary of the fact that this decision is very often made before there is full evidence to be considered. In *Re Q (Children)*[18] the trial judge early in the proceedings had expressed his preliminary view that the local authority would find it difficult to make out the s 31 threshold. He said:

> '... it seems to me that the local authority could be, I am using that word advisedly, could be in some difficulty in getting over the threshold in this case ... at the moment, on the basis of what I have read in those police papers, I very much

---

[16] *Lesage v Mauritius Commercial Bank Ltd* [2012] UKPC 41.
[17] *Lesage v Mauritius Commercial Bank Ltd* [2012] UKPC 41 at [51].
[18] *Re Q (Children)* [2014] EWCA Civ 918.

doubt, and I put it no higher than this, but I very much doubt that threshold would be made out. I can put it no higher than that at the moment, because obviously I need to give the parties an opportunity to investigate that, and the local authority, perhaps, to file further threshold documents.'

**4.48** McFarlane LJ gave the lead judgment and observed that:[19]

'There is, therefore, a real and important difference between the judge at a preliminary hearing inviting a party to consider their position on a particular point, which is permissible and to be encouraged, and the judge summarily deciding the point then and there without a fair and balanced hearing, which is not permissible.'

**4.49** He goes on to say, referring to the particular comments of the trial judge that:[20]

'Such expressions of judicial opinion, given the need for the judge to manage the case and be directive, are commonplace and would not be supportive of an appeal to this court based upon apparent judicial bias. The question in the present appeal is whether the other observations made by the judge, and the stage in the overall court process that those observations were made, establishes circumstances that would lead a fair-minded and informed observer to conclude that there was a real possibility that the judge was biased in the sense that he had formed a concluded view on the mother's allegations and her overall veracity.'

**4.50** A decision as to whether to make an application for a judge to recuse themselves from the proceedings is very much lead by the facts of the case. Any application for the judge to recuse themselves should be carefully considered.

## Right to respect of private and family life

**4.51** The interference of a public authority in family life, is a very serious matter, and one that should be considered carefully and thoroughly. The investigation and involvement of the local authority in family life is intrusive, but the way in which it is managed and the decisions made must have full consideration to Art 8. Both the way in which the decisions are made and the impact that this process has on the family and child are relevant when considering any infringements of this Convention right.

**4.52** HRA 1998, Sch 1 recites Art 8 of the Convention and provides:

'1. Everyone has the right to respect for his private and family life, his home and his correspondence.

2. There shall be no interference by a public authority with the exercise of this right except such as is in accordance with the law and is necessary in a democratic society in the interests of national security, public safety or the economic

---

[19] *Re Q (Children)* [2014] EWCA Civ 918 at [48].
[20] *Re Q (Children)* [2014] EWCA Civ 918 at [50].

well-being of the country, for the prevention of disorder or crime, for the protection of health or morals, or for the protection of the rights and freedoms of others.'

**4.53** There is no clear definition as to what constitutes 'private' or 'family life', it is essentially a question of fact but 'family life' importantly does not require a biological relationship between a parent and a child.[21]

**4.54** Article 8 does not specify any procedural requirements but it is clear that the decision making leading to the interference must be fair. In *McMichael v UK*[22] it was emphasised that:[23]

> 'the decision-making process leading to the measures of interference must be fair and such as to afford due respect to the interests safeguarded by Art 8.'

**4.55** The local authority must therefore fully involve the parents in the decision making as to their involvement and where necessary issue proceedings with the court to ensure that there is sufficient independent overview of the local authority's inference.

**4.56** In the same way as delay in coming before the court is an infringement of the Art 6 right to a fair trial, it is also an infringement of the right to private and family life. The speed at which the local authority makes firm plans for a child can impact upon the possibility of a child accessing support and ultimately being able to be a member of a 'forever family'. The longer a child remains outside of their birth family and in temporary foster care they remain in limbo. The age of the child could mean that their prospects of being adopted and therefore ceasing to be a looked after child, if that is the path endorsed by the court, could diminish or disappear. Similarly, if there is delay in assessments and support being offered to the birth family which results in the child spending time in foster care when they may otherwise have been able to return home, this too impacts upon the child and the parents' right to a family life. Foster care is widely accepted to be no substitute to a 'forever family' and the longer that there is uncertainty for the child as to where they will live, the longer they are deprived of a family life.

**4.57** In terms of the interference in private and family life of an adoption order, there must be a high degree of justification as to why an adoption order is the only order that will secure the child and safeguard their interests. The UK is distinct from a number of other countries in that in the UK it is possible for a child to be made the subject of an adoption order without the consent of the birth parents.

**4.58** In *Re B-S (Children)*, the President provided a clear outline for courts when considering a care plan for adoption. This case followed the Supreme

---

[21] *Singh v Entry Clearance Officer, New Delhi* [2005] 1 FLR 308, CA at [58]–[80].
[22] *McMichael v UK* (1995) 20 EHRR 205, ECtHR.
[23] *McMichael v UK* (1995) 20 EHRR 205, ECtHR at [87].

Court's decision in *Re B (A Child)* and highlighted the Court of Appeal's concern as to how matters involving adoption had been dealt with following four cases being referred to the Court of Appeal within the last ten days of July 2013.

**4.59** The President emphasised the remarks of Baroness Hale in *Re B*:[24]

'The language used in Re B is striking. Different words and phrases are used, but the message is clear. Orders contemplating non-consensual adoption – care orders with a plan for adoption, placement orders and adoption orders – are "a very extreme thing, a last resort", only to be made where "nothing else will do", where "no other course [is] possible in [the child's] interests", they are "the most extreme option", a "last resort – when all else fails", to be made "only in exceptional circumstances and where motivated by overriding requirements pertaining to the child's welfare, in short, where nothing else will do": see *Re B* paras 74, 76, 77, 82, 104, 130, 135, 145, 198, 215.'

**4.60** He continued, highlighting the considerations of McFarlane J in *Re G*:[25]

'A process which acknowledges that long-term public care, and in particular adoption contrary to the will of a parent, is "the most draconian option", yet does not engage with the very detail of that option which renders it "draconian" cannot be a full or effective process of evaluation.'

**4.61** The term 'nothing else will do' should not be considered in isolation. McFarlane LJ in *Re W (A Child)* said:[26]

'The phrase is meaningless, and potentially dangerous, if it is applied as some freestanding, shortcut test divorced from, or even in place of, an overall evaluation of the child's welfare. Used properly, as Baroness Hale explained, the phrase "nothing else will do" is no more, nor less, than a useful distillation of the proportionality and necessity test as embodied in the ECHR and reflected in the need to afford paramount consideration to the welfare of the child throughout her lifetime.'

**4.63** It is clear that the court must consider all other possibilities before proposing adoption, in order to ensure that no lesser order that will preserve family ties, is available. This consideration must be reflected clearly in the final judgment handed down by the court.

# INFRINGEMENT OF RIGHTS AND REMEDIES

**4.64** Once it has been determined that there has been an infringement of a Convention right, the court will make a declaration of incompatibility. This declaration will lead to consideration as to what remedy should be awarded to

---

[24] *Re BS (Children)* [2013] EWCA Civ 1146 at [22].
[25] *Re BS (Children)* [2013] EWCA Civ 1146 at [41].
[26] *Re W (A Child)* [2016] EWCA Civ 793 at [68].

provide 'just satisfaction' for the infringement. The basis of claim may arise out of the action of a local authority or inaction.

**4.65** Section 6(1) of the HRA 1998 provides that:

'It is unlawful for a public authority to act in a way which is incompatible with a Convention right.'

**4.66** A claim is available to a party to care proceedings pursuant to s 7(1)(b) of the HRA 1998 which states:

'A person who claims that a public authority has acted (or proposes to act) in a way which is made unlawful by section 6(1) may –

(a) bring proceedings against the authority under this Act in the appropriate court or tribunal, or
(b) rely on the Convention right or rights concerned in any legal proceedings but only if he is (or would be) a victim of the unlawful act.'

**4.67** HRA 1998, s 8 provides for 'judicial remedies' in the event that the court determines that there has been an infringement of Convention rights.

'(1) In relation to any act (or proposed act) of a public authority which the court finds is (or would be) unlawful, it may grant such relief or remedy, or make such order, within its powers as it considers just and appropriate.

(2) But damages may be awarded only by a court which has power to award damages, or to order the payment of compensation, in civil proceedings.

(3) No award of damages is to be made unless, taking account of all the circumstances of the case, including –

(a) any other relief or remedy granted, or order made, in relation to the act in question (by that or any other court), and
(b) the consequences of any decision (of that or any other court) in respect of that act,

the court is satisfied that the award is necessary to afford just satisfaction to the person in whose favour it is made.

(4) In determining –

(a) whether to award damages, or
(b) the amount of an award,

the court must take into account the principles applied by the European Court of Human Rights in relation to the award of compensation under Article 41 of the Convention.'

**4.68** In relation to actions that have not yet occurred, the court's power includes the power to grant injunctions which is vested by the High Court by s 37(1) of the Senior Courts Act 1981, in the county court by s 38 of the County Courts Act 1984 and now in the family court by virtue of s 31E of the Matrimonial and Family Proceedings Act 1984 as amended by Sch 10 to the Crime and Courts Act 2013. This remedy may provide just satisfaction in the event that the local authority seeks to separate of a parent and child unlawfully.

**4.69** This remedy was considered in *Re DE (A Child)*[27] when the local authority sought to remove a child from his parents after the child had been placed with them under a care order. Baker J determined that:[28]

> 'To my mind, where a care order has been granted on the basis of a care plan providing that the child should remain at home, a local authority considering changing the plan and removing the child permanently from the family is obliged in law to follow the same approach. It must have regard to the fact that permanent placement outside the family is to be preferred only as a last resort where nothing else will do. Before making its decision, it must rigorously analyse all the realistic options, considering the arguments for and against each option. This is an essential process, not only as a matter of good practice, but also because the local authority will inevitably have to demonstrate its analysis in any court proceedings that follow the change of care plan, either on an application for the discharge of the care order or an application for placement order under the Adoption and Children Act 2002. This process of rigorous analysis of all realistic options should be an essential feature of all long-term planning for children. And, as indicated by Munby J in *Re G*, the local authority must fully involve the parents in its decision-making process.'

**4.70** In this situation the court of first instance had no alternative but to award the injunction to prevent the unlawful act from occurring.

**4.71** The court also has the power to award damages against the local authority in the event that a declaration of incompatibility if made. In *Anufrijeva v Southwark London Borough Council*,[29] Lord Woolf CJ sets out the following:[30]

> 'The remedy of damages generally plays a less prominent role in actions based on breaches of the articles of the Convention, than in actions based on breaches of private law obligations where, more often than not, the only remedy claimed is damages ... Where an infringement of an individual's human rights has occurred, the concern will usually be to bring the infringement to an end and any question of compensation will be of secondary, if any, importance.'

**4.72** In *Regina v Secretary of State for the Home Department (Respondent) ex parte Greenfield*[31] Lord Bingham provided at [9]:

> 'The routine treatment of a finding of violation as, in itself, just satisfaction for the violation found reflects the point already made that the focus of the Convention is on the protection of human rights and not the award of compensation.'

---

[27] *Re DE (A Child)* [2014] EWFC 6.
[28] *Re DE (A Child)* [2014] EWFC 6 at [34].
[29] *Anufrijeva v Southwark London Borough Council* [2003] EWCA Civ 1406, [2004] QB 1124.
[30] *Anufrijeva v Southwark London Borough Council* [2003] EWCA Civ 1406, [2004] QB 1124 at [52] and [53].
[31] *Regina v Secretary of State for the Home Department (Respondent) ex parte Greenfield* [2005] UKHL 14, [2005] 1 WLR 673.

Nevertheless, there are occasions when damages are awarded following a declaration of incompatibility and the awards have not been insubstantial.[32]

## Section 20 and human rights claims

**4.73** The use and management of s 20 accommodation has come under a lot of scrutiny recently and applications have been considered by the court with regard to infringements of Art 6 (fair trial) and Art 8 (the respect of private and family life) rights. Article 6 considerations regarding s 20 accommodation have been discussed above. The second implication of s 20 accommodation is with regard to the right to the respect of family and private life. Section 20 accommodation is discussed fully in chapter 5 of this book.

**4.74** If the local authority form the view that a child cannot return home, the matter must be bought before the court to enable this decision to be carefully scrutinised within the proper judicial process. Under s 20 the child is effectively left in limbo. This cannot, and should never be, a situation that continues for any length of time.

**4.75** There are a number of elements of s 20 accommodation that warrant careful consideration. Practice guidance is given by Hedley J in *Coventry City Council v C, B, CA and CH*:[33]

    'i)    Every parent has the right, if capacitous, to exercise their parental responsibility to consent under Section 20 to have their child accommodated by the local authority and every local authority has power under Section 20(4) so to accommodate provided that it is consistent with the welfare of the child.

    ii)    Every social worker obtaining such a consent is under a personal duty (the outcome of which may not be dictated to them by others) to be satisfied that the person giving the consent does not lack the capacity to do so.

    iii)    In taking any such consent the social worker must actively address the issue of capacity and take into account all the circumstances prevailing at the time and consider the questions raised by Section 3 of the 2005 Act, and in particular the mother's capacity at that time to use and weigh all the relevant information.

    iv)    If the social worker has doubts about capacity no further attempt should be made to obtain consent on that occasion and advice should be sought from the social work team leader or management.

    v)    If the social worker is satisfied that the person whose consent is sought does not lack capacity, the social worker must be satisfied that the consent is fully informed:

        a)    Does the parent fully understand the consequences of giving such a consent?

        b)    Does the parent fully appreciate the range of choice available and the consequences of refusal as well as giving consent?

---

[32] *Kent County Council v M and K (Section 20: Declaration and Damages)* [2016] EWFC 28.
[33] *Coventry City Council v C, B, CA and CH* [2013] 2 FLR 987 at [46].

    c) Is the parent in possession of all the facts and issues material to the giving of consent?

vi) If not satisfied that the answers to a) – c) above are all "yes", no further attempt should be made to obtain consent on that occasion and advice should be sought as above and the social work team should further consider taking legal advice if thought necessary.

vii) If the social worker is satisfied that the consent is fully informed then it is necessary to be further satisfied that the giving of such consent and the subsequent removal is both fair and proportionate.

viii) In considering that it may be necessary to ask:
    a) what is the current physical and psychological state of the parent?
    b) If they have a solicitor, have they been encouraged to seek legal advice and/or advice from family or friends?
    c) Is it necessary for the safety of the child for her to be removed at this time?
    d) Would it be fairer in this case for this matter to be the subject of a court order rather than an agreement?

ix) If having done all this and, if necessary, having taken further advice (as above and including where necessary legal advice), the social worker then considers that a fully informed consent has been received from a capacitous mother in circumstances where removal is necessary and proportionate, consent may be acted upon.

x) In the light of the foregoing, local authorities may want to approach with great care the obtaining of Section 20 agreements from mothers in the aftermath of birth, especially where there is no immediate danger to the child and where probably no order would be made.'

**4.76** Whilst this is guidance and not a statutory provision, it is useful nonetheless when considering whether an agreement to s 20 accommodation has impacted upon the Convention right.

**4.77** A number of cases have come before the court since the guidance provided in *Coventry City Council v C, B, CA and CH* (set out above). It is important however, to note that there is no statutory requirement for the local authority to obtain positive consent from a parent in order for s 20 accommodation to be appropriate as long as the placement otherwise satisfies the statutory provisions. In *London Borough of Hackney v Williams & Anor*[34] Sir Brian Leveson P comments at [77]:

'Before passing from the issue of s. 20 of the 1989 Act and consideration of the guidance given by Sir James Munby P, Hedley J and others in the Family Division cases to which I have referred, I wish to stress that nothing that is said in this judgment is intended to, or should be read as, altering the content and effect of that guidance in family cases. The focus of the court in the present appeal is on the bottom-line legal requirements that are established by s 20 and within which a local authority must act. The guidance given in the family court, which has built upon that bottom-line in the period since the Williams' children were removed, identifies clear, cooperative and sensible ways in which a voluntary arrangement can be made between a parent and a local authority when a child may need to be

---

[34] *London Borough of Hackney v Williams & Anor* [2017] EWCA Civ 26.

accommodated; it is, in short, good practice guidance and a description of the process that the family court expects to be followed. For reasons of good administration, the practice guidance should continue to be followed, notwithstanding the limits of the underlying legal requirements in s 20 that I have identified but a failure to follow it does not, of itself, give rise to an actionable wrong, or found a claim for judicial review.'

**4.78** In this case both parents were unable to provide their children with accommodation due to bail conditions preventing them for caring for the children. This situation came within s 20(7)(b)(ii), in that the parents were unable to provide accommodation, and therefore the local authority was entitled to use s 20 accommodation following the expiry of police protection. In a situation such as this the matter must immediately come before the court for the issue regarding the children's care to be dealt with.

**4.79** Claims that have been successful against local authorities have tended to centre around lack of consent and significant delay in issuing proceedings once it has become clear that the child could not return home.[35]

**4.80** Whilst there is no time limit on providing s 20 accommodation in the statute each case must be considered on its own facts, with active consideration being given as to whether proceedings should be issued.

## PROCEDURE FOR APPLICATIONS UNDER HUMAN RIGHTS ACT 1998

**4.81** An application pursuant to the HRA 1998 can be made within care proceedings or as a freestanding application following the conclusion of the proceedings. The conclusion of care proceedings does not impact on the ability to make a claim subject to the usual time limitations. Any application made pursuant to HRA 1998 will attract the Civil Procedure Rules and not the Family Procedure Rules.

**4.82** In *SW & TW (Human Rights Claim: Procedure) (No 1)*[36] Mr Justice Cobb considered the procedure for dealing with human rights claims within family proceedings. Within his judgement he outlines at [27] the comments of the President in *Re L (Care Proceedings: Human Rights Claims)*[37] and drew particular attention to the following paragraphs:[38]

---

[35] *Re N (Children) (Adoption: Jurisdiction)* [2015] EWCA Civ 1112; *Re P (A child: Use of section 20)* [2014] EWFC 775; *Northamptonshire County Council v AS and Others* [2015] EWHC 199; *Newcastle City Council v WM & Others* [2015] EWFC 42; *Medway Council v M & T* [2015] EWFC B164; *Kent County Council v M and K (Section 20: Declaration and Damages)* [2016] EWFC 28.
[36] *SW & TW (Human Rights Claim: Procedure) (No 1)* [2017] EWHC 450 (Fam).
[37] *Re L (Care Proceedings: Human Rights Claims)* [2003] EWHC 665 (Fam), [2003] 2 FLR 160.
[38] Emphasis by underlining added.

'[23] There is, however, in my judgment ... an important distinction to be drawn between: (a) those cases in which a European Convention issue arises whilst care proceedings are still on foot; and (b) those cases in which a European Convention issue arises after a final care order has been made and when the care proceedings have accordingly come to an end.

[24] In the latter class of case – that is, where the care proceedings have come to an end – the appropriate remedy may well be a freestanding application under s 7(1)(a) of the Human Rights Act 1998. Such an application can be made either on its own or in conjunction with some other application, for example (as in *Re M (Care: Challenging Decisions by Local Authority)* [2001] 2 FLR 1300, *C v Bury Metropolitan Borough Council* [2002] EWHC 1438 (Fam), [2002] 2 FLR 868 and *Re G (Care: Challenge to Local Authority Decision)* [2003] EWHC 551 (Fam), [2003] 2 FLR 42 an application under s 39 of the Children Act 1989 for discharge of the care order. In such a case, as the President emphasised in *C v Bury*, the application should be heard in the Family Division and, if possible, by a judge with experience of sitting in the Administrative Court. *C v Bury*, it should be noted, was a case where the care proceedings had come to an end.

[25] In the other class of case – that is, where the care proceedings are still on foot – the position, in my judgment, is quite different. <u>Here there is no need for any freestanding application under s 7(1)(a). Section 7(1)(b) will provide an appropriate remedy within the care proceedings themselves. Accordingly, Human Rights Act complaints arising before the making of a final care order can, and in my judgment normally should, be dealt with within the context of the care proceedings and by the court which is dealing with the care proceedings.</u> I might point out that *Re L (Care: Assessment: Fair Trial)* [2002] EWHC 1379 (Fam), [2002] 2 FLR 730 is an example, albeit in the Family Division, showing just that procedure being adopted. In that case, the mother's complaints of numerous breaches of Art 8 were litigated within the care proceedings and without any separate application being issued under the Human Rights Act 1998.'

**4.83** Considering the timing of an application Cobb J goes on to say:[39]

'Munby J in the passage underlined above ([2003] EWHC 665 (Fam) [2003] 2 FLR 160 [25]) advises that a HRA 1998 claim arising in the context of ongoing family proceedings can and should ordinarily be dealt with "by the court" dealing with the care proceedings and "within the context" of those proceedings. This is apposite where the relief to be awarded under section 8 HRA 1998 coincides in large measure with the relief or orders which the court may wish to make in the CA 1989 proceedings. But where declarations of unlawfulness and damages are sought which do <u>not</u> have an impact on the outcome of the CA 1989 proceedings, there is much less justification for uniting them. There is a real risk that in doing so, the CA 1989 proceedings become bogged down. A HRA 1998 claim should never be permitted (as it has in this case, I believe) to prolong the CA 1989 litigation.

---

[39] *SW & TW (Human Rights Claim: Procedure) (No 1)* [2017] EWHC 450 (Fam) at [28] and [29].

Keehan J analyses *Re L* in *H v Northamptonshire* at [115] in a way with which I entirely associate myself, thus:[40]

> "I respectfully agree with Munby J's general proposition that a court hearing public law proceedings should deal with any associated HRA claim brought by one of the parties to the care proceedings. His concern was to prevent the proliferation of satellite litigation in respect of HRA claims. The judgment should not be read, and was plainly not intended to be read, as requiring a party seeking HRA damages to issue his or her claim within the existing public law care proceedings. On this basis the decision in *Re L*, and the decision in *Re V*, may be distinguished from proceedings in which a HRA claim is pursued <u>and damages are sought. Therefore, where the remedy sought in the HRA claim is not limited to injunctive or declaratory relief but includes a claim for damages, it is almost inevitable that those representing the Claimant will be well advised to issue separate proceedings and to seek the issue of a separate public funding certificate because of the potential applicability of the statutory charge in respect of any HRA damages awarded</u>".'

**4.84** However, there is a word of caution in relation to applications for damages against local authorities as a result of the funding of any such applications. It is possible for public funding to be obtained for such applications, but careful consideration should be given as to how any damages awarded will be viewed by the Legal Aid Agency (LAA) and any statutory charge that may be applied. Any statutory charge may also include the costs incurred by that party during the care proceedings as well as any freestanding application for damages.

**4.85** The costs of the applicant for the HRA claim will 'follow the event' and therefore the applicant will be awarded these costs in the event that the application is successful. The LAA, however, may seek to recover the costs incurred throughout the care proceedings by way of statutory charge if 'the factual basis of the HRA claim is "connected with" the factual basis of the concurrent publicly funded care proceedings and thus whether the statutory charge is applicable' pursuant to s 25 of the Legal Aid, Sentencing and Punishment of Offenders Act 2012.

**4.86** In *H (A Minor) v Northamptonshire County Council & Anor*[41] Keehan J summarises his conclusions at para 117:

> '117. Where damages are sought in just satisfaction of a HRA claim during the currency of public law proceedings, I provide the following guidance:
>
> (a) Alleged breaches of Convention rights by a local authority must be set out with particularity in a letter before action as soon as ever possible;

---

[40] Emphasis by underlining added.
[41] *H (A Minor) v Northamptonshire County Council & Anor* [2017] EWHC 282 (Fam).

(b) Every effort should be made by the claimant and the local authority to settle the issues of liability and the quantum of damages before and without the need to issue proceedings;

(c) Where liability and quantum are agreed prior to the issue of proceedings, it will invariably be in the interests of the child to issue a Part 8 claim to secure the court's approval of the proposed settlement pursuant to CPR r 21.10;

(d) The local authority should, save in exceptional circumstances, pay the reasonable costs of the claimant's HRA claim/proceedings;

(e) Where it is necessary for a party to issue a formal HRA claim, proceedings should be issued separately from the care proceedings and a separate public funding certificate should be sought from the LAA in respect of the same;

(f) Well in advance of the final hearing of the HRA claim the LAA should be invited to make a decision on whether it asserts that the statutory charge will be applicable to any award of HRA damages. Where:

i) The basis of threshold and the material facts of the case are agreed or the court has made findings of fact and given a judgment establishing the factual matrix of the public law proceedings; and

ii) Liability is agreed and the material facts relied upon to establish the breach or breaches of the claimant's Convention rights are agreed or have been determined by the court; I see no reason in law or on public policy grounds or in practical terms why the LAA could not and should not notify the court and the parties of its decision on the applicability of the statutory charge prior to the final hearing and well in advance of the submission of the claimant's solicitor's final bill(s); and

(g) With the benefit of the LAA's decision, the court should have the necessary information to assess the quantum of damages or, as the case may be, to approve the settlement, and to consider what are the appropriate orders for costs.'

**4.87** The prospect of a successful applicant losing all damages awarded to the statutory charge must be considered when looking at what action should be taken and what remedy should be sought.

# Part 2

# CHILD PROTECTION MEASURES SHORT OF CARE PROCEEDINGS

# CHAPTER 5

# LOCAL AUTHORITY SUPPORT, INVESTIGATION AND INTERVENTION

## LOCAL AUTHORITY SUPPORT FOR CHILDREN AND THEIR FAMILIES

**5.1** The local authority has a statutory duty to provide assistance, support and services to children and families in their area. They must provide both adult and children's services to those in their locality, but these services must remain separate as per the Children Act 2004. Each local authority must appoint a director of children's services who is responsible for the provision of services including education and children's healthcare (those elements not already covered by the NHS). In governmental guidance issued to local authorities, it is made clear that 'providing early help is more effective in promoting the welfare of children than reacting later'.[1]

**5.2** The Children Act 1989 ('CA 1989') makes provision for the local authority provision of mandatory and discretionary support services for children and their families within their area. Part III of the CA 1989 sets out the support that should be in place and imposes certain duties on local authorities in respect of the families in their area. Where there is a duty that the local authority provides services they must act accordingly; where there is a power to provide a service, the local authority should exercise its discretion in deciding whether to exercise that power. The discretion must be exercised reasonably and is subject to judicial review.

**5.3** Section 17(1) of the CA 1989 provides:

'It shall be the general duty of every local authority (in addition to the other duties imposed on them by this Part) –

(a) to safeguard and promote the welfare of children within their area who are in need; and
(b) so far as is consistent with that duty, to promote the upbringing of such children by their families,

by providing a range of services appropriate to those children's needs.'

**5.4** Section 17(2) sets out that the specific duties and powers which are established in Part I, Sch 2 of the CA 1989. The duty established in s 17(1) is an

---

[1] *Court Orders and Pre-Proceedings*, (Department for Education, April 2014).

overriding duty and the range of services in a particular local authority's area must be sufficient to ensure their duty is discharged. However, this duty does not extend to providing a particular service for a particular need of a child.

## Children in need

**5.5** The duty that is imposed on the local authority by s 17(1) requires that the welfare of a child is to be safeguarded and promoted when a child is 'in need'. Once a child is assessed to be 'in need' a number of services become open to them and the local authority becomes under a clear duty to the child. The decision as to whether a child is 'in need' is a matter to be assessed by the local authority. Section 17(3) of the CA 1989 provides that:

> 'Any service provided by an authority in the exercise of functions conferred on them by this section may be provided for the family of a particular child in need or for any member of his family, if it is provided with a view to safeguarding or promoting the child's welfare.'

**5.6** A child in need is defined in s 17(10) as a child:

> '(a) Who is likely to achieve or maintain a reasonable standard of health or development without the provision of support services by the local authority;
> (b) Whose health or development is likely to be significantly impaired without the provision of such services; or
> (c) Who is disabled.'

**5.7** Section 17(11) specifies that for the purposes of the CA 1989, 'development' extends to physical, intellectual, emotional, social or behavioural development, and 'health' includes both physical and mental health.

**5.8** The definition of a 'disabled child' for the purposes of the CA 1989 is a child who is blind, deaf or dumb, suffers from any mental disorder or is substantially and permanently handicapped by illness, injury or congenital deformity.[2]

**5.9** Importantly, the court does not play a role in the determination of whether a child is a 'child in need', although the local authority's assessment can be judicially reviewed. Even then, the court's only function is to decide whether the local authority has fulfilled its legal obligation under the CA 1989 and whether they have exercised their discretion reasonably and in conjunction with public law principles.[3] The court cannot substitute the local authority's decision for another one, but can only remit it back to the authority for a fresh assessment. The structure of all assessments of children should be based on the outline of a good assessment set out in the *Working Together to Safeguard Children 2015* at para 35.

---

[2] CA 1989, s 17(11).
[3] *R (LH and MH) v London Borough of Lambeth* [2006] 2 FLR 1275.

**5.10** When looking at the provision of services available to a 'child in need', s 17(1)(b) sets out a duty 'to promote the upbringing of such children by their families'. The purpose of Part III is to provide services that will enable children to remain at home with their parents, as is clear from the Sch 2(7) which places an obligation on local authorities to take reasonable steps to reduce the need for care proceedings. The services that a local authority shall make available to a 'child in need' while living at home are set out in Sch 2(8) and include:

> '(a)  advice, guidance and counselling;
> (b)  occupational, social, cultural or recreational activities;
> (c)  home help (which includes laundry facilities);
> (d)  facilities for, or assistance with, travelling to and from home for the purpose of taking advantage of any other service provided under this Act or of any similar service;
> (e)  assistance to enable the child concerned and his family to have a holiday.'

**5.11** Under s 17(4A) a child's wishes and feelings should be obtained when considering which services are appropriate, and consideration should be given to those wishes and feelings, in line with the child's age and understanding.

**5.12** It is important to note that whilst the statute requires the local authority to make services available, whether the services are *provided* remains at the discretion of the local authority alone. Again, such discretion is subject to judicial review.

## LOCAL AUTHORITY INVESTIGATION

**5.13** The local authority may become aware of a child in their area whose circumstances may require investigation through a variety of mechanisms. Serious cases will come to light following the making of an emergency protection order or situations where a child has been taken into police protection. For non-emergent cases, referrals may be received from other professionals working with the child, such as health professionals or teachers.

**5.14** Unless the child is thought to be in immediate danger, the local authority must decide within one working day whether the referral they have received requires a response. Clearly if there is a concern that the child may be in immediate danger, urgent action should be considered (see chapters 8 and 9). If it is decided that the referral requires a response, the local authority must carry out their initial assessment within 7 days. This should include making enquires of other agencies that have had dealings with the child, visiting and speaking to the child and speaking to other family members. Once completed, the local authority must assess this information and decide whether they have reasonable cause to suspect that the child is suffering or is likely to suffer significant harm.[4] The local authority must also consider whether the child should be identified as a 'child in need' as discussed above.

## Section 47 investigations

**5.15** If, following their initial assessment, the local authority considers the child may be suffering or likely to suffer significant harm, the local authority must investigate their situation fully under s 47 of the CA 1989. Section 47(1) provides:

> 'Where a local authority –
>
> (a) are informed that a child who lives, or is found, in their area –
>   (i) is the subject of an emergency protection order; or
>   (ii) is in police protection;
>
> the authority shall make, or cause to be made, such enquiries as the consider necessary to enable them to decide whether they should take any action to safeguard or promote the child's welfare.'

**5.16** An assessment under s 47 takes the form of a detailed child protection assessment designed to enable the local authority to consider whether the child's welfare requires intervention. As with the 'child in need' assessment mentioned above, the structure of the assessment should comply with the *Framework for the Assessment of Children in Need and their Families*.[5]

**5.17** Section 47 imposes a duty to undertake investigations so that the local authority can make decisions as to the child's welfare. In the event that the local authority attempts to make the necessary enquiries, but is prevented from accessing the child, s 47(6) requires the local authority to consider whether it is necessary to apply for an emergency protection, child assessment, care or supervision order. An application under s 47(6) should be made unless the local authority is of the view that the child's welfare can be safeguarded without it.

**5.18** The adequacy of a s 47 investigation and the decision reached at its conclusion can only be challenged by way of judicial review which again, is capable only of remitting the decision back to the local authority for a fresh assessment.

## Section 37 Children Act 1989

**5.19** In private law proceedings, an assessment can be triggered under s 37 of the CA 1989 if the court considers a care or supervision order may be appropriate. Section 37 provides:

---

[4] The timescales for assessments are set out in *Working Together to Safeguard Children* (2015), paras 57–64 and can also be found in *Court Orders and Pre-Proceedings*, (Department for Education, April 2014).

[5] *Framework for the Assessment of Children in Need and their Families* (see above).

'Where, in any family proceedings in which a question arises with respect to the welfare of any child, it appears to the court that it may be appropriate for a care or supervision order to be made with respect to him, the court may direct the appropriate authority to undertake an investigation of the child's circumstances.'

**5.20** The court has the power to make this direction against the local authority in whose area the child is ordinarily resident, or in whose area the concerns have arisen.[6]

**5.21** As part of the s 37 report prepared for the court, the local authority must consider the matters set out in s 37(2), including:

'Where the court gives a direction under this section the local authority concerned shall, when undertaking the investigation, consider whether they should –

(a) apply for a care order or for a supervision order with respect to the child;
(b) provide services or assistance for the child or his family; or
(c) take any other action with respect to the child.'

**5.22** In the event that following the assessment, the local authority does not intend to take any of the actions set out in s 37(2) the report should set out:[7]

'(a) their reasons for so deciding;
(b) any service or assistance which they have provided, or intend to provide, for the child and his family; and
(c) any other action which they have taken, or propose to take, with respect to the child.'

**5.23** In addition, in accordance with s 37(6) the local authority must consider whether it is appropriate to review the situation at a later date and, if so, the date upon which the review should occur. The assessment and report must be completed and filed with the court within eight weeks from the making of the direction unless the court directs a different date.[8]

**5.24** Making a s 37 direction represents a significant step for the court given it may result in an application for a care or supervision order. Where such a direction is made by the court, the local authority should be informed as quickly as possible and provided with all relevant information and a full reason as to why the direction has been made. A full note or transcript of the relevant judgment should be made available to the local authority.[9]

**5.25** A s 37 direction is not to be used by the court in order to simply find out information regarding local authority investigations into the family. If such information is considered necessary within private law proceedings, the most appropriate route is to make an order under s 7 of the CA 1989 for a report to be prepared. A s 37 direction should only be made if the court forms the view that a care or supervision order may be necessary in the case.

---

[6] CA 1989, s 37(5).
[7] CA 1989, s 37(3).
[8] CA 1989, s 37(4).
[9] *Re M (Intractable Contact Dispute: Interim Care Order)* [2003] 2 FLR 636.

**5.26** Best practice guidance for the making of a s 37 direction can be found in the annual report of the Children Act Advisory Committee 1992/93.

**5.27** In the event that the s 37 direction has been granted by the court and was not opposed by any of the parties to the proceedings, the local authority cannot appeal the making of the direction. The three considerations set out in s 37(1) (ie. that there is a child, in family proceedings, where there is a concern for that child's welfare), are for the court to determine.

**5.28** Once a direction is made under s 37, the proceedings become 'specified' proceedings within the meaning of s 41(6)(b) of the CA 1989 which means that a children's guardian will be appointed and the child becomes party to the proceedings. This is discussed further at chapter 12.

**5.29** At the same time as making a s 37 direction, the court can make an interim care or supervision order to cover the period during which the investigation is undertaken.[10] Before doing so, the court must have reasonable grounds to believe that the child is suffering or is likely to suffer significant harm during the period of the investigation and assessment. The order will last until the report is concluded, the assessment provided and the matter has returned to court.

**5.30** The decision as to whether or not an application for a care or supervision order is made following the assessment is the decision of the local authority alone. The court has no power to force the local authority to make the application, and cannot make a further interim care order of its own motion past the end of the assessment process.

## Child assessment orders

**5.31** In the event that the local authority has significant concerns about for a child and it has not been possible to get access to the child in order to complete the necessary assessment, it can make an application to the court for a child assessment order. Section 43(1) of the CA 1989 provides:

> 'On the application of a local authority or authorised person for an order to be made under this section with respect to a child, the court may make the order if, but only if, it is satisfied that –
>
>    (a)   the applicant has reasonable cause to suspect that the child is suffering, or is likely to suffer, significant harm;
>
>    (b)   an assessment of the state of the child's health or development, or of the way in which he has been treated, is required to enable the applicant to determine whether or not the child is suffering, or is likely to suffer, significant harm; and
>
>    (c)   it is unlikely that such an assessment will be made, or be satisfactory, in the absence of an order under this section.'

---

[10] CA 1989, s 38(1).

**5.32** This is an order that is very rarely used, but if made requires that any person, who is in the position to do so, produces the child to the person named in the order for the purposes of assessment.[11]

**5.33** The court will consider the matter in the same way as an application for an emergency protection order and must not make a child assessment order if it is felt that an emergency protection order should be made. There must be a risk of immediate harm to the child, as is necessary when applying for an emergency protection order, unless the local authority have access to the child for the purposes of making the necessary enquiries.[12] For discussion in relation to the application and making of emergency protection orders, see chapter 9.

**5.34** A child assessment order will specify the date upon which the assessment is to begin and have effect for a period not exceeding 7 days.[13]

**5.35** In the event that it is necessary for the child to be kept away from their home for the purposes of this assessment, there must be a direction in the order specifying the period that the child must be kept away and contact with the parents must be considered and included in any order (where contact is deemed appropriate).[14]

**5.36** In the event that the child is of sufficient age and understanding, they are able to refuse to submit to a psychiatric or medical assessment, so it is essential that information as to the views of the child and their age and understanding is available if at all possible.[15] Although the local authority does not acquire parental responsibility for the child, it but can make all necessary arrangements for assessment.

**5.37** Every reasonable steps are to be taken to provide notice of this application to:

(a) the child's parents;
(b) any person who is not a parent of his but who has parental responsibility for him;
(c) any other person caring for the child;
(d) any person named in a child arrangements order as a person with whom the child is to spend time or otherwise have contact;
(e) any person who is allowed to have contact with the child by virtue of an order under s 34; and
(f) the child.

---

[11] CA 1989, s 43(6).
[12] CA 1989, s 43(3).
[13] CA 1989, s 43(5).
[14] CA 1989, s 43(9)–(10).
[15] CA 1989, s 43(8).

Such notice should be given before the hearing of the application.[16]

**5.38** As mentioned above, this order is rarely made as it is difficult to see when there would be a situation when an emergency protection order would not be made in the event that the criteria of immediate risk is fulfilled. However, in the event that the local authority is unable to gain access to a child for the purposes of assessment, this order is available.

## LOCAL AUTHORITY INTERVENTION

**5.39** In the event that it is necessary for the local authority to intervene in order to safeguard the welfare of a child, there are a number of different levels of intervention aimed at assisting children and their families. In the event that the assistance provided cannot secure the welfare of the child, the local authority must consider taking whatever further action is necessary.

### Children protection plans

**5.40** All local authorities are required to register the steps necessary to protect a child by creating a 'child protection plan'. The duty is established by the *Working Together to Safeguard Children* guidance reissued in April 2010.[17] A record must be kept of all the children subject to 'child protection plans' on the local authority's database, recorded under one or more of the following categories:

- physical abuse;

- emotional abuse;

- sexual abuse; or

- neglect.

Prior to the reissued guidance in 2010, children were known as being on the 'child protection register'.

**5.41** The registration process is monitored by the Safeguarding Children Board, a multi-agency group set up to facilitate communication and information-sharing between the relevant agencies involved in child protection. The system is intended to ensure that all agencies have access to information relating to children considered to be in need of a protection plan whether during or outside office hours.

---

[16] CA 1989, s 43(11).
[17] *Working Together to Safeguard Children* (see above).

## Child protection conference

**5.42** The process to identify a child as requiring a 'child protection plan' involves the consideration of the circumstances of the child at a child protection conference. The local authority will convene the conference, inviting all of the agencies involved with the child who should either attend and/or provide information to the conference. The purpose of the conference is to ensure that all of the relevant information is before it so that it can determine whether the child has suffered or is at risk of suffering harm under the four categories set out above.

**5.43** The conference should include the child's parents and, if appropriate, other family members, social services, health practitioners (including health visitors), the police and the school. In the event that there are any other professionals involved with the parents (such as mental health services, substance misuse workers, etc), they too should be included.

**5.44** The social worker allocated to the child should prepare a report for the conference which collates all of the information received from all of the relevant agencies. The information for this report may include information collected during the s 47 investigation (see above for more detail). The agencies will also be asked to provide brief reports setting out their involvement with the child or family. These reports are intended to provide as full a picture as possible of the circumstances for the child.

**5.45** The parents should have an opportunity to see and have the reports explained to them by the social worker before the conference, as well as meeting the conference chairperson who will further explain the reports and the process involved. The parents should then be able to attend the conference to have their views heard. In the event it is considered that one or both parents present a risk to the child or another person, that parent may be excluded from the conference as long as they have the opportunity to meet with the chair and put forward their views in advance.

**5.46** During the child protection conference, the attendees will consider the reports prepared and will comment on any other relevant information that they have. Once the information has been shared, the attendees will be asked to consider whether in their view, the child is at risk of suffering significant harm and if so, under which categories. If the attendees consider the child is at risk of suffering significant harm, they must vote in favour of the child protection plan being formulated under one or more of the relevant categories.

**5.47** Once the plan is formulated, a 'core group' will be set up to meet and discuss the progress of the plan. The core group will usually consist of the parents, foster cares and wider family as well as the social worker and professionals that have direct contact with the child.

**5.48** The first core group meeting is to take place within 10 working days of the case conference and a report should be prepared for any review case conferences that occur. There should be a subsequent review conference in 3 months, and then at 6 monthly intervals thereafter. The review conferences should continue to consider the reports prepared by the professionals as well as the views of the core group as to whether the child should remain subject to the child protection plan.

**5.49** In the event that there are ongoing legal proceedings in relation to the family, the legal representatives of the parents and the local authority can attend the conferences. However, their attendance is for observation only and they should not intervene unless a legal issue arises. If appointed, the child's guardian should also be invited to attend.

**5.50** Minutes of all of the case conferences should be prepared and provided to the parents and the other professionals and agreed by all in attendance as an accurate record. This document may also be filed in any legal proceedings that are ongoing or occur in the future.

**5.51** In the event that a child is subject to a child protection plan and their circumstances do not improve, the local authority should consider taking the matter further and should take legal advice. The purpose of the child protection plan is to ensure that the family has the assistance it needs to improve the care given to the child. If the assistance does not succeed in improving matters, the local authority must, in the interests of the child, consider further intervention.

## Section 20 accommodation

**5.52** Section 20 imposes a duty on local authorities to accommodate children in need in their area if it appears to them that the child requires accommodation and their parent(s)' consent. Parental consent can be dispensed with if the conditions in s 20(1) are met:

'(a) there being no person who has parental responsibility for him;
(b) his being lost or having been abandoned; or
(c) the person who has been caring for him being prevented (whether or not permanently, and for whatever reason) from providing him with suitable accommodation or care.'

**5.53** Furthermore, s 20(4) provides:

'A local authority may provide accommodation for any child within their area (even though a person who has parental responsibility for him is able to provide him with accommodation) if they consider that to do so would safeguard or promote the child's welfare.'

**5.54** Where a local authority provides accommodation to a child who is ordinarily resident in the area of another local authority, the child's home local authority may take over the accommodation of the child. This should be done within three months of the notification to the child's home local authority that the child is being accommodated.[18]

**5.55** Section 21 of the CA 1989 makes it clear that the local authority has a duty to accommodate a child who has been removed subject to police protection, as discussed in more detail at chapter 9.

**5.56** The use of s 20 accommodation has come under a lot of scrutiny recently. The President in *Re N (Children) (Adoption: Jurisdiction)* commented that:[19]

> 'There has in recent months been a litany of judgments in which experienced judges of the Family Court have had occasion to condemn local authorities, often in necessarily strong, on occasions withering, language, for misuse, and in some cases plain abuse, of section 20.'

**5.57** The President identifies four separate problems outlined by the recent case law:

- the failure of the local authority to obtain informed consent from the parent(s) at the outset;
- the form in which the consent of the parent is recorded;
- that arrangements under s 20 are allowed to continue for far too long; and
- the seeming reluctance of local authorities to return the child to the parent(s) immediately upon a withdrawal of parental consent.

## *Parental consent*

**5.58** A child cannot be accommodated under s 20 of the CA 1989 without the consent of all people holding parental responsibility for the child, save in the circumstances set out at s 20(1)(a)–(c). Section 20(7) stipulates:

> 'A local authority may not provide accommodation under this section for any child if any person who –
>
> (a) has parental responsibility for him; and
> (b) is willing and able to –
>     (i) provide accommodation for him; or
>     (ii) arrange for accommodation to be provided for him,
>
> objects.'

---

[18] CA 1989, s 20(2).
[19] *See*, for example, *Re P (A Child: Use of S.20 CA 1989)* [2014] EWFC 775, a case involving the London Borough of Redbridge, *Re N (Children)* [2015] EWFC 37, a case involving South Tyneside Metropolitan Borough Council, *Medway Council v A and ors (Learning Disability: Foster Placement)* [2015] EWFC B66, *Gloucestershire County Council v M and C* [2015] EWFC B147, *Gloucestershire County Council v S* [2015] EWFC B149, *Re AS (Unlawful Removal of a Child)* [2015] EWFC B150, a case where damages were awarded against the London Borough of Brent, and *Medway Council v M and T (By Her Children's Guardian)* [2015] EWFC B164.

**5.59** The issue of consent is very important. In the event that a child has been accommodated under s 20 without parental consent, the local authority will have removed the child unlawfully and could be subject to an application for compensation under the Human Rights Act 1998.

**5.60** Some of the criticisms that have been made of local authorities recently by the courts include; failing to ensure that parents have the capacity to provide the necessary consent, placing parents under duress when obtaining their agreement; and failing to properly inform parents of the meaning of s 20 and their rights. Ultimately, the local authority <u>must</u> ensure that social workers understand what constitutes valid parental consent for the purposes of s 20.

## Capacity to provide parental consent

**5.61** Hedley J sets out guidance on capacity in *Coventry City Council v C, B, CA and CH*, namely that:[20]

> '(ii) every social worker obtaining consent from a parent is under a personal duty to be satisfied that the person giving the consent does not lack the required capacity.
>
> (iii) [...] the social worker must actively address the issue of capacity, take into account all the prevailing circumstances and must consider the questions raised by the Mental Capacity Act 2005, s 3 and in particular the mother's capacity to use and weigh all the relevant information.
>
> (iv) if the social worker has doubts about capacity, no further attempt should be made to obtain consent on that occasion. Advice should be sought from the social work team leader or management.'

**5.62** In *Newcastle City Council v WM & Others,* the mother was assessed as having severe learning difficulties and found not to have capacity to litigate in the proceedings and in need of assistance from the Official Solicitor. Cobb J considered that:[21]

> 'There is a significant question whether she *ever* had capacity to consent to the accommodation of her children (it is said, per Dr. Thorpe, consultant psychiatrist, that "she did not appear to understand the reasons why her children had been placed in foster care"), and whether, in the circumstances, the children were for the extended period referred to above lawfully accommodated.'

**5.63** Cobb J concluded that by virtue of this and the local authority's failure to take into consideration the guidance of Hedley J in *Coventry City Council v C, B, CA and CH* 'for a significant period of time, the children have been accommodated unlawfully'.[22]

---

[20] *Coventry City Council v C, B, CA and CH* [2013] 2 FLR 987 at [46].
[21] *Newcastle City Council v WM & Others* [2015] EWFC 42 at [3].
[22] *Newcastle City Council v WM & Others* [2015] EWFC 42 at [46].

## Ensuring parental consent is freely given

**5.64** The local authority must be careful to ensure that a parent does not feel under duress to provide consent to accommodation. The consent must be clearly and freely given and it is not possible for the local authority to equate any lack of objection to consent.

**5.65** In *Coventry City Council v C, B, CA and CH*, Hedley J stressed that the use of s 20 'must not be compulsion in disguise'[23] and that any such agreement requires genuine consent, not a mere 'submission in the face of asserted State authority'.[24]

**5.66** In *Re W (Children)*, Lord Tomlinson raised concern regarding the approach of the local authority of using the agreement to control the mother and her children without commencing care proceedings:[25]

> 'There must be a suspicion that the reason why the mother did not object was because she was made to understand that if her agreement was not forthcoming, public law proceedings would have been instigated. I cannot believe that section 20 was enacted in order to permit a local authority to assume control over the lives of the mother and her children in this way.'

**5.67** It is clear that a parent must not feel that they have no alternative but to agree to the accommodation. Whilst it may be the case that the local authority would intend to issue care proceedings in the event that the child could not be accommodated under s 20, this should not be used as a coercive factor to make a parent feel that they have no other choice but to consent. Clearly if the local authority did issue proceedings, it would be a question for the court as to whether a child would be removed on the basis of the evidence adduced, and by no means a foregone conclusion.

## Information given to parents as to the meaning of s 20

**5.68** A parent should always be informed that they are at liberty to take legal advice before consenting to accommodation provision under s 20. Just because a parent wishes to take legal advice does not mean that they are withholding consent, and they should be informed as such and not treated any differently.

**5.69** A parent should be informed that they are able to withdraw consent to accommodation at any time. In *Coventry City Council v C, B, CA and CH* Hedley J set out:[26]

> 'v) If the social worker is satisfied that the person whose consent is sought does not lack capacity, the social worker must be satisfied that the consent is fully informed:

---

[23] *Coventry City Council v C, B, CA and CH* [2013] 2 FLR 987 at [27].
[24] *Re G v Nottingham City Council and Nottingham University Hospital* [2008] EWHC 400 (Admin) at [61].
[25] *Re W (Children)* [2014] EWCA Civ 1065 at [41].
[26] *Coventry City Council v C,B,CA and CH* [2013] 2 FLR 987 at [46].

a) Does the parent fully understand the consequences of giving such a consent?
b) Does the parent fully appreciate the range of choice available and the consequences of refusal as well as giving consent?
c) Is the parent in possession of all the facts and issues material to the giving of consent?

vi) If not satisfied that the answers to a) – c) above are all 'yes', no further attempt should be made to obtain consent on that occasion and advice should be sought as above and the social work team should further consider taking legal advice if thought necessary.'

**5.70** The need to ensure that a parent does not feel under duress when being provided with the request for accommodation from the local authority is essential. Failure to do so can have significant consequences.

## Ability of a parent to withdraw their consent to s 20 accommodation

**5.71** There is a continuing right for a parent to withdraw their consent to the accommodation of the child. Section 20(8) provides:

'Any person who has parental responsibility for a child may at any time remove the child from accommodation provided by or on behalf of the local authority under this section.'

**5.72** Furthermore, in *Re N (Adoption: Jurisdiction)* the President made it clear that:[27]

'A local authority which fails to permit a parent to remove a child in circumstances within section 20(8) acts unlawfully, exposes itself to proceedings at the suit of the parent and may even be guilty of a criminal offence. A parent in that position could bring a claim against the local authority for judicial review or, indeed, seek an immediate writ of habeas corpus against the local authority.'

This right cannot be restricted, either by agreement with the parents or by any other mechanism.

## Proper use of s 20 accommodation

**5.73** In *Re N (Adoption: Jurisdiction)*, the President made clear that:[28]

'Accommodation of a child under a section 20 agreement deprives the child of the benefit of having an independent children's guardian to represent and safeguard his interests and deprives the court of the ability to control the planning for the child and prevent or reduce unnecessary and avoidable delay.'

---

[27] *Re N (Adoption: Jurisdiction)* [2016] 1 FLR 621 at [169].
[28] *Re N (Adoption: Jurisdiction)* [2016] 1 FLR 621 at [158].

**5.74** He continued:[29]

> 'The misuse and abuse of section 20 in this context is not just a matter of bad practice. It is wrong; it is a denial of the fundamental rights of both the parent and the child; it will no longer be tolerated; and it must stop. Judges will and must be alert to the problem and pro-active in putting an end to it. From now on, local authorities which use section 20 as a prelude to care proceedings for lengthy periods or which fail to follow the good practice I have identified, can expect to be subjected to probing questioning by the court. If the answers are not satisfactory, the local authority can expect stringent criticism and possible exposure to successful claims for damages.'

**5.75** Guidance has been provided by the President in *Re N (Adoption: Jurisdiction)* to assist the local authority in the use of s 20 accommodation:

> 'It follows, in my judgment, that for the future good practice requires the following, in addition to proper compliance with the guidance given by Hedley J which I have set out above:
>
> i) Wherever possible the agreement of a parent to the accommodation of their child under section 20 should be properly recorded in writing and evidenced by the parent's signature.
> ii) The written document should be clear and precise as to its terms, drafted in simple and straight-forward language that the particular parent can readily understand.
> iii) The written document should spell out, following the language of section 20(8), that the parent can "remove the child" from the local authority accommodation "at any time".
> iv) The written document should not seek to impose any fetters on the exercise of the parent's right under section 20(8).
> v) Where the parent is not fluent in English, the written document should be translated into the parent's own language and the parent should sign the foreign language text, adding, in the parent's language, words to the effect that "I have read this document and I agree to its terms".'

**5.76** The full guidance for social workers in respect of obtaining consent under s 20 (referred to throughout this chapter but provided below in full) is as per Hedley J in *Coventry City Council v C, B, CA and CH*:[30]

> 'i) Every parent has the right, if capacitous, to exercise their parental responsibility to consent under Section 20 to have their child accommodated by the local authority and every local authority has power under Section 20(4) so to accommodate provided that it is consistent with the welfare of the child.
> ii) Every social worker obtaining such a consent is under a personal duty (the outcome of which may not be dictated to them by others) to be satisfied that the person giving the consent does not lack the capacity to do so.

---

[29] *Re N (Adoption: Jurisdiction)* [2016] 1 FLR 621 at [171].
[30] *Coventry City Council v C, B, CA and CH* [2013] 2 FLR 987 at [46].

iii) In taking any such consent the social worker must actively address the issue of capacity and take into account all the circumstances prevailing at the time and consider the questions raised by Section 3 of the 2005 Act, and in particular the mother's capacity at that time to use and weigh all the relevant information.
iv) If the social worker has doubts about capacity no further attempt should be made to obtain consent on that occasion and advice should be sought from the social work team leader or management.
v) If the social worker is satisfied that the person whose consent is sought does not lack capacity, the social worker must be satisfied that the consent is fully informed:
   a) Does the parent fully understand the consequences of giving such a consent?
   b) Does the parent fully appreciate the range of choice available and the consequences of refusal as well as giving consent?
   c) Is the parent in possession of all the facts and issues material to the giving of consent?
vi) If not satisfied that the answers to a) – c) above are all "yes", no further attempt should be made to obtain consent on that occasion and advice should be sought as above and the social work team should further consider taking legal advice if thought necessary.
vii) If the social worker is satisfied that the consent is fully informed then it is necessary to be further satisfied that the giving of such consent and the subsequent removal is both fair and proportionate.
viii) In considering that it may be necessary to ask:
   a) what is the current physical and psychological state of the parent?
   b) If they have a solicitor, have they been encouraged to seek legal advice and/or advice from family or friends?
   c) Is it necessary for the safety of the child for her to be removed at this time?
   d) Would it be fairer in this case for this matter to be the subject of a court order rather than an agreement?
ix) If having done all this and, if necessary, having taken further advice (as above and including where necessary legal advice), the social worker then considers that a fully informed consent has been received from a capacitous mother in circumstances where removal is necessary and proportionate, consent may be acted upon.
x) In the light of the foregoing, local authorities may want to approach with great care the obtaining of Section 20 agreements from mothers in the aftermath of birth, especially where there is no immediate danger to the child and where probably no order would be made.'

**5.77** The guidance provided is not intended to undermine or curtail the use of s 20 accommodation but rather to emphasise the intention behind the drafting of the legislation. Parliament never intended the accommodation provision available under s 20 to be anything more than a short-term arrangement. As confirmed by the President in *Re N (Children) (Adoption: Jurisdiction)*:[31]

> 'Section 20 may, in an appropriate case, have a proper role to play as a short-term measure pending the commencement of care proceedings.'

---

[31] *Re N (Adoption: Jurisdiction)* [2016] 1 FLR 621 at [157].

**5.78** Section 20 does not provide the child with any stability or permanency. Their parents remain the only holders of parental responsibility and there will have been no judicial scrutiny of their removal from the family. A children's guardian can only be appointed within care proceedings, and it is only then that the child's position will be considered separately from the local authority's position and the position of the parents.

**5.79** If the local authority form the view that the child cannot return home, the matter must be bought before the court to enable this decision to be carefully scrutinised within the proper judicial process. Under s 20 the child is effectively left in limbo. This cannot and should never be a situation that continues for any length of time.

# CHAPTER 6

# THE PRE-PROCEEDINGS PROCESS

## INTRODUCTION

**6.1** The local authority's decision to issue proceedings and intervene in a family's life of has far-reaching implications for that family and, most importantly, the child. As a result, any such decision should be a last resort and there are a number of steps that should be taken before it is made.

**6.2** Following the provisions in the Children and Families Act 2014 ('CFA 2014') and the changes to the public law children process set out in the Family Justice Review,[1] local authorities have been issued with guidance from the Department of Education to assist with the steps that should now be taken prior to issuing an application for a care or supervision order.[2]

**6.3** Duties have been placed on local authorities to ensure the early identification of potential concerns and, where possible, to provide support for children and their families to address these issues.[3]

**6.4** Earlier chapters of this book have considered the duties and powers of the local authority to assist families that they have identified as 'in need', and to promote the care of children by and within their families. Assessments are provided for so that appropriate investigations can take place to enable the local authority to determine exactly what their concerns are and what assistance should be provided to the family and the child to address them. It is clear then, that there are a number of steps the local authority must take before escalating the situation to the point where proceedings are issued.

**6.5** It may not be possible for all of the pre-proceedings steps to be taken before commencing. In the event that a child needs immediate protection, proceedings must be issued and documents and assessments can be carried out at a later stage. However, wherever possible, the local authority should undertake and complete the pre-proceedings steps as described in PD12A.

---

[1]  *Family Justice Review*, (Ministry of Justice, November 2011).
[2]  *Court Orders and Pre-Proceedings*, (Department for Education, April 2014).
[3]  See chapter 5.

## Parents who may have learning difficulties or mental health issues

**6.6** It will often be the case that parents who are involved in the pre-proceedings process will have some difficulties in relation to their mental health, or perhaps a specific a learning difficulty. For those parents whose disabilities are sufficiently severe to suggest that they may lack the capacity to conduct legal proceedings, extra care should be taken pre-proceedings to ensure they are dealt with appropriately.

**6.7** The detailed guidance issued in 2007 entitled *Good Practice in Working with Parents with a Learning Disability* sets broad standards for local authorities to follow when working with parents who have learning difficulties in order to enable them to engage with the process. It is essential that each parent's particular difficulties are recognised and properly taken into account right from the beginning of any local authority involvement.

**6.8** An early cognitive functioning assessment may be particularly helpful in enabling the local authority to undertake parenting and other social work assessments on an informed basis, particularly during the pre-proceedings process. If a parent's difficulties are not recognised and accommodated, any assessment conducted by the local authority is open to be challenged if the matter proceeds to court, and may have to be completed again.

**6.9** In *RP v Nottingham City Council and the Official Solicitor*,[4] the court gave guidance on the steps that should be taken before and during care proceedings where there is an issue as to a parent's capacity to engage in those proceedings. If there are concerns held by those working with the parents that they might not be able to engage and understand the proceedings fully, they should refer that parent to the adult disability team within the local authority at the earliest opportunity.

## Wider family

**6.10** During the assessment process, it is important that wider family members are identified and involved as early as possible. The wider family can play a key role in supporting the child and helping the parents to address any identified problems. In the event that the problems escalate and children cannot live safely with their parents, local authorities should seek to place children with suitable, wider family members where possible.

**6.11** Wider family members may attend the case conference for a child and can also be involved in the assessment process, but only with the parents' agreement. Involving wider family members in the decision-making process where there are child protection or welfare concerns is an important part of pre-proceedings planning. This extends to decisions that a child cannot remain

---

[4] *RP v Nottingham City Council and the Official Solicitor* [2008] 2 FLR 1516.

safely with their birth parents. Family group conferences are an important way of involving the family at an early stage so that they can provide support to ensure the child is able to remain at home, or as part of the examination of alternative, permanent options for the child.

**6.12** Often parents will not wish for the wider family to be involved. The problems that these parents experience are sometimes not fully understood or completely unknown by their wider family. It is important for social workers to work closely with parents to assist them to seek help from the wider family where appropriate.

## *Family group conference*

**6.13** Local authorities should consider referring the family to a 'family group conference' service if they believe that there is a possibility the child may not be able to remain with their parents, unless such a meeting would pose a risk to the child. Parental consent is required before any such conference can be convened.

**6.14** The conference itself takes the form of a meeting involving the wider family and, where relevant, friends. The purpose of this is to assist the family members to understand the severity of the situation and the specific concerns the local authority have in respect of the child. Whilst the meeting is facilitated by the social worker, the family can prepare their own plan detailing how they could provide support to enable the child to remain with their parents. It is also an opportunity for the family and friends to consider whether they might be in a position to provide care for the child, if the child cannot safely remain with their parents.

**6.15** The guidance produced by the Department for Education sets out that the key features of a successful family group conference should include:[5]

> '• Having an independent coordinator to facilitate the involvement of the child, family network and professionals in the family group conference process;
> • Allowing the family private time at the family group conference to produce their plans for the child or young person; and
> • Agreeing and resourcing the family's plan unless it places the child at risk of significant harm.'

**6.16** A 'family plan', formulated and agreed by the conference attendees, should be produced at the end of the conference, and the local authority should then assist the family in putting their plan into action if it is considered to be in the best interests of the child.

---

[5] *Court Orders and Pre-Proceedings* (Department for Education, April 2014), para [24].

## Pre-proceedings meeting

**6.17** Once all assessments are completed and information gathered, proceedings may be avoided if the parents can demonstrate they can safeguard their child by working with the relevant services to improve their parenting ability. However, in light of all of the information gathered, the local authority may form the view that the child requires a protective placement with relatives or foster carers under s 20 of the Children Act 1989 ('CA 1989'). In the event that such a placement is considered necessary but the parents will not consent, the local authority should issue proceedings immediately without taking any further steps.

### *Legal planning meeting*

**6.18** In the event that the social worker has reached the decision that matters need to escalate to commencing proceedings, a legal planning meeting should be convened. This decision to issue will be taken if it is felt that the parents have not been able to address the concerns enough in order to protect the child from significant harm. Legal advice will be obtained from the local authority lawyer and a decision will be reached as to whether the circumstances meet the 'threshold' for proceedings, considering whether the child is suffering or at risk of suffering significant harm as a result of the care that that is being provided by the parents. For a full discussion of the threshold test, see chapter 13, for interim orders, and chapter 20 for final orders.

**6.19** In the event that either parent is likely to have potential difficulties understanding by virtue of their intellectual or mental capacity, this should be raised at this meeting to ensure that the necessary assessments are undertaken if they have not been completed already.

### *Letter before proceedings and pre-proceedings meetings*

**6.20** Unless the local authority considers that the level of risk requires an immediate application to be issued, the local authority should send a letter before proceedings to parents and anyone with parental responsibility for the child.

**6.21** The letter is the formal, written notification that proceedings are likely to occur and should set out the following:

- a summary, in simple language, of the local authority's concerns;
- a summary of what support has already been provided to the parents;
- what parents need to do and what support will be provided to them, in order to avoid proceedings (including timescales); and
- information on how to obtain legal advice and advocacy, along with a clear warning as to the importance of seeking legal representation and an up-to-date list of solicitors in the local area who specialise in public law children matters.

**6.22** The letter should invite the parents and holders of parental responsibility to a pre-proceedings meeting to examine the problems that have led to the concerns about the welfare of the child and how they can be addressed. The parents and holders of parental responsibility should attend the meeting with their legal representatives who will assist with their participation. The solicitor for the local authority should also attend.

**6.23** If the parents' first language is not English, consideration should be given as to whether an interpreter may be needed during this meeting, and the letter before proceedings should being sent to the parents in their own language as well as in English.

**6.24** The guidance from the Department for Education sets out the local authority's obligations at this meetings as follows:

- To agree a revised plan for the child, which should be subsequently confirmed in writing to the parents, setting out what the parents and the local authority must do to safeguard the child. It should indicate the steps the local authority will take to support the parents and the timescales within which progress must be made for proceedings to be avoided.
- To outline the steps that the local authority will take at the end of this period, depending on whether progress has been demonstrated.
- To review arrangements for identifying potential family carers, and/or for assessments with the parents, particularly where these require letters of instruction to assessment services.

**6.25** The local authority will also confirm whether any further assessments are considered necessary, such as psychological or psychiatric assessments. The parents will need to consent to these assessments and they cannot be forced to participate. Consideration must also be given as to whether a parent has the capacity to consent to such an assessment, in the event that there is a concern about their capacity to consent, the matter should be considered carefully by the local authority and the parent should be assisted in accessing specialist legal advice.

**6.26** It is hoped that by setting out clear expectations and the timescales for improvement that the potential for delay will be reduced, and proceedings may be avoided.

**6.27** It is recommended that the local authority should review the child's plan within 6 weeks of the meeting to ensure sufficient progress is being made. It is possible to organise a further meeting, in the same form as the initial meeting, with the legal representatives for the local authority and the parents present.

**6.28** If the parents' first language is not English, consideration should be given to the use of an interpreter during this meeting and the letter before proceedings being given to the parents in their own language as well as English.

## DECISION TO COMMENCE PROCEEDINGS

**6.29** Where the local authority is of the view that the parents cannot address their parenting within the required timescale and the 'threshold' for care proceedings has been met, it should decide whether to issue proceedings as quickly as possible.

**6.30** To ensure that the welfare of a child is safeguarded, the local authority must issue proceedings for a care or supervision order as soon as it becomes clear that there is no other alternative. In some cases, this will be clear from the child's immediate need for protection. In other cases, the decision to issue will be made once the local authority has seen that the assistance afforded to the family has not resulted in the necessary improvements in the care provided.

**6.31** In the event that a pre-proceedings meeting has occurred, the parent will have been provided with clear expectations and timescales in relation to the changes that are expected of them. If these issues have not been addressed and the local authority believe that the child remains at risk of significant harm, they will have no alternative but to issue care proceedings.

**6.32** The decision to commence proceedings will be taken with legal advice from the local authority lawyer at a further legal planning meeting.

## Preparation in readiness for proceedings

**6.33** All evidence and assessments on which the local authority intends to rely on in support of its application to the court should be up-to-date and prepared in advance. This includes any specialist assessments, whether commissioned as part of the early help assessments or later in the process, including those intended to inform the local authority's final decision on the initiation of proceedings.

**6.34** The CFA 2014 made changes to Part 12 of the FPR 2010 (discussed in more detail at chapter 10), including providing for a pre-proceedings checklist which should be considered prior to the issue of the proceedings. This checklist makes reference to all of the documents that the court will require when it considers the case; including:

- the social work chronology;
- the social work statement and genogram;
- the current assessments relating to the child and/or the family and friends of the child to which the social work statement refers and on which the local authority relies;
- the care plan; and
- the index of checklist documents.

**6.35** The following documents should also be available, but do not need to be sent with the application:

(1) Evidential documents including:
- previous court orders, including foreign orders and judgments/reasons;
- any assessment materials relevant to the key issues including capacity to litigate, s 7 and 37 reports;
- single, joint or inter-agency materials (eg, health and education/Home Office and Immigration Tribunal documents).

(2) Decision-making records including:
- records of key discussions with the family;
- key local authority minutes and records for the child;
- pre-existing care plans (eg, child in need plan, looked after child plan and child protection plan)
- letters before proceedings.

For full discussion the Public Law Outline, see chapter 10.

## Preparation prior to proceedings involving new-borns

**6.36** Care proceedings can only be started after a child's birth. Where the local authority is considering bringing proceedings for an unborn child, the pre-proceedings process provides an effective framework for social work with the parents before the birth of their child, ensuring fairness by enabling parents to get access to free, non-means-tested legal advice relating to:

- pre-birth assessments;
- the agreement of arrangements for support of the parents before and after the birth;
- the agreement of arrangements after the baby's discharge from hospital, if required, and
- assessment of parental care following the birth.

**6.37** The local authority may need to consider whether the parents should be invited to agree to s 20 accommodation once the baby is born. If this is being considered, the social worker involved must be careful to follow the guidance given by the President in *Re N (Adoption: Jurisdiction)*[6] on s 20 accommodation, dealt with fully at chapter 5.

---

[6] *Re N (Children) (Adoption: Jurisdiction)* [2016] 1 FLR 621.

# CHAPTER 7

# THRESHOLD CRITERIA

## INTRODUCTION

**7.1** When deciding whether to make an application for a care or supervision order, the local authority must consider whether the child's circumstances indicate that they are suffering or are likely to suffer significant harm. In the event that this cannot be established, the application will not succeed before the court.

**7.2** The harm suffered or likely to be suffered must be as a result of the parenting that the child is receiving. That parenting must fall below what is expected of a reasonable parent, or the child must be found to be beyond parental control.

**7.3** These criteria are contained in s 31(2) of the Children Act 1989 ('CA 1989') and are known as the 'threshold criteria' or 'threshold test':

'A court may only make a care order or supervision order if it is satisfied –

(a) that the child concerned is suffering, or is likely to suffer, significant harm; and
(b) that the harm, or likelihood of harm, is attributable to –
   (i) the care given to the child, or likely to be given to him if the order were not made, not being what it would be reasonable to expect a parent to give to him; or
   (ii) the child's being beyond parental control.'

**7.4** Section 31(2) of the CA 1989 essentially provides a two-stage test to establish 'threshold'. The first limb requires demonstrating that the child has suffered or is likely to suffer significant harm. The second limb requires that the harm must be attributable to the care provided to them, being below that of the standard that would be expected of a reasonable parent.

**7.5** A court cannot make a care or supervision order unless satisfied that the threshold criteria have been met. Emergency protection and child assessment orders do not require the threshold criteria to be met, but the court must still be satisfied that there is reasonable cause to believe that the child is likely to suffer significant and immediate harm.[1]

---

[1] See chapter 7.

**7.6** As part of the evidence before the court, the local authority will prepare a 'threshold document'. Practice differs: the threshold document can either be a standalone document or contained within the application made by the local authority for the care or supervision order.

**7.7** Once significant harm is established, compulsory intervention into family life, in the best interests of the child, is justified. The existence of, or potential for significant harm is considered throughout child protection procedures from considering the need for assessment, to the need to formulate a child protection plan, through to the issue of care proceedings.

**7.8** This chapter will consider the threshold criteria and what evidence is required to establish that it has been crossed. Discussions in relation to any of the orders that can be made and the interventions possible following the finding that the threshold is met can be found in other chapters.

## THE FIRST LIMB: WHAT IS 'SIGNIFICANT HARM'?

**7.9** When considering what amounts to 'significant harm', it is necessary to first consider what 'harm' means within the CA 1989. Section 31(9) of the CA 1989 sets out the definition of 'harm' as follows:

> '"harm" means ill-treatment or the impairment of health or development including, for example, impairment suffered from seeing or hearing the ill-treatment of another;
> "development" means physical, intellectual, emotional, social or behavioural development;
> "health" means physical or mental health; and
> "ill-treatment" includes sexual abuse and forms of ill-treatment which are not physical.'

From this definition it is clear that 'harm' includes all areas of a child's health and development, including impairment resulting from witnessing someone else being harmed.[2]

**7.10** The definition does not seek to specify exactly what amounts to 'significant harm'. Section 31(10) of the CA 1989 provides that:

> 'Where the question of whether harm suffered by a child is significant turns on the child's health or development, his health or development shall be compared with that which could reasonably be expected of a similar child.'

**7.11** This provision constitutes a yard stick by which the impairment to the child's health or development can be measured, but still does not provide clarity as to what might amount to 'significant harm'.

---

[2] Amended to include reference to 'seeing or hearing the ill-treatment of another' via the Adoption and Children Act 2002, s 120.

**7.12** In *Re B (A Child)* Lord Wilson was clear that the court should avoid providing a strict definition as to what amounts to 'significant harm'. He said:[3]

> 'In my view this court should avoid attempting to explain the word "significant". It would be a gloss; attention might then turn to the meaning of the gloss and, albeit with the best of intentions, the courts might find in due course that they had travelled far from the word itself.'

**7.13** He considered what was included in the White Paper preceding the CA 1989, *The Law on Child Care and Family Services (Cm 62, January 1987)*, and quoted:[4]

> 'It is intended that "likely harm" should cover all cases of unacceptable risk in which it may be necessary to balance the chance of the harm occurring against the magnitude of that harm if it does occur.'

**7.14** In *Re C and B (Care Order: Future Harm)*, Hale LJ, as she then was, explained that:[5]

> 'A comparatively small risk of really serious harm can justify action, while even the virtual certainty of slight harm might not.'

**7.15** It is clear that the question of whether the existing or likely harm is 'significant' is very much dependent on the facts of the case itself. In *Re L (Care: Threshold Criteria)*, Hedley J reiterated that:[6]

> 'Society must be willing to tolerate very diverse standards of parenting, including the eccentric, the barely adequate and the inconsistent.'

**7.16** He continued:[7]

> 'Significant harm is fact-specific and must retain the breadth of meaning that human fallibility may require of it [...] It is clear that it must be something unusual; at least something more than the commonplace human failure or inadequacy.'

Importantly, 'significant harm' does not only result from an intentional or deliberate action or inaction.

**7.17** In *Re A (A Child)* the President expressly approved the judgement of HHJ Jack in *North East Lincolnshire Council v G & L* and quoted:[8]

---

[3] *Re B (A Child)* [2013] UKSC 33 at [26].
[4] *Re B (A Child)* [2013] UKSC 33 at [26].
[5] *Re C and B (Care Order: Future Harm)* [2000] EWCA Civ 3040 at [28].
[6] *Re L (Care: Threshold Criteria)* [2007] 1 FLR 2050 at [50].
[7] *Re L (Care: Threshold Criteria)* [2007] 1 FLR 2050 at [51].
[8] *Re A (A Child)* [2015] EWFC 11 at [16].

'The courts are not in the business of providing children with perfect homes. If we took into care and placed for adoption every child whose parents had had a domestic spat and every child whose parents on occasion had drunk too much then the care system would be overwhelmed and there would not be enough adoptive parents. So we have to have a degree of realism about prospective carers who come before the courts.'

**7.18** It is worth noting that in the matter of *Re MA (Care Threshold)*, Ward LJ commented that:[9]

'The harm must, in my judgment, be significant enough to justify the intervention of the State and disturb the autonomy of the parents to bring up their children by themselves in the way they choose.'

**7.19** What is evident from the case law is that consideration of what amounts to 'significant harm' is a matter to be assessed on an objective basis in light of the facts of the case. Such assessment should be realistic and take into account any 'commonplace human failure or inadequacy'.[10] Ultimately, any concern that a child is at risk of significant harm compels the local authority and indeed the court to intervene in family life by virtue of the CA 1989, and therefore the 'harm' must be identifiable and significant.

## SUFFERING OR LIKELY TO SUFFER

**7.20** Having considered what is meant by 'significant harm', it is prudent to consider the second aspect of the first part of the threshold criteria: 'suffering or likely to suffer'. Section 31(2) of the CA 1989 allows the court to make a care or supervision order if it is satisfied that the child is 'suffering or likely to suffer significant harm'. When considering the local authority's assessment and the need for a child protection plan, the potential difference between any current and/or future harm is important in order to assess risk and plan how to safeguard the child. In essence, this is about risk management: what harm has there been, what harm could there be and how can all of this be managed?

**7.21** In the context of care proceedings, the court must be satisfied that at the point of the application, or when continuous protective measures were taken, the child was suffering or was likely to suffer significant harm. This is known as the 'relevant date' and is discussed in more detail at chapter 13.

**7.22** The question then, is how 'likely' does harm have to be in order to cross the threshold outlined in s 31(2)? Lord Nicholls in *Re H and Others (Minors) (Sexual Abuse: Standard of Proof)* described 'likelihood' as follows:[11]

---

[9] *Re MA (Care Threshold)* [2010] 1 FLR 431 at [54].
[10] *Re L (Care: Threshold Criteria)* [2007] 1 FLR 2050 at [50].
[11] *Re H and Others (Minors) (Sexual Abuse: Standard of Proof)* [1996] AC 563, [1996] 1 FLR 80 at [585F].

'In my view, therefore the context shows that in s. 31(2)(a) likely is being used in the sense of a real possibility, a possibility that cannot sensibly be ignored having regard to the nature and gravity of the feared harm in the particular case.'

**7.23** The importance of the likelihood of harm is not equal to the severity of the harm and it is worth repeating Hale LJ in *Re C and B (Care Order: Future Harm)* to that effect:[12]

'A comparatively small risk of really serious harm can justify action, while even the virtual certainty of slight harm might not.'

**7.24** In this context, the seriousness of potential harm is relevant when considering whether intervention is necessary. The more serious the harm, the more likely it is that it an intervention is required to safeguard the child.

## THE SECOND LIMB: ATTRIBUTABLE TO THE CARE PROVIDED

**7.25** The question as to whether the harm that the child has suffered or is likely to suffer is as a result of the care provided by a parent falls within the second limb of the threshold test.

**7.26** In *Re B (A Child)* Lord Wilson considered this point and found:[13]

'Section 31 (2)(b)(i) requires only that the harm or likelihood of harm should be "attributable" to the care given or likely to be given to the child not being what it would be reasonable to expect a parent to give to him. Such is a requirement only of causation as between the care and the harm. The provision was prefigured in the White Paper, Cm 62, cited above, also at para 60:

"The court will also have to make a decision as to whether the harm was caused or will in future be caused by the child not receiving a reasonable standard of care or by the absence of adequate parental control. This is not intended to imply a judgment on the parent who may be doing his best but is still unable to provide a reasonable standard of care".'

**7.27** In this case it was submitted that the character of a parent was the underlying reason for concern, not their parenting capacity. Lord Wilson was clear that character is relevant at every stage of consideration insofar as it impacts upon the parent's ability to provide adequate care. He reiterated:[14]

'There is no requisite mental element to accompany the actions or inactions which have caused, or are likely to cause, significant harm to the child.'

---

[12] *Re C and B (Care Order: Future Harm)* [2000] EWCA Civ 3040 at [28].
[13] *Re B (A Child)* [2013] UKSC 33 at [31].
[14] *Re B (A Child)* [2013] UKSC 33 at [31].

**7.28** As articulated by Lady Hale in *Re B (A Child) (Care Proceedings: Threshold Criteria):*[15]

> 'We are all frail human beings, with our fair share of unattractive character traits, which sometimes manifest themselves in bad behaviours which may be copied by our children. But the State does not and cannot take away the children of all the people who commit crimes, who abuse alcohol or drugs, who suffer from physical or mental illnesses or disabilities, or who espouse antisocial political or religious beliefs.'

## A reasonable parent

**7.29** The final element of the second limb of the threshold test is the assessment as to whether the care being given is in line with what would be reasonable to expect a parent to give. The obvious question follows: who is a 'reasonable parent'?

**7.30** The President, in *Re A (A Child)*, emphasised that:[16]

> 'The courts are not in the business of providing children with perfect homes. If we took into care and placed for adoption every child whose parents had had a domestic spat and every child whose parents on occasion had drunk too much then the care system would be overwhelmed and there would not be enough adoptive parents. So we have to have a degree of realism about prospective carers who come before the courts.'

**7.31** Following the welfare checklist, discussed in chapter 2, the court must consider the age, sex, background and any characteristics of a child. Similarly, Munby J, as he then was, said in *Re K, A Local Authority v N and Others*, that when considering the care afforded to the child:[17]

> 'the court must always be sensitive to the cultural, social and religious circumstances of the particular child and family.'

**7.32** However, the parents subject to child protection procedures are often vulnerable themselves. Their vulnerability might be as a result of a learning difficulty or physical impairment, or simply as a result of their age, life experiences or lifestyle (such as substance misuse). However, the test is not whether the harm is attributable to the care that is reasonable to expect of *this* parent but rather *a* parent. It is an objective test and does not take into consideration the vulnerability of the parent themselves. Moreover: there is no requisite mental element to accompany the actions or inactions of a parent: a parent does not need to intentionally cause the harm, the issue rests solely on whether harm has been caused or is likely to be caused to the child.

---

[15] *Re B (A Child) (Care Proceedings: Threshold Criteria)* [2013] UKSC 33 at [143].
[16] *Re A (A Child)* [2015] EWFC 11 at [16].
[17] *Re K, A Local Authority v N and Others* [2005] EWHC 2956 (Fam), [2007] 1 FLR 399 at [26].

## BEYOND PARENTAL CONTROL

**7.33** This limb of the threshold test is rarely employed. Section 31(2)(b)(ii) provides that if a child is putting themselves at risk of harm, through no fault of their parents, the court can make a care or supervision order. Again, when local authorities are considering whether a child is suffering or likely to suffer significant harm prior to proceedings, this should be a consideration when deciding what measures may be necessary to safeguard the child.

**7.34** The question as to whether a child is beyond parental control is a question of fact. This limb of the threshold test is usually pleaded in cases of older children with behaviours or difficulties that are causing them significant harm. It is usually clear from the facts as to whether it can be successfully demonstrated that the child has suffered significant harm as a result of being beyond parental control.

**7.35** It is unclear as to whether, when a child is found to beyond parental control, it is then necessary to attribute that fact to the care given to them by their parent(s).

**7.36** There is very little case law on this important distinction. In *Lancashire County Council v Barlow,* Lord Nicholls observed that:[18]

> '[...] the phrase "attributable" in s 31(2)(b) connotes a causal connection between the harm or likelihood of harm on the one hand and the care or likely care of the child's being beyond parental control on the other[...]. The connection need not be that of a sole or dominant or direct cause and effect, a contributory causal connection suffices.'

**7.37** It would seem then, that at the very least *some* link will need to be established in order for threshold to be crossed and a public law order made, although that may be as simple as demonstrating that the parents are unable to prevent the child from behaving in the way they are.

## Difference between interim and final threshold

**7.38** In order for the court to make an interim care or supervision order under s 38 of the CA 1989, the court must be satisfied that there are 'reasonable grounds for believing that the circumstances with respect to the child are as mentioned in section 31(2)'.[19] The court will therefore need to set out in its judgment what evidence there is to demonstrate that there are reasonable grounds to believe that the child is suffering or likely to suffer significant harm.

---

[18] *Lancashire County Council and Another v Barlow and Another* [2000] UKHL 16 at [5].
[19] CA 1989, s 38(2).

**7.39** When considering the final threshold before making a public law order, as set out in s 31(2), the court must have clear evidence that the threshold has been crossed beyond 'reasonable grounds for believing'. This is discussed later in this book.

# Part 3

# EMERGENCY INTERVENTION

# CHAPTER 8

# POLICE PROTECTION: SECTION 46 OF THE CHILDREN ACT 1989

## THE ROLE OF THE POLICE IN CHILD PROTECTION

**8.1** The police are frequently the first agency to respond to child protection concerns, as they are for so many other social problems, and their role goes beyond the statutory power to remove children for their protection discussed in this chapter. As an example of the approach of the police to child protection issues, one may take the published policy of the Kent Police on the use of this power:[1]

> 'The priorities of Kent Police in responding to child abuse and neglect are as follows:
>
> - To protect the lives of children and ensure that in the policing of child abuse, the welfare of all children is paramount.
> - To investigate all reports of child abuse and neglect and to protect the rights of child victims of crime.
> - To take effective action against offenders so they can be held accountable through the criminal justice system, whilst safeguarding the welfare of the child.
> - To adopt a proactive multi-agency approach to preventing and reducing child abuse in line with the agreed arrangements of the Local Safeguarding Children Boards (LSCBs) of Kent and Medway.'

**8.2** The dual responsibility of the police to protect children but also to investigate crime and act against offenders sets them apart from other agencies. The balancing of these roles makes it particularly important that paramountcy is accorded to the welfare of children and that an effective multi-agency approach is taken to child protection issues; these are issues that are discussed elsewhere in this work.

## POLICE POWERS TO REMOVE CHILDREN

**8.3** The power of the police to protect a children by removing them to a, 'place of safety' (an evocative phrase that continued to feature in child

---

[1] Kent Police Policies: O37 Police Protection, Section 46 Children Act 1989. Kent Police website (kent.police.uk) accessed 25 July 2016.

protection legislation until the 1989 Act) was first introduced in 1889.[2] This power is now found in s 46 of the Children Act 1989.

## A unique, emergency, power

**8.4** It is noteworthy that s 46 provides the only instance of a power to remove children from their parents without an order from a court of competent jurisdiction. As Munby J (as he then was) pointed out in the case of *R (G) v Nottingham City Council*:[3]

> '[15] The law is perfectly clear but perhaps requires re-emphasis. Whatever the impression a casual reader might gain from reading some newspaper reports, no local authority and no social worker has any power to remove a child from its parent or, without the agreement of the parent, to take a child into care, unless they have first obtained an order from a family court authorising that step: either an emergency protection order in accordance with s 44 of the Children Act 1989 or an interim care order in accordance with s 38 of the Act or perhaps, in an exceptional case (and subject to s 100 of the Act), a wardship order made by a judge of the Family Division of the High Court.
> 
> [16] Section 46 of the Children Act 1989 permits a police constable to remove a child where he has reasonable cause to believe that the child would otherwise be likely to suffer significant harm, and that power can be exercised without prior judicial authority. But the powers conferred on the police by s 46 are *not* given to either local authorities or social workers.
> 
> [17] Local authorities and social workers have no power to remove children from their parents unless they have first obtained judicial sanction for what they are proposing to do. Only a court can make a care order. Only if a court has authorised that step, whether by making an emergency protection order or by making a care order or an interim care order or in some other way, can a local authority or a social worker remove a child from a parent ...'[4]

**8.5** The section's heading refers to its use, 'in cases of emergency' and Home Office guidance issued to the police emphasises that:[5]

> 'Police protection is an emergency power and should only be used when necessary, the principle being that whenever possible the decision to remove a child/children from a parent or carer should be made by a court.'

---

[2] Prevention of Cruelty to, and Protection of, Children Act 1889, s 4(1). Immediately prior to the coming into force of the 1989 Act the corresponding power was found in s 28(2) of the Children and Young Persons Act 1969 under which a child could be detained for up to 8 days (s 28(5)).

[3] [2008] 1 FLR 1660.

[4] His Lordship did add two qualifications to this statement. The first (see para [21]) referred to the general power of any person to intervene to prevent an actual or threatened assault and the second (para [23]) to the general power of a person who has care of a child to act to safeguard or promote their welfare conferred by s 3(5) of the 1989 Act.

[5] Home Office Circular 017/2008 (referred to below as 'Home Office Guidance'), para 15.

**8.6**  As the power does not derive from a court decision it is wrong to refer to a, 'police protection order':[6] s 46(2) provides that child in respect of whom the power has been exercised is referred to for the purposes of the Act as, 'having been taken into police protection'.

## Police protection and voluntary accommodation

**8.7**  In the case of *R (G) v Nottingham City Council* Munby J (as he then was) refers to a child being taken into care with the agreement of their parents. Local authorities have a duty to provide accommodation for children when the person who has care of them is prevented from doing so[7] and either no person with parental responsibility who is willing and able to provide or arrange accommodation objects[8] or a person named in a child arrangements order as being a person with whom the child is to live or who holds a special guardianship order agrees.[9] This procedure is commonly referred to as the child placed in 'voluntary' or 'section 20' accommodation. A number of reported cases have emphasised that such arrangements must be truly voluntary, that there must be no element of coercion used to induce parents to agree to their children being looked after and that the safeguards in the Act should be observed.[10]

**8.8**  There is a danger that when police become involved their very presence can act as a coercive factor. This can in turn contribute to the sort of abuse of the voluntary accommodation procedure that was described and condemned by Theis J in the case of *Re E (A Child)*:[11]

> '[60] What the LA should have done was apply for either an EPO or interim care order on short notice (as set out in the clear guidance from McFarlane J (as he then was) in *Re X* [2006] EWHC 510 Fam). This would have required the LA to set out its evidence in statement form and the parents would have had an opportunity to be properly represented and challenge the LA case. The LA, in their written submissions, realistically accepts the procedure adopted by them that evening cannot be justified. They are right to do so. To use the section 20 procedure in circumstances where there was the overt threat of a police protection order if they did not agree, re-enforced by the physical presence of uniformed police officers, was wholly inappropriate. By adopting this procedure the LA sought to circumvent the test any court would have required them to meet if they sought to secure an order, either by way of an EPO or interim care order.'

---

[6]  Although this phrase is often used and appears in several reported judgments.
[7]  Section 20(1) of the 1989 Act.
[8]  Section 20(7) of the 1989 Act.
[9]  Section 20(9), which also applies to a person who has care of the child by virtue of an order made in the High Court under its inherent jurisdiction.
[10]  See, for a recent example, the comments of, and review of the case law by, Sir James Munby P in the case of *Re N (Adoption: Jurisdiction)* [2015] EWCA Civ 1112, [2016] 1 FLR 621 at paras [157]–[171].
[11]  [2013] EWHC 2400 (Fam).

**8.9** The Home Office Guidance[12] reminds officers that emergency protection orders can be obtained speedily and outside normal court hours and is clear that, '[p]olice protection powers should only be used when this is not possible'. It is suggested that if police officers keep this guidance in mind they will avoid being drawn into playing a role in an inappropriate, and probably unlawful, removal of children by way of an agreement for them to be accommodated that is tainted by duress.

## The power and the decision to exercise it

**8.10** Section 46(1) of the Act defines the power of the police and the grounds for exercising it and does so in following terms:

> '(1) Where a constable has reasonable cause to believe that a child would otherwise be likely to suffer significant harm, he may –
>
> (a) remove the child to suitable accommodation and keep him there; or
> (b) take such steps as are reasonable to ensure that the child's removal from any hospital, or other place, in which he is then being accommodated is prevented.'

**8.11** The concepts of, 'reasonable cause' and, 'significant harm' receive detailed treatment elsewhere but in construing this subsection it is important to bear in mind the observation of Dyson LJ (as he then was) in the case of *Langley v Liverpool City Council* that:[13]

> 'The relevant provisions of the Act should be construed so as to further the manifest object of securing the protection of children who are at risk of significant harm. A construction of the Act which prohibits a constable from removing a child under s 46 where he has reasonable cause to believe that the child would otherwise be likely to suffer significant harm would frustrate that object.'

**8.12** However, the draconian nature of a power to remove a child without court authority must always be borne in mind. As Hedley J put it in the case of *A v East Sussex County Council and Chief Constable of Sussex Police*:[14]

> '[23] It is essential to stress that even in an emergency it is desirable, where possible, to work in partnership with a parent. Parents can with careful and sympathetic explanation be brought to agree to regimes of supervision, or to the child remaining in hospital or even to voluntary accommodation under Part III of the Act for a brief period. Where parents have access to a solicitor (particularly where, as here, he or she is available), then the solicitor should be apprised of the

---

[12] Paragraph 16.
[13] [2006] 1 FLR 342, CA, at para [32]. *Langley* as an unusual case in which the police had taken a child into protection when an emergency protection order had already been made. The Court of Appeal held (reversing the trial judge) that the existence of an Emergency Protection Order did not of itself render the use of the s 46 power unlawful but went on to hold that the use of the power to remove under the court order should be preferred, that there was, on the facts of that case, no 'compelling reason' to use s 46 powers and that the removal was therefore unlawful.
[14] [2010] 2 FLR 1596, CA.

local authority's concerns and proposals and then be invited (if the solicitor thinks it proper to do so) to give advice to the parent. Even where emergency powers are obtained under s 44 or exercised under s 46, least interventions are best. For example the police have power to prevent a removal from hospital. In the circumstances of this case it would have been surprising had the hospital, if pressed, refused to keep the child for an extra 2 days. The removal of the child to a known destination (eg a relative) is to be preferred to removal to a stranger. If, however, there is removal to a stranger, the parent should, in the absence of good reason (eg abusive or irrational behaviour) be informed of the fact and be allowed to pass relevant information to the carer and speedy arrangements be made for contact. If a court order has not been obtained or obtained ex parte, an inter partes hearing should be arranged as soon as possible. The judge described a hearing 2 days hence as "creditable" but it should also be the norm. It goes without saying that where practicable an order of the court should be sought in preference to the use of s 46 powers.'

**8.13** Inappropriate use of the power can expose the police force and local authority concerned to claims that the removal of the child amounted to an unlawful interference with family life protected by Art 8 of the European Convention for the Protection of Human Rights and Fundamental Freedoms 1950 and to damages claims under s 7 of the Human Rights Act 1998.[15]

**8.14** The police's power under s 46 is not limited to the removal of children from neglectful or abusive carers. It includes taking into protection lost or abandoned children, unaccompanied migrant children and even, in one reported case, a 16 year old who was out late at night at a fast food outlet in the company of an, 'inappropriate' adult.[16]

**8.15** A constable who is not a 'Home Office' police officer (the most numerous being officers of the British Transport Police) can take a child into protection but should then hand the child over to the local Home Office police force.[17]

## The consequences of a child being taken into police protection

### Accommodating the child

**8.16** The primary consequence of a child becoming police protected is that they are either removed to 'suitable accommodation' or are prevented from being removed from a 'hospital or other place' where they are accommodated. Section 46 does not in terms define the, 'suitable accommodation' to which the child may be removed. However, s 46(3)(f) places a duty on, 'the constable concerned':

'(W)here the child was taken into police protection by being removed to accommodation which is not provided –

---

[15] Both the *Langely* and *East Sussex* cases involved claims of this nature.
[16] *A (A Child) v Chief Constable of Dorset Police* [2011] 1 FLR 11.
[17] Home Office Guidance, para 13.

(i) by or on behalf of a local authority; or
(ii) as a refuge, in compliance with the requirements of section 51,

secure that he is moved to accommodation which is so provided.'

**8.17** The Home Office Guidance states[18] that, 'suitable accommodation' would normally mean local authority accommodation, a registered children's home or foster care but that if the 'designated officer'[19] and children's social care consider it appropriate the child may be placed with, 'relatives or other appropriate carers'.[20] A police station is not, 'suitable accommodation' but a child may be taken there for a short period in exceptional circumstances (such as lack of available local authority accommodation) and subject to safeguards: however a child under police protections must, '*on no account*'[21] be taken to the cellblock area of a police station.[22]

## Duration of, and discharge from, police protection

**8.18** No child may be kept in police protection for more than 72 hours;[23] there is no provision for extension of this period.

**8.19** The Home Office Guidance provides:[24]

'It should be extremely rare that a child remains under police protection for 72 hours. Normally arrangements for children's social care to provide accommodation for the child or to apply for an EPO [Emergency Protection Order] should be undertaken within a few hours of the child being taken into police protection. The continuation of a child's placement in police protection should be subject to regular review by the designated officer.'

**8.20** The designated officer is under a positive duty to release the child on completing his enquiries unless he considers that there is, '. . . still reasonable cause for believing that the child would be likely to suffer significant harm if released'.[25] Home Office guidance provides that any decision to release a child from police protection should be taken, 'following discussion with the relevant personnel in the Children's Social Care'[26] and that a child should only be discharged from police protection if they are considered by the designated officer to be no longer at risk, an emergency protection order has been obtained or the child has been accommodated by the local authority under s 20 of the Act and is no longer considered to be at risk of significant harm.[27]

---

[18] Paragraph 25.
[19] An officer of at least the rank of inspector designated by the chief officer of police to investigate cases where s 46 powers are executed: see s 46(3)(e) and Home Office Guidance, para 9.
[20] Paragraph 25.
[21] Emphasis in original.
[22] Paragraphs 28 and 29.
[23] Section 46(6).
[24] Paragraph 40.
[25] Section 46(5).
[26] Paragraph 39.
[27] Paragraph 38.

## Parental responsibility

**8.21** In keeping with the principle that protection under s 46 is a short term, emergency measure, it does not supplant the parental responsibility of parents or others who hold parental responsibility and gives the police only limited power to take action in relation to the child. Section 46(9) provides:

> '(9) While a child is being kept in police protection –
>
> (a) neither the constable concerned nor the designated officer shall have parental responsibility for him; but
>
> (b) the designated officer shall do what is reasonable in all the circumstances of the case for the purpose of safeguarding or promoting the child's welfare (having regard in particular to the length of the period during which the child will be so protected).'

**8.22** It is noteworthy that the power to act in s 46(9)(b) is expressed in exactly the same terms as that conferring a right to act on any person who has care of a child without having parental responsibility contained in s 3(5) of the act; to that extent police officers have no special status or power to act without a court order. The Home Office guidance comments that, 'in practical terms' acting to safeguard the child's welfare may not extend beyond providing food and shelter and makes the point that in the event of a medical emergency a doctor would act in the patient's best interests (ie in accordance with s 3(5)) without express consent as an officer could not give consent as they lack parental responsibility.[28]

## Communication with parents and contact with a child in police protection

**8.23** Section 46(4) imposes on the constable who takes a child into protection a duty, 'as soon as is reasonably practicable' to inform the child's parents, any other person with parental responsibility and any person with whom the child was living before being taken into protection of the steps that have been taken under the section, the reasons for taking those steps and the further steps that may be taken in respect of the child under the section. A similar duty to inform the child, 'if he appears capable of understanding' arises under s 46(3)(c).

**8.24** Section 46(10) requires the, 'designated officer' to allow such contact ('if any') with the child by his parents and other persons as listed in the subsection as, 'in the opinion of the designated officer, is both reasonable and in the child's best interests'. The decision to allow contact between a child under police protection and a parent (who may be implicated in abuse or serious neglect of the child) can be a difficult one, as can that of identifying safeguards that should be put in place around contact. The Home Office guidance recommends that wherever possible any issues regarding contact should be jointly agreed with children's social care.[29]

---

[28] Paragraph 43.
[29] Paragraph 46.

## What follows police protection of a child?

### Involvement of the local authority

**8.25** The Act requires the constable who takes a child into protection to inform, '(a)s soon as is reasonably practicable' the local authority within whose area the child is found of the fact and circumstances of this being done[30] and the local authority in whose area the child is ordinarily resident of the place where the child is being accommodated.[31] When a local authority receives such notification it has a duty to:[32]

> 'make, or cause to be made, such enquiries as they consider necessary to enable them to decide whether they should take any action to promote or safeguard the child's welfare.'

**8.26** In practice the local authority will at this stage be concerned to form a view as to whether:

- the child can return to their parents or other usual carers (and, if so, with what local authority support and monitoring); or
- there are other family members (or members of the child's social circle) who can look after the child if the parents or (other persons with parental responsibility) agree; or
- the parents or (other persons with parental responsibility) should be asked to give agreement to the child being accommodated by the local authority under s 20 of the Act; or
- the local authority should apply to the court for an emergency protection order.

**8.27** In deciding which course to take the local authority's paramount concern will be the welfare of the child and they will also have to have regard to the principle that the course that involves the least state interference in family life consistent with the child's welfare should be preferred. However, given the very short duration of police protection for a child, there is inevitably a tendency to err on the side of caution by seeking an emergency protection order so that the child's safety can be ensured whilst other options are investigated.

**8.28** Local authority applications for emergency protection orders are considered in the next chapter.

---

[30] Section 46(3)(a).
[31] Section 46(3)(b).
[32] Section 47(1).

## Applications by the police

**8.29** Section 46(7) provides that the designated officer may themselves apply for an emergency protection order, 'on behalf of the appropriate authority' and may do so, 'whether or not the authority know of it or agree to it being made'.[33]

**8.30** These subsections would allow the police to make an application if the local authority decided not to do so but is difficult to imagine circumstances in which the police would do so. The Home Office Guidance described these circumstances as, 'rare' (without suggesting examples) and recommends that the local Clerk to the Justices be consulted if such an application is to be made.[34]

## Evidence in subsequent proceedings

**8.31** As with other aspects of police operations, there is a requirement to record observations made and actions taken in exercising powers under s 46 and the Home Office guidance provides for this and has attached a checklist of matters that need to be recorded.[35] This record, made contemporaneously by a trained observer, can be a valuable source of information, and be of evidential use, in subsequent emergency protection order or care order proceedings.

**8.32** Other, potentially valuable, records are kept by the police as part of their general procedures and in accordance with the requirements of the Police and Criminal Evidence Act 1984.

---

[33] Section 46(8).
[34] Paragraphs 53 and 54.
[35] Paragraph 10 and Appendix A.

# CHAPTER 9

# EMERGENCY PROTECTION ORDERS

## THE NATURE OF AN EMERGENCY PROTECTION ORDER
### 'A terrible and drastic remedy'[1]

**9.1** An emergency protection order made under s 44 of the Children Act 1989 is a court order that authorises the taking of urgent steps to protect a child. These steps will almost invariably involve the separation of the child from its parents.[2] Whilst such an order is in force, parental responsibility for the child can be exercised (subject to limitations) by a non-parent (generally, a local authority)[3] and contact between parent and child can be restricted or withheld entirely.[4] Furthermore, a person (including a parent) may be guilty of a criminal offence if they obstruct a removal of the child that is authorised by the order.[5]

**9.2** An order producing these serious consequences can be made at a hearing of which parents have been given very little notice, or indeed one of which they have deliberately not been notified, and can even be made over the telephone.[6] Before the introduction of the single family court in 2014 applications for such orders were required (unless the child was already the subject of proceedings in the county court or the High Court) to be made to a magistrates court[7] and so would generally be heard by lay justices. An order can be made by a single lay justice.[8] There is no right to appeal against the making of the order.[9]

**9.3** A number of reported cases have commented on the draconian nature of these orders and the caution that should be exercised when a court is asked to make one. These comments are usually made in the context of criticism of the

---

[1] Per Munby J (as he then was) in *X Council v B (Emergency Protection Orders)* [2005] 1 FLR 341, para 57.
[2] Section 44(4)(b).
[3] Section 44(4)(c).
[4] Section 44(6) and (13).
[5] Section 44(15) and (16).
[6] Family Procedure Rules 2010 ('FPR 2010'), r 12.6.
[7] See Allocation and Transfer of Proceedings Order 2008, art 5(2) (revoked). The Family Court (Composition and Distribution of Business) Rules 2014, art 16(3) now allocates applications to, 'the first available judge of the family court'.
[8] FPR 2010, r 2.6(1)(a).
[9] Section 45(10): however, see remarks of Munby J (as he then was) in *X Council* (paras 40 and 41) as to the possible use of judicial review as mechanism for challenging such orders.

making of such orders at the outset of cases in which subsequent care proceedings are before the higher courts.[10]

**9.4** For example, in the Court of Appeal case of *Re C and B (Care Order: Future Harm)*[11] Hale LJ (as she then was) comments on the granting of an emergency protection order in the context of long standing concerns about the parents' capacity to care for their children:[12]

> 'I am bound to comment. I find it quite impossible to see how that could be justified under the terms of s 44(1) of the Children Act 1989. They require that there is a risk of significant harm to the child if the child is not removed or kept where the child is now. Such orders are intended to be made when there is an emergency and it can be shown that unless emergency action is taken that child will be at risk of significant harm during the period of the order. As I have already pointed out, there was no evidence of any immediate risk of harm to either of these children. I appreciate that there may have been a worry, resulting from the mother's failure from time to time to keep appointments and sometimes the difficulty of finding out where she was. But this was not a case in which that risk should be put too high.'

**9.5** In the well-known case of *X Council v B (Emergency Protection Orders)*[13] Munby J (as he then was) expresses similar views whilst emphasising the importance of considering alternative measures to promote the child's welfare:[14]

> 'An EPO, summarily removing a child from his parents, is a "draconian" and "extremely harsh" measure, requiring "exceptional justification" and "extraordinarily compelling reasons". Such an order should not be made unless the FPC is satisfied that it is both necessary and proportionate and that no other less radical form of order will achieve the essential end of promoting the welfare of the child. Separation is only to be contemplated if immediate separation is essential to secure the child's safety: "imminent danger" must be "actually established".'

**9.6** In the later (and perhaps rather confusingly named) case of *Re X (Emergency Protection Orders)*[15] McFarlane J (as he then was) quotes at length from Munby J's comments but also sets consideration of making of emergency protection orders in the context of guidance issued at the time that the 1989 Act came into force:

---

[10] It is important both in considering procedural issues and in legal analysis of s 44 to bear in mind that an application for an emergency protection order is a free-standing set of proceedings and not an interlocutory step in any care proceedings under Part IV of the 1989 Act that may be taken in relation to the same child arising from the same of related concerns as to their welfare.
[11] [2001] 1 FLR 611.
[12] At para 19.
[13] [2005] 1 FLR 341.
[14] At para 57(i).
[15] [2006] 2 FLR 701.

'[62] Where an EPO is in force the applicant may only exercise the power given to remove or detain the child in order to safeguard the welfare of the child and shall only take such action under the order as is reasonably required to safeguard and promote the welfare of the child (s 44(5) of the CA 1989).

[63] The government guidance issued prior to the introduction of the Children Act 1989 states with respect to EPOs:

> "The purpose of the new order, as its name suggests, is to enable the child in a genuine emergency to be removed from where he is or be kept where he is, if and only if this is what is necessary to provide immediate short-term protection." (*Children Act 1989 – Guidance and Regulations* (HMSO, 1991), vol 1, p 51)

The words "genuine emergency" and "only what is necessary to provide immediate short-term protection" cannot, in my view, be stressed enough.'

**9.7** The themes of the existence of a genuine emergency, the gravity of the risk, the proportionality of the intervention, and consideration alternative protective measures should be central to any consideration of the making or continuation of an emergency protection order.

**9.8** With these principles in mind, the statistics as to the use made of emergency protection orders are striking. In the calendar year 2016 1,287 children were made subject to such orders and in the second quarter of 2017 the comparable figure is 278 children. By way of comparison, in the same periods the figures for children made subject to care orders are 13,953 and 3,629.[16]

## *The effect of an emergency protection order*

**9.9** The primary mechanism for achieving the 'emergency protection' of a child where this is indeed required is set out in s 44(4), which provides as follows:

> 'While an order under this section ("an emergency protection order") is in force it –
>
> (a) operates as a direction to any person who is in a position to do so to comply with any request to produce the child to the applicant;
> (b) authorises –
>   (i) the removal of the child at any time to accommodation provided by or on behalf of the applicant and his being kept there; or
>   (ii) the prevention of the child's removal from any hospital, or other place, in which he was being accommodated immediately before the making of the order; and
> (c) gives the applicant parental responsibility for the child.'

---

[16] Ministry of Justice: Family Court Statistics Quarterly, England and Wales April to June 2017, Table 4.

**9.10** These provisions should be read in conjunction with the following limitations set out in s 44(5):

> '(5) Where an emergency protection order is in force with respect to a child, the applicant –
>
> (a) shall only exercise the power given by virtue of subsection (4)(b) in order to safeguard the welfare of the child;
> (b) shall take, and shall only take, such action in meeting his parental responsibility for the child as is reasonably required to safeguard or promote the welfare of the child (having regard in particular to the duration of the order); and
> (c) shall comply with the requirements of any regulations made by the Secretary of State for the purposes of this subsection.'

**9.11** Experience suggests[17] that the removal of a child to accommodation, 'provided by or on behalf of the applicant' (the applicant will usually be a local authority, but see below for exceptions to this) is the object of the great majority of emergency protection order applications. As noted above, it is a criminal offence to intentionally obstruct any person exercising the power to remove a child.[18]

## THE APPLICATION FOR AN EMERGENCY PROTECTION ORDER

### Applicants and applications

**9.12** Section 44(1) refers to applications being made by, 'any person'. In practice, applications are normally made by a local authority but the section makes specific provision for applications by an, 'authorised person' (ie an officer of the National Association for the Prevention of Cruelty to Children or other person authorised in accordance with s 31(9) of the Act[19]) and applications by others are not unknown.[20] Special provisions apply for applications by the police when a child has been taken into police protection.[21]

**9.13** The application is made on Form C110A. The respondents[22] are any person whom the applicant believes to have parental responsibility for the child or, in the event that the child is the subject of a care order, any person who had parental responsibility before the care order was made[23] and the child. In addition, notice must be given any local authority providing accommodation for the child, any person caring for the child at the commencement of the

---

[17] There appear to be no specific statistics available.
[18] Section 44(15).
[19] Section 44(2)(a).
[20] A colleague of the writer's has experience of an application being made by a children's guardian.
[21] See s 46(7), discussed in chapter 8 above.
[22] See FPR 2010, r 12.3.
[23] This would be relevant where a child who is in the care of one local authority is in need of protection whilst living in the area of another local authority.

proceedings, any person providing a refuge for the child in accordance with s 51 of the 1989 Act, and, importantly, every person whom the applicant believes to be a parent of the child even if they do not have parental responsibility.[24]

**9.14** Applications for emergency protection orders are, 'specified proceedings' for the purposes of s 41 of the 1989 Act[25] and an officer of Cafcass or a Welsh family proceedings officer will normally be appointed as children's guardian for any child in respect of whom an order is sought.

**9.15** The application is made to the family court and will be allocated to the first available judge authorised to conduct emergency applications.[26] The provisions of the FPR 2010 as to transfer to another court or to another area and allocation to another level of judge apply.[27]

## Without notice applications

**9.16** An application can be made without notice, in which case the provisions of FPR 2010, r 12.16 and PD12E apply. The power to make such a draconian order without giving notice to the persons affected by it should be used with great caution. In *X Council v B (Emergency Protection Orders)*[28] Munby J (as he then was) said:[29]

> 'An ex parte application will normally be appropriate only if the case is genuinely one of emergency or other great urgency – and even then it should normally be possible to give some kind of albeit informal notice – or if there are compelling reasons to believe that the child's welfare will be compromised if the parents are alerted in advance to what is going on.'

**9.17** In the same case His Lordship referred to his observations on the conduct of without notice applications in the cases of *Re W (Ex Parte Orders)*,[30] *Kelly v British Broadcasting Corporation*[31] and *Re S (Ex Parte Orders)*[32] and comments that, '... these principles ... might be thought to be particularly applicable, and the need for meticulous compliance to be all the more pressing, in the context of relief as draconian as an ex parte EPO'.[33]

**9.18** It is particularly important that persons affected by the order, and in particular the parents of the child concerned, should have proper information

---

[24] FPR 2010, PD12C, para 3.1.
[25] See s 41(6)(g).
[26] See Family Court (Composition and Distribution of Business) Rules 2014, art 16(3) and FPR 2010, r 12.2(c).
[27] See FPR 2010, rr 29.17, 29.18, and 29.19.
[28] See above.
[29] At para 53.
[30] [2000] 2 FLR 927.
[31] [2001] 1 FLR 197.
[32] [2001] 1 FLR 308.
[33] At para 54.

as to why the court has taken this drastic step. This point was emphasised by McFarlane J (as he then was) in the case of *Re X (Emergency Protection Orders)*[34] in which he said:[35]

> 'It seems to me that the following two steps should be undertaken whenever an application is made without notice for an EPO:
>
> (a) the hearing ought to be tape recorded. Most magistrates' courts are not wired up for regular recording, but in my view resources ought to be made for the introduction of a small portable tape recorder (or even a dictation recorder). In the absence of such provision then a dedicated note taker, in addition to the clerk, should attend the hearing with the task of compiling a verbatim note;
> (b) paragraph (xi) of the *B Council* guidance limits the requirement to provide information to parents, where the hearing has taken place without notice, to cases where the parents ask for the information. I would go further and say that unless there is very good reason to the contrary, the parents should always be given a full account of the material submitted to the court, the evidence given at the hearing, the submissions made to support the application and the justices reasons whether they ask for this information or not.'

**9.19** A useful practice is for the court to record on the face of an emergency protection order made without notice the reasons why the court decided that a without notice order was justified and the information upon which that decision was based.

**9.20** The FPR 2010 provide for service of the application and order within 48 hours of the order being made at a without notice hearing.[36]

## Evidence

**9.21** An application for an emergency protection order must be supported by evidence and Munby J (as he then was) commented in *X Council v B (Emergency Protection Orders)*[37] that:[38]

> 'The evidence in support of an application for an EPO must be full, detailed, precise and compelling. Unparticularised generalities will not suffice. The sources of hearsay evidence must be identified. Expressions of opinion must be supported by detailed evidence and properly articulated reasoning.'

**9.22** Note, however, the very sweeping terms of s 4(7):

---

[34] Above
[35] Paragraph 66.
[36] Rules 12.16(4) and (5) respectively.
[37] See above.
[38] At para 57(vi).

'Regardless of any enactment or rule of law which would otherwise prevent it from doing so, a court hearing an application for, or with respect to, an emergency protection order may take account of –

(a) any statement contained in any report made to the court in the course of, or in connection with, the hearing; or
(b) any evidence given during the hearing,

which is, in the opinion of the court, relevant to the application.'

This would allow the court an unfettered discretion as to as to the material that can be taken into account in deciding to make an order.

**9.23** Nevertheless, evidence should normally be provided in statement form and the maker of the statement should attend court to give oral evidence if required. Even if an application is being made without notice, and hence without an opportunity for respondents cross-examine the maker of the statement, the court will often require clarification or additional information as to the circumstances leading to the making of the application and the plans for the children should an order be made. Any such additional information provided to the court must be recorded in accordance with the guidance above.

## *The X Council v B (Emergency Protection Orders)* factors

**9.24** In the case of *X Council v B (Emergency Protection Orders)*[39] Munby J (as he then was) reviewed the domestic and European jurisprudence and produced a list of some 14 factors that must be considered by any court asked to make an emergency protection order.[40] This is widely acknowledged as a definitive statement of the matters that should be considered on such an application and in *Re X (Emergency Protection Orders)*[41] McFarlane J (as he then was) said:[42]

'I regard this list of 14 factors to be "required reading" for every magistrate and justices' clerk involved in any EPO application. The list should be copied and placed before the court on every occasion that an application is made for an EPO, so that the bench may consider its applicability to the case that is before them. Applicants for an EPO and their legal advisers should consider themselves under a duty to the court to ensure that this list is expressly and in terms drawn to the attention of the bench.'

These factors are set out in full as Appendix 7 to this work.

---

[39] Above.
[40] See para 57 of his judgment.
[41] Above.
[42] At para 65.

## THE DECISION TO MAKE AN EMERGENCY PROTECTION ORDER

### The grounds for making an order

**9.25** The statutory grounds for making an order are set out in s 44(1) of the Act and are as follows:

'(1) Where any person ("the applicant") applies to the court for an order to be made under this section with respect to a child, the court may make the order if, but only if, it is satisfied that –

   (a) there is reasonable cause to believe that the child is likely to suffer significant harm if –
      (i) he is not removed to accommodation provided by or on behalf of the applicant; or
      (ii) he does not remain in the place in which he is then being accommodated;
   (b) in the case of an application made by a local authority –
      (i) enquiries are being made with respect to the child under section 47(1)(b); and
      (ii) those enquiries are being frustrated by access to the child being unreasonably refused to a person authorised to seek access and that the applicant has reasonable cause to believe that access to the child is required as a matter of urgency; or
   (c) in the case of an application made by an authorised person –
      (i) the applicant has reasonable cause to suspect that a child is suffering, or is likely to suffer, significant harm;
      (ii) the applicant is making enquiries with respect to the child's welfare; and
      (iii) those enquiries are being frustrated by access to the child being unreasonably refused to a person authorised to seek access and the applicant has reasonable cause to believe that access to the child is required as a matter of urgency.'

**9.26** Applications are most commonly made on the grounds of, 'reasonable cause to believe' that the child is, 'likely to suffer' 'significant harm'. These concepts are discussed in detail elsewhere in this work but it is important to bear in mind that they are by their nature fact specific.[43] An evaluation of the basis for asserting that these three factors are present is an essential first step in the court's decision making.

**9.27** In considering the making of an emergency protection order, the child's welfare is the court's paramount consideration[44] but the 'welfare checklist' in s 1(3) does not apply as the making of an order under Part V of the Act (which includes s 44) is not one of the circumstances specified by s 1(4). The, 'no order'

---

[43] See, for example, the discussion of the meaning of, 'significant harm' by the Supreme Court in the case of *Re B (Care Proceedings: Appeal)* [2013] 2 FLR 1075.
[44] Section 1(1) of the Act.

principle in s 1(5) of the Act applies as does the principle that any state interference in family life must be proportionate to the object of protecting the child from harm.

**9.28** As part of the exercise of determining if a child's welfare requires the making of an order the court will need to consider whether some lesser form of intervention in the child's life would meet the concerns that are being expressed. In practice, contested hearings of emergency protection order applications generally resolve themselves into an argument as to whether the making of an order and removal is, 'essential to secure the child's safety'[45] or whether some other measures proposed by the family (or the children's guardian) would achieve that end.

**9.29** If the court decides that the criteria for the grant of an emergency protection order are not satisfied, the applicant local authority will frequently apply for the early listing for hearing of an application for interim care order and this should be done. In the case of *Re B-C (A Child)*[46] a decision to refuse to list such an application for hearing following dismissal of an application for an emergency protection order was set aside.[47]

## Alternatives to making an order: cooperation and voluntary arrangements

**9.30** The first, and possibly most important, stage of the process of deciding if an order is necessary is the assessment of the extent to which the child's parents (or other carers) are able to cooperate in implementing measures that are necessary to secure the child's safety without the need for an order of any sort. Good practice and judicial comment both emphasise the need for local authorities to work with families and to attempt to meet concerns by doing so before resort is had to statutory powers.

**9.31** As an example guidance as to good practice one can take the statement in the Department of Education's 2014 Guidance for local authorities *Court Orders and Pre-Proceedings*:[48]

> 'The Children Act 1989 is based on the principle that, where consistent with children's welfare, local authorities should promote the upbringing of the child by their families. Where concerns do arise and are identified by a local authority, the local authority is under a duty to act. The guidance in this chapter highlights the requirement that local authorities work closely with families to ensure that key steps are taken to help parents address problems in a timely way.'

---

[45] Per Munby J (as he then was) in *X Council v B* (above) at para 57(i).
[46] [2016] EWCA Civ 970.
[47] See comments of McFarlane LJ at para [19].
[48] Page 11.

**9.32** A typical judicial comment is that of Hedley J who said, when considering the steps that should be taken to ensure the safety of a new born baby:[49]

> 'It is, of course, incumbent on the local authority where practicable to act in partnership with a parent and to devise a process (whether by supervision, retention in hospital or removal) which commands at least the acquiescence of the parent. That accords both with the spirit of the [Children Act 1989] and with the European Convention for the Protection of Human Rights and Fundamental Freedoms 1950 requirement of proportionality.'

**9.33** Measures to protect a child are generally based on an agreement to cooperate with social workers that will usually involve a regime of announced and unannounced visits to the family home to monitor the care the child is receiving. In other cases, as Hedley J notes, a child may be removed from their home on a temporary basis to be cared from by relatives or local authority foster carers on the basis of an agreement under s 20 of the 1989 Act.[50]

## Alternatives to making an order: family assessment orders

**9.34** As is noted above, a specific ground for the making of an emergency protection order is that enquiries into a child's welfare by a local authority or authorised person are being frustrated by access to the child being, 'unreasonably refused'.[51] In addition to these provisions, the Act contains a specific remedy for use in such cases in the shape of a child assessment order under s 43 of the Act, which allows an order to be made compelling a person who is in a position to produce the child to do so and to comply with any directions of the court as to the assessment.[52] This provision was controversial and gave rise to some of the lengthiest parliamentary exchanges during the passage of the Children Bill, no doubt because of a number of notorious cases of children coming to harm whilst social workers were being denied access to them. It was clearly regarded by legislators as a central feature of the new statutory system of child protection.[53]

**9.35** In *X Council v B* Munby J (as he then was) draws attention to this power and says:[54]

> 'If the real purpose of the local authority's application is to enable it to have the child assessed then consideration should be given to whether that objective cannot

---

[49] *A v East Sussex County Council and Chief Constable of Sussex Police* [2010] 2 FLR 1596, para 9.
[50] Note, however, the need for caution in the use of agreements under s 20: see for example comments of Munby P in *Re N (Adoption: Jurisdiction)* [2016] 1 FLR 621 at paras 157–171 and Theis J in *Medway Council v M, F and G (By Her Children's Guardian)* [2014] 2 FLR 982 at para 11.
[51] Section 44(b)(ii) and (iii).
[52] Section 43(6).
[53] See notes to the subsection in *Current Law Statutes Annotated* 1989, Volume 4.
[54] Paragraph 57(iv).

equally effectively, and more proportionately, be achieved by an application for, or by the making of, a CAO under s 43 of the Children Act 1989.'

**9.36** Despite the apparent intention of Parliament and such judicial encouragement, this provision is relatively little used, with applications being made in relation to only 10 children during 2016 and 1 child in the second quarter of 2017.[55] This is probably because in practice local authorities perceive there to be relatively little scope for such an order being as it would be of use only in the relatively narrow band of cases where a family will not agree, or at least acquiesce, to the assessment process but where concerns are not of such a level that the full protective powers of the emergency protection order are required. It is noteworthy that s 43(3) allows the court to treat an application for a child assessment order as one for an emergency protection order and that s 43(4) prohibits the court from making a child assessment order if it is satisfied both that there are grounds for making an emergency protection order and that it should make the latter order.

## Alternatives to removal of children: exclusion requirements and undertakings

**9.37** A sadly common set of facts giving rise an application for an emergency protection order is that of children who receive adequate (often indeed good and loving) care from a parent with whom they live (generally their mother) but are at risk of harm from another member of the household (typically, mother's new partner). Such cases present a particularly difficult task in balancing the needs to protect the children from a risk of harm against the likely emotional harm to them arising from separation from their primary carer.

**9.38** Sections 44A and 44B of the Act, inserted by the Family Law Act 1996, provide, in suitable cases, a solution to this dilemma by enabling the court to order that the person whose presence creates a risk to a child can be excluded from the child's home (or can give an undertaking to vacate). It is important to note that in cases where these provisions are used an emergency protection order is still made and indeed they are included in the order; their effect is to provide a safeguard for the child without the need to use the power of removal set out in s 44(4)(b)(i).[56]

**9.39** The key provision is s 44A(2), which sets out the conditions that must be satisfied before an exclusion requirement can be incorporated in an emergency protection order:

'The conditions are –

    (a)    that there is reasonable cause to believe that, if a person ('the relevant person') is excluded from a dwelling-house in which the child lives, then

---

[55] Ministry of Justice: Family Court Statistics Quarterly, England and Wales April to June 2017, Table 4.
[56] Corresponding provisions apply when an interim care order is sought: see ss 38A and 38B.

(i) in the case of an order made on the ground mentioned in section 44(1)(a), the child will not be likely to suffer significant harm, even though the child is not removed as mentioned in section 44(1)(a)(i) or does not remain as mentioned in section 44(1)(a)(ii), or
(ii) in the case of an order made on the ground mentioned in paragraph (b) or (c) of section 44(1), the enquiries referred to in that paragraph will cease to be frustrated, and

(b) that another person living in the dwelling-house (whether a parent of the child or some other person) –
(i) is able and willing to give to the child the care which it would be reasonable to expect a parent to give him, and
(ii) consents to the inclusion of the exclusion requirement.'

**9.40** A power of arrest may be attached to an exclusion requirement[57] but not to an undertaking.[58]

**9.41** The terms of s 44A(2)(b) focus the court's attention on the child's carer. In hearings where imposing an exclusion requirement is raised as a credible option the crucial issue is generally that of whether the carer can be relied upon to 'police' the requirement by not allowing the excluded person to return and reporting any attempts to do so to social services or the police (where there is a power of arrest).

**9.42** A person to whom an exclusion requirement applies has a right to apply for the exclusion requirement and any power of arrest to be varied or discharged.[59]

## THE CONSEQUENCES OF MAKING AN EMERGENCY PROTECTION ORDER

### Parental responsibility

**9.43** As noted above, the making of an emergency protection order gives the applicant parental responsibility[60] for the child concerned but the extent to which this can be exercised is severely limited by the terms of s 44(5)(b), which provides that the applicant:

'shall take, and shall only take, such action in meeting his parental responsibility for the child as is reasonable required to safeguard or promote the welfare of the child as is reasonably required to safeguard or promote the welfare of the child (having regard in particular to the duration of the order.'

---

[57] Section 44A(5).
[58] Section 44B(2).
[59] Section 45(8A) and (8B) respectively.
[60] Section 44(4)(c).

**9.44** Specific provision is made for the court to give to have power to give directions in respect of the, 'medical or psychiatric examination or other assessment of the child'.[61]

## Removal of the child

**9.45** Although in practice applications for emergency protection orders almost always involve the court being asked to sanction the removal of a child from their carers (or the prevention of their removal from a safe place) the court does not in fact order removal but rather authorises the applicant to remove or prevent removal.[62] Munby J (as he then was) puts the point in this way:[63]

> 'The [court] decides to make an EPO. But the local authority decides whether to remove. The local authority, even after it has obtained an EPO, is under a duty to consider less drastic alternatives to emergency removal.'

**9.46** The exercise of this power is subject to the important safeguard of subs (10), which provides that:

> 'Where an emergency protection order is in force with respect to a child and –
>
> (a) the applicant has exercised the power given by subsection (4)(b)(i) but it appears to him that it is safe for the child to be returned; or
> (b) the applicant has exercised the power given by subsection (4)(b)(ii) but it appears to him that it is safe for the child to be allowed to be removed from the place in question,
>
> he shall return the child or (as the case may be) allow him to be removed.'

**9.47** However, in these circumstances the emergency protection order, including the authorisation of removal, remains in force and the applicant has the power to remove the child again if, 'it appears to him that a change in the circumstances of the case makes it necessary for him to do so'.[64]

**9.48** Subsection (11) sets out the persons to whom the child can be returned in accordance with this subsection and this includes: 'such other person as the applicant (with the agreement of the court) considers appropriate'.[65]

**9.49** This would open the possibility of the child being returned to the care of a family member even if care by a parent presents an unacceptable risk. It is also unusual, within the overall scheme of child protection under the Children Act 1989,[66] in requiring court approval for placement decisions taken by a local authority with parental responsibility.

---

[61] Section 44(6)(b).
[62] Section 44(4)(b).
[63] *X Council v B (Emergency Protection Orders)* (above) at para 57(xii).
[64] Section 44(12).
[65] Section 44(11)(b)(iii).
[66] ie the provisions for the making of care and supervision orders under Part IV of the Act as well as 'Protection of Children' under Part V of the Act.

**9.50** Section 48 of the Act supplements the mechanisms to protect the child by setting out a number of provisions to ensure that the child concerned is found and secured. These include a power to require disclosure of information as to a child's whereabouts,[67] to authorise the applicant to enter and search premises,[68] and to issue a warrant authorising a constable to assist in doing so.[69] The provisions of ss 49 and 50 of the Act creating a criminal offence of abduction of a child in care and making provision for recovery of an abducted child in care apply to a child who is the subject of an emergency protection order.[70]

## Contact with children who are subject to emergency protection orders

**9.51** Section 44(13) makes provision for contact with children who are subject to an emergency protection order in the following terms:

> 'Where an emergency protection order has been made with respect to a child, the applicant shall, subject to any direction given under subsection (6), allow the child reasonable contact with –
>
> (a) his parents;
> (b) any person who is not a parent of his but who has parental responsibility for him;
> (c) any person with whom he was living immediately before the making of the order;
> (d) any person named in a child arrangements order as a person with whom the child is to spend time or otherwise have contact;
> (e) any person who is allowed to have contact with the child by virtue of an order under section 34; and
> (f) any person acting on behalf of any of those persons.'

**9.52** The list with whom contact is to be allowed is similar to, but not identical with, that set out in the corresponding provision in relation to children who are the subject of care orders, s 34.[71] Notably, it includes, as s 34(1) does not, any person with whom the child lived prior to the making of the order irrespective of whether they are a parent, held parental responsibility or is named in a child arrangements order and the very broad class of any person, 'acting on behalf' of the persons named.

**9.53** The court has, as noted in s 44(13), a power to give such directions, 'as it considers appropriate' in relation to: 'the contact which is, or is not, to be allowed between the child and any named person'.[72]

---

[67] Section 48(1).
[68] Section 48(4).
[69] Section 48(9).
[70] Sections 49(2)(b) and 50(2).
[71] See s 34(1).
[72] Section 44(6)(a).

**9.54** Such a direction would be appropriate to regulate contact between the child and, for example, a parent who is believed to present a risk and could include provision for such contact to be supervised.

**9.55** Section 44(9) provides that such directions may be:

'(a) given when the emergency protection order is made or at any time while it is in force; and
(b) varied at any time on the application of any person falling within any class of person prescribed by rules of court for the purposes of this subsection.'

**9.56** The welfare principle set out in s 1 of the Act would apply to any decision to give or vary such a direction.

## DURATION, EXTENSION AND DISCHARGE OF EMERGENCY PROTECTION ORDERS

**9.57** The stated purpose emergency protection orders of providing, 'immediate short-term protection'[73] is reflected in the provisions as to the duration of such orders and related issues set out in s 45 of the Act.

### Duration and extension of order

**9.58** Section 44(1) provides that an emergency protection order shall have effect: '... for such period, not exceeding eight days, as may be specified in the order'.

**9.59** When the court would make an order for the full period eight days allowed but the eighth day is a public holiday[74] the court may specify a period that ends at noon on the first later day that is not a public holiday.[75]

**9.60** An important practical factor in deciding the duration of an order will be the earliest possible date upon which the court can hear an application for an interim care order,[76] since an application for such an order is very likely to follow close upon the removal of children from their parents, if that is the object of seeking an emergency protection order.

**9.61** In the unusual cases when an application for an emergency protection order is made by the police in relation to a child who has already been taken into police protection under s 46 of the Act,[77] the period of eight days commences with the first day on which the child was taken into protection.[78]

---

[73] *Children Act 1989 – Guidance and Regulations* (HMSO, 1991), vol 1, p 51
[74] Defined as Christmas day, Good Friday, a bank holiday or a Sunday.
[75] Section 45(2).
[76] Under s 38 of the Act.
[77] See s 46(7) and (8), discussed in chapter 8 above.
[78] Section 45(3).

**9.62** An application can be made to extend the term of an emergency protection order by any person who has parental responsibility for the child as a result of the order being made or who is entitled to apply for a care order in relation to the child.[79] On such an application, the court can extend the period during which the order is to have effect by, 'such period not exceeding seven days as it thinks fit' but may do so, 'only if it has reasonable cause to believe that the child concerned is likely to suffer significant harm if the order is not extended'.[80]

**9.63** An emergency protection order can only be extended once.[81] Note that the maximum period of extension is fixed at seven days, even if the original order was for less than the allowable total of 8 days.

## Applications to discharge an emergency protection order

**9.64** Although the Act expressly excludes an appeal against the making of an emergency protection order[82] an application can be made to discharge the order by:[83]

'(a) the child;
(b) a parent of his;
(c) any person who is not a parent of his but who has parental responsibility for him; or
(d) any person with whom he was living immediately before the making of the order.'

**9.65** There are important limitations to this right as set out in s 45(11):

'Subsection (8) does not apply –

(a) where the person who would otherwise be entitled to apply for the emergency protection order to be discharged –
   (i) was given notice (in accordance with rules of court) of the hearing at which the order was made; and
   (ii) was present at that hearing; or
(b) to any emergency protection order the effective period of which has been extended under subsection (5).'

**9.66** This creates a dilemma for a respondent (generally, a parent) as to whether they should appear at the hearing of the application to oppose an order being made or stay away[84] with a view to making an application to discharge

---

[79] Section 45(4): persons entitled to apply, for a care order are defined by s 31(1) as, 'any local authority' or an, 'authorised person'.
[80] Section 45(5).
[81] Section 45(7).
[82] Section 45(10), which also excludes any appeal against the refusal to make an order, against the extension or refusal to extend an order, and against the discharge or refusal to discharge an order.
[83] Section 45(8).
[84] It is not entirely clear whether a party who is legally represented at the hearing of an application but does not attend in person is, 'present' for the purposes of this subsection: see note to the subsection in the *Family Court Practice*.

the order when their case is better prepared. One has to say that the latter is so transparently 'tactical' a position to take that an application to discharge made by a party who failed to appear after having had notice of the hearing of the application would attract little sympathy from most tribunals.

## Consequences of the expiry of an emergency protection order

**9.67** Upon the expiry of the emergency protection order, the powers it confers to accommodate the child, to prevent its removal from accommodation, and to exercise parental responsibility all lapse.

**9.68** In the absence of the granting of an interim care order[85] before the expiry of the emergency protection order or an agreement for the child to be accommodated,[86] a retention of care of the child by a person (generally, of course, a local authority) who has exercised the power of removal under the order is unlawful and will expose that person to civil proceedings for damages under the Human Rights Act 1998, s 8, and at common law.

---

[85] See s 38.
[86] See s 20.

# Part 4

# CARE PROCEEDINGS: FROM ISSUE TO FINAL HEARING

# CHAPTER 10

# PROCEDURAL STAGES OF AN APPLICATION FOR A CARE ORDER: AN OVERVIEW

## PUBLIC LAW OUTLINE

**10.1** The Public Law Outline ('PLO') was introduced in 2008 in an attempt to streamline care proceedings, avoid delay and encourage a cultural change amongst professionals and the court in relation to timescales. It came into force on 1 April 2008 and applied to all new applications for a care or supervision order from that point onwards.

**10.2** Prior to the introduction of the PLO, the timescales for care proceedings varied greatly across the country, with some proceedings lasting more than 2 years. The overuse of experts and delays in proceedings were identified as major issues that undermined the 'no delay' principle contained in the Children Act 1989 ('CA 1989'), and therefore the welfare of a child.

**10.3** The President of the Family Division issued the *Guide to Case Management in Public Law Proceedings* at the same time, replacing the protocol of 2003 and was intended to be implemented in all care proceedings save in exceptional circumstances. The Practice Direction incorporated an overriding objective, 'enabling the court to deal with cases justly, having regard to the welfare issues involved'.

**10.4** The Practice Direction stated that it included factors such as fairness and expedition, proportionality, saving expense and ensuring that the parties are on an equal footing. The overriding objective was to be the focus for all of the parties to the proceedings, and the court is to ensure that it was followed.

## Revised Public Law Outline 2014

**10.5** The revised PLO was issued in 2014 and came into force on 22 April 2014 following feedback from professionals during the pilot and consultation period. The Children and Families Act 2014 (the 'CFA 2014') made changes to Part 12 of the Family Procedure Rules 2010 ('FPR 2010') and specified that all care and supervision order proceedings must be completed within a maximum of 26 weeks. PD12A of FPR 2010 clearly sets out the provisions that now apply and provides a helpful guide.

**10.6** This revision was a further attempt to ensure that matters are concluded proportionately and expeditiously, whilst ensuring that the court has all the evidence it needs to make a final determination in the best interest of the child and on a fully informed basis.

**10.7** The diagram below depicts the revised PLO and each stage is considered in this chapter.

*Procedural Stages of an Application for a Care Order: An Overview* 141

## Public Law Outline 2014 (26 weeks)

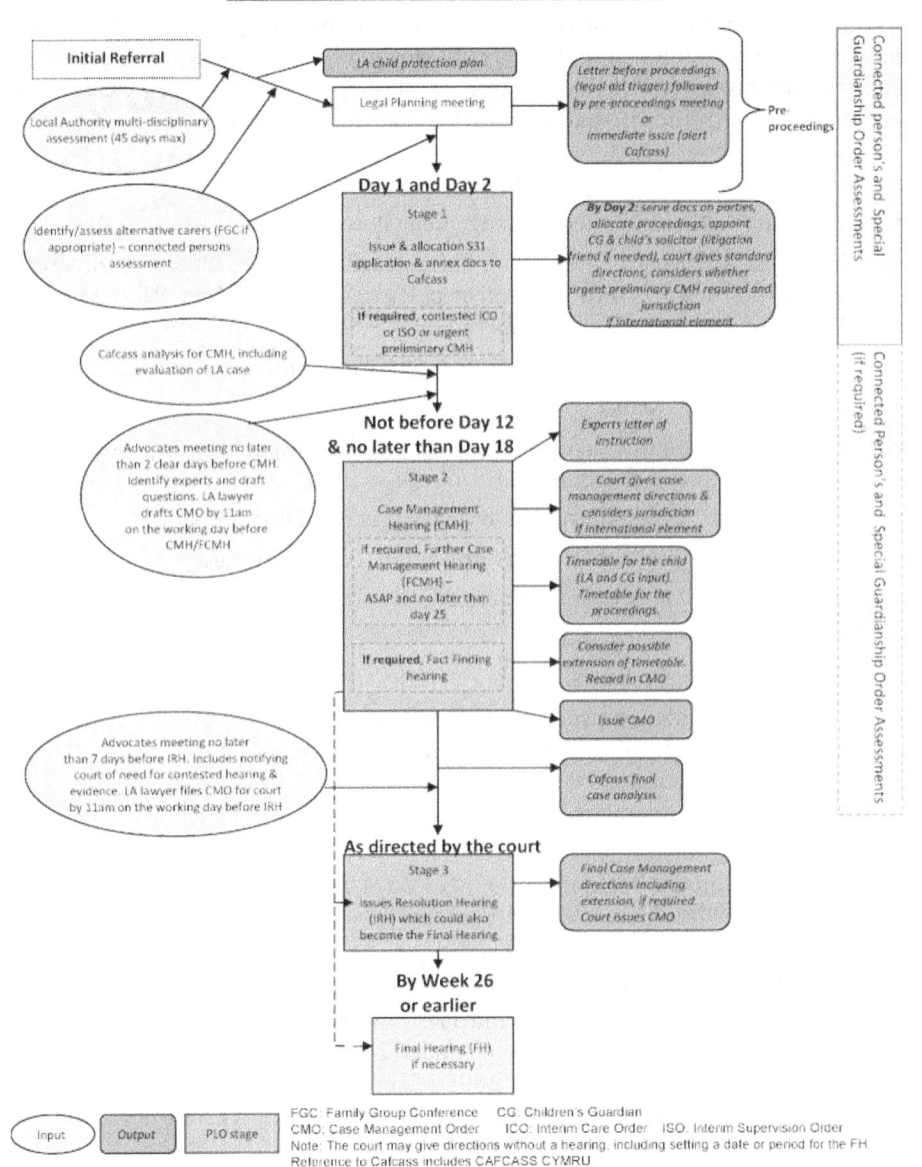

**Initial Referral**

Local Authority multi-disciplinary assessment (45 days max)

Identify/assess alternative carers (FGC if appropriate) – connected persons assessment

LA child protection plan

Legal Planning meeting

Letter before proceedings (legal aid trigger) followed by pre-proceedings meeting *or* immediate issue (alert Cafcass) — Pre-proceedings

### Day 1 and Day 2

**Stage 1**
Issue & allocation S31 application & annex docs to Cafcass

If required, contested ICO or ISO or urgent preliminary CMH

*By Day 2:* serve docs on parties, allocate proceedings, appoint CG & child's solicitor (litigation friend if needed), court gives standard directions, considers whether urgent preliminary CMH required and jurisdiction if International element.

Cafcass analysis for CMH, including evaluation of LA case

### Not before Day 12 & no later than Day 18

Advocates meeting no later than 2 clear days before CMH. Identify experts and draft questions. LA lawyer drafts CMO by 11am on the working day before CMH/FCMH

**Stage 2**
Case Management Hearing (CMH)

If required, Further Case Management Hearing (FCMH) – ASAP and no later than day 25

If required, Fact Finding hearing

Experts letter of instruction

Court gives case management directions & considers jurisdiction if international element

Timetable for the child (LA and CG input). Timetable for the proceedings.

Consider possible extension of timetable. Record in CMO

Issue CMO

Advocates meeting no later than 7 days before IRH. Includes notifying court of need for contested hearing & evidence. LA lawyer files CMO for court by 11am on the working day before IRH

Cafcass final case analysis

### As directed by the court

**Stage 3**
Issues Resolution Hearing (IRH) which could also become the Final Hearing

Final Case Management directions including extension, if required. Court issues CMO

### By Week 26 or earlier

Final Hearing (FH) if necessary

Connected person's and Special Guardianship Order Assessments

Connected Person's and Special Guardianship Order Assessments (if required)

Input | Output | PLO stage

FGC: Family Group Conference   CG: Children's Guardian
CMO: Case Management Order   ICO: Interim Care Order   ISO: Interim Supervision Order
Note: The court may give directions without a hearing, including setting a date or period for the FH
Reference to Cafcass includes CAFCASS CYMRU

## FPR 2010: PART 12, CHAPTER 3

**10.8** Part 12, Chapter 3 of the FPR 2010 contains the special provisions for public law proceedings and the way in which they should be conducted. In applying the provisions of Part 12 and the PLO, PD 12A FPR 2010 clearly sets out that the court and the parties must also have regard to:

- FPR Part 1 (Overriding objective);
- FPR Part 4 (General Case Management Powers);
- FPR Part 15 (Representation of Protected Parties) and Practice Direction 15B (Adults Who May Be Protected Parties and Children Who May Be Protected Parties in Family Proceedings);
- FPR Part 18 (Procedure for Other Applications in Proceedings);
- FPR Part 22 (Evidence);
- FPR Part 24 (Witness, dispositions generally and taking of evidence in Member States of the European Union);
- FPR Part 25 (Experts) and the Experts Practice Directions;
- FPR Part 27.6 and Practice Direction 27A (Court Bundles);
- FPR Part 30 (Appeals) and Practice Directions 30A (Appeals);
- the Allocation Rules; and
- the Justices Clerks Rules.
- President's Guidance issued from time to time on:
  * Distribution of business of the family court;
  * Judicial continuity and deployment; and
  * Prescribed templates and orders.
- International instruments:
  * The Council Regulation (EC) No 2201/2003 (Brussels II revised); and
  * The 1996 Hague Convention.
- Guidance relating to protected parties and other with a disability:
  * Protected Parties in Family Proceedings: Checklist for the Appointment of a Litigation Friend (including the Official Solicitor) (published in Family Law (January 2014); and
  * The Mental Capacity Act 2005 (Transfer of Proceedings) Order 2007 SI 2007/1899, relating to young people over 16 where they are likely to lack decision-making capacity at age 18.[1]

**10.9** The PLO envisages three interim hearings in care proceedings: a case management hearing ('CMH'), a further case management hearing ('FCMH') and an issues resolution hearing ('IRH'). It is hoped that by the IRH the issues will have been narrowed sufficiently to allow some cases to conclude without any further hearings. If that is not possible, the matter will be listed for a final hearing ('FH') so that the matter can be fully heard and concluded.

---

[1] FPR 2010, PD12A, para 1.3.

## TIMETABLE FOR THE PROCEEDINGS

## 26 weeks rule

**10.10** The CA 1989 was amended by s 14 of the CAFA 2014 to provide a statutory timescale within which applications for care and supervision orders must be concluded without delay and within a default timetable of 26 weeks, running from the date of the local authority's application.[2] Rule 12.22 of the FPR 2010 also provides that care and supervision order applications should be concluded within 26 weeks (excluding emergency protection orders or recovery orders).

**10.11** Section 32(1) of the CA 1989 requires the court to draw up a timetable with a view of disposing of the application without delay and within 26 weeks from the date of issue, ensuring the court grapples with the timetable head on and enforces the spirit of the 'no delay' principle.

**10.12** The question of whether it is possible for the matter to conclude within the timescales has been the subject of much discussion since the amendments to the CA 1989 came into force. The statutory timescale and can only be extended in exceptional circumstances, as per s 32(5) of the CA 1989:

> 'A court in which an application under this part is proceeding may extend the period that is for the time being allowed under subsection (1)(a)(ii) in the case of the application, but may do so only if the court considers that the extension is necessary to enable the court to resolve the proceedings justly.'

**10.13** The court may extend the timetable beyond 26 weeks, but this is only possible with reference to the child's welfare and the impact on the duration and conduct of the proceedings. Section 32(6) of the CA 1989 stipulates:

> 'When deciding whether to grant an extension under subsection (5), a court must in particular have regard to –
> 
> (a) the impact which any ensuing timetable revision would have on the welfare of the child to whom the application relates, and
> (b) to the impact which any ensuing timetable revision would have on the duration and conduct of the proceedings;
> 
> and here "ensuing timetable revision" means any revision, of the timetable under subsection (1)(a) for the proceedings, which the court considers may ensue from the extension.'

**10.14** An extension can only be made following a fully-reasoned application (usually made orally) for the court to adjudicate. The court cannot extend the proceedings of its own motion. Helpful guidance has emerged as to when an extension to the timetable can be agreed between the parties. The frequently argued concept of 'planned and purposeful delay'[3] is no longer acceptable, however, there is clearly a very delicate balance to be struck between

---

[2] CA 1989, s 32.
[3] *C v Soulihull MBC* [1993] 1 FLR 290.

proceeding without delay whilst accommodating for situations which may require the proceedings to last beyond the 26 weeks imposed by statute.

**10.15** The President, Sir James Munby, in his judgment in *Re M-F (Children)* made clear that the 26 week rule should not be applied at the expense of justice:[4]

> 'is not, and must never be allowed to become, a straightjacket, least of all if rigorous adherence to an inflexible timetable risks putting justice in jeopardy', and my endorsement (para 29) of Pauffley J's warning in *Re NL (A child) (Appeal: Interim Care Order: Facts and Reasons)* [2014] EWHC 270 (Fam), [2014] 1 FLR 1384, that "Justice must never be sacrificed upon the altar of speed".'

**10.16** An extension of time will not, however, be granted routinely.[5] In the matter of *Re S (A Child)*[6] the President identified three areas in which an extension may be 'necessary' in accordance with s 32(5):[7]

> 'i) The first is where the case can be identified from the outset, or at least very early on, as one which it may not be possible to resolve justly within 26 weeks. Experience will no doubt identify the kind of cases that may fall within this category. Four examples which readily spring to mind (no doubt others will emerge) are (a) very heavy cases involving the most complex medical evidence where a separate fact finding hearing is directed in accordance with *Re S (Split Hearing)* [2014] EWCA Civ 25, [2014] 2 FLR (forthcoming), para 29, (b) FDAC type cases (see further below), (c) cases with an international element where investigations or assessments have to be carried out abroad and (d) cases where the parent's disabilities require recourse to special assessments or measures (as to which see *Re C (A Child)* [2014] EWCA Civ 128, para 34).
>
> ii) The second is where, despite appropriately robust and vigorous judicial case management, something unexpectedly emerges to change the nature of the proceedings too late in the day to enable the case to be concluded justly within 26 weeks. Examples which come to mind are (a) cases proceeding on allegations of neglect or emotional harm where allegations of sexual abuse subsequently surface, (b) cases which are unexpectedly "derailed" because of the death, serious illness or imprisonment of the proposed carer, and (c) cases where a realistic alternative family carer emerges late in the day.
>
> iii) The third is where litigation failure on the part of one or more of the parties makes it impossible to complete the case justly within 26 weeks (the type of situation addressed in *In re B-S*, para 49).'

**10.17** It is clear then, that all practitioners and the court must to work to the 26 week timetable, and this will only be extended if the court considers that it is 'necessary'. The timetable should only be extended 'for the imperative demands of justice, namely fair process, or the child's welfare'. The President

---

4   *M-F (Children)* [2014] EWCA Civ 991 at [26].
5   CA 1989, s 32(7).
6   *Re S (A Child)* [2014] EWCC B44 (Fam).
7   *Re S (A Child)* [2014] EWCC B44 (Fam) [33]. *Re B-S* is explored fully in later chapters.

was very careful in *Re M-F* (above) to emphasise that the list provided within his judgment should not be viewed as additional text to supplement the statute.[8]

**10.18** In the event that the timetable is extended by the court, s 32 of the CA 1989 also sets out the blocks of time that the proceedings may be extended by. Section 32(8) provides that:

'Each separate extension under subsection (5) is to end no more than eight weeks after the later of

(a)   the end of the period being extended; and
(b)   the end of the day on which the extension is granted.'

**10.19** In the event that one of the parties considers the timetable needs extending further, another application must be made to the court, with the court undertaking the same exercise as per the original application for an extension.

**10.20** Cases with concurrent criminal proceedings are often prime examples where there is an obvious need to extend the timetable early on. Any trial in criminal proceedings is likely to be listed outside of 26 week timetable for the care proceedings and the court will need to consider whether a fact finding hearing is listed in care proceedings to determine whether the offence too place. The general rule in this situation is that each case will be considered on its merits. The court must weigh up any risk of prejudice to the accused and any risk of delay to the child of undertaking a fact finding prior to the determination of the criminal trial.[9] The welfare of the child will always take precedence over the detriment to the family facing criminal proceedings, in accordance with the welfare principle.

## *Timetable for the child*

**10.21** PD12A, para 5.3 provides for the court to set a 'timetable for the child'. This timetable takes into account dates which are important to the child's welfare and development and will inform the timetable for proceedings which will be reviewed regularly.[10] Where there is more than one child subject to proceedings, the court will set a timetable for each of the children individually.[11] The timetable for the child will be recorded in each case management order made by the court and considered at every hearing.

**10.22** Examples of the dates that the court will record and take into account when setting the timetable for the child are the dates of:

---

[8]   *M-F (Children)* [2014] EWCA Civ 991.
[9]   *Re TB (Care Proceedings: Criminal Trial)* [1995] 2 FLR 801.
[10]  FPR 2010, PD12A, para 5.4.
[11]  FPR 2010, PD12A, para 5.7.

- any formal review by the local authority of the case of the looked after child (within the meaning of s 22(1) of the CA 1989);
- any significant educational steps, including the child taking up a place at a new school and, where applicable. Any review by the local authority of a statement of the child's especial educational needs;
- any health care steps, including assessment by a paediatrician or other specialist;
- any review of the local authority plans for the child, including any plans for permanence through adoption, special guardianship or placement with parents or relatives;
- any change or proposed change of the child's placement;
- any significant change in the child's social or family circumstances; or
- any timetable for the determination of an issue in the case with an international element.[12]

**10.23** Any parallel criminal proceedings will obviously impact upon the timetable for the care proceedings and also the timetable for the child.

## PD12A

**10.24** PD12A supplements Part 12 and sets out the timescales for the key stages of the court process in care or supervision order proceedings. An outline is provided in tabula form containing an overview of:

(1) the order of the different stages of the process;

(2) the matters to be considered at the main case management hearings;

(3) the latest point at which the main stages of the process should take place in order to resolve the proceedings within 26 weeks.

### Pre-proceedings checklist

**10.25** The duties of a local authority and work to be undertaken prior to proceedings is considered in full in chapter 5 of this book. As can be seen from the PLO table above, there is a clear list of documents that should either be filed by the local authority when they issue care proceedings, or should be made available to the parties upon request. Only the following checklist documents are to be filed with the application:

- previous court orders including foreign orders and judgements / reasons;
- any assessment materials relevant to the key issues including capacity to litigate, s 7 and s 37 reports; and
- single, joint or inter-agency materials (eg health and education / Home Office and Immigration Tribunal documents).

---

[12] FPR 2010, PD12A, para 5.5.

The other documents specified in section (b) of the table should only be disclosed upon request (see chapter 10).

**10.26** It is clear that in some cases, especially where the welfare of the child might be jeopardised by any delay, it might not have been possible to complete the pre-proceedings process prior to issuing the application. If this is the case, proceedings should be issued in the absence of the documents to ensure the welfare and safety of the child. Nothing in the PLO prevents local authorities acting appropriately to safeguard children, and the PLO should not be viewed as an inflexible instrument that must be rigidly adhered to at the expense of the welfare principle.

**10.27** In the event that any of the documents prescribed in the pre-proceedings checklist above are not available, the court will make directions for the documents to be filed when issuing the application. There is an expectation that there will be a good reason explaining why the documents are not available, and an explanation may be required in the event that the process has not been followed and reasons for explaining why are unclear.

**10.28** The aim of the pre-proceedings checklist is to ensure that the court has clear and full information before it at the first hearing so that it can deal with any immediate issues, such as applications for interim care orders with a plan for removal. It is designed to avoid any delay as a result of information not being available, or alternative placements or family support for the child not having been investigated.

**10.29** Again, an application for an emergency protection order is not subject to the pre-proceedings provisions. This is a separate application and discussed at chapter 9 of this book.

## Day 1: issue and allocation

**10.30** For the purposes of the 26 week timetable and the Public Law Outline, day 1 is the day the local authority files their application for a public law order. The process of issuing an application and the formal requirements for doing so are discussed fully at chapter 11 of this book.

**10.31** The local authority will file their application and supporting documents with the court and they must inform the court in the event that an urgent preliminary hearing is necessary to determine whether a child should be removed from the care of their parents immediately.

**10.32** The court must issue the application and make any directions that are necessary to take the matter through to the first hearing date. The court must also consider whether there are any jurisdictional issues to be determined (see chapter 3) and make whatever directions it considers necessary to enable the court to determine jurisdiction as soon as possible and preferably as a preliminary issue. This may include allocating the matter to a circuit judge or High Court judge. This will be considered at chapter 11 of this book.

**10.33** The court will also set a timetable for the child as discussed above. Future timetabling and directions should be considered in conjunction with the timetable for the child to ensure that matters proceed expeditiously, yet fairly, and in the best interests of the child.

## Days 12–18: case management hearing

**10.34** Case management is at the heart of the PLO, and the CMH is usually the first hearing that the court will list and must be listed between days 12 and 18.

**10.35** In the event that the local authority is of the view that the child requires immediate protection and the parents do not consent to the placement of the child in foster care or with a family member, a contested interim care order hearing will be necessary. If this hearing needs to take place prior to the date of the CMH, it should be listed as such. An earlier hearing may also be necessary to consider matters such as jurisdiction, parentage, party status, capacity to litigate and disclosure.[13]

**10.36** At the CMH, the court will examine the timetable and give detailed case management directions. As set out in the table above at stage 2, the court must also consider jurisdictional issues as well as any application by a party to instruct an expert to undertake an assessment.

**10.37** In the event that there is an early hearing listed to determine the interim placement of a child, the CMH should remain listed between day 12 and 18 and should not be vacated unless all of the parties are in the position to deal with the case management issues. It is not anticipated that an earlier hearing will delay the CMH.

**10.38** An advocates meeting should take place prior the CMH to enable the parties to discuss what evidence is required and whether there is a need for expert evidence to be requested.

## Further case management hearing

**10.39** It may not always be possible to deal with all of the case management issues at the first CMH. In the event that there are other matters which need to be considered at a later hearing, the court will list an FCMH.

**10.40** It is useful to have a FCMH if evidence needs to be considered prior to further decisions being made. For example, it may be necessary for police disclosure to be obtained before deciding whether an expert report is required.

---

[13] FPR 2010, PD12A, para 2.4.

**10.41** As with all timetabling decisions, the court will consider the need for an FCMH in conjunction with the timetable for the child as well as the timetable for the matter in general.

## Issues resolution hearing

**10.42** The IRH is intended to narrow the issues in dispute. The parties and the court must also consider whether the matter can be concluded at the IRH or whether a final, contested hearing is required. The IRH is the final interim hearing that is provided for in the PLO.

**10.43** No later than 7 days prior to the IRH, there should be an advocates meeting to ensure that the remaining issues that are agreed and in dispute are clear, and the parties' positions crystalised.

**10.44** It is possible for oral evidence to be heard at the IRH in the event that the issues are so narrow that only short evidence is necessary and all other evidence is before the court. In the event that the contested matter requires longer than the time estimate for the IRH, a final hearing will need to be listed. A witness template should be available at the IRH with all parties confirming how long they will require to cross examine the witnesses, to enable the court to allocate sufficient time to the final hearing without wasting court time.

## EVIDENCE TO BE GATHERED IN CARE PROCEEDINGS

**10.45** The evidence to be placed before the court within the course of care proceedings must enable the court to decide whether it is necessary for a final care or supervision order to be.

**10.46** Given the magnitude of the decision before it, the court requires the best evidence possible to determine such applications and the local authority should ensure that the evidence they produce is based on clear information that can be tested by the court.

**10.47** In *Re A (A Child)*, the President clearly set out the evidential basis upon which the local authority should rely in order for the court to properly consider making a care or supervision order.

**10.48** The President reminded practitioners of the importance of three fundamental principles within all s 31 applications:

(1) Fact finding and proof.
(2) The need to establish the link between facts relied upon in a threshold document and the conclusion that the child has suffered, or is at risk of suffering, significant harm.

(3) The temptation of social engineering and the need to recognise the inevitable diverse and unequal standards of parenting.[14]

**10.49** For the local authority to prove, on the balance of probabilities, the facts upon which it seeks to rely, findings of fact must be based on evidence and not on suspicion or speculation. The President endorsed the judgment in *Re A (A Child) (No 2)*.[15]

**10.50** Reliance is often placed upon material found in local authority case records, or social work chronologies. This is hearsay. A local authority which is unwilling or unable to produce witnesses who can speak of matters first-hand, may find itself in difficulties if a parent goes into a witness-box to deny the allegations.

**10.51** It is a common feature of care cases that a local authority asserts that a parent 'does not admit, recognise or acknowledge' something or 'does not recognise or acknowledge the local authority's concern'. The local authority must prove both that an event or incident happened, and that it is significant in relation to the care given to the child by the parent.

**10.52** Threshold should not include reference to things that various people have 'stated' or 'reported'. The relevant allegations should concern events that have *happened*, not something that has merely been reported. Furthermore, the local authority's evidence and submissions must set out their argument and explain explicitly why the conclusion follows from the facts adduced. The President highlighted the judgment of Macur LJ in *Re Y (A Child)* in a judgment agreed by both Arden and Ryder LJJ:[16]

> 'No analysis appears to have been made by any of the professionals as to why the mother's particular lies created the likelihood of significant harm to these children and what weight should reasonably be afforded to the fact of her deceit in the overall balance.'

**10.53** Given the burden of proof is on the local authority to establish, with evidence, that a child has or may suffer significant harm, it is vital that the evidence adduced must be prepared thoroughly by the local authority and responded to carefully by the respondents.

## What constitutes evidence?

**10.54** Part 22 of the FPR 2010 provides for the preparation, filing and form of evidence (both oral and written) placed before the court.

**10.55** Pursuant to r 22.1, the court has the power to control the evidence that is filed within the proceedings:

---

[14] *Re A (A Child)* [2015] EWFC 11.
[15] *Re A (A Child) (No 2)* [2011] EWCA Civ 12.
[16] *Re Y (A Child)* [2013] EWCA Civ 1337 at [7].

'(1) The court may control the evidence by giving directions as to –

(a) the issues on which it requires evidence;
(b) the nature of the evidence which it requires to decide those issues; and
(c) the way in which the evidence is to be placed before the court.'

**10.56** Rule 22.2 continues:

'(1) The general rule is that any fact which needs to be proved by the evidence of witnesses is to be proved –

(a) at the final hearing, by their oral evidence; and
(b) at any other hearing, by their evidence in writing.'

**10.57** The form of a person's witness statement is clearly provided for in PD22A of the FPR 2010, which includes requirements as to the statement's structure and the inclusion of a 'statement of truth' alongside the witness's signature.

**10.58** It is important that when this document is prepared, the person signing it is fully aware that they are asserting that the information therein is true and stands as their evidence before the court. Witnesses will be cross-examined on their statement so care should be taken to ensure that everything that appears in it is true, accurate and fully understood by the person providing the statement.

## Documentation from previous proceedings

**10.59** The local authority is required to identify whether there have been any previous proceedings in relation to the child or their parents in their application form. The local authority should also file any previous orders made by the court with their application.

**10.60** If there have been previous proceedings, the evidence filed within them may be of use in the current application. The court will consider whether the evidence from the previous proceedings should be disclosed into the current proceedings and may make a direction for this at the gatekeeping stage, although it is usually considered at the CMH.

**10.61** In the event that the parties are the same across previous and current proceedings, the court can order the papers from earlier proceedings to be disclosed into the current ones. If the parties are not the same, consent will need to be obtained from all the parties to the previous proceedings before the papers can be disclosed. The local authority will need to give notice that the evidence from the previous proceedings is sought, and the parties to those proceedings must have an opportunity to object or consent to this. If they object to the papers being disclosed, the court will need to consider an application for disclosure before they determine whether the documents should be disclosed.

**10.62** Only the relevant documents from any previous proceedings should be disclosed, and typically an index of the proposed documents will be provided to all parties in an attempt to agree can which documents will be relevant and which will not. Again, this is something that will normally be directed at the CMH.

**10.63** As set out above, the local authority must provide evidence based on more than mere supposition and it must be capable of being tested by the court.

## Parenting assessments

**10.64** By the time the matter comes before the court, the local authority will have filed the documents required by the PLO, including any assessments that have been undertaken prior to the issue of proceedings. The court will need clear evidence as to the parenting capacity of the parents involved and consideration will be given during the proceedings as to whether there are any deficits in the initial work carried out to assess parenting capacity, and whether any further assessments should be undertaken.

**10.65** The court generally will not prescribe who undertakes the social work assessments unless there is an application under Part 25 of the FPR 2010 for an independent social worker ('ISW') to undertake work in opposition to, or instead of, the case holding social worker completing the assessment. In *Re W (Assessment of Child)*,[17] it was held that the court has jurisdiction to direct a named social worker to carry out a s 38(6) assessment, but that applications to name specific social workers should not be encouraged.

**10.66** When a parenting assessment is to be carried out, the same care should be taken by the local authority as with pre-proceedings assessments to ensure that the social worker involved is able to sufficiently address any learning difficulties or mental health problems the parent may have. The court requires a thorough and carefully prepared parenting assessment and consideration should be given to any specific needs that a parent or child has whilst undertaking it.

## Independent expert evidence

**10.67** Part 25 of the FPR 2010 deals with applications for expert reports within care and supervision order proceedings. A direction will usually be made at the gatekeeping stage, requiring any party who seeks to instruct an expert to make application to the court to be considered at the CMH. In the event that an application is not made in accordance with the direction, parties can seek an extension of time to make the application at the CMH, supported with an explanation as to why the application has not already been made.

**10.68** Pursuant to r 25.4(2) of the FPR 2010, expert evidence can only be adduced with permission of the court. The court may give permission for the

---

[17] *Re W (Assessment of Child)* [1998] 2 FLR 130.

instruction of an expert and the filing of a report, only if 'the court is of the opinion that the expert evidence is necessary to assist the court to resolve the proceedings'.[18]

**10.69** Permission is not necessary if the expert report was completed prior to the commencement of the proceedings. If a report has been prepared pre-proceedings, it should be filed with the court and served on the other parties with the initial application, as set out in the pre-proceedings checklist.

**10.70** When an application is made to instruction an expert, consideration should be given to PD25C which supplements Part 25. Paragraph 3 of PD25C sets out the preparations required for the permission hearing in a Part 25 application. The Part 25 applicant should, as soon as possible after the issue of proceedings, notify the other parties that they will be making an application for an expert to be appointed, and providing a list of the names of one or more experts in the relevant speciality whom they consider suitable to be instructed.[19] Within 5 working days of notification, the other parties should confirm whether they agree to the instruction of the expert or not. If there is disagreement as to the identity of the expert, or a disagreement as to whether an expert is necessary, the court will hear submissions at the CMH and make a decision as to whether the assessment should be undertaken and by whom.[20]

**10.71** The application form should be prepared together with details of the expert sought, a draft letter of instruction and details of timescales and costs. A draft order should also be prepared and attached to the application specifying the issues the expert will address, which party will be responsible for taking the lead in the expert's instruction, the timetable for the report to be completed and how the cost of the assessment will be met.

**10.72** The making of a Part 25 application and the court's approach will be considered at chapter 15 of this book.

## Guardian's reports

**10.73** The guardian will meet with the parties and the child in order to investigate the circumstances of the family and provide their analysis to the court. The role of the guardian is discussed in chapter 12 of this book.

**10.74** In the exercise of their duties, the children's guardian has the right to access the documents held by the local authority under s 42 of the CA 1989.

**10.75** PD16A, para 6.6 requires that:

> The children's guardian must advise the court on the following matters –

---

[18] FPR 2010, r 25.4(3).
[19] FPR 2010, PD25C, para 2.1.
[20] FPR 2010, PD25C, para 2.4.

(a) whether the child is of sufficient understanding for any purpose including the child's refusal to submit to a medical or psychiatric examination or other assessment that the court has the power to require, direct or order;
(b) the wishes of the child in respect of any matter relevant to the proceedings including that child's attendance at court;
(c) the appropriate forum for the proceedings;
(d) the appropriate timing of the proceedings or any part of them;
(e) the options available to it in respect of the child and the suitability of each such option including what order should be made in determining the application; and
(f) any other matter on which the court seeks advice or on which the children's guardian considers that the court should be informed.

**10.76** A guardian must attend all court hearings unless directed otherwise[21] and must provide a written report to the court advising on the interests of the child in accordance with the timetable set by the court.[22]

**10.77** As a result of the guardian's investigation and analysis, the guardian may come to a position that is in opposition to that of the wishes and feelings of the child they represent. It may be that the guardian will support the long-term removal of the child away from the parents but the child does not agree. The guardian has a duty to inform the court of the child's wishes and feelings, but will ultimately form their own recommendations for the court based on all of the circumstances of the case. This is discussed later in the book at chapter 12.

## Application for the withdrawal of care proceedings

**10.78** In the event that during the course of the proceedings, the local authority wishes to withdraw their application, they must obtain permission from the court.[23] In accordance with r 29.4(3) of the FPR 2010, the application must be made in writing detailing why they seek leave to withdraw.

**10.79** If the threshold criteria[24] has been found not to have been met, permission will usually be granted. However, if the court considers that the threshold criteria could be established, the court will need to consider the local authority's application to withdraw in accordance with s 1(5) of the CA 1989: the 'no order' principle.[25]

---

[21] FPR 2010, PD16A, para 6.5.
[22] FPR 2010, PD16A, para 6.8.
[23] FPR 2010, r 29.4.
[24] CA 1989, s 31(2).
[25] *Redbridge LBC v B and C and A (through his Children's Guardian)* [2011] 2 FLR 117.

# CHAPTER 11

# APPLICATION FOR A CARE OR SUPERVISION ORDER AND CASE MANAGEMENT

## LOCAL AUTHORITY'S APPLICATION

**11.1** As discussed in chapter 10, when the local authority files their application with the court, this constitutes day 1 of the Public Law Outline ('PLO'). The local authority must include the pre-proceedings documents with their application form and send copies to Cafcass / Cafcass Cymru. The application for a care or supervision order should be made on court form C110, which requires the details of all of the parties and any legal representatives the local authority is aware of. The local authority should provide a brief summary of the case, which will be expanded upon in greater detail within the supporting documents.

### Threshold document

**11.2** The threshold document (or threshold statement) prepared by the local authority forms the basis on which the court will decided if a care or supervision order should be made.[1]

**11.3** Practice varies across the country, and in some cases the 'threshold findings' that the local authority relies upon to prove that the child has suffered, or is likely to suffer significant harm, are contained in the C110 form only. In other areas a separate document is prepared.

**11.4** The threshold statement should be a succinct, document, confined to two pages. A template has been provided, which envisages a brief introductory paragraph drafted in accordance with the wording in the template. If the local authority's application is based on a number of heads of significant harm and/or the likelihood of significant harm, these should be set out under separate headings (eg neglect, physical abuse, sexual abuse).

**11.5** Specific incidents should be presented briefly, in bullet point form, under each heading and in chronological sequence if practicable. The issues raised in the local authority's letter before proceedings[2] should be based on the threshold

---

[1] See chapters 13 and 20 for a full discussion of the threshold criteria.
[2] See chapter 6 for a discussion of the letter before proceedings.

concerns and areas of concern contained in the letter should be reproduced in the threshold document to ensure that the parents are clear why the local authority are taking the action that they are.

**11.6** If the parents accept or do not oppose the threshold statement, there should be no need for any further or 'final' threshold statement to be prepared. However, the local authority should be mindful that in order for the interim threshold to be satisfied there needs to be reasonable grounds to believe that the threshold id cross, whereas for a final threshold determination the court must be satisfied that the facts are found on the balance of probabilities. If there is a dispute in relation to the threshold statement, this will be dealt with in the evidence of all parties, and a further document will be produced prior to the issues resolution hearing ('IRH'). This document will either be an agreed final document or will fall to be determined at the final hearing.

## Initial social work evidence

**11.7** The initial social work evidence that should be filed with the application form should include the chronology, statement and genogram. Any assessments that have been undertaken will also need to be filed, together with the care plan for each child detailing the proposed placement for the child and the contact envisaged between the child and their parents.[3]

**11.8** The *Key Elements of Good Practice for Local Authorities' Contribution to Care Proceedings* provides an expectation that the social worker will prepare a chronology of significant events. This should be filed by way of background information to the local authority evidence. The social work chronology should contain all of the significant and relevant information in relation to the circumstances of the case, from incidents of concern to examples of good parenting and details of the services offered and work undertaken with the child and their family.

**11.9** The social worker's statement should expand on the detail of the significant events and set out their concerns about the care provided. It is essential that this document is as balanced as possible, and should acknowledge the parents' positive parenting abilities as well as their negatives. This will give the court a clear picture of the work that has been undertaken with the family, as well as the concerns that remain.

**11.10** There should be a clear link between the evidence provided in the social work statement and the points included in the threshold document, so that the court can identify the evidence supporting the local authority's threshold concerns.

---

[3] All evidence filed with the court must comply with FPR 2010, r 22.4 and PD22A.

**11.11** In the event that the social worker's statement refers to any documents not already disclosed as per the pre-proceedings checklist,[4] these documents should be made available to the parties upon request.

## ISSUING AN APPLICATION FOR A CARE OR SUPERVISION ORDER

**11.12** When issuing their application for a care or supervision order, the local authority must notify the court if there is a need for an urgent case management or contested interim care order ('ICO') hearing. It may also be necessary for there to be an urgent case management hearing ('CMH') to consider matters such as jurisdiction, parentage, party status or capacity to litigate. If any of these issues are relevant, they should be highlighted in the application form. Unless the matter needs to be listed urgently, a CMH should be listed between 12 and 18 days after the application has been issued.

## GATEKEEPING

**11.13** *Guidance on Allocation and Gatekeeping* was issued by the President of the Family Division in 2014 and applies to the allocation of all relevant proceedings to judges of the Family Court, including lay justices working with Justices' Clerks or Assistant Justices' Clerks (referred to in this guidance as 'legal advisers').[5]

**11.14** The purpose of this guidance is to ensure that all new care, supervision and other Part IV proceedings are allocated to the appropriate level of judge and, where appropriate, to a named case management judge (or case manager) who is to provide continuity for the proceedings in accordance with the *President's Guidance on Judicial Continuity and Deployment (Public Law)*.

**11.15** Under the PLO, the court must first consider the local authority's application on day 2 of the proceedings (ie the first day after it has been issued). Within the guidance, it is provided that each designated family judge ('DFJ') will lead a gatekeeping team in every designated family centre:[6]

> 'A gatekeeping team will consist of the Designated Family Judge, his nominated deputy, the Justices' Clerk (or his nominated legal adviser) and an equal number of District Judges nominated by the Designated Family Judge, and legal advisers who will be identified by the Justices' Clerk in agreement with the Designated Family Judge. The number of legal advisers and District Judges is to be consistent with the needs of the business and the expertise of those who are available. Members of the gatekeeping team are referred to in this guidance as "gatekeepers".'

---

[4] See chapter 6 for the pre-proceedings checklist.
[5] *President's Guidance on Allocation and Gatekeeping for Care, Supervision and other Proceedings under Part IV of the Children Act 1989 (Public Law)*, 22 April 2014.
[6] Ibid, para 3.

**11.16** All applications for care, supervision and other Part IV orders which are received by the court for issue by 4pm will be issued by HMCTS and placed before gatekeepers for their joint consideration on the next working day. Anything issued after 4pm will be considered the next day.

## Allocation to appropriate level of judge

**11.17** In determining allocation, the gatekeepers are required to consider each application individually having regard to the information provided in the application form, from which it shall determine the appropriate level of judge. Considerations on the allocation of an application will include:

(1) the need to make the most effective and efficient use of the local judicial resources that is appropriate, given the nature and type of application;
(2) the need to avoid delay;
(3) the need for judicial continuity;
(4) the location of the parties or of any child relevant to the proceedings; and
(5) complexity.[7]

**11.18** Allocation to a specific level of judge at gatekeeping does not prevent the parties applying for the matter to be heard by a more senior judge later on. There is also an expectation that magistrates will not hear any contested hearing where the time estimate for the hearing is in excess of 3 days, without this being approved from time to time by the Justices' clerk (or his nominated deputy) in consultation with the DFJ.[8]

## Directions and case management at gatekeeping

**11.19** At gatekeeping, the court will give standard directions, including:

- checking compliance with pre-proceedings checklist including service of any missing Annex documents;
- appointing a children' guardian (to be allocated by Cafcass / Cafcass Cymru);
- appointing a solicitor for the child (only if necessary);
- appointing (if the person to be appointed consents) of a litigation friend for any protected party or any non-subject child who is a party, including the Official Solicitor where appropriate;
- identifying whether a request has been made or should be made to a central authority or other competent authority in a foreign state or a consular authority in England and Wales in cases with an international element;

---

[7] Ibid, para 14.
[8] Ibid, para 19.

- filing and service of a local authority case summary and a case analysis by the children's guardian;
- filing and serving the parent's response;
- sending a request for disclosure to e.g. the police or health service body;
- filing and serving an application for permission relating to experts under Part 25 of the Family Procedure Rules 2010 (the 'FPR 2010') on a date prior to the advocates meeting for the CMH;
- directing the advocates meeting to take place no later than 2 business days before the CMH; and
- listing of the CMH.

**11.20** In the event that the matter is to be listed for an urgent hearing, directions will also be made for that to take place. The CMH will still be listed between day 12 and day 18 unless all parties agree at the urgent hearing that it is no longer necessary.

## JURISDICTION

**11.21** The issue of jurisdiction must be considered by the court as soon as soon as possible after public law proceedings have been issued, normally when gatekeeping. In their application, the local authority must whether they think there is a potential international element that the court will need to consider. There may be limited information available at the time of the application being made, however, if there is a connection to another country, this must be specified on the application form so that the court is alerted as soon as possible. The court may list an urgent hearing for this issue to be determined, or seek directions for specific information to be made available.

**11.22** As discussed in chapter 3 of this book, it is essential that the court considers whether it has jurisdiction to hear the matter and this must be dealt with at the earliest opportunity. Consideration should also be given at gatekeeping as to whether a central authority or other competent authority in a foreign state, or a consular authority in England and Wales should be notified of the application. Again directions should be made at this stage for any relevant, outstanding information.

## DOCUMENTS REQUIRED FOR THE CMH

### Local authority case summary

**11.23** The local authority will draft the case summary for each hearing which should be drafted as neutrally as possible if it cannot be agreed between the parties.

**11.24** There is a template case summary available as an example of good practice. The case summary should provide information about any previous proceedings so the court can give early directions for any relevant documents to be extracted from previous bundles and disclosed into the current proceedings. If the previous proceedings did not have the same parties as the current application (for example, a different father), the parties to the previous proceedings must be notified of any application for disclosure, and will need to have the opportunity to oppose it, as discussed below.

**11.25** The case summary should include a summary of key events and a case update. It should provide a brief summary in one or two sentences of the circumstances giving rise to the application in order to appraise the court of the steps already taken in the proceedings to date, if any.

**11.26** The timetable for the child should also be set out in this document and should contain relevant information about how the timescale of the care proceedings will impact upon outcomes for the child. This is to enable the court to consider the timescales for the child when looking at the timetabling of the matter as a whole, to ensure that the court timetable is compatible with the child's timetable.

## Case analysis from the children's guardian

**11.27** Once a children's guardian is appointed, considered below, it is anticipated that they will meet the child and prepare an initial case analysis prior to the CMH to ensure that the court has all of the relevant information and analysis of the evidence available at CMH and can timetable the matter effectively and seek the appropriate evidence.

**11.28** The guardian will consider the local authority's evidence, meet the child, and preferably the parents, prior to the hearing, and consider whether they support the local authority's application or hold a different position. The guardian will also be able to identify any missing or outstanding information that is necessary.

## Parents' response document

**11.29** This will be the first piece of evidence before the court from the parents and should summarise their response to the local authority's initial evidence and their position in relation to the application before the court. This document should be filed before the CMH.[9]

**11.30** This is intended to be a short document, responding to the threshold statement and confirming where the parents wish the child to live, as well as identifying any relatives or friends they want to be assessed as potential carers in the event that the court decides the child cannot live with one or both of their parents. There will usually be a direction for a full narrative statement made at the CMH, but the response document should enable the extent of any

---

[9] All evidence filed with the court must comply with FPR 2010, r 22.4 and PD22A.

disagreement to become clear and for the proposals as to where the child should live to be available to the court.

**11.31** Practically, this is a document that will need to be completed quickly. The CMH will be listed after day 12 of the application being received by the court, and the parents' solicitors will need to take instructions and provide the response document before then. As a result of the tight timescale for this document being completed, it is only intended to be a short, just to ensure that all parties and the court know the issues at the CMH.

## Disclosure

**11.32** There are a number of different types of disclosure that will need to be considered at the onset of proceedings. It is essential that the court has all information that is necessary before it, but limited to what is relevant. The bundle should not be filled with unnecessary information.[10]

### *Documentation from previous proceedings*

**11.33** From C110 requires the local authority to identify whether there have been any previous proceedings in relation to the child or the parents involved, and file any previous orders made by the court.

**11.34** In the event that there have been previous proceedings, the evidence filed within these proceedings may relevant to the current application. The court will consider whether the evidence from the previous proceedings can be disclosed into the current proceedings, and if so, the court may make a direction for this at gatekeeping, although it is more commonly dealt with at the CMH.

**11.35** In the event that the parties are the same across the previous and current proceedings, the court can order the papers be disclosed. In the event that one or more of the parties involved in the previous proceedings are not involved the current ones, their consent must be obtained before the materials are disclosed.

**11.36** The local authority will need to give notice that the evidence from the previous proceedings is sought, and the parties to those proceedings must have an opportunity to object to this. If they object to the papers being disclosed, the court will need to consider an application for disclosure before they determine whether the documents should be disclosed.

**11.37** Only the relevant documents from any previous proceedings should be disclosed, and typically an index of the proposed documents will be provided to all parties in an attempt to agree can which documents will be relevant and which will not. Again, this is something that will normally be directed at the CMH.

---

[10] See chapter 19 for discussion of the size of the bundle.

## Police disclosure

**11.38** If the local authority is aware of police involvement with the family, an application will need to be made for the disclosure of police records. It is not uncommon for a direction to be made for a print out from the Police National Computer ('PNC') to confirm whether the parents involved have any previous convictions or cautions.

**11.39** When considering applying for police disclosure, practitioners should be aware of the protocol arrangements in place with the police service. A request should be made in accordance with the protocol to the police service in the area in which the parents live, have lived, or an incident took place. Each police service has their own protocol arrangement which should be followed.[11]

**11.40** As part of *Working Together to Safeguard Children* arrangements,[12] the police must share information with the other agencies for the purposes of child protection. They will also be a member of the case conference convened by the local authority, as discussed in chapter 5. As a result, the local authority and the police are likely to have already shared a great deal of information prior to the application being made.

**11.41** The police should be notified in writing, prior to the direction for disclosure being sought from the court. Failure to notify the police will not prevent the court from making an order, but may delay access to the documents.

**11.42** Police disclosure can be sought in respect of any party to the proceedings, with or without their consent, and the court will direct as such if it is of the view that the documents are necessary. If the local authority seeks police disclosure in relation to a non-party, for example, one of the parents' partners, the non-party will need to have an opportunity to oppose this information being provided. If the non-party has not been consulted, the court can make the direction for information to be disclosed, but must also provide for liberty to apply back to the court to vary or discharge the direction within a specified period of time. The relevant order must then be served on the non-party so that they are aware of the information that has been requested.

**11.43** Regardless of the individual protocol arrangements, all police services are clear that any request for disclosure must be clear and detailed as to what is required. The local authority should specify which records are sought so that resources are not wasted. The date of birth of the person subject to the disclosure request is required, together with their address(es) and the dates of any relevant incidents.

---

[11] See *Protocol and Good Practice Model: Disclosure of information in cases of alleged child abuse and linked criminal and care directions hearings* (2013).
[12] *Working Together to Safeguard Children* (2015).

**11.44** Police disclosure can provide essential information for the court when determining an application for a care or supervision order, and therefore it is vital that relevant information is identified as quickly as possible. In *Cumbria County Council v M & Others*, Peter Jackson J commented:[13]

> 'The efficient process of disclosure between the criminal and family jurisdictions is essential to the proper administration of justice. It is governed by protocols and on occasions reinforced by court orders. The criminal and family courts must be able to rely on assurances that all relevant material has been disclosed, though in some cases they may have to resolve claims of public interest immunity.'

**11.45** Any issues in relation to police disclosure should be identified quickly so that the court can deal with this appropriately and ensure the information is made available.

## *Medical disclosure*

**11.46** This is a matter that will need to be considered at the CMH, not at gatekeeping. There are a number of types of disclosure that may be sought from medical professionals within care proceedings. It may be necessary to seek medical information relevant to the questions before the court in respect of the child, or the physical or mental health of a parent.

**11.47** In order for medical records to be obtained, the person to whom they relate will need to provide their consent for them to be disclosed. If this concerns a child, it is the holders of parental responsibility who will need to consent.

**11.48** As with the police above, health professionals are members of the case conference convened by the local authority, so the local authority will, in most cases, already have some information that will assist them when considering what disclosure may be necessary.

**11.49** In the event that an expert, such as a psychiatrist or psychologist, is instructed within the proceedings under Part 25, parents' medical notes will need to be provided to them to assist with their report. It is possible for parents' medical notes to be sent directly to the expert only without filing and serving them on the court and the parties. Privacy is important and all parties and the court should have that at the forefront of their minds when deciding what information is essential to resolving the application.

## Appointing an expert

**11.50** Part 25 of the FPR 2010 deals with applications for expert reports within care and supervision order proceedings. A direction will usually be made at the gatekeeping stage, requiring any party who seeks to instruct an expert to make application to the court to be considered at the CMH. In the event that

---

[13] *Cumbria County Council v M & Others* [2016] EWFC 27 at [15].

an application is not made in accordance with the direction, parties can seek an extension of time to make the application at the CMH, supported with an explanation as to why the application has not already been made.

**11.51** Pursuant to r 25.4(2) of the FPR 2010, expert evidence can only be adduced with permission of the court. The court may give permission for the instruction of an expert and the filing of a report, only if 'the court is of the opinion that the expert evidence is necessary to assist the court to resolve the proceedings'.[14]

**11.52** Permission is not necessary if the expert report was completed prior to the commencement of the proceedings. If a report has been prepared pre-proceedings, it should be filed with the court and served on the other parties with the initial application, as set out in the pre-proceedings checklist.

**11.53** When an application is made to instruction an expert, consideration should be given to PD25C which supplements Part 25. Paragraph 3 of PD25C sets out the preparations required for the permission hearing in a Part 25 application. The Part 25 applicant should, as soon as possible after the issue of proceedings, notify the other parties that they will be making an application for an expert to be appointed, and provide a list of the names of one or more experts in the relevant speciality whom they consider suitable to be instructed.[15] Within 5 working days of notification, the other parties should confirm whether they agree to the instruction of the expert or not. If there is disagreement as to the identity of the expert, or a disagreement as to whether an expert is necessary, the court will hear submissions at the CMH and make a decision as to whether the assessment should be undertaken and by whom.[16]

**11.54** The application form should be prepared together with details of the expert sought, a draft letter of instruction and details of timescales and costs. A draft order should also be prepared and attached to the application specifying the issues the expert will address, which party will be responsible for taking the lead in the expert's instruction, the timetable for the report to be completed and how the costs of the assessment will be met.

**11.55** The making of a Part 25 application and the court's approach will be considered further at chapter 15 of this book.

## Advocates meeting

**11.56** The court will direct that an advocates meeting shall occur no later than 2 business days before the CMH, including any litigants in person where a party is not represented. The meeting can take place over the telephone or face-to-face, depending on what is convenient for the attendees.

---

[14] FPR 2010, r 25.4(3).
[15] FPR 2010, PD25C, para 2.1.
[16] FPR 2010, PD25C, para 2.4.

**11.57** At the meeting, the following points should be considered in accordance with the stage 2 of the PLO:

- information on the application form and annex document, the local authority's case summary, and the case analysis;
- identify the parties' positions to be recited in the draft case management order;
- identify the parties' position on jurisdiction, in particular arising out of any international element;
- if necessary, identify proposed experts and draft questions in accordance with Part 25 and the relevant practice directions;
- identify any disclosure that, in the advocates' view, is necessary; and
- immediately notify the court of the need for a contested ICO hearing and any issues arising from allocation.

**11.58** Following the meeting, the advocate for the local authority will compose and file with the court a draft case management order on the prescribed form by 11am on the business day before the CMH.

**11.59** The aim of this stage is to ensure that all of the necessary information and the parties' positions clear so that the CMH is effective.

## DECISION TO LIST AN APPLICATION FOR AN INTERIM CARE ORDER

**11.60** Whether the matter needs to be listed for an ICO hearing depends the local authority's position in relation to the care of the child. If the local authority seek an ICO so that they can remove the child from their parents, or keep the child in accommodation away from the parents, and the parents do not agree, the court will need to determine the local authority's application quickly.

**11.61** When the local authority notifies the court in their application that an ICO hearing is necessary, the court will make directions at gatekeeping for the filing of any evidence before the contested hearing, but will still list the CMH as prescribed in the PLO (between days 12 and 18).

**11.62** The local authority cannot lawfully remove or keep a child away from the care of a parent without the parent's consent. It is possible to place a child away from a parent under s 20 of the Children Act 1989, but only by consent and not for an extended period of time.[17]

**11.63** If the parents oppose the removal of their child or seek their child's return in circumstances where s 20 accommodation was previously agreed, the

---

[17] See chapter 5.

court will need to determine the local authority's application for an ICO as a matter of urgency. The local authority cannot accommodate a child without parental consent unless an ICO is in place and the local authority shares parental responsibility with the parents, or they are granted an emergency protection order.

**11.64** The parents must be served with the ICO application and given 3 working days' notice prior to the hearing.[18] The court can abridge the notice period between service and the hearing, but only when it is satisfied that this is necessary to safeguard the child. It must leave sufficient time for the parent to obtain legal advice either prior to or at the hearing.

**11.65** An ICO cannot be made on a without notice basis: the correct application in circumstances where the local authority wish to have a without notice hearing is for an emergency protection order. ICO hearings are considered further at chapter 15 of this book.

---

[18] In accordance with the Civil Procedure Rules 1998, r 23.7(b).

# CHAPTER 12

# REPRESENTATION OF THE RESPONDENTS IN CARE PROCEEDINGS

## WHO IS PARTY TO PUBLIC LAW PROCEEDINGS?

**12.1** There is a very useful table provided at r 12.3 of the Family Procedure Rules 2010 ('FPR 2010') setting out who can apply for various orders and who the automatic respondents will be. A respondent must be provided with notice of the proceedings together with all documentation filed with the court.

**12.2** In care or supervision order applications, anyone who holds parental responsibility for a child will automatically become a respondent (parental responsibility is discussed at chapter 2).

**12.3** The birth mother of a child automatically holds parental responsibility for them, as will a married father. If the father is not married to the child's mother, he will only hold parental responsibility for the child if he is named as the father on the child's birth certificate, as long as the child was born after December 2003. If the child was born before December 2003 and the mother and father are unmarried, the father will not hold parental responsibility, even if he is on the birth certificate.[1]

**12.4** If the biological father does not have parental responsibility, he must still be given notice of the proceedings but will not receive any of the other documents. Only a party is entitled to receive the documents filed in the proceedings. The notice should enable the father to take steps to attend court and make an application to be joined to the proceedings, if he so wishes.

**12.5** If a mother disputes the legitimacy of a child, the father with parental responsibility must still be served with notice of the proceedings so that the issue can be determined.[2] In exceptional circumstances it may be appropriate to exclude a father with parental responsibility from care proceedings, but only when it is found that the father would present a real and substantial risk to the children and the mother.[3]

---

[1] Fathers named on a child's birth certificate after December 2003 were conferred parental responsibility by virtue of the Adoption and Children Act 2002.
[2] *Re AB (Care Proceedings: Service on Husband Ignorant of Child's Existence)* [2004] 1 FLR 527.
[3] *Re M (Children)* [2010] 1 FLR 1355.

**12.6** A step-parent, or the partner of a parent, will not automatically become a party unless they have parental responsibility for a child by virtue of a parental responsibility agreement or order. If the facts of the case rely on the conduct of a step-parent, or allegations are made against them, there will need to be consideration as to whether that person should intervene in the proceedings, as discussed below, or granted full party status.

**12.7** If an application is made in relation to a child who is named as 'living with' someone under a child arrangements order, that person will hold parental responsibility for them for the duration of the order and will automatically become a party. However, if an interim care order is made, the child arrangements order will be discharged and that person's parental responsibility, lost. They will remain a party to the proceedings unless an application is made for them to be discharged.

**12.8** Similarly, in the event that the child is subject to a special guardianship order, the special guardian will automatically be a party to the proceedings. Unlike child arrangements orders, a special guardianship order will not be discharged by an interim care order and the special guardian will retain their parental responsibility.

**12.9** If the child was living with someone immediately prior to the issue of proceedings, but that person does not hold parental responsibility for the child, that person is only entitled to notice of the proceedings, after which they can apply to be joined.

## Joinder

**12.10** An application for a non-party to be joined to proceedings must be made on form C2.[4] An oral application can also be made to the court by another party, but it is best practice for the application to be made formally and in writing first, so that the court has all of the information it needs before it.

**12.11** There is no guidance provided by the Children Act 1989 ('CA 1989') as to how the court should consider an application by someone to become party to the proceedings. The court must apply the overriding objective set out in r 1.1 of the FPR 2010:

> '(1) These rules are a new procedural code with the overriding objective of enabling the court to deal with cases justly, having regard to any welfare issues involved.
>
> (2) Dealing with a case justly includes, so far as is practicable –
>
>     (a)    ensuring that it is dealt with expeditiously and fairly;
>     (b)    dealing with the case in ways which are proportionate to the nature, importance and complexity of the issues;
>     (c)    ensuring that the parties are on an equal footing;

---

[4] FPR 2010, rr 18.1–18.13 and PD18A.

(d) saving expense; and
(e) allotting to it an appropriate share of the court's resources, while taking into account the need to allot resources to other cases.'

**12.12** This is also relevant to any application to discharge a party to proceedings.

## An application by a father who does not hold parental responsibility

**12.13** There is a presumption that the biological father of a child who does not have parental responsibility will be made party to care or supervision order proceedings, if an application is made.

**12.14** Article 8 of the ECHR recognises the right to respect for a person's private and family life. A father without parental responsibility still has that right, and must have access to the court. He also has a right to a fair trial under Art 6. Without having access to the courts as a party to the proceedings, neither of these rights can be protected.

**12.15** However, the court will also consider whether there is a justifiable reason as to why a father without parental responsibility should _not_ be party to the proceedings. The court will consider any impact upon the welfare of the child resulting from the father being a party, as well as any impact upon the proceedings as a whole, such as delay.[5] The child's welfare is an important but not a paramount consideration for the court in this instance.[6]

**12.16** It is within the court's power to decide that the local authority does not have a duty to provide information to a parent, or consult them in relation to the care of the child, if it is contrary to the child's best interests. However, this is only in exceptional cases.[7] Furthermore, the court will not sanction the withholding of information about the existence of a child from a parent, or dispense with service on the parents.

## An application by a grandparent

**12.17** The Court of Appeal in *Re B (Paternal Grandmother: Joinder as Party)*[8] provides guidance as to how an application by a grandparent to be joined as a party to care proceedings should be considered by the court. Black LJ determined that in the absence of specific guidance in the CA 1989 or the FPR 2010 on this issue, it was appropriate to consider s 10(9) of the CA 1989.

**12.18** Section 10(9) sets out the considerations the court must have when an application is made for leave to apply for a s 8 (ie private law) order:

---

[5] *Re P (Care Proceedings: Father's Application to be Joined as Party)* [2001] 1 FLR 781.
[6] *North Yorkshire County Council v G* [1993] 2 FLR 732.
[7] *Re C (Care: Consultation with Parents not in Child's Best Interests)* [2006] 2 FLR 787.
[8] *Re B (Paternal Grandmother: Joinder as Party)* [2012] 2 FLR 1358.

'(9) Where the person applying for leave to make an application for a section 8 order is not the child concerned, the court shall, in deciding whether or not to grant leave, have particular regard to –

- (a) the nature of the proposed application for the section 8 order;
- (b) the applicant's connection with the child;
- (c) any risk there might be of that proposed application disrupting the child's life to such an extent that he would be harmed by it; and
- (d) where the child is being looked after by a local authority –
    - (i) the authority's plans for the child's future; and
    - (ii) the wishes and feelings of the child's parents.'

**12.19** Black LJ summarised the position in case law and concluded that s 10(9) did not contain a specific test, but rather picked out some of the factors to which the court should have particular regard, whilst acknowledging that there may be others. These factors will vary from case-to-case and all applications should be dealt with individually.

**12.20** If the grandparent making the joinder application does not have an independent or separate view from one of the other parties, the application may not be granted. The court will guard against unnecessary delay and will attempt to protect costs from escalating. If it is possible that the position of the grandparent applying to be joined can be argued by an existing party, the court will allow them to be called as a witness rather than making them a party.

## Leave for a person to intervene in the proceedings for a specific purpose

**12.21** Rather than joining a party to the whole of the proceedings, it might be more appropriate for the court to give leave for a person to intervene for a specific purpose. Leave is usually granted when a non-party is the subject of findings of fact that the local authority wishes the court to determine, and as such the non-party may be involved in order to put their own case forward on that specific issue. See chapter 19 for further discussion of this.[9]

**12.22** There is no 'right' for a person against whom findings are sought to intervene in the proceedings, and each application to intervene in such circumstances must be considered on the facts.[10] The overriding objective contained in r 1.1 of the FPR 2010 and discussed above, will evidently be relevant to the court's considerations.

**12.23** If it is clear that someone may need to have the opportunity to intervene in the proceedings for a particular purpose, the court will invite the person to attend court to confirm whether they intend to become involved. In the event that they do wish to intervene, the court will then make consequential directions to enable evidence to be placed before the court for the provision of evidence.

---

[9] Re H (Children) (Care Proceedings: Sexual Abuse) [2000] 2 FCR 499.
[10] Re H (Care Proceedings: Intervener) [2000] 1 FLR 775.

# REPRESENTATION OF PARENTS AND PEOPLE WITH PARENTAL RESPONSIBILITY

**12.24** Once an application has been made for a care or supervision order, the respondents will need the opportunity to obtain legal representation. Respondents to care proceedings may decide to represent themselves (as is their right), but if they have parental responsibility for the child they will be entitled to non-means/merits tested legal aid. Parties should be encouraged to obtain legal representation where at all possible.

## Parents with parental responsibility

**12.25** As above, a birth mother automatically holds parental responsibility for a child, as does any father married to the mother or, if unmarried, named on the birth certificate (see chapter 2 for the position on same-sex families).[11]

**12.26** If there is no conflict of interest, both parents can be represented by the same solicitor. There will be a conflict of interest if the court needs to consider matters on which the parents have different positions. Evidently, in situations where there are allegations of domestic abuse, parents will have their own instructions and will need separate representation. Because care proceedings invariably turn on the parenting a child has received, parents usually have separate representation to ensure that any conflicts of interest do not come to light late in proceedings, causing delay.

## Fathers without parental responsibility

**12.27** The biological father of a child who does not have parental responsibility will not be an automatic respondent, but must still be given notice of the proceedings and then may apply to be joined as a party (see above). In any event, the father will still be eligible for non-means/merits tested legal aid, even without parental responsibility, as is consistent with their Art 6 right to a fair trial.

**12.28** In reality, the local authority's duty to consider alternative family placements and the court's obligation to decide whether it is necessary to remove a child from their natural family, means that any father without parental responsibility should be assessed and heard within the proceedings.

## Holders of parental responsibility by virtue of a child arrangements order

**12.29** If an application is made in relation to a child who is 'living with' someone under a child arrangements order, that person will have parental responsibility for the child for the life of the order and will therefore qualify for

---

[11] CA 1989, s 4(1A). Unmarried fathers will only obtain parental responsibility by virtue of being named on their child's birth certificate if that child was born after December 2003.

non-means/merits tested legal aid. However, if the court makes an interim care order, the pre-existing child arrangements order will be discharged and the person will lose their parental responsibility as well as their entitlement to public funding.

**12.30** The person can remain a party to the proceedings if they so wish, but they will have to make a fresh application to the legal aid agency, which will now be both means and merits tested. This may result in the party not having representation, unless they can afford to fund it privately.

**12.31** The funding position of this person cannot be a reason preventing an interim order from being made, although it is essential that the parties and the court assist them in the event that they lose their representation. The Bar Pro Bono Unit, a charity which arranges for barristers to represent individuals on a pro bono basis, may also be able to assist with representation in court.[12]

## Holder of parental responsibility by virtue of a special guardianship order

**12.32** Special guardianship orders confer responsibility on special guardians, and therefore they will be automatic respondents to the proceedings and eligible for non-means/merits tested legal aid.

**12.33** Unlike child arrangements orders, a special guardianship order will not be discharged by the making of an interim care order, so special guardians will continue to be eligible for non-means/merits tested legal aid.

## Other carers without parental responsibility

**12.34** If a child is being cared for by a family member or friend without an order of the court, or parental responsibility agreement, they will not have parental responsibility and will not be an automatic party to the proceedings. They will not be entitled to non-means/merits tested legal aid and must make a formal application to the Legal Aid Agency for funding based on their means and the merits of their case.

**12.35** They can, of course, apply to be joined to the proceedings without legal representation, and if such an application is successful the other parties and the court must assist them so that they can engage fully. The Bar Pro Bono Unit may also be able to assist.

## Representation of intervenors

**12.36** As discussed above, a person may intervene in the proceedings for a specific purpose, rather than becoming a party. They will not be entitled to non-means/merits tested legal aid and will need to make a formal application to

---

[12] Include Bar Pro Bono Unit's details?

the Legal Aid Agency for funding, fund their representation privately or attend the court in person. The other parties and the court must assist them so that they can engage fully and the Bar Pro Bono Unit may be able to offer free representation in court.

## Litigation capacity of an adult party or intervener

**12.37** If an adult party or intervenor is known or suspected to have a disability that may affect their ability to participate fully in the proceedings, it is essential that this is identified at the earliest possible opportunity. A person who is under a disability is described in Part 15 of the FPR 2010 as a protected party. Rule 2.3(1)[13] of the FPR 2010 provides that a 'protected party' means "a party, or an intended party, who lacks capacity (within the meaning of Mental Capacity Act 2005) to conduct the proceedings"'.

**12.38** Local authorities are under a duty to consider whether a parent is a protected party, and therefore potentially unable to engage fully in proceedings without assistance, at the earliest opportunity. For instance, a parent may suffer from a learning difficulty or mental health issue which could impact on their understanding of the proceedings and/or their ability to engage with professionals.

**12.39** Pre-proceedings, the local authority should consider the potential issues and arrange for an expert report to be commissioned. This will inform their work with the parent and allow them to assess that parent's ability to consent to s 20 accommodation, for example.

**12.40** If the local authority have concerns about a parent's capacity to litigate, or their ability to engage in their proceedings (for example, because of a hearing, language or sight issue), they must make this clear in their initial application to the court. This will enable everyone to take the necessary steps to ensure that the parent can participate fully in the proceedings, especially when there is the possibility of early removal of a child from a parent's care.

**12.41** The same considerations should be given to other parties to the application as well as any potential interveners. Access to justice requires that all participants are able to fully engage with the proceedings.

**12.42** Whilst an assessment is being undertaken to determine a person's litigation capacity, the proceedings cannot progress and no further directions should be made until this question is answered.[14]

---

[13] See also FPR 2010, PD15B.
[14] FPR 2010, r 15.3(2) and (3), PD12A, para 8.

## Assessing capacity to conduct proceedings

**12.43** The general principle is that a person must be assumed to have capacity unless it is established otherwise.[15] Section 2(1) of the MCA 2005 describes 'lacking capacity' as follows:

> 'A person lacks capacity in relation to a matter if, at the material time, he is unable to make a decision for himself in relation to the matter because of an impairment of or disturbance in the functioning of the mind or brain.'

**12.44** Having, or lacking, capacity is not necessarily a lifelong, or even long-term state. A person may lack capacity temporarily, and regain capacity as their health improves. Litigation capacity may fluctuate throughout the proceedings, if the person is suffering from an acute mental illness or following a brain injury for example. Lifelong lack of litigation capacity will usually result from profound learning difficulties or a degenerative illness.

**12.45** Section 3(1) of the MCA 2005 provides that a person is unable to make a decision for himself if they are unable to understand information relevant to a decision, retain it, use or weigh it up as part of the decision-making process or communicate their decision.

**12.46** It is essential that a capacity assessment is undertaken as soon as possible and the local authority must be alive to this pre-proceedings. If this has not been raised in pre-proceedings, an assessment must be arranged as a matter of urgency at the first hearing, by way of an application for an expert report in accordance with Part 25 of the FPR 2010 as discussed in chapter 15.

**12.47** There are essentially three categories of person who may come within the definition of a protected party: people who suffer from a mental illness, learning difficulties or brain damage. Psychologists should be appointed where the concerns surround learning disabilities or cognitive understanding, and psychiatrists should be appointed in respect of individuals with mental health issues. In all circumstances, the expert will confirm whether the individual has the capacity to litigate, or what support can be put in place to assist them to participate in the proceedings.

**12.48** The expert instructed will then prepare the following capacity certificate:

---

[15] MCA 2005, s 1.

# CERTIFICATE AS TO CAPACITY
# TO CONDUCT PROCEEDINGS

[Ref:          ]

*You should read the whole of this form and the attached notes for guidance before completing this form.*
*Please answer all questions as fully as you can.*

Name of person concerned:

Date of birth:

The proceedings are ................................................. (and see paragraph 3 below)

| Insert your full name and address (including postcode)  Give your professional Qualifications | I  of |
|---|---|
| For a definition of 'a person who lacks capacity' see note 2 attached | 1. Nature of your professional relationship with the person concerned:  - I have acted as practitioner for the person concerned since ........................... and last assessed him/her on ........................  or  - I assessed the person concerned on ........................... following a referral from ...........................................................  AND in my opinion............................................  - **is capable** (within the meaning of the Mental Capacity Act 2005) of conducting the proceedings*  or  - **lacks capacity** (within the meaning of the Mental Capacity Act 2005) to conduct the proceedings*  (*strike through as appropriate)  If in your opinion ............................................ is a person who lacks capacity to conduct the proceedings please answer questions 2-8 below |

2. The person concerned has the following impairment of, or disturbance in the functioning of, the mind or brain (see note 2):

this has lasted since:..............................................................................

3. As a result, the person concerned is incapable of conducting the proceedings described below and/or in the attached letter of instructions.

**because (please tick as many boxes as apply)**

☐ the person is unable to understand the following relevant information (please give details):

**and/or**

☐ the person is unable to retain that information (please give details)

**and/or**

☐ the person is unable to use or weigh the following information as part of the process of making the decisions in the conduct of the proceedings:

**or**

☐ for cases where the person can in fact understand, retain and use / weigh the information the person is unable to communicate their decisions by any means at all (please give details):

4. Do you consider that the person concerned might regain or develop capacity to conduct the proceedings in the future -

☐ Yes - please state why and give an indication of when this might happen

☐ No - please state why

5. Is the person concerned able to discuss the proceedings with my representative or with a solicitor instructed by me?

☐ YES    ☐ NO

Please comment

6. If so, is such discussion likely to affect the person detrimentally and if so, in what way?

☐ YES ☐ NO

Please comment

7. Has the person concerned made you aware of any views in relation to the proceedings and / or in relation to their capacity to conduct the proceedings?

8. Any additional comments

Statement of Truth:

I confirm that insofar as the facts stated in this certificate are within my own knowledge I have made clear which they are and I believe them to be true and that the opinions I have expressed represent my true professional opinion.

Signed  _____

Dated  _____

**12.49** This certificate addresses all the provisions included in the MCA 2005. If the expert concludes that the person lacks capacity, the court must direct a litigation friend is appointed on their behalf.[16]

---

[16] FPR 2010, r 15.2.

**12.50** This assessment is crucial. If the court determines that a party lacks capacity, they will not have the ability to give their instructions directly to the court, so the matter will be conducted on their behalf, considering their wishes and feelings. However, the litigation friend may disagree with the protected party's views and provide instructions contrary to them.

## *Ability of a party to contest their assessment as to capacity*

**12.51** A person may wish to contest an outcome stating that they lack capacity. They may not agree might want to conduct the proceedings without the assistance of a litigation friend.

**12.52** The court will hear evidence from the expert who has undertaken the assessment and the individual in question will have the opportunity to explain why they do not agree with the assessment of them. The court is the ultimate arbiter of capacity and will make their decision after hearing all of the evidence. In light of the consequences of determining a person lacks capacity, this is a decision that the court will make with the utmost care.

## *Litigation friend*

**12.53** If a person is assessed as lacking litigation capacity, they will become a protected party and appointed a litigation friend as per r 15.2 of the FPR 2010. There are no exceptions to this rule, but the court may waive the requirement if it sees fit.[17]

**12.54** A litigation friend is someone who conducts the proceedings on behalf of the protected party. Therefore, any steps that have been taken by the court prior to the appointment of a litigation friend, other than the steps set out in r 15.3, will have no effect. However, the court can decide that steps taken prior to the appointment of a litigation friend remain in place. If urgent orders have been made prior to the appointment of the litigation friend, the court must be in possession of all of the relevant information as to the circumstances.

**12.55** In the event that a litigation friend has been appointed but the protected party is assessed as having regained capacity, the litigation friend will be discharged by a court order.[18]

**12.56** FPR 2010, r 15.6 provides that the court may appoint the Official Solicitor or another person as a litigation friend, providing they consent and are an adult who can 'fairly and competently conduct proceedings on behalf of the protected party' and have 'no interest adverse to that of the protected party'.

---

[17] FPR 2010, r 15.3.
[18] FPR 2010, r 15.9.

**12.57** If there is no one other than the Official Solicitor that could act as the litigation friend, the Official Solicitor will be invited to act by court order. If the Official Solicitor is invited to act, they will usually consent subject to:

- satisfactory evidence in the form of an expert's opinion accepted by the party that they lack capacity to conduct the proceedings, or a finding of the court that the party is a protected party;
- confirmation that the Official Solicitor is litigation friend of last resort; and
- confirmation that there is security for the costs of legal representation.

**12.58** The Official Solicitor will consider the papers and instruct the solicitor on behalf of the party directly. The party's wishes and feelings will be obtained, but the Official Solicitor's instructions will be final and a position will be put forward on their behalf, even if it is against the protected party's wishes.

## Ability to give written and oral evidence

**12.59** Any statement that is prepared on behalf of the protected party will be completed by the Official Solicitor according to a template. Whilst it will contain the wishes and feelings of the protected party, the position put forward will be that of the position held by the Official Solicitor, after having considered all of the evidence.

**12.60** If the protected party is required to give oral evidence, there will need to be a further assessment as to whether they are capable of doing so. As before, the assessment must consider whether there are any measures that can be put in place to assist the protected party in giving their best evidence. For example, an intermediary.

**12.61** In the event that the protected party does not have the capacity to give evidence, especially as to facts that the local authority seeks to prove, they will not be compelled to give evidence as this will clearly not assist the court.

### Intermediary assessment

**12.62** An expert report may recommend that an intermediary service is approached. An intermediary service will then undertake an assessment of the person before deciding whether they can assist.

**12.63** This may be necessary if a party or intervener requires assistance in order to give oral evidence to the court, or to understand the evidence given. They will assess and determine whether the individual would benefit from assistance when giving oral evidence and can recommend measures that will enable the person to give live evidence and minimise the risk of confusion or inaccurate information resulting from a person's functioning and understanding.

**12.64** Measures could include screens to enable the person to avoid looking at one of the parties, or a video link facility to prevent the person from having to be in the same room as a party. An intermediary will also advise the court and the advocates on how best to put questions, as well as ensuring that there are frequent breaks to make sure the person can have a rest and collect their thoughts.

## REPRESENTATION OF CHILDREN

**12.65** A child is automatically a respondent to a local authority's application for a care or placement order. Part 16 of the FPR 2010 provides for the representation of children in family proceedings. Under r 16.3, the court must appoint a children's guardian for the child who is the subject or party to specified proceedings (including care and supervision orders by virtue of s 41(6)(a) CA 1989), unless they are satisfied that it is not necessary to do so to safeguard the interests of the child.

**12.66** This must be done within one day of the application being issued.[19] A children's guardian must be an officer of Cafcass, or a Welsh family proceedings officer. Their role is to represent the best interests of the child and they will appoint a solicitor who will take instructions from the guardian on behalf of the child.[20]

## POWERS AND DUTIES OF A CHILDREN'S GUARDIAN

**12.67** Rule 16.20 of the FPR 2010 provides as follows:

> '(1) The children's guardian is to act on behalf of the child upon the hearing of any application in proceedings to which this Chapter applies with the duty of safeguarding the interests of the child.
>
> (2) The children's guardian must also provide the court with such other assistance as it may require.
>
> (3) The children's guardian, when carrying out duties in relation to specified proceedings, other than placement proceedings, must have regard to the principle set out in section 1(2) and the matters set out in section 1(3)(a) to (f) of the 1989 Act as if for the word "court" in that section there were substituted the words "children's guardian".'

**12.68** Section 41(2)(b) of the CA 1989 confers a duty on a children's guardian to safeguard the interests of the child in the manner prescribed by the rules of the court. In *Re R v Cornwall County Council*, it was emphasised that a children's guardian must be independent in the performance of their duties. The local authority cannot restrict the work of a guardian.[21]

---

[19] FPR 2010, r 12.6.
[20] FPR 2010, PD16A, para 6.2.
[21] *Re R v Cornwall County Council ex parte G* [1992] 1 FLR 270.

**12.69** The guardian has certain duties in relation to the child. PD16A provides:

> 'The children's guardian must make such investigations as are necessary to carry out the children's guardian's duties and must, in particular –
>
> a. contact or seek to interview such persons as the children's guardian thinks appropriate or as the court directs; and
> b. obtain such professional assistance as is available which the children's guardian thinks appropriate or which the court directs be obtained.'

**12.70** The guardian will meet with the parties as well as the children in order to investigate the circumstances of the family and provide an analysis of this to the court, to assist the court to determine the application in the best interests of the children. In the exercise of their duties, the children's guardian has the right to access the documents held by the local authority under s 42 of the CA 1989.

**12.71** PD16A, para 6.6 provides that:

> 'The children's guardian must advise the court on the following matters –
>
> a. whether the child is of sufficient understanding for any purpose including the child's refusal to submit to a medical or psychiatric examination or other assessment that the court has the power to require, direct or order;
> b. the wishes of the child in respect of any matter relevant to the proceedings including that child's attendance at court;
> c. the appropriate forum for the proceedings;
> d. the appropriate timing of the proceedings or any part of them;
> e. the options available to it in respect of the child and the suitability of each such option including what order should be made in determining the application; and
> f. any other matter on which the court seeks advice or on which the children's guardian considers that the court should be informed.'

**12.72** The guardian must attend all if the hearings unless directed otherwise,[22] and must provide a written report to the court advising on the interests of the child in accordance with the timetable set by the court.[23]

**12.73** As a result of the guardian's investigation and analysis of the circumstances of the family, the guardian may come to a position that is in opposition to that of the child they represent. For example, it may be that the guardian will support the long term removal of the child from their parents, but the child does not agree. The guardian must inform the court of the child's wishes and feelings in relation to matters such as contact and the long term plans for them, but ultimately will come to their own conclusions on the recommendations to be made to the court.

---

[22] FPR 2010, PD16A, para 6.5.
[23] FPR 2010, PD16A, para 6.8.

## Separate representation of a child

**12.74** A child will be represented through their guardian, unless the child is considered to be of sufficient age and understanding to provide instructions separately. This situation can arise in the event that the child disagrees with the guardian and is considered able to provide instructions directly to the solicitor.

**12.75** PD16A, para 6.3 provides that in the event that the child wishes to instruct a solicitor directly and the guardian and the court are of the view that the child is of sufficient age and understanding to do so, the child can instruct a solicitor independently of their guardian. The children's solicitor will undertake their own assessment as to whether a child has sufficient understanding to instruct them directly, possibly assisted by a Part 25 appointed expert.

**12.76** If a child does instruct a solicitor directly, the guardian will remain involved in the proceedings and will normally instruct another solicitor. The guardian retains their duty to investigate the circumstances of the application and advise the court as to the best interest of the child.

# CHAPTER 13

# INTERIM CARE ORDERS (PART 1): GENERAL PRINCIPLES OF INTERIM ORDERS AND INTERIM THRESHOLD

## INTRODUCTION: THE NEED FOR AN INTERIM ORDERS REGIME

### The basis for applying for a care order: protection from significant harm

**13.1** It should never be forgotten that in making an application for a care order or a supervision order the applicant, almost always a local authority,[1] asserts that:[2]

> 'the child concerned is suffering, or is likely to suffer, significant harm.'

and that:[3]

> 'the harm, or likelihood of harm, is attributable to –
> 
> (i) the care given to the child, or likely to be given to him if the order were not made, not being what it would be reasonable to expect a parent to give him: or
> (ii) the child being beyond parental control.'

**13.2** If the court is satisfied that this is in fact the case, the child can be protected from such actual or likely suffering by the making of a range of orders that can include ones that have the effect not only of removing the child from an inadequate home but also severing the legal relationships between child and birth family.[4] Even if such drastic orders are not made, a finding that this assertion is justified is likely to result in children and their families experiencing, often for many years, levels of interference by public authorities in their lives that would not otherwise be countenanced in a free and democratic society.[5]

---

[1] See Children Act 1989, s 31(1).
[2] Section 31(2)(a).
[3] Section 31(2)(b).
[4] ie adoption orders, for the effect of which see Adoption and Children Act 2002, Part 1, Chapter 4.
[5] See Convention for the Protection of Human Rights and Fundamental Freedoms, Art 8.

**13.3** As is discussed elsewhere in this work, the making of such 'draconian' orders requires the utmost care. It is likely to involve detailed examination of oral and written evidence, including expert evidence, and the court often requires the assistance of independent experts in a wide range of disciplines. All this takes time and begs the question of what happens to a child in relation to whom there are such serious concerns whilst the court process moves towards the stage when a final decision can be made.

**13.4** The Children Act 1989 ('CA 1989) answers this question by providing for the making of interim orders to provide protection for children pending the court's final decisions. In this context, the interim order will usually be an interim care order under s 38 of the CA 1989 but interim supervision orders also have a place in the statutory scheme.

## The timescale of proceedings and possible duration of interim orders

**13.5** At the time that the CA 1989 was enacted it was envisaged that care proceedings would generally be concluded within 8 weeks of them coming before the court. The White Paper that preceded the Children Bill accordingly proposed that the maximum duration of an interim care order should be eight weeks with the possibility of extensions of up to 14 days, 'in exceptional circumstances'.[6]

**13.6** As originally enacted, the CA 1989 allowed for interim orders to be made for a period of up to 8 weeks and thereafter renewed for successive periods of 4 weeks,[7] but with no statutory requirement for, 'exceptional circumstances' for renewal nor any limit on the number of extensions that could be granted. The unintended effect of these provisions was that as care proceedings increased in duration and complexity as a result of such factors as the recognition of the need to carry out assessments of parents by observation of their parenting over time, the limited availability of suitably qualified experts and the need to find court time for increasingly lengthy hearings, children could be the subject of interim orders for many months and in some cases years.[8]

**13.7** Over recent years, revisions of legislation and relevant court rules and sustained judicial action in the form of increasingly robust case management have reduced the overall duration of care cases but the timespan of proceedings can still amount to a substantial proportion of a child's life. According to the

---

[6] See for example the White Paper: *The Law on Child Care and Family Services*, 1987 (CM 62), para 61.

[7] See ss 38(4)(a) and (b) and 38(5); all now repealed, see Children and Families Act 2014, s 14(4).

[8] Having said that, the need for four weekly renewal of the interim care order, done 'on paper' by judicial consideration of a written application to renew (unless the expiry of a four-week period happened to coincide with a hearing listed for another reason), did provide a measure of judicial monitoring of the progress of an application even if no court hearing was due to take place: see comments as to the importance of this judicial oversight from the Court of Appeal in the case of *Re G (Minors) (Interim Care Order)* [1993] 2 FLR 839.

most recently published statistics[9] the average time for disposal of such proceedings stood at 28.3 weeks for cases disposed of in the second quarter of 2017 and the median time for disposal for the same period was 25.4 weeks, with only 56 per cent of cases being disposed of within the statutory time frame of 26 weeks.[10]

**13.8** These statistics should now be seen in the context of s 32 of the CA 1989 (as amended by s 14 of the Children and Families Act 2014), which imposes a duty on the court to draw up a timetable with a view to disposing of an application, 'without delay' and:[11]

> 'in any event within twenty-six weeks beginning with the day on which the application was issued.'

**13.9** This 26-week time limit can be extended if the court, '... considers that the extension is necessary to ... resolve the proceedings justly',[12] although this power is itself subject to stringent criteria.[13]

**13.10** The repeal of the requirement that an interim order be renewed every four weeks means that such orders will generally continue from the time that they first granted until, 'the disposal of the application'.[14] The effect of this is that they can continue in force for up to 26 weeks and thereafter are automatically continued in accordance with any extension to the period allowed for disposal of the application. Conversely, an interim care order may be discharged before the final disposal of the proceedings if circumstances change and this level of intervention in the family is no longer required to secure the child's welfare; an example would be where the child is, in the course of proceedings, placed with family members under a child arrangements order under s 8 of CA 1989.[15]

## The circumstances in which the court can make an interim order

### The statutory provision for making interim orders

**13.11** The statutory provision allowing for the making of interim care and supervision orders is s 38(1) of CA 1989, which provides as follows:

'Where –

(a) in any proceedings on an application for a care order or a supervision order, the proceedings are adjourned; or

(b) the court gives a direction under section 37(1)

---

[9] Ministry of Justice *Family Court Statistics Quarterly* April to June 2017.
[10] Figure 5 and commentary.
[11] Section 32(1)(a)(ii).
[12] Section 32(5)
[13] Section 32(6), (7) and (8).
[14] Section 38(4)(b), which provides for other circumstances in which an order will cease to have effect.
[15] In these circumstances, an interim supervision order will normally be made in accordance with s 38(3) of the Act (see below).

the court may make an interim care order or interim supervision order with respect to the child concerned.'

**13.12** As can be seen, CA 1989 envisages two quite different scenarios that may give rise to the making of an interim care or supervision order, i.e. when proceedings for a substantive care or supervision order have been commenced or, alternatively, when then court makes a direction under s 37(1) when no such application is before the court.

**13.13** Note that s 31(3) of the CA 1989 Act provides that:

'No care order or supervision order may be made with respect to a child who has reached the age of seventeen (or sixteen, in the case of a child who is married).'

This prohibition also applies to interim care or supervision orders under s 38 of CA 1989.[16]

## Orders made when a s 31 application is before the court

**13.14** As can be seen from the discussion below, interim care or supervision orders can be made in pending proceedings where the court is satisfied that there are, 'reasonable grounds' to believe that 'threshold'[17] is made out and that the child's welfare requires the making of an order before the court carries out its full investigation of the case. In other words, this power addresses directly the dilemma of how a child can be protected from possible harm whilst the court process determines whether harm has actually been suffered or is likely to be suffered. The court's further dilemma of how to identify what protective measures are in fact needed before that determination is made and other relevant investigations carried out is the subject of the next chapter.

**13.15** The making of an interim order under s 38(1)(a) requires consideration by the court of, first, the existence of 'interim threshold', secondly, whether the child's welfare requires an order to be made and, thirdly and in cases when it is proposed to remove a child from their family on an interim basis, whether such a removal is justified before a full consideration of the case.[18]

**13.16** Note that there is no requirement that any interim order, whether a care order or a supervision order, is made pending final determination of the case.

**13.17** However, s 38(3) provides that:

'Where, in any proceedings on an application for a care order or supervision order, a court makes a child arrangements order with respect to the living

---

[16] Section 31(11).
[17] See s 31(2).
[18] See inter alia: *Re GR (Children)* [2010] EWCA Civ 871 at paras 35 and 42, *Re L (A Child)* [2013] EWCA Civ 489 at paras 38–42 (both judgments of Black LJ) and *Re L (Children)* [2016] EWCA Civ 1110 at paras 20–22 (judgment of King LJ).

arrangements of the child concerned,[19] it shall also make an interim supervision order with respect to him unless satisfied that his welfare will be satisfactorily safeguarded without an interim order being made.'

**13.18** This provision is relevant in the frequent cases where a child cannot stay at home but can be adequately cared for by relatives or family friends for the duration of the proceedings. It will generally be prudent to regularise this placement by making a child arrangements order (not least because it allows the carer to exercise parental responsibility: see s 12(2) of CA 1989).[20] The making of a child arrangements order is these circumstances is a very different step from making one when this is tantamount to a premature determination that there is no basis for the making of a public law, as was the case with the order set aside in *Re B (Children) (residence: interim care order)*.[21]

**13.19** Section 38(3) requires the making of an interim supervision order to provide a statutory basis for support of the placement unless the court is satisfied that this is unnecessary. When making an interim supervision order under this subsection, the court must be satisfied that 'threshold' is established in accordance with s 38(2) as that subsection applies to all interim orders made under s 38.

## A special case: interim orders and appeals

**13.20** If an interim care order or interim supervision order has been made but the substantive application is dismissed, the court has a further power to, in effect, extend the interim order by making an order that has effect pending the determination of an appeal against that decision. This power is set out in s 40(1) and (2) of CA 1989, which provide as follows:[22]

'(1) Where –

   (a) a court dismisses an application for a care order; and
   (b) at the time when the court dismisses the application, the child concerned is the subject of an interim care order,

the court may make a care order with respect to the child to have effect subject to such directions (if any) as the court may see fit to include in the order.

(2) Where –

   (a) a court dismisses an application for a care order, or an application for a supervision order; and

---

[19] i.e. determining with whom the child is to live: s 38(3A).
[20] Such a placement can also be achieved by making an interim care order and the local authority then placing with the family carer (referred to as a 'connected person') as a foster carer but this would require them being temporarily approved as foster carers, see Care Planning, Placement and Case Review (England) Regulations 2010, regs 24 and 25, which may cause a difficulty. It would mean that the local authority hold parental responsibility, which may not always be necessary or desirable.
[21] [2002] 3 FCR 562, a, 'difficult and unusual' (per Thorpe LJ at para 32) case where the Court of Appeal accepted that the decision under appeal was flawed in several respects.
[22] A similar power exists to extend a care or supervision order pending appeal against the grant of an application to discharge the order: s 40(3) of the Act.

(b)  at the time when the court dismisses the application, the child concerned is the subject of an interim supervision order,

the court may make a supervision order with respect to the child to have effect subject to such directions (if any) as the court sees fit to include in the order.'

**13.21** An order made under these subsections has effect for, 'such period as may be specified in the order' but this period may not exceed the, 'appeal period'.[23] The appeal period is defined by s 40(6) as:

'(a)  where an appeal is made against the decision in question, the period between the making of that decision and the determination of the appeal; and
(b)  otherwise, the period during which an appeal may be made[24] against the decision.'

**13.22** Orders pending appeal made under s 40 can be viewed as an exception to the requirement that, 'reasonable grounds' to believed that threshold is established must exist before even an interim order can be made as orders can be made under this section even if the court has dismissed the substantive application because it declined to find that threshold was established.

**13.23** If no order under s 40 is made by the trial court any interim orders are discharged by the dismissal of the substantive application but the appellate level within the family court has jurisdiction to make an interim order under s 38 of CA 1989.[25] However, the Court of Appeal does not have this power as it is does not fall within the definition of, 'the court' in s 38.[26]

## Cases where a direction under s 37(1) has been made

**13.24** Section 37 is entitled, 'Powers of court in certain family proceedings' but s 37(1) itself refers to, 'any family proceedings' thus incorporating the very broad definition of such proceedings set out in s 8(3) and (4) of CA 1989. Consideration of s 37 usually becomes relevant where a child's parents (or other persons entitled to be parties to an application) have brought an issue before the court by applying for a child arrangements order[27] or other 'private law' order under Part II of CA 1989. Such cases often bring to the court's attention concerns about a child that require investigation above and beyond that which takes place in the normal course of private law proceedings and s 37 provides a vehicle for the court to require that such investigations take place.[28]

---

[23]  Section 40(4).
[24]  This period is 21 days from the date of the decision, subject to any specific direction as to time for filing the appellant's notice made by the lower court or variation granted by the appellate court: see FPR 2010, rr 30.4(2) and 30.7(1) respectively.
[25]  *Croydon London Borough Council v A (No 2)* [1992] 2 FLR 348.
[26]  See s 92(7).
[27]  Section 8 of the Act
[28]  The procedure to be followed when such a direction is made is set out in FPR 2010, r 12.17.

**13.25** The key provisions of s 37 are subss (1) and (2), which provide as follows:

> '(1) Where, in any family proceedings in which a question arises with respect to the welfare of any child, it appears to the court that it may be appropriate for a care or supervision order to be made with respect to him, the court may direct the appropriate authority to undertake an investigation of the child's circumstances.
>
> (2) Where the court gives a direction under this section the local authority concerned shall, when undertaking the investigation, consider whether they should –
>
> > (a) apply for a care order or for a supervision order with respect to the child;
> > (b) provide services or assistance for the child or his family; or
> > (c) take any other action with respect to the child.'

**13.26** The local authority to whom the direction is addressed (which may, of course, have no previous knowledge of the child) is the authority in whose area the child is ordinarily resident or, if the child is not ordinarily resident in any local authority area, the authority in whose area the circumstances giving rise to the referral arose.[29]

**13.27** In the event that the relevant local authority decides not to apply for a public law order, they must provide to the court within eight weeks of the direction being made[30] with information as to the reasons for so deciding, any services they are providing or intend to provide for the child and any other action taken or proposed.[31]

**13.28** As when an application is made in pending public law proceedings, there is no obligation on the court to make an interim order when giving a s 37 direction, nor any presumption that it should do so. The terms of s 37(1) and s 38(1) and (2) make it clear that the decisions to make a direction and to make an interim order are separate and sequential. There is to an extent a tension between the court on the one hand saying that it needs the child's circumstances to be investigated so as to ascertain if an order is necessary and yet on the other making such an order before such an investigation has even begun and cases where orders are made tend to be unusual on their facts and to involve an urgent need for intervention to safeguard a child's welfare.[32] Once the court is satisfied that need does exist, the court is unlikely to give much weight to arguments that it is procedurally irregular or impermissible to reach the stage of

---

[29] See provisions as to naming that local authority in subs (5).
[30] Section 37(4): this period can be varied if the court so directs.
[31] Section 37(3).
[32] See for example the extremely difficult history and family dynamics that led to the making of such an order in the case of *Re L (Interim Care Order: Extended Family)* [2013] 2 FLR 302, CA. The writer was involved in a case at District Judge level where an interim care order was made following a s 37 direction in circumstances where no person having parental responsibility was in a position to exercise it and the court considered it essential that the local authority step into this gap.

considering an interim order under by way of the making of a s 37 direction; as McFarlane LJ observes in *In Re L (Interim Care Order: Extended Family)*:[33]

'[74] In circumstances where, as I have held, the judge was justified in holding that this child's safety required immediate protection by means of compulsory removal from her home, a submission that the procedural path chosen by the judge was technically not available to her is only likely to succeed if there is no escaping the procedural points that are made. This is not such a case. The course adopted by the judge is not excluded by any provision in the CA 1989, the FPR 2010 or elsewhere.'

**13.29** It is important to note that if a court has decided to make a s 37 direction and is going on to consider making an interim order it must still consider whether the, 'threshold' for making such an order is satisfied in accordance with s 38(2) and only then can it consider whether an order should in fact be made. In *Re L (Interim Care Order: Extended Family)*,[34] a case in which the relevant child had been in the care of her grandparents under a special guardianship order until the making of a s 37 direction and an interim care order, McFarlane LJ describes the sequential decision making process in the following terms:

'[62] The statutory jurisdictional thresholds applicable to s 37 and to the making of an interim care order are:

"… it appears to the court that it may be appropriate for a care or supervision order to be made …' [s 37(1)]

… [the court] is satisfied that there are reasonable grounds for believing that the circumstances with respect to the child are as mentioned in s 31(2)" [s 38(2)].

The "circumstances … mentioned in s 31(2)" are that the court is satisfied:

'(a) that the child concerned is suffering, or is likely to suffer, significant harm; and

(b) that the harm, or likelihood of harm, is attributable to—

(i) the care given to the child, or likely to be given to him if the order were not made, not being what it would be reasonable to expect a parent to give to him; or

(ii) the child's being beyond parental control.'

The threshold in s 37(1) is necessarily low ("may be appropriate"). The threshold in s 38(2) is higher ("reasonable grounds for believing") but not as high as that in s 31(2). The task facing [counsel for the appellant] on appeal is the need to establish that the judge was plainly wrong in holding that the thresholds in s 37(1)

---

[33] See above.
[34] See above.

and in s 38(2) were met on the facts of this case as they were known to be on [the date when the interim care order was made].

...

[65] For present purposes it is only necessary to conclude that the finding of emotional harm, or likelihood of emotional harm, to the extent required by s 37(1) and s 38(2) was reasonably open to the judge on the totality of the evidence. In my view that is plainly the case and it is not open to this court to hold that the judge was wrong in these two conclusions made in relation to these two relatively low interim thresholds.

[66] The next stage was for the judge to consider whether an interim care order was justified and, as a separate conclusion, that under it M's welfare required her immediate removal from her grandparents' home. The test here ... is that set out by this court in *Re LA (Care: Chronic Neglect)* [2009] EWCA Civ 822, [2010] 1 FLR 80 where Thorpe LJ stated at para [7] that:

> "... separation is only to be ordered if the child's safety demands immediate separation' and '... is not to be sanctioned unless the child's safety requires immediate protection."

[67] In *Re B (Care Proceedings: Interim Care Order)* [2009] EWCA Civ 1254, [2010] 1 FLR 1211, Wall LJ rightly concluded that, in this context, "safety" should be given a broad construction to include a child's psychological welfare.

[68] The question for this court is: was the judge plainly wrong to conclude that M's emotional and psychological welfare were at risk of harm to the extent that her safety demanded immediate protection by means of separation from her home and her grandparents' care?'

**13.30** In other words, even though the court has decided that a s 37 direction should be made because it, 'may be appropriate' to make an interim order it must go through the same process in deciding whether such an order should be made as it would have to carry out were an application under s 31 to be before the court.

## Interim threshold

### *The court's enquiry as to threshold at the interim stage: 'reasonable grounds for believing'*

**13.31** As noted at the beginning of this chapter, the making of an application for a care or supervision order involves an assertion by the applicant that the child concerned is suffering or is likely to suffer significant harm that is attributable to deficiencies in parenting. It has been repeatedly emphasised by the courts that it is only if this is in fact the case that state intervention in the family can be justified.³⁵ Since the validity of this assertion can only be finally determined by a full examination of all the relevant circumstances it follows that if intervention in the family is to take place at an interim stage is to be allowed a different approach to the question of actual or likely harm and its attribution has to be taken.

**13.32** The White Paper proposed that the court should have power make interim orders, 'under strict rules as to grounds' and that those grounds should be that there has to be, 'reasonable cause to believe' that the grounds for making an order that now appear in s 31(2), 'may exist'.³⁶ This approach is reflected in CA 1989, although the wording is slightly different.

**13.33** Section 38(2) of CA 1989 provides:

> 'A court shall not make an interim care order or interim supervision order under this section unless it is satisfied that there are reasonable grounds for believing that the circumstances with respect to the child are as are as mentioned in section 31(2).'

It is important to be clear that it is the court that must be satisfied as to the existence of reasonable grounds, not the applicant (whom one must assume believes that such grounds exist in order to launch proceedings) nor the children's guardian.

## On what basis can 'reasonable grounds' be found to exist?

**13.34** In contrast to the very extensive case law on the proper approach to the 'welfare' stage of the court's consideration of an application for an interim care order (see the following chapter) there is relatively little direct authority on the application of s 38(2). In particular, these is little guidance from the higher courts on the central issue of what amounts to, 'reasonable grounds' for the purposes of this subsection.

**13.35** A case in which this issue did arise is that of *Re M (Interim Care Order: Removal)*.³⁷ In this case the Court of Appeal had to consider an appeal against the making of an interim care on the basis that, as it put by Thorpe LJ giving the judgement of the court, '… essentially, there was insufficient evidence of risk of harm to satisfy the statutory test'.³⁸ In finding that the test was satisfied the trial judge had based himself, '… principally, if not exclusively, on the evidence of the guardian'³⁹ as to his concerns. It is worth looking in detail at

---

[35] See for example the much quoted comments of Hedley J in *Re L (Care: Threshold Criteria)* [2007] 1 FLR 2050.
[36] See the White Paper: *The Law on Child Care and Family Services*, 1987 (CM 62), para 61.
[37] [2006] 1 FLR 1043.
[38] Paragraph 12: there was a further ground of appeal in that it was said that the trial judge had failed to carry out the necessary exercise of balancing the risk of harm to the child from returning home (there had already been a removal in circumstances that were themselves procedurally problematic: see paras 2–5 and 19 of Thorpe LJ's judgment) against the risk of harm flowing from the child's distress at being separated from her parents, siblings and home.
[39] Paragraph 14.

the comments of Thorpe LJ on some of the concerns expressed by the guardian, and accepted by the trial judge, in this case as they illustrate the limitations of the court's examination of threshold issues at an interim stage and some of the problems that can arise from those limitations (the 'headings' are the present author's).

*(1) Inadequate base in primary evidence:*

**13.36** The guardian reported that the child to whom the application related showed, 'an acceptance of chaos' when professionals arrived to remove his siblings (in respect of whom orders had been made earlier). However, '… the guardian himself was not present … all he was doing was repeating a concern apparently expressed by an unnamed social worker who did not give evidence at the hearing'.[40]

*(2) Inadequate analysis of evidence as to the existence of a risk of harm:*

**13.37** The trial judge had also given weight to the guardian's observation of the child's, 'muted reaction' to the family at contact from which the guardian drew an opinion that there was, 'a real risk to [the child] in the short term'.[41] However, it was valid to observe, in His Lordship's view, that the guardian had only observed contact once, that social workers who had observed contact had not expressed concern and that in any event the interpretation of the contact observed by the guardian was, 'by no means straightforward and thus was flimsy foundation for the conclusion drawn by the guardian of a real risk of harm in the short-term'.[42]

*(3) Inadequate analysis of evidence for there being a risk of harm in the short as opposed to the long term:*

**13.38** The guardian had expressed concern that the family home was, 'a volatile and intermittently violent household' and that the child was therefore at risk of the effects of violence.[43] His Lordship's accepted that this was an understandable concern in terms of the long-term effects on the child but continued, '… it is hard to see the risk of short term harm unless it is expressed in terms of the possibility of [the child] being caught in some physical crossfire. There is no evidence of anything of that sort having occurred in the past. It seems to me to be a relatively insignificant risk in relation to a further period of approximately 4 months'.[44]

**13.39** His Lordship's summarised the appellant's submissions on this aspect of the appeal as follows:[45]

---

[40] Paragraph 16.
[41] Paragraph 20.
[42] Paragraph 21.
[43] Paragraph 18.
[44] Paragraph 18.
[45] Paragraph 22.

'... the guardian was expressing speculative concerns ("may suffer", "might suffer") and nowhere is there any concrete evidence that a risk of harm from return was established. [Counsel] makes the point that the guardian, in his oral evidence, has taken as his compass direction that there should be, if any error, an error on the side of caution. Although the judge does not himself adopt this approach, insofar as it was the guardian's standpoint, the judge should have been careful to recognise that speculative concerns expressed by the guardian were, or might be, tainted by an unprincipled approach.'

**13.40** This submission was accepted and His Lordship concluded that he did not believe that, 'the very high standards that must be established to justify the continuing removal of a child from home were made good in this case, simply on the basis of the somewhat speculative evidence of the guardian'.[46] (The separate submission that the judgment below was also flawed as it failed to balance the risk found to exist in letting the child return home against the risk of emotional harm from continued separation also succeeded.[47])

**13.41** The emphasis in *Re M (Interim Care Order: Removal)* on the need for an evidential base for an assertion that there is a risk of harm and for a proper analysis of how a risk of harm in fact arises from the facts established resonates with subsequent case law on the proper approach to the issue of whether the 'threshold' for the making of final orders is established. For example, in the case of *Re A (Fact Finding: Disputed Findings)*[48] Munby P observed that:

'[7] In the light of the way in which this case has been presented and some of the submissions I have heard, it is important always to bear in mind in these cases, and too often, I fear, they are overlooked, three fundamentally important points. The present case is an object lesson in, almost a textbook example of, how not to embark upon and pursue a care case.

[8] The first fundamentally important point relates to the matter of fact-finding and proof. I emphasise, as I have already said, that it is for the local authority to prove, on a balance of probabilities, the facts upon which they seek to rely. I draw attention to what, in *Re A (Fact-Finding: Disputed Findings)* [2011] EWCA Civ 12, [2011] 1 FLR 1817, at [26], I described as:

"the elementary proposition that findings of fact must be based on evidence (including inferences that can properly be drawn from the evidence) and not on suspicion or speculation."

This carries with it two important practical and procedural consequences.

[9] The first is that the local authority, if their case is challenged on some factual point, must adduce proper evidence to establish what they seek to prove. Much material to be found in local authority case records or social work chronologies is hearsay, often second or third-hand hearsay. Hearsay evidence is, of course, admissible in family proceedings. But, and as the present case so vividly

---

[46] Paragraph 27.
[47] See paras 23, 24 and 27.
[48] [2016] 1 FLR 1.

demonstrates, a local authority which are unwilling or unable to produce the witnesses who can speak of such matters first-hand, may find themselves in great, or indeed insuperable, difficulties if a parent not merely puts the matter in issue but goes into the witness box to deny it. As I remarked in my second *View from the Presidents Chambers* [2013] Fam Law 680:

> "Of course the court can act on the basis of evidence that is hearsay. But direct evidence from those who can speak to what they have themselves seen and heard is more compelling and less open to cross-examination. Too often far too much time is taken up by cross-examination directed to little more than demonstrating that no one giving evidence in court is able to speak of their own knowledge, and that all are dependent on the assumed accuracy of what is recorded, sometimes at third or fourth hand, in the local authority's files."

It is a common feature of care cases that a local authority assert that a parent does not admit, recognise or acknowledge something or does not recognise or acknowledge the local authority's concern about something. If the "thing" is put in issue, the local authority must both prove the "thing" and establish that it has the significance attributed to it by the local authority.

[10] The second practical and procedural point goes to the formulation of threshold and proposed findings of fact. The schedule of findings in the present case contains, as we shall see, allegations in relation to the father that "he appears to have" lied or colluded, that various people have "stated" or "reported" things, and that "there is an allegation". With all respect to counsel, this form of allegation, which one sees far too often in such documents, is wrong and should never be used. It confuses the crucial distinction, once upon a time, though no longer, spelt out in the rules of pleading and well understood, between an assertion of fact and the evidence needed to prove the assertion. What do the words 'he appears to have lied' or "X reports that he did Y" mean? More important, where does it take one? The relevant allegation is not that "he appears to have lied" or "X reports"; the relevant allegation, if there is evidence to support it, is surely that "he lied" or "he did Y".

[11] Failure to understand these principles and to analyse the case accordingly can lead, as here, to the unwelcome realisation that a seemingly impressive case is, in truth, a tottering edifice built on inadequate foundations.

[12] The second fundamentally important point is the need to link the facts relied upon by the local authority with their case on threshold, the need to demonstrate *why*, as the local authority assert, facts A + B + C justify the conclusion that the child has suffered, or is at risk of suffering, significant harm of types X, Y or Z. Sometimes the linkage will be obvious, as where the facts proved establish physical harm. But the linkage may be very much less obvious where the allegation is only that the child is at risk of suffering emotional harm or, as in the present case, at risk of suffering neglect. In the present case, as we shall see, an important element of the local authority's case was that the father "lacks honesty with professionals", "minimises matters of importance" and "is immature and lacks insight of issues of importance". Maybe. But how does this feed through into a conclusion that A is at risk of neglect? The conclusion does not follow naturally from the premise. The local authority's evidence and submissions must set out the argument and explain

explicitly why it is said that, in the particular case, the conclusion indeed follows from the facts. Here, as we shall see, the local authority conspicuously failed to do so.'

**13.42** Although the learned President was not considering the making of interim orders in the case of *Re A (Fact Finding: Disputed Findings)* it is the present author's view that these observations are also highly relevant to the way in which the court approaches applications for interim orders.

**13.43** This is for two reasons. First, for the court to be satisfied that there are, 'reasonable grounds for believing' that the circumstances are as mentioned in s 31(2) of CA 1989 there must be at least some basis for that belief derived both from sufficient evidence of the existence of relevant primary facts and from an analysis of those facts. It was a failure to have sufficient regard to these issues that led Thorpe LJ to allow the appeal of the parents in the case of *Re M (Interim Care Order: Removal)*.[49] An interesting analogy may be drawn with guidance on the meaning of the expression, 'reasonable grounds for suspicion' used in the Police and Criminal Evidence Act as the basis for the exercise of, for example, police powers of, 'stop and search'.[50] The statutory guidance as to what amounts to, reasonable grounds' for search is that:[51]

> '... the suspicion that the object will be found must be reasonable. This means that there must be an *objective* basis for that suspicion based on facts, information and/or intelligence which are relevant to the likelihood that the object in question will be found, so that a reasonable person would be entitled to reach the same conclusion based on the same facts and information and/or intelligence.'

**13.44** Whilst, 'reasonable grounds for believing' that a child is, 'suffering or is likely to suffer significant harm' may often be based on information that would fall well short of what would be required to prove such suffering or likelihood of suffering, in order to be 'reasonable' those grounds must arise from sufficient evidence of the existence to primary facts and proper analysis of the facts evidenced. The subjective belief of a social worker or other professional that, 'reasonable grounds for believing' a fact or state of affairs exist is not of itself sufficient to satisfy a court that such reasonable grounds exist, as is apparent from the observations of Thorpe LJ in *Re M (Interim Care Order: Removal)*.[52] The need to consider the basis for asserting that grounds exist leads directly and unavoidably to the question of the quality of the evidence on which that belief could be based and to the issues about the quality of evidence identified by the learned President.

---

[49] See above.
[50] See s 1(3) of that Act.
[51] Code of Practice A, 2015 edn: https://www.gov.uk/government/publications/**pace-code**-a-2015 (emphasis in original).
[52] See above. Those who remember studying Constitutional Law may be reminded of Lord Atkin's famous excoriation of the majority in the House of Lords for their acceptance of the proposition that, '... the words "if the Secretary of State has reasonable cause" merely mean "if the Secretary of State thinks that he has reasonable cause."': see *Liversedge v Anderson* [1943] UKHL 1, [1941] 3 All ER 338 at 349H.

**13.45** The second reason why it is suggested that *Re A (Fact Finding: Disputed Findings)* is relevant when considering interim threshold issues is that of the nature of a threshold finding. In *Re A (Fact Finding: Disputed Findings)* the learned President is at pains to emphasise the need to, firstly, identify facts asserted and, secondly, to demonstrate how those facts lead to the conclusion that the child is, 'suffering or is likely to suffer significant harm'. Whilst, 'reasonable grounds for believing' that the circumstances are as mentioned in in s 31(2) may fall well short of proving that those circumstances exist there is no basis in CA 1989 to say that the circumstances are themselves any different at the two stages and it must, it is suggested, follow that the same criteria apply when considering whether the matters relied on are in any event, when exposed to a *Re A* analysis, capable of establishing threshold.

## Looking at all the 'circumstances'

**13.46** A point to note is that when considering whether, 'circumstances with respect to the child are as mentioned in s 31(2)' the court has to look at the whole of the circumstances, including any other relevant legal processes.

**13.47** This point is illustrated by the decision of MacDonald J in the case of *London Borough of Camden v RZ and Others*.[53] Here the two children concerned were in the care of their father. They were made the subject to forced marriage protection orders[54] and subsequently taken into police protection. They were then made subject to interim care orders pending a substantive hearing, which was delayed due to disclosure issues. Although the background to proceedings was complex, and heavily contentious (much of the local authority's case relied on disputed allegations made by mother, who was out of the country and did not give evidence), the basic issue was whether interim care orders, on the basis of the children remaining in foster care, should be made when the principle harm alleged was that the children were at risk of being removed from the country for the purpose of undergoing forced marriage. Whilst he acknowledged that there might be cases in which both an interim care order and a forced marriage protection order should be made,[55] MacDonald J was clear that this was not such a case:

> '[96] ... in circumstances where the local authority concede that the matters it relies on above and beyond the forced marriage application do not meet the interim threshold, and in circumstances where I am satisfied that, contrary to the submission of the local authority,[56] the pre-existing forced marriage protection order sufficiently protects DZ against the elevated risk of forced marriage and sufficiently protects SZ against an elevated risk of removal, I am not persuaded that it can, in fact, be said in this case that, pursuant to s 38(2) of the Children Act 1989, there are reasonable grounds for believing that the circumstances of DZ

---

[53] [2017] 1 FLR 873.
[54] See Family Law Act 1996, ss 63A, 63B and 63R.
[55] See para [86].
[56] He was impressed with neither the general case advanced that such orders were ineffective nor the 'anecdotal' evidence of a police officer as to the ease with orders restricting a person under protection from leaving the country could be evaded: see paras [84] and [86].

and SZ are such that they are suffering, or are likely to suffer significant harm attributable to the care given to them, or likely to be given by the father if an interim care order were not made where the 'circumstances in respect of' DZ and SZ for the purposes of s 38(2) include the fact that there is already in place a forced marriage protection order, which order is, as I find, effective to meet the risks.'

**13.48** His Lordship went on to say that even had he been satisfied that the interim threshold criteria were met, it would not have been open to him, given this background, to conclude that the children's safety required their continued removal from father's care under an interim care order.[57]

**13.49** The general point that can be drawn from this case is that account should be taken of any other protective measures in force when considering the s 38(2) test. As a hypothetical example, it would seem arguable that if the sole perpetrator[58] of harm to child A had been excluded from a household by effective Family Law Act 1996 orders or police action then it would be impermissible to say that there were, 'reasonable grounds' for believing that child B in that household is, 'likely to suffer significant harm'.

## Likelihood of harm as the basis for interim threshold

**13.50** Despite all that is said above, the exercise of determining whether there are or are not, 'reasonable grounds for believing' that a child is actually suffering significant harm is generally relatively straightforward as the nature of the harm asserted to be suffered can be clearly identified and the evidence can then be tested (in whichever way is appropriate[59]) to see if the requisite, 'reasonable grounds' are made out.

**13.51** A more difficult exercise has to be carried out when it is not alleged that harm is being suffered but that the relevant child is, 'likely to suffer' significant harm. In other words, the effect of the interaction of s 38(2) and 31(2)(a) requires the court to consider whether there are reasonable grounds to believe that a state of affairs that does not now exist may come to exist in the future, and to do so with an eye to the need to be satisfied that this future state of affairs is not merely possible but, 'likely'.

**13.52** This was one of the issues that the Court of Appeal had to consider in the case *Re W (Interim Care Order)*.[60] Here the child was, by agreement, living in the care of his father within a specialist foster care placement whilst assessments were carried out and plans for the long term care of the child were considered. As a result of, '... a series of events, each not necessarily very significant in its own right, but cumulatively indicating that the father was

---

[57] Paragraph [97].
[58] See below as to the issues that arise when it is only possible to identify a, 'pool of possible perpetrators'.
[59] See below.
[60] [2012] 2 FLR 240.

unable adequately and safely to supervise [the child] in that setting'[61] the local authority concluded that it should seek an interim care order on the basis of separation of father and child with then child to remain in foster care with a view to adoption. In these circumstances, interim threshold could only be found on the basis that there were reasonable grounds to believe the child was likely to suffer harm. The trial judge so found and made the interim care order sought.

**13.53** Sir Nicholas Wall P dealt with the issue of the proper approach to the issue of likely harm and did so in these terms:[62]

> 'The judge was making an interim order and the question he had to ask himself under s 38 of the Act was whether or not there were reasonable grounds for believing that threshold criteria under s 31(2) were met. In this context that must mean whether there was a likelihood of significant harm. Were there grounds for believing there was a likelihood of significant harm? In my judgment, it was open to the judge to find that there were. In my judgment "likely" in this context is to be read as interpreted by Lord Nicholls in *Re H (Minors) (Sexual Abuse: Standard of Proof)* [1996] AC 563, [1996] 2 WLR 8, [1996] 1 FLR 80, namely a possibility that cannot sensibly be ignored in relation to the nature and gravity of the feared harm in a particular case, a real possibility, and in my judgment the judge was inclined to find there was a real possibility this child would come to significant harm if unsupervised. That in my judgment was sufficient to enable him to make an interim care order removing the child from the father's care.'

**13.54** It is indicative of the difficult judgments involved at both the 'threshold' and 'welfare' stages when a case turns on an assessment of the likelihood of future harm that both Wall P and McFarlane LJ were at pains to emphasise[63] that in dismissing the appeal (as the unanimous court did, the other member being Ryder J) they were in no way indicating a likely outcome of the substantive proceedings and McFarlane LJ commented that even at the interim stage a decision by the judge not to grant an interim care order, 'would have been difficult to appeal'.[64]

## A reminder: 'interim threshold' is still 'threshold'

**13.55** In considering the issue of whether there are, 'reasonable grounds for believing that the circumstances of the child are as mentioned in s 31(2)' it is important to remember that the question of the circumstances that are, or are not, capable of falling within the definition in s 31(2) has itself been the subject of extensive judicial analysis (discussed elsewhere in this work). Whilst there may be reasonable grounds for concern about a child, s 38(2) can only be satisfied if those concerns are, as facts or as a matter of law, capable of falling with the terms of s 31(2) as interpreted in the leading authorities.

---

[61] Per McFarlane LJ at para [7]: the incidents causing concern are detailed at para [9] but did not include any in which it was asserted the child had suffered actual harm.
[62] Paragraph [44].
[63] At paras [38] and [45] respectively.
[64] Paragraph [37].

**13.56** This point is illustrated by the argument put forward by the appellant mother in the case of *E (A Child)*.[65] This case concerned two children, 'C' and 'M'. C had suffered serious physical injuries and at a fact finding hearing the trial judge concluded that these were the result of the way in which he had been handled, 'by either or both of his parents'; as it is commonly put the, 'pool of possible perpetrators' was comprised of the two parents. There were no specific concerns about the care that M had received. At a separate hearing a few days later the same judge found on the basis of the previous findings that s 38(2) was satisfied in respect of M and made an interim care order.

**13.57** The mother appealed on the basis that the findings in respect of C amounted only to finding a that she might have been responsible for the injuries, which logically carried with it an implicit finding that she might not have been responsible, and that as this was in law incapable of establishing that M was 'likely' to suffer harm in her care there could not be reasonable grounds for believing such a likelihood. This argument was derived from a series of House of Lords and Supreme Court cases that establish that a finding of, 'likelihood of harm'[66] must be based on established facts[67]. It follows from this that where a finding had been made that a parent was, 'within the pool' of possible perpetrators but not one that they were in fact the perpetrator of an injury to one child (the specific findings in the case before the Supreme Court in *Re J*) it was:[68]

> '... impermissible ... to make this, and this alone, the basis for predicting that the mother was likely to harm [another child] in the future.'

**13.58** Giving the main judgment in the Court of Appeal, McFarlane LJ said that his initial approach to the case was, 'to be in substantial sympathy with the arguments put forward on behalf of the mother'.[69] However, on a close examination of a not particularly clearly expressed judgment (and subsequent clarifications by the trial judge in response to requests from the parties) His Lordship identified further findings as to the culpability of whichever parent was not responsible for the injuries in the form of failing to protect the child by failing to be aware of the injuries and taking action and that on this basis s 38(2) was satisfied.[70] In approaching the case in this way McFarlane LJ emphasised that 'one issue' cases of the type presented to the Supreme Court in

---

[65] [2014] EWCA Civ 1754.
[66] See s 31(2)(b).
[67] The cases are *Re M (A Minor) (Care Order: Threshold Conditions)* [1994] 2 AC 424, [1994] 3 WLR 558, [1994] 2 FLR 577; *Re H (Minors) (Sexual Abuse: Standard of Proof)* [1996] AC 563, [1996] 2 WLR 8, [1996] 1 FLR 80; *Lancashire County Council v B* [2000] 2 AC 147, [2000] 2 WLR 590, [2000] 1 FLR 583; *Re O and N; Re B* [2003] UKHL 18, [2003] 1 FLR 1169; *Re B (Care Proceedings: Standard of Proof)* [2008] UKHL 35, [2009] 1 AC 11, [2008] 3 WLR 1, [2008] 2 FLR 141; *Re S-B (Children) (Care Proceedings: Standard of Proof)* [2009] UKSC 17, [2010] 1 AC 678, [2010] 2 WLR 238, [2010] 1 FLR 1161 and *Re J (Care Proceedings: Possible Perpetrators)* [2013] UKSC 9, [2013] 1 FLR 1373.
[68] Per Baroness Hale of Richmond in *Re J* at para [50].
[69] Paragraph [31].
[70] See paras [35], [37] and [38]. In expressing his agreement with this conclusion Briggs LJ puts it succinctly; the mother's failing was that she, ' . . . did not realise what the baby was telling her'.

*Re J* are highly unusual;[71] in most cases a range of information about both specific incidents and the whole of the family's circumstances is before the court and has to be considered when deciding whether the test in s 38(2) is satisfied.

## The limitations of the court's investigation of interim threshold

**13.59** A theme of this chapter has been the inherent tension between the need to act protect children's welfare by making orders prior to the court's full investigation of the case and the inevitability of basing the decision to make such orders on what must by definition be an incomplete and is also often an imperfect understanding of the relevant circumstances. Both the perceived need for urgent action and the exigencies of the court process in terms of available hearing time, witness availability and other factors tend to limit the extent to which the court can examine the basis on which it is said that, 'reasonable grounds' are established as required by s 38(1). However, the section makes it clear that it is the court that must be, 'satisfied' that this is the case and there is an irreducible minimum of investigation that must be carried out by the court before this can be said. What that irreducible minimum amounts to will vary according to the facts of each case but reported cases give some guidance.

## *The nature and conduct of an interim hearing: 'a line beyond which it is impermissible for the court to go'?*[72]

**13.60** An authority from the very earliest days of the Children Act 1989 (it was decided on 13 October 1992, not even a year after the main part of CA 1989 came into force on 14 October 1991) has proved of lasting relevance in giving guidance as to the management of interim hearings. This is the decision of Cazalet J in the case of *Hampshire County Council v S*.[73] The substantive issue in this case was whether contact previously ordered between a child in care and its parents (as part of a plan for the child's rehabilitation into the parents' care) should be substantially reduced due to problems that had arisen and the immediate issue in the appeal was whether magistrates had correctly approached an application to make that reduction on an interim basis pending a full hearing.

**13.61** His Lordship was critical of most aspects of the procedure adopted by the lay justices and their clerk (the phrase, 'on a learning curve' comes inescapably to mind) and summarised his guidance (given with the approval of the then President of the Family Division, Sir Stephen Brown[74]) as to the

---

[71] A point also made by Baroness Hale in *Re J*, see in particular at paras [5], [52] and [53].
[72] Per McFarlane LJ in *Re N (Care Proceedings: Adoption)* [2013] 1 FLR 1244 (see below).
[73] [1993] 1 FLR 559.
[74] It was also expressly approved, and held to be equally applicable to hearings in the County Court, by the Court of Appeal in the case of *Re W (A Minor)(Interim Care Order)* [1994] 2 FLR 892.

conduct of interim hearings in eight points[75] of which points 1, 3 and 5 are particularly relevant to the issues under discussion here. So far as is relevant, these points read as follows:

> '1. Justices should bear in mind that they are not, at an interim hearing, required to make a final conclusion; indeed it is because they are unable to reach a final conclusion that they are empowered to make an interim order. An interim order or decision will usually be required so as to establish a holding position, after weighing all the relevant risks, pending the final hearing ...
>
> ...
>
> 3. At the start of a hearing which is concerned with interim relief, justices will usually be called upon to exercise their discretion under r 21(2)[76] as to the order of speeches and evidence. Circumstances prevailing will almost certainly not permit full evidence to be heard. Accordingly, in such proceedings, justices should rarely make findings as to disputed facts. These will have to be left over for the final hearing.
>
> ...
>
> 5. When an interim order may be made which will lead to a substantial change in a child's position, justices should consider permitting limited oral evidence to be led and challenged by way of cross-examination. However, it will necessarily follow that, in cross-examination, the evidence will have to be restricted to the issues which are essential at the interim stage. To this end the court may well have to intervene to ensure that this course is followed and that there is not a 'dress rehearsal' of the full hearing.'

**13.62** Although the specific issue before the His Lordship concerned an application in respect of contact under s 34 of CA 1989 his observations are accepted as being of general application to interim hearings[77] and continue to be routinely referred to in submissions and judgments. In practice, they continue to provide the basic structure for case management decisions on the handling of interim applications under s 38.

**13.63** *Hampshire County Council v S* supports the proposition that interim hearings should be limited and focused in scope and, in particular, should rarely make findings as to disputed fact. This point was reiterated by Black J (as she then was in the case of *Re B (Interim Care orders: Renewal)*[78] in which she said:[79]

> '... it is plain that an interim hearing is bound to be circumscribed in its ambit. It is an interim hearing precisely because (and there may be many reasons why this is

---

[75] Pages 567–568.
[76] Of the Family Proceedings Courts (Children Act 1989) Rules 1991: the equivalent provision of the current rules is FPR 2010, r 12.21.
[77] See, for example, notes to section 38 in the *Family Court Practice* 2016, p 552.
[78] [2001] 2 FLR 1217.
[79] At p 1222.

so) it is too soon to have a full and final hearing. It is, as Cazalet J pointed out in *Hampshire County Council v S* [1993] Fam 158, [1993] 1 FLR 559, a limited hearing required to establish a holding position pending the final hearing. The judge's observations in that case were made with the then President's approval and remain, in my view, as valuable today as they were then. Amongst them is the observation that circumstances prevailing in an interim hearing will almost certainly not permit full evidence to be heard and therefore findings of fact on disputed issues should rarely be made at an interim stage, and that when oral evidence is permitted, cross-examination should be restricted to the issues which are essential at the interim stage so that the interim hearing is not a dress rehearsal of the full hearing.'

**13.64** However, it has to be remembered that although it is for the court to determine how to approach its consideration an application, natural justice and the Art 6 and Art 8 rights of parents and children dictate that the procedure adopted in a particular hearing is appropriate and fair. McFarlane LJ puts the point in this was in the case of *Re N (Care Proceedings: Adoption)*[80] (a case concerning the conduct of an issues resolution hearing):

'[10] . . . Equally, as the words of Butler-Sloss LJ[81] make plain, there is a spectrum of procedure in these cases, and in my view where on the spectrum a particular case sits on a particular day, and what is permissible or impermissible in terms of a court's approach will vary from case to case, and must be proportionate to the issues. In this case, the court was considering making orders at the most Draconian end of the spectrum of orders open to a family court, the permanent removal by adoption of a child from, not only the care of his parents, but also legally from their family.

[11] The overriding objective in the FPR is to discharge the determination of these cases justly and fairly; that is the requirement also borne in by Art 6. There is a line beyond which it is impermissible for the court to go; that line will vary from case to case and will be dependent on the facts of the case and the proportionate approach to procedure.'

## *The problem of oral evidence*

**13.65** A frequent problem in case managing interim hearings, and one that is particularly relevant to issues of interim threshold, is that of the extent to which oral evidence is allowed. A common scenario is that the applicant local authority relies, to establish, 'reasonable grounds for believing' that the circumstances of the case are as set out in s 31(2), on information in statements or records that the parents say is untrue, or which they wish to rebut by their own oral evidence.

**13.66** The problem that arises is twofold. First, there is the issue of principle as to whether it is appropriate to allow this examination of the facts at an interim stage in accordance with point 3 of the *Hampshire County Council v S*

---

[80] [2013] 1 FLR 1244.
[81] In *Re B (Minors) (Contact)* [1994] 2 FLR 1 (not an interim order case): Her Ladyship sets out a number of considerations relevant to deciding an appropriate procedure at p 6.

guidance. Secondly, there are the purely practical issues of whether the required witnesses can be brought to court for hearings that, by their nature, are treated as urgent and listed at relatively short notice and whether enough court time is available for the hearing of oral evidence.

**13.67** Despite these problems, it is sometimes necessary for a court considering an application under s 38 to hear oral evidence in order to dispose of the application fairly. The key issue when a court is considering allowing oral evidence will generally be that of the relevance of the disputed issue to which oral evidence would go in the context of the court's overall decision making.

**13.68** A good example of this approach in practice can be seen from the judgment of McFarlane LJ in *Re W (Interim Care Order)*.[82] One of the grounds of appeal in that case was that the trial judge had refused to allow oral evidence. His Lordship analyses in some detail how that issue was considered and decided by the court below with particular reference to the relatively limited areas of factual dispute raised by the father as to matters relevant at the interim stage[83] and goes on to say:[84]

> 'The judge deals with the application for oral evidence at 6 of the transcript:
>
>> "JUDGE LEVEY: Well, I think the central point really is that it is not for the court to make findings of fact on interim hearings. So in those circumstances, it would really mostly be pointless to hear oral evidence because the purpose of that is to enable findings to be made. It seems to me it is a matter I can deal with properly on submissions. That is the way it was set up and whilst I take the points that are made on behalf of the second respondent, those points can equally be well made on the basis of submissions and those are matters that I will simply have to take into account and weigh in the balance.
>>
>> I will take into account the fact that the allegations are disputed, but that will be a matter for the trial judge not for me. So in those circumstances, I will deal with it as was originally envisaged by hearing submissions from the parties."
>
> In effect the judge declines to hear oral evidence for the reasons that I have already summarised. Insofar as the application was made on behalf of the father because of the interpretation that was put on the events by the social worker, the judge indicated that that could be dealt with by way of comments during the course of submissions.'

This approach was approved by the Court of Appeal.

---

[82] [2012] 2 FLR 240: see above.
[83] Paragraph 24.
[84] Paragraph 27.

# CHAPTER 14

# INTERIM CARE ORDERS (PART 2): WELFARE DECISIONS AT THE INTERIM ORDER STAGE

## INTRODUCTION

**14.1** As is discussed in the preceding chapter, the court's power to make interim care and supervision orders under s 38 of the Children Act 1989 enables it to act on concerns about a child's welfare without having to await the outcome a full investigation and before a full court process is undertaken. Very often, acting to protect a child can mean removing them from their home and authorising a local authority to place them in foster care; a decision of the utmost magnitude taken, by definition, without full knowledge of the circumstances that may make this necessary or full consideration of those circumstances by the court.

**14.2** The draconian nature of this power means that the decision to exercise is always a difficult one and the way in which courts should approach doing so has been the subject of numerous reported cases.[1] Most of these reported cases involve, as do most contested hearings encountered in practice, the issue of whether an interim care order should be made where the plan is to remove children to foster care and this chapter deals in the main with the approach that should be taken when this is the order being sought.

### The court's dilemma when considering an interim order

**14.3** A consistent theme in the case law on interim care orders is that the court must focus its attention on the welfare of a child in the period between the interim application being made and the court's full consideration of the application for a care order. In part this principle derives from the very nature of the interim decision as defined by s 38 of the Act and hence of the interim hearing. Black LJ explains this point in these terms in the case of *Re L (Interim Care Order: Prison Mother and Baby Unit)*:[2]

---

[1] Over 80 cases are noted in the entry for s 38 in the 'Statutes Considered' section of *Family Law Reports: Cumulative Index 1995 to 2015*. This includes the extensive case law on applications for directions in respect of assessment under s 38(6) discussed in: Farrington and Johnson *Assessment of Parents within Care Proceedings* (Family Law, 2014), Chapters 2 and 3.
[2] [2014] 1 FLR 807.

'[54] The reasons why the interim care hearing has to be limited in this way are likely to vary from case to case but I will give examples.'

[55] One obvious reason is that the threshold affords a lesser protection to parents and children against the State's intrusion into their family life than there is with a final care order; all that need be shown is that 'there are reasonable grounds for believing that circumstances with respect to the child are as mentioned in s 31(2)' (s 38(2) of the Children Act 1989).

[56] Another reason is that the evidence is unlikely to be complete by the time of the interim care hearing. The hearing in this case took place rather later in the process than may often be the case so there was perhaps more material available than there may sometimes be. But there were still be important gaps and it is surprising how the complexion of a care case sometimes changes as more evidence becomes available.'

**14.4** However, the difficulty of deciding whether to make an interim order separating children from their family goes beyond the caution that courts will always instinctively exercise when asked to make a decision on the basis of incomplete information and without a full court process. As will be discussed below, the court's approach to interim care order applications will turn on an assessment of the child's welfare and although that welfare is always, 'the court's paramount consideration'[3] recent case law reminds us that:[4]

'... the court must never lose sight of the fact that [the child's] interests include being brought up by the natural family, ideally by the natural parents, or at least one of them, unless the overriding requirements of the child's welfare make that not possible.'

**14.5** It must also be remembered that the human rights of both the parents and their children are at stake when a court is asked to separate them. As Baroness Hale of Richmond puts it in *Re B (Care Proceedings: Appeal)*:[5]

'It is well-established in the case-law of the ECHR that "the mutual enjoyment by parent and child of each other's company constitutes a fundamental element of family life, and domestic measures hindering such enjoyment amount to an interference with the right protected by Art 8 of the Convention" (*Johansen v Norway*,[6] among many others). However, such measures may be justified if aimed at protecting the "health or morals" and "the rights and freedoms" of children. But they must also be "necessary in a democratic society".'

**14.6** Furthermore, the fact of separation from parents, however problematic their care may be, will almost certainly be traumatic for a child and may in some cases result in real and serious emotional harm. This was the case in for

---

[3] Section 1(1) of the Children Act 1989.
[4] Per Munby P in *Re B-S (Adoption: Application of section 47(5))* [2014] 1 FLR 1035, citing Lord Neuberger of Abbotsbury in *Re B (Care Proceedings: Appeal)* [2013] 2 FLR 1075 at para 104.
[5] Above, at para 195.
[6] *Johansen v Norway* (Application No 17383/90) (1996) 23 EHRR 33, ECtHR.

the child, 'E', whose removal from her mother was the subject of an appeal to the Court of Appeal in the case of *Re C (Interim Care Order)*.[7] Ward LJ described the consequences of this decision and the dilemma it presented to the trial judge in graphic terms:

> '[31] ... Is there enough reason to believe that E's welfare would demand the making of an interim care order? This is the issue which seemed so stark to us when the matter was before us for the grant of permission to appeal. The contrast between the happy child who went into care and the deeply traumatised child in need of a special therapeutic placement was tragic. Her deterioration was to be measured by the breakdown of two placements ...
>
> [His Lordship then read into the judgement extracts from a chronology of the child's disturbed behaviour since her removal into foster care.]
>
> [33] That is a catalogue of disaster, unmitigated disaster, in the life of this 5-year-old child. Given that state of affairs one can well understand why the mother asks us what is being gained by being kept in care. The judge was hardly unmindful of the problem, although I wonder whether he was as apprised of the full horror of E's distress ... He "readily acknowledged that harm is done to E by keeping her in foster care" but he had to balance that harm against the harm she was likely to suffer if returned to the care of her mother.'

**14.7** The Court of Appeal had earlier drawn attention to the need, when considering the making of an interim care order on the basis of removal of the child from their home, to consider as part of the balancing exercise both the harm that the child is at risk of suffering at home and the emotional harm that will be suffered as a result of removal.[8] As Thorpe LJ put it, 'harm' should be seen as a, 'two-sided coin'.[9]

**14.8** It also has to be acknowledged that there are cases where, on the facts, the separation of children and parents at an interim stage will in reality be determinative of the ultimate outcome of the case.[10] This reinforces the gravity of the decision that the court is asked to make.

**14.9** It is the need not only to respect the interests of a child in being brought up by their own parents and the rights to family life of child and parents but also to balance the harm that may be suffered by the child by being removed against the risk of harm if they remain at home that makes decisions on interim care order applications so difficult.

---

[7] [2012] 2 FLR 251.
[8] *Re M (Interim Care Order: Removal)* [2006] 1 FLR 1043.
[9] At para 23.
[10] See for example *Re H (a child) (interim care order)* [2002] EWCA Civ 1932, per Thorpe LJ at para 39, a case discussed in more detail below.

# THE COURT'S APPROACH TO THE MAKING OF AN ORDER

## The welfare principle

**14.10** The principle set out in s 1(1) of the Children Act that the child's welfare is the court's 'paramount consideration' applies when the making of an interim care order is being considered and the welfare checklist set out in s 1(3) is expressly applied to such decisions by operation of s 1(4)(b). The principle that delay is, 'likely to prejudice' the welfare of the child' (s 1(2)) applies and has significant implications for the listing and case management of application s for interim orders.

**14.11** Importantly, the principle set out in s 1(5) of the Act that the court should not make an order, 'unless it considers that doing so would be better for the child than making no order at all' applies. One way of viewing the case law on welfare decisions at the interim order application hearings considered below is that it amounts to an extended discussion of what features of a case may make it better for a child to make an interim care order, despite the limitations of the court process and the risks involved, rather than to make no order.[11]

## The nature of an interim care order

**14.12** The starting point for considering the court's approach to the making of an interim care order is an appreciation of the nature of these orders, which in turn flows from the difficulties that they present discussed above.

**14.13** As long ago as 1993 the Court of Appeal (Sir Thomas Bingham MR, Waite and Steyn LJJ) was, in the case of *Re G (Minors) (Interim Care Order)*,[12] invited to set aside the refusal of a trial judge to make an interim care order on the basis that he had misunderstood the nature of the order he was asked to make. Giving the judgment of the court Waite LJ said:[13]

> 'The judge rightly regarded this as a complex and difficult case, in which it was important in the children's interests to demonstrate at this early interlocutory stage that the mind of the court was entirely open to all possibilities and to avoid taking any step which might appear to pre-judge the issues. I am, for myself, persuaded, however ... that the judge fell into error in regarding an interim care order as being a step which involved any advance judgment on the part of the court. Given the acceptance of all parties that this was a case in which the threshold requirements of s 31 of the Act are satisfied, the making of an interim care order, far from inhibiting the status quo, was a neutral, and arguably the most effective, way of preserving it. The regime of interim care orders laid down by s 38 of the Act (with its limitation to maximum periods of 8 weeks in the first instance and 4 weeks

---

[11] The propositions set out in these two paragraphs derive from the text of the Act; see also the judgments of Thorpe LJ in *Re LA (Care: Chronic Neglect)* [2010] 1 FLR 80 at para 5 and Black LJ in *Re GR (Care Order)* [2011] 1 FLR 669 at para 35.
[12] [1993] 2 FLR 839.
[13] At pp 844–845 (emphasis added).

thereafter) is designed to leave the court with the ability to maintain strict control of any steps taken or proposed by a local authority in the exercise of powers that are by their nature temporary and subject to continuous review. *The making of an interim care order is an essentially impartial step, favouring neither one side nor the other, and affording to no one, least of all the local authority in whose favour it is made, an opportunity for tactical or adventitious advantage.*'

(These remarks were made against the background of agreement between parents and local authority that the child should remain in foster care for the immediate future, however, the Court of Appeal accepted that their welfare required the making of an order to enable the local authority to have control over ongoing assessment and parental contact.)

**14.14** In the 2002 case of *Re H (A Child) (Interim Care Order)*[14] Thorpe LJ had to consider an appeal against the making of an interim care order in circumstances where, so he held (Lawrence Collins J agreed with his judgment without further comment), an expert giving evidence before the trial judge had:[15]

'... strayed beyond the essential question: would B be safe in his parents' charge between 17 December [the date when the family would have to leave their then residential placement for reasons that were not relevant at the appeal hearing] and the hearing on 7 April fixed to consider long-term risks? That diversion led the judge to found himself on a consideration of the long-term rather than the interim.'

**14.15** The error that the judge fell led to the order being set aside. Thorpe LJ explained the essential point in these terms:[16]

'[38] There can be no doubt that the events of 19/26 July [when a rehabilitation plan, "lurched off the rails" in Thorpe LJ's words] are crucial and fall to be assessed judicially and were as well able to be assessed at an interim hearing as at a final hearing. But I think it is important to recognise that they are all within the context of the complex relationship between these two adults and focus on the frustration and sadness of a fragile mother, coping with a 15-month old child under constant monitoring and suffering from some level of clinical depression. The performance of the mother, qua mother, and of the father, qua father, since, is acknowledged to have been excellent. *Above all it seems to me important to recognise the purpose and the bounds of an interim hearing. There can be no doubt that a full and profound trial of the local authority's concerns is absolutely essential. But the interim hearing could not be allowed to usurp or substitute for that trial. It had to be properly confined to control the immediate interim before the court could find room for the essential trial.*

[39] I would accept the analysis that in this instance the interim hearing exceeded its proper bounds in the evidence of [the expert] which undoubtedly invited the judge to reach present conclusion on her assessment of long-term future prospects.

---

[14] Above.
[15] Paragraph 32.
[16] Emphasis added.

There can be no doubt that to some extent, and perfectly understandably, the judge, in accepting the evidence of' [the expert] was drawn into the same boundary breach. The judge at the end of his judgment during the course of exchanges between counsel offered some reassurance that the parents' case would be fully judged on 7 April despite the conclusions that he had reached. But with all due respect that seems to me an unrealistic reassurance. [Counsel for the local authority's] concession that an order sanctioning separation was effectively determinative of the parents' long-term case seems to me to be the realistic view. *In my judgment, the Articles 6 and 8 rights of the parents required the judge to abstain from premature determination of their case for the future beyond the final fixture, unless the welfare of the child demanded it. In effect, since removal from these lifelong parents to foster parents would be deeply traumatic for the child, and of course open to further upset should the parents' case ultimately succeed, that separation was only to be contemplated if B's safety demanded immediate separation.*'

**14.16** Whilst the making of an interim care order may be, 'an essentially impartial step'[17] the responsibility of the court to avoid, 'diversion' and, 'boundary breach' and to concentrate on the immediate welfare needs of the child has proved to be an important safeguard for parents and children.

## Decisions to authorise removal of children at the interim order stage: the requirement for interim protection

**14.17** As the learned editors of the Family Court Practice 2017 note in their commentary on s 38 of the Children Act no less than eight reported Court of Appeal authorities set out the test the court should apply when asked to authorise removal of a child from their parents at an interim stage. The effect of these authorities is summarised by Pauffley J in the case of *Re NL (Appeal: Interim Care Order: Facts and Reasons)*[18] where she refers (as she notes the justices whose decision came before her on appeal failed to do) to:

'... the three well-known propositions derived from the Court of Appeal's decision in *Re LA (Care; Chronic Neglect)* [2009] EWCA Civ 822, [2010] 1 FLR 80 applicable to interim care orders. First, that the decision taken by the court must necessarily be limited to issues that cannot await the substantive hearing and must not extend to issues that are being prepared for determination at that fixture. Secondly, that *separation is only to be ordered if the child's safety demands immediate separation* (my emphasis). And thirdly, that a local authority in seeking to justify the removal of a child from home necessarily must meet a very high standard – reiterating what had been said in *Re K and H* [2006] EWCA Civ 1898, [2007] 1 FLR 2043, namely that "...at an interim stage the removal of children from their parents is not to be sanctioned unless the child's safety requires interim protection".'

---

[17] Not always a concept easily grasped by parents whose children have been made the subject of such orders.
[18] [2014] 1 FLR 1384 at para 48.

**14.18** In *Re L (Interim Care Order: Prison Mother and Baby Unit)*[19] Black LJ summarises the effect of the main authorities in the following terms:

> '[33] In *Re GR (Care Order)* [2010] EWCA Civ 871, this court gathered together a number of the authorities on how to approach the welfare stage of an application for an interim care order (see particularly §§35 – 42) and I do not propose to repeat what I said there. The authorities not only give guidance as to the sort of factual situation that justifies an interim care order but also deal with the nature and purpose of the interim care process.
>
> [34] As to the nature and purpose of the interim care process [counsel for the mother] rely upon *Re G (Minors) (Interim Care Order)* [1993] 2 FLR 839 in which the Court of Appeal said:
>
>> "The making of an interim care order is an essentially impartial step, favouring neither one side nor the other, and affording to no one, least of all the local authority in whose favour it is made, an opportunity for tactical or adventitious advantage."
>
> [35] In *Re H (A Child) (Interim Care Order)* [2002], Thorpe LJ said:
>
>> "[38] ... Above all it seems to me important to recognise the purpose and the bounds of an interim hearing. There can be no doubt that a full and profound trial of the local authority's concerns is absolutely essential. But the interim hearing could not be allowed to usurp or substitute for that trial. It had to be properly confined to control the immediate interim before the court could find room for the essential trial.
>>
>> [39] ... In my judgment, the Arts 6 and 8 rights of the parents required the judge to abstain from premature determination of their case for the future beyond the final fixture, unless the welfare of the child demanded it."
>
> [36] He restated this proposition later in *Re LA* (supra) as follows:
>
>> "The decision taken by the court on an interim care application must necessarily be limited to issues that cannot await the fixture and must not extend to issues that are being prepared for determination at that fixture."
>
> [37] [Counsel for the respondent local authority] "did not seek to undermine these passages from the authorities but rightly invited our attention to the qualification that Thorpe LJ incorporated in what he said in §39 of *Re H* (above) to the effect that the judge should abstain from a final determination of the case 'unless the welfare of the child demanded it". As she observed, the course that the court has to take on an interim care application may sometimes unavoidably have long term consequences. However, this does not, in my view, detract from the court's duty to do its best to make decisions which respect the "purpose and bounds of an interim hearing" and not to "usurp or substitute for [the] trial" (*Re H* §38).

---

[19] [2014] 1 FLR 807, see above.

[38] The guidance as to when an interim care order is appropriate can be found in *Re H (A Child) (Interim Care Order)* [2002] EWCA Civ 1932 ("separation was only to be contemplated if [the child's] safety demanded immediate separation"), *Re M (Interim Care Order: Removal)* [2005] EWCA Civ 1594 ("the very high standards that must be established to justify the continuing removal of a child from home"), *Re K and H* [2006] EWCA Civ 1898 ("interim ... removal ... is not to be sanctioned unless the child's safety requires interim protection"), *Re L-A (Care: Chronic Neglect)* [2009] EWCA Civ 822 (endorsing the earlier authorities), *Re B (Care Proceedings: Interim Care Order)* [2009] EWCA Civ 1254 and *Re B (Interim Care Order)* [2010] EWCA Civ 324.'

**14.19** In this passage Her Ladyship provides an invaluable 'reading list' of judicial comment on the making of interim care orders. However, it is important never to lose sight of the extent to which cases are fact specific and that, as she points out later in her judgment:[20]

'A court considering what is in a child's best interests must take account of all the circumstances and will concern itself with the reality of the child's situation.'

**14.20** The facts of *Re L (Interim Care Order: Prison Mother and Baby Unit)* are a stark reminder of how complex and unusual (or at least atypical) the circumstances of a case and the reality of a child's situation may be. The mother was serving a prison sentence when she gave birth and wished to be placed with the child in a prison, 'mother and baby' unit whereas the local authority sought and obtained at first instance an interim care order sanctioning the continued removal of the child to foster care (the unsatisfactory circumstances in which this removal took place before any order was granted were the subject of findings and a separate appeal: see paras [2] and [6] of Black LJ's judgment). It was acknowledged that there would be no danger to the child's physical safety in the placement sought by mother but it was said by the local authority (and accepted by the trial judge) that the poor long term prognosis of mother making necessary changes made it contrary to the child's welfare to remove her from her settled foster placement (para [17] of the judgment). The Court of Appeal held that it was inappropriate to give such weight to long term issues, discharged the interim care order and substituted an interim supervision order: see para [60] of the judgment, in which Black LJ also makes the important observation that the relationship of mother and child should be preserved pending a final adjudication.

## Welfare considerations and sibling groups

**14.21** It is important always to have in mind the basic principle where applications for interim care orders are made in respect of groups of siblings the application in respect of each child is a separate application and that each child's welfare has to be considered separately (as does the existence of interim threshold).[21] For an example of a case where a judge's consideration of one

---

[20] Paragraph 47.
[21] See, for example, *B (Children)* [2012] EWCA Civ 1275 at para 30.

child's welfare resulted in the making an interim care order and removal from the home whilst such an order was refused in respect of a sibling, see *Re B (Care Proceedings: Interim Care Order)*,[22] although that decision was found to have been wrongly made on the facts following a review of the evidence by the Court of Appeal.

## 'SAFETY' OR 'WELFARE': A DISTINCTION WITHOUT A DIFFERENCE? OR ALL A QUESTION OF PROPORTION?

**14.22** It will be noted that many of the cases discussed above speak of the child's, 'safety' requiring separation from their parents whereas s 1(1) of the Act refers to the child's, 'welfare' as the court's paramount consideration. Section 1 contains no express reference to a child's, 'safety' as a matter the court should consider although s 1(3)(e) directs the court to have, 'regard in particular' to, 'any harm he has suffered or is at risk of suffering' when deciding whether to make, inter alia, a care order (including an interim care order). 'Safety' is similarly absence from the text of ss 31 and 38 of the Act.

**14.23** The use of this terminology immediately suggests the question of whether the requirements of the child's, 'safety' implies a different and higher test than that of its, 'welfare'. The short answer, on the authorities, is 'no' but in the course of resolving this point a series of cases in the Court of Appeal have provided important clarification of what is meant by, 'safety' and, 'harm' in this context and have also established the important and overarching principle that the need to consider whether the making of an interim care order authorising separation of parent and child is a, 'proportionate' response to the concerns identified.

### *Re L (Care Proceedings: Removal of Child)*: 'safety' and 'imminent risk of really serious harm'

**14.24** The issue of the significance of the expression, 'safety' (and its meaning) in the case law first came to prominence as a result of the reporting of the judgment of Ryder J, as he then was, in the case of *Re L (Care Proceedings: Removal of Child)*.[23] In this case the hearing before magistrates had been, 'blighted with procedural problems some of which had the potential to raise serious complaints under Art 6 of the European Convention for the Protection of Human Rights and Fundamental Freedoms 1950'.[24] An interim care order was eventually made on the basis of concerns about the risks posed by the child's father and as to mother's ability to separate from him whereas the mother's case was that she should be placed in a residential assessment unit where her ability to separate from the father could be assessed and her asserted determination to do so supported. The mother appealed.

---

[22] [2010] 1 FLR 1211: see also below.
[23] [2008] 1 FLR 575.
[24] Per Ryder J at para [4].

**14.25** Ryder J had this to say about the approach of the local authority (supported by the guardian and ultimately accepted by the justices):

> '[8] There is no question but that an interim threshold in accordance with s 38 of the Children Act 1989 is made out by the local authority, ie there is cogent evidence that more than adequately demonstrates a prima facie case justifying an interim care order being renewed on the local authority's application ... As to whether an interim order is proportionate and necessary, there would equally be no real dispute as to that question (or at least no discernible case that would have a reasonable prospect of success at an interim hearing) were it not for the local authority's plan to remove L.
>
> [9] It has been the local authority's assumption and, in my judgment, that of the guardian, that all that needs to be demonstrated is that an interim threshold exists for the local authority to succeed in persuading the court that L should be removed. That is explicit in the documentation filed before this court including the local authority's statement of facts. That is a profound error of perception that regrettably on the facts of this case amounts also to an error of law. Nowhere is there a recognition that removal is a separate consideration from the existence of the interim threshold or the need for an interim order.
>
> [10] Even more stark is the failure to acknowledge the need to consider on the alleged facts of this case whether:
>
> (a) there is an imminent risk of really serious harm, ie whether the risk to L's safety demands immediate separation (per Thorpe LJ in *Re H (A Child) (Interim Care Order)* [2002] EWCA Civ 1932, [2003] 1 FCR 350); and
>
> (b) if not, the question whether the mother is able to provide good enough long term care should be a matter for the court to decide at a final hearing not to be litigated at an interim hearing which effectively pre-judges the full and profound trial of the local authority's case and the parents' response to the same thereby usurping or substituting for the function of the final hearing or issues resolution processes: *Re G (Minors) (Interim Care Order)* [1993] 2 FLR 839 at 845 and *Re H* (above) at para 38.'

**14.26** Later in his judgment His Lordship comments that a concern as to, 'insecurity of attachment' between mother and child (emphasised by the guardian), 'does not present an acute safety question necessitating the child's removal'[25] and that the local authority's concern as to meetings between the parents was only one of a risk of harm that might not occur, 'within the proceedings if adequate arrangements can be put in place'.[26] In His Lordship's view neither concern justified removal and he declined to authorise this, making instead an interim care order coupled with a direction under s 38(6) for mother and child to be placed together in a residential assessment unit.

**14.27** The judgment of Ryder J was in truth an entirely orthodox restatement of what were already well established principles and his decision clearly flowed from an application of those principles. However, it was his coinage of the,

---

[25] Paragraph [15].
[26] Paragraph [16].

'snappy phrase',[27] 'imminent risk of really serious harm' that caught the attention of commentators,[28] advocates seeking to oppose removal of children from their parent clients and some first instance judges.

## Chronic neglect: risk, safety and welfare

**14.28** It took almost 2 years for the issue of whether Ryder J's phrase truly encapsulated the test that had to be applied came to be considered by the Court of Appeal.

**14.29** The facts of *Re LA (Care: Chronic Neglect)*[29] were typical of a very common type of case that always causes difficulty at both the interim and final order stages of care proceedings; namely those where there is a known history of, 'chronic neglect' of children and social workers, and ultimately the court, have to make a judgment as to whether the point has been reached where, 'enough is enough' and removal of the children is justified. In *Re LA (Care: Chronic Neglect)* proceedings had been issued and were proceeding (via a number of directions hearings) to a hearing in July 2009. However:[30]

> ' . . . on 7 May a social worker visiting the mother and children in the home found a state of affairs that suggested that chronic neglect was deteriorating into something more serious, which, even in the short term, placed the children in jeopardy. Accordingly, the local authority decided to seek the court's leave to remove the four children into foster care pending the final hearing.'

**14.30** At the interim hearing in July 2009 the judge took the view (reluctantly but feeling he was bound to follow the decision of Ryder J) that the expression, 'imminent risk of really serious harm' had 'set the bar' for the making of the order sought and that this test was not met.[31] He accordingly made an interim care order (as he felt the local authority should share parental responsibility) but required an amendment to the care plan to allow the children to remain at home. The local authority supported by the guardian, appealed.

**14.31** Before the Court of Appeal (Thorpe LJ, who gave the only substantive judgment, and Maurice Kay LJ) it was common ground that Ryder J had not intended to alter the approach to interim applications set out by the Court of Appeal in the cases he mentions. However, Thorpe LJ continues:

---

[27] Per His Honour Judge Donald Hamilton in the judgment considered on appeal in the case of *Re B (Care Proceedings: Interim Care Order)* [2010] 1 FLR 1211.
[28] See for example articles by Darren Howe ('Removal of Children at Interim Hearings: is the test now set too high?' [2009] Fam Law 321) and Jacqui Gilliatt ('The Interim Removal of Children from their Parents Updated: Emergency Protection Orders, Interim Care Orders, Re L & the Baby P Effect' [2008] Family Law Week: www.familylawweek.co.uk › Home › Articles › 2008 archive).
[29] [2010] 1 FLR 80.
[30] Per Thorpe LJ at para [2] of his judgment.
[31] In taking this view the learned Judge was reflecting the commonly expressed view amongst practitioners that it was difficult if not impossible to satisfy the, 'an imminent risk of really serious harm' test in a case where the concern for the child was that they were experiencing continuing, chronic, neglect albeit with some fluctuations in the quality of care.

'[8] In his review of these authorities Ryder J coined a phrase which according to Mr Baker [counsel for the local authority] has given rise to considerable problems. The phrase is to be found in the first line of para [10](a), namely: "an imminent risk of really serious harm". Mr Baker says that it has been the experience of practitioners and local authorities that this is the phrase within all these reported cases that is being emphasised as the key phrase, the key definition of the standard that must be achieved to justify the making of an interim care order. So for me the question today is: did His Honour Judge Cleary construe these paragraphs in the judgment of Ryder J as simply restating the test defined in the appellate cases, or as the definition of the new standard to be applied to future cases? As a matter of principle it is transparent to me that a judge as experienced as Ryder J would not have been seeking to break fresh ground that was not for him. He was bound by the authorities in the Court of Appeal. He plainly recognised that and so expressed himself.

...

[10] In my judgment, it is clear beyond argument that His Honour Judge Cleary construed para [10] of the decision in *Re L* as a decision that altered the law and that raised the bar against the applicant local authority. By that evolution he was bound and only the Court of Appeal could unbind him. For the reasons already sketched, that, in my view, was a misdirection. Plainly the judge was wrong to think that the words of Ryder J that there should be an imminent risk of really serious harm prevented him from doing what he instinctively felt the welfare of the children required. That that was his instinct seems to me to be plain from para [160] of his judgment.'

In the light of this misdirection, a rehearing of the interim application was ordered.

## Interim protection of the child's psychological welfare

**14.32** The import of the decision in *Re LA (Care: Chronic Neglect)* was itself considered by the Court of Appeal (Wall and Thorpe LJJ) in the case of *Re B (Care Proceedings: Interim Care Order)*.[32] The facts of this case were unusual but certainly not unique in that a child of mother's by a previous relationship ('TA') suffered horrific neglect and physical abuse whilst another child ('KB'), whose father was mother's present partner, was historically favoured as to her physical care but was, in the view of the local authority and guardian, at risk of harm and in particular psychological harm. The trial judge had no difficulty making an interim care order authorising TA's removal to foster care but did not consider the risk of harm to KB was sufficient to justify the same course and left her at home on the basis that she could be adequately protected by an interim supervision order.

**14.33** The Court of Appeal criticised the trial judge for expressing the view that the only significance of *Re LA (Care: Chronic Neglect)* was to disapprove Ryder J's, 'snappy phrase' and generally for his, 'dismissive' approach to the

---

[32] [2010] 1 FLR 1211.

Court of Appeal authorities.[33] Having said that, his self-direction that, having found interim threshold to be made out, he must ask himself:

> 'whether the continued removal of KB from the care of her parents is proportionate to the risk of harm to which she will be exposed if she is allowed to return to her parents' care?'

was described as Wall LJ as, 'immaculate'.[34]

**14.34** However, the decisive factor in the Court of Appeal's decision to intervene was the failure of the judge to follow this self-direction by carrying out an adequate, 'balancing exercise'[35] that included an adequate analysis of the concerns of the local authority and the Guardian or to give any explanation of how he envisaged the interim supervision order he made would protect the child he allowed to remain at home.[36] Wall LJ ended his judgement with a general overview of the authorities on interim care orders, with particular reference to *Re LA (Care: Chronic Neglect)*.[37] Paragraph [56] of His Lordship's judgment is particularly important:

> 'Speaking for myself, I find *Re LA* helpful. I agree with the judge that the s 38 criteria were plainly met in relation to both children, but it is equally clear to me that KB's welfare did demand her immediate removal from her parents' care, and that there was abundant material (not least the views of the police) which warranted that course of action. In my judgment, KB's safety, using that word in a broad sense to include her psychological welfare, did require interim protection.'

**14.35** His Lordship's recognition of the relevance of a child's, 'psychological welfare' has proved highly significant in the way applications for interim care orders are presented.

## Threshold, welfare and the burden of proof

**14.36** Wall LJ, again sitting with Thorpe LJ (they were joined by Aikens LJ), returned to these issues 3 months later in another '*Re B*', *Re B (Interim Care Order)*.[38] Here a mother appealed against the making of an interim care order on the grounds that the trial judge (the same first instance judge as in *Re L*, above) had not applied the correct legal test for removal and that he had approached his decision on the basis that the onus was on the mother to show why the children should not be placed in foster care.[39]

---

[33] See judgment of Wall LJ, as he then was, at paras [10]–[13].
[34] Paragraphs [31]–[32].
[35] Wall LJ at para [15].
[36] Paragraphs [15] and [50].
[37] Paragraphs [52]–[59].
[38] [2010] 2 FLR 283.
[39] See Wall LJ's summary at para [16].

**14.37** In the course of dealing with these arguments Wall LJ made a number of important points about the approach to be taken to applications of this nature:[40]

> '[17] In my judgment, neither ground is sustainable, as I think is plain from the extensive citation from the judge's judgment which I have provided. Taking the second ground first, it does not seem to me that, on a fair reading of his judgment, the judge did reverse the burden of proof as the appellant seeks to allege. He rightly found the threshold established. In this respect, the burden of proof was on the local authority, although the point was conceded. The judge rightly then decided that the question was whether it would be "better for the child to make an order than to make no order" and that he had to consider "the child's welfare pursuant to the subsection" to which he had already referred. This is a clear reference back to an earlier passage in his judgment in which he had specified, in particular, ss 1(3), 1(5), 31 and 38 of the Children Act 1989, as well as Arts 6 and 8 of the European Convention for the Protection of Human Rights and Fundamental Freedoms 1950 and the United Nations Convention on the Rights of the Child 1989.
>
> [18] In summary, therefore, the judge was rightly considering a welfare question, and within that welfare question the test was whether or not there was what he described as "an urgent need to keep the children from their mother for the weeks to which I have referred". In my judgment, this is not an approach which can be faulted. *As the judge noted, the burden of proof was on the local authority to satisfy the court that the threshold criteria were met: whether or not interim care orders were made then became a welfare issue.*
>
> [19] His Honour Judge Cleary was, of course, the judge at first instance in *Re LA (Care: Chronic Neglect)* [2009] EWCA Civ 822, [2010] 1 FLR 80. I note in passing the tribute which Thorpe LJ paid to him in this court in para [5] of his judgment, a tribute which I would seek to echo in relation to the current extempore judgment under appeal in the instant case. In particular, the judge was careful to avoid falling into the trap identified in that case (and in *Re H (A Child) (Interim Care Order)* [2002] EWCA Civ 1932, [2002] 1 FCR 350), namely that the interim order should last until the final hearing and be thus determinative of outcome. In my judgment, moreover, and given the nature of the threshold, the *Re LA* test was plainly met in this case.
>
> [20] In my judgment, therefore, the judge did not apply the wrong test.
>
> [21] Although he does not mention it, we understand that the judge was referred to the decision of this court in *Re B (Care Proceedings: Interim Care Order)* [2009] EWCA Civ 1254, [2010] 1 FLR 1211, which had been handed down on 25 November 2009. In that case, this court approved the test enunciated by the trial judge namely (on the basis that the threshold criteria for an interim order were satisfied): *"whether the continued removal of (the child) from the care of her parents is proportionate to the risk of harm to which she will be exposed if she is allowed to return to her parents care"*: see para [31]. Had Judge Cleary referred to this passage or applied this test the answer would, in my judgment, once again, have been obvious. Furthermore, as it seems to me, the test approved in *Re B* is

---

[40] Emphasis added.

one which can be universally applied, and which addresses the judge's observation that "it is difficult if not impossible to find a rule to which all cases can be compared when faced with these unhappy applications".

[22] I have, accordingly, reached the very clear conclusion that the mother's attack on the judgment fails ...'

**14.38** These passages reinforce the point that it is the child's, 'welfare' that determines whether an interim order should be made and that at the stage when the court is considering welfare it is inappropriate to address that issue in terms of the, 'burden of proof' lying on the local authority.

## Black LJ reviews the authorities: The court's paramount consideration and the need to determine if removal is proportionate

**14.39** Further comment on the first *Re B* case came from Black LJ in the case of *Re GR (Care Order)*[41] where she says, in the course of dismissing the local authority's appeal against then refusal to make an order:[42]

'[42] It may do no harm to invite particular attention to Wall LJ's definition of 'safety' in this passage in *Re B*. The concept of a child's safety, as referred to in the authorities which I have cited, is not confined to his or her physical safety and includes also his or her emotional safety or, as Wall LJ put it, psychological welfare. Indeed, *it may be helpful to remember that the paramount consideration in the court's decision as to whether to grant an interim care order is the child's welfare, as s 1 of the Children Act 1989 requires*, and as Wall LJ shows when he says that in his view "KB's welfare did demand her immediate removal from her parents' care".

[43] The recorder correctly took the view, as he said at the outset of his judgment, that the test he had to apply was that set out by Wall LJ in *Re B* and he referred to para [55] of that decision in which Wall LJ had quoted Thorpe LJ's restatement of the principles in *Re LA*. In my view, a complete reading of his judgment shows that he took into account not only physical risk to C and G but also emotional risk and was conscious that an interim care order could, in a proper case, be required to protect a child's psychological safety/welfare, not just his or her physical safety ...'

**14.40** Finally, Black LJ again commented on Wall LJ's observations in the course of her judgment in *Re L (Interim Care Order: Prison Mother and Baby Unit)*[43] where she says:

'[39] The focus of M's case was upon the authorities which talk in terms of removal not being justified unless the child's safety requires it whereas the local authority preferred to look at the issue in terms used in the two *Re B* cases I have cited above.

---

[41] [2011] 1 FLR 669: see also above.
[42] Emphasis added.
[43] [2014] 1 FLR 807: see also above.

[40] In the first *Re B (Care Proceedings: Interim Care Order)*, Wall LJ said that the trial judge's direction to himself as to the law could not be faulted. That direction was as follows:

> '... whether the continued removal of KB from the care of her parents is proportionate to the risk of harm to which she will be exposed if she is allowed to return to her parents' care.' (Para [31].)

[41] Wall LJ referred back to this with approval in the later *Re B* (see para [21] of that decision), saying that it seemed to him a test which can be universally applied. However, it is important to note that in the first *Re B* Wall LJ did not stop with that direction of the trial judge's. He went on to review the authorities on interim care orders, endorsing what was said in *Re LA (Care: Chronic Neglect)* and, therefore, affirming the earlier authorities which I cited above. His ultimate conclusion was expressed in the sort of terms that were used in those earlier authorities as he said:

> 'I agree with the judge that the s 38 criteria were plainly met in relation to both children, but it is equally clear to me that KB's welfare did demand her immediate removal from her parents' care ... In my judgment, KB's safety, using that word in a broad sense to include her psychological welfare, did require interim protection.' (Para [56].)

[42] Accordingly, I do not consider that Wall LJ's approval of the proportionality approach was intended to alter the import of what had been said by the earlier authorities. Their description of the circumstances in which an interim care order is justified assists in determining *whether removal is proportionate* and vice versa.'

## The other side of the equation: The consequences of removal and interim care plans

**14.41** In *Re GR (Care Order)* Black LJ also pointed out that when deciding whether to order the removal of children from their family at an interim stage it was necessary to have regard to the possible negative consequences of that removal. As she puts it:[44]

> 'The discretionary exercise that had to be carried out in this case was a delicate and difficult one. That is often so where an application is made for an interim care order, and not least when the application comes when care proceedings are finally launched after a very long history of difficulties. Into the balance must come not only the harm that may befall children in their home but also the harm that may be occasioned to them by removal from home.'

**14.42** The decision as to where this balance falls is made more difficult when (as is often the case at an interim stage) a child's needs are not well understood, the effect on them of removal is hard to assess and the way in which their needs can be met away from the family is unclear.

---

[44] At para [61].

**14.43** These problems are illustrated by the decision of the Court of Appeal in the case of *Re L (Children)*.[45] In this case, there were long standing concerns as to home conditions, mental health and guidance issues, and alleged inter-sibling sexual abuse. Autistic traits were, 'prevalent within the family'[46] and exhibited to a marked degree by the child with whom the court was mainly concerned ('PL'), although there had not been a formal diagnosis. It was common ground that an expert assessment of the family was required. The local authority sought an interim care order, although it was unable to identify an immediately available foster placement that could cope with the child's needs and behaviour. The judge, contrary to the advice of the children's guardian, made an order but provided that it:

> 'Shall not come into effect until a suitable placement has been identified by the local authority that can accommodate PL on a longer term basis.'

The parents appealed. The first ground was that the test of 'imminent risk' justifying removal had not been satisfied and the Court of Appeal agreed.

**14.44** However, the parents were also given permission to appeal in relation to the ground that the judge had, '... erred in making the order sanctioning removal in the absence of any viable care plan being before the court'.[47] In answer to this, the local authority pointed out that whilst s 31A of the CA 1989 required the preparation of a 'care plan' in any case where an application for a care order was made s 31A(5) expressly excluded interim care orders from this statutory requirement. King LJ had this to say about this argument:[48]

> 'With respect to the local authority, to rely on that provision for justification for the making of the order made by this judge might be regarded as somewhat disingenuous. In considering the making of an interim care order, PL's welfare is paramount. Whilst there is no statutory requirement, and it would undoubtedly be premature in many cases to file a care plan which complies with the stringent conditions now found in section 31A and the Family Procedure Rules 2010, nevertheless, in order for the court to conduct its welfare analysis it is essential that the judge has adequate information in relation to the local authority's proposals for placement, particularly where, as here, a child has particular difficulties or presents particular challenges. A judge must be aware of the viability of and timescales for identifying such a placement.'

**14.45** Applying these principles to the facts of the case, Her Ladyship said:

> '35. In my judgment, in order for the judge to balance the longstanding issues in relation to this family the court needed to be in a position to evaluate the risk of distress and emotional damage to P which would be caused by his precipitate

---

[45] [2016] EWCA Civ 1110.
[46] Per King LJ at para 4: she notes that the father, who was wheelchair bound, had for a number of years lived in a shed in the garden of the family home and had mainly communicated with his family by using an intercom system.
[47] Paragraph 24.
[48] Paragraph 27.

removal from his family. Further, the court would need to be satisfied before making that decision that a placement was achievable and which could cater for what the judge himself referred to as PA's "unusual and multiple needs".

36. In my judgment, the judge was wrong to make what amounted to a suspended removal order, as not only was there no evidence that the local authority would be able to identify an appropriate placement, but, more than that, the judge wholly failed to take into account the guardian's understandable view that absent the psychologist's assessment in relation to PL's autistic traits the local authority were not in a position adequately to identify such carers or properly to equip those carers with the information and understanding of PL they would require if they were to cope with his significant difficulties and the inevitable distress he would suffer being removed from the care of his mother.

37. The issue, therefore, is not the absence of a formal care plan. Neither is it a case where the court could be seen to be trespassing on the territory of the local authority in respected of identifying a foster placement, but rather it was a critical part of the balancing exercise for and against the making of an interim care order.'

**14.46** The facts of *Re L (Children)* presented in an unusually severe form the difficulties that can arise when seeking to balance, at an interim stage, the risks to children of remaining in their homes against those of removal. However, the general point that the decision re-emphasises is that the court's needs to know what placements are available for children if removal is authorised in order to assess the effect of removal on them. Whilst s 31A(5) excludes a requirement to provide a full care plan[49] on an application for an interim care order, it is good practice to provide the court with as much information as possible and to do so within the usual format of a care plan. Issues that commonly arise as requiring particular scrutiny when carrying out the balancing exercise referred to by Her Ladyship include those of whether siblings can be placed together, whether it is feasible for the children to remain in their existing schools, and the implications of the location of a proposed placement for contact arrangements.

## Some conclusions on the test for removal

**14.47** The line of authority that starts with Ryder J's decision in *Re L (Care Proceedings: Removal of Child)* is of great interest in showing the way in which the courts have approached the task of applying the framework provided by the Children Act 1989, as explained and commented on in the extensive case law, to the inevitably very diverse facts presented by troubled families so as to produce the correct outcome for individual children.

**14.48** Two fundamental conclusions emerge from these cases:

(1) Once it is established that interim threshold is made out within the terms of s 38(2) of the Act, the court the court's decision as to whether to make an order is based on consideration of the child's welfare in accordance

---

[49] As to the prescribed content of which, see the Care Planning, Placement and Case Review (England) Regulations 2010, Part 2.

with s 1 of the Act. The expressions, 'safety' or 'imminent risk of harm' (or similar) do not imply any separate or higher test to be applied.

(2) However, and crucially for the court's decision making process, the decision to remove must always be, 'proportionate' to the harm or risk of harm identified. If the welfare of the child in question can be adequately protected without making an order, or by making an order less drastic than one that leads to the child's removal, then that is the course that should be taken.[50] Furthermore, in carrying out the balancing exercise necessary in deciding if removal is proportionate, regard must be had to any adverse effects on the children that would flow from a removal.

---

[50] In the writer's experience, by far the most common course for a contested interim care order application hearing to take is that of arguments as to the sufficiency of available 'alternative protective measures', as they are commonly referred to, to protect the child's welfare over the timescale of the proceedings up to the making of final decisions.

# CHAPTER 15

# INTERIM CARE ORDERS (PART 3): CASE MANAGEMENT OF INTERIM CARE ORDER APPLICATIONS

## CASE MANAGEMENT FOR AN INTERIM CARE ORDER HEARING

**15.1** The local authority cannot lawfully remove a child from the care of a parent, or keep a child away from the care of a parent, without the parent's consent. A child can be placed away from a parent under s 20 of the Children Act 1989 ('CA 1989'), but this must be with the consent of the parents and cannot be for an extended period of time. See chapter 5 for a full discussion of s 20 accommodation.

**15.2** If a parent opposes the removal of a child, or seeks the return of a child to their care following a s 20 agreement, the local authority will need the court to make an interim care order ('ICO') as a matter of urgency. The local authority cannot accommodate a child without consent unless an ICO is in place and the local authority shares parental responsibility with the parents, or an emergency protection order has been obtained.

**15.3** Section 38 of the CA 1989 provides:

'(1) Where –

(a) in any proceedings on an application for a care order or supervision order, the proceedings are adjourned; or
(b) the court gives a direction under section 37(1),

the court may make an interim care order or an interim supervision order with respect to the child concerned.

(2) A court shall not make an interim care order or interim supervision order under this section unless it is satisfied that there are reasonable grounds for believing that the circumstances with respect to the child are as mentioned in section 31(2).'

**15.4** The interim threshold test can be found at s 31(2) of the CA 1989:

'A court may only make a care order or supervision order if it is satisfied –

(a) that the child concerned is suffering, or is likely to suffer, significant harm; and
(b) that the harm, or likelihood of harm, is attributable to—

(i) the care given to the child, or likely to be given to him if the order were not made, not being what it would be reasonable to expect a parent to give to him; or
(ii) the child's being beyond parental control.'

**15.5** An ICO is designed to maintain the balance for a child, ensuring they are caused the least possible harm and afforded essential protection.[1] The court should not be asked to deal with issues that can properly await the final determination of care proceedings at an interim stage.[2] The court can only decide to remove a child from their parents' care at an interim stage if there is no other option to ensure their welfare of the child at that stage. An ICO does not pre-empt the outcome of the proceedings, and parents will need to be reassured that assessments will continue even if the child is accommodated with foster carers. For a full discussion of the circumstances in which an ICO can be made, see chapter 14.

**15.6** If the need for an ICO is evident at the beginning of proceedings, the local authority must notify the court in their application. In the absence of a request for an urgent hearing, the first hearing that will take place will be the case management hearing ('CMH') between days 12 and 18 of the PLO. It is possible to apply for an ICO at the CMH, but the time estimate for this hearing is usually fairly short. If the local authority notifies the court at the start of proceedings that they wish to apply for an ICO and therefore require an urgent hearing, the court will make directions at gatekeeping for the filing of any evidence before the contested hearing and will continue to list the CMH.

**15.7** If an urgent hearing is required, the court will list it as soon as possible. If there is a real and immediate risk to the safety of a child, the local authority should apply for an emergency protection order.

**15.8** If an ICO application is made during the course of proceedings, the court will make whatever directions are necessary for evidence to be filed to determine the application, either at a directions hearing or by way of a paper exercise following correspondence between the local authority and the other parties.

**15.9** In order for the court to consider making an ICO, the parents must have been served with the application and given 3 working days' notice prior to the hearing.[3] It is possible for the court to abridge the notice period but only if satisfied that this is necessary. In any event the parent must be able to obtain legal advice either prior to or at the hearing.

---

[1] *B v B (Interim Contact with Grandparents)* [1993] Fam Law 393; *Hampshire County Council v S* [1993] 1 FLR 559.
[2] *Re H (A Child) (Interim Care Order)* [2002] EWCA Civ 1932.
[3] In accordance with r 23.7(b) of the Civil Procedure Rules 1998.

**15.10** An ICO cannot be made on a without notice basis. If the local authority considers the situation is so serious it would warrant a without notice hearing, they should apply for an emergency protection order.

## Directions and case management

**15.11** As set out in chapter 11, the court will give standard directions at gatekeeping when the local authority's application for a care or supervision order is issued, even if an urgent ICO hearing has been requested. These directions include:

- checking compliance with pre-proceedings checklist including service of any missing annex documents;
- appointing a children' guardian (to be allocated by Cafcass / Cafcass Cymru) and a solicitor for the child (but only if necessary);
- appointing (if the person to be appointed consents) a litigation friend for any protected party or any non-subject child who is a party, including the Official Solicitor where appropriate;
- identifying whether a request has been made or should be made to a Central Authority or other competent authority in a foreign state or a consular authority in England and Wales in a case with an international element;
- filing and service of a local authority case summary; a case analysis by the children's guardian and the parents' responses;
- sending a request for disclosure to the police or health service body, for example;
- filing and serving an application for permission relating to experts under Part 25 of the Family Procedure Rules 2010 ('FPR 2010') on a date prior to the advocates meeting for the CMH;
- directing the advocates meeting to take place no later than 2 business days before the CMH; and
- listing of the CMH.

**15.12** If an urgent hearing is listed, directions will also be made in respect of that. Even if an urgent hearing is required, the CMH will still be listed for between days 12 and 18.

**15.13** It is likely that very little evidence will be available at the interim hearing if it is listed urgently. Usually the parents will not have had the opportunity to file a response to the local authority's evidence and, if they have, it is likely to be a short document. Whilst the guardian should make all efforts to see the child prior to the urgent hearing, it is unlikely that they would have had enough time to prepare an initial analysis.

**15.14** If the local authority seeks an ICO during the course of the proceedings, the court will make whatever directions are necessary, which may include an updating statement from the local authority, responses to the evidence from the parents and a guardian's report or position statement.

## JURISDICTION AND ICO APPLICATIONS

**15.15** The issue of jurisdiction must be considered by the court as soon as possible upon the issuing of public law proceedings, and this is discussed fully at chapter 3.

**15.16** At an interim stage, especially in a situation where there is an urgent need for an ICO application, it may not be clear whether the child is habitually resident in the UK, but this does not prevent the court from assuming jurisdiction for the purposes of considering the welfare of the child urgently.

**15.17** In the event that urgent action is necessary and jurisdiction has not yet been determined, Art 20 of Brussels II Revised provides that:[4]

> 'In urgent cases, the provisions of this Regulation shall not prevent the court of a Member State from taking such provisional, including protective, measures in respect of persons or assets in that State as may be available under the law of that Member State, even if, under this Regulation, the court of another Member State has jurisdiction as to the substance of the matter.'

**15.18** This court can assume jurisdiction for a matter to ensure that protective measures can be taken to safeguard a child. The substantive question as to jurisdiction and habitual residence must then be dealt with as soon as possible thereafter.

## EVIDENCE AVAILABLE AT AN ICO HEARING

**15.19** The evidence that should be available for an ICO hearing is dependent on what the local authority are seeking to establish. They will need to demonstrate both that there is reasonable cause to believe that the child is at risk of, or has suffered, significant harm, and that there are no steps that can be taken to protect the child other than removing them from the care of the parents, or keeping them in the accommodation they are currently in.

### At the beginning of proceedings

**15.20** The local authority must file a statement with their initial application for a care or supervision order, setting out their concerns supported by the annex documents required. If an ICO is necessary at the beginning of proceedings, the application documents filed by the local authority will be sufficient for the hearing unless there is any further updating information they wish to rely upon.

---

[4] Article 11 of the Hague Convention 1996 contains a similar provision.

**15.21** The local authority must be careful to ensure that the evidence before the court considers what other examples of practical support could be put in place to prevent the removal, or continued removal, so that the court can consider all of the options available. The local authority must provide this information even if the provision of this support is not part of their plan for the child.

**15.22** Directions will have been made for a response document to be filed by the parents. However, if the ICO hearing was listed urgently the response may not have been completed. If a response document cannot be provided, those representing the parents will file a position statement on their behalf. This is a document prepared by the legal representatives following instructions from the person they are representing, which sets out their position. As this is not a document that is signed by the parent with a statement of truth, it will not form part of their evidence but is an efficient way of ensuring that the court and the other parties are aware of their position.

**15.23** The guardian also may not be in a position to file their initial analysis prior to the ICO hearing, but should take steps to investigate the circumstances of the child as fully as possible in the time allowed. They may instruct the child's legal representatives to prepare a position statement setting out their position in relation to the application before the court.

## During proceedings

**15.24** If local authority applies for an ICO as the proceedings progress, there is likely to be a significant amount of evidence before the court already including the parties' statements, expert reports and police and medical disclosure.

**15.25** The local authority will need to file a separate statement in support of their ICO application, detailing the concerns that have arisen and explaining why they assert that there is reasonable cause to believe that the child has suffered or is at risk of suffering, significant harm. The local authority must explain why they consider that there are no other steps that can be taken to protect the child, other than removing them from the care of the parents or keeping them in the accommodation they are currently in. This may include filing documents from other agencies, such as the child's school or GP, to support their application. The local authority must provide details of what support services are available to the parent and why they consider that they would not adequately support the placement of the child at home.

**15.26** The parents will need to be able to respond to the local authority's statement in support of their application and set out what they do and do not accept, and their position in relation to the local authority's concerns. The parents can also set out what support they feel could be made available to them and why this would alleviate the concerns held.

**15.27** The guardian may have already filed an initial analysis and recommendation report, but will need to update their position on the local authority's application by way of a further report or position statement. In the event that the child is of an age where they can express their wishes and feelings, the guardian should obtain the wishes and feelings of the child in preparation to inform the court.

## THE ICO HEARING

**15.28** The court will list a hearing to determine the ICO application, ensuring the time estimate is sufficient to enable the application to be dealt with justly. In order for the court to consider making an ICO, the parents must be served with the application and given 3 working days' notice prior to the court hearing.[5] The court can abridge the notice period if deemed necessary, although parents must be given some notice of the hearing, even if such notice is short. If the matter is considered so serious that no notice should be given, then the local authority should apply for an emergency protection order under s 44 of the CA 1989, as discussed in chapter 9.

### Documents to be made available to the court

**15.29** As set out in chapter 19, PD27A provides for bundles to be lodged for the use of the court prior to hearings. The local authority is responsible for the lodging of the bundles and PD27A clearly sets out what is necessary. PD27A, para 4.1 provides:

> 'The bundle shall contain copies of only those documents which are relevant to the hearing and which it is necessary for the court to read or which will actually be referred to during the hearing.'

**15.30** This prevents large bundles being sent to the court unless necessary, and ensures that only relevant documents are before the court. This can cause difficulties if it becomes necessary to consider other documents within the course of the hearing, and so the local authority should ensure that any potentially relevant document is available at court. If a party wishes to rely on a particular document during the course of the hearing, they should ensure that it is included in the bundle.

**15.31** PD27A, para 4.2 describes how the bundle should be arranged and what should be contained within it:

> 'The documents in the bundle shall be arranged in chronological order from the front of the bundle, paginated individually and consecutively (starting with page 1 and using Arabic numbering throughout), indexed and divided into separate sections (each section being separately paginated) as follows –

---

[5] In accordance with r 23.7(b) of the Civil Procedure Rules 1998.

a. preliminary documents (see paragraph 4.3) and any other case management documents required by any other practice direction;
b. applications and orders;
c. statements and affidavits (which must be dated in the top right corner of the front page) but without exhibiting or duplicating documents referred to in para 4.1;
d. care plans (where appropriate);
e. experts' reports and other reports (including those of a guardian, children's guardian or litigation friend); and
f. other documents, divided into further sections as may be appropriate.

All statements, affidavits, care plans, experts' reports and other reports included in the bundle must be copies of originals which have been signed and dated.'

**15.32** Furthermore, PD27A, para 4.3 provides that:

'At the commencement of the bundle there shall be inserted the following documents (the preliminary documents) –

a. an up to date case summary of the background to the hearing confined to those matters which are relevant to the hearing and the management of the case and limited, if practicable, to four A4 pages;
b. a statement of the issue or issues to be determined (1) at that hearing and (2) at the final hearing;
c. a position statement by each party including a summary of the order or directions sought by that party (1) at that hearing and (2) at the final hearing;
d. an up to date chronology, if it is a final hearing or if the summary under (i) is insufficient;
e. skeleton arguments, if appropriate;
f. a list of essential reading for that hearing; and
g. the time estimate (see paragraph 10.1).

Copies of all authorities relied on must be contained in a separate composite bundle agreed between the advocates.'

**15.33** For the purposes of an ICO hearing, the court should have all of the evidence that is available to assist with the question of whether there is reasonable cause to believe that the child has or is likely to suffer significant harm, and whether there are any provisions that can be put in place to protect the child without removing them from their parents' care. If there is a piece of evidence outstanding, such as an expert report or parenting assessment, consideration should be given as to whether the application can await the outcome of that report, or whether it is of such urgency that the application should be considered without it.

## Live evidence or submissions

**15.34** When being asked to make an ICO, the court must be satisfied that there are reasonable grounds to believe that the child is suffering or is likely to suffer significant harm as a result of the care provided to them by their parents.

This is known as interim threshold.[6] The object of an interim order should normally be to maintain the balance and cause the least possible harm to the child,[7] and the court should not be asked to determine matters of fact or welfare that can await the determination of the proceedings.[8]

**15.35** Parents may attend at the ICO hearing without opposing the local authority's application. Even without parental opposition, the court must still consider whether it is satisfied that the interim threshold is met and whether the order sought is necessary.

**15.36** If the application is contested by any of the respondents, the court will consider how best to deal with the application. The parties may agree for the matter to proceed on submissions alone, with the advocates for the parties summarising their respective positions and inviting the court to make a determination without hearing live evidence.

**15.37** Rule 22.2 of the FPR 2010 contains the general rule that evidence is not required for ICO applications. Furthermore, r 22.7 provides that:

'(1) Subject to paragraph (2), the general rule is that evidence at hearings other than the final hearing is to be by witness statement unless the court, any other rule, a practice direction or any other enactment requires otherwise.

(2) At hearings other than the final hearing, a party may rely on the matters set out in that party's

(a) application form;
(b) application notice; or
(c) answer,

if the application form, application notice or answer, as the case may be, is verified by a statement of truth or if the court gives that party permission to do so without such verification.'

**15.38** There may be occasions when the court is asked to hear evidence and declines to do so. If the court refrains from making any findings of fact at an interim stage, it is within its discretion to refuse to hear oral evidence.[9] However, if a disputed fact is at the heart of the application and the court must determine the truth, or otherwise of the fact in order to establish the need for an ICO, the court must hear oral evidence.

**15.39** In *Re W (A Child)*, the Court of Appeal held that the judge in an ICO application had not erred in declining to hear oral evidence. It found that there was no procedural unfairness because there was no direct challenge to the factual reports submitted by the foster carers, and the father's position was not that the events as presented did not happen, but that his lapses in supervision

---

[6] CA 1989, s 38.
[7] *B v B (Interim Contact with Grandparents)* [1993] Fam Law 393; *Hampshire County Council v S* [1993] 1 FLR 559.
[8] *Re H (A Child) (Interim Care Order)* [2002] EWCA Civ 1932.
[9] *W (A Child)* [2012] EWCA Civ 106.

were understandable or explicable. It was held that the trial judge would not have gained any radical insight if the foster carers had been called to give oral evidence and as a result, it was not necessary for oral evidence to be heard.[10]

**15.40** It is not unusual for a court to say that on the balance of the evidence, it is satisfied there are reasonable grounds to believe that a child has suffered or is likely to suffer significant harm. The court does not have to make findings in relation to disputed facts if they do not go to the heart of the case at an interim stage, and the test for an ICO is one of 'reasonable grounds'. Refusing to hear evidence will not automatically render the proceedings unfair.[11]

**15.41** The perception of the fairness of the proceedings is something that should be considered carefully. The interim removal of a child from its parents, whilst legally has no impact on the final outcome, practically is a serious step to take and must be treated as such by the court. The court should not make an ICO without being satisfied that it has all of the available information before it, be it written or oral evidence. If the court is of the view that oral evidence will assist in the determination of the application, then it should hear such evidence. If time constraints mean that there is insufficient court time to hear the ICO application, the court must either adjourn the application to a later date when there is sufficient time, or invite the parties to agree an ICO for a very short time until the matter can come back to court. If the parents do not wish to agree to the order and any of necessary evidence is not available, the order cannot be made.

**15.42** If an ICO is made, the court cannot dictate a care plan for the child to the local authority. If the local authority seek an ICO and the plan is for placement in foster care, the court is unable to make the order unless they are of the view that the care plan is in the best interests of the child. If the court disagrees with the local authority as to what the plan should be for the child, the court can invite the local authority to consider amending their plan, but if the local authority refuses the court will have to consider whether to make the order with the plan as presented. The only occasion that this does not apply is when an application is made under s 38(6) of the CA 1989 for an assessment of the child, discussed below.

## SECTION 38(6) OF THE CA 1989

**15.43** If an ICO is made, the court can also make an order under s 38(6) of the CA 1989, directing the medical, psychiatric or other assessment of the child if it considers it necessary to do so. If the child is of sufficient understanding, they may refuse to submit to the assessment directed.

**15.44** An assessment under s 38(6) can include assessing the child along with their parents, and has frequently been used to enable the child and a parent to

---

[10] W (A Child) [2012] EWCA Civ 106 at [31].
[11] Re N (Care proceedings: Adoption) [2013] 1 FLR 1244.

be placed in a residential unit. Upon the granting of an ICO, the local authority assumes control of the child, save where the court intervenes under s 38(6). An ICO can be made alongside a s 38(6) direction, stipulating that the child should not be removed from their parents' care but rather placed in a facility for the purposes of the assessment of the child. In *Re B (Interim Care Order: Directions)*, it was made clear that upon an application for a direction under s 38(6), the court is able to make such a direction even if in opposition to the local authority's position.[12]

**15.45** Any assessment must be a clear examination or assessment of the child, including their relationship with a parent where appropriate, and the risk that the parent may present to them and ways in which those risks can be addressed. The assessment must be proposed as a means of providing the evidence required by the court to determine the application and must not stray into therapy for the parent. In *Re G (Interim Care Order: Residential Assessment)*, the House of Lords limited the scope of this subsection to work of which the primary purpose is assessment; it is not to be used where the primary purpose is to impose 'treatment' or therapy.[13]

**15.46** A direction under s 38(6) does not have to involve a placement in a residential unit, but can include directions for a non-residential psychiatric or psychological report together with social work assessments.

**15.47** When considering an application for a direction under s 38(6), the court must have consideration to the matters set out in s 38(7A) and (7B):

'(7A) A direction under subsection (6) to the effect that there is to be a medical or psychiatric examination or other assessment of the child may be given only if the court is of the opinion that the examination or other assessment is necessary to assist the court to resolve the proceedings justly.

(7B) When deciding whether to give a direction under subsection (6) to that effect the court is to have regard in particular to –

- (a) any impact which any examination or other assessment would be likely to have on the welfare of the child, and any other impact which giving the direction would be likely to have on the welfare of the child,
- (b) the issues with which the examination or other assessment would assist the court,
- (c) the questions which the examination or other assessment would enable the court to answer,
- (d) the evidence otherwise available,
- (e) the impact which the direction would be likely to have on the timetable, duration and conduct of the proceedings,
- (f) the cost of the examination or other assessment, and
- (g) any matters prescribed by Family Procedure Rules.'

**15.48** The cost of an assessment under s 38(6) of the CA 1989 can very often be high, especially if the child and parent are being placed in a residential unit.

---

[12] *Re B (Interim Care Order: Directions)* [2002] 1 FLR 545.
[13] *Re G (Interim Care Order: Residential Assessment)* [2006] 1 FLR 601.

The court can order that the cost of the assessment is to be borne solely by the local authority. If the local authority wishes to oppose the funding on the basis that they lack the financial resources, the court will require evidence from someone who can speak directly on the financial situation of the local authority.

## Part 25 of the FPR 2010

**15.49** Part 25 of the FPR 2010 governs the procedure for any application within care and supervision order proceedings for an expert report to be provided under s 38(6) of the CA 1989. If a party seeks to instruct an expert, a direction will be made at gatekeeping requiring them to make their application prior to the CMH. In the event that the application is not made in accordance with the gatekeeping directions, a party can seek an extension of time to make the application at the CMH. However, an explanation as to why the application was not been made in time will need to be provided to the court as part of the extension request.

**15.50** Once an application has been made, no party can place any expert evidence before the court without permission.[14] An application must be made to the court before an independent expert undertakes an assessment of the child or a party in the proceedings and the court may only give permission for the instruction of an expert if it considers it necessary to assist the court to resolve the proceedings.[15]

**15.51** Permission is not required if the report was made during the pre-proceedings process. Any such report should be filed with the court and served on the other parties as part of the initial application, in conjunction with the pre-proceedings checklist.

**15.52** PD25C, para 3 sets out the preparations required for a Part 25 permission hearing for the instruction of an expert. The party who wishes to instruct an expert should, as soon as possible after the issue of proceedings, notify the other parties of their intention to make an application under Part 25, providing a list of the names of one or more experts in the relevant speciality whom they consider suitable to be instructed.[16] Within 5 working days of notification, the other parties should confirm whether they agree to the instruction of the expert or not. If there is disagreement as to the identity of the expert, or a disagreement as to whether the expert is necessary at all, the court will hear submissions at the CMH and make the necessary decisions.[17]

**15.53** An application form should be prepared together with details of the expert sought, a draft letter of instruction and details of time scales and anticipated cost of the assessment. A draft order should also be prepared and

---

[14] FPR 2010, r 25.4(2).
[15] FPR 2010, r 25.4(3).
[16] FPR 2010, PD25C, para 2.1.
[17] FPR 2010, PD25C, para 2.4.

attached to the application specifying the issues that the expert is to address, the party who will be responsible for taking the lead in the instruction, the time table for the report to be completed and how the cost of the assessment will be met.

# CHAPTER 16

# INTERIM CARE ORDERS (PART 4): THE INTERIM CARE ORDER

## PURPOSE OF AN INTERIM CARE ORDER

**16.1** An interim care order ('ICO') is designed to maintain the balance for a child, ensuring they are caused the least possible harm and afforded essential protection.[1] At an interim stage, the court should not be asked to deal with issues that can properly await the final determination of the care proceedings.[2]

**16.2** When being asked to make an ICO, the court must be satisfied that there are reasonable grounds to believe that the child is suffering or is likely to suffer significant harm as a result of the care afforded to them by their parents.[3] This is known as the interim threshold test and is contained within s 31(2) of the Children Act 1989 ('CA 1989').

**16.3** Section 38 of the CA 1989 governs interim care orders. It provides:

'(1) Where –

(a) in any proceedings on an application for a care order or supervision order, the proceedings are adjourned; or
(b) the court gives a direction under section 37(1),

the court may make an interim care order or an interim supervision order with respect to the child concerned.

(2) A court shall not make an interim care order or interim supervision order under this section unless it is satisfied that there are reasonable grounds for believing that the circumstances with respect to the child are as mentioned in section 31(2).'

**16.4** After deciding whether the interim threshold has been met, the court must then proceed to balance the impact of the child remaining in their current situation without an order, against the impact of being removed from their parents and placed in the accommodation proposed by the local authority. This is known as the balance of harm.

---

[1] *B v B (Interim Contact with Grandparents)* [1993] Fam Law 393; *Hampshire County Council v S* [1993] 1 FLR 559.
[2] *Re H (A Child) (Interim Care Order)* [2002] EWCA Civ 1932.
[3] CA 1989, s 38.

**16.5** Once an ICO has been made, it will remain in force until the conclusion of the final hearing or another date as specified by the court.[4] If the court has not been able to hear a contested ICO hearing, a short ICO may be made until the court can hear the matter fully.

## Parental responsibility under a care order

**16.6** An ICO invests parental responsibility with the local authority, which is then shared with the parents. Whilst a parent does not lose their parental responsibility when an ICO is made, the local authority can act contrary to the wishes of the parent in the event of a disagreement.

**16.7** Section 33(3) of the CA 1989 provides:

'(3) While a care order is in force with respect to a child, the local authority designated by the order shall –

    (a)   have parental responsibility for the child; and
    (b)   have the power (subject to the following provisions of this section) to determine the extent to which
        (i)   a parent, guardian or special guardian of the child; or
        (ii)  a person who by virtue of section 4A has parental responsibility for the child,
may meet his parental responsibility for him.'

**16.8** The local authority may only exercise its power under s 33(3) in the event 'that it is satisfied that it is necessary to do so in order to safeguard or promote the child's welfare'.[5]

**16.9** Whilst the subject of an ICO or care order, the local authority must not cause the child to be bought up in any religious persuasion that the child would not have been bought up in had the order not been made.[6]

**16.10** Once an ICO is granted, any private law order made under s 8 of the CA 1989 that is in force will automatically be discharged. This means that anyone who holds parental responsibility for a child via a child arrangements order will lose their parental responsibility once an ICO is made.

## Exclusion requirement

**16.11** Section 38A of the CA 1989 allows for an exclusion requirement to be attached to an ICO.[7] It provides:

'(1) Where –

---

[4]   CA 1989 s 38(4).
[5]   CA 1989, s 33(4).
[6]   CA 1989, s 33(6).
[7]   See also the Family Procedure Rules 2010 ('FPR 2010'), r 12.28 and PD12K.

(a) on being satisfied that there are reasonable grounds for believing that the circumstances with respect to a child are as mentioned in section 31(2)(a) and (b)(i), the court makes an interim care order with respect to a child, and
(b) the conditions mentioned in subsection (2) are satisfied,

the court may include an exclusion requirement in the interim care order.

(2) The conditions are –
(a) that there is reasonable cause to believe that, if a person ("the relevant person") is excluded from a dwelling-house in which the child lives, the child will cease to suffer, or cease to be likely to suffer, significant harm, and
(b) that another person living in the dwelling-house (whether a parent of the child or some other person) –
(i) is able and willing to give to the child the care which it would be reasonable to expect a parent to give him, and
(ii) consents to the inclusion of the exclusion requirement.'

**16.12** Exclusion requirements are designed to secure the child in the placement proposed by the local authority, where there are risks posed by a person living in the home, or a person attending the home. This can assist in keeping a child with a parent, if the risk is presented by a violent partner who can be excluded. It can also secure a child away from a parent to a new placement, if the only risk to that placement is a person's attendance at the property.

**16.13** Section 38A(3) of the CA 1989 provides:

'(3) For the purposes of this section an exclusion requirement is any one or more of the following –

(a) a provision requiring the relevant person to leave a dwelling-house in which he is living with the child,
(b) a provision prohibiting the relevant person from entering a dwelling-house in which the child lives, and
(c) a provision excluding the relevant person from a defined area in which a dwelling-house in which the child lives is situated.'

**16.14** An ICO must be in force before an exclusion requirement can be attached. Any exclusion requirement must be served on the person being excluded to ensure they are aware of the provisions. If the order has not been served; it cannot be enforced.

**16.15** A power of arrest can be attached to the exclusion requirement by virtue of s 38A(5) of the CA 1989. If the exclusion requirement is breached, the 'relevant person' responsible for the breach can be arrested without a warrant.

**16.16** If the child is removed from the accommodation covered by the exclusion requirement for a continuous period of more than 24 hours, the exclusion requirement will no longer take effect.[8]

---

[8] CA 1989, s 38A(10).

**16.17** Section 38B provides that the court may accept an undertaking from a party in the place of making an exclusion requirement, although a party cannot be compelled to offer an undertaking. No power of arrest can be attached to the undertaking and, in order for the undertaking to be given, the person must be at court and have received advice on the consequences of breaching an undertaking. They can be fined, imprisoned or both.

## Local authority duties under an interim care order

**16.18** The local authority must provide information to the parents and anyone with parental responsibility for the child about where the child is being accommodated. This duty only extends to providing information insofar as it is reasonably practicable, having regard to the child's circumstances. The court can decide, on an application by the local authority, that it is not in the child's best interests for a holder of parental responsibility to be notified of their whereabouts. If the local authority is of the view that it is appropriate to withhold details of the placement, the court must be informed and the parents should have the opportunity to contest this decision.

**16.19** The local authority also have a duty to allow and promote reasonable contact between the child and their family when they are being looked after under an ICO. This duty must be weighed against the local authority's responsibility to safeguard the child's welfare.

**16.20** The local authority must also allocate an independent person to visit the child on a regular basis to ensure they are progressing well in their placement.

## INTERIM CARE PLANS

**16.21** When applying for a care order, the local authority has a statutory duty to provide a care plan in accordance under s 31A of the CA 1989. This does not apply if the local authority is only applying for an ICO, but the court will still need to see what provisions are being suggested for the child's care in order to undertake the welfare balancing exercise. The court must be able to assess whether the harm caused to the child in removing them from their family, is less than the harm that they may suffer if they remain with their parent(s).

**16.22** Section 31A(1) provides:

> 'Where an application is made on which a care order might be made with respect to a child, the appropriate local authority must, within such time as the court may direct, prepare a plan ("a care plan") for the future care of the child.'

**16.23** During the course of the proceedings, the local authority must keep any care plan under review and revise it if necessary.[9] Revised care plans should be presented to the allocated judge.[10]

**16.24** The Care Planning, Placement and Case Review (England) Regulations 2010 (the 'CPPCR Regulations 2010') specify what a care plan should contain. Schedule 2 provides that the care plan should include:

'1. How on a day to day basis the child ("C") will be cared for and C's welfare will be safeguarded and promoted by the appropriate person.

2. Any arrangements made for contact between C and any parent of C's and any person who is not C's parent but who has parental responsibility for C, and between C and any other connected person including, if appropriate –

(a) the reasons why contact with any such person would not be reasonably practicable or would not be consistent with C's welfare,
(b) if C is not in the care of the responsible authority, details of any order made under section 8,
(c) if C is in the care of the responsible authority, details of any order relating to C made under section 34,
(d) the arrangements for notifying any changes in the arrangements for contact.

3. The arrangements made for C's health (including physical, emotional and mental health) and dental care including –

(a) the name and address of C's registered medical and dental practitioners and, where applicable, any registered medical or dental practitioner with whom C is to be registered following the placement,
(b) any arrangements for the giving or withholding of consent to medical or dental examination or treatment for C.

4. The arrangements made for C's education and training including –

(a) the name and address of any school at which C is a registered pupil,
(b) the name of the designated teacher at the school (if applicable),
(c) the name and address of any other educational institution that C attends, or of any other person who provides C with education or training,
(d) where C has a statement of special educational needs, details of the local authority that maintains the statement.

5. The arrangements made for the representative of the local authority ("R") to visit C in accordance with Part 5, the frequency of visits and the arrangements made for advice, support and assistance to be available to C between visits in accordance with regulation 31.

6. If an independent visitor is appointed, the arrangements made for them to visit C.

7. The circumstances in which the placement may be terminated and C removed from the appropriate person's care in accordance with regulation 14.

8. The name and contact details of –

---

[9] CA 1989, s 31A(2).
[10] *Re A (Care Plan)* [2008] 2 FLR 1183.

(a) the IRO,
(b) C's independent visitor (if one is appointed),
(c) R, and
(d) if C is an eligible child, the personal adviser appointed for C.'

**16.25** When considering making an ICO, the court will require information about the placement in order to decide whether the plan is in the best interests of the child.

## Placement of the child

**16.26** On an ICO is granted, the local authority assumes control of the child. Whilst it does not follow that once the interim threshold is crossed a child should be removed from their parents as a matter of course, the local authority has the ability to remove the child from the parents' care, save in specific circumstances. This ability is only fettered where the court has the power to intervene under s 38(6) of the CA 1989 (discussed below).

**16.27** Apart from when making a s 38(6) direction, it is not possible for the court to make an ICO specifying that a child is to be placed in a particular placement or should remain with their parents. If the court is satisfied that an ICO is required, unless the local authority agree with the court's specific view as to placement, the court cannot stipulate one. The court can either make an ICO based on the interim care plan provided, or refuse to make the order full stop.

### Placement of the child with local authority foster carers

**16.28** When an ICO is made, the local authority will usually try to place the child in local authority foster care. It is possible to place the child with their parent in a 'parent and child' foster placement. This may be the best course of action if the court is not persuaded that a child should be separated from a parent, but there are sufficient concerns to warrant an ICO being made. However, it is not possible for the court to order a specific placement for the child other than via a s 38(6) direction.

**16.29** Whilst the foster carer has the day-to-day care of the child, they will not be able to make any major decision in relation to the child without consulting the local authority, who must in turn inform anyone with parental responsibility for the child.

**16.30** The foster carer will keep a daily log of the care given to the child and this will include any issues that arise, progress that the child makes and any other matters which they consider important to note. The foster carer will be supported by their own fostering social worker who will assist them with any difficulties that arise.

**16.31** Regulation 22 of the CPPCR Regulations 2010 provides that foster carers must be registered before a child can be placed with them. Foster carers are usually employed by the local authority or by independent fostering agencies, known as IFAs.

**16.32** Regulation 22 provides:[11]

'(1) This regulation applies where the responsible authority proposes to place C with F.

(2) The responsible authority may only place C with F if –

    (a) F is approved by –
        (i) the responsible authority, or
        (ii) provided that the conditions specified in paragraph (3) are also satisfied, another fostering service provider,
    (b) the terms of F's approval are consistent with the proposed placement, and
    (c) F has entered into a foster care agreement either with the responsible authority or with another fostering service provider in accordance with regulation 28(5)(b) of the 2002 Regulations.

(3) The conditions referred to in paragraph (2)(a)(ii) are that –

    (a) the fostering service provider by whom F is approved consents to the proposed placement, and
    (b) where any other local authority currently have a child placed with F, that local authority consents to the proposed placement.'

**16.33** The assessment and approval of foster carers is governed by the Care Planning, Placement and Case Review and Fostering Services (Miscellaneous Amendments) Regulations 2013 amending the Fostering Services (England) Regulations 2011. This guidance covers the assessment and approval process, including detailing the process itself, the sharing of information for the purposes of the assessment, independent review mechanism, and reviews and termination of approval.

## *Placement with friends or family members*

**16.34** If the local authority wishes to place, or continue the placement of a child, with a family member or a friend under an ICO, they local authority must have assessed the family member or friend as a suitable local authority foster carer, in accordance with the Fostering Services Regulations 2002. A family member or friend is known as a 'connected person' for the purposes of a placement under these Regulations.[12]

**16.35** Regulation 24 of the CPPCR Regulations 2010 provides for the temporary approval of a connected person so that a child can be placed with them prior to the full assessment being completed. Temporary approval only

---

[11] In the regulations, 'C' refers to the child, 'P' to the parent, 'F', foster carer and 'R', the representative of the local authority.
[12] CPPCR Regulations 2010, reg 24(3).

lasts for 16 weeks, after which the full assessment must have been completed or the child must be placed elsewhere. Regulation 24 provides:

'(1) Where the responsible authority is satisfied that –

(a) the most appropriate placement for C is with a connected person, notwithstanding that the connected person is not approved as a local authority foster parent, and

(b) it is necessary for C to be placed with the connected person before the connected person's suitability to be a local authority foster parent has been assessed in accordance with the 2002 Regulations, they may approve that person as a local authority foster parent for a temporary period not exceeding 16 weeks ("temporary approval") provided that they first comply with the requirements of paragraph (2).

(2) Before making a placement under paragraph (1), the responsible authority must –

(a) assess the suitability of the connected person to care for C, including the suitability of –
  (i) the proposed accommodation, and
  (ii) all other persons aged 18 and over who are members of the household in which it is proposed that C will live, taking into account all the matters set out in Schedule 4,

(b) consider whether, in all the circumstances and taking into account the services to be provided by the responsible authority, the proposed arrangements will safeguard and promote C's welfare and meet C's needs set out in the care plan, and

(c) make immediate arrangements for the suitability of the connected person to be a local authority foster parent to be assessed in accordance with the 2002 Regulations ("the full assessment process") before the temporary approval expires.

**16.36** If the local authority does not have the information required by reg 24, or the full assessment has not been completed within the 16 weeks of the placement, the child cannot be placed or continue to be placed with the connected person under an ICO. In such circumstances, the court may consider placing the child with the connected person under a child arrangements order rather than an ICO, alongside an interim supervision order to ensure that the local authority remains involved and can offer some security.

## *Placement with parents*

**16.37** Part 4 of CPPCR Regulations 2010 provides for the placement of a child with a parent under an ICO. Local authorities are often reluctant to place a child with a parent under an ICO. For interim threshold to be met, the court must be satisfied that the care the parent has provided has placed the child at risk of suffering significant harm, and that it is necessary for the local authority to share parental responsibility to safeguard the child. As such, the child is often removed whilst assessments are completed, however, it is possible for the children to remain with their parent if the regulations are complied with.

**16.38** In some circumstances, the necessary protection can be afforded by attaching an exclusion requirement to the ICO, excluding a person from the home and allowing the child to remain there (as long as the staying parent consents). If this is an option, the court will need to be satisfied that the staying parent can be relied upon to report any breach of the exclusion requirement before it is attached to the ICO.

**16.39** Regulation 17 contains the requirements for the thorough assessment the local authority must undertake before placing a child with a parent under an ICO:

'17. Before deciding to place C with P, the responsible authority must –

(a) assess the suitability of P to care for C, including the suitability of –
(i) the proposed accommodation, and
(ii) all other persons aged 18 and over who are members of the household in which it is proposed that C will live,

(b) take into account all the matters set out in Schedule 3 in making their assessment,

(c) consider whether, in all the circumstances and taking into account the services to be provided by the responsible authority, the placement will safeguard and promote C's welfare and meet C's needs set out in the care plan, and

(d) review C's case in accordance with Part 6.'

**16.40** Schedule 3 of the Regulations sets out the issues that must be assessed by the local authority when considering whether a child should be placed with a parent under an ICO. Schedule 3 specifies:

'1. In respect of P –

(a) P's capacity to care for children and in particular in relation to C to –
(i) provide for C's physical needs and appropriate medical and dental care,
(ii) protect C adequately from harm or danger, including from any person who presents a risk of harm to C,
(iii) ensure that the home environment is safe for C,
(iv) ensure that C's emotional needs are met and C is provided with a positive sense of self, including any particular needs arising from C's religious persuasion, racial origin and cultural and linguistic background, and any disability C may have,
(v) promote C's learning and intellectual development through encouragement, cognitive stimulation and the promotion of educational success and social opportunities,
(vi) enable C to regulate C's emotions and behaviour, including by modelling appropriate behaviour and interactions with others, and
(vii) provide a stable family environment to enable C to develop and maintain secure attachments to P and other persons who provide care for C,

(b) P's state of health including P's physical, emotional and mental health and medical history including any current or past issues of domestic violence, substance misuse or mental health problems,

- (c) P's family relationships and the composition of P's household, including particulars of –
  - (i) the identity of all other members of the household, including their age and the nature of their relationship with P and with each other, including any sexual relationship,
  - (ii) any relationship with any person who is a parent of C,
  - (iii) other adults not being members of the household who are likely to have regular contact with C, and
  - (iv) any current or previous domestic violence between members of the household, including P,
- (d) P's family history, including –
  - (i) particulars of P's childhood and upbringing including the strengths and difficulties of P's parents or other persons who cared for P,
  - (ii) P's relationships with P's parents and siblings, and their relationships with each other,
  - (iii) P's educational achievement and any specific learning difficulty or disability,
  - (iv) a chronology of significant life events, and (v) particulars of other relatives and their relationships with C and P,
- (e) particulars of any criminal offences of which P has been convicted or in respect of which P has been cautioned,
- (f) P's past and present employment and other sources of income, and
- (g) the nature of the neighbourhood in which P's home is situated and resources available in the community to support C and P.

2. In respect of members of P's household aged 18 and over, so far as is practicable, all the particulars specified in paragraph 1 except sub-paragraphs (d), (f) and (g).'

**16.41** The assessment set out above is clearly an in-depth piece of work and will take some time. Under reg 19, the local authority can place a child with a parent before the reg 17 assessment has been completed in circumstances where the local authority considers it 'necessary and consistent' with the child's welfare to do so. Regulation 19 provides:

'19. Where the nominated officer considers it to be necessary and consistent with C's welfare, the responsible authority may place C with P before their assessment under regulation 17 ("the assessment") is completed provided that they –

- (a) arrange for P to be interviewed in order to obtain as much of the information specified in Schedule 3 about P and the other persons living in P's household who are aged 18 and over as can be readily ascertained at that interview,
- (b) ensure that the assessment and the review of C's case are completed in accordance with regulation 17 within ten working days of C being placed with P, and
- (c) ensure that a decision in accordance with regulation 18 is made and approved within ten working days after the assessment is completed, and—
  - (i) if the decision is to confirm the placement, review the placement plan and, if appropriate amend it, and
  - (ii) if the decision is not to confirm the placement, terminate the placement.'

**16.42** If a child is placed with a parent, the local authority has a duty to provide such services and support that is necessary to safeguard and promote the child's welfare and must record those services in the care plan.

## CONTACT

**16.43** The local authority is under a statutory duty to facilitate reasonable contact between the child in their care and their family. Section 34 of the CA 1989 provides:

> '(1) Where a child is in the care of a local authority, the authority shall (subject to the provisions of this section) and their duty under section 22(3)(a) allow the child reasonable contact with –
>
> (a) his parents;
> (b) any guardian or special guardian of his;
> (ba) any person who by virtue of section 4A has parental responsibility for him;
> (c) where there was a child arrangements order in force with respect to the child immediately before the care order was made, any person named in the child arrangements order as a person with whom the child was to live; and
> (d) where, immediately before the care order was made, a person had care of the child by virtue of an order made in the exercise of the High Court's inherent jurisdiction with respect to children, that person.'

This provision must be read alongside s 22(3)(a) of the CA 1989, which provides that a local authority has a duty to 'safeguard and promote' the child's welfare.

**16.44** When considering whether contact between the child and any of the persons described in s 34(1) of the CA 1989 should take place, reg 8ZA of the CPPCR Regulations 2010 states that the local authority must have regard to the child's care plan.

**16.45** The local authority must consider the child's views on contact if they are of a sufficient age and understanding to have an input. The child's views will normally be communicated via the children's guardian. If the guardian's recommendations for contact are at odds with the views of the child themselves, it may be necessary to consider separate representation of the child (see chapter 12).

**16.46** The court can make a direction in relation to contact under s 34(2) of the CA 1989. If any person listed in s 34(1) does not agree with the level, or type of contact provided by the local authority provides, an application can be made to the court under s 34(3) of the CA 1989.

**16.47** If the contact is in dispute, the court will list a contested interim contact hearing so that evidence can be heard and the matter fully considered. The court will need evaluate any risk that may be posed to the child as a result of the contact proposed, and may be assisted by any assessments that are ongoing in the proceedings. Timing is important when it comes to contact hearings: the court might struggle to deal with the matter if there are outstanding assessments that go to the question of contact.[13]

**16.48** The court will need to balance any risk that may be posed to the child from the contact sought by the parent versus that offered by the local authority. The local authority must consider what arrangements can be put into place to minimise any potential risk, such as supervising the contact or prescribing the venue.

**16.49** Supervised contact may be provided when there are concerns surrounding the way the child is parented; what the parent(s) might say to the child during contact, and physical or emotional harm. It should only be employed where the local authority are clear that it is necessary to safeguard and promote the welfare of the child.

**16.50** Local authorities will usually have access to contact centres in which contact can be supervised. Resources are scarce for local authorities, so they will need to ensure that the contact is in the child's best interests whilst managing the scant resources available for supervision.

**16.51** If contact is supervised, contact notes will be prepared by the supervisor which can be useful to the court later on when considering the standard of care afforded to the child by their parent during the sessions, and more generally the relationship between the child and their parents. These notes will be provided to the parties but should only be included in the court bundle if they are relevant to the decision that the court must make.

**16.52** The local authority should also consider whether any other family members are able to supervise contact as part of their duty to consider all measures that could enable contact to take place. Obviously the relevant family member must be content to be involved in this way, and should be sensitive to the issues raised in the proceedings. Contact notes will not be available if supervised by a family member.

**16.53** The child's foster carer can also supervise contact if they and their own social worker consents. Contact notes are unlikely to be available: whilst foster carers must keep a diary of the care given to the child, these are rarely provided to the parties or the court unless specifically requested. Careful consideration will need to be given as to how any feedback will be provided so that the relationship between the foster carer and the parent is not damaged. If that is not possible, it is unlikely to be suitable for the foster carer to supervise contact.

---

[13] *Re A (A Child)* [2013] EWCA Civ 543.

## No contact

**16.54** If the local authority or children's guardian are of the view that there should be no contact between a child and a holder of parental responsibility, they must make an application to the court under s 34(4) of the CA 1989 to refuse contact.

**16.55** Whilst the local authority is under a statutory duty to arrange reasonable contact for the child, they may refuse to do so under s 34(6) if they are satisfied that it is necessary to do so in order to safeguard or promote the child's welfare, and the refusal is decided upon as a matter of urgency and does not last for more than 7 days.

**16.56** If the local authority wishes to suspend contact prior to a court hearing, the parent must be notified in writing that contact has been suspended, and the local authority must provide reasons for their decision.[14] The local authority must issue an application if they intend to suspend contact for more than 7 days and this is not agreed by the person with whom the child is supposed to have contact.

**16.57** The local authority's duty is limited to *offering* reasonable contact. If a parent does not take up the contact sessions offered, the local authority is under no obligation to take any further steps save to assist the parent in engaging in the contact proposed. The local authority cannot require a parent to contact the contact centre or social worker prior to the planned session to notify them of their attendance.

## SECTION 38(6) ASSESSMENTS

**16.58** When an ICO or an interim supervision order (ISO) is made, the court can also make an order under s 38(6) of the CA 1989, directing the medical, psychiatric or other assessment of the child if it considers it necessary to do so. If the child is of sufficient understanding, they may refuse to submit to the assessment directed. A s 38(6) assessment can only be made if an ICO or ISO is in place.

**16.59** When an ICO is granted, the local authority assumes control of the child, save where the court intervenes under s 38(6). An assessment under s 38(6) can include assessing the child along with their parents, and has frequently been employed to enable a parent and child to be placed in a residential unit, together. A s 38(6) direction can be made alongside any ICO granted, stipulating that the child should not be removed from their parents' care but rather placed in a facility for the purposes of the assessment of the

---

[14] CPPCR Regulations 2010, reg 8.

child. In *Re B (Interim Care Order: Directions)*, it was made clear that the court can make such a direction even if this is not the local authority's position.[15]

**16.60** A direction under s 38(6) must comprise of a clear examination or assessment of the child, including their relationship with a parent; the risk that the parent may pose to them and any ways in which those risks can be addressed.

**16.61** A s 38(6) direction is primarily evidential in purpose. Any assessment must be proposed as a means of providing the evidence necessary for the court to determine the application and must not stray into therapy for the parent. In *Re G (Interim Care Order: Residential Assessment)*, the House of Lords limited the scope of this subsection: it is not to be used where the primary purpose is to impose treatment or therapy, although evidently there may be a therapeutic consequence of the assessment or examination ordered.[16]

**16.62** A direction under s 38(6) can also include directions for a non-residential psychiatric or psychological report, together with social work assessments.

**16.63** When considering an application for a direction under s 38(6), the court must have regard to the matters set out in s 38(7A) and (7B):

> '7A A direction under subsection (6) to the effect that there is to be a medical or psychiatric examination or other assessment of the child may be given only if the court is of the opinion that the examination or other assessment is necessary to assist the court to resolve the proceedings justly.
>
> 7B When deciding whether to give a direction under subsection (6) to that effect the court is to have regard in particular to –
>
> (a) any impact which any examination or other assessment would be likely to have on the welfare of the child, and any other impact which giving the direction would be likely to have on the welfare of the child,
> (b) the issues with which the examination or other assessment would assist the court,
> (c) the questions which the examination or other assessment would enable the court to answer,
> (d) the evidence otherwise available,
> (e) the impact which the direction would be likely to have on the timetable, duration and conduct of the proceedings,
> (f) the cost of the examination or other assessment, and
> (g) any matters prescribed by Family Procedure Rules.'

**16.64** The cost of an assessment under s 38(6) of the CA 1989 can very often be high, especially if the child and parent are being placed in a residential unit. The court can order that the cost of the assessment is to be borne solely by the local authority. If the local authority seeks to oppose the funding on the basis

---

[15] *Re B (Interim Care Order: Directions)* [2002] 1 FLR 545.
[16] *Re G (Interim Care Order: Residential Assessment)* [2006] 1 FLR 601.

that they lack the financial resources, the court will require evidence from someone who can speak directly on the financial situation of the local authority.

# CHAPTER 17

# INTERIM ORDERS ALTERNATIVES

## INTRODUCTION

**17.1** As is discussed in chapter 14 above, the court's decision to make an interim care order involves a decision as to whether the making of an order is a proportionate response to the concerns about the family and a balancing exercise as to the harm that may be suffered by the children if an order is or is not made. A crucial factor in carrying out this decision-making process is that of considering what alternative there is to the making of an order removing the children from their family.

**17.2** In order to decide if an interim care order based on removal of a child is proportionate it is necessary for the court to consider less interventionist alternatives. This is not only a clear requirement flowing from the guidance given in reported cases such as those discussed in the preceding chapter but also, it should be remembered, a specific statutory imperative as s 1(3)(g) of the CA 1989 requires the court the court to have regard to, 'the range of powers available to the court under this Act in the proceedings in question'. It is also a consequence of the court's statutory duty not to make any order, ' . . . unless it considers that doing so would be better for the child than making no order at all'.[1] As Glidewell LJ put it in one of the earliest reported cases on interim care orders:[2]

> '... the joint effect of s 38 and s 31 of the Act is that before making an interim order, the court must be satisfied that there are reasonable grounds for believing that the criteria set out in s 31(2) are satisfied, which are the same criteria for care orders and for supervision orders. However, if the court is so satisfied, it must then go on to decide, first, whether it is necessary to make any order at all. That obligation is placed on the court by s 1(5) of the Act. If it decides that an order is necessary, the court must then decide whether to make a supervision order or a

---

[1] Section 1(5) of the CA 1989.
[2] *Re W (A Minor) (Interim Care Order)* [1994] 2 FLR 892: although dated this case also remains of interest for Glidewell LJ's criticisms of the rushed and unfair procedures adopted that led to interim care orders being made without the parents having a proper opportunity to challenge the case put forward: these orders were set aside by the Court of Appeal, as was an 'invalid' (Glidewell LJ's term) emergency protection order that had also been made. The Court of Appeal ordered an urgent re-hearing in the County Court of the interim care order application (a date was obtained in the following week) and made a short term interim care order to hold the position pending that hearing.

care order. If it appears to the court that the risk of harm is such that it can probably be met or obviated by a supervision order, then that is the appropriate order to be made.

It is only if the supervision order appears unlikely to be sufficient to obviate the risk that the court should go on to make a care order.'[3]

This chapter considers the main alternatives to removal of children that fall to be considered by the courts.

## INTERIM CARE ORDER WITHOUT REMOVAL TO FOSTER CARE

### The roles of the local authority and the court

**17.3** The making of an interim care order puts on the local authority the same duty as it has under a full care order to, 'receive the child into their care and to keep him in their care while the order remains in force'.[4] It also has the effect of granting them parental responsibility for the child[5] and giving them power to determine the extent to which a parent, guardian or special guardian may meet their parental responsibility.[6]

**17.4** Whilst the court cannot direct[7] where a child who is received into the care of the local authority is to be placed[8] it can express a view as to the appropriate placement, require (as a matter of case management) the local authority to provide information as to placement options and adjourn a hearing to allow the local authority to reflect on the court's expressed views and/or provide better information as to placements.

### Alternatives to separation from the parents

**17.5** On seeking an interim care order, the local authority will generally propose that the child is separated from their parents and placed with foster carers provided by the local authority. There are two obvious alternatives to this removal from the parents in cases where an interim care order has been made.

---

[3] At p 898.
[4] Section 33(1) of the CA 1989.
[5] Section 33(3)(a); but see restrictions in the exercise of parental responsibility by a local authority set out in s 33(6).
[6] Section 33(3)(b).
[7] Save for the purposes of assessment pursuant to s 38(6) of the Act.
[8] Section 22C(5) of the Act, inserted by the Children and Young Persons Act 2008 and amended by the Children and Families Act 2014, provides that if a child looked after by the local authority (which includes a child in their care) is not placed with a parent they must be placed in placement which, in the opinion of the local authority, is the most appropriate available. There may be rare cases in which the local authority's placement decision can be challenged by judicial review: see, for example, *R (H) v Kingston Upon Hull City Council* [2014] 1 FLR 1094, discussed below.

*(1) The child remains at home with their parents but subject to the interim care order*

**17.6** This is seldom agreed by local authorities as they take the view that although it gives them overriding parental responsibility it does not enable them to exercise adequate oversight of the child's welfare on a day to day basis. Such a placement would, in formal terms, be made in accordance with s 22C(2) and (3) of the 1989 Act[9] and the local authority would need to follow the procedure set out in in the Care Planning, Placement and Case Review (England) Regulations 2010, Part 4, Chapter 1. For the purposes of considering such placements 'parent' includes other persons with parental responsibility and persons named in a child arrangements order before the care order was made as being a person with whom the child was to live.[10] In circumstances where an individual who would normally frequent the child's home presents a risk to the child and this risk is the only factor that prevents the child remaining at home, the court has power to exclude that individual by making an order[11] or accepting an undertaking.[12]

*(2) The child is placed with one or both parents in a, 'parent and child' foster placement or specialist residential facility*

**17.7** These placements are more common and are often proposed by local authorities on the basis that they protect the child but also provide an opportunity to monitor parenting skills whilst at the same time providing some element of support and of training to enhance those skills. The difficulty is often that no suitable placement is said to be available and courts should be, and generally are, vigilant to ensure that proper enquiries as to availability of places are made. This should include the availability of places provided by independent agencies as well as within the local authority's own pool of foster carers and facilities.[13] The court does have power to direct a placement of this nature, upon making an interim care order, by way of a direction for assessment pursuant to s 38(6) but the limitations of this power set out by the House of Lords in the case of *Re G (Interim Care Order: Residential Assessment)*[14] must be borne in mind when considering making such a direction.

## Placement with a 'connected person'

**17.8** If the circumstances do not allow the child to remain with their parents, either at home or in a placement they can still be placed with an individual who

---

[9] Inserted by the Children and Young Persons Act 2008 and amended by the Children and Families Act 2014.
[10] Section 22C(3), as inserted and amended.
[11] See s 38A.
[12] See s 38B. These powers closely correspond to those connected to the making of emergency protection orders, see chapter 9 above.
[13] Placements in the independent sector invariability come at a substantial cost to the local authority.
[14] [2006] 1 FLR 601.

is, 'a relative, friend or other person connected with [the child] and who is a local authority foster carer'[15] as an alternative to being placed in foster care.

**17.9** The facility to place a child, on a temporary basis, with a relative or family friend can be invaluable as a way of protecting the child's welfare from concerns that arose when they were in the care of their parents whilst minimising the disruption caused by removal from their usual home and wider family. Such placements are subject to the Care Planning, Placement and Case Review (England) Regulations 2010, Part 4, Chapter 2, and the proposed carers must be approved as foster carers (albeit that they only seek to care for a specific child) in accordance with the Fostering Services (England) Regulations 2011, which provide the assessment of prospective foster carers (reg 26) and their approval (reg 27)[16].

## Changes to the local authority's plan

**17.10** There are, of course, cases where an interim placement under a care order with parents or connected persons breaks down or, in the view of the local authority, ceases to be compatible with either the child's welfare or the local authority's statutory duties towards the child in their care. When this occurs, consideration will need to be given to a change in placement. Typically, this will mean moving the child to foster care but a move within the family may be possible, for example from the care of parents to that of grandparents, and this course should be preferred if this is the minimum level of intervention that meets the concerns and the child's needs.

## The need to refer to the court

**17.11** It is well established that in the event that a local authority seeks to remove a child placed with parents or other family members, but subject to an interim care order, that change in the care plan should be referred to the court. This point was made as long ago as 1994 in the case of *Re W (A Minor) (Interim Care Order)*[17] in which Glidewell LJ said:[18]

> '... if there is a material change in the nature of the order sought, then in my judgment it is necessary for the court to satisfy itself about the change in circumstances which it is said justifies a different order. That, in my view, will mean that normally on a hearing where an application is being made or for an order of a different kind from that previously made, the court will normally be required to allow some cross-examination as to the material matters which lead to the application for a new form of order, and it will require to hear at least briefly the necessary evidence, including that of the mother if she wishes to give evidence.'

---

[15] Section 22C(6)(a), as inserted and amended.
[16] In cases where the proposed 'connected person' has not been approved, or cannot be approved, as a foster carer the court may consider using its powers in wardship to achieve the desired placement: see decision of Hedley J in *Re W and X (Wardship: Relatives Rejected as Foster Carers)* [2004] 1 FLR 415.
[17] Above.
[18] At p 902.

**17.12** These comments were made in the context of dealing with submissions as to the extent to which the court should enquire into the circumstances of a case when considering periodical renewal of an interim care order as then required by required by s 38(4)(b) (now repealed). The removal of the requirement for renewal by the Children and Families Act 2014, s 14(4)[19] does not, it is submitted, remove the necessity for a reference to the court when there is change in the placement plan. This would follow from the principle, derived from the case law discussed in the previous chapter, that the decision to remove a child is separate from that to make an order and should only be made if the child's welfare requires it. It would also follow from the terms of s 33(4) of the Act and Art 8 of the European Convention for the Protection of Human Rights and Fundamental Freedoms 1950 ('ECHR'). In the case of *Re DE (Child Under Care Order: Injunction Under Human Rights Act 1998)*[20] Baker J explains why this is the case:

> '[35] ... under s 33(4) of the CA 1989, the local authority may not exercise its powers under a care order to determine how a parent may exercise his or her parental responsibility for the child unless satisfied it is necessary to do so to safeguard or promote the child's welfare. For a local authority to remove a child in circumstances where its welfare did not require it would be manifestly unlawful and an unjustifiable interference with the family's Art 8 European Convention rights.
>
> [36] In submissions before the district judge, and before this court, it was argued on behalf of the local authority that its removal of D from the family home was lawful simply by reason of the care order. That submission is fundamentally misconceived. The local authority's removal of the child would only be lawful if necessary to safeguard or promote his welfare. Any other removal, or threatened removal, of the child is prima facie unlawful and an interference of the Art 8 European Convention rights of the parents and child. In such circumstances, the parents are entitled to seek an injunction under s 8 of the HRA 1998.'

**17.13** *Re DE* was a case in which the child had been placed with parents under a final care order but some 18 months later the local authority became concerned as to the care it was receiving and sought removal. In these circumstances the parents' remedy was to apply to discharge the care order.[21] The central issue on appeal was whether the District Judge had been right to hold that he had no jurisdiction to grant an injunction under the Human Rights Act 1998 to prevent removal of the child from the parents pending the hearing of that application. Baker J held that there was such jurisdiction[22] and the case was remitted for rehearing. Although not directly concerned with an interim care order, it is submitted that His Lordship's comments are equally applicable to such cases and re-inforce the need for such a change in plan to be referred to the court.

---

[19] Discussed in chapter 13 above.
[20] [2015] 1 FLR 1001: His Lordship was hearing an appeal from a District Judge.
[21] See at para [10].
[22] Following *Re S (Minors) (Care Order: Implementation of Care Plan); Re W (Minors)) Care Order: Adequacy of Care Plan)* [2002] 1 FLR 815.

**17.14** It is a common, and useful, practice for interim care orders made on the basis of the child remaining in a family placement to include a recital by which the local authority agree not to seek to change the placement without causing the case to be listed for reconsideration by the court save in an emergency, and that if an emergency leads to the child being removed the case will be listed as soon as possible thereafter for further consideration.[23]

**17.15** If for any reason the local authority that has removed or intends to remove the child do not bring the case before the court promptly, the usual remedy of the parents would be to apply for an injunction under s 8 of the Human Rights Act 1998 to prevent removal of the child or compel the local authority to return the child.

**17.16** An application under s 39 of the Act to discharge the interim care order is possible but rarely if ever appropriate. Thorpe LJ explained the reasons for this in the case of *Re W (Removal into Care)*[24] (a case concerning the removal of children placed with parents under a final care order). Commenting on the parents' attempt to challenge this decision by way of an application to discharge, His Lordship said:

> '[25] In conclusion, with the huge advantage of hindsight, it is clear to me that the remedy that the parents selected on 13 May was quite simply the wrong remedy. There was nothing in the history between 23 February and 13 May to render an application for discharge of the care orders either plausible or arguable. What the parents essentially needed was a challenge to the lawfulness of the local authority's decision to remove. The appropriate challenge was the application for an injunction. Had that been issued on 13 May, given the misgivings which His Honour Judge Ticehurst expressed on the 18th, there is a possibility – indeed perhaps a probability – that it would have succeeded, at least on a short-term basis until the court could investigate further and arrive at a confident conclusion as to the necessity and proportionality of the removal. If there is a lesson to be learned from this litigation history, it is that parents in similar circumstances must issue the Human Rights Act challenge at the earliest possible opportunity. It should be issued prior to the removal of the children and not as a reaction to removal. The obligation on the local authority to involve and consult with the parents, and the obligation on the local authority to give due notice to the parents of an intention to remove, gives the parents just that opportunity. If it is not taken in advance of removal as a protective measure it is simply that much harder to mount and succeed, given that the children will have suffered the experience of removal and will have been placed into some neutral environment.'

**17.17** These remarks have perhaps even greater force when considering an application to discharge an interim care order since such an order can only have been made if the court was satisfied of the necessity of doing so pending the

---

[23] The inclusion of similar provisions in a final care order where the child remains at home is one of the measures set out in guidance given by Baker J, with the approval of the President of the Family Division, in *Re DE*: see at para [49].

[24] [2005] 2 FLR 1022.

outcome of a full investigation of the case. In rare and unusual cases, an application for judicial review may be appropriate.[25]

## Challenging a decision to remove

**17.18** In the Court of Appeal case of *Re S (Authorising Children's Immediate Removal)*[26] a decision by a trial judge to approve removal of children under an existing interim care order was successfully challenged. In allowing the appeal, the court (Wilson LJ, as he then was, gave the only substantive judgment) gave an insight into the way in which courts that are asked to approve a change in interim care plan so as to remove children from their parents should approach that application.

**17.19** In this case, an interim care order had been made in August 2009 (and periodically renewed, most recently on 4 December) on the basis that the children would remain at home with their mother. The local authority became concerned that mother was not complying with requirements to maintain a separation from the children's father (who had in the meantime been found at a fact finding hearing to present a serious risk to the children) and on 23 December 2009, at a hearing originally only listed to consider father's committal for breach of an injunction preventing contact with the children, sought the judge's approval to removal the children, which was given. The mother appealed.

**17.20** Allowing the appeal and remitting the case for a re-hearing (pending which the children would remain in short term foster care) Wilson LJ was critical of a number of aspects of the way in which the court below had reached its decision and which rendered the process unfair.[27] He was also critical of more substantive aspects of the decision. He concluded that although the mother had not argued the appeal under the ECHR, the removal of the children, 'represented a clear infringement of the rights of the children and the mother under Arts 6 and 8 of the Convention'.[28]

**17.21** The substantive failings of the judgment below identified by Wilson LJ are of particular interest. These were:

(1) The grounds for the change in care plan did not appear to demonstrate that, 'the safety of the children demanded immediate separation':[29] on this point he referred to the observations of Thorpe LJ in *Re LA (Care: Chronic Neglect)*.[30]

---

[25] See *R (H) v Kingston Upon Hull City Council* [2014] 1 FLR 1094, discussed below.
[26] [2010] 2 FLR 873.
[27] Paragraphs [31] and [33].
[28] Paragraph [30].
[29] Paragraph [32].
[30] [2010] 1 FLR 80 at para [7].

(2) The judgment, 'reflected no proper balancing of the pros and cons of leaving the children in mother's care'.[31]
(3) There was no proper discussion of an alternative way of protecting the children without removal (return of the family to a refuge).[32]
(4) There was no proper consideration of what contact was to take place between mother and children if they were removed.[33]

**17.22** It is significant that these issues are also amongst the main considerations that would be considered by the court if asked to make an interim care plan where the care plan is from the outset for removal, as discussed in the previous chapter.

**17.23** His Lordship also made the important observation that if the removal of the children was necessary, the judge should still have recognised, 'the summary nature of the enquiry which was all that he had been able to conduct'. This should have led him to give directions for a further hearing, 'as a matter of extreme urgency' at which the local authority could properly put its case and mother have an opportunity to challenge it.[34]

## The nature of the court's decision

**17.24** Another interesting aspect of Wilson LJ's judgment is his consideration of what the court is actually determining when it is asked to approve a change in care plan under a continuing care order and hence what an appeal would be against. The 'technical conundrum' (as he describes it) that troubled His Lordship arises from the principal that once a care order has been made the court has no power to direct the local authority as to where a child is placed[35] and so any 'decision' ('expression of opinion' might be more strictly accurate) of the court as to where a child in care should be placed cannot be viewed as an enforceable order to that effect within the family proceedings.

**17.25** His Lordship sets out his thinking, and conclusion, on this interesting point as follows:[36]

> '[3] ... The conundrum is whether, in seeking to protest to this court about the removal of the children, the mother should be appealing against the interim care orders dated 4 December 2009 or even perhaps the interim care orders now in force in relation to the children; or whether, rather, she should be appealing against the judge's judgment dated 23 December, albeit that it did not lead to any orders. While they hold an interim care order over a child, the local authority have power to remove the child from the mother or from any other person caring for the child, irrespective of any endorsement on the part of a judge of their changed plans for

---

[31] Paragraph [34].
[32] Paragraph [35].
[33] Paragraph [36].
[34] Paragraph [37].
[35] Save where the placement is for assessment under s 38(6), as discussed above.
[36] Emphasis in original.

the child. It is thus arguable that it was not the judge's judgment dated 23 December which led to the removal of the children into care. When we asked Miss Compton-Rickett, who appeared before us on behalf of the local authority whether, had the judge on 23 December not endorsed the amended care plans, the local authority would in any event have proceeded to remove the children from the mother, she politely responded that it was a hypothetical question to which she could not give a definite answer. In our private discussions, however, Baron J has persuaded me that reality is better served by treating the mother as appealing against the judge's judgment dated 23 December. Although this court usually hears an appeal against an *order* rather than a *judgment*, it has specific power, under r 52.10(2)(a) of the Civil Procedure Rules 1998, to set aside or vary not only an *order* but also a *judgment* made or given by the lower court; and, when we hear an appeal against findings of fact made by a judge at a bespoke interim hearing of care proceedings at which no particular order has been made, we are of course considering whether to set aside not an order but a judgment or part thereof. The fact is that, as responsible professionals, local authorities always hesitate long and hard before declining to adjust their plans for a child in their care so as to accord with the views of the court; and, however problematical its play in many circumstances, the trump card is, ultimately, in the hands of the court in that it can discharge the care order, interim or otherwise, from which the local authority derive their power. I therefore consider the present proceedings to be an appeal by the mother against the judgment of HHJ Dodds dated 23 December 2009.'

## Injunctions under Human Rights Act 1998

**17.26** The possibility of the making of an injunction under the Human Rights Act 1998, as discussed in the subsequent case of *Re DE (Child Under Care Order: Injunction Under Human Rights Act 1998)*[37] was not referred to in *Re S (Authorising Children's Immediate Removal)*. To an extent, the approach of courts to the granting of such injunctions within interim care proceedings has not been definitively set out.

**17.27** However, the observations of McFarlane J (as he then was) in the case of *G v N County Council*[38] (in the context of removal of a child ('A') placed with mother under a final care order) are likely to be highly relevant if such an application is made. In this case, having concluded that the way in which the local authority took its decision to remove the child was unlawful both in procedure and in substance and amounted to a breach of the Convention rights of mother and child,[39] His Lordship went on to consider the question of the appropriate remedy and, in particular, whether there should be an interim injunction requiring the child to be returned to mother's care pending a full consideration of the child's future by the court. He had this to say on this issue:

'[45] What is the approach of the court to be to the question of whether or not there should be an interim injunction requiring A to be placed back in his mother's

---

[37] Above.
[38] [2009] 1 FLR 774.
[39] See at paras [26] and [27] where he makes the interesting observation that the case law on the approach to granting an emergency protection order is, 'not wholly irrelevant to the process that should be adopted in these cases', [29] and [34].

care? The starting point must be that there has been a finding that the local authority acted unlawfully in removing him from her care. Section 8(1) of the Human Rights Act says this: "In relation to any act of a public authority which the court finds is unlawful, it may grant such relief or remedy or make such order within its powers as it considers just and appropriate". I regard the local authority's unlawful act as a serious failure by them to afford due regard to the rights of the mother and A.

[46] In looking to achieve a remedy which, at this interim stage, is "just and appropriate", I have to have some regard to the total justice of the case, and part of that must be to take account of the fact that the local authority has acted unlawfully. The remedy that the court imposes, if it is an injunction, is not punishment of the local authority or a penalty for its actions. There may be other remedies that would be. But this is to do with the important question of what happens to A over the coming few weeks and months.

[47] Having canvassed the issue with counsel, I am of one mind with them, to the extent that A's welfare is not my paramount consideration in determining whether or not an interim injunction should be granted. A's circumstances and his welfare are undoubtedly an important part of the considerations that the court has, but they are not the only consideration or the overriding or paramount consideration. A question which it seems to me is helpful to ask is to consider what the situation would be if the local authority had acted properly and had given the mother due notice of what it was proposing and she had applied to the court under the Human Rights Act to prevent the removal taking place before the local authority took action. What would the result have been on the basis of the information that the local authority put forward to this court which mother's counsel accepts is the basis upon which the matter has to be determined at this stage?

...

[50] The question that I posed, which was what the result would be if the local authority had undertaken the process properly, and I was considering the issue before a removal took place, is answered, in my view, on balance, in favour of A being removed from the mother's care. It is a case which, on the material before me, probably would justify the making, in another context, of an interim care order and probably, as I say, would justify a decision after a proper process of removal even pending an assessment process.'

**17.28** His Lordship's comment that the child's welfare is not the court's, 'paramount consideration' is important in the context of the judgment's overall theme of the importance of acting lawfully towards, and respecting the convention rights of, parents. However, to the extent that the ultimate question posed by His Lordship is, 'what would the result be if the local authority had undertaken the process properly' welfare considerations are bound to play a substantial part in the decision to grant or refuse an injunction particularly when, as in this case, doing so would involve a further move for the child.[40]

---

[40] His Lordship notes that it would be unfair to attach, 'substantial weight' to the fact that the child had been out of mother's care for a period as this was result of an unlawful removal but notes this as a factor in his decision: paras [50] and [52].

## Judicial review

**17.29** Although such cases are very rare and likely to be unusual on their facts, there is no doubt that decisions of local authorities in respect of children in care can be challenged by way of judicial review.[41]

**17.30** *R(H) v Kingston Upon Hull City Council*,[42] decided by His Honour Judge Jeremy Richardson QC sitting in the Queen's Bench Division, Administrative Court, illustrates when such a challenge may be made and, it should also be noted, the limitations of this procedure.

**17.31** In this case, the family court had made an interim care order on the basis that the children would be placed with their paternal grandparents, implicitly under reg 24(1) of the Care Planning, Placement and Case Review (England) Regulations 2010. Subsequently, concerns emerged as to the care the children were receiving and the local authority decided,[43] without consulting parents, grandparents or children's guardian (although it later emerged that they in fact also had concerns) that the children should be removed. When the parents were informed of that decision on the following day the father's reaction was said (no findings had been made at the time that judgment was given in the Administrative Court proceedings) to have been so concerning that a further decision to remove the children immediately was taken. The mother commenced judicial review proceedings in respect of the two decisions; in the meantime, the family proceedings proceeded to further hearings before the same judge.

**17.32** The learned judge had this to say as to the circumstances in which judicial review proceedings might arise in relation to an interim care order:

> '[56] There have not been – insofar that counsel and I have been able to determine – any reported case of judicial review proceedings in relation to ICO's. It was felt by counsel – and I am inclined to agree – that challenges whilst care proceedings are in train are usually made within the confines of the family court when an application to revoke the ICO is made or a renewal application is made. Ordinarily, the Administrative Court will not countenance judicial review proceedings when there is an alternative remedy – especially so when that alternative is a judicial remedy. However, that does not mean that judicial review cannot apply to decisions made by local authorities whilst care proceedings are in train. I am of the view that there are limited – perhaps very limited circumstances – where an application can be made justly. This would be so when a person affected by a decision is not actually a party to the care proceedings and might not have a sufficiently good reason to be made an intervener in those proceedings. It

---

[41] See, for example, comments of Lord Nicholls of Birkenhead in *Re S (Minors) (Care Order: Implementation of Care Plan); Re W (Minors) (Care Order: Adequacy of Care Plan)* [2002] 1 FLR 815 at para 43, discussed by Munby J (as he then was) in *Re G (Care: Challenge to Local Authority's Decision)* [2003] 2 FLR 42 at paras [47]–[51].
[42] [2014] 1 FLR 1094.
[43] The learned judge was at some pains to emphasise that he made an express finding that this was a concluded decision and not a proposal that would be discussed with other relevant parties: paras [30], [67] and [68].

might equally apply where (as here) a party (the mother) does not wish to challenge the basis of the ICO, but merely a decision made by the LA as to its implementation. It may be that a local authority has reached a conclusion in respect of which it refuses to alter (despite the request of the family court). All the family court can do is to exhort (it usually works – but it does not always) or revoke the ICO. The family court is not exercising the jurisdiction of the High Court in, the now infrequently used, wardship procedure whereby the court makes all important decisions about all aspects of a child's life as used to be the case. In my judgment the circumstances whereby judicial review is applicable whilst care proceedings are in progress (and there is an extant ICO) are likely to be rare and distinctly fact specific. The Administrative Court is very alive to the concept of an alternative remedy.'

**17.33** Having recognised that this was one of the unusual cases where judicial review was an appropriate forum to adjudicate on the issues, he went on the make a declaration that the first decision to remove was unlawful ('comprehensively unlawful'[44]) by reason of lack of consultation and he would have quashed it had it not been overtaken by the events of the following day, which gave rise to a lawful removal that had by then been approved in the family jurisdiction.

**17.34** Although the family in question may have found this result to be rather academic, the case does illustrate the role of judicial review as providing a remedy for defective local authority decision making in cases where this is not available within the family court proceedings.

## VOLUNTARY ACCOMMODATION

**17.35** In some cases, it may be appropriate for the court to approve an arrangement whereby the parents give consent for a child who is the subject of proceedings to be accommodated by the local authority in accordance with s 20 of CA 1989. The effect of this is that a child is placed in foster care but without a care order and hence without the local authority obtaining parental responsibility.

**17.36** The inappropriate use of such, 'voluntary accommodation' has been criticised in a number of reported cases[45] but one of the main concerns, that of a child remaining in accommodation for an extended period without proceedings being issued and so without the safeguards that proceedings involve for the child and family or proper court oversight, will not be present if the case has reached the stage of the considering an interim order.

**17.37** In any case where voluntary accommodation is being considered, careful regard should be had to the detailed guidance as to the use of this provision

---

[44] Paragraph [71].
[45] See, for example, the judgments Theis J in *Medway Council v M, F and G (By Her Children's Guardian)* [2014] 2 FLR 982 and *Kent County Council v M and K (Section 20: Declaration and Damages)* [2016] EWFC 28.

given by Munby P (sitting in the Court of Appeal) in the case of *Re N (Adoption: Jurisdiction)*.[46] In particular, it should be noted that at para 170 of his judgment His Lordship makes it clear that the previously common practice of requiring parents to agree to give a specified period of notice when withdrawing consent to a child continuing to be accommodated is wrong and contrary to s 20(8) of the Act, which provides any person with parental responsibility may, 'at any time' remove the child from accommodation provided by the local authority under the section.[47]

## INTERIM SUPERVISION ORDERS

**17.38** Section 38(1) of the Act provides that an interim supervision order may be made in any case where a care or supervision order has been applied for and the proceedings are adjourned so there is no need for an express provision equivalent to s 31(5), which gives the court power to make a supervision order when a care order has been applied for and vice versa.

**17.39** Section 31(11) of the Act provides that the expression, 'supervision order' in s 31 includes an interim supervision order except, 'where express provision to the contrary is made' and the general provisions as to supervision orders set out in Sch 3 of the Act apply to interim orders.[48]

**17.40** Interim supervision orders do not vest the local authority with parental responsibility and will generally involve a lower level of monitoring and control of the child's life than would a care order.

**17.41** An interim supervision order can provide a valuable vehicle for social services' support of a family and protection of children from risks that are real but in respect of which removal would be a disproportionate response. They may be particularly appropriate where the risks in question arise from neglectful parenting and poor home conditions but where parents have at least some capacity to raise their standards and they need to be supported and monitored to ensure they do so.

**17.42** There is no requirement in the Act to make an interim supervision order if the court concludes that interim threshold is established but goes on, at the welfare stage, to conclude that an interim care order should not be made and the children are accordingly to remain in the care of their parents. However, since to reach this point the court would have been satisfied that there were

---

[46] [2016] 1 FLR 621; see paras 157–171.
[47] Note, however, that s 20(9) provides an exception to this if any person with whom the child is to live by operation of a child arrangements, special guardianship or order made by the High Court in its inherent jurisdiction agrees to the child being accommodated.
[48] Save for paras 4 and 5 of the Schedule, which relate to medical examination and treatment, which are disapplied to interim orders by s 38(9) of the Act.

reasonable grounds for believing that the child is suffered or is at risk of suffering harm there would seem to be a logical inconsistency in not then making an interim supervision order.

## CHILD ARRANGEMENTS ORDERS

**17.43** It is fairly common in practice for family or friends of the parents to come forward to offer to care for children on an interim basis. As noted above, this can be achieved by way of them acting as foster carers under a care order but in many cases this will involve a disproportionate level of local authority involvement (not to mention the time and resources necessary to go through the required assessment and approval process). An alternative is to place the children with the alternative carers under the auspices of a child arrangements order under s 8 of the CA 1989.

**17.44** No formal application by the proposed carers, or indeed any-one else, is required before such an order can be made. This is because and application for a care or supervision falls within the definition of, 'family proceedings' in s 8(4) of the Act and in any such proceedings the court is expressly empowered to make an order, 'if it considers that an order should be made even though no such application has been'.[49]

**17.45** The Act does not impose any requirement for assessment of alternative carers before a child arrangements order is made. However, a court will require information as to the suitability of proposed carers before it can be satisfied it should make an order and is highly unlikely to place a child without there being some assessment provided by the local authority. Identification of possible alternative carers is an essential part of the pre-proceedings process.[50] Standard directions provide for the identification of possible alternative carers once proceedings have started and the court is entitled to expect that the local authority will contact and assess the persons identified.

**17.46** As noted in chapter 13 above, s 38(3) requires the court to make an interim supervision order when a child arrangements order is made at an interim stage in care proceedings, 'unless satisfied that his welfare will be satisfactorily safeguarded without an interim order being made'. In these circumstances, there is still a requirement for interim threshold to be established before making an interim supervision order as this requirement applies to all interim orders made under s 38.[51]

**17.47** The court would also have power to make a family assistance order under s 16 of the Act since its power to do so arises in any, 'family proceedings'

---

[49] Section 10(1)(b)
[50] Often by way of a Family Group Conference.
[51] Section 38(2).

where there is power to make a child arrangements.[52] It is not necessary for the court to find that threshold is established when making a family assistance order.

---

[52] See ss 8(3) and 10(1)(b) discussed above.

# CHAPTER 18

# CONTACT WITH CHILDREN IN CARE

## CONTACT WITH CHILDREN IN CARE: BASIC PRINCIPLES

### The importance of contact for children and the need for planning

**18.1** The *Children Act 1989 Guidance and Regulations Volume 2: Care Planning and Case Review* (referred to in this section as 'the Guidance') takes as the starting point for its discussion of the issue of contact with children in care the following:[1]

> 'The interests of the majority of looked after children are best served by sustaining or creating links with their birth families including wider family members. Consideration of contact is an essential element in the planning process. Managing contact can place emotional and practical strains on all parties involved, which is why there should be a clear understanding from the outset about the arrangements for contact and what is expected of the parents, the responsible authority and the child's carers in connection with those arrangements.'

**18.2** The Guidance goes on to make the point that:[2]

> 'Contacts, however occasional, may continue to have a value for the child even when there is no question of return to his/her family. These contacts can keep alive for a child a sense of his/her origins and may keep open the options for family relationships to be re-established when the child is older.'

**18.3** An appreciation of these principles should underpin any consideration by the local authority and, if necessary, the court, of issues in relation to contact between a child in care and their parents and others.

### The statutory framework: the local authority's duties in relation to contact and the supervisory role of the court

**18.4** Section 34(1) of the 1989 Act provides that:

---

[1] Paragraph 2.78.
[2] Paragraph 2.86.

'(1) Where a child is in the care of a local authority, the authority shall (subject to the provisions of this section and their duty under section 22(3)(a)[3] or, where the local authority is in Wales, under section 78(1)(a) of the Social Services and Well-being (Wales) Act 2014[4]) allow the child reasonable contact with –

(a) his parents;
(b) any guardian or special guardian of his;
(ba) any person who by virtue of section 4A has parental responsibility for him;
(c) where there was a child arrangements order in force with respect to the child immediately before the care order was made, any person named in the child arrangements order as a person with whom the child was to live; and
(d) where, immediately before the care order was made, a person had care of the child by virtue of an order made in the exercise of the High Court's inherent jurisdiction with respect to children, that person.'

**18.5** Furthermore, Sch 2,[5] para 15 of the Act provides that:[6]

'(1) Where a child is being looked after by a local authority, the authority shall, unless it is not reasonably practicable or consistent with his welfare, endeavour to promote contact between the child and –

(a) his parents;
(b) any person who is not a parent of his but who has parental responsibility for him; and
(c) any relative, friend or other person connected with him.'

**18.6** Contact can take many forms, ranging from regular overnight (or longer) stays with the family to infrequent written or electronic communication, depending on the circumstances of the case and the dictates of the child's welfare. However, the Guidance makes the point that:[7]

'Contact in the sense of personal meetings and visits will generally be the most common and, for both families and children, the most satisfactory way of maintaining their relationship.'

**18.7** In the context of the local authority's specific duty to allow contact under s 34(1), it was held by Ewbank J in *Re P (Minors) (Contact with Children in Care)*[8] that:[9]

---

[3] Which provides that the local authority's duty to safeguard and promote the welfare of a child in care includes, 'in particular, a duty to promote the child's educational attainment'.
[4] This provision imposes a duty to, 'promote and safeguard' the welfare of a child in the care of a local authority in Wales.
[5] The Schedule is entitled: 'Support for Children and Families provided by Local Authorities in England'.
[6] Paragraph 16 of Sch 2 gives concrete form to this duty to promote contact by allowing a local authority to make payments in respect of expenses incurred by, inter alia, parents in having contact with a child who is in the authority's care if, '(a) it appears to the authority that the visit in question could not otherwise be made without undue financial hardship; and (b) the circumstances warrant the making of the payments' (see para 16(3) of Sch 2).
[7] Paragraph 2.86.
[8] [1993] 2 FLR 156.

'"Reasonable" implies access[10] which is agreed between the local authority and the parents or, if there is no such agreement, access which is objectively reasonable.'

**18.8** In *Re W (Section 34(2) Orders)*[11] the Court of Appeal held that there was no jurisdiction within s 34 to make an order inhibiting a local authority's discretion in carrying out its statutory duty by making an order prohibiting contact that the local authority considered to be advantageous to the child and hence, 'reasonable'. In this case, the child's guardian made an application under s 34(2) seeking an order prohibiting the local authority from allowing staying contact between a child in their care and its mother.

**18.9** *Re W (Section 34(2) Orders)* is important not only in relation to the specific issue before the court but also for the light it sheds on the relationship between court and local authority in dealing with contact issues. Giving the judgment of the Court of Appeal, Thorpe LJ drew attention to the two, 'cornerstones' of Part IV of the Children Act, namely the, 'shifting of power from the court to the local authority on or after the making of the care order'[12] and the imposition of a, 'clearer and higher duty to promote contact'[13] and goes on to say:[14]

> '... we are of the opinion that the primary purpose of s 34 is to impose obligations and restraints on local authorities with children in care. The obligation is the duty to promote contact. The restraint is upon their discretion to refuse contact unless they have first persuaded a judge that such a refusal is necessary. The power of the judge to supervise and control is the power to require the local authority to go further in the promotion of contact than the authority itself considers appropriate. The other power is to monitor the local authority's proposal to refuse contact in order to ensure that its proposal is not excessive. We do not believe that the legislation ever intended the jurisdiction of the judge under s 34 to be deployed so as to inhibit the local authority in the performance of its statutory duty by preventing contact which the local authority considers advantageous to welfare.'

**18.10** Returning to the issue determined in *Re W (Section 34(2) Orders)*, this clarification of the court's jurisdiction under s 34 is of considerable practical importance. Whilst local authorities will always give great respect to the views of a child's guardian as to the proper contact arrangements, and may wish to defer implementing arrangements pending consideration of those views and discussion with the guardian, the ultimate decision is that of the authority. Furthermore, it is not uncommon to find that one parent will object to the other parent (or another family member) having that contact with a child who is in care that the local authority has decided to be in the child's best interests.

---

[9] At page 161.
[10] Sic: in fairness to His Lordship he was giving judgment in July 1992, less than a year after the change in terminology in the 1989 Act that replaced 'access' with 'contact' came into force.
[11] [2000] 1 FLR 502.
[12] At page 506, as to which His Lordship cites dicta of Butler-Sloss LJ (as she then was) in *Re L (Sexual Abuse: Standard of Proof)* [1996] 1 FLR 116 at p 124.
[13] At p 507.
[14] Also at p 507.

Thorpe LJ's judgment in *Re W (Section 34(2) Orders)* makes it clear that in these circumstances there is no jurisdiction in the court under s 34 to prohibit those contact arrangements being put in place.[15]

## A note on terminology: 'contact at the discretion of the local authority'

**18.11** The expression, 'contact at the discretion of the local authority' (or similar) sometimes appears in care plans, agreements between local authority's and parents and in court orders. In *Re P (Minors) (Contact with Children in Care)*, indeed in the sentence immediately preceding that quoted above, Ewbank J remarked that reasonable access is not the same as access at the discretion of the local authority. However, he says this in the context of his reference to the pre-Children Act practice of awarding 'access' at the discretion of the local authority.

**18.12** In *L v London Borough of Bromley*[16] Wilson J (as he then was) had this to say about the meaning to be attached to, 'contact at the discretion of the local authority:[17]

> 'I cannot read the order for contact with the mother to be at the discretion of the local authority as in any way eroding the obligation cast upon the local authority under s 34(1)(a) to allow these children reasonable contact with the mother. The only way in which a court can erode that obligation is when it makes an order under s 34(4) of the Act, authorising the authority to refuse to allow contact between the child and any person mentioned in s 34(1). No such order, of course, was made. So I read the order for contact in favour of the mother at the discretion of the local authority to mean first that there is no inroad into the obligation of s 34(1); secondly that there is to be no definition by the court of contact between the mother and the children under s 34(2) or (3); and thirdly that the quantum of contact, together with the other arrangements for reasonable contact that must take place under s 34(1), is specifically placed to be determined by the local authority in the exercise of their discretion.'

**18.13** It is suggested that this construction is correct and that a local authority cannot lawfully use a 'discretion' to put in place contact arrangements that are not, 'objectively reasonable' (or agreed by the parents) and that if it seeks to do so in the face of a challenge to the reasonableness of its proposals it must seek authority under s 34(4). In practice, courts often take up the suggestion made by Wilson J in the Bromley case that it is '... often helpful for a court to express

---

[15] The court may, of course, express a view as to contact arrangements in these circumstances, which the local authority will take into account. The only remedies (both theoretical rather than practical in virtually all foreseeable circumstances) for the dissatisfied parent would be to apply to discharge the care order on the basis that the proposed contact was so inimical to the child's welfare that the s 1 welfare balance tipped back against the continuation of the care order or to seek a judicial review as to the reasonableness of the local authority's process of planning for contact.
[16] [1998] 1 FLR 709.
[17] At p 714.

some sort of indication as to the amount of contact which, even if it is leaving the matter in the discretion of the authority, it envisages that the authority may favour'[18] by setting out expectations as to minimum levels of contact in a recital to the care order.

## THE ROLE OF THE COURT
### Section 34 Children Act 1989: available orders

**18.14** Section 34 sets out a comprehensive, self-contained,[19] code providing for the court's adjudication on disputed issues as to contact with children in care. There are two aspects to the court's jurisdiction under s 34: it has power to determine what contact should be allowed between a child in care and other persons[20] and, conversely, it can authorise that contact that the local authority would otherwise be required to facilitate be refused.[21] The court can impose, 'such conditions as the court considers appropriate' to an order under the section[22] and has power to vary or discharge an order.[23]

**18.15** As noted in *Re S (Minors) (Care Order: Implementation of Care Plan); Re W (Minors) (Care Order: Adequacy of Care Plan)*[24] and other cases discussed elsewhere in this work, the court's power to make orders under this section continue to exist so long as the care order is in force and, therefore, represents the sole exception within the Children Act to the principle that the making of a final care order passes responsibility for decisions about a child from the court to the local authority.

**18.16** The clear and succinct statement of the purpose of s 34 and the court's role within its scheme given by Thorpe LJ in the case of *Re W (Section 34(2) Orders)*[25] and set out above is a good starting point for any consideration of the question of whether the court can, or should, become involved in determining issues as to contact with children in care.

**18.17** The Ministry of Justice's published statistics provide an interesting insight into the extent to which the court is actually involved in making decisions about contact with children in care. In the calendar year 2016 care orders were made in respect of a total of 13,472 children. Orders for contact were made in respect of only 71 children during that year whereas orders giving the local authority permission to refuse contact were made in respect of 440

---

[18] At p 715.
[19] Section 9(1) of the Act prohibits the making of an order providing for contact under s 8(1) of the Act in respect of a child who is in the care of a local authority.
[20] Sections 34(2) and 34(3).
[21] Sections 34(4), 34(6), 34(6A) and 34(6B).
[22] Section 34(7).
[23] Section 34(9).
[24] [2002] 1 FLR 815.
[25] [2000] 1 FLR 502.

children.[26] During that year applications for contact were made in respect of 443 children whilst applications for permission to refuse contact were made in respect of 491 children. These figures suggest that in the relatively small proportion of care cases in which the court makes formal decisions it generally accept local authority arguments as to the need for withhold contact whereas parents and connected persons have a significantly more difficult task in persuading the court to overrule local authority decisions as to what contact is in a child's interests.[27]

## Orders for contact: types of contact and conditions

**18.18** The court can make, 'such order as it considers appropriate' with respect to contact between the child and, 'any named person'.[28] The persons who may be named in such an order are not limited to those with an established, legal, relationship with the child and may well extend to encompass the wider class of, 'relative, friend or other person connected with him' envisaged in Sch 2, para 15.[29]

**18.19** The wide scope of the court's discretion as to the orders that can be made as to contact will be noted. Contact ordered by the court can take many forms ranging from indirect contact by way of written communication only through various permutations of direct contact in the controlled environment of a contact centre or 'in the community' and with or without supervision (which can be provided by social work professionals, lay volunteers or family members) to extended periods of staying contact.[30] The court may also, of course, decline to make an order if it does not consider this to be appropriate or make an order that there be no contact between the child and the named person.[31]

---

[26] These orders are not necessarily in respect of the same children who are the subject of care orders.

[27] See *Family Court Statistics Quarterly, England and Wales* October to December 2016, Tables 3 (applications) and 4 (orders). Note that Table 4 does not distinguish between the figures for orders made following a specific and those made of the court's own motion in accordance with s 34(5) as discussed below. Nor do the statistics specifically enumerate those cases (undoubtedly the great majority) where contact is dealt with by way of arrangements agreed to, or at least acquiesced in, by all relevant parties being incorporated in a care plan without the need for a separate order as to contact issues.

[28] See s 34(2) and (3).

[29] For example, in *L v London Borough of Bromley* [1998] 1 FLR 709 Wilson J (as he then was) held that both a 'de facto' step father and a half sibling fell within the definition in the Schedule. On a strict reading of the Act, there is power to name in an order for contact a person who does not fall within either s 34(1) or Sch 2, para 15 but it is difficult to image circumstances in which a child's welfare would require that they be provided with contact with a person who did not fall into one or other of these classes.

[30] Staying contact, even in a home that has been determined to be unsuitable as a permanent placement, is often considered appropriate for older children who are in long term foster care or where a plan for rehabilitation of children into the care of their parents is being implemented.

[31] *Kent County Council v C* [1993] 1 FLR 308.

**18.20** Section 34(7) enables to the court to, 'impose such conditions as the court considers appropriate' to any order under s 34. This would enable it further to regulate any contact ordered by, for example, ordering that that contact allowed between the child and family member 'A' but on condition that family member 'B' is not present or that the child is not taken to the home of family member 'C'.

## Orders authorising the refusal of contact: powers of the local authority

**18.21** Conversely, the court can make an order authorising the local authority to refuse contact between the child and any person, 'who is mentioned in paragraphs (a) to (d) of subs (1) and is named in the order'.[32]

**18.22** Such an order relieves the local authority of its obligation to allow the child, 'reasonable contact' with the persons named. What amounts to, 'reasonable' contact will depend on the circumstances of each case but in practice a local authority that proposes that there should be no direct contact between a child and a person in one of the classes defined in subs (1) is, in the absence of that person's agreement, very likely to seek the approval of the court by an application under subs (4) rather than leave it to the person being denied contact to apply under subs (3).

**18.23** The local authority has strictly limited power to act, without prior reference to the court, to refuse to allow contact required to be provided either by subs (1) or by an order of the court. They can do this if:[33]

'(a) they are satisfied that it is necessary to do so in order to safeguard or promote the child's welfare; and
(b) the refusal –
  (i) is decided upon as a matter of urgency; and
  (ii) does not last for more than seven days.'

**18.24** This is a draconian power and, in the writer's experience, local authority internal procedures require authorisation at a senior level before it is invoked. Regulation 8 of the Care Planning, Placement and Case Review (England) Regulations 2010 requires the local authority to, 'immediately give written notification' of its decision to use this power to parents and others affected[34] and to include in such notification specified information, which includes a statement of the reasons for the step being taken and the remedies available in the case of dissatisfaction.[35] Having said that, s 34(6) serves the important purpose of allowing a pause in contact when difficulties have arisen and whilst alternative arrangements are considered and, if possible, agreed.

---

[32] Section 34(4).
[33] Section 34(6).
[34] Regulation 8(2).
[35] Regulation 8(3).

**18.25** Where an order under s 34 authorises the refusal of contact between the child and a parent, guardian, special guardian, step-parent with parental or former holder of a child arrangements order providing that the child live with that person,[36] or where s 34(6) applies, the local authority is not required to endeavour to promote contact with that person in accordance with para 15(1) of Sch 2 of the Act.[37]

## THE COURT'S DECISION MAKING PROCESS

### The decision to make an order as to contact: welfare and the balancing exercise

**18.26** In determining issues arising under s 34 the welfare of the child whose contact arrangements are in issue[38] is the court's paramount consideration and regard has to be had to the checklist in s 1(3) of the Act.[39] As Hale J (as she then was) put it in the case of *Berkshire County Council v B*:[40]

> 'The Children Act 1989 deliberately gave the court wide powers over the contact that there was to be between children in care, their parents and, indeed, other people. It made that contact subject to the paramount consideration of the child's welfare, together with the checklist and other considerations set out in s 1 of the 1989 Act.'

**18.27** In carrying out its assessment of the child's welfare the court has to balance the potential benefits for the child of contact against other relevant welfare considerations and these can include any danger that continuing contact would frustrate long term plans to place the child in an alternative home by way of adoption or otherwise.[41]

### The balancing exercise: relevant considerations and the welfare of the individual child

**18.28** The nature of this balancing exercise is explained by Hale J in *Berkshire County Council v B* in the following terms:[42]

---

[36] i.e. the persons with whom the local authority are required to allow the child 'reasonable contact': see s 34(1)(a), (b), (ba) and (c).
[37] Section 34(6A) (England) and (6B) (Wales).
[38] See *Birmingham City Council v H (No 3)* [1994] 1 FLR 224 in which the House of Lords held that it was the welfare of the child subject to then proceedings that was the court's paramount concern and not that of the child's 16 year mother, who was herself a child in care. For the nature of the welfare enquiry when a child in care seeks contact with a child not in care (in this case, her siblings living at home) see the judgment of Wilson J (as he then was) in the case of *Re F (Contact: Child in Care)* [1995] 1 FLR 510.
[39] Section 1(4)(b).
[40] [1997] 1 FLR 171 at p 174.
[41] See the decisions of the Court of Appeal in the cases of *Re B (Minors) (Care: Contact: Local Authority's Plans)* [1993] 1 FLR 543 and *Re E (A Minor) (Care Order: Contact)* [1994] 1 FLR 146.
[42] At p 176.

'The question, therefore, becomes one of balancing the respective factors in the welfare of the child. At one end of the spectrum there must be cases where the child clearly needs a new family for life and contact with his family of birth will bring little or no benefit and is likely to impede this. At the other end of the spectrum are cases where the child is likely to return home in the short to medium term and contact is essential to enable this to take place.

There are also many cases in the middle where the child is unlikely to be able to return home in the short to medium term and so needs a long-term stable placement but where the relationships with his family of origin are so important to him that they must be maintained. One reason for this may well be that adoption is unlikely to succeed so that a child must not be deprived of his existing relationships which matter to him for the sake of putative ones which may never be found.

In these very difficult cases the court has to balance these various advantages against the difficulties that contact is likely to cause in finding and sustaining an appropriate placement for the child. Obviously contact, however important, cannot be pursued to a level which makes a successful placement impossible to find because the child needs a home and to be properly looked after, and that must be the first priority.

The local authority are not entitled to approach the case in a "take it or leave it" manner, for two reasons: first, because, as I have already explained, the court retains control over the relationship between the child and his parents through the issues of contact and adoption. The court therefore has to balance the various factors and so must the local authority. Secondly, while I accept that local authorities are entitled to have a general approach based on their appreciation of what is in general best for children – and we are all aware of the many reasons why adoption may well provide the best solution for most young children who have to be looked after for a long time away from their family of birth – they have a statutory duty to make decisions in the interests of the individual child in their care. They cannot approach decision-making in any particular case as if it were governed by general principles alone. It is trite law that those exercising a statutory discretion are not entitled to fetter their discretion by a reference to a general policy of which they will not admit departures in appropriate cases.'

**18.29** The last paragraph quoted above is particularly important in practice. In cases where the care plan presented to the court is for children to be adopted or placed in long term foster care it is generally argued by the local authority (often with the support of the children's guardian) that it follows that parental contact should be severely restricted. Typically, if the plan is for the children to be adopted it will be proposed that the parents have indirect contact only and if it is for long term foster care the parents will be offered direct contact between 2 and 6 times per year. Her Ladyship's observations make it clear that it is not sufficient, when advancing such a plan, to rely on general propositions (albeit ones derived from research and experience) that more extensive contact will, 'limit the pool of prospective adoptive placements' or 'destabilise the foster placement': the court has to consider the individual circumstances of the child whose future is being considered and make an evidence based welfare decision as to the contact arrangements necessary to advance that particular child's welfare.[43]

## THE CIRCUMSTANCES IN WHICH ORDERS UNDER S 34 MAY BE MADE

### When can orders under s 34 may be made?

**18.30** An order under s 34 may be made, 'either at the same time as the care order itself or later'.[44] In this context, 'care order' includes an interim care order.[45]

**18.31** Although there is no requirement to make an order under s 34 when a care order is made,[46] s 34(11) provides that:

> 'Before making, varying or discharging an order under this section or making a care order with respect to any child the court shall –
> 
> (a) consider the arrangements which the authority have made, or propose to make, for affording any person contact with a child to whom this section applies; and
> 
> (b) invite the parties to the proceedings to comment on those arrangements.'

**18.32** The effect of s 31(3A)(b) is that contact arrangements are now the only aspect of the local authority's care plan going beyond the, 'long term plan for the upbringing of the child'[47] that the court is required to consider before making a care order.

**18.33** Conversely, there is nothing in the Act to suggest that the court's power to make orders under s 34 is affected by the effluxion of time since the making of the care order in issue. The court retains its powers under the section so long as the child in question remains the subject of a care order. If an application is made to change contact arrangements that have been in place for some time the court is likely to have to give, when applying the welfare test, particular consideration to the effect of a change in arrangements on the child.[48] On the other hand, as a child in care gets older changes in contact arrangements may well be justified as they become more independent.

---

[43] An interesting analogy can be drawn with the increasing openness of the courts to the possibility of post-adoption contact shown by such cases as *Re G (Adoption: Contact)* [2003] 1 FLR 270 and *Down Lisburn Health and Social Services Trust v H* [2007] 1 FLR 121: see also ACA 2002, ss 46(6) and 51A.
[44] Section 34(10).
[45] Section 31(11).
[46] Note that the s 1(5) applies to s 34 orders and accordingly the court should not make an order, 'unless it considers that doing so would be better for the child than making no order at all'.
[47] Section 31(3B).
[48] Section 1(3)(c) of the Act.

## Applications and orders made of the court's own motion

**18.34** Applications for orders, 'making provision regarding contact under s 34(2) to (4) of the 1989 Act or an order varying or discharging such an order under s 34(9) of that Act' follow the procedure set out in Part 12 of the Family Procedure Rules 2010.[49] They are, 'specified proceedings'[50] so the child is an automatic respondent to the application[51] and the court is required to appoint an officer of Cafcass (or a Welsh family proceedings officer where applicable) as the child's guardian unless satisfied that this is not necessary.[52] The, 'person whose contact with the child is the subject of the application' is also an automatic respondent.[53]

**18.35** An application for an order for allowing contact between the child and any named person may be made on an application by the local authority or by the child.[54] A person named in s 34(1)(a) to (d) or any other person who has obtained leave[55] to make an application may apply for an order that contact be allowed between the child and the person applying.[56]

**18.36** The court has power to vary or discharge an order under s 34 on the application of, 'the local authority, the child concerned or the person named in the order'.[57]

**18.37** However, s 91(17) of the Act provides that:

'Where –

(a) a person has made an application for an order under section 34;
(b) the application has been refused; and
(c) a period of less than six months has elapsed since the refusal,

that person may not make a further application for such an order with respect to the same child, unless he has obtained the leave of the court.'

**18.38** Furthermore, in *Re T (Termination of Contact: Discharge of Order)*[58] the Court of Appeal held that there must be a, 'material change of circumstances' between the making of an order and the application for it to be discharged if that application is to be granted. As Simon Brown LJ put it:

---

[49] See r 12.2.
[50] Section 41(6)(f) of the 1989 Act.
[51] Rule 12.3.
[52] Section 41(1) of the 1989 Act.
[53] Rule 12.3.
[54] Section 34(2).
[55] See below as to the grant of leave.
[56] Section 34(3)
[57] Section 34(9).
[58] [1997] 1 FLR 517.

'Clearly such an application[59] must be considered by the court, and considered indeed with the child's welfare in mind as the paramount consideration – save only in the very limited circumstances provided for by s 91(17) when the court's leave is required.

That said, it is plain that there must be demonstrable some material change of circumstance between the making of the s 34(4) order and the application to discharge it: the courts are obviously entitled to screen out what are essentially no more than disguised appeals against the original orders.'[60]

**18.39** In addition to its power to determine an application for an order, the court has a wide power to make orders under s 34 of its own motion. Section 34(5) provides that:

'When making a care order with respect to a child, or in any family proceedings in connection with a child who is in the care of a local authority, the court may make an order under this section, even though no application for such an order has been made with respect to the child, if it considers that the order should be made.'

**18.40** This mirrors the court's power to make child arrangements (including as to contact), prohibited steps and specific issue orders despite there being no application before the court.[61] Note that it allows the court to make any order under the section, which could include an order authorising the refusal of contact under s 34(4).

## Leave to apply for contact

**18.41** A person seeking contact with a child in care who does not fall within the terms of s 34(1)(a) to (d) requires leave of the court to make an application in accordance with s 34(3)(b). Any such application should be made in accordance with the procedure set out in Part 18 of the Family Procedure Rules 2010. Section 34 does not contain a statutory test for the grant of leave to make an application for contact.

**18.42** In the well-known case of *Re M (Care: Contact: Grandmother's Application for Leave)*[62] the Court of Appeal held that although the test for leave to make a s 8 order set out in s 10(9)[63] of the CA 1989 does not govern

---

[59] In the case before the court, mother sought to discharge an order under s 34(4) authorising a refusal to allow her to have contact with the child, that order being made some 2 years previously at the time of the final order in care proceedings.
[60] At p 526.
[61] Section 10(1)(b) of the 1989 Act.
[62] [1995] 2 FLR 86.
[63] Which provides that:
'Where the person applying for leave to make an application for a s 8 order is not the child concerned, the court shall, in deciding whether or not to grant leave, have particular regard to
(a) the nature of the proposed application for the s 8 order;
(b) the applicant's connection with the child;
(c) any risk there might be of that proposed application disrupting the child's life to such an

an application for leave to apply for contact with a child in care the factors set out in that subsection are relevant to such an application. Ward LJ explains why in the following terms:[64]

> 'It is equally clear, however, from s 10(9)(d) that children in care may be the object of s 10(9) applications and that must include an application for a residence order. If the court were faced with an application by a grandparent for leave to apply for a residence order, alternatively a contact order, it would be anomalous, in my judgment, were the court not to take into account for the exercise of the s 34(3) discretion the criteria specifically laid out for consideration in s 10(9). Those particular factors seem to me to be also apposite for s 34(3).'

**18.43** His Lordship went on to observe that the court must, 'have regard to all the circumstances of the case' and to make observations as to what circumstances might lead to the grant or refusal of leave.[65]

**18.44** The Court of Appeal returned to the issue of leave to make applications in relation to a child in care in the case of *Re J (Leave to Issue Applications for Residence Order)*.[66] As the name of the case indicates, the issue before the Court of Appeal was as to the grant of leave to make a residence[67] application. However, the observations of Thorpe LJ are important in considering an application for leave to apply for contact. He has this to say about the approach to leave applications in general set out by Ward LJ, in particular having regard to the increased recognition of both the importance to a child of their wider family and of human rights considerations:

> '[15] The decision of this court in *Re M (Care: Contact: Grandmother's Application for Leave)* was centred upon a consideration in another section of the statute, s 34(3), where the court is required to determine an application in relation to contact with children in care made by a person defined by subs (1). But in the course of his judgment, Ward LJ, recognising that s 10(9) did not directly govern applications for contact for a child in care, held that, nonetheless, it would be anomalous if the court, in exercising its discretion under s 34, did not have in mind the criteria contained in s 10(9). He held that those criteria were also apposite for applications brought under s 34(3). He went on to say that, in exercising the discretion under s 34, the court must have regard to: (a) the nature of the contact sought; (b) the applicant's connection to the child; (c) any disruption or risk to the child or risk to the child brought about by the proposed application; and (d) the wishes of the parents and the local authority on the issue. By that route, Ward LJ was importing into the s 34 exercise the four statutory criteria that Parliament had applied in s 10(9).

---

    extent that he would be harmed by it; and
    (d) where the child is being looked after by a local authority –
      (i) the authority's plans for the child's future; and
      (ii) the wishes and feelings of the child's parents.'
[64] At p 95.
[65] Pages 95–97 and 98–99.
[66] [2003] 1 FLR 114.
[67] Now a 'live with' child arrangements order: s 8(1)(a).

[16] Ward LJ went on to say that, in weighing up the factors, the court should apply the following test:

"(1) If the application is frivolous or vexatious or otherwise an abuse of the process of the court, of course it will fail.

(2) If the application for leave fails to disclose that there is any eventual real prospect of success, if those prospects of success are remote so that the application is obviously unsustainable, then it must also be dismissed: see *W v Ealing London Borough Council* [1993] 2 FLR 788, approving *Cheshire County Council v M* [1993] 1 FLR 463.

(3) The applicant must satisfy the court that there is a serious issue to try and must present a good arguable case . . ."

[17] I would observe that all that is said directly in relation to the discharge of the judicial task under s 34(3) and not directly in relation to the discharge of the judicial task under s 10(9). In my experience, trial judges have interpreted the decision in *Re M (Care: Contact: Grandmother's Application for Leave)* as requiring them, in the determination of applications under s 10(9) to apply the three-fold test formulated by Ward LJ which has the laudable purpose of excluding from the litigation exercise applications which are plainly hopeless.

[18] I am particularly anxious at the development of a practice that seems to substitute the test, 'has the applicant satisfied the court that he or she has a good arguable case' for the test that Parliament applied in s 10(9). That anxiety is heightened in modern times where applicants under s 10(9) manifestly enjoy Art 6 rights to a fair trial and, in the nature of things, are also likely to enjoy Art 8 rights.

[19] Whilst the decision in *Re M (Care: Contact: Grandmother's Application for Leave)* no doubt served a valuable purpose in its day and in relation to s 34(3) applications, it is important that trial judges should recognise the greater appreciation that has developed of the value of what grandparents have to offer, particularly to children of disabled parents. Judges should be careful not to dismiss such opportunities without full inquiry. That seems to me to be the minimum essential protection of Arts 6 and 8 rights that Mrs J enjoys, given the very sad circumstances of the family.'

**18.45** Although *Re J (Leave to Issue Application for Residence Order)* is, as His Lordship is careful to point out, not concerned with an application for leave to apply under s 34 it is suggested that his observations as to the recognising importance of wider family, the need to protect Art 6 and 8 rights and to be cautious not to dismiss the possibility of wider family having a role without, 'full inquiry' are all highly relevant to applications for permission to apply under s 34.

**18.46** Sumner J drew together the observations of Ward and Thorpe LJJ in the case of *Re W (Care Proceedings: Leave to Apply)*.[68] In this case the appellant, a

---

[68] [2005] 2 FLR 468.

maternal aunt of the child in question, had not made a specific application for leave to apply for contact but did seek to be joined as a party so as to be heard by the court on the issue of contact. Sumner J held that the same test should apply whether or not a separate application was made.[69] As to that test he had this to say:

> '[28] Before me all counsel have agreed and I accept that the test in s 10(9) applies in considering applications under s 34(3). The decision in *Re M* remains good law for that proposition. The test is as set out in the first two propositions identified by Ward LJ in *Re M*. In particular the second proposition is not intended, on a proper construction, to set any positive merits test. That second test, it will be recalled, is in these terms:
>
>> "If the application for leave fails to disclose that there is any eventual real prospects of success, if those prospects of success are remote so that the application is obviously unsustainable, then it must also be dismissed."
>
> [29] I suggested to counsel that it is really the two different sides of the same coin. It does not require a party to show that there is any eventual real prospect of success. What it does require is for the court to say that, if the prospects of success are remote so that the application is obviously unsustainable, then it must be dismissed. Accordingly, the proper test is the particular matters referred to under s 10(9) and the two matters to which Ward LJ referred in *Re M*.
>
> [30] Section 10(9) speaks of the court having particular regard to four different matters. In my judgment, that means that the court, in considering an application for leave under s 10(9) or s 34(3), is exercising a discretion. The fact that the court is to have regard to certain specified matters does not mean that other considerations are not to be considered. It is only that the four matters mentioned are to be those to which the court has a particular regard. Thus it follows that the full inquiry to which Thorpe LJ referred in *Re J* would be part of the exercise of that discretion.
>
> [31] Equally, the two tests proposed by Ward LJ also would fall under the same category of the exercise of discretion. The first is whether the application is frivolous or vexatious, the second is whether the application is obviously unsustainable.
>
> [32] There are other considerations to which the reported cases refer. One of those is whether any application which the applicant has in mind has any independent or separate point of view to be put forward. In other words, is it an application where the interests identified are identical to those of another person who is a party to the proceedings?
>
> [33] One can envisage that in some cases this may amount to a positive disadvantage to join someone as a party. It could come under s 10(9)(c):

---

[69] See at para [47]: His Lordship commented that he was satisfied that behind her application to be joined as a party there lay a wish to obtain an order for contact that was more extensive than proposed by the local authority.

"any risk that might be of that proposed application disrupting the child's life to such an extent that he would be harmed by it;"

I am satisfied that where a person has no independent or separate point of view or is putting forward an interest identical to another person who is a party to proceedings, then it is unlikely that the court would permit them to become a party in their own right.'

**18.47** In the light of Thorpe LJ's comments about the need for a, 'full inquiry', His Lordship goes into the background in some detail, notes that it was envisaged that the aunt would have joint contact along with the maternal grandmother (who was already a party) and concludes that the appellant aunt did not have a separate position that required separate representation before the court. He accordingly dismissed the appeal.

**18.48** His Lordship's point about the need to show an, 'independent and separate' position is an important one in any application to become party to a care case[70] and, as he makes clear, is a factor in the court's discretionary exercise in granting or refusing leave to apply for an order in respect of contact. However, it is salutary to note that the aunt's motives for seeking to become a party to the case were that she feared that if she was not she would be, 'shunned by the local authority' and marginalised in the child's life.[71] Disputes of this nature should be capable of being avoided if local authorities have proper regard to their duties in promoting contact with important family members and to the principles of working in collaboration with a child's family whenever possible.[72]

## Variation of contact arrangements without reference to the court

**18.49** Although not strictly speaking matters of the court's powers, this is a convenient point to note that the Care Planning, Placement and Case Review (England) Regulations 2010, reg 8, provide that:

'(4) The responsible authority may depart from the terms of any order made under section 34 by agreement with the person in relation to whom the order is made, provided that –

(a) C[73], being of sufficient age and understanding, also agrees, and
(b) written notification of the specified information is given within five working days to the persons listed in paragraph (2).[74]

---

[70] The authorities that His Lordship cites for this very well established proposition are *Re M (Minors) (Sexual Abuse: Evidence)* [1993] 1 FLR 822 and *North Yorkshire County Council v G* [1993] 2 FLR 732.
[71] Her concerns as set out by Sumner J at para [20].
[72] It is interesting to note that in *Re W* the local authority agreed to a recital in the court's order as to consideration of the wishes of the aunt as to contact and communication with her: see at para [54].
[73] The child concerned.
[74] These persons are the child, any parent, any person who had care of the child before the care

(5) Where the responsible authority has decided to vary or suspend any arrangements made (otherwise than under an order under section 34) with a view to affording any person contact with C, the responsible authority must immediately give written notification containing the specified information[75] to the persons listed in paragraph (2).'

**18.50** Whilst courts have commented on the usefulness of the flexibility to agree changes in contact arrangements allowed by reg 8(4)[76], the importance of reg 8(5) should not be underestimated. As noted above, court statistics show that orders under s 34 regulate contact for only a relatively small percentage of all children in care. For other children, and therefore their parents, wider family and other connected persons, contact occurs as a result of 'arrangements' made outside of the structure of s 34 orders. Regulation 8(5) imposes a clear duty on the local authority to act openly and transparently should it decide that such arrangements should be changed and to provide parents and others with the basic information they need in order to consider seeking a remedy under s 34. As noted above, a decision to suspend contact between the child and a person with whom the local authority has a duty to allow them, 'reasonable contact' in accordance with s 34(1) of the Act will in practice be followed by an application for authority for permission to refuse such contact under s 34(4).

---

order was made by virtue of an order made under the Inherent Jurisdiction of the High Court, 'any other person whose wishes and feelings the responsible authority consider to be relevant' and the Independent Reviewing Officer.

[75] See reg 8(3).
[76] See for example comments of Thorpe LJ in *Re W (Section 34(2) Orders)* (above) at p 509.

# Part 5

# CARE PROCEEDINGS: FINAL HEARINGS AND FINAL ORDERS

# CHAPTER 19

# PREPARATION FOR FINAL HEARINGS

## SEPARATE FACT FINDING OR THRESHOLD HEARING

**19.1** In exceptional cases, it may be decided prior to the issues resolution hearing ('IRH') that a separate threshold or fact finding hearing is necessary. Such a hearing will be completed prior to the final hearing, in order to decide disputed facts that cannot await the final determination of the matter. Incorporating a separate fact finding or threshold hearing is known as having a 'split' hearing.

**19.2** Once a fact has been determined by the court to be true, it can then be relied upon when looking at assessments or plans for the child. If it is found to be false, it cannot. Consideration should be given to whether a separate hearing is needed as early as possible so as to ensure that the final hearing can be concluded within the 26 weeks required by statute. If the issues to be resolved are extensive, and the matter is complicated, it may be necessary to consider whether the 26-week timetable will need to be extended (see chapter 10 for further discussion of this).

### Decision to undertake a split hearing

**19.3** The President of the Family Division issued guidance in relation to split hearings in 2010, following a series of cases in which the Court of Appeal had expressed growing concern at the delay and complications arising in cases with split hearings. Prior to the President's Guidance on the matter, it was not unusual for hearings to be split and for the court to adjudicate the facts relied upon by the local authority to establish threshold, separate from the 'welfare' hearing to consider what arrangements (if any) should be in place. The Guidance defines a split hearing as follows:[1]

> 'A hearing divided into two parts, during the first of which the court makes findings of fact on issues either identified by the parties or the court, and during the second part of which the court, based on the findings which it has made, decides the case.'

**19.4** PD12J of the Family Procedure Rules 2010 ('FPR 2010') supersedes the President's guidance and applies equally to public and private law matters.

---

[1] *Guidance in Relation to Split Hearings* [2010] 2 FCR 271 at [4].

**19.5** The decision as to whether there should be a split hearing is a decision for the court alone, not for the parties. When an application is made for a split hearing, the court will consider contained the factors set out in para 17 of PD12J.

**19.6** The President's guidance is clear that 'a fact finding hearing should only be ordered if the court takes the view that the case cannot properly be decided without such a hearing'. It continues:[2]

> 'Even when the court comes to the conclusion that a fact finding hearing is necessary, it by no means follows that such a hearing needs to be separate from the substantive hearing. In nearly every case, the court's findings of fact inform its conclusions. In my judgment it will be a rare case in which a separate fact finding hearing is necessary.'

**19.7** In *Re S (A Child)*, Ryder LJ considered split hearings in the context of the overriding objective, stating:[3]

> 'A split hearing is only justifiable where the delay occasioned is in furtherance of the overriding objective in rule 1 FPR 2010.'

**19.8** He further commented that:[4]

> 'Unless the basis for such a decision is reasoned so that the inevitable delay is justified it will be wrong in principle in public law children proceedings. Even where it is asserted that delay will not be occasioned, the use of split hearings must be confined to those cases where there is a stark or discrete issue to be determined and an early conclusion on that issue will enable the substantive determination (i.e. whether a statutory order is necessary) to be made more expeditiously.'

**19.9** In the past, local authorities have pursued split hearings so that they could use the determinations as the basis for their applications for assessments. Ryder LJ addressed this directly and said:[5]

> 'The oft repeated but erroneous justification for them, that a split hearing enables a social care assessment to be undertaken is simply poor social work and forensic practice …
>
> In so far as it is necessary to express a risk formulation as a precursor to an analysis or a recommendation to the Court, that can be done by basing the same on each of the alternative factual scenarios that the Court is being asked to consider.'

**19.10** In some cases it will be fairly obvious that a split hearing will be necessary. In cases such as *Re S (A Child)* which concerned non-accidental

---

[2] *Guidance in Relation to Split Hearings* [2010] 2 FCR 271 at [7].
[3] *Re S (A Child)* [2014] EWCA Civ 25 at [31].
[4] *Re S (A Child)* [2014] EWCA Civ 25 at [27].
[5] *Re S (A Child)* [2014] EWCA Civ 25 at [29]–[30].

injuries, it was clear that a split hearing was required so that the court could be satisfied as to how the injuries had been sustained before the court moving on to the second part of its assessment.

**19.11** The Court of Appeal in *Re S* provided the following guidance:

(1) Split hearings should occur only within:
   (a) the most complex cases, where death or very serious medical issues had arisen and where accurate medical diagnosis is integral to the future care of the child concerned;
   (b) cases where there is only one factual issue to be decided and where the threshold criteria would not be satisfied if a finding could not be made, thereby concluding proceedings.
(2) Local authorities must take extra care in how they draft their threshold documents in cases where the subject child has received an injury.
(3) A decision as to whether a split hearing is necessary should be reasoned in court at the case management hearing and the reasons should be recorded on the face of the case management order.

**19.12** The court must take care to ensure that only the facts are dealt with at a split hearing. The court should not stray into considering matters that go to welfare decisions for the child and must be careful not to prejudge the outcome of the care proceedings, no matter how clear things may appear at the end of the fact finding.[6]

## *Preparation for a split hearing*

**19.13** Paragraph 19 of PD12J of the FPR 2010 sets out what directions must be made in preparation of the hearing. Most importantly, the local authority must provide a schedule of the findings sought, detailing the facts that they wish to establish. This document must make reference to the evidence before the court, in accordance with Munby P's comments in *Re A (A Child)*.[7]

**19.14** Parents must have the opportunity to respond to the local authority's schedule of findings sought, and their response will assist the court in deciding what evidence is necessary for the matter to be conducted fairly.

**19.15** The judge is not bound by the schedule prepared by the local authority and can find facts that have not been explicitly sought after hearing the evidence. It goes without saying, that the court must ensure that any additional findings are securely founded in the evidence heard and that the fairness of the fact finding process has not compromised.[8]

---

[6] *Re L (Care Proceedings: Risk Assessment)* [2010] 1 FLR 790.
[7] *Re A (A Child)* [2015] EWFC 11.
[8] *Re G and B (Fact-Finding Hearing)* [2009] 1 FLR 1145.

## Parties in a split hearing

**19.16** On occasion, findings may be sought against individuals who are not party to the proceedings, for example, the partner of one of the parents. If findings are being sought against a non-party, this must be established as early as possible, the non-party given notice that findings are sought against them, and invited to intervene in the proceedings. The court will usually invite the individual to attend court to confirm whether they intend to become involved or not.

**19.17** There is no right for a non-party against whom findings are sought to intervene in the proceedings, and each case must be determined on its own facts.[9] The overriding objective contained in r 1.1 of the FPR 2010 will form part of this determination.

**19.18** Intervenors do not have access to non-means, non-merits tested legal aid, and it may be that an intervenor will not be represented at the fact finding hearing if they cannot afford legal representation (see chapter 12 for further discussion on representation).

## CASE MANAGEMENT FOR A FINAL HEARING

**19.19** If matters cannot be concluded at the IRH, then the court will make case management decisions in preparation for the final hearing. The court will consider the length of the hearing, any further evidence that needs to be filed and what live evidence will be required.

## Issue resolutions hearing

**19.20** The purpose of an IRH is to see whether matters can be concluded without continuing to a final hearing, and if not, narrow the issues that need to be determined. This is the final interim hearing that is provided for in the PLO.[10]

**19.21** PD12A sets out in tabular form, how the court and the parties should approach the IRH. Pursuant to PD12A, there should be an advocates' meeting no later than 7 days prior to the IRH. This is to ensure that the remaining key issues are clear and the parties' positions crystalised so at the IRH, that the court can be fully appraised of what is agreed and what still needs to be determined. At the meeting, the advocates should:

(1) Review evidence and the positions of the parties.
(2) Identify the advocates' views of:
    (a) the remaining key issues and how the issues may be resolved or narrowed at the IRH including by the making of final orders;

---

[9] *Re H (Care Proceedings: Intervener)* [2000] 1 FLR 775.
[10] FPR 2010, r 12.25(3).

(b) the further evidence which is required to be heard to enable the key issues to be resolved or narrowed at the IRH;
(c) the evidence that is relevant and the witnesses that are required at the final hearing;
(d) the need for a contested hearing and/or time for oral evidence to be given at the IRH.
(3) Local authority advocate to:
 (a) notify the court immediately of the outcome of the discussion at the meeting;
 (b) file a draft case management order with the court by 11a.m. on the business day before the IRH.

**19.22** It is possible to hear oral evidence at the IRH if the issues are so narrow that only short evidence is necessary and all of the written evidence is before the court. If the contested matter requires longer than the time estimate for the IRH, a final hearing will need to be listed.

**19.23** At the IRH the court will consider the following issues and make directions accordingly:

(1) the key issues (if any) to be determined, and the extent to which those issues can be resolved or narrowed at the IRH;
(2) whether the IRH can be used as a final hearing;
(3) whether it is possible to resolve or narrows the issues by hearing evidence within the IRH time estimate;
(4) what evidence is to be heard on the issues which remain to be resolved at the final hearing;
(5) what final case management directions are required including:
 (a) any extension of the timetable for the proceedings which is necessary;
 (b) filing of the threshold agreement or a statement of facts/issues remaining to be determined;
 (c) filing of:
  (i) final evidence and care plan;
  (ii) case analysis for final hearing (if required);
  (iii) witness templates;
  (iv) skeleton arguments;
 (d) judicial reading list/reading time, including time estimate and an estimate for judgment writing time;
 (e) ensuring compliance with PD27A ('the Bundles Practice Direction');
 (f) listing the final hearing.

**19.24** At the conclusion of the IRH then, the matter will have been concluded, either by way of agreement or short evidence, or listed for a final hearing.

## Final decisions for the child

**19.25** If there has been a separate fact finding hearing, the final hearing will be limited to considering the welfare of the child and the plans for their long term care. If there has been no fact finding, at the final hearing the court will need to consider whether there are any factual disputes that need to be determined to establish threshold, as well as considering the long term welfare and care of the child. At the IRH the issues should have been narrowed sufficiently to make the remaining differences between the parties clear.

## FILING EVIDENCE

**19.26** The evidence placed before the court must enable it to determine whether a final care order or supervision order should be made.

**19.27** The court requires the best evidence possible to determine the application before it and the local authority should ensure that the evidence that they produce is based on clear information that is able to be tested by the court.[11]

### Preparation of evidence

**19.28** In *Re A (A Child)*, Munby P reminded practitioners of the evidential basis that the local authority must meet in order for a court to properly consider making a care order or supervision order.[12]

**19.29** There are three, fundamental principles that must be adhered to in s 31 applications:

(1) It is for the local authority to prove, on the balance of probabilities, the facts upon it which it seeks to rely, adducing proper evidence to that end.
(2) In doing so, they must establish the link between facts relied upon in a threshold document and the conclusion that the child has suffered, or is at risk of suffering, significant harm.
(3) Society must be willing to tolerate very diverse standards of parenting and the courts are not in the business of social engineering.

**19.30** For the local authority to prove, on the balance of probabilities, the facts upon which it seeks to rely must be based on evidence and not on suspicion or speculation. The President endorsed the judgment in *Re A (A Child) (No 2)*.[13]

**19.31** Reliance is often placed upon material found in local authority case records or social work chronologies. This is hearsay. A local authority which is

---

[11] In accordance with *Re A (A Child)* [2015] EWFC 11.
[12] *Re A (A Child)* [2015] EWFC 11.
[13] *Re A (A Child) (No 2)* [2011] EWCA Civ 12.

unwilling or unable to produce the witnesses who can speak of matters first-hand, may find itself in difficulties if a parent goes into a witness box and denies it.

**19.32** It is a common feature of care proceedings that a local authority will assert that a parent does not admit, recognise or acknowledge something that is of concern to the local authority. In such cases, the local authority must prove both that the incident in question actually happened, and that it has the significance they have attributed to it in terms of the impact upon the care afforded to the child is concerned.

**19.33** Threshold documents should not include references to things that various people have 'stated' or 'reported'. Allegations must be limited to things that have happened; not merely reported to have happened.

**19.34** Moreover, the local authority's evidence and submissions must explain explicitly *why* a significant risk of harm follows from the facts. In *Re A (A Child) (No 2)*, the President endorsed the judgment of Macur LJ in *Re Y (A Child)*, agreed by both Arden and Ryder LJJ:[14]

> 'No analysis appears to have been made by any of the professionals as to why the mother's particular lies created the likelihood of significant harm to these children and what weight should reasonably be afforded to the fact of her deceit in the overall balance.'

**19.35** Since the burden of proof rests firmly on the local authority, it is clear that their evidence must be prepared thoroughly and responded to carefully by the respondents.

**19.36** Part 22 of the FPR 2010 rules provides for the preparation, filing and form of evidence placed before the court. The court has the power under r 22.1 to control the evidence that is filed within the proceedings, giving directions as to the issues on which it requires evidence, and the nature and way in which such evidence should be placed before the court. This includes written and oral evidence provided from the parties.

**19.37** The general rule contained within r 22.2 of the FPR 2010 is that any fact which needs to be proved by witness evidence should be done so via oral evidence at a final hearing; and written evidence at any other hearing.

**19.38** PD22A of the FPR 2010 provides for the form a witness statement should take. The provisions include how the statement should be structured as well as the signing of the document and the 'statement of truth' that should be included along with the person's signature.

**19.39** It is important that the person signing the witness statement is fully aware that the information they are providing must be true and will stands as

---

[14] *Re A (A Child) (No 2)* [2011] EWCA Civ 12 at [13].

their evidence before the court. Witnesses giving evidence will be cross-examined on the matters contained within their statement and so care should be taken to ensure that everything that appears in the statement is true.

## Local authority evidence

**19.40** In preparation for the final hearing, the local authority must prepare a final statement together with a final care plan for the children. For a full discussion of the final care plan, see chapter 22.

**19.41** The local authority's final evidence will contain a proposal for the final plan for the child including an analysis of the child's situation based on the evidence before it, with reasons for the proposals.

**19.42** The local authority's final statement must consider the possible alternative plans for the child and set out why they have concluded that the support available cannot adequately safeguard the child. The pros and cons of each potential plan for the child must be set out with a balanced analysis of each option.

**19.43** If the local authority's care plan is for adoption, the matter must have been considered by the local authority's decision maker and a decision made that adoption is in the best interests of the child (see chapter 28).

**19.44** The level of analysis required when the court is being asked to consider making a care order for adoption is clearly set out in *Re BS (Children)* in which the President voiced concerns:[15]

> 'We have real concerns, shared by other judges, about the recurrent inadequacy of the analysis and reasoning put forward in support of the case for adoption both in the materials put before the court by the local authorities and guardian and also in too many judgments.'

**19.45** Earlier in the same judgement, the President emphasised the remarks of Baroness Hale in *Re B*:[16]

> 'The language used in *Re B* is striking. Different words and phrases are used, but the message is clear. Orders contemplating non-consensual adoption – care orders with a plan for adoption, placement orders and adoption orders – are "a very extreme thing, a last resort", only to be made where "nothing else will do", where "no other course [is] possible in [the child's] interests", they are "the most extreme option", a "last resort – when all else fails", to be made "only in exceptional circumstances and where motivated by overriding requirements pertaining to the child's welfare, in short, where nothing else will do": see *Re B* paras 74, 76, 77, 82, 104, 130, 135, 145, 198, 215.'

---

[15] *Re BS (Children)* [2013] EWCA Civ 1146 at [30].
[16] *Re BS (Children)* [2013] EWCA Civ 1146 at [22].

**19.46** He continued, highlighting the considerations of McFarlane J in *Re G*:[17]

'A process which acknowledges that long-term public care, and in particular adoption contrary to the will of a parent, is "the most draconian option", yet does not engage with the very detail of that option which renders it "draconian" cannot be a full or effective process of evaluation.'

**19.47** It is clear then, that since non-consensual adoption represents a draconian step, the court must consider all other possibilities before it to ensure that no lesser order which does not involve the severance of all family ties by way of adoption, is available.

**19.48** In the absence of this analysis, the court will not be in a position to conclude that no other options are not available for the child.

## Evidence of the guardian

**19.49** The guardian will meet with the parties and the children to investigate the circumstances of the family, and provide an analysis to assist the court in determining the application. In the exercise of their duties, the children's guardian has the right to access the documents held by the local authority under s 42 of the Children Act 1989 ('CA 1989').

**19.50** PD16A, para 6.6 provides that:

'The children's guardian must advise the court on the following matters –

a. whether the child is of sufficient understanding for any purpose including the child's refusal to submit to a medical or psychiatric examination or other assessment that the court has the power to require, direct or order;
b. the wishes of the child in respect of any matter relevant to the proceedings including that child's attendance at court;
c. the appropriate forum for the proceedings;
d. the appropriate timing of the proceedings or any part of them;
e. the options available to it in respect of the child and the suitability of each such option including what order should be made in determining the application; and
f. any other matter on which the court seeks advice or on which the children's guardian considers that the court should be informed.'

**19.51** As a result of the guardian's investigation and analysis of the circumstances of the family, the guardian may come to a position that is in opposition to that of the child they represent. For example, it may be that the guardian will support the long term removal of the child from their parents, but the child does not agree. The guardian must inform the court of the child's wishes and feelings in relation to matters such as contact and the long term plans for them, but ultimately will come to their own conclusions on the recommendations to be made to the court.

---

[17] *Re BS (Children)* [2013] EWCA Civ 1146 at [41].

**19.52** For a discussion as to the implications of the guardian's recommendations when at odds with the child's views, see chapter 12.

## BUNDLES

### Practice Direction 27A

**19.53** The local authority is responsible for lodging bundles prior to court hearings according to the requirements contained in PD27A of the FPR 2010. PD 27A, para 4.1 provides:

> 'The bundle shall contain copies of only those documents which are relevant to the hearing and which it is necessary for the court to read or which will actually be referred to during the hearing.'

**19.54** This prevents large bundles containing all of the documents ever produced in a case being sent to the court. However, this can cause difficulties in the event that it becomes necessary to consider other documents throughout the course of the hearing, so the local authority should ensure that anything potentially relevant is available.

**19.55** PD27A, para 4.2 sets out how the bundle should be arranged and what should be contained within it:

> 'The documents in the bundle shall be arranged in chronological order from the front of the bundle, paginated individually and consecutively (starting with page 1 and using Arabic numbering throughout), indexed and divided into separate sections (each section being separately paginated) as follows –
>
> a. preliminary documents (see paragraph 4.3) and any other case management documents required by any other practice direction;
> b. applications and orders;
> c. statements and affidavits (which must be dated in the top right corner of the front page) but without exhibiting or duplicating documents referred to in para 4.1;
> d. care plans (where appropriate);
> e. experts' reports and other reports (including those of a guardian, children's guardian or litigation friend); and
> f. other documents, divided into further sections as may be appropriate.
>
> All statements, affidavits, care plans, experts' reports and other reports included in the bundle must be copies of originals which have been signed and dated.'

**19.56** Furthermore, PD27A, para 4.3 provides that:

> 'At the commencement of the bundle there shall be inserted the following documents (the preliminary documents) –

a. an up to date case summary of the background to the hearing confined to those matters which are relevant to the hearing and the management of the case and limited, if practicable, to four A4 pages;
b. a statement of the issue or issues to be determined (1) at that hearing and (2) at the final hearing;
c. a position statement by each party including a summary of the order or directions sought by that party (1) at that hearing and (2) at the final hearing;
d. an up to date chronology, if it is a final hearing or if the summary under (i) is insufficient;
e. skeleton arguments, if appropriate;
f. a list of essential reading for that hearing; and
g. the time estimate (see paragraph 10.1).

Copies of all authorities relied on must be contained in a separate composite bundle agreed between the advocates.'

**19.57** The local authority will prepare the case summary as well as the statement of issues and chronology. Each of the respondents will prepare a position statement, which is a document prepared by the legal representatives of the respondents based on the instructions received from their clients. It should set out the parties' positions and outline what the party seeks the court to determine. In the event a respondent is a litigant in person, they must prepare a document and may have assistance in doing so.

**19.58** PD27A, para 5.1 specifies that the bundle should be contained in one A4 size ring binder or lever arch file, and should not exceed 350 sheets of A4 paper and 350 sides of text. The bundles should also be printed on one side of the paper unless agreed otherwise by the court.

**19.59** The bundle should be lodged with the court 2 working days prior to the hearing[18] and all parties should have a paginated index 4 working days prior to the hearing in order to enable the bundles to be prepared.[19]

---

[18] FPR 2010, PD27A, para 6.3.
[19] FPR 2010, PD27A, para 6.1.

# CHAPTER 20

# THE FINAL HEARING: PRACTICAL CONSIDERATIONS

**20.1** The final hearing represents the point at which the court will consider all of the evidence adduced against the relevant legal tests and considerations, in order to make final decisions about the long-term plans for the children that accord with their best interests and the family's human rights.

## THE COURT'S CONSIDERATIONS: THRESHOLD AND WELFARE

**20.2** The first stage of the court's task at a final hearing is to consider whether threshold has been met. The court must consider the test set out at s 31(2) of the Children Act 1989 ('CA 1989'):

'A court may only make a care order or supervision order if it is satisfied –

(a) that the child concerned is suffering, or is likely to suffer, significant harm; and
(b) that the harm, or likelihood of harm, is attributable to –
   (i) the care given to the child, or likely to be given to him if the order were not made, not being what it would be reasonable to expect a parent to give to him; or
   (ii) the child's being beyond parental control.'

**20.3** Once the court is satisfied that the threshold has been crossed, it must then proceed to the second stage of its task: considering the long-term plan for the child. The care plan must be in the child's best interests, in accordance with the welfare checklist set out at s 1(3) of the CA 1989 (for a full discussion of welfare considerations see chapters 14 and 21).

**20.4** 'Welfare' is not confined to a child's minority. Munby LJ (as he then was) has previously endorsed Sir Thomas Bingham's comments in *Re O (Contact: Imposition of Conditions)*, that a child's welfare should be considered throughout the child's minority and 'into and through adulthood'.[1] Although *Re O* was a private law matter, Munby P considered that it had a *'wider resonance'*, but how far into the future one looks, will depend on the question before the court.

---

[1] *Re G* [2012] EWCA Civ 1233 at [26].

**20.5** 'Welfare' is a difficult thing to pin down, and one person's idea of the standard of welfare to be applied might be different from another. Munby LJ held that the standard to be applied by the court is that of reasonable men and women in today's world:[2]

> '[...] not by the standards of their parents in 1970, and having regard to the ever changing nature of our world: changes in our understanding of the natural world, technological changes, changes in social standards and, perhaps most important of all, changes in social attitudes.'

**20.6** Moreover, he held that, the court must take a holistic approach to the evaluation of a child's welfare:[3]

> 'Evaluating a child's best interests involves a welfare appraisal in the widest sense, taking into account, where appropriate, a wide range of ethical, social, moral, religious, cultural, emotional and welfare considerations. Everything that conduces to a child's welfare and happiness or relates to the child's development and present and future life as a human being, including the child's familial, educational and social environment, and the child's social, cultural, ethnic and religious community, is potentially relevant and has, where appropriate, to be taken into account.'

**20.7** By extension then, he held that it is important to recognise that a child's welfare cannot be assessed in isolation:[4]

> 'It is only by considering the child's network of relationships that their well-being can be properly considered. So a child's relationships, both within and without the family, are always relevant to the child's interests; often they will be determinative.'

**20.8** It is upon this basis that the Children Act 1989 operates. However, as Thorpe LJ remarked in *Re S (Adult Patient: Sterilisation)* 'it would be undesirable and probably impossible to set bounds to what is relevant to a welfare determination'.[5] The court must and will always consider all cases on their own facts.

## Threshold and the burden of proof

**20.9** Full discussion in relation to the final threshold document required can be found at chapter 19. The burden of proof rests with the local authority and their case must be established on the civil standard of proof: the balance of probabilities. In *Re BR (Proof of Facts)*,[6] Jackson J reiterated that there is no special standard of proof in care proceedings:

---

[2] *Re G* [2012] EWCA Civ 1233 at [33].
[3] *Re G* [2012] EWCA Civ 1233 at [27].
[4] *Re G* [2012] EWCA Civ 1233 at [30].
[5] *Re S (Adult Patient: Sterilisation* [2001] Fam 15.
[6] *Re BR (Proof of facts)* [2015] EWFC 41.

'The standard of proof is the balance of probabilities: is it more likely than not that the event occurred? Neither the seriousness of the allegation, nor the seriousness of the consequences, nor the inherent probabilities alters this.'

**20.10** In *Re A (A Child)*, Munby P reminded practitioners of the evidential basis that the local authority must meet in order for a court to properly consider making a care order or supervision order.[7]

**20.11** There are three, fundamental principles that must be adhered to in s 31 applications:

(1) It is for the local authority to prove, on the balance of probabilities, the facts upon it which it seeks to rely, adducing proper evidence to that end.
(2) In doing so, they must establish the link between facts relied upon in a threshold document and the conclusion that the child has suffered, or is at risk of suffering, significant harm.
(3) Society must be willing to tolerate very diverse standards of parenting and the courts are not in the business of social engineering.

**20.12** For the local authority to prove, on the balance of probabilities, the facts upon which it seeks to rely must be based on evidence and not on suspicion or speculation. The President endorsed the judgment in *Re A (A Child) (No 2)*.[8]

**20.13** Reliance is often placed upon material found in local authority case records or social work chronologies. This is hearsay. A local authority which is unwilling or unable to produce the witnesses who can speak of matters first-hand, may find itself in difficulties if a parent goes into a witness box and denies it.

**20.14** It is a common feature of care proceedings that a local authority will assert that a parent does not admit, recognise or acknowledge something that is of concern to the local authority. In such cases, the local authority must prove both that the incident in question actually happened, and that it has the significance they have attributed to it in terms of the impact upon the care afforded to the child is concerned.

**20.15** Threshold documents should not include references to things that various people have 'stated' or 'reported'. Allegations must be limited to things that have happened; not merely reported to have happened.

**20.16** Moreover, the local authority's evidence and submissions must explain explicitly *why* a significant risk of harm follows from the facts. In *Re A (A*

---

[7] *Re A (A Child)* [2015] EWFC 11.
[8] *Re A (A Child) (No 2)* [2011] EWCA Civ 12.

*Child) (No 2)*, the President endorsed the judgment of Macur LJ in *Re Y (A Child)*, agreed by both Arden and Ryder LJJ:[9]

> 'No analysis appears to have been made by any of the professionals as to why the mother's particular lies created the likelihood of significant harm to these children and what weight should reasonably be afforded to the fact of her deceit in the overall balance.'

**20.17** Since the burden of proof rests firmly on the local authority, it is clear that their evidence must be prepared thoroughly and responded to carefully by the respondents.

## Jurisdiction

**20.18** By the time the matter has reached final hearing, issues as to whether the English and Welsh court has jurisdiction should have already been determined (see chapter 3 for further discussion on jurisdiction).

**20.19** If the care plan for the child is placement outside of the UK, the court will need to consider what orders can be made here to secure the child and whether there are any 'mirror orders' that should be sought in the receiving jurisdiction.

**20.20** These considerations are often complex and full consideration of them are outside the scope of this book, however, the court must ensure that any order made is not unenforceable. If the order is not enforceable overseas, it may not protect and secure the child in the placement proposed by the local authority.

**20.21** Consideration may be given to transferring the matter to another jurisdiction if the planned placement is outside of the UK and the final orders would be better dealt with in that jurisdiction.

## WITNESS ATTENDANCE

**20.22** The general rule on witness attendance is contained within r 22.2 of the Family Procedure Rules 2010 ('FPR 2010'). Any fact which needs to be proved by witness evidence must be done so by oral evidence at a final hearing, and by writing at any other hearing. This general rules does not apply if a practice direction or a court order states otherwise.[10]

**20.23** If the evidence is contested, the court will consider whether live evidence is necessary to enable the issues to be fully tested. If the oral evidence of a party or expert is not required, the evidence in the statement or report before the court will stand and will be treated as accepted by the parties. If a witness or

---

[9] *Re A (A Child) (No 2)* [2011] EWCA Civ 12 at [13].
[10] FPR 2010, r 22.2(2)(b).

expert is not available to give oral evidence and the evidence is challenged, the court will be invited to place limited reliance, if any reliance at all, on the evidence.

**20.24** Rule 22.6 of the FPR 2010 provides that if a party has served a witness statement that they wish to rely on, that witness must be called to give oral evidence unless the court directs otherwise or the party puts the statement in as hearsay evidence.

**20.25** A person's written statement will stand as their evidence-in-chief in a family matter and the court will need to give leave for additional questions to be asked in examination-in-chief. It is important that any errors in the written evidence before the court are highlighted and corrected in examination-in-chief, and with the court's leave extra questions may be asked to cover matters that have not been addressed in the written statements.

## Hearsay evidence

**20.26** Hearsay evidence is permitted in proceedings concerning the upbringing, maintenance or welfare of a child by virtue of Children (Admissibility of Hearsay Evidence) Order 1993.[11] However, s 4 of Civil Evidence Act 1995 provides:

> '(1) In estimating the weight (if any) to be given to hearsay evidence in civil proceedings the court shall have regard to any circumstances from which any inference can reasonably be drawn as to the reliability or otherwise of the evidence.
>
> (2) Regard may be had, in particular, to the following –
>
> > (a) whether it would have been reasonable and practicable for the party by whom the evidence was adduced to have produced the maker of the original statement as a witness;
> >
> > (b) whether the original statement was made contemporaneously with the occurrence or existence of the matters stated;
> >
> > (c) whether the evidence involves multiple hearsay;
> >
> > (d) whether any person involved had any motive to conceal or misrepresent matters;
> >
> > (e) whether the original statement was an edited account, or was made in collaboration with another or for a particular purpose;
> >
> > (f) whether the circumstances in which the evidence is adduced as hearsay are such as to suggest an attempt to prevent proper evaluation of its weight.'

**20.27** It is important to remember the President's words in *Re A (A Child)*.[12] Reliance is often placed upon material found in local authority case records or social work chronologies. This is hearsay. A local authority which is unwilling or unable to produce the witnesses who can speak of matters first-hand, may find itself in difficulties if a parent goes into a witness box and denies it.

---

[11] SI 1993/623.
[12] *Re A (A Child)* [2015] EWFC 11.

## Parents' evidence

**20.28** A parent may wish to resist giving evidence at a hearing. If a parent refuses to give evidence or to answer a particular question, the court can draw an inference that the allegation made against the parent is true.[13]

**20.29** Section 98 of the CA 1989 provides that no person is excused from giving evidence within care proceedings on the basis that they may incriminate themselves, their spouse or civil partner, of an offence. This is an exception to the general protection against self-incrimination. Section 98(2) further provides that a statement or admission made within care proceedings will not stand as evidence against the person in any criminal matter, save for a charge of perjury.

**20.30** Despite the provisions of s 98(2) of the CA 1989, the judge in *Re EC (Disclosure of Material)*[14] assured all of the witnesses who were suspected of causing the injuries sustained by a child that the evidence they gave in the care proceedings could not be disclosed into the criminal proceedings. The Court of Appeal said that the judge in such circumstances should point out that guarantees of confidentiality cannot be given. The judgment in care proceedings and transcripts of evidence can be sought by the police and may be disclosed to them to be used in the preparation of the prosecution and defence case, including when questioning witnesses during the course of the police investigation. However, these documents cannot be shown to a jury in any trial.

**20.31** Any parent that continues to refuse to answer a question or give evidence, should be warned that they may be committed to prison for contempt of court.[15]

## Children giving evidence

**20.32** The court will weigh up a number of factors when considering an application for a child to give evidence in proceedings, looking at the case as a whole but also the welfare of the child who is to give evidence, although this is not a paramount consideration.

**20.33** Section 96 of the CA 1989 considers evidence given by, or with respect to, children. It provides:

> '(1) Subsection (2) applies where a child who is called as a witness in any civil proceedings does not, in the opinion of the court, understand the nature of an oath.
>
> (2) The child's evidence may be heard by the court if, in its opinion –
>
>     (a)   he understands that it is his duty to speak the truth; and
>     (b)   he has sufficient understanding to justify his evidence being heard.'

---

[13] *Re O (Care Proceedings: Evidence)* [2004] 1 FLR 161.
[14] *Re EC (Disclosure of Material)* [1996] 2 FLR 725.
[15] *Re L-R (Children)* [2013] EWCA Civ 1129.

**20.34** In *Re W*, the Supreme Court established that there is no presumption within family proceedings that a child should not give evidence.[16] This was reiterated recently by the Court of Appeal in *Re E (A Child)*.[17]

**20.35** In *Re W*, it was acknowledged that, whilst the risk of harm to a child of giving evidence is present in every case, it will vary from case-to-case. The risk to each particular child must be evaluated by the court, with the relevant assessments discussed below.

**20.36** Guidelines in relation to children giving evidence in family proceedings were issued in *Working Party of the Family Justice Council Guidelines* by the Family Justice Council and endorsed by the President of the Family Division.[18]

## Assessment of the child

**20.37** Before a decision is made as to whether a child should give evidence in the proceedings, an assessment must be undertaken. The court must have enough information to be able to decide whether the child has sufficient understanding and whether it is in the child's interests to give evidence. This must then be balanced against the impact upon the parties' ability to have a fair trial without the child's evidence, and the impact upon the subject child in the proceedings.

**20.38** *Re E (A child)* clarified that it is the guardian who should undertake this assessment of the child.[19] The court must balance any potential harm caused to the child in giving evidence, with the impact upon the fairness of the trial if the child does not. In most cases, the child in line to give evidence will be the subject of the proceedings. If the court is concerned with a different child, consideration must be given as to whether it is appropriate for the guardian to undertake the assessment. It may be that an independent social worker is better placed to undertake this work and this decision should be made on a case-by-case basis, according to the particular facts.

**20.39** *Re E (A Child)* provides helpful guidance on what an assessment should consider in order to assist the court in reaching its decision. The court will need to weigh up the following considerations:

- the advantages that calling the child will bring to the determination of the truth; and
- the damage it may do to the welfare of this, or any, child.

**20.40** The court must balance the welfare of the child giving evidence alongside the parties' rights to a fair trial, and the court's ability to get to the

---

[16] *Re W* [2010] UKSC 12.
[17] *Re E (A Child)* [2016] EWCA Civ 473.
[18] *Working Party of the Family Justice Council Guidelines December 2011* [2012] Fam Law 79.
[19] *Re E (A Child)* [2016] EWCA Civ 473.

truth. The impact upon the subject child of the court being unable to make certain findings is something that the court will consider carefully as part of its balancing exercise. Any harm caused to the child in giving evidence may be short-lived, whilst the impact upon that child and others of the facts not being determined might be felt long into the future.

**20.41** When assessing the child, consideration should be given to whether special measures are required to enable the child to give best evidence. The provision of special measures is discussed below.

## The court's decision

**20.42** There are a number of factors that the court must have regard to when considering calling a child to give evidence, including:

- the issues that are required in order to determine the case;
- does the child need to give evidence in order to determine the issues;
- the quality of the ABE interview;
- the nature of the challenge made against the child's evidence;
- the age and maturity of the child;
- the length of time since the events occurred.

**20.43** In addition to the issues set out above, the court may also consider:

- the support (or lack of it) that the child has from family or other sources;
- the child's wishes and feelings about giving evidence;
- the views of the children's guardian (if any) and (where appropriate) those with parental responsibility;
- the potential for delay
- where the child is to give evidence in parallel criminal proceedings, or has done so, the potential for harm in also giving evidence in the family court.

## Quality of the ABE interview

**20.44** In the majority of cases, the child will have been interviewed in accordance with the Achieving Best Evidence ('ABE') guidelines beforehand. If the child does give evidence, this interview will stand as the child's statement and evidence-in-chief.

**20.45** During the course of an ABE interview, the child must be asked the difference between truths and lies and should be given an example of this to ascertain whether they are able to understand the importance of telling the truth. McFarlane LJ recognised in *Re E (A Child)* that the absence of the truth and lies questions in phase one of an ABE interview was a serious breach of the guidelines, and in that case, rendered the ABE material unreliable.[20] It is necessary to consider the whole of the ABE interview when deciding whether it is of good enough quality to be relied upon by the court.

**20.46** Just because an ABE has not been conducted properly it does not mean that all of the evidence should be rejected. However, a bad ABE can impact hugely on the reliability of the account taken and this may mean that the need for a child to give evidence is greater in order for the court to determine the truth.

## Witnesses requiring special measures

**20.47** Special measures are available to all vulnerable witnesses to support them in giving their best evidence and so it is essential that consideration is given at the earliest opportunity as to whether a witness would be considered as vulnerable.

**20.48** The need for special measures should form part of the assessment of a child's ability to give evidence.

**20.49** There is no definition in the family court of who should be considered 'vulnerable', however, in accordance with the considerations set out in ss 16 and 17 of Youth Justice and Criminal Evidence Act 1999, indicators of vulnerability include:

- mental health issues;
- learning disabilities;
- victims of domestic violence and abuse;
- victims of sexual abuse;
- disclosure of medical history;
- deafness;
- sexuality and gender identity;
- addiction;
- children and young people.

**20.50** Guidance is also available in *Achieving Best Evidence in Criminal Proceedings: Guidance on interviewing victims and witnesses, and guidance on using special measures* (March 2011).

**20.51** There is no definition of special measures in family proceedings as yet, but special measures that are commonly available include:

- screens
- live video link

---

[20] *Re E (A Child)* [2016] EWCA Civ 473 at [36].

- video-recorded interview
- examination of the witness through an intermediary
- aids to communication

**20.52** A child's assessment may recommend that an intermediary service is approached to assess the child before deciding whether they can assist. There are specialist intermediary services that work with children which may be able to assist with the initial balancing exercise undertaken by the court.

**20.53** An intermediary is trained to assess individuals and determine whether they would benefit from assistance when giving oral evidence, in order to ensure that they can give their best, possible evidence to the court. If an intermediary service is of the view that their service will be of assistance, they will recommend measures to enable the person to give live evidence and minimise the risk of confusion or any inaccurate information resulting from a person's functioning and understanding.

**20.54** Intermediaries will also advise the court and the advocates on how best to ask questions of the individual as well as ensuring that there are frequent breaks.

**20.55** An intermediary's function is limited to assisting the person giving evidence, they will not carry out any other role in the proceedings.

**20.56** When special measures are considered by the court, the judge evaluating the resulting evidence will need to assess the degree (if any) to which the process may have affected the ability of the court to rely on the witness's evidence.[21]

## Ground rules hearing

**20.57** Whilst a ground rules hearing is not yet a requirement under the FPR 2010, it is good practice for such a hearing to take place before a witness relying on special measures, gives evidence. Ground rules hearings are required in criminal proceedings and take the form of a case management hearing at which all parties consider how questions should be put and managed. This allows the parties to agree a way forward, with the assistance of the court, to ensure that the evidence being obtained from the witness is the best evidence that can be achieved.

**20.58** One consideration for the ground rules hearing is whether the witness should undergo a memory refreshing exercise. Witnesses who give recorded evidence-in-chief, for example via an ABE interview, are entitled to refresh their memory of the interview before trial. When this should happen will need to be decided, and the witness will need to feel as settled as possible when giving evidence. Decisions about how, when and where memory refreshing should take place should be made on a case-by-case basis.

---

[21] *Re J (A Child)* [2014] EWCA Civ 875 at [93].

**20.59** The parties should also consider whether the witness should have an opportunity to see the courtroom or the room in which they will give evidence via video link, so that the environment is familiar to them. Information as to who sits where in the courtroom, as well as the possibility of meeting the advocates so that they know who will be asking the questions, may also assist.

**20.60** Another issue that will need to be considered is the ability of the vulnerable witness to understand and give the oath. Section 96 of the CA 1989 provides that:

> '(1) Subsection (2) applies where a child who is called as a witness in any civil proceedings does not, in the opinion of the court, understand the nature of an oath.
>
> (2) The child's evidence may be heard by the court if, in its opinion –
>
> (a) he understands that it is his duty to speak the truth; and
> (b) he has sufficient understanding to justify his evidence being heard.'

**20.61** These issues are commonly dealt with in the context of criminal proceedings. Children under the age of 14 should not give the oath,[22] neither should witnesses who are unable to understand the meaning its meaning. Any such impediment should be raised at the ground rules hearing so an appropriate way forward can be decided.

## Cross-examination of experts

**20.62** Once an expert has prepared a report for the court in accordance with Part 25 of the FPR 2010, the parties will need to consider whether it is necessary for the expert to attend court to give evidence. The court will be reluctant for an expert to attend unless the questions the parties have cannot be dealt with by way of further written questions to the expert. Once the responses to the further questions are received, it may be that the attendance of the expert is still necessary and a direction from the court should be obtained to that effect.

**20.63** The court will be mindful of the costs and inconvenience of the expert attending court, but if the findings in the report are contested and the issues cannot be dealt with by way of further questions, there will be no alternative but for the expert to attend.

**20.64** It may be possible for the expert to give evidence via video or audio link to try and minimise the costs and time required. This should be considered at the IRH when the arrangements for the final hearing are being finalised.

---

[22] Criminal Justice Act 1988, s 33A.

## ORAL EVIDENCE

**20.65** Rule 12.21 of the FPR 2010 provides that the court may give directions about the order of speeches and the evidence in the hearing.

**20.66** When considering what order the evidence should be heard in, r 12.21(2) states:

> 'Subject to any directions given under paragraph (1), the parties and the children's guardian must adduce their evidence at a hearing in the following order –
> 
> (a) the applicant;
> (b) any party with parental responsibility for the child;
> (c) other respondents;
> (d) the children's guardian;
> (e) the child, if the child is a party to proceedings and there is no children's guardian.'

## SUBMISSIONS

**20.67** Once all of the evidence has been heard by the court, the parties will have the opportunity to summarise their positions in relation to the application and the evidence that has been heard. They will outline the legal basis for their arguments and cite any guidance found in case law that may assist the court. Legal representatives are under a duty to bring to the attention of the court any case law that is relevant, even if it undermines their position. Submissions can be made orally or in writing, depending on what the court requires.

**20.68** If it has previously been agreed by the parties and the court that no oral evidence is necessary, submissions will be made on the basis of the parties' positions and the written evidence before the court. It is important to note that if a matter does go forward on submissions alone, it will be on the basis that the written evidence is not challenged by the parties.

**20.69** If a party disputes evidence that has been filed with the court, it must have been challenged in oral evidence before it can be challenged in submissions. If it has not been possible to challenge evidence because the individual has attended to give oral evidence, the court will be invited in to place little, if any, weight on the disputed evidence.

**20.70** When considering the evidence given by a parent, it is important that the court is reminded of the 'Lucas directions':[23]

> 'If a court concludes that a witness has lied about a matter, it does not follow that he has lied about everything. A witness may lie for many reasons. For example out of shame humiliation misplaced loyalty panic fear distress confusion and emotional pressure.'

---

[23] *R v Lucas* [1981] QB 720.

**20.71** It is essential that this is considered by the court when weighing up all of the evidence and deciding whether threshold has been met and what decision best promotes the welfare of the child.

## JUDGMENT

**20.72** At the end of the proceedings, the court will provide a judgment, or in the case of lay magistrates: facts and reasons. The court must set out in its judgment, the evaluation of the evidence and the reasons for the decision it has made. This document must fully address the evidence filed, the oral evidence heard and the findings that the court has made on any disputed evidence. The judgment must also cite the reasons why it has made the decision it has, in accordance with the provisions in the CA 1989 as well as the Human Rights Act 1998.

**20.73** The judge must demonstrate that they have kept the elements of the welfare checklist in mind when making the final orders, although they do not need to address each element of the welfare checklist. It must be clear that they have considered the individual elements of s 1(3) CA 1989,[24] and that the court's approach is compatible with the law.[25]

**20.74** If a decision is challenged, it is challenged on the basis of the judgment and the facts that the court has relied upon and the legal basis for the decision. The judgment must be clear and thorough enough for the family, and the child, to understand the reasons why the court has reached the decision that it has, as well as addressing the legal and welfare basis for the decision.

---

[24] *P (A Child)* [2016] EWCA Civ 3.
[25] *Re E (Adoption Order: Proportionality of Outcome to Circumstances)* [2014] 2 FLR 514.

# CHAPTER 21

# WELFARE TEST FOR MAKING A FINAL CARE ORDER

**21.1** If the court is satisfied that the threshold criteria has been made out on the evidence before it, it must then consider whether it is in the child's best interests to make a care order according to the care plan filed by the local authority. The court should not make the care order simply because the facts of a case crosses the threshold criteria.

**21.2** The court cannot dictate what the local authority's care plan is, and so the welfare consideration must be limited to the implications of the specific care plan filed (see chapter 22 for a full discussion of final care plans).

**21.3** The term 'welfare' will be familiar to family practitioners and pervades all children law proceedings. Section 1 of the Children Act 1989 ('CA 1989') stipulates that:

> 'When a court determines any question with respect to –
>
> (a) the upbringing of a child; or
> (b) the administration of a child's property or the application of income arising from it,
>
> the child's welfare shall be the court's paramount consideration.'

**21.4** This is echoed in the Adoption and Children Act 2002 ('ACA 2002') which specifies in s 1(2) that when considering an application for a placement or adoption order:

> 'The paramount consideration of the court or adoption agency must be the child's welfare, throughout his life.'

**21.5** It is clear from the legislation then, that the court's primary concern when making decisions about a child's future must be the 'welfare' of that child. However, what 'welfare' means on a practical level; and how the 'welfare' of a child can be quantified, are just two of the difficult questions that the family court has grappled with over the years. Defining 'welfare' is of particular importance when considering the gravity of the decisions that courts are required to make within care and adoption proceedings. Promoting and prioritising a child's welfare goes to the heart of all decisions made which will affect children not just in their minority, but into adulthood and throughout the rest of their lives.

**21.6** In *Re G*, Lord Justice Munby, as he then was, sitting in the Court of Appeal, considered what 'welfare' meant in the context of the CA 1989. He considered the importance of the developments of the welfare principle in the late nineteenth and early twentieth centuries and examined the current understanding of 'welfare'. Accepting that the paramountcy of welfare is undeniably enshrined in statue, he considered two crucial questions:[1]

> 'First, what do we mean by welfare; and, second, by reference to what standard or yardstick is welfare to be assessed?'

## WHAT DO WE MEAN BY WELFARE?

**21.7** Munby LJ addressed the first question by reiterating the understanding of welfare as articulated by Lord Hailsham LC in *Re B (A Minor) (Wardship: Sterilisation)* and commenting:[2]

> '"Welfare", which in this context is synonymous with "well-being" and "interests" (see Lord Hailsham LC in *Re B (A Minor) (Wardship: Sterilisation)* [1988] AC 199, 202), extends to and embraces everything that relates to the child's development as a human being and to the child's present and future life as a human being.'

**21.8** Munby LJ emphasised Sir Thomas Bingham MR's comments in *Re O (Contact: Imposition of Conditions)*,[3] that is that a child's welfare is to be considered throughout the child's minority and 'into and through adulthood'.[4] *Re O* was again, a private law matter, but Munby LJ considered it held a 'wider resonance', and added that how far one is required to look into the future will depend on the question before the court. For example, a change in school may require less of a 'forward-looking' approach versus that required in the context of the far-reaching ramifications of making a placement or adoption order.

## WHAT STANDARD, OR YARDSTICK, IS WELFARE TO BE ASSESSED BY?

**21.9** In answer to the second question posed, Munby placed the standards to be applied squarely in the context of the here and now, that is:[5]

> '[...] the standards of reasonable men and women in 2012, not by the standards of their parents in 1970, and having regard to the ever changing nature of our world: changes in our understanding of the natural world, technological changes, changes in social standards and, perhaps most important of all, changes in social attitudes.'

---

[1] *Re G* [2012] EWCA Civ 1233 at [25].
[2] *Re G* [2012] EWCA Civ 1233 at [26].
[3] *Re O (Contact: Imposition of Conditions)* [1995] 2 FLR 124 at 129.
[4] *Re G* [2012] EWCA Civ 1233 at [26].
[5] *Re G* [2012] EWCA Civ 1233 at [33].

**21.10** Moreover, he held that the court must take a holistic approach to the evaluation of a child's welfare:[6]

> 'Evaluating a child's best interests involves a welfare appraisal in the widest sense, taking into account, where appropriate, a wide range of ethical, social, moral, religious, cultural, emotional and welfare considerations. Everything that conduces to a child's welfare and happiness or relates to the child's development and present and future life as a human being, including the child's familial, educational and social environment, and the child's social, cultural, ethnic and religious community, is potentially relevant and has, where appropriate, to be taken into account.'

**21.11** By extension then, he held that it is important to recognise that a child's welfare cannot be assessed in isolation:[7]

> 'It is only by considering the child's network of relationships that their well-being can be properly considered. So a child's relationships, both within and without the family, are always relevant to the child's interests; often they will be determinative.'

**21.12** It is upon this basis that the CA 1989 operates. However, the 'yardstick of welfare' does not set a restrictive framework in which children law proceedings must be resolved, nor does it prescribe in any detail what factors or situations should be viewed as 'good' or 'bad' in the context of a child's welfare. As Thorpe LJ remarked in *Re S (Adult Patient: Sterilisation)*, 'it would be undesirable and probably impossible to set bounds to what is relevant to a welfare determination'.[8] The court must and will always consider every case on its own facts, however, the ever-evolving concept of 'welfare' has been bought into the present day by *Re G* and has remained strong and clear ever since.

## WELFARE CHECKLIST

**21.13** When considering making a final care order, the court must have regard to the matters set out in s 1(3) of the CA 1989: the 'welfare checklist'. The 'welfare checklist' contained in the ACA 2002 will be considered in chapter 28.

**21.14** Section 1(3) of the CA 1989 provides:

> 'In circumstances mentioned in subsection (4) [whether to make an order or not], a court shall have regard in particular to –
>
> (a) the ascertainable wishes and feelings of the child concerned (considered in the light of his age and understanding)
> (b) his physical, emotional and educational needs
> (c) the likely effect on his of any change in his circumstances
> (d) his age, sex, background and any characteristics of his which the court considers relevant;
> (e) any harm which he has suffered or is at risk of suffering;

---

[6] *Re G* [2012] EWCA Civ 1233 at [27].
[7] *Re G* [2012] EWCA Civ 1233 at [30].
[8] *Re S (Adult Patient: Sterilisation* [2001] Fam 15.

(f) how capable each of his parents, and any other person in relation to who the court considers the question to be relevant, is of meeting his needs;
(g) the range of powers available to the court under this Act in the proceedings in question.'

**21.15** Evidently, both checklists encompass the meaning and standard of 'welfare' set out by Munby LJ in *Re G*.[9] The paramountcy of welfare is clear and must be specifically considered when determining what orders (if any) the court should make in relation to the arrangements for the children it is concerned with.

**21.16** The court must demonstrate that the elements of the checklist are at the forefront of its mind when making final orders. The judge does not need to address each element of the checklist in the judgment provided, but they must make it clear that they have considered the elements,[10] and that the court's approach is compatible with the law.[11]

**21.17** The Senior President of the Tribunals, Lord Justice Vos, addressed the issue of how thoroughly a judge is required to address the welfare checklist in judgments in the matter of *P (A Child)*:[12]

> 'We are entitled to assume that a judge of the experience of Judge Ansell knew how to perform the welfare review, and knew which matters he should take into account, unless he has demonstrated the contrary. There was no need for him laboriously to rehearse each item of the checklist as if a pilot conducting his pre-flight checks (see Staughton LJ in *H v H (Residence Order: leave to remove from the jurisdiction)* [1995] 1 FLR 529), even if, in a difficult or finely balanced case, it is a great help to address each of the factors in the list, along with any others which may be relevant, so as to ensure that no particular feature of the case is given more weight than it should properly bear.'

**21.18** The checklist serves as a balancing exercise for the court when considering the range of potential outcomes available, and whether any order should be made.[13] However, the court is not bound to solely consider the issues raised by the parties and may highlight other issues it considers relevant. Importantly, no one element of the checklist is more important than another.

## Ascertainable wishes and feelings of the child

**21.19** Whilst the court will consider the wishes and feelings of a child, their views will not be determinative. Wishes and feelings will be considered in light of the child's age and understanding and balanced against what best promotes their welfare.[14]

---

[9] *Re G* [2012] EWCA Civ 1233.
[10] *P (A Child)* [2016] EWCA Civ 3.
[11] *Re E (Adoption Order: Proportionality of Outcome to Circumstances)* [2014] 2 FLR 514.
[12] *P (A Child)* [2016] EWCA Civ 3 at [48].
[13] *B v B (Residence Order: Reasons for decision)* [1997] 2 FLR 602.
[14] *Re H (A Child)* [2014] EWCA Civ 271.

**21.20** The court's powers in care proceedings are enormous: it can completely sever a child's ties with their family if it sees fit. Clearly then, acknowledging the child's age and understanding is essential when considering their wishes and feelings, but the court will not dismiss a child's wishes without careful consideration.

**21.21** The child will be represented by a children's guardian during care proceedings. It is part of the role of the children's guardian to ensure that the court is aware of a child's wishes and feelings. Pursuant to PD16A, para 7.7, a guardian must advise the court of the child's wishes and feelings, the options available to the court and the suitability of each of these options.

**21.22** In the event that a child has been assessed as competent and is being separately represented from the guardian, the child will have the opportunity of communicating their views directly to the court (see chapter 12 for further discussion on representation).

## *Seeing the judge*

**21.23** It is not uncommon for older children to want to go to court and meet the judge deciding their fate. The President issued *Guidelines for judges meeting children who are subject to family proceedings* in 2010 which provides for how the court should conduct meetings with the child and the practical arrangements that should be made to enable the child to attend court. The Court of Appeal considered the guidance in *Re KP (Abduction: Child's Objections)* in which Moore-Bick LJ offered further points of guidance and clarification:[15]

> '(i) During that part of any meeting between a young person and a judge in which the judge is listening to the child's point of view and hearing what they have to say, the judge's role should be largely that of a passive recipient of whatever communication the young person wishes to transmit.
>
> (ii) The purpose of the meeting is not to obtain evidence and the judge should not, therefore, probe or seek to test whatever it is that the child wishes to say. The meeting is primarily for the benefit of the child, rather than for the benefit of the forensic process by providing additional evidence to the judge. As the Guidelines state, the task of gathering evidence is for the specialist CAFCASS officers who have, as Mr Gupta submits, developed an expertise in this field.
>
> (iii) A meeting, such as in the present case, taking place prior to the judge deciding upon the central issues should be for the dual purposes of allowing the judge to hear what the young person may wish to volunteer and for the young person to hear the judge explain the nature of the court process. Whilst not wishing to be prescriptive, and whilst acknowledging that the encounter will proceed at the pace of the child, which will vary from case to case, it is difficult to envisage circumstances in which such a meeting would last for more than 20 minutes or so.

---

[15] *Re KP (Abduction: Child's Objections)* [2014] 2 FLR 660 at [56].

(iv) If the child volunteers evidence that would or might be relevant to the outcome of the proceedings, the judge should report back to the parties and determine whether, and if so how, that evidence should be adduced.

(v) The process adopted by the judge in the present case, in which she sought to 'probe' K's wishes and feelings, and did so over the course of more than an hour by asking some 87 questions went well beyond the passive role that we have described and, despite the judge's careful self-direction, strayed significantly over the line and into the process of gathering evidence (upon which the judge then relied in coming to her decision).

(vi) In the same manner, the judge was in error in regarding the meeting as being an opportunity for K to make representations or submissions to the judge. The purpose of any judicial meeting is not for the young person to argue their case; it is simply, but importantly, to provide an opportunity for the young person to state whatever it is that they wish to state directly to the judge who is going to decide an important issue in their lives.'

**21.24** Judges are not under any obligation to see the children subject to care proceedings and it is for the judge to decide if they should meet with the child or not. If they do meet with the child, the judge cannot promise them their meeting will be confidential. And agreement should be reached as to who will be present during the interview to take a note.

## LOCAL AUTHORITY'S CARE PLAN

**21.25** The local authority must prepare a final statement together with a final care plan for the child prior to the final hearing. For a full discussion of the final care plan see chapter 22. Within their final evidence, they must include an analysis of the child's situation, weigh up the pros and cons of each option for the child and set out the reasons for their proposals with reference to the child's future.

**21.26** The potential care plans available are as follows:

- no order (the child being left with the parent);
- private law orders, ie child arrangements order or special guardianship order, placing with a parent of extended family (see chapters 26 and 27);
- a supervision order (see chapter 25);
- a care order with a plan for the child to live with a parent; in long-term foster care or to be placed for adoption.

## NO ORDER

**21.27** Prior to the final hearing and when making its initial application, the local authority will have considered whether an order is necessary, and if so what order should be made. The court must also consider whether an order is necessary, in light of all of the evidence before it.

**21.28** Section 1(5) of the CA 1989 provides:

> 'Where a court is considering whether or not to make one or more orders under this Act with respect to a child, it shall not make the order or any of the orders unless is considers that doing so would be better for the child than making no order at all.'

**21.29** There is an expectation that parents should and will exercise their parental responsibility to promote the welfare of their children and this remains at the heart of the 'no order' principle.[16] Furthermore, Art 8 of the European Convention on Human Rights (as per Sch 1 of the Human Rights Act 1998) provides that everyone has a right to respect for their private and family life.

**21.30** McFarlane LJ in the matter of *Re W (Direct Contact)* expanded on this further:[17]

> 'It is the parents, rather than the court or more generally the State, who are the primary decision makers and actors for determining and delivering the upbringing that the welfare of their child requires [...] the courts are entitled to look to each parent to use their best endeavours to deliver what their child needs, hard or burdensome or downright tough though that may be. The statute places the primary responsibility for delivering a good outcome for a child upon each of his or her parents, rather than upon the courts or some other agency.'

**21.31** In the event that the court is called upon to interfere in arrangements for children, this interference must be no more than is necessary to safeguard the child and promote their welfare and should be proportionate.

**21.32** It is not unusual for a parent to invite the court to make no order at a final hearing, and the court will need to consider this potential outcome of such a step for the child, balancing it against the welfare considerations set out in the welfare checklist.

## CARE PLAN FOR ADOPTION

**21.33** If a child is adopted, they will cease to be a member of their birth family. This is the most draconian order that can be made and the court will need to consider the impact of adoption on a child throughout their life very carefully.

**21.34** In *Re B-S (Children)*, the President provided a clear outline for courts when considering a care plan for adoption. This case followed the Supreme Court's decision in *Re B (A Child)* and highlighted the Court of Appeal's

---

[16] *Re D (Withdrawal of Parental Responsibility)* [2015] 1 FLR 166.
[17] *Re W (Direct Contact)* [2012] EWCA Civ 999 at [74], [76].

concern as to how matters involving adoption had been dealt with following four cases being referred to the Court of Appeal within the last ten days of July 2013.

**21.35** The President emphasised the remarks of Baroness Hale in *Re B*:[18]

> 'The language used in *Re B* is striking. Different words and phrases are used, but the message is clear. Orders contemplating non-consensual adoption – care orders with a plan for adoption, placement orders and adoption orders – are "a very extreme thing, a last resort", only to be made where "nothing else will do", where "no other course [is] possible in [the child's] interests", they are "the most extreme option", a "last resort – when all else fails", to be made "only in exceptional circumstances and where motivated by overriding requirements pertaining to the child's welfare, in short, where nothing else will do": see *Re B* paras 74, 76, 77, 82, 104, 130, 135, 145, 198, 215.'

**21.36** He continued, highlighting the considerations of McFarlane J in *Re G*:[19]

> 'A process which acknowledges that long-term public care, and in particular adoption contrary to the will of a parent, is "the most draconian option", yet does not engage with the very detail of that option which renders it "draconian" cannot be a full or effective process of evaluation.'

**21.37** The term 'nothing else will do' should not be considered in isolation. McFarlane LJ in *Re W (A Child)* said:[20]

> 'The phrase is meaningless, and potentially dangerous, if it is applied as some freestanding, shortcut test divorced from, or even in place of, an overall evaluation of the child's welfare. Used properly, as Baroness Hale explained, the phrase "nothing else will do" is no more, nor less, than a useful distillation of the proportionality and necessity test as embodied in the ECHR and reflected in the need to afford paramount consideration to the welfare of the child throughout her lifetime.'

**21.38** It is clear then, that the court must consider all other possibilities before proposing adoption, in order to ensure that no lesser order that will preserve family ties, is available.

## Realistic options

**21.39** The court will need to consider what other realistic options may be available as an alternative to adoption. It should not simply use the term 'nothing else will do' as a broad brush. The President said in *Re B-S (Children)*:[21]

---

[18] *Re BS (Children)* [2013] EWCA Civ 1146 at [22].
[19] *Re BS (Children)* [2013] EWCA Civ 1146 at [41].
[20] *Re W (A Child)* [2016] EWCA Civ 793 at [68].
[21] *Re B-S (Children)* [2013] EWCA Civ 1146 at [34].

'First, there must be proper evidence both from the local authority and from the guardian. The evidence must address *all* the options which are realistically possible and must contain an analysis of the arguments for and against each option. As Ryder LJ said in *Re R (Children)* [2013] EWCA Civ 1018, para 20, what is required is:

> "Evidence of the lack of alternative options for the children and an analysis of the evidence that is accepted by the court sufficient to drive it to the conclusion that nothing short of adoption is appropriate for the children".'

**21.40** Within the local authority's final evidence and the guardian's final analysis, all realistic options for the long-term care of a child should be considered so that the court can weigh up and balance the welfare of the child in each alternative situation.

**21.41** Frequently, it will be the parents' position that there is a realistic alternative to the local authority's care plan and that the interests of the child are better served by the alternative plan. The parents' evidence should set out whichever option(s) they say the court should take.

**21.42** However, in *Re R*, the President clarified that:[22]

> '*Re B-S* does not require the further forensic pursuit of options which, having been properly evaluated, typically at an early stage in the proceedings, can legitimately be discarded as not being realistic. *Re B-S* does not require that every conceivable option on the spectrum that runs between "no order" and "adoption" has to be canvassed and bottomed out with reasons in the evidence and judgment in every single case. Full consideration is required only with respect to those options which are "realistically possible".'

**21.43** Options must be realistic possibilities, not just potential ways forward for a child. If something has been considered early on in the proceedings and discarded on the basis of the evidence available, it will not be necessary for the court to reconsider it at a final hearing.

## Holistic approach

**21.44** When considering the options available for the child, the President in *Re B-S (Children)* went on to emphasise the importance of employing a holistic approach to its decision making:[23]

> 'In relation to the nature of the judicial task we draw attention to what McFarlane LJ said in *Re G (A Child)* [2013] EWCA Civ 965, paras 49–50:
>
>> "In most child care cases a choice will fall to be made between two or more options. The judicial exercise should not be a linear process whereby each option, other than the most draconian, is looked at in isolation and then

---

[22] *Re R* [2015] 1 FLR 715 at [59].
[23] *Re B-S (Children)* [2013] EWCA Civ 1146 at [43].

rejected because of internal deficits that may be identified, with the result that, at the end of the line, the only option left standing is the most draconian and that is therefore chosen without any particular consideration of whether there are internal deficits within that option.

The linear approach ... is not apt where the judicial task is to undertake a global, holistic evaluation of each of the options available for the child's future upbringing before deciding which of those options best meets the duty to afford paramount consideration to the child's welfare".'

**21.45** In order to undertake a 'global, holistic evaluation', the court must consider any potential difficulties associated with one option, along with what support could be made available to address such difficulties. Just because the local authority does not propose an option for a child, it does not mean that they have ignored support that could be made available to the family. Clearly, if the court is to evaluate the options carefully, this information must be provided.[24]

**21.46** When considering the potential support available, the local authority should also consider what support external agencies such as housing and mental health services may be able to offer.

## Proportionality and the 'least interventionist' approach

**21.47** After considering the realistic options available for the child, and conducting the global, holistic evaluation of the potential options, the court must then consider the proportionality of the suggested order.

**21.48** This involves a careful analysis of the placement options and consideration as to whether the proposed interference of the local authority is justified.[25] The President in *Re B-S (Children)* stated:[26]

'Behind all this there lies the well-established principle, derived from s 1(5) of the 1989 Act, read in conjunction with s 1(3)(g), and now similarly embodied in s 1(6) of the 2002 Act, that the court should adopt the 'least interventionist' approach. As Hale J, as she then was, said in *Re O (Care or Supervision Order)* [1996] 2 FLR 755, 760:

"the court should begin with a preference for the less interventionist rather than the more interventionist approach. This should be considered to be in the better interests of the children [...] unless there are cogent reasons to the contrary".'

**21.49** Ryder LJ cautioned in *W (A Child) v Neath Port Talbot County Borough Council*:[27]

---

[24] *Re Y (A Child)* [2013] EWCA Civ 1337.
[25] *Surrey County Council v S* [2014] EWCA Civ 601.
[26] *Re B-S (Children)* [2013] EWCA Civ 1146 at [23].
[27] *W (A Child) v Neath Port Talbot County Borough Council* [2013] EWCA Civ 1227 at [80].

'The courts powers extend to making an order other than that asked for by a local authority. The process of deciding what order is necessary involves a value judgment about the proportionality of the State's intervention to meet the risk against which the court decides there is a need for protection. In that regard, one starts with the court's findings of fact and moves on to the value judgments that are the welfare evaluation. That evaluation is the court's not the local authority's, the guardian's or indeed any other party's. It is the function of the court to come to that value judgment. It is simply not open to a local authority within proceedings to decline to accept the court's evaluation of risk, no matter how much it may disagree with the same. Furthermore, it is that evaluation which will inform the proportionality of the response which the court decides is necessary.'

**21.50** The court's evaluation is also essential in considering the proportionality of the order sought, bearing in mind the principle that making the least interventionist order is in the child's best interest.

## BALANCE OF WELFARE CONSIDERATIONS

**21.51** When considering the proportionality, and the need to make an order, in accordance with a child's welfare, the court must ensure that the evaluation of their welfare is undertaken in a realistic manner. The decision for the court represents a careful balancing act between the various options for the child.

**21.52** In *Re A (A Child)*, Sir James Munby P emphasised that:

'The courts are not in the business of providing children with perfect homes. If we took into care and placed for adoption every child whose parents had had a domestic spat and every child whose parents on occasion had drunk too much then the care system would be overwhelmed and there would not be enough adoptive parents. So we have to have a degree of realism about prospective carers who come before the courts.'

When considering the risk posed to the child, the court will consider what harm the child is at risk of suffering, and balance that against the whole picture.

**21.53** In *Re C and B (Care Order: Future Harm)*, Hale LJ (as she then was) noted:[28]

'A comparatively small risk of really serious harm can justify action, while even the virtual certainty of slight harm might not.'

**21.54** It is clear that the question as to whether the existing or likely harm is significant is very much dependent on the facts of the case itself. In *Re L (Care: Threshold Criteria)*[29] Hedley J reiterated that:[30]

---

[28] *B (A Child)* [2013] UKSC 33 at [28].
[29] *Re L (Care: Threshold Criteria)* [2007] 1 FLR 2050.
[30] *Re L (Care: Threshold Criteria)* [2007] 1 FLR 2050 at [50]–[51].

'Society must be willing to tolerate very diverse standards of parenting, including the eccentric, the barely adequate and the inconsistent [...] Significant harm is fact-specific and must retain the breadth of meaning that human fallibility may require of it ... it is clear that it must be something unusual; at least something more than the commonplace human failure or inadequacy.'

# CHAPTER 22

# FINAL CARE PLANS

## INTRODUCTION

**22.1** Once threshold has been satisfied and when deciding whether to make a final care order, the court must consider the care plan that the local authority has proposed for the child. The contents of the care plan must be considered carefully by all parties when the court is asked to make a final care order. When the court undertakes its balancing exercise in relation to the long-term welfare of a child, the details contained in the care plan are crucial. It is possible for a care plan to provide for a child to be placed at home with a parent, placed in long term foster care, or placed for adoption. All of these represent significant steps in a child's life.

**22.2** The court has no jurisdiction to dictate a care plan, and can only make a care order if it determines that the care plan proposed is in the best interests of the child. It is therefore essential for all of the relevant information to be included in the care plan to ensure that the court is able to consider the matter thoroughly. Whilst the court can ask the local authority to reconsider their care plan, especially if elements are missing, the local authority cannot be compelled to change or add to it.

**22.3** If a final care order is made, the care plan will travel with the child and is the document upon which the independent reviewing officer will rely to ensure that the plan is followed.

## FORMAL REQUIREMENTS

**22.4** Section 31A(1) provides:

> 'Where an application is made on which a care order might be made with respect to a child, the appropriate local authority must, within such time as the court may direct, prepare a plan ("a care plan") for the future care of the child.'

**22.5** This does not apply when the court is considering making an interim care order, although it is common practice for the local authority to provide an interim care plan so that the court is aware of the proposed arrangements for the child if the interim order is granted (see chapter 16 for further discussion).

**22.6** During proceedings, the local authority must keep any care plan under review and revise the plan if necessary.[1] If the care plan is revised, it should be presented to the allocated judge.[2]

**22.7** The Care Planning, Placement and Case Review (England) Regulations 2010 (the 'CPPCR Regulations 2010')[3] specify what the care plan should contain. Schedule 2 provides that the care plan should include:

'(1) How on a day to day basis C will be cared for and C's welfare will be safeguarded and promoted by the appropriate person.

(2) Any arrangements made for contact between C and any parent of C's and any person who is not C's parent but who has parental responsibility for C, and between C and any other connected person including, if appropriate –

- (a) the reasons why contact with any such person would not be reasonably practicable or would not be consistent with C's welfare,
- (b) if C is not in the care of the responsible authority, details of any order made under section 8,
- (c) if C is in the care of the responsible authority, details of any order relating to C made under section 34,
- (d) the arrangements for notifying any changes in the arrangements for contact.

(3) The arrangements made for C's health (including physical, emotional and mental health) and dental care including –

- (a) the name and address of C's registered medical and dental practitioners and, where applicable, any registered medical or dental practitioner with whom C is to be registered following the placement,
- (b) any arrangements for the giving or withholding of consent to medical or dental examination or treatment for C.

(4) The arrangements made for C's education and training including –

- (a) the name and address of any school at which C is a registered pupil,
- (b) the name of the designated teacher at the school (if applicable),
- (c) the name and address of any other educational institution that C attends, or of any other person who provides C with education or training,
- (d) where C has a statement of special educational needs, details of the local authority that maintains the statement.

(5) The arrangements made for R to visit C in accordance with Part 5, the frequency of visits and the arrangements made for advice, support and assistance to be available to C between visits in accordance with regulation 31.

(6) If an independent visitor is appointed, the arrangements made for them to visit C.

(7) The circumstances in which the placement may be terminated and C removed from the appropriate person's care in accordance with regulation 14.

---

[1] CA 1989, s 31A(2).
[2] *Re A (Care Plan)* [2008] 2 FLR 1183.
[3] In the Regulations, 'C' refers to the child, 'P' to the parent, 'F', foster carer, 'R', the representative of the local authority, and 'IRO', the independent reviewing officer.

(8) The name and contact details of –
   (a)   the IRO,
   (b)   C's independent visitor (if one is appointed),
   (c)   R, and
   (d)   if C is an eligible child, the personal adviser appointed for C.'

**22.8** In practice, a number of local authorities do not prepare the care plan in a separate document, instead relying on the information contained in the social work statement, which can make it difficult to piece together the plan itself. If this is the local authority's approach, they must ensure that all information pertaining to the care plan is contained within the statement. Any deficits in this information must be dealt with before any care order is made.

## PARENTAL RESPONSIBILITY UNDER A CARE ORDER

**22.9** A care order invests parental responsibility in the local authority, which is then shared with the parents. Although a parent does not lose their parental responsibility by virtue of a care order being made, in the event of a disagreement about the discharge of parental responsibility, the local authority can act against the wishes of the parent if 'it is satisfied that it is necessary to do so in order to safeguard or promote the child's welfare'.[4]

**22.10** Section 33(3) of the CA 1989 provides:

'(3) While a care order is in force with respect to a child, the local authority designated by the order shall –
   (a)   have parental responsibility for the child; and
   (b)   have the power (subject to the following provisions of this section) to determine the extent to which
      (i)    a parent, guardian or special guardian of the child; or
      (ii)   a person who by virtue of section 4A has parental responsibility for the child,
      may meet his parental responsibility for him.'

**22.11** Whilst the subject of a care order, the local authority cannot cause the child to be bought up in any religious persuasion that the child would not have been bought up in had the order not been made.[5] This applies whether the order is an interim or full care order.

**22.12** Once any care order is granted, any child arrangements order or any order made under s 8 of the CA 1989 that is in force at the time will be automatically discharged. This will result in the holder of a child arrangements order having their parental responsibility removed, if their parental responsibility is limited to the duration of that order.

---

[4]   CA 1989, s 33(4).
[5]   CA 1989, s 33(6).

## PLACEMENT

**22.13** The proposed placement of a child is the crucial piece of information in the care plan. There may be a number of potential placements for the child and the details of those, as well as what should happen if the proposed placement breaks down, should all be included within the care plan.

### Placement of the child with local authority foster carers

**22.14** Whilst the foster carer has the day-to-day care of the child, they will not be able to make any major decision in relation to the child without consulting the local authority, who must in turn inform anyone with parental responsibility for the child.

**22.15** The foster carer will keep a daily log of the care given to the child and this will include any issues that arise, progress that the child makes and any matters which they consider important to note. The foster carer will be supported by their own fostering social worker who will assist them with any difficulties that arise.

**22.16** Regulation 22 of the CPPCR Regulations 2010 provides that foster carers must be registered before a child can be placed with them. Foster carers are usually employed by the local authority or by independent fostering agencies, known as IFAs.

**22.17** Regulation 22 provides:

'(1) This regulation applies where the responsible authority propose to place C with F.

(2) The responsible authority may only place C with F if –

    (a) F is approved by –
        (i) the responsible authority, or
        (ii) provided that the conditions specified in paragraph (3) are also satisfied, another fostering service provider,
    (b) the terms of F's approval are consistent with the proposed placement, and
    (c) F has entered into a foster care agreement either with the responsible authority or with another fostering service provider in accordance with regulation 28(5)(b) of the 2002 Regulations.

(3) The conditions referred to in paragraph (2)(a)(ii) are that –

    (a) the fostering service provider by whom F is approved consents to the proposed placement, and
    (b) where any other local authority currently have a child placed with F, that local authority consents to the proposed placement.

**22.18** The assessment and approval of foster carers is governed by the Care Planning, Placement and Case Review and Fostering Services (Miscellaneous Amendments) Regulations 2013 amending the Fostering Services (England)

Regulations 2011. This guidance covers the assessment and approval process, including detailing the process itself, the sharing of information for the purposes of the assessment, independent review mechanism, and reviews and termination of approval. The guidance also covers the number of children that can be placed with a carer.

## Placement with friends or family members

**22.19** If the local authority wishes to place, or continue the placement of a child, with a family member or a friend under an ICO, they local authority must have assessed the family member or friend as a suitable local authority foster carer, in accordance with the Fostering Services Regulations 2002. A family member or friend is known as a 'connected person' for the purposes of a placement under these regulations.[6]

**22.20** Regulation 24 of the CPPCR Regulations 2010 provides for the temporary approval of a connected person so that a child can be placed with them prior to the full assessment being completed. Temporary approval only lasts for 16 weeks, after which the full assessment must have been completed or the child must be placed elsewhere. This should normally have been completed by the time the court is asked to consider making a final order. A full discussion of temporary approval can be found at chapter 16.

**22.21** If the outcome of the connected person's assessment is negative, the child cannot be placed with them. Notwithstanding the negative assessment, if placement with the connected person is preferred to local authority care, the parties and the court will need to consider whether a special guardianship order or child arrangements order should be made instead. The court must always consider all of the orders available when considering the long-term plan for a child, and it may be that a less invasive order will secure the child in a placement that meets the child's needs. Supervision orders can still be made alongside a special guardianship order or child arrangements order.

## Placement with parents

**22.22** Part 4 of the CPPCR Regulations 2010 provides for the placement of a child with a parent under a care order. In order for a care order to be made, the court must be satisfied that the care the parent has provided has placed the child at such risk that it is necessary for the local authority to share parental responsibility. Unsurprisingly, local authorities are often reluctant to place a child with a parent under a care order, and the court cannot force the local authority to do so. If the child is placed with the parent, the local authority has a duty to provide such services and support that is necessary to safeguard and promote the child's welfare and must record the services in their care plan.

---

[6] CPPCR Regulations 2010, reg 24(3).

**22.23** The assessment that needs to be in place for a child to be placed with a parent under a care order is very thorough for obvious reasons. Regulation 17 provides:

'17. Before deciding to place C with P, the responsible authority must –

(a) assess the suitability of P to care for C, including the suitability of –
  (i) the proposed accommodation, and
  (ii) all other persons aged 18 and over who are members of the household in which it is proposed that C will live,
(b) take into account all the matters set out in Schedule 3 in making their assessment,
(c) consider whether, in all the circumstances and taking into account the services to be provided by the responsible authority, the placement will safeguard and promote C's welfare and meet C's needs set out in the care plan, and
(d) review C's case in accordance with Part 6.'

**22.24** Schedule 3 of the regulations sets out the issues that must be assessed by the local authority when considering whether a child should be placed with a parent under a care order:

'1. In respect of P –

(a) P's capacity to care for children and in particular in relation to C to –
  (i) provide for C's physical needs and appropriate medical and dental care,
  (ii) protect C adequately from harm or danger, including from any person who presents a risk of harm to C,
  (iii) ensure that the home environment is safe for C,
  (iv) ensure that C's emotional needs are met and C is provided with a positive sense of self, including any particular needs arising from C's religious persuasion, racial origin and cultural and linguistic background, and any disability C may have,
  (v) promote C's learning and intellectual development through encouragement, cognitive stimulation and the promotion of educational success and social opportunities,
  (vi) enable C to regulate C's emotions and behaviour, including by modelling appropriate behaviour and interactions with others, and
  (vii) provide a stable family environment to enable C to develop and maintain secure attachments to P and other persons who provide care for C,
(b) P's state of health including P's physical, emotional and mental health and medical history including any current or past issues of domestic violence, substance misuse or mental health problems,
(c) P's family relationships and the composition of P's household, including particulars of –
  (i) the identity of all other members of the household, including their age and the nature of their relationship with P and with each other, including any sexual relationship,
  (ii) any relationship with any person who is a parent of C,
  (iii) other adults not being members of the household who are likely to have regular contact with C, and

(iv) any current or previous domestic violence between members of the household, including P,
(d) P's family history, including –
   (i) particulars of P's childhood and upbringing including the strengths and difficulties of P's parents or other persons who cared for P,
   (ii) P's relationships with P's parents and siblings, and their relationships with each other,
   (iii) P's educational achievement and any specific learning difficulty or disability,
   (iv) a chronology of significant life events, and (v) particulars of other relatives and their relationships with C and P,
(e) particulars of any criminal offences of which P has been convicted or in respect of which P has been cautioned,
(f) P's past and present employment and other sources of income, and
(g) the nature of the neighbourhood in which P's home is situated and resources available in the community to support C and P.

2. In respect of members of P's household aged 18 and over, so far as is practicable, all the particulars specified in paragraph 1 except sub-paragraphs (d), (f) and (g).'

**22.25** The assessment set out above is clearly an in-depth piece of work and will take some time. A child can still be placed with their parent prior to the assessment being completed, pursuant to reg 19:

'19. Where the nominated officer considers it to be necessary and consistent with C's welfare, the responsible authority may place C with P before their assessment under regulation 17 ("the assessment") is completed provided that they –

(a) arrange for P to be interviewed in order to obtain as much of the information specified in Schedule 3 about P and the other persons living in P's household who are aged 18 and over as can be readily ascertained at that interview,
(b) ensure that the assessment and the review of C's case are completed in accordance with regulation 17 within ten working days of C being placed with P, and
(c) ensure that a decision in accordance with regulation 18 is made and approved within ten working days after the assessment is completed, and—
   (i) if the decision is to confirm the placement, review the placement plan and, if appropriate amend it, and
   (ii) if the decision is not to confirm the placement, terminate the placement.'

**22.26** If the result of the assessment is negative, the child cannot be placed with their parent unless successfully challenged. Again however, the court cannot force the local authority to provide a particular placement for the child and if the assessment of the parents is negative, they will not propose the placement.

**22.27** *Re DE (A Child)* contains guidance as to what should be included in a care order placing a child with their parents. Baker J specifies the following:[7]

> 'In every case where a care order is made on the basis of a care plan providing that a child should live at home with his or her parents, it should be a term of the care plan, and a recital in the care order, that the local authority agrees to give not less than fourteen days' notice of a removal of the child, save in an emergency. I consider that fourteen days is an appropriate period, on the one hand to avoid unnecessary delay but, on the other hand, to allow the parents an opportunity to obtain legal advice.'

For further discussion of the discharge of care orders, see chapter 24.

## CONTACT WITH CHILDREN IN CARE

**22.28** The local authority is under a statutory duty to facilitate reasonable contact between the child in care and their family. Section 34 of the CA 1989 provides:

> '(1) Where a child is in the care of a local authority, the authority shall (subject to the provisions of this section) and their duty under section 22(3)(a) allow the child reasonable contact with –
>
> (a) his parents;
> (b) any guardian or special guardian of his;
> (ba) any person who by virtue of section 4A has parental responsibility for him;
> (c) where there was a child arrangements order in force with respect to the child immediately before the care order was made, any person named in the child arrangements order as a person with whom the child was to live; and
> (d) where, immediately before the care order was made, a person had care of the child by virtue of an order made in the exercise of the High Court's inherent jurisdiction with respect to children, that person.'

This provision must be read alongside s 22(3)(a) of the CA 1989, which provides that a local authority has a duty to 'safeguard and promote' the child's welfare.

**22.29** When considering whether contact between the child and any of the persons described in s 34(1) of the CA 1989 should take place, reg 8ZA of the CPPCR Regulations 2010 states that the local authority must have regard to the child's care plan.

**22.30** If a local authority or a child themselves wishes to seek an order in respect of contact, the court has the power to make such an order as it considers appropriate under s 34(2) of the CA 1989. If any person listed in s 34(1) does not agree with the level, or type, of contact that the local authority

---

[7] *Re DE (A Child)* [2015] 1 FLR 1001 at [49].

provides for, then an application can be made to the court under s 34(3) of the CA 1989. This application can be made outside of care proceedings if a care order is in place before the dispute arises. The parents will not receive automatic public funding will need to complete a means and merits tested application with the legal aid agency. Unless there are very special reasons for the application, the parents are unlikely to secure public funding.

**22.31** Any disputes surrounding the contact contained in the care plan should be dealt with at the final hearing. The court will need to consider any risk that may be posed to the child as a result of contact and may be assisted by any assessments completed during the proceedings.

**22.32** The court will need to balance any risk that may be posed to the child from the contact sought by the parent versus that offered by the local authority. The local authority must consider what arrangements can be put into place to minimise any potential risk, such as supervising the contact or prescribing the venue.

**22.33** Supervised contact may be provided when there are concerns surrounding the way the child is parented; what the parent(s) might say to the child during contact, and physical or emotional harm. It should only be employed where the local authority are clear that it is necessary to safeguard and promote the welfare of the child.

**22.34** Local authorities will usually have access to contact centres in which contact can be supervised. Resources are scarce for local authorities, so they will need to ensure that the contact is in the child's best interests whilst managing the scant resources available for supervision.

**22.35** It may be possible for a family member to supervise contact, if supervision is necessary. The local authority should consider all measures that could enable contact to happen in as natural setting as possible. Obviously the relevant family member must be content to be involved in this way before this is proposed. The child's foster carer can also supervise contact if they and their own social worker consents.

**22.36** The local authority must consider the child's views on contact if they are of a sufficient age and understanding to have an input. The child's views will normally be communicated via the children's guardian. If the guardian's recommendations for contact are at odds with the views of the child themselves, it may be necessary to consider separate representation of the child (see chapter 12).

**22.37** The level of contact proposed in the final care plan should accord with the child's best interests in light of the proposed final orders.

## No contact

**22.38** If the local authority or children's guardian are of the view that there should be no contact between a child and a holder of parental responsibility, they must make an application to the court under s 34(4) of the CA 1989 to refuse contact.

**22.39** Whilst the local authority is under a statutory duty to arrange reasonable contact for the child, they may refuse to do so under s 34(6) if they are satisfied that it is necessary to do so in order to safeguard or promote the child's welfare, and the refusal is decided upon as a matter of urgency and does not last for more than 7 days.

**22.40** If the local authority wishes to suspend contact prior to a court hearing, the parent must be notified in writing that contact has been suspended, and the local authority must provide reasons for their decision.[8] The local authority must issue an application if they intend to suspend contact for more than 7 days and this is not agreed by the person with whom the child is supposed to have contact.

**22.41** The local authority's duty is limited to *offering* reasonable contact. If a parent does not take up the contact sessions offered, the local authority is under no obligation to take any further steps save to assist the parent in engaging in the contact proposed. The local authority cannot require a parent to contact the contact centre or social worker prior to the planned session to notify them of their attendance.

## INDEPENDENT REVIEWING OFFICER

**22.42** If a child is looked after by the local authority, an independent reviewing officer ('IRO') must be appointed. The function of an IRO is to participate in the review process for a child, to chair review meetings and to monitor the local authority functions in accordance with the child's care plan. The IRO should refer the matter to Cafcass if they have concerns about how the local authority is exercising their duty to the child. If the IRO refers the matter to Cafcass following concerns, it is possible for Cafcass to appoint a guardian and make an application to the court on behalf of the child, bringing the deficiencies in the local authority's actions to the court's attention.[9]

**22.43** At the conclusion of care proceedings and in the event that a care order is made, the children's guardian will write or speak to the IRO in relation to the care plan and any provisions that the guardian considers are essential in the future planning for the child. Once a care order is made, the guardian's role ceases and the overview of the care plan becomes the responsibility of the IRO.

---

[8] CPPCR Regulations 2010, reg 8.
[9] The IRO handbook contains guidance for IROs in the exercise of their duties.

## CARE PLAN FOR ADOPTION

**22.44** In the event that the local authority's care plan is one of adoption, the local authority must also make an application for a placement order. It is not possible to be place a child with the local authority for adoption without either parental consent or a placement order first having been made (see chapter 29). Within a care plan where the proposal is adoption, there must be consideration of the transition plan for the child in the event that an adoptive placement is found for them, and what reduction there will be in contact between the child and their natural parent. Information should also be given as to what contact (if any) is proposed in the event a placement order is made.

**22.45** Before a placement order application can be made, the local authority's decision maker must consider whether it is in the child's best interest to be placed for adoption. A placement order application can only be made if the local authority is of view that it is in the best interests of the child to be placed for adoption. For a full discussion of placement orders, see chapter 29.

# CHAPTER 23

# THE EFFECT OF A FINAL CARE ORDER

## PRELIMINARY: THE ROLES OF THE FAMILY COURT AND OF THE LOCAL AUTHORITY

### 'A cardinal principle'

**23.1** It is a fundamental principle of the Children Act 1989 ('CA 1989') that once a final care order has been made in respect of a child the court ceases, with very limited exceptions, to have a role in taking decisions about that child.

**23.2** The classic statement of this principle, the reasoning behind it, and the exceptions to it is found in the speech of Lord Nicholls of Birkenhead in the case of *Re S (Minors) (Care Order: Implementation of Care Plan); Re W (Minors) (Care Order: Adequacy of Care Plan)*[1] where His Lordship says:

> '[23] ... First, a cardinal principle of the Children Act 1989 is that when the court makes a care order it becomes the duty of the local authority designated by the order to receive the child into its care while the order remains in force. So long as the care order is in force the authority has parental responsibility for the child. The authority also has power to decide the extent to which a parent of the child may meet his responsibility for him: s 33. An authority might, for instance, not permit parents to change the school of a child living at home. While a care order is in force the court's powers, under its inherent jurisdiction, are expressly excluded: s 100(2)(c) and (d). Further, the court may not make a contact order, a prohibited steps order or a specific issue order: s 9(1).
>
> [24] There are limited exceptions to this principle of non-intervention by the court in the authority's discharge of its parental responsibility for a child in its care under a care order. The court retains jurisdiction to decide disputes about contact with children in care: s 34 of the Children Act 1989. The court may discharge a care order, either on an application made for the purpose under s 39 or as a consequence of making a residence order (ss 9(1) and 91(1)). The High Court's judicial review jurisdiction also remains available.
>
> [25] These exceptions do not detract significantly from the basic principle. The Children Act 1989 delineated the boundary of responsibility with complete clarity. Where a care order is made the responsibility for the child's care is with the

---

[1] [2002] 1 FLR 815.

authority rather than the court. The court retains no supervisory role, monitoring the authority's discharge of its responsibilities. That was the intention of Parliament.

...

[28] The Children Act 1989, embodying what I have described as a cardinal principle, represents the assessment made by Parliament of the division of responsibility which would best promote the interests of children within the overall care system. The court operates as the gateway into care, and makes the necessary care order when the threshold conditions are satisfied and the court considers a care order would be in the best interests of the child. That is the responsibility of the court. Thereafter the court has no continuing role in relation to the care order. Then it is the responsibility of the local authority to decide how the child should be cared for.'

23.3 Although the primary responsibility for making decisions about a child passes to the local authority on making of a final care order, that decision making takes place in the context of a statutory framework. The nature of that framework is the subject of this chapter. This subject is important not only because of the imperative need for local authorities to act within the law, and with respect to the rights of parents and others, when exercising their powers in relation to children in care but also because an appreciation of the legal and practical consequences of committing a child to the care of a local authority is an essential element in the balancing exercise that has to be undertaken in deciding whether or not the child's welfare requires the making of a care order.

## The care plan

23.4 An important part of the court's balancing exercise in deciding whether or not to make a care order is its consideration of the local authority's proposals for the future care of the child. The Adoption and Children Act 2002 inserted a new section[2] into the CA 1989 requiring a formal statement of those proposals to be provided to the court.[3] This section provides that:[4]

'Where an application is made on which a care order might be made with respect to a child, the appropriate local authority must, within such time as the court may direct, prepare a plan ("a care plan") for the future care of the child.'

23.5 A care plan must contain any, 'prescribed information and do so in the prescribed manner'.[5] The Care Planning, Placement and Case Review (England) Regulations 2010,[6] Part 2 and Sch 1 set out in great detail the prescribed information, which cover such issues as the long-term plan for the child, the

---

[2] Section 31A.
[3] This formalised what had long been regarded as good practice.
[4] Section 31A(1).
[5] Section 31A(3).
[6] SI 2010/959.

placement proposed, the arrangements proposed for meeting the child's educational needs, and arrangements for contact between the child and their birth family.[7]

**23.6** The Adoption and Children Act 2002 also inserted a new subs (3A) into s 31 of the CA 1989. This prohibited the making of a care order until the court had, 'considered a section 31A plan'. However, the Children and Families Act 2014 sought to limit significantly the scope of the court's enquiry into a care plan by replacing subs (3A) as enacted in 2002 with the following:

'(3A) A court deciding whether to make a care order –

(a) is required to consider the permanence provisions of the section 31A plan for the child concerned, but
(b) is not required to consider the remainder of the section 31A plan, subject to section 34(11).

(3B) For the purposes of subsection (3A), the permanence provisions of a section 31A plan are such of the plan's provisions setting out the long-term plan for the upbringing of the child concerned as provide for any of the following –

(a) the child to live with any parent of the child's or with any other member of, or any friend of, the child's family;
(b) adoption;
(c) long-term care not within paragraph (a) or (b).'

**23.7** The legislature returned to s 31, and the issue of the extent of the court's scrutiny of the care plan in 2017 when the Children and Social Work Act 2017 substituted the following for subs (3B):[8]

'In section 31 of the Children Act 1989 (care and supervision orders), for subsection (3B) substitute –

"(3B) For the purposes of subsection (3A), the permanence provisions of a section 31A plan are –
(a) such of the plan's provisions setting out the long-term plan for the upbringing of the child concerned as provide for any of the following –
  (i) the child to live with any parent of the child's or with any other member of, or any friend of, the child's family;
  (ii) adoption;
  (iii) long-term care not within sub-paragraph (i) or (ii);
(b) such of the plan's provisions as set out any of the following –
  (i) the impact on the child concerned of any harm that he or she suffered or was likely to suffer;
  (ii) the current and future needs of the child (including needs arising out of that impact);
  (iii) the way in which the long-term plan for the upbringing of the child would meet those current and future needs."'

---

[7] These Regulations are supplemented by *The Children Act 1989 Guidance and regulations Volume 2: Care Planning, Placement and Case Review*, HM Government, March 2010, see in particular, ch 2.

[8] See s 8 of the 2017 Act, which came into force on 31 October 2017: see Children and Social Work Act 2017 (Commencement No 1) Regulations 2017, SI 2017/918.

**23.8** The clearly intended effect of the provisions of the 2014 Act is to focus the court's attention on the decisions needed as to the child's permanent placement and to limit the extent to which the court concerned itself with the detailed plans of the local authority. However, they should be read in the light of the observations of King LJ in the case of *Re S-W (Care Proceedings: Case Management Hearing)*:[9]

> 'It can be seen that a court is "required" to consider permanence plans but, save as to contact (CA 1989, s 34(11)), it is "not required" to consider the remainder of the care plan. The fact that the court is 'not required' to consider certain other aspects of the plan does not mean it is prohibited from doing so; one can imagine any number of situations where a particular child's individual identified needs will mean that the court, whilst not seeking to trespass on the exercise of parental responsibility of the local authority, forms the view that the child's welfare necessitates the court satisfying itself in relation to certain important aspects of the care plan not found within the permanence provisions themselves.'[10]

**23.9** Courts remain, in practice, rigorous in examining all aspects of a care plan and in pressing applicant local authorities to amend, clarify or expand upon its contents. A commonly encountered example is where an expert reporting in the proceedings has identified therapeutic needs of the child and the court considers that the care plan should contain a clear, detailed and credible statement of how those needs will be met. In such cases, the new s 31(3B)(b) seems to provide statutory authority for a rigorous examination of the local authority's plan.

**23.10** In the event that the court considers that the care plan is deficient, it can invite the local authority to reconsider its plan. It can also require, in the exercise of its case management powers, the local authority to present evidence as to matters that it does not propose, or indeed would actively oppose, being included in the plan so that the court can carry out a proper welfare evaluation of all available options. The relevant legislation and case law on this issue was comprehensively reviewed by Ryder LJ in the case of *Re W (Care Proceedings: Functions of Court and Local Authority)*.[11] His Lordship summarised the principles he identified, and the consequences that should follow from an irreconcilable difference between the court and the local authority, in the following terms:

> 'The local authority is required to provide the evidence to enable the judge to undertake the welfare and proportionality evaluations. That includes a description of the services that are available and practicable for each placement option and each order being considered by the court. It may be convenient for that to be put into the form of the s 31A care plan in the alternative so that the court may expressly undertake its statutory function to consider the same or in evidence filed in support. There should be no question of an authority declining to file its evidence or proposed plans in response to the court's evaluations. None of this

---

[9] [2015] 2 FLR 136.
[10] Paragraph [34].
[11] [2014] 2 FLR 431.

strays into the impermissible territory of seeking to bind the local authority's care planning and review processes once a full order is made. If a local authority makes it clear that it will not implement a care plan option about which evidence has been given and which the judge prefers on welfare and proportionality grounds, then in a rare case it can be subjected to challenge in the High Court within the proceedings.[12] If and insofar as the local authority is of the opinion that it needs to change a care plan option approved by the court once the proceedings are complete, it is entitled to do so and must do so in accordance with the processes laid out in the regulations. If it does so without good reason it will risk an appropriate challenge including on behalf of the child after a referral from an IRO[13] to Cafcass or a Welsh family proceedings officer.'[14]

The judgment of Ryder LJ was strongly endorsed by Sir James Munby P, who observed that it, '... explains and elucidates the respective functions of the court and the local authority in care cases' and will (along with the complementary principles set out in *Re B-S*[15]), '... inform practice in all care cases'.[16]

**23.11** Once a final care plan has been approved by the court, responsibility for implementing it passes to the local authority. In the event that the local authority fail to follow the provisions of the plan in their care for the child, or decide that the plan should be changed, that decision can be challenged by way of an application to discharge the care order, judicial review, and/or an application for injunctive relief under the Human Rights Act 1998.

## THE DUTIES OF THE LOCAL AUTHORITY

### Receiving the child into care

**23.12** Section 33(1) of the CA 1989 provides that:

'Where a where a care order is made with respect to a child it shall be the duty of the local authority designated by the order to receive the child into their care and to keep him in their care while the order remains in force.'

**23.13** There is no separate definition of what is meant by a local authority receiving a child, 'into their care' but the remaining subsections of s 33 set out the effects of making a care order. The most important of these effects is the acquisition by the local authority of, 'overriding parental responsibility';[17] this issue is discussed in detail below.

---

[12] See, for example, the decision of Munby J (as he then was) in *Re X; Barnet London Borough Council v Y and X* [2006] 2 FLR 998, discussed by Ryder LJ at para [84] of his judgment.
[13] 'Independent Reviewing Officer': for the appointment and functions of the Independent reviewing Officer, see CA 1989, ss 25A, 25B and 25C and the Care Planning, Placement and Case Review Regulations 2010, reg 36 and Part 8.
[14] At para [101].
[15] [2014] 1 FLR 1035.
[16] Paragraph [114].
[17] A phrase that appears nowhere in the CA 1989 but is often used as shorthand to describe the effects of s 33(3) and (4) of the Act: see for example its use by Munby J (as he then was) in *Re F: F v Lambeth London Borough Council* [2002] 1 FLR 217 at para [52].

**23.14** Other sections in the Act impose specific duties on local authorities in relation to children in their care; notable examples are a duty to provide the child with accommodation[18] and the duty to allow contact between children in care and their parents and other persons.[19] These duties are also considered below and elsewhere in this work.[20]

## Designation of local authority: 'these undoubtedly difficult subsections'[21]

**23.15** Clearly, the first question that has to be answered when considering the duties of a local authority towards a particular child is that of which local authority owes those duties. Section 31(1) of the Act is explicit in stating that whilst an application for a care order may be made by, 'any local authority' the order made is for the child to be placed, 'in the care of[22] a designated local authority'.[23] It is by no means uncommon for the local authority applying for a care order to propose that another authority be designated, should an order be made. An example of a case when this would be appropriate is where a child already lives with family members who live in the area of another local authority and the plan is that they remain in that placement under the auspices of a care order. In such a case, it makes obvious sense for the local authority responsible for providing services for a child to be the authority local to where the child lives. However, not all cases are as straight forward or clear cut as this and regard has to be had to the provisions of the Act as they apply to the facts of each case.[24]

**23.16** The issue of which local authority is to be, 'designated' to receive a child into their care is governed by s 31(8) of the Act. This subsection reads as follows:

> 'The local authority designated in a care order must be –
> 
> (a) the authority within whose area the child is ordinarily resident; or
> (b) where the child does not reside in the area of a local authority, the authority within whose area any circumstances arose in consequence of which the order is being made.'

**23.17** This has to be read in conjunction with s 105(6), which provides that:

---

[18] Section 22A of the Act, which should be read with reference to the provisions as to the ways in which children are to be accommodated set out in s 22C.
[19] Section 34.
[20] See detailed consideration of contact issues in chapter 18.
[21] Per Thorpe LJ in *Northamptonshire County Council v Islington London Borough Council* [1999] 2 FLR 881 at 885.
[22] Or under the supervision of: s 31(1)(b).
[23] Section 31(1)(a).
[24] It also has to be acknowledged that a factor in 'designation' disputes between local authorities is the fact that there are very significant resource implications for a local authority that is 'designated' under a care order. For example, Kent County Council's budget for the financial year 2016/7 allowed for spending of £30,736,100 on the net cost of providing accommodation in foster care (both 'in-house' and provided by independent agencies) for 1,127 children: *Budget Book 2016/7*, available at kent.gov.uk (accessed 25 April 2017).

'In determining the "ordinary residence" of a child for any purpose of this Act, there shall be disregarded any period in which he lives in any place –

(a) which is a school or other institution;
(b) in accordance with the requirements of a supervision order under this Act
(ba) in accordance with the requirements of a youth rehabilitation order under Part 1 of the Criminal Justice and Immigration Act 2008; or
(c) while he is being provided with accommodation by or on behalf of a local authority.'

**23.18** These provisions have caused a surprising amount of difficulty over the years. They have given rise to differences of opinion between eminent Family Division judges[25] and continue to be the subject of litigation.[26] As recently as May 2012, some 21 years after the provisions came into force, their proper interpretation divided the Court of Appeal in the, 'nice, tricky, little case' of *Re D (Local Authority Responsibility)*.[27]

**23.19** The proper approach to the provisions, as they had been construed in the relevant reported cases, was set out by David Hershman QC (sitting as a Deputy Judge of the Family Division) in the following much cited passage in his judgment in the case of *London Borough of Redbridge v Newport City Council*:[28]

'I extract the principles that I must apply to the instant case:

(1) the first question the court must consider in determining an issue of designated authority under the Children Act 1989, s 31(8) is "ordinary residence" of the child concerned. This is to be determined at the time of the hearing (per Thorpe LJ in *Northamptonshire County Council v Islington London Borough Council* [2001] Fam 364, [1999] 2 FLR 881 at 370 and 887 respectively);

(2) when determining ordinary residence at the date of the hearing the court shall, by virtue of the Children Act 1989, s 105(6), disregard any period of time during which the child was provided with accommodation by the local authority (per Bracewell J in *Re BC (A Minor) (Care Order: Appropriate Local Authority)* [1995] 3 FCR 598 and per Thorpe LJ in *Northamptonshire County Council v Islington London Borough Council* at 372 and 889 respectively) described as the 'stop-the-clock approach' or extending the period of ordinary residence in the authority from where the child has moved (Area A) and delaying the notional period of residence to the area where the child moved to (Area B);

---

[25] See for example the views of Bracewell J in *Re BC (A Minor) (Care Order: Appropriate Local Authority)* [1995] 3 FCR 598, Wilson J (as he then was) in *Gateshead Metropolitan Borough Council v L and another* [1996] 2 FLR 179 and Singer J in *Re R (Care Order: Jurisdiction)* [1995] 1 FLR 711: these and other cases are discussed by Thorpe LJ in *Northamptonshire County Council v Islington London Borough Council* [1999] 2 FLR 881.
[26] For a recent example, see *Sheffield City Council v Bradford City Council* [2013] 1 FLR 1027.
[27] [2013] 2 FLR 673: the description of the case is that of Ward LJ at para [1]. This case is essential reading in considering the designation issue in cases where the mother of the child who is the subject of proceedings is herself in the care of a local authority.
[28] [2004] 2 FLR 226.

(3) the "stop-the-clock approach" does not apply when the child is with a parent (per Wall J in *Re C (Care Order: Appropriate Local Authority)* [1997] 1 FLR 544 and per Thorpe LJ in *Re H (Care Order: Appropriate Local Authority)* [2003] EWCA Civ 1629, [2004] 1 FLR 534), relative, friend or other person connected with him (per Thorpe LJ in *Re H (Care Order: Appropriate Local Authority)*) because the child is not being provided with accommodation by or on behalf of a local authority under the Children Act 1989, s 105(6)(c);

(4) another exception to the 'stop-the-clock approach' is if there are "exceptional circumstances" to justify looking at the history during this period of time (per Thorpe LJ in *Northamptonshire County Council v Islington London Borough Council* [2001] Fam 364, [1999] 2 FLR 881 and in *Re C (A Child) v Plymouth City Council* [2000] 1 FLR 875 at 879). The Court of Appeal has made it clear that exceptional means more than a child having acquired a new ordinary residence (in Area B) and severing all links (in Area A) (see Swinton Thomas LJ in *Re C (A Child) v Plymouth City Council* at 880 and Thorpe LJ in *Re H (Care Order: Appropriate Local Authority)* at paras [9]–[14]);

(5) if after having carried out this analysis the conclusion of the court is that the child is not ordinarily resident in any local authority area the court must determine the designated authority in accordance with the Children Act 1989, s 31(8)(b) (per Thorpe LJ in *Northamptonshire County Council v Islington London Borough Council* at 371 and 888 respectively);

(6) the test to be applied in determining the "circumstances arose in consequence of which the order is being made" under the Children Act 1989, s 31(8)(b) means the primary circumstances that carry the case over the s 31 threshold (per Thorpe LJ in *Northamptonshire County Council v Islington London Borough Council* at 373 and 890 respectively). At this point there is no consideration of 'exceptional circumstances' or of intervening events.'[29]

**23.20** However, Mr Hershman QC's point (3) now needs to be revised as the effect of s 22C of the CA 1989 (inserted by the Children and Young Persons Act 2008) is that accommodation of the child with a, 'relative, friend or other person connected with [the child]'[30] is expressly declared to be a placement made by the local authority and hence would fall within his point (2): see comments of Bodey J in *Sheffield City Council v Bradford City Council*[31] at paras [15]–[19].

## The duty to provide accommodation for a child in care

**23.21** Section 22 of the CA 1989 imposes on local authorities[32] a duty in relation to any child looked after by them[33] to 'safeguard and promote his welfare'.[34] This general duty is now supplemented by specific provisions in

---

[29] At para 24.
[30] Section 22C(6)(a): parents and certain others fall in a different category, see s 22C(3).
[31] Above.
[32] For equivalent provisions in Wales, see Social Services and Well-Being (Wales) Act 2014, Part 6.
[33] Defined by s 22(1)(a) as including a child in the care of the local authority.
[34] Section 22(3)(a).

relation to the accommodation and maintenance of looked after children that were inserted by the Children and Young Persons Act 2008.[35]

**23.22** As noted above, s 22A straightforwardly provides that when a child is in the care of a local authority 'it is their duty to provide the child with accommodation'.

**23.23** The ways in which this duty can be met are set out in detail in s 22C.[36] This section is interesting as on its face it expresses a clear preference for placement of children with their parents or, if this is not possible with family members,[37] and it is also in other ways quite prescriptive as to the nature of placement permitted in an individual case. However, on a closer reading both these features are heavily qualified.

**23.24** The key subsections of s 22C are as follows:

'(2) The local authority must make arrangements for C to live with a person who falls within subsection (3) (but subject to subsection (4)).

(3) A person ("P") falls within this subsection if –

(a) P is a parent of C;
(b) P is not a parent of C but has parental responsibility for C; or
(c) in a case where C is in the care of the local authority and there was a child arrangements order in force with respect to C immediately before the care order was made, P was a person named in the child arrangements order as a person with whom C was to live.

(4) Subsection (2) does not require the local authority to make arrangements of the kind mentioned in that subsection if doing so –

(a) would not be consistent with C's welfare; or
(b) would not be reasonably practicable.

(5) If the local authority are unable to make arrangements under subsection (2), they must place C in the placement which is, in their opinion, the most appropriate placement available.

(6) In subsection (5) "placement" means –

(a) placement with an individual who is a relative, friend or other person connected with C and who is also a local authority foster parent;
(b) placement with a local authority foster parent who does not fall within paragraph (a);
(c) placement in a children's home in respect of which a person is registered under Part 2 of the Care Standards Act 2000; or
(d) subject to section 22D, placement in accordance with other arrangements which comply with any regulations made for the purposes of this section.

---

[35] Sections 22A–22G.
[36] Which applies equally to children, 'looked after' other than under a care order, see s 22(1)(b).
[37] Hence acknowledging the rights of children, parents and wider family to a 'family life' in accordance with Art 8 of the Convention for the Protection of Human Rights and Fundamental Freedoms 1950.

(7) In determining the most appropriate placement for C, the local authority must, subject to subsection (9B) and the other provisions of this Part (in particular, to their duties under section 22) –

    (a) give preference to a placement falling within paragraph (a) of subsection (6) over placements falling within the other paragraphs of that subsection;

    (b) comply, so far as is reasonably practicable in all the circumstances of C's case, with the requirements of subsection (8); and

    (c) comply with subsection (9) unless that is not reasonably practicable.

(8) The local authority must ensure that the placement is such that –

    (a) it allows C to live near C's home;

    (b) it does not disrupt C's education or training;

    (c) if C has a sibling for whom the local authority are also providing accommodation, it enables C and the sibling to live together;

    (d) if C is disabled, the accommodation provided is suitable to C's particular needs.

(9) The placement must be such that C is provided with accommodation within the local authority's area.'

**23.25** Section 22(9A), (9B) and (9C) make special provision for placement of children in respect of whom the local authority is either considering adoption or where the local authority is satisfied that the child ought to be placed for adoption but is not authorised to place under the Adoption and Children Act 2002.[38] In such cases the local authority must consider placement with a person falling within s 22(6)(a) and, where it decides that this is not the most appropriate placement, must consider placing the child 'with a local authority foster parent who has been approved as a prospective adopter'.

**23.26** This provision is particularly important in relation to children who are the subject of interim care orders, to which it applies by operation of the provisions of s 31(11).[39] In such cases it gives statutory authority, and indeed encouragement, for the practice of 'parallel planning' whereby a child who is removed from their family is placed with alternative carers who could become its adoptive parents should a plan for permanent removal with a view to adoption ultimately be approved by the court.

**23.27** Further provisions as to placement of children in care are set out in Parts 3 and 4 of the Care Planning, Placement and Case Review (England) Regulations 2010.

**23.28** It is important to remember that decisions as to placement following the making of a final care order are for the local authority, not the family court.[40]

---

[38] See s 22C(9A)(a) and (b) of the 1989 Act, as amended.

[39] Which provides that, 'except where express provision to the contrary is made' the expression, 'care order' includes an interim care order.

[40] See the well-known decision of the House of Lords in in *Re S (Minors) (Care Order: Implementation of Care Plan); Re W (Minors) (Care Order: Adequacy of Care Plan)* [2002] 1 FLR 815.

However, such decisions may be the subject of judicial review.[41] They may also be challenged by way of an application to discharge the care order.[42] In cases where the local authority proposes a change in the child's placement following the making of a final care order, there is jurisdiction to grant an injunction under s 8 of the Human Rights Act 1998 to prevent implementation of that decision pending the determination of a challenge to that decision.[43]

## Duration of care orders and the problem of the 17 year old 'child'

**23.29** The duration of a care order, and hence of a duty of the local authority to receive the child into their care, is determined by s 91(12). This provides that:

> 'Any care order, other than an interim care order,[44] shall continue in force until the child reaches the age of eighteen, unless it is brought to an end earlier.'

**23.30** However, s 31(3) of the Act prohibits the making of a care or supervision order in respect of a child who has reached the age of seventeen, or sixteen in the case of a child who is married.

**23.31** In the case of *Re M (Children)*[45] the Court of Appeal considered the relationship between s 31(3) and the court's inherent jurisdiction and jurisdiction in wardship[46] in relation to a child who had attained the age of 17 years during the proceedings. It was common ground before the court that no care order could be made.[47] It was further held that the court does not have jurisdiction to exercise its inherent jurisdiction so as to grant authority to a local authority to provide care for a child where the local authority would not otherwise have power to do so under the statutory scheme. However, the court may make orders to support arrangements that are, 'otherwise legitimately in place' if they are not contrary to s 100;[48] in the instant case this rendered legitimate the trial judge's order that the child, 'remain a ward of court' without any requirement for them to be accommodated by the local authority.[49]

---

[41] See comments of Lord Nicholls of Birkenhead in *Re S (Minors) (Care Order: Implementation of Care Plan); Re W (Minors)(Care Order: Adequacy of Care Plan)* (above) at para 43, discussed by Munby J (as he then was) in *Re G (Care: Challenge to Local Authority's Decision)* [2003] 2 FLR 42 at paras [47]–[51].
[42] See below.
[43] For an example of such a case, see the decision of Baker J in *Re DE (Child Under Care Order: Injunction Under Human Rights Act 1998)* [2015] 1 FLR 1001, which also contains detailed guidance (approved by Sir James Munby P) on the procedure to be adopted in dealing with such applications.
[44] For the duration of interim care orders, see s 38(4) of the 1989 Act, as amended; discussed in detail in chapter 13.
[45] [2016] EWCA Civ 937.
[46] The use of wardship and the inherent jurisdiction being subject to restrictions set out in s 100 of the 1989 Act.
[47] Judgment of McFarlane LJ, para [10].
[48] Judgment of McFarlane LJ, paras [30]–[41]
[49] Such a requirement would be contrary to s 100(2) of the 1989 Act.

**23.32** For consideration of the issues that arise when a child can in law be made the subject of either a care order or an order of the Court of Protection,[50] including the use of the court's power to transfer of proceedings to the Court of Protection[51] see the judgment of Hedley J in *B (A Local Authority) v RM, MM AND AM*.[52]

## Applications to discharge care orders

**23.33** Section 39 of the Act makes provision for applications for the discharge of a care order. Such applications can be made by:[53]

'(a) any person who has parental responsibility for the child;
(b) the child himself; or
(c) the local authority designated by the order.'

**23.34** The court has power to substitute a supervision order for a care order on the application of any person entitled to apply for discharge of the care order.[54]

**23.35** Applications for discharge of care orders follow the same procedure, set out in Part 12 of the Family Procedure Rules 2010, as is laid down for the making of such orders.[55] They are, 'specified proceedings'[56] so the child is an automatic respondent to the application[57] and the court is required to appoint an officer of Cafcass (or a Welsh family proceedings officer where applicable) as the child's guardian unless satisfied that this is not necessary.[58]

**23.36** There is no requirement for the child to obtain permission of the court to make an application. Section 39 of the Act contains no equivalent provision to s 10(8), which imposes a requirement for the child to obtain leave to make a s 8 application.[59]

**23.37** When considering an application to discharge a care order, the child's welfare is the court's paramount consideration and regard has to be had to the checklist in s 1(3) of the Act.[60] The burden is on the applicant to show that the

---

[50] This jurisdiction can be exercised in relation to a person who lacks capacity once they have reached the age of 16 years: Mental Capacity Act 2005, s 2(5).
[51] See Mental Capacity Act 2005 (Transfer of Proceedings) Order 2007, arts 2 and 3.
[52] [2011] 1 FLR 1635.
[53] Section 39(1) of the 1989 Act.
[54] Section 39(4) of the 1989 Act.
[55] See r 12.2.
[56] Section 41(6)(c) of the 1989 Act.
[57] Rule 12.3.
[58] Section 41(1) of the 1989 Act.
[59] *Re A (Care: Discharge Application by Child)* [1995] 1 FLR 599.
[60] Section 1(4)(b).

child's welfare requires the discharge of the order.[61] However, there is no obligation on the applicant to show that the threshold criteria no longer apply.[62]

**23.38** When an application for discharge of a care order has been disposed of, no further application may be made in respect of the child concerned without leave of the court, unless the period between disposal of the application and the further application exceeds 6 months.[63] The court's general power to impose, on disposing of an application, a requirement that leave of the court is obtained before an application for an order of a specified kind is made[64] is also available to it on disposing of an application to discharge a care order.

## Duties to children leaving care

**23.39** In the case of older children subject to care orders who are, 'looked after' by the local authority[65] but cease to be so, the local authority retains certain duties to provide support and assistance.[66]

**23.40** In the case of children aged 16 or 17 when they cease to be looked after (ie they move to independent living although a care order may still be in effect) these duties arise under s 23A. In the case of children who have attained the age of 18, so that the care order has ceased to be in force, these duties arise under s 23C and subsist until the child's twenty first birthday (or later if a programme of education or training is being pursued).[67]

**23.41** Younger children who cease to be the subject of care orders may still be treated as, 'children in need' and provided with services in accordance with the local authority's general duty under s 17 of the CA 1989.

# PARENTAL RESPONSIBILITY FOR CHILDREN IN CARE

**23.42** The making of a care order does not remove the parental responsibility of parents and others who hold it[68] but results in it being shared between those persons and the local authority. However, as was said by the responsible minister, David Mellor QC MP, during the committee stage of the Children Bill the intention of the legislation is that, 'the local authority must be in the driving seat'.[69] This aim is achieved by the terms of s 33(3) of the Act.

---

[61] *Re MD and TD (Minors) (No 2)* [1994] Fam Law 489, FD per Wall J (as he then was).
[62] *Re S (Discharge of Care Order)* [1995] 2 FLR 639 CA.
[63] Section 91(15) of the 1989 Act.
[64] Section 91(14) of the 1989 Act.
[65] In accordance with s 22(1)(a) of the 1989 Act.
[66] See ss 23A–23D and Sch 2, paras 19A–19C of the CA 1989, all inserted by the Children (Leaving Care) Act 2000 and subsequent amending legislation.
[67] Sections 23C(6) and (7).
[68] Save where it is held by a person who does so solely by virtue of being named in a child arrangements order that is discharged by the making of the care order: see below.
[69] Quoted in the commentary to s 33 of the Act in *Current Law Statutes Annotated* 189, Vol 4:

**23.43** The court's decision to make a care order, once the threshold criteria in s 31 of the Act are found to be met is always, of course, dependent on an analysis of the child's welfare in accordance with s 1 of the Act. Cases occasionally arise where the decisive factor in the court's welfare analysis is the need to vest parental responsibility in the local authority. An example is the case of Re M (Care Order: Parental Responsibility)[70] in which Cazalet J made a care order in relation to an abandoned baby whose family were untraceable[71] on the basis that his welfare required the that the local authority have the power to make decisions about him that flows from holding parental responsibility.

## The core statutory concepts

**23.44** There are two aspects to the provisions of s 33 in relation to parental responsibility for children in care. These are, firstly, the granting of parental responsibility to the local authority, subject to certain restrictions as to the way in which it can be exercised, and, secondly, the granting to the local authority of the power to determine the extent to which a parent, guardian, special guardian or step-parent[72] can meet their parental responsibility.[73]

**23.45** The relevant subsection reads as follows:

> '(3) While a care order is in force with respect to a child, the local authority designated by the order shall –
> 
> (a) have parental responsibility for the child; and
> (b) have the power (subject to the following provisions of this section) to determine the extent to which –
> (i) a parent, guardian or special guardian of the child; or
> (ii) a person who by virtue of section 4A has parental responsibility for the child
> may meet his parental responsibility for him.'

**23.46** Both the parental responsibility held by the local authority and its power to determine the extent the which another person meets their parental responsibility are the subject of important restrictions or, one might prefer to say, safeguards set out elsewhere in s 33.

---

this note also summarises the argument of one prominent commentator for the complete removal of parental responsibility from the parents of children in care.

[70] [1996] 2 FLR 84.
[71] It is poignant to note that this child will have celebrated his birthdays on a date that represents only the best estimate of the medical experts as to his actual date of birth.
[72] See s 4A of the Act.
[73] Only persons in these classes can hold parental responsibility for a child who is the subject of a care order as the automatic discharge of any child arrangements order in respect of the child that occurs on the making of the care order (see s 91(2) of the Act, discussed below) also brings to an end the holding of parental responsibility by a person named in such an order as provided for in s 12(2) and (2A) of the 1989 Act.

## The limits of a local authority's parental responsibility

**23.47** Section 33(6) sets out three specific prohibitions as to the exercise of parental responsibility by a local authority in relation to a child in their care. This subsection (as amended by the Adoption and Children Act 2002) reads as follows:

> '(6) While a care order is in force with respect to a child, the local authority designated by the order shall not –
>
> (a) cause the child to be brought up in any religious persuasion other than that in which he would have been brought up if the order had not been made; or
> (b) have the right –
>   (i) ...
>   (ii) to agree or refuse to agree to the making of an adoption order, or an order under section 84 of the Adoption and Children Act 2002, with respect to the child;[74] or
>   (iii) to appoint a guardian for the child.[75]'

**23.48** Statutory provisions as to the religious upbringing of children removed from the care of their parents have a long history: the Prevention of Cruelty to, and Protection of, Children Act 1889 imposed a duty on the court to, 'endeavour to ascertain' the religious persuasion to which the child belongs and, if possible, to place them in the care of a person of the same persuasion (s 5(2) of the 1889 Act). The, 'subtle and careful' language of s 33(6)(a) receives detailed analysis, in the context of modern thinking as to the overriding importance of the child's welfare, in the judgment of Baker J in the case of *Re A and D (Local Authority: Religious Upbringing)*.[76]

**23.49** Section 33(7) imposes two further restrictions on the taking of steps that could otherwise be within the scope of the holding of parental responsibility for a child by providing that:

> 'While a care order is in force with respect to a child, no person may –
>
> (a) cause the child to be known by a new surname; or
> (b) remove him from the United Kingdom,
>
> without either the written consent of every person who has parental responsibility for the child or the leave of the court.'

**23.50** These prohibitions would apply not only to the local authority but to a foster carer or other person with whom a child is placed in accordance with

---

[74] In arranging for children in care to be adopted, a local authority will act as an 'adoption agency' as defined by s 2(1) of the Adoption and Children Act 2002 and will follow the procedure for placement set out in Chapter 3 of the 2002 Act.
[75] ie a guardian appointed in accordance with s 5 of the 1989 Act.
[76] [2011] 1 FLR 615: see in particular at paragraphs [73] to [75]. This very interesting case is discussed in detail in Simon Johnson's article, *Religion, Children and the Family Courts* [2013] Fam Law 574.

s 22C(3) or (6) of the Act. They mirror provisions that apply when a child is the subject of a child arrangements order or a special guardianship order.[77]

**23.51** In the case of *Re M, T, P, K and B (Care: Change of Name)*[78] it was held that an application for permission to change the surname of a child in care should be approached in the same way and in accordance with the same principles as are applied in private law cases.[79] The child's welfare is the court's paramount consideration and the welfare checklist[80] applies. In *Re M, T, P, K and B (Care: Change of Name)* permission to change the children's surname was granted on the basis that this step, which the children themselves wished to have taken, was necessary in order to protect the children, who were in foster care, from the risk posed by the extremely violent behaviour of their father should he or his family discover their whereabouts.

**23.52** Section 33(8)(a) permits the authority with care of a child to allow removal from the United Kingdom for a period of less than one month and this will allow carers to go overseas for holidays, with the agreement of the local authority. This again corresponds to the position where child arrangements or special guardianship orders are in place.[81]

**23.53** A local authority's plan for a child in their care to live outside England and Wales[82] requires the approval of the court in accordance with Sch 2, para 19 of the Act,[83] which sets out detailed criteria for the giving of such approval. If such approval has been given by the court, the prohibition on removal of the child from the United Kingdom does not apply.[84]

## The local authority's power to determine the extent to which others may meet their parental responsibility

**23.54** The local authority's power under s 33(3)(b) to control the exercise by others of their parental responsibility for a child is subject to the crucial qualification set out in s 33(4) that:

> 'The authority may not exercise the power in subsection (3)(b) unless they are satisfied that it is necessary to do so in order to safeguard or promote the child's welfare.'

**23.55** Furthermore, s 33(9) provides that:

---

[77] Sections 13(1) and 14C(3) of the 1989 Act respectively.
[78] [2000] 2 FLR 645.
[79] For these principles, see the decision of the House of Lords in *Dawson v Wearmouth* [1999] 1 FLR 1167.
[80] Section 1(3) of the Act.
[81] Sections 13(2) and 14C(4) respectively: in the case of a special guardianship order the period of removal authorised is 3 months.
[82] For example, by way of a permanent placement with relatives who live out of the jurisdiction.
[83] For children in the care of local authorities in Wales the corresponding provision is the Social Services and Well-Being (Wales) Act 2014, s 124.
[84] Section 33(8)(b).

'The power in subsection (3)(b) is subject (in addition to being subject to the provisions of this section) to any right, duty, power, responsibility or authority which a person mentioned in that provision has in relation to the child and his property by virtue of any other enactment.'

**23.56** Whilst s 33(3)(b) clearly envisages limits to the local authority's power to determine the extent to which others holding parental responsibility can exercise that responsibility,[85] the Act itself does not provide for a mechanism for adjudicating on disputes.[86] Nor does it provide a remedy to the parents or others holding parental responsibility who seek to challenge the local authority's determination as to how they can use it short of an application to discharge the care order, which is likely to face great difficulty if a court has already determined that the child's welfare requires the order to be made.[87]

## Remedies: local authority powers in respect of parental responsibility and human rights issues

**23.57** In their speeches in the case of *Re S (Minors) (Care Order: Implementation of Care Plan); Re W (Minors) (Care Order: Adequacy of Care Plan)*[88] both Lord Nicholls of Birkenhead and Lord Mackay of Clashfern discuss the remedies available should the local authority fail to act properly in exercising its parental responsibility. Lord Nicholls makes the following comments in the context of his consideration of the relationship between care proceedings under the CA 1989 and the rights of parents under the European Convention for the Protection of Human Rights and Fundamental Freedoms 1950 and, in particular, the right to family life protected by Art 8 of the Convention:

> '[62] ... if a local authority fails to discharge its parental responsibilities properly, and in consequence the rights of the parents under Art 8 are violated, the parents may, as a longstop, bring proceedings against the authority under s 7. I have already drawn attention to a case where this has happened. I say "as a longstop", because other remedies, both of an administrative nature and by way of court proceedings, may also be available in the particular case. For instance, Bedfordshire Council[89] has an independent visitor, a children's complaints officer and a children's rights officer. Sometimes court proceedings by way of judicial

---

[85] Baker J puts the point unequivocally in his judgment in *Re DE (Child Under Care Order)* [2015] 1 FLR 1001 (dealing with a removal of a child placed with parents under a care order): '... the local authority may not exercise its powers under a care order to determine how a parent is to exercise his or her parental responsibility unless satisfied it is necessary to safeguard or promote the child's welfare. For a local authority to remove a child in circumstances where its welfare did not require it would be manifestly unlawful and an unjustifiable interference with the family's Article 8 European Convention rights.' (at para [35]).

[86] Note that s 9(1) prohibits the making of prohibited steps or specific issue orders in respect of a child in care.

[87] See the discussion of applications to discharge care orders above, and in particular note that those applying for discharge of the order would need to show that this was justified on welfare grounds.

[88] [2002] 1 FLR 815.

[89] The local authority concerned in one of the case before their lordships.

review of a decision of a local authority may be the appropriate way to proceed. In a suitable case an application for discharge of the care order is available. One would not expect proceedings to be launched under s 7 of the Human Rights Act 1998 until any other appropriate remedial routes have first been explored.'

**23.58** Lord Mackay, who as Lord Chancellor had played a prominent role in the Parliamentary process leading to the enactment of the CA 1989, added these observations:

> '[109] When the Children Act 1989 was enacted the UK was a party to the European Convention for the Protection of Human Rights and Fundamental Freedoms 1950 although at that time the Convention was not incorporated into our domestic law. Accordingly the Act was framed in a way which took account of the terms of the Convention as then understood. For example, s 34 of the Children Act 1989 is a reflection of the requirement that a dispute relating to access is for decision by the court. In my opinion, the fundamental change brought about by the Act placing the responsibility for looking after children who are the subject of care orders squarely on the local authorities is not in any way incompatible with the Convention. In discharging its responsibility the local authority has the duty of respecting the Convention rights of the child and of each member of the child's family. If a dispute arises whether this duty has been breached in any particular case the person aggrieved can now invoke the court's jurisdiction to determine it, under s 7 of the Human Rights Act 1998, if no other route is available.'

**23.59** The judgment of Baker J in the case of *Re DE (Child Under Care Order)*[90] sets out in detail the steps that lead him to conclude, following *Re S (Minors) (Care Order: Implementation of Care Plan); Re W (Minors) (Care Order: Adequacy of Care Plan)* and other cases, that there is jurisdiction to grant an injunction under s 8 of the Human Rights Act 1998:

> '[24] Under s 33(4) of the CA 1989 ...
>
>> "The authority may not exercise the power in subsection (3)(b) unless they are satisfied that it is necessary to do so in order to safeguard or promote the child's welfare."
>
> It follows, therefore, that, when a child is placed at home under a care order, the local authority may not remove him from home unless satisfied that such a step is necessary to safeguard or promote his welfare.
>
> [25] Furthermore, under s 33(9) of the CA 1989:
>
>> "The power in subsection (3)(b) is subject (in addition to being subject to the provisions of this subsection) to any right, duty, power, responsibility or authority which a person mentioned in that provision has in relation to the child at his property by virtue of any other enactment."

---

[90] [2015] 1 FLR 1001: the substantive issue in this case was that of what remedy was available to the parents to prevent the local authority implementing a change in care plan from one of placement of the child at home with parents to removal of the child to foster care.

[26] The European Convention for the Protection of Human Rights and Fundamental Freedoms 1950 (the European Convention) was incorporated into the law of England and Wales by the HRA 1998. Under Art 8 of the European Convention:

> "(1) Everyone has the right to respect for his private and family life, his home and his correspondence.
>
> (2) There should be no interference by a public authority with exercise of this right except such as in accordance with the law and is necessary in a democratic society in the interests of national security, public safety or the economic wellbeing of the country for the prevention of disorder or crime, for the protection of health of morals, or the protection of the rights and freedoms of others."

[27] Under s 6(1) of the HRA 1998, it is unlawful for a public authority to act in a way which is incompatible with a right under the European Convention. The local authority is a public authority. In exercising its powers under a care order, the local authority must therefore comply with its obligations under Art 8 of the European Convention not to interfere with the rights of the child and his parents to respect for their private and family life.

[28] Previous decisions have identified that the local authority's duties under Art 8 of the European Convention are not confined to substantive obligations to refrain from inappropriate interference with the rights to family and private life but also incorporate procedural safeguards.

...

[30] Under s 7(1) of the HRA 1998, a parent who claimed that a local authority has acted, or is proposing to act, in a way that is made unlawful by s 6(1) may either bring proceedings under the HRA 1998 or rely on the European Convention right in any other legal proceedings. Under s 8(1) of the HRA 1998:

> "In relation to any act (or proposed act) of a public authority which the court finds is (or would be) unlawful, it may grant such relief or remedy, or make such order, within its powers as it considers just and appropriate."

This includes the power to grant injunctions which is vested in the High Court by s 37(1) of the Senior Courts Act 1981, in the county court by s 38 of the County Courts Act 1984 and now in the Family Court by virtue of s 31E of the Matrimonial and Family Proceedings Act 1984 as amended by Sch 10 to the Crime and Courts Act 2013.'

**23.60** The court below had proceeded on the erroneous basis that there was no jurisdiction to grant an injunction in the circumstances of the case[91] and the case was accordingly remitted for further consideration. A salutatory reminder

---

[91] See discussion at paras [37]–[39]; a further error, that of giving weight to the prospects of success of the parents' application to discharge the care order rather than focusing on the question of the necessity to make an injunction to protect the parents' Article 8 rights, also vitiated the decision below: see at para [41].

of the need for swift and effective action when a local authority is proposing to act in manner contrary to parents Convention rights comes in His Lordship's decision, made with some hesitation, not to make an interim injunction to secure the return of the child to then parents pending that further hearing.[92]

## CONTACT WITH CHILDREN IN CARE

**23.61** This important subject is given separate consideration in chapter 18.

## THE RELATIONSHIP BETWEEN CARE ORDERS AND OTHER ORDERS

### The effect of care orders on other orders

**23.62** Section 91 of the CA 1989 contains a number of provisions concerning the effect of the making of a care order on other orders. These effects are as follows:

(1) The making of a care order discharges any existing s 8 order, including a child arrangements order providing for contact between the child and another person[93] (s 34 of the Act provides the only route regulating contact between the child and others).

(2) The making of a care order discharges any existing activity direction[94] with respect to the child.[95]

(3) The making of a care order discharges any existing supervision order.[96]

(4) The making of a care order with respect to child who is a ward of court brings that wardship to an end.[97] Furthermore, s 100(2)(c) prohibits the court from making a child who is the subject of a care order a ward of court.

(5) The making of a care order discharges any existing school attendance order under s 437 of the Education Act 1996.[98]

### The effect of other orders on care orders

**23.63** The continuing operation of a care order may be affected by the making of certain other orders. These effects are as follows:

---

[92] See at paras [45] and [46]. The judgment concludes with guidance, endorsed by the President, as to the proper management of proposed changes to care plans so as to remove children from a placement with parents under a care plan.
[93] Section 91(2).
[94] ie a direction made under s 11A of the act in relation to a child arrangements order.
[95] Section 91(2A).
[96] Section 91(3)
[97] Section 91(4).
[98] Section 91(5).

(1) A care order is discharged by the making of a child arrangements order determining with whom a child who is the subject of a care order is to live and when they are to do so.[99] Such an order is the only s 8 order that the court has power to make in relation to a child in care: see s 9(1) and 9(6B) of the CA 1989.

(2) The making of a special guardianship order in relation to a child who is the subject of a care order discharges the care order.[100]

(3) The making of an adoption order in relation to a child who is the subject of a care order discharges the care order.[101]

(4) When a placement order is made, the care order does not have effect (but is not discharged) whilst the placement order is in force.[102]

(5) Where an emergency protection order is made in respect of a child who is the subject of a care order, the care order shall have effect subject to the emergency protection order.[103]

**23.64** In addition, a care order will cease to have effect if the child concerned is lawfully removed to Northern Ireland, the Isle of Man or the Channel Islands, provided that the conditions set out in regulations are satisfied.[104]

## Care orders and the inherent jurisdiction of the court

**23.65** One important consequence of the passage of the CA 1989 was to put in place a clear division between on the one hand the statutory regime for state intervention in families represented by, primarily, Part IV of the Act and on the other hand the jurisdiction of the High Court in Wardship and under its inherent jurisdiction.[105] In particular, it removed the court's power to place a ward of court in the care of the local authority and placed strict limits on the making of applications under the inherent jurisdiction by local authorities.

**23.66** This was achieved by the enactment of s 100 of the CA 1989, which reads as follows:

> '(1) Section 7 of the Family Law Reform Act 1969 (which gives the High Court power to place a ward of court in the care, or under the supervision, of a local authority) shall cease to have effect.
>
> (2) No court shall exercise the High Court's inherent jurisdiction with respect to children –

---

[99] Sections 91(1) and (1A) of the 1989 Act.
[100] Section 91(5A) of the 1989 Act.
[101] Section 46(2)(b) of the Adoption and Children Act 2002.
[102] Section 29(1) of the 2002 Act.
[103] Section 91(6).
[104] Section 101(4) of the 1989 Act: the relevant regulations are the Children (Prescribed Orders – Northern Ireland, Guernsey and Isle of Man) Regulations 1991, SI 1991/2032 (as amended by SI 2006/837).
[105] The issues that could arise under the pre-1989 law are well illustrated by the House of Lords case of *A v Liverpool City Council* (1981) 2 FLR 222.

(a) so as to require a child to be placed in the care, or put under the supervision, of a local authority;
(b) so as to require a child to be accommodated by or on behalf of a local authority;
(c) so as to make a child who is the subject of a care order a ward of court; or
(d) for the purpose of conferring on any local authority power to determine any question which has arisen, or which may arise, in connection with any aspect of parental responsibility for a child.

(3) No application for any exercise of the court's inherent jurisdiction with respect to children may be made by a local authority unless the authority have obtained the leave of the court.

(4) The court may only grant leave if it is satisfied that –

(a) the result which the authority wish to achieve could not be achieved through the making of any order of a kind to which subsection (5) applies; and
(b) there is reasonable cause to believe that if the court's inherent jurisdiction is not exercised with respect to the child he is likely to suffer significant harm.

(5) This subsection applies to any order –

(a) made otherwise than in the exercise of the court's inherent jurisdiction; and
(b) which the local authority is entitled to apply for (assuming, in the case of any application which may only be made with leave, that leave is granted).'

**23.67** It is in the nature of applications to invoke the inherent jurisdiction that they arise from grave, unusual and possibly novel circumstances.[106] However, reported cases do give some guidance as to circumstances in which a local authority should make an application for the court to exercise its inherent jurisdiction.

**23.68** A number of cases deal the issues that arise when the local authority and the parents disagree as to the medical care that should be given to[107] a child in care and the local authority seek the approval of the court for a course of action that at first sight would be within their powers in the exercise of their parental responsibility. Cases on this subject are comprehensively reviewed by Macdonald J in the case of *Re SL (Permission to Vaccinate)*.[108] In this case, His Lordship notes previous case law to the effect that there are, 'a small group of

---

[106] For a comprehensive discussion of the current law on The Inherent Jurisdiction and Wardship, see Michael D Jones *Children: The Inherent Jurisdiction and Wardship: A Family Practitioner's Handbook* (Family Law, 2016).
[107] Or in some particularly harrowing cases withheld from: see for example the decision of Sir James Munby in *Re Jake (A Child) (Withholding of Medical Treatment)* [2015] EWHC 2442 (Fam).
[108] [2017] EWHC 125 (Fam).

important decisions' that ought not to be carried out by one person with parental responsibility but require specific approval form the court.[109] He goes on to say:

> '[32] In this case the court is concerned with the issue of vaccinations in the context of children who are the subject of care orders and thus the dispute is between the local authority sharing parental responsibility for the child and the parent with parental responsibility. In the circumstances where SL is in the care of the local authority, by virtue of s 9(1) of the Children Act 1989 the local authority cannot apply for a specific issue order with respect to the issue of vaccination. Further, given the gravity of the issue in dispute, it is not appropriate for the local authority simply to give its consent to immunisation pursuant to the provisions of s 33(3) of the Children Act 1989 on the basis of its shared parental responsibility for SL under the interim care order (see *A Local Authority v SB, AB & MB*) [2010] 2 FLR 1203 and *Re Jake (Withholding Medical Treatment)* [2015] EWHC 2442 (Fam)).
>
> [33] In the circumstances, as in *Re A, B, C and D (Welfare of Children: Immunisation)* [2011] EWHC 4033 (Fam), and whilst the C2 application made by the local authority on 21 October 2016 is for an order in existing Children Act proceedings, the application the local authority pursues before this court must in fact be an application for relief under the inherent jurisdiction of the High Court. The local authority requires leave to make such an application, which application for leave is to be considered against the criteria set out in s 100(4) of the Children Act 1989. Being satisfied that the relief sought by the local authority does not contravene s 100(2) of the Children Act 1989 and that the criteria for granting leave to the local authority to make an application under the inherent jurisdiction set out in s 100(4) of the Act are met, I granted permission for the local authority to make an application for relief under the inherent jurisdiction of the High Court.'

**23.69** He went on to consider the arguments (the child's welfare being his paramount consideration) and to make an order giving permission for the local authority to arrange for the child to receive the vaccination proposed.

**23.70** The rather more unusual case of *Re C (Children)*[110] is authority for the corresponding proposition that there are some instances where the gravity of the issue under consideration makes it inappropriate for the local authority to simply use its power under s 33(3)(b) of the Act to control the way in which others exercise their parental responsibility. In this case a mother, who had a history of mental health problems, wished to register the names of her twin children (who had been made the subject of an interim care order shortly after birth) as 'Cyanide' and 'Preacher'. The judge below proceeded on the basis that s 33(3)(b) gave the local authority power to prevent this, made a declaration (superfluously, as the Court of Appeal held) that they could exercise that power

---

[109] See, for example, dicta of Dame Elizabeth Butler-Sloss P in *Re J (Specific Issue Orders: Child's Religious Upbringing and Circumcision)* [2000] 1 FLR 571 at 577D, cited by Thorpe LJ in *Re C (Welfare of Child: Immunisation)* [2003] 2 FLR 1095, and quoted by Macdonald J at para [26].
[110] [2016] EWCA Civ 374.

and granted an injunction to prevent the mother from registering the birth of her daughter in her chosen name.[111] The mother appealed.

**23.71** King LJ's judgment addresses in detail the, 'somewhat labyrinthine technicalities'[112] of the procedural route necessary to establish that the court has power to intervene to prevent a parent with parental responsibility registering their child with an inappropriate name. In the course of doing so she makes the important observation that:[113]

> '[77] In my judgment notwithstanding that a local authority may have the statutory power under section 33(3)(b) CA 1989 to prevent the mother from calling the twins "Preacher" and "Cyanide", the seriousness of the interference with the Article 8 rights of the mother consequent upon the local authority exercising that power, demands that the course of action it proposes be brought before and approved by the court.'

**23.72** She then goes on to review the case law on the use of the inherent jurisdiction and continues:

> '[104] I have reached the conclusion that there is a small category of cases where, notwithstanding the local authority's powers under section 33(3)(b) CA 1989, the consequences of the exercise of a particular act of parental responsibility are so profound and have such an impact on either the child his or herself, and/or the Article 8 rights of those other parties who share parental responsibility with a local authority, that the matter must come before the court for its consideration and determination.

> '[105] It follows that I am also satisfied that there may be rare cases, where a local authority believes that the forename chosen by a parent, and by which he or she intends to register a child, goes beyond the unusual, bizarre, extreme or plain foolish, and instead gives the local authority reasonable cause to believe that by calling him or her that name he or she is likely to be caused significant harm. In those highly unusual circumstances, the proper route by which the local authority seek to ensure that the course it proposes is necessary and in the child's interests is (as was held by Butler-Sloss LJ in *Re D, L, and LA* supra[114]) by putting the matter before the High Court by way of an application to invoke its inherent jurisdiction.'

**23.73** Whilst cases in which the High Court is asked to exercise its inherent jurisdiction in respect of children in care are and will remain rare, the cases noted above show that it remains an important mechanism for bringing particularly difficult issues before the court when local authority and parents disagree. King LJ's reference to the need to consider the seriousness of the interference with the Art 8 rights of a parent in deciding whether an issue in

---

[111] His order prohibited the use of 'Cyanide' but not of 'Preacher': the Court of Appeal ultimately decided that the use of neither name should be allowed.
[112] At para [2].
[113] This follows an interesting passage in the judgment in which the observations of Baker J in *Re DE (A Child)* [2014] EWFC 6 as to use of injunctions under the *Human Rights Act* 1998 are noted, without, 'commenting upon the decision'.
[114] *Re D, L and LA (Care: Change of Forename)* [2003] 1 FLR 339.

dispute is so important that the local authority should bring it before the court rather than really on its s 33(3) powers is particularly important.

# CHAPTER 24

# APPLICATIONS TO DISCHARGE A CARE ORDER

## DISCHARGE OF A CARE ORDER

**24.1** Whilst care orders cannot be varied, they can be discharged (via an application to the court), or replaced with a supervision order.

**24.2** The child's welfare is the paramount consideration in any such decisions, and the court will have careful regard to the welfare checklist factors. This consideration will not only include whether the child should continue to be cared for away from a parent, but also what arrangements could be made for them if the order is discharged, and the impact upon the child of any change of plan.

**24.3** If a care order is not discharged, it will last until the child reaches 18.

## Procedure

**24.4** Section 39(1) of the Children Act 1989 ('CA 1989') provides that a care order may be discharged by the court upon application of:

'(a) Any person who has parental responsibility for the child;
(b) The child himself; or
(c) The local authority designated by the order.'

**24.5** The application must be made using Form C110A and once issued, will be served on all parties to the original care proceedings.

**24.6** If a parent wishes to apply to discharge a care order, they will not receive non-means / merits tested public funding for this application, as they will have done for the original proceedings. They will be means and merits tested by the Legal Aid Agency and if funding is not available, they will have to represent themselves.

**24.7** An application to discharge a care order is an application under Part IV of the CA 1989 and therefore operates under the same structure as the PLO as care proceedings, in accordance with PD12A of the Family Procedure Rules 2010 ('FPR 2010'), as discussed in chapter 10. The proceedings must be completed within 26 weeks and the court is under the same robust case management duties.

**24.8** A children's guardian will be appointed in accordance with s 41 of the CA 1989.[1] It is clearly preferable for the same guardian that was involved in the original care proceedings to be appointed as they will have an established relationship with the family and knowledge of the case.

**24.9** As with care proceedings generally, the burden of proof in the application rests with the applicant.

## Local authority as applicant

**24.10** A local authority will seek to discharge a care order if they decide that it is no longer necessary for the order to be in place because the child's welfare no longer requires it to be in place.

**24.11** It may be that there has been a programme of rehabilitation in place and the parent has shown that they can now provide adequate care for their child without the local authority sharing parental responsibility. Similarly, if the child is in the care of another family member, the local authority may consider that a less invasive order can be made.

**24.12** If a child has been placed with a foster carer who wishes to apply for a more long-term order for a child, such as a special guardianship order, the local authority may apply to discharge the care order and invite the court, within the same application, to make a special guardianship order in its place.

**24.13** If the local authority makes an application to discharge the care order, they will need to comply with the pre-proceedings protocol regarding the required documentation as set out in PD12A of the FPR 2010 so that the court has the fullest information at the outset.

## Parent as applicant

**24.14** A parent may wish to apply to discharge the care order if they feel that it is no longer in the child's best interests for the care order to remain in force, or if the care plan for the child has changed during the course of the care order and the parent is concerned that this change is not in their child's best interests. The local authority is entitled to change their care plan for a child during the course of the order, but any proposed change must be considered at the 'child in care' reviews that take place, and the child's independent reviewing officer ('IRO') must be informed. For a full discussion of the IRO's responsibilities, see chapter 22. Parents continue to share parental responsibility for a child subject to a care order and so must be informed of any major decisions that are being made with regards to the child.

---

[1] Section 41(6)(c) provides that an application to discharge a care order amounts to specified proceedings and as such the child should become a party and a guardian appointed.

**24.15** A parent can make representation to the local authority in relation to their concerns about the change care plan via the 'child in care' review meetings. However, the local authority has the power to act against the parents' wishes if they consider it necessary to safeguard the child's welfare in accordance with s 33 of the CA 1989. A parent will only be able to change this balance of parental responsibility if the care order is discharged and they are afforded sole parental responsibility again.

## Removal from a parent

**24.16** If the care order was made with a care plan for the child to remain with their parent, the local authority may later decide that it is necessary to remove the child. A parent does not lose their parental responsibility when a care order is made, but in the event of a disagreement, the local authority can act against the wishes of the parent but only when the local authority 'is satisfied that it is necessary to do so in order to safeguard or promote the child's welfare'.[2]

**24.17** Section 33(3) of the CA 1989 provides:

> '(3) While a care order is in force with respect to a child, the local authority designated by the order shall –
>
> (a) have parental responsibility for the child; and
> (b) have the power (subject to the following provisions of this section) to determine the extent to which
>    (i) a parent, guardian or special guardian of the child; or
>    (ii) a person who by virtue of section 4A has parental responsibility for the child, may meet his parental responsibility for him.'

**24.18** In *Re DE (A Child)*, Baker J, in a decision approved by the President of the Family Division, gave further guidance as to the proper approach in circumstances where a local authority seeks to remove a child placed in the care of a parent under a care order This case was further complicated by the fact that both parents had been diagnosed with learning difficulties which compounded the problems they had faced when informed that the local authority sought to remove the child.

**24.19** Human Rights Act 1998:s 8

Baker J specified that:[3]

> '(1) In every case where a care order is made on the basis of a care plan providing that a child should live at home with his or her parents, it should be a term of the care plan, and a recital in the care order, that the local authority agrees to give not less than fourteen days' notice of a removal of the child, save in an emergency. I consider that fourteen days is an appropriate period, on the one hand to avoid unnecessary delay but, on the other hand, to allow the parents an opportunity to obtain legal advice.

---

[2] CA 1989, s 33(4).
[3] *Re DE (A Child)* [2015] 1 FLR 1001 at [49].

(2) Where a care order has been granted on the basis of a care plan providing that the child should remain at home, a local authority considering changing the plan and removing the child permanently from the family must have regard to the fact that permanent placement outside the family is to be preferred only as a last resort where nothing else will do and must rigorously analyse all the realistic options, considering the arguments for and against each option. Furthermore, it must involve the parents properly in the decision-making process.

(3) In every case where a parent decides to apply to discharge a care order in circumstances where the local authority has given notice of intention to remove a child placed at home under a care order, the parent should consider whether to apply in addition for an injunction under s.8 of the HRA to prevent the local authority from removing the child pending the determination of the discharge application. If the parent decides to apply for an injunction, that application should be issued at the same time as the discharge application.

(4) When a local authority, having given notice of its intention to remove a child placed at home under a care order, is given notice of an application for discharge of the care, the local authority must consider whether the child's welfare requires his immediate removal. Furthermore, the authority must keep a written record demonstrating that it has considered this question and recording the reasons for its decision. In reaching its decision on this point, the local authority must again *inter alia* consult with the parents. Any removal of a child in circumstances where the child's welfare does not require immediate removal, or without proper consideration and consultation, is likely to be an unlawful interference with the Article 8 rights of the parent and child.

(5) On receipt of an application to discharge a care order, where the child has been living at home, the allocation gatekeeper at the designated family centre should check whether it is accompanied by an application under s.8 of HRA and, if not, whether the circumstances might give rise to such an application. This check is needed because, as discussed below, automatic legal aid is not at present available for such applications to discharge a care order, and it is therefore likely that such applications may be made by parents acting in person. In cases where the discharge application is accompanied by an application for an order under s.8 HRA, or the allocation gatekeeper considers that the circumstances might give rise to such an application, he or she should allocate the case as soon as possible to a circuit judge for case management. Any application for an injunction in these circumstances must be listed for an early hearing.

(6) On hearing an application for an injunction under s.8 HRA to restrain a local authority removing a child living at home under a care order pending determination of an application to discharge the care order, the court should normally grant the injunction unless the child's welfare requires his immediate removal from the family home.'

Baker J highlights the need for an application to be allocated to a circuit judge level as soon as possible.

**24.20** Within the guidance is reference to an application for an injunction under s 8 of the Human Rights Act 1998 ('HRA 1998') to prevent the local authority from removing a child pending the determination of their application to discharge the care order. The use of this application is only briefly considered here, but under s 6(1) of the HRA 1998, it is unlawful for a public authority to act in a way which is incompatible with a right under ECHR. The local authority is a public authority and in exercising its powers under a care order, the local authority must therefore comply with its obligations under Art 8 not to interfere with the rights of the child and his parents to respect for their private and family life.

**24.21** When considering the application for an injunction under s 8 of the HRA 1998 in *Re DE*, Baker J emphasised:[4]

> 'The procedural element includes the duty to ensure that the processes by which decisions about children are made are fair and that the parents (and the child, depending on his age and level of understanding) are sufficiently involved in that process: see *Re L (Care: Assessment: Fair Trial)* [2002] EWHC 1379 (Fam) [2002] 2 FLR 730, *Re G (Care: Challenge to Local Authority's Decision)* [2003] EWHC 551 (Fam) [2003] 2 FLR 42, and *Re W (Removal into Care)* [2005] EWCA Civ 642 [2005] 2 FLR 1022. As Munby J (as he then was) observed in *Re G*, Article 8
>
>> "requires that the parents are properly involved in the decision-making not merely before the care proceedings are launched, and during the period when the care proceedings are on foot ....but also ... after the care proceedings have come to an end and whilst the local authority is implementing the care order ..."'

**24.22** If the local authority seeks to remove the child before the determination of their discharge application, the parent should apply for an injunction to prevent the removal, and enabling the situation for the child to be carefully considered before a move. Where the local authority has been given notice of an intention to apply to discharge a care order, the local authority must consider whether the child's welfare requires his immediate removal. Any removal of a child, where the child's welfare does not require immediate removal, or if there has not been proper consultation with the parents, is likely to constitute an unlawful interference with the Art 8 rights of the parent and child.

**24.23** A parent must obtain legal advice as a matter of urgency if the local authority seeks to remove a child from their care, and any applications should also be made swiftly.

## *Return to a parent*

**24.24** If a parent wishes to have a child returned to their care once a care order has been made, they must apply for the care order to be discharged. If discharged, the local authority will no longer share parental responsibility for the child and the parents will be free to make all decisions about the care of the child.

---

4    *Re DE (A Child)* [2015] 1 FLR 1001 at [28].

**24.25** This application does not attract automatic public funding and will require a means and merits tested application to the Legal Aid Agency, which will not be an easy application to make. If the local authority does not agree that the care order should be discharged, the merits aspect of the application will have to be prepared very carefully in light of their position.

**24.26** A parent will understandably be upset at the conclusion of care proceedings if a care order is made for the child to remain away from them. Careful advice should be given to a parent seeking to apply to discharge a care order to ensure that they have made sufficient changes themselves, or that there are significant concerns as to the child's placement pursuant to the local authority's care plan.

## Child as applicant

**24.27** It is possible for an application to be made to discharge a care order on behalf of the child. This may be as a result of direct instructions from a child who is old enough to make their views known, or as a result of the independent reviewing officer ('IRO') referring the matter to Cafcass if they consider the local authority have not acted in the interests of the child and in accordance with the care plan.

**24.28** If a child wishes to apply for the discharge of the care order, it is necessary for the solicitor to assess whether the child is of sufficient age and understanding to make such an application. An application to discharge a care order commences specified proceedings and, in accordance with s 41 of the CA 1989, a guardian will be appointed in any event. The child's ability to provide instructions independently of the guardian will be considered and if the child does have capacity, and there is a difference of opinion between the child and the guardian, they will be separately represented.

**24.29** If an IRO refers the matter to Cafcass, they must then make a decision as to whether an application should be made on behalf of the child. Currently, there are no reported cases in which this procedure has been followed, but the application will be allocated and case managed in the same way as a parent or local authority application would.

## Another person as applicant

**24.30** Section 39(1) of the CA 1989 lists the people who are able to apply to discharge a care order. This includes the child themselves, the local authority or a person with parental responsibility. However, there may be occasions when another significant person in the child's life may wish to apply to discharge the care order. This person will not be able to apply automatically, and may need to pursue another application first.

**24.31** Section 91(1) of the CA 1989 provides that if a child arrangements order is made in relation to a child subject to a care order, the care order is discharged. A person who is entitled to apply for a child arrangements order is specified in s 10(5) of the CA 1989 as:

- '(a) any party to a marriage (whether or not subsisting) in relation to whom the child is a child of the family;
- (aa) any civil partner in a civil partnership (whether or not subsisting) in relation to whom the child is a child of the family;
- (b) any person with whom the child has lived for a period of at least three years;
- (c) any person who –
    - (i) in any case where a child arrangements order in force with respect to the child regulates arrangements relating to with whom the child is to live or when the child is to live with any person, has the consent of each of the persons named in the order as a person with whom the child is to live;
    - (ii) in any case where the child is in the care of a local authority, has the consent of that authority; or
    - (iii) in any other case, has the consent of each of those (if any) who have parental responsibility for the child.
- (d) any person who has parental responsibility for the child by virtue of provision made under section 12(2A).'

**24.32** Furthermore, s 10(5A) provides that a local authority foster parent is entitled to apply for a child arrangements order with respect to a child if the child has lived with them for a period of at least one year immediately before the application. Section 10(5B) specifies that a relative of a child is entitled to apply for a child arrangements order as to where a child should live, if the subject child has lived with the relative for a period of at least one year immediately preceding the application.

**24.33** Anyone who is not entitled to apply for a child arrangements order by virtue of s 10 can apply for leave to apply for the order pursuant to s 10(2) of the CA 1989.

## Substitution of a care order for a supervision order

**24.34** It may be possible for an application to be made to discharge a care order and replace it with a supervision order. Section 39(4) of the CA 1989 provides:

> 'Where a care order is in force with respect to a child the court may, on the application of any person entitled to apply for the order to be discharged, substitute a supervision order for the care order.'

**24.35** The court does not need to reconsider the threshold criteria set out in s 31 of the CA 1989, and will instead consider the child's welfare as its paramount concern in accordance with s 1(1) of the CA 1989 and will apply the factors in the welfare checklist when considering any such application.

## VARIATION OR DISCHARGE OF A SUPERVISION ORDER

**24.36** In the same way that an application can be made to discharge a care order, it is also possible to apply to discharge a supervision order. Unlike a care order, however, it is also possible to apply to vary a supervision order with the variation usually being in relation to requirements attached to it.

**24.37** Section 39(2) of the CA 1989 specifies that:

'A supervision order may be varied or discharged by the court on the application of –

(a) Any person who has parental responsibility for the child;
(b) The child himself; or
(c) The supervisor.'

**24.38** A person who is not entitled to apply by virtue of s 39(2) of the CA 1989 may still apply to vary the supervision order if it imposes a requirement which affects that person.[5]

**24.39** Again, as with an application to discharge a care order, these proceedings are specified proceedings in accordance with s 41 a guardian will be appointed for the child. As an application under Part IV of the CA 1989, the proceedings are subject to FPR 2010, PD12A and the PLO contained therein, see chapter 10 for further discussion.

**24.40** If the local authority wishes to extend the length of the supervision order, their application should be made pursuant to Sch 3, para 6(3) of the CA 1989 and not under the more general power contained in s 39(2) to vary.

---

[5] CA 1989, s 39(3).

# Part 6

# ALTERNATIVES TO THE MAKING OF A FINAL CARE ORDER

# CHAPTER 25

# SUPERVISION ORDERS

## INTRODUCTION

**25.1** This chapter considers an order that allows state intervention in family life but, crucially, does not vest state authorities with parental responsibility for children, as is the case when a care order is made. Still less do these orders give state authorities the power to determine the extent to which those who ordinarily have parental responsibility may exercise that responsibility, the existence of this power being one of the defining features of a care order.[1]

**25.2** Supervision orders under s 31(1)(b) of the Children Act 1989 ('CA 1989') can be appropriately made where there are general concerns as to deficiencies in the care of the child. They are not to be confused with Education supervision orders under s 36 of the CA 1989, which are restricted to cases where the court is specifically satisfied that the child concerned is, 'not being properly educated'.[2] The narrower scope of s 36 is illustrated by published statistics for the number of children involved in orders made under the two provisions. In the calendar year 2016 supervision orders were made that affected 7,676 children whereas only 106 were affected by education supervision orders (a further three were involved in orders extending education supervision orders).[3]

### The significance of holding parental responsibility

**25.3** The fundamental importance of the vesting or not of parental responsibility in state authorities was explained by His Honour Judge Coningsby QC in one of the early reported cases on the approach to be taken when deciding whether to make a care order or supervision order:[4]

> 'We tend to look at supervision orders and care orders under the same umbrella because the threshold criteria for the coming into operation of the two is the same. But when we actually look at the content of the two orders we find that they are wholly and utterly different. This is because of s 22[5] and because of the passing of

---

[1] Section 33(3) of the CA 1989.
[2] Section 36(3).
[3] Ministry of Justice: Family Court Statistics Quarterly, England and Wales April to June 2017, Table 4. By way of comparison, 13,953 children were made the subject of care orders in the same period.
[4] Re S(J) (A Minor) (Care or Supervision Order) [1993] 2 FLR 919.
[5] The section that sets out the general duty of a local authority in respect of a child, 'looked after' by them.

parental responsibility. Supervision should not in any sense be seen as a sort of watered down version of care. It is wholly different.'[6]

**25.4** Supervision orders can, therefore, be viewed as allowing a proportionate response to concerns about the care that children are receiving within their families that require state intervention but are not so serious as to require the appointment of a, 'statutory parent' to act in the place of those who ordinarily have responsibility for by virtue of a biological relationship[7] or by operation of the various sections in the CA 1989 that provide for the acquisition of parental responsibility.[8] The consequences of the making of a care order and of the passing of parental responsibility to the local authority are considered in detail in chapter 23 above.

# SUPERVISION ORDERS

## Supervision orders and proportionality in a post *Re B-S* world

**25.5** The need for state intervention in family life, to be, 'proportionate' to the concerns found by the court to exist has been emphasised in recent case law.[9] This is particularly the case when that intervention in is the form of the making of care and placement orders. This search for proportionality, often referred to as *the Re B-S* exercise (although the much quoted observations of Sir James Munby P in that case[10] have to be read with an awareness of subsequent judicial comment[11]), has led to increased interest in, and use of, supervision orders as a means of achieving that proportionate intervention.[12] This can be seen, for example, in a doubling in the making of supervision orders to accompany special guardianship orders.[13] This represents something of a change from the previous perception of supervision orders as being relatively ineffectual[14] as instruments for remedying deficiencies in parenting and protecting children's welfare. Further study of this change in perception and its implications is underway.[15]

---

[6] At 950F–G: this passage was cited with approval by Dillon LJ in *Re V (Care or Supervision Order)* [1996] 1 FLR 776 at p 788; see also comments of Waite LJ in that case at p 783.
[7] CA 1989, s 2.
[8] See ss 4, 4ZA, 4A, 5, 12 and 14C.
[9] See, for example, *Re B (Care Proceedings: Appeal)* [2013] 2 FLR 1075 and *Re B-S (Adoption: Application of s 47(5))* [2014] 1 FLR 1035.
[10] See at paras [23]–[29] of his judgment
[11] See for example, *Re R* [2015] 1 FLR 715 and *Re W (A Child)* [2016] EWCA Civ 793.
[12] It has also led to some re-consideration of the usefulness of family assistance orders under s 16 of the CA 1989 in cases where the outcome of public law proceedings is placement of the child under a child arrangements order or special guardianship order: see article by Gabrielle Jan Posner in *Family Law Week*: http://www.familylawweek.co.uk/site.aspx?i=ed161390. The circumstances in which such orders can be made are considered in more detail later in this chapter.
[13] This orders are considered in detail in chapter 27.
[14] Some of the reasons for this perception are discussed below. It is interesting to note that the provision for supervision orders set out in the 1989 Act were themselves in part designed to remedy features of the similarly named orders under the Children and Young Persons Act 1969

## The nature of a supervision order

**25.6** As will be seen below, s 31(1) of the CA 1989 provides for a child to be, 'placed under the supervision' of a local authority. The meaning of this is explained by s 35(1) of the CA 1989:

> 'While a supervision order is in force it shall be the duty of the supervisor –
> 
> (a) to advise, assist and befriend the supervised child;
> (b) to take such steps as are reasonably necessary to give effect to the order; and
> (c) where –
>   (i) the order is not wholly complied with; or
>   (ii) the supervisor considers that the order may no longer be necessary, to consider whether or not to apply to the court for its variation or discharge.'

**25.7** In this context, 'the supervisor' will be the designated local authority.[16] Schedule 3, para 9 of the Act provides for the identification of the local authority to be designated in the following terms:

> '(1) A supervision order shall not designate a local authority as the supervisor unless –
> 
> (a) the local authority agree; or
> (b) the supervised child lives or will live within their area.'

**25.8** Although the paragraph does not provide in terms that a potential supervising authority must agree to or even be consulted before designation if the supervised child, 'lives or will live within their area' in practice it is highly desirable that they are at least notified that such an order may be made so that consideration can be given to how the order will be put into effect and any necessary planning done. It also allows, in an appropriate case, the relevant local authority can be represented when the making of the order is being considered by the court. A failure to notify the authority that may be designated may result in practical difficulties in supplying services to the family and unnecessary further court proceedings.[17]

**25.9** Note that this test for identifying the local authority to be designated is not the same as that for designation in a care order.[18]

**25.10** Parts I and II of Sch 3 to the CA 1989 make further provision as to supervision orders and these will be considered below.

---

that led to such orders been regarded as ineffectual and hence seldom made: see commentary to s 35 of the 1989 Act in *Current Law Statutes Annotated* 1989, Volume 4.

[15] See article 'Spotlight on supervision orders: what do we know and what do we need to know?' by Professor Judith Harwin and others [2016] Fam Law 365, from which the comment as to the increased use of supervision orders in conjunction with special guardianship orders is also drawn.

[16] Acting, for most purposes, by an allocated social worker.

[17] Personal experience of the writer.

[18] Set out in s 31(8) of the CA 1989.

**25.11** Although it is one of the salient features of a supervision order that it does not vest the supervising local authority with parental authority, a supervision order is an order of the court made under the CA 1989 and accordingly the provisions of s 2(8) would be relevant to any dispute between the supervisor and those persons holding parental responsibility. This subsection reads as follows:

> 'The fact that a person has parental responsibility for a child shall not entitle him to act in any way which would be incompatible with any order made with respect to the child under this Act.'

**25.12** In addition, paragraphs within Parts I and II of Sch 3 provide for the giving of directions, imposition of obligations and provision of information.

**25.13** The nature, and limitations, of a supervision order were explained by Bracewell J, sitting in the Court of Appeal, in the case of *Re T (A Minor) (Care or Supervision Order)*[19] in the following terms:[20]

> 'The nature of a supervision order is to help and assist a child where the parents have full responsibility for the care and upbringing. It does not involve any statutory level of monitoring and it does not give the local authority parental responsibility. Any conditions attached to a supervision order cannot in themselves be enforced by the court. That was made clear in the case of *Croydon London Borough Council v A (No. 3)* [1992] 2 FLR 350; breaches can only be evidence in further proceedings.
>
> The essence of a supervision order is to advise, assist and befriend the supervised child. The directions which may be attached under Sch 3 to the Children Act 1989 are restricted to requiring a responsible person, that is the parent in this case, to take reasonable steps to ensure the child lives at a specified place, presents to a specified person, participates in specified activities and submits to various examinations where appropriate. The limits of such requirements do not, in my judgment, begin to address the problems of these parents who continue, to date, to exercise their parental responsibilities in a way which still merits some criticism.
>
> The contract drawn up between the parents and the local authority cannot be enforced without further court proceedings, whereas a care order places on the local authority a positive duty to ensure the welfare of the child and protect her from inadequate parenting. That is the framework and essence of the Act.'

**25.14** In the case of *Re T (Care Order)*[21] Sir Mark Potter P, sitting in the Court of Appeal, cited this passage and passages to the same effect in other cases with approval but went on to say:[22]

---

[19] [1994] 1 FLR 103.
[20] At pp 106–107.
[21] [2009] 2 FLR 574.
[22] At para 31.

'Since the advent of the Human Rights Act 1998 it is necessary also to emphasise and have regard to the issue of proportionality when contemplating the removal of parental responsibility from, or its enforced sharing by, those otherwise entitled to exercise it exclusively.'

**25.15** As will be seen below, the issue of 'proportionality' is central to any consideration of the making of a supervision order or an alternative order.

## The consequences of failure to co-operate with a supervision order

**25.16** A supervision order is by its nature not intended to be a coercive measure and no enforcement mechanism is provided for in the CA 1989. In the event of a serious failure by the child's parents or carers to accept advice or otherwise cooperate with the supervisor, the appropriate course of action is for the supervisor to apply to court to discharge the order. However, such an application will very often be accompanied by an application to substitute a care order on the basis that the 'lesser' measure of protection has failed to secure the child's welfare and that doing so requires the passing of parental responsibility to the local authority. In the event that such an application is made some comments of Hale LJ (as she then was) in the case of *Re O (Supervision Order)*[23] should be borne in mind:[24]

> 'Nobody should be in any doubt that a supervision order is compulsory. The parents' failure to co-operate is very cogent evidence indeed that something more stringent may be needed, or, at the very least, that there is a continuing risk of harm to the child.'

**25.17** The *evidential* significance in future proceedings of any failure to co-operate is something that should always be emphasised when advising parents, particularly where they are being invited to agree to the making of a supervision order.

**25.18** The limitations on the power of the court to ensure compliance with a plan to deal with concerns about a child's care under the auspices of a supervision order are illustrated and explained by the decision of the Court of Appeal in the particularly sad case of *Re V (Care or Supervision Order)*.[25]

**25.19** In this case the child concerned, who had been adopted as a baby and was now 17 years of age, suffered from cerebral palsy leading to spastic quadriplegia and he also had learning difficulties. He was enrolled in a specialist school, ultimately as a weekly boarder, and the advice of professionals was that this was beneficial to him. His adoptive parents, who remained together and whose devotion to the child was unquestionable, differed in their response to this advice. His father accepted that the child should attend this

---
[23] [2001] 1 FLR 923.
[24] At para 23.
[25] [1996] 1 FLR 776.

school but his mother felt that, 'too much pressure' was placed on her son at the school and started to keep him away from school on what were described as, 'slight medical pretexts'. The absence of the stimulation provided at the school led the child to regress and the local authority made an application initially (interestingly) for a supervision order and then for a care order. The making of a care order, with the aim of vesting the local authority with parental responsibility and enabling them to secure the child's attendance at school, was supported by the guardian ad litem but opposed by both parents.

**25.20** The trial judge accepted that being kept off school put the child, 'at risk of significant harm' and hence that the threshold for making a public law order was established. However, he declined to make a care order, in large part because of the strain this would place on the parents' relationship, and instead attempted to achieve the desired end by making, 'a supervision order with conditions' (as he described it),[26] the 'conditions' being designed to ensure that the child attended school. The guardian and the local authority appealed.

**25.21** The first point taken on appeal was that there is simply no basis in the CA 1989 for the court having jurisdiction to attach 'conditions' to a supervision order and the Court of Appeal agreed with this.[27] However, Sch 3 of the CA 1989 does allow the inclusion in a supervision order of, 'requirements' provided any 'responsible person' agrees[28] and the parents' secondary position was that they would agree to the judge's 'conditions' being re-cast as 'requirements' in accordance with this paragraph. In the view of Waite LJ (with whom Dillon LJ agreed) this would still fail to meet the child's welfare needs by ensuring he attended school. As His Lordship explained:[29]

> 'Even if the supervision order were to be so corrected, however, and thus given validity as a matter of form, that would still fail to eliminate the essential difficulty arising from the fact that a supervision order rests primarily upon the consent of the parent affected by it. Any provisions incorporated into a supervision order, either by direction of the supervisor or by requirements directly stated by the judge, are incapable of being enforced directly through any of the ordinary processes by which courts of law enforce obedience to their directions. The only sanction, when any infringement of the terms of a supervision order, or of directions given under it, occurs is a return by the supervisor to court. There the ultimate sanction will be the making of a care order under which the local authority will be given the necessary legal powers to enforce its will.'

**25.22** The judge's misconception as to the options available to him invalidated his conclusions and the Court of Appeal went on to decide that a care order should be made.

---

[26] See at p 785 of the Court of Appeal report.
[27] See judgment of Waite LJ at p 785.
[28] See Sch 3, para 1, discussed in more detail below: a 'responsible person is defined by para 1 of the Schedule as being any person with parental responsibility for the child and also any person with whom the child is living.
[29] At p 786.

**25.23** As *Re V (Care or Supervision Order)* and other cases make clear, the fact that a supervision order does not provide a legal basis for ensuring that a plan made for a child is implemented is a fundamental difference between that order and a care order. In many cases, this is a crucial consideration at the 'welfare' stage of the court's decision making and this issue is discussed in detail below.

## When can a supervision order be made?

**25.24** Section 31(1) of the CA 1989 provides, in relation to a child, that:

'On the application of any local authority or authorised person,[30] the court may make an order –

...

(b) putting him under the supervision of a designated local authority.'

**25.25** In addition to granting a specific, free-standing, application for an order the court also has power to make a supervision order under s 31(5)(a), which provides that the court may 'on an application for a care order, make a supervision order'.[31]

**25.26** This is an important provision in practice as it enables a court to give effect to a conclusion that although a child is suffering or at risk of suffering harm[32] the circumstances do not require the making of a care order. The extensive use made of it is illustrated by the statistic that whilst specific applications for supervision orders involved only 2,149 children in respect of whom public law orders were sought in the calendar year 2016, supervision orders were actually made in respect of 7,676 children involved in orders ultimately made by courts. By way of comparison, in the same period applications involving 25,691 children were made for care orders (or orders substituting care orders for supervision orders) and care orders involving 13,953 children were made.[33]

**25.27** The court's power under s 31(5)(a) to make a supervision order is particularly useful in cases where an application for a care order is made but during the course of the proceedings the family demonstrate an ability to work with professionals. If this is to an extent that makes the less interventionist order adequate to meet the remaining concerns this may lead the local authority to change its plan to one of seeking a supervision order only, or the court to decide that this is the appropriate order even if a care order is still sought.

---

[30] The only such person being an officer of the National Society for the Prevention of Cruelty to Children: s 31(9).
[31] Conversely, s 31(5)(b) allows the court to make a care order on an application for a supervision order: for an example of then use of this power, see the decision of the Court of Appeal in the case of *Re T (Care Order)* [2009] 2 FLR 574 discussed below.
[32] See below.
[33] All statistics in this paragraph drawn from: Ministry of Justice: Family Court Statistics Quarterly, England and Wales April to June 2017, Tables 3 and 4.

**25.28** The court also has power to make a supervision order by way of substitution for an existing care order on an application to discharge that order made by any person entitled to do so.[34]

**25.29** The court's powers to make interim supervision orders under s 38(1) and (3) of the CA 1989 are considered in chapter 13 above, as are its powers under s 40(2) and (3) to make orders pending appeal.

**25.30** Section 31(3) of the 1989 Act provides that:

> 'No care order or supervision order may be made with respect to a child who has reached the age of seventeen (or sixteen, in the case of a child who is married).'

This prohibition also applies to interim supervision orders made under s 38 of the CA 1989.[35]

## The responsibility of the court to determine the appropriate order

**25.31** Although it is the local authority (or authorised person) who makes an application for a care or supervision order the court is not bound by the applicant's decision as to which order is sought at final hearing.[36] As can be seen from the statistics above, supervision orders are commonly made when care orders have been sought, indeed it is very often the parents' primary case at the welfare stage to argue that a supervision order should be made in preference to a care order as it is a sufficient and proportionate measure to ensure the child's welfare is safeguarded. Conversely, cases occur where the applicant seeks a supervision order only but another party (in practice, this will almost inevitably be the children's guardian) argues that this is an insufficient protection for the child and that a care order is required: this occurred in a number of the cases discussed below.[37] Moreover, it is clearly established that it is the court's responsibility to decide what order is appropriate and even the agreement of all parties to the proceedings cannot bind the court as to the way in which it exercises that responsibility.

**25.32** The ultimate responsibility of the court to decide what order to make was examined by Sir Mark Potter P (sitting in the Court of Appeal) in the case of *Re T (Care Order)*.[38] In this case the child concerned had suffered a serious head injury that the trial judge concluded, at a fact-finding hearing, had been inflicted by one of the parents (he was unable to say which) whilst the other

---

[34] Section 39(4).
[35] Section 31(11)(b).
[36] This is also the case at an interim hearing.
[37] However, it is well established that there must be, 'cogent and strong' reasons to force upon a local authority a more draconian order than it has sought: see for example the observations of Hale J (as she then was) in the case of *Oxfordshire County Council v L* [1998] 1 FLR 70, at p 73; these comments were cited with approval by Sir Mark Potter P in the case of *Re T (Care Order)* [2009] 2 FLR 574.
[38] [2009] 2 FLR 574.

parent had been guilty of a failure to protect the child. In spite of this unpromising start to proceedings, the parents had done so well in various assessments and in working with professionals that by the time of the final hearing all parties agreed that the child could be placed in the care of the parents, subject to a supervision order being made.

**25.33** The trial judge was not prepared to accept that this was the correct outcome for the child. He summarised his concerns as follows:[39]

> 'I do not like to reject the view urged upon me, or the evidence before me. I feel however that its approach misses the real point of this case, which is the protection of B if he is to live with one of the persons responsible for his injuries, the true reason for which will never be known. I also bear in mind the way that this case has developed and the changes of stance (apart from that of the parents regarding acknowledgment of findings) which have characterised it and which might auger uncertainties. It is appropriate in such circumstances to place responsibility for B's safety on the authority rather than on his parents.'

He accordingly made a care order on the basis that the child would remain at home with the parents.[40]

**25.34** The local authority appealed; as the other parties were unlikely to resist the appeal (indeed, no other party was represented before the Court of Appeal) Cafcass Legal was requested, at the time of the grant of permission to appeal, to assist the court by instructing counsel to act as amicus curiae and they did so.[41]

**25.35** In giving the only judgment in the Court of Appeal the learned President recognised that the decision of the trial judge was unusual but he had no doubt that it lay within his powers to take that course. As he remarks:[42]

> 'There appears to be no reported case in which the court has made a care order despite the unanimous agreement of the parties to the making of a supervision order. The authorities directly concerned with the question whether or not, in given circumstances, a care order is to be preferred have all involved adjudication of opposing cases advanced by the parties. Nonetheless, it seems to me clear that, even when that is not so, the power in s 31(5) to make a care order on an application for a supervision order cannot be neutered by an agreement reached between the parties outside the court, particularly where, as here, the proceedings have originated in an application for a care order which has become 'diluted' by

---

[39] Quoted by Sir Mark Potter P at para 25.
[40] Such a placement is now governed by s 22C of the 1989 Act (inserted by the Children and Young Persons Act 2008, as amended by the Children and Families Act 2014) and Care Planning, Placement and Case Review (England) Regulations 2010, Part 4. Although the lawfulness placement of a child who is the subject to a care order with their parents (or one parent) has never been in issue the writer's experience is that such placements are not popular with local authorities as they are concerned that they are placed in a position of having, so to speak, 'responsibility without power'. A court will be concerned to look into how parents' compliance with the care plan will be monitored if such a placement is proposed.
[41] Paragraph 39.
[42] Paragraph 44.

the time of the final hearing. The decision to end proceedings and to make the appropriate statutory order is and remains the responsibility of the court. Indeed, the duty of the court to treat the welfare of the child as the paramount consideration requires the court to make an appropriate judicial investigation.'

**25.36** He goes on to explain how a judge should approach the question of whether or not to adopt a course of action approved by the parties:

'[48] This provision [section 31(5) of the Act] expressly confers upon the judge discretion on an application for either type of order to refuse one and substitute the other. There is no suggestion that the court is fettered in its powers under this section by reason of any agreement which the parties may have reached as to which is the more appropriate. What is important when the court addresses this question whether or not to reflect the agreement of the parties in its order or to take some different course, is that the court should examine the background facts as well as the reasoning underlying the agreement and come to a measured conclusion, taking the relevant considerations into account. I would add that human rights considerations dictate that, when faced with a choice between the making of a care order and the less draconian provisions of a supervision order supported by the agreement of all the parties, the court should, so far as is consistent with the paramountcy of the child's welfare, favour the making of a supervision order, as the sufficient and proportionate response to any risk presented to the child, in preference to the protection afforded by a care order, given the potentially greater inroad into the parents' (and indeed the child's) rights to respect for their family and private life which the latter represents.

[49] Additionally, as a broad proposition, where the decision which the judge is disposed to make would result in rejecting the unanimous approach of the parties, it is important that the judge should justify with some precision the reasoning for taking his proposed course, involving as it will a departure from professional assessment and guidance, often from a number of sources, such as the guardian, council social workers and, in this case, an independent social worker.'

**25.37** His Lordship went on to draw an analogy with the approach that the court should take when considering departing from the opinion of experts in care cases as elucidated by Thorpe LJ in the case of *Re M (Residence)*.[43]

**25.38** Having set out these principles His Lordship then reviewed the trial judge's reasons for making a care order[44] and concluded that the necessary, 'strong and cogent' reasons for the more draconian order were not in fact made out. The appeal was accordingly allowed. A twelve-month supervision order was substituted for the care order but subject to the provisos that the order should recite the detailed written agreement that the parents had entered into as to working with the local authority[45] and that the order should include a

---

[43] [2002] 2 FLR 1059.
[44] Paragraphs 56–63.
[45] The agreement is set out at para 17 of the judgment and, incidentally, can be seen as a model of the matters that such an agreement needs to cover.

requirement that the parents, 'as responsible persons, take all reasonable steps to ensure compliance with any direction given by the supervisor under Sch 3'.[46]

**25.39** The approach to be taken when local authority and children's guardian disagree as to the appropriate order was recently considered by Moor J in the case of *I County Council v TD and Others*.[47] In this case, the local authority and children's guardian agreed that the children should reside with their mother but whilst the local authority proposed that this be under the auspices of a supervision order the Guardian argued that a care order was necessary (they also differed as to then provision for father's contact). Moor J's judgment contains the following summary of the approach to be taken to such an issue:

> '[8] I make it clear that I can make a care order notwithstanding the current Local Authority care plans. Indeed, Mr AD on behalf of the Local Authority has acknowledged that, if I were to do so, the care plans would be changed. It is for me to decide which is more appropriate. The case of *Oxfordshire County Council v L* [1998] 1 FLR 70 is authority for the proposition that I should not make an order that the Local Authority does not seek unless I am satisfied that very cogent reasons exist for doing so. On the other hand, there is authority for the proposition that I must give full reasons if I am to disagree with the recommendation of a Guardian. In this case, I have to do one or the other.
>
> [9] The protection of the child is the decisive factor when deciding whether to make a care order or a supervision order (*Re D* [1993] 2 FLR 423). A care order should be made only if the stronger order is necessary for the protection of the child (*Re B* [1996] 2 FLR 693). If the balance between the two is equal, I should adopt the least interventionist approach (*Re D* [2000] Fam Law 600). The key in each case is to decide whether a supervision order is proportionate as a response to the risk presented (*Re O* [2001] 1 FLR 923).'

Adopting this approach, he concluded that a supervision order was appropriate.

## Threshold and supervision orders

**25.40** A court may only make a supervision order if it is satisfied:

'(a) that the child concerned is suffering, or is likely to suffer, significant harm; and
(b) that the harm, or likelihood of harm, is attributable to –
　(i) the care given to the child, or likely to be given to him if the order were not made, not being what it would be reasonable to expect a parent to give to him; or
　(ii) the child's being beyond parental control.'

This provision, usually referred to as setting out the 'threshold' for the making of an order, is the same as that applies to the making to the making of a care order and is considered in detail in chapter 7.

---

[46] ie Schedule 3 of the 1989 Act, considered below.
[47] [2017] EWHC 379 (Fam).

## The welfare decision: 'proportionality ... is the key'[48]

**25.41** If the court is satisfied that the threshold for making a supervision order is established it then has to consider whether to make such an order. In doing so the court's 'paramount consideration' is the welfare of the child.[49] The 'checklist' of matters to which the court has to have particular consideration in deciding to make an order[50] applies,[51] as does the principle set out in s 1(5) that a court should not make an order:

'... unless it considers that doing so would be better for the child than making no order at all.'

**25.42** Note that in deciding to make a supervision order the court has to, 'have regard in particular' to:[52]

'... the range of powers available to the court under this Act in the proceedings in question.'

**25.43** A supervision order is by its nature something of a 'half-way house' between the full force of state intervention in family life that is represented by a care order and support for families[53] that does not involve any court sanctioned state interference with the right of parents and children to respect for their, 'private and family life'.[54] It is, therefore, not surprising that there are two distinct strands to the reported case law on the welfare stage of the decision to make a supervision order, namely cases that consider whether a supervision order offers adequate protection to the children concerned and those where the issue is whether any public law order at is required at all.

## Supervision order or care order?

**25.44** In the course of giving judgment in the case of *Re O (Supervision Order)*[55] Hale LJ (as she then was) explained the three main differences between a care order and a supervision order that are relevant when deciding which of the two is appropriate. In this case it was agreed that the child should stay at home with the parents but the local authority (supported by the guardian) sought a care order, primarily to enable them to protect the child from the risk of future harm should mother's (historically fragile) mental health deteriorate whereas the parents opposed any order on the basis that their record of co-operation and acceptance of support showed that an order to be unnecessary. The judge took, so to speak, the middle course of making a

---

[48] Per Hale LJ (as she then was) in *Re O (Supervision Order)* [2001] 1 FLR 923 at para 28.
[49] Section 1(1
[50] Section 1(3).
[51] See s 1(4)(b).
[52] Section 1(3)(g).
[53] The statutory basis for which can be found in Part III of the 1989 Act.
[54] Convention for the Protection of Human Rights and Fundamental Freedoms, Art 8(1) and (2).
[55] [2001] 1 FLR 923.

supervision order and the Court of Appeal[56] held that he was right to do so when the local authority appealed. Hale LJ had this to say about the differences between the two orders:

> '(24) A care order is ... very different from a supervision order. There are three main points. First, it gives a local authority power to remove the child without recourse even to a family proceedings court for an emergency protection order. The parents' only means of challenging that removal is by an application to discharge the care order,[57] which usually takes some time to be heard, especially if, as in this case, it would have to be transferred to a higher court. Given the judge's findings as to the nature of risk, the slowness of any deterioration, the level of protection available from other sources including the father, it is very difficult to say that the local authority need to have this power. The care plan itself, as I have already indicated, does not suggest that they do.
>
> (25) Secondly, it gives the local authority parental responsibility for the child coupled with the power to control the parents' exercise of that responsibility. Again, the care plan does not suggest that the local authority wish to exercise parental responsibility or control the parents' exercise of it. It expressly states, for example, 'that A's social, moral and academic education will be the responsibility of his parents'. Under "Health" it points out that he "continues to be in good health and he will need to receive the usual check-ups and vaccinations via the local health visitor and GP service". This is not indicative of the suggestion that the local authority need to be in a position to arrange that for him. In any event, that could be done by inserting appropriate requirements in the supervision order.
>
> (26) The third difference is one of timing. [Counsel for the guardian] in particular has argued that it might be difficult to achieve a further order in 3 years' time, but of course that difficulty would only arise if by then the risk of harm had disappeared or almost disappeared, or the need for an order had disappeared or almost disappeared. If that were not the case, the local authority would have to investigate and take any action which was thought appropriate to protect the child.'

**25.45** Her ladyship went on to say to this about the application of the overarching principle of 'proportionality', derived from the European Convention for the Protection of Human Rights and Fundamental Freedoms, in such cases:

> '(27) All of these considerations, therefore, suggest that the judge, far from being plainly wrong to make a supervision order, was absolutely right so to do. [Counsel for the local authority] has not relied upon earlier case law on the choice between care and supervision orders. He was probably wise to do so. Each case is an exercise of discretion on its own particular facts and earlier case law may be of

---

[56] Hale LJ and Cresswell J.
[57] Since the passing of the Human Rights Act 1998, parents in this position can apply for an injunction to prevent removal of the child pending proper judicial consideration: see *Re S (Minors) (Care Order: Implementation of Care Plan); Re W (Minors))Care Order: Adequacy of Care Plan)* [2002] 1 FLR 815 and other authorities usefully reviewed by Baker J in the case of *Re DE (Child under Care Order: Injunction under Human Rights Act 1998)* [2015] 1 FLR 1001. This subject is considered in more detail in chapter 4 above.

limited help in this context. But, in any event, it has to be considered in the light of the Human Rights Act 1998 and Art 8 of the European Convention for the Protection of Human Rights and Fundamental Freedoms 1950. As I said in the case of *Re C and B (Care Order: Future Harm)* [2001] 1 FLR 611, paras (33)–(34) at 620–621:

> "I do note that under Art 8 of the Convention both the children and the parents have the right to respect for their family and private life. If the state is to interfere with that there are three requirements: first, that it be in accordance with the law; secondly, that it be for a legitimate aim (in this case the protection of the welfare and interests of the children); and thirdly, that it be 'necessary in a democratic society'."

There is a long line of European Court of Human Rights jurisprudence on that third requirement, which emphasises that the intervention has to be proportionate to the legitimate aim.'

(28) Proportionality, therefore, is the key. It will be the duty of everyone to ensure that, in those cases where a supervision order is proportionate as a response to the risk presented, a supervision order can be made to work, as indeed the framers of the Children Act 1989 always hoped that it would be made to work. The local authorities must deliver the services that are needed and must secure that other agencies, including the health service, also play their part, and the parents must co-operate fully.'

**25.46** Whilst bearing in mind Her Ladyship's note of caution as to the limited assistance that can be gained from previously reported cases, *Re O (Supervision Order)* was one of a number of reported cases in which the issue is whether the court should make a care order or a supervision order and which turn on a concern as to whether a supervision order will provide adequate protection for the child. These cases show that the court has to carry out a balancing exercise between the risks found to be present and the harm that may be caused by the more extensive intervention in the family represented by the making of a care order, and that the final decision is always subject to the test of 'proportionality'.

**25.47** This point is well illustrated by the Court of Appeal decision in the case of *Re S (Care or Supervision Order)*.[58] In this case, each parent had children by other relationships. Although their care for the child with whom the court was concerned was good there were serious concerns about the father as a finding had been made in other proceedings that he had sexually abused one of his other children, a finding that he continued to dispute (he had been acquitted at a related Crown Court trial). The local authority considered that the risk of sexual harm to the child was such that a care order was required and their plan was to place the child with a grandparent. At final hearing, the circuit judge declined to make a care order and, 'instead made a supervision order attaching certain conditions which he considered were appropriate to provide such

---

[58] [1996] 1 FLR 753: all quotations are from the judgment of Beldam LJ, who sat with Johnson J.

protection as was possible' for the child.[59] The trial judge invited counsel to draw up an order that he reflected this preferred outcome but despite their 'ingenuity' in seeking to frame the judge's requirements in terms compatible with paras 2 and 3 of Sch 3 of the CA 1989, 'the altered requirements clearly fell some way short of the protection that had apparently weighed with the judge when he decided that a supervision order was appropriate';[60] the result was, 'unsatisfactory and had all the hallmarks of an unhappy compromise'.[61] The inability of the court to attach 'conditions' to a supervision order had, of course, been identified by the Court of Appeal in the case of *Re V (Care or Supervision Order)*[62] and the trial judge's failure to appreciate this was held by then Court of Appeal to vitiate his decision and re-hearing was ordered. Beldam LJ defined the task of the judge in a case of this nature in the following terms:[63]

> 'I am far from saying that this was a case in which only a care order was appropriate, nor should I be taken to be expressing a view that a supervision order was inappropriate, but in my view the case demanded a careful assessment of the degree of likelihood of harm to [the child]. That required consideration of the likelihood that the father would abuse him at some time in the future and the ability of the mother to protect him against it. The court then, having assessed the likelihood of harm, would need to weigh that likelihood against the undoubted harm of S being removed from the care of his mother and father and brought up by his maternal grandmother. That balancing exercise was never properly carried out, and in my opinion it should be.'

**25.48** Balancing exercises of the type identified in *Re S* continues to dominate the court's approach to deciding between care and supervision orders.

**25.49** An example of a case where such a balancing exercise resulting the making of a supervision order can be seen in the decision of Sumner J (sitting as trial judge in the Family Division) in the case of *Re C (Care Order or Supervision Order)*.[64] Here the child had suffered severe injuries at the hands of the father[65] but the mother[66] was not implicated in this assault, had co-operated with enquiries and in other respects had been positively assessed, including as to her willingness to work with professionals and seek help when she needed it. The local authority agreed that the child should remain in the care of the mother but sought, with the support of the child's guardian, a care order on the basis that mother remained isolated and vulnerable, because she might again become involved with a violent partner, and had shown a serious lack of judgment in leaving the child alone with father. Having reviewed the

---

[59] At p 756.
[60] At p 759.
[61] At p 760.
[62] [1996] 1 FLR 776, discussed above: Johnson J drew attention to this case during argument in *Re S*.
[63] At pp 760–761.
[64] [2001] 2 FLR 466.
[65] He was convicted of inflicting grievous bodily harm and sentenced to eight years imprisonment.
[66] Herself the victim of a number of assaults by the father.

evidence[67] of the risks to the child and the positive indicators for mother's capacity to protect Sumner J concluded that he regarded the risks to the child as, 'not significant or very low' and accordingly that, 'a supervision order is proportionate to the risks presently presented'.[68]

## Supervision order or no order?

**25.50** In the case of *T (A Child) v Wakefield Metropolitan District Council*[69] Thorpe LJ observed of supervision orders that:[70]

> 'Usually they are made where there is a real risk that the child's carers, ordinarily the child's parents, will fail or falter unless supported by a supervisor. Thus the supervision order where the risks indicate the need for statutory intervention is less intrusive than a care order.'

**25.51** This begs the questions of how real the risk of the parents failing or faltering needs to be and whether the support has to be provided by a supervisor under the terms of a supervision order.[71]

**25.52** In considering whether a supervision order is to be preferred to the making of no order, it is helpful to look the question from the starting point of asking what support the parents would receive if the order were not to be made and whether that support would meet the identified need to ameliorate the identified risk. This in turn gives rise to the need to consider the nature of the duty to provide support that is laid on local authorities.

**25.53** Part III of the CA 1989 sets out the provisions of the CA 1989 in relation to, 'support for children and families provided by local authorities'. Its key provision, which sets out the general duty to provide support, is s 17(1), which provides as follows:

> 'It shall be the general duty of every local authority (in addition to the other duties imposed on them by this Part) –
>
> (a) to safeguard and promote the welfare of children within their area who are in need; and
> (b) so far as is consistent with that duty, to promote the upbringing of such children by their families,
>
> by providing a range and level of services appropriate to those children's needs.'

**25.54** The provision of services for, 'children in need' represents the level of support for families and safeguarding for children that should be made available by all local authorities to families in their area. It is not a coercive

---

[67] See at paras 42–48 and 52.
[68] At para 52.
[69] [2008] EWCA Civ 199: this case is concerned with the court's powers to determine the duration of a supervision order and is discussed in that context below.
[70] Paragraph 2.
[71] Remembering always the 'no order' principle in s 1(5) of the 1989 Act.

step[72] and does not involve any compulsory intervention in the family's life[73] nor any assessment that the child is or may be suffering or at risk of suffering harm. Conversely, there is limited scope for challenge to the way in which a local authority chooses to discharge this general duty. A local authority's decision as to whether or not a particular child is, 'in need' is one of evaluation, not fact, and can only be challenged by judicial review[74] and this is also the case in the case in the event of any dispute between the local authority and the child's family as to the services being provided or offered to a child. It is in any event wrong to make a s 31 order solely in order to induce a local authority to provide services that would fall within the ambit of Part III support. As Wall J comments in *Re K (Supervision Order)*:[75]

> 'In [*Oxfordshire County Council v L (Care or Supervision Order)*[76]] Hale J made the point that it would be wrong to make a care order which was not in the interests of the children simply to encourage the local authority to perform its statutory duties towards children in need. The same observation applies, in my judgment, mutatis mutandis, to the making of a supervision order where the duties imposed under Part III would be sufficient to meet the children's needs. I equally bear in mind Hale J's observation in both cases that the court should start with 'a preference for the less interventionist approach rather than the more interventionist approach'. In essence, therefore, the matter, it seems to me, comes down to the duty imposed upon the court by s 1(5).'[77]

**25.55** In *Re K (Supervision Order)* Wall J considered some of factors that would lead a court to make a supervision order rather than leave the child to be supported by the local authority as a child in need. This case concerned three children whose younger sibling had died (at the age of seven days) in circumstances that were 'suspicious' but where the evidence was, it was accepted, insufficient to justify any findings as to cause of death or of wrongdoing against the mother (the parents separated before the deceased child's birth and the children's father was not involved in the case). The local authority asserted that the remaining children had suffered significant harm for reasons unconnected with their sibling's death and whilst mother denied this, she accepted that the children were at risk of harm. Generally speaking, mother's care for the children was satisfactory. At final hearing the local authority and mother agreed that threshold was established and that the children should remain in mother's care but subject to a supervision order. The children's guardian disagreed and argued that in the absence of findings as to the child's death threshold was not established and that even if it were met only on the basis agreed by local authority and mother then no order was necessary

---

[72] 'Part III imposes duties on local authorities but, as I understand it, no duties on parents or persons with parental responsibility': per Wall J (as he then was) in *Re K (Supervision Order)* [1999] 2 FLR 303 at p 317.
[73] Although in reality a refusal to accept advice or assistance will often be the factor that leads a local authority to consider the need to commence proceedings for a care or supervision order.
[74] See the decision of the Supreme Court in *R (A) v Croydon London Borough Council; R (M) v Lambeth London Borough Council* [2010] 1 FLR 959.
[75] At p 318.
[76] [1998] 1 FLR 70.
[77] At page 317.

as the children would remain in mother's care and would in any event remain subject to local authority monitoring as they would continue to be on the child protection register.

**25.56** In these circumstances and after considering authorities to which he had been referred,[78] Wall J concluded that he should hear short evidence from social workers and the guardian. Having done so, he concluded that threshold was indeed made out and went on to consider whether a supervision order was appropriate on the facts of the case.

**25.57** After considering various authorities, which he comments deal in the main with the situation where the court has to decide whether a care or a supervision order should be made, and considering the terms of s 35, Sch 3 and Part II of the CA 1989,[79] he concluded that it was appropriate to make a supervision order. He said that he reached this decision for the following reasons:[80]

> 'The local authority accepts in this case that, in the absence of a supervision order, and provided the children remain on the child protection register, the level of services to be provided to the family will remain very much the same. However, the reasons for a supervision order which weigh with me in this case are the following:
>
> (1) I share the local authority's concern that in the absence of a supervision order the mother will not continue to co-operate with the local authority. There is abundant evidence for this conclusion. A supervision order represents a means of ensuring continuing co-operation which is not available under Part III.
>
> (2) The court has found there is a likelihood of the children suffering significant harm. Whilst not of itself predetermining the need for an order, the satisfaction of the threshold criteria means, in my judgment, that the concerns for the children are serious and warrant the making of an order, that there is a need for careful monitoring of this family over the next 12 months to ensure that the welfare of the children is safeguarded.
>
> (3) With a supervision order the local authority will, as a matter of practice, allocate a social worker and an assistant social worker, and will generally accord a higher degree of priority to children who are the subject of such orders as opposed to children who are on the child protection register, and not subject to any order.
>
> (4) Whilst it lacks teeth, a supervision order does nonetheless impose obligations on the mother, none of which are imposed under Part III.
>
> (5) The family's situation is fragile. A supervision order guarantees proper local authority involvement for 12 months, with the prospect of renewal if necessary. That involvement needs, in my judgment, to be guaranteed by the court in fulfilment of its duty to these children under s 1 of the Children Act, and should not be left to the internal workings of the local authority.

---

[78] *Re G (A Minor) (Care Proceedings)* [1994] 2 FLR 69 and *Stockport Metropolitan Borough Council v D* [1995] 1 FLR 873: neither in fact on all fours with the case before Wall J, see his discussion at pp 311–313.
[79] See discussion at pp 316–318.
[80] At p 319.

(6) The mother herself agrees to a supervision order, and it is recommended by Dr E[81] in the circumstances which I have found to exist. I therefore accept Dr E's reasoning on this point.

In all these circumstances, I conclude that a supervision order in this case is better for the children than no order. I am not making the order to persuade a reluctant local authority to fulfil its duties to these children. Both local authorities involved have acted responsibly throughout, and both take the view that supervision orders are the best way of fulfilling their statutory obligations to the family.'

**25.58** Whilst they are obviously fact specific, some or all of the six factors enumerated by Wall J are generally referred to when a court is being urged to make a supervision order rather than no order.[82]

**25.59** A factor that is likely to have great weight in the court's consideration is that of the harm that a child has suffered and the need to avoid or ameliorate that harm in the future. This point is illustrated by the case of *Wiltshire County Council v F*,[83] decided by Baker J.

**25.60** The facts of this case were highly unusual in that the child ('B') had been brought into the United Kingdom by two people, 'F' and 'C', who claimed to be his father and mother respectively and who stated that B was 5 years and 7 months old when he entered the country. Social services became involved because the child's school raised concerns as they thought that he was significantly older than his stated age and proceedings were commenced. DNA testing showed that B was unrelated to his 'mother' but was almost certainly his 'father's' full brother whilst paediatric evidence was to the effect that he was at least 5 years older than his claimed age and Baker J made findings of fact accordingly.[84] He went on to find that the child had suffered significant emotional harm as a result of the deceptions practiced by the 'parents' as to his age and relationships but, crucially, that their physical care of him was good and that it would not be in his interests to be 'uprooted' from his home.[85] In these circumstances, His Lordship decided that the child's welfare did require the making of a supervision order. He explained his reasons for this in the following terms:

'[38] In those circumstances, it seems to me imperative that the local authority should remain involved with this family for the time being. At the outset the local

---

[81] A Consultant Child and Adolescent Psychiatrist who had reported on the family.
[82] His points (1), (2), (3) and (5) are specifically reflected in the often cited summary of the reasons why a court may decide that a child's welfare requires the making of a supervision order in *Hershman and McFarlane Children Law and Practice*, Part C, para 1506, where reference is made to the judgment.
[83] [2014] 2 FLR 336.
[84] These findings, which ultimately included one that the child was 14 years of age (and undergoing puberty) and not 7, as claimed by his 'parents' were made on the balance of probabilities and represented His Lordship's best attempt to construct a true history of the child's life, a task hampered by the continued denials of the 'parents', whose evidence on almost every relevant issue was rejected by the learned judge.
[85] At para [36].

authority proposed that there should now be no order but, rather, that B should continue to be supported under a child in need plan under s 17 of the Children Act 1989. As the hearing progressed, and the extent of the deception and its impact on B became more apparent, it became clear that this was an inadequate response and the local authority sensibly amended its plan to fall in line with that advocated on behalf of the guardian, namely that there should be a supervision order. F and C also now accept that a supervision order should be made. The only issue is the length of that supervision order. The guardian argued for 12 months, the local authority for 6.

[39] As stated above, in deciding what order to make I apply s 1 of the Children Act 1989, the paramountcy principle in s 1(1) and the welfare checklist in s 1(3), together with the principle that the court should only make an order when satisfied that to do so is better than making no order at all. In this case, I am satisfied that an order is required. I bear in mind the principle that the court should favour the least interventionist order consistent with meeting B's needs. Although B has suffered emotional and psychological harm as a result of the deceptions perpetrated by F and C, it is important to stress that their physical care of him has been good, so it would be contrary to his interests for him to be removed from their care. Accordingly, there is no question in this case over a care order being made and I will renew the residence order in favour of F and C.

[40] In this case the magnetic factors in the welfare checklist seem to me to be B's background, his emotional needs, the harm he has suffered and the harm he is likely to suffer in the future. As set out above, I consider it likely that the emotional and psychological harm will continue for some time to come. In those circumstances I conclude that a supervision order for 12 months is the least interventionist order that meets B's current needs and that is the order that I propose to make.'

His Lordship went on to note, and approve, the proposal that a 'care plan' should be produced specifying the support that the child would receive.[86]

**25.61** The first factor mentioned by Wall J when setting out his reasons for making a supervision order in *Re K (Supervision Order)* was the need to ensure continued cooperation by the parent or parents. In other cases, this can be a factor weighing against the making of an order. This was the case in *Re K: A Local Authority v N and Others*,[87] decided by Munby J (as he then was).

**25.62** In this case a young woman (she was 16 years old at time of the final hearing), 'K', had been party to an arranged (but not, it was found, forced) purported marriage at the age of 15 years in accordance with the religious practice and custom of her family's country of origin. When this came to light, by way of disclosures she made to her general practitioner that included allegations of physical abuse against her father (which were not found to be

---

[86] This would include counselling and/or therapy and life story work: see at para [41]. Note that although commonly referred to as 'care plans' plans setting out support to be given under a supervision order fall outside the requirements for production of care plans set out in s 31A of the CA 1989.
[87] [2007] 1 FLR 399.

substantiated) and her 'husband', proceedings were commenced. Concerns also emerged as to her mental health. Over a period of 7 months she was placed in foster care and secure accommodation but by the time of the final hearing she had lived in her family home for 8 months without any court order and without incident. The local authority sought a supervision order as being, 'not only proportionate but necessary'[88] to ensure the K's well-being by providing a statutory basis of continued involvement in the family. This was opposed by K's parents, her guardian and, very significantly, by K herself (she saw the judge to express her strongly held views) and K and her family made it clear that they would not accept the proposed involvement of the local authority.

**25.63** Munby J decided that no order should be made. His conclusions on this aspect of the case were as follows:

'[55] The guardian agrees that the threshold criteria are met but, on the basis of the "no order" principle, opposes the making of a supervision order. She considers that for the following reasons it would be better for there to be no order than a supervision order:

(i) K has indicated a clear opposition to the making of an order. The guardian does not consider that it will assist the local authority in supporting K if an order is made against her expressed wishes. The guardian believes that if such an order were to be made it would undermine the limited but positive support the social worker has been able to provide to K over the last nine months.

(ii) On the assumption that the parents are also in opposition to the orders sought by the local authority, the guardian is concerned that the making of a supervision order will be counter productive to the family working with social services in the future. While the family has not welcomed the involvement of social services the family has, over the last 9 months when there has been no order, co-operated to enable the social worker to meet with K at the family home. They have also attended, to a limited extent, the CAMHS services offered, and facilitated K's attendance for counselling. The guardian is concerned that the making of an order against the parents' wishes will make them less likely to seek and utilise the support of social services in the future.

(iii) Without some co-operation from K and her parents the local authority will be in difficulties fulfilling its responsibilities to K under the supervision order. The guardian is mindful that the local authority has worked with the family without an order since 17 January 2005.

(iv) The guardian has detailed in her report the future support she recommends the social worker provides to K and her family. The guardian considers that these limited services could be provided by the local authority under Part III of the 1989 Act rather than under Part IV. The guardian notes in this context that the local authority will continue to try to have K's case allocated to the existing social worker and that there is in any event no guarantee that the social worker will continue to be allocated even if there is a supervision order.

---

[88] Paragraph [41].

[56] I agree with the guardian, and essentially for the reasons she gives, that there should not be a supervision order.

[57] I have to face the realities. They are that I have a girl aged almost 17, and her parents, who are unwilling to co-operate with public authorities if required by order to do so. Compulsion was recognised as long ago as January 2005 to be no longer appropriate. K has been living at home for some time now, without the local authority having the benefit of any kind of public law order at all. It is clear that, whatever may remain to be done, things are much better for K now than they have been for quite some time. Relations between K and her parents seem much improved. There has been no recent repetition of the florid episodes of a year ago. To an extent, K and her family have been able to co-operate with the local authority despite the absence of any formal order. That co-operation is much less than might be thought desirable, but I do not think that a supervision order is going to improve matters, or increase the chances of co-operation; if anything the reverse.

[58] The local authority has rightly disavowed compulsion by means of secure accommodation; it has rightly concluded that it is not appropriate for it to share parental responsibility. I do not in any way criticise it for seeking a supervision order, but on balance I agree with the guardian that a supervision order is unlikely to achieve anything and that it may even be counter-productive.'

**25.64** A striking feature of the two *Re K* cases is the way in which the court's balancing exercise resulted in different conclusions as to the desirability of a supervision order when considering the issue of how to secure the cooperation of family and indeed child. Wall J concluded that an order should be imposed in order, in part, to secure cooperation whilst Munby J accepted that cooperation would only be obtained if an order were not made. This perhaps illustrates the highly fact specific nature of the welfare exercise and the delicacy of the balancing exercise that is required. Munby J's decision is also a useful reminder of the need of the court to, 'face reality' when deciding on the appropriate level of state intervention in the family, particularly when older children express strongly held, 'wishes and feelings' on this question.

## The terms and effect of the supervision order: directions, obligations and requirements and the extent of the court's powers

**25.65** In addition to the general duties of the supervisor under s 35(1) of the CA 1989[89] Sch 3 allows specific provisions as to the matters specified to be incorporated by way of imposing a requirement for a supervised child to comply with directions given by the supervisor[90] and for persons with parental responsibility, or with whom the child is living,[91] to abide by requirements, which may include ensuring that a child comply with any direction given. Furthermore, paras 4 and 5 of Sch 3 make specific provision for the

---

[89] See above.
[90] Paragraph 2 of Sch 3.
[91] See definition of 'responsible person' in para 1.

incorporation in a supervision order of requirements that a child undergo medical or psychiatric examination or treatment. It is important to emphasise the limited role of the court in determining the way in which an order is to operate in terms of controlling the way in which the supervisor and responsible person conduct themselves.

**25.66** The matters in respect of which directions can be given are specified para 2 are as follows:

> 'A supervision order may require the supervised child to comply with any directions given from time to time by the supervisor which require him to do all or any of the following things –
>
> (a) to live at a place or places specified in the directions for a period or periods so specified;
> (b) to present himself to a person or persons specified in the directions at a place or places and on a day or days so specified;
> (c) to participate in activities specified in the directions on a day or days so specified.'[92]

**25.67** Although a court can include in a supervision order a requirement that the child concerned comply with any directions within the scope of the paragraph that may be given, the court has no power to specify what directions should in fact be given. This is clear from para 2(2) of Sch 3, which provides that:

> 'It shall be for the supervisor to decide whether, and to what extent, he exercises his power to give directions and to decide the form of any directions which he gives.'

**25.68** Paragraph 3 of Sch 3 deals with the placing of obligations on a, 'responsible person' and has the effect of putting further distance between the court and the operation of the supervision order by providing that the consent of the responsible person is required before a 'requirement' is incorporated in the order. Paragraph 3(1) provides that:

> 'With the consent of any responsible person, a supervision order may include a requirement –
>
> (a) that he take all reasonable steps to ensure that the supervised child complies with any direction given by the supervisor under paragraph 2;
> (b) that he take all reasonable steps to ensure that the supervised child complies with any requirement included in the order under paragraph 4 or 5;
> (c) that he comply with any directions given by the supervisor requiring him to attend at a place specified in the directions for the purpose of taking part in activities so specified.'

**25.69** As Bracewell J remarked in the case of *Re H (Supervision Order)*:[93]

---

[92] Paragraph 2(1).
[93] [1994] 2 FLR 979.

'However, it appears to me that the imposition of obligations on a responsible person falls into a completely different category.[94] The consent of the responsible person is required and that is present in this case. However, para 3 goes on to state that a supervision order may include a requirement that he comply with any directions given by the supervisor requiring him to attend at a place specified in the directions for the purposes of taking part in activities so specified. Such a direction may specify the time at which the responsible person is to attend, and whether or not the supervised child is required to attend with him.

I am satisfied that in relation to that paragraph the directions are entirely a matter for the supervisor and it is not open to the court to order that the local authority should give any such directions. The responsible person may be ordered by the court to comply with any such directions, but that is an entirely different matter from the court imposing an obligation to do specific thing.'[95]

**25.70** Similarly, in the Court of Appeal case of *Re B (Supervision Order: Parental Undertaking)*[96] (a case in which the main issue of appeal was as to whether a county court had jurisdiction to accept and incorporate in a supervision order a mother's undertaking that she would accept treatment for her own mental health issues) Neill LJ emphasised the need both for the supervisor to decide to give a direction and the responsible person to agree to it being reflected in a requirement:[97]

'I have considered whether the matter could be dealt with by including in the supervision order a requirement that the mother should comply with any directions given by the supervisor requiring her to attend at a specified hospital for medical treatment. I am satisfied, however, that even if in some circumstances such a requirement could be included in a supervision order under para 3(1)(c) of Sch 3 (which I find it unnecessary to decide), such a requirement would be quite inappropriate in the present case. There is no evidence as to what the supervisor might require the mother to do with regard to receiving medical treatment. Nor is there any information as to whether the mother would be willing to consent to any such directions. Thus it is important to emphasise that the requirements included in a supervision order pursuant to para 3(1) can only be made with the consent of the responsible person concerned.'

**25.71** As Bracewell J notes in *Re H (Supervision Order)*[98] the position is somewhat different in relation to the provisions of paras 4 and 5 of Sch 3.

**25.72** Paragraph 4(1) provides that a supervision order:

'... may require the supervised child –

    (a)    to submit to a medical or psychiatric examination; or
    (b)    to submit to any such examination from time to time as directed by the

---

[94] From the provisions as to imposing requirements that the child submit to medical or psychiatric assessment or treatment in accordance with paras 4 and 5 of Sch 3: see below.
[95] At p 980.
[96] [1996] 1 FLR 676.
[97] At p 685.
[98] Above.

supervisor.'

**25.73** Such an examination can take place at a hospital or care home that the child is attending or will attend as a residential placement.[99] The court is required to receive medical evidence as to the child's condition and the necessity of the child being assessed as a residential patient before incorporating such a requirement in a supervision order.[100]

**25.74** Paragraph 5 of Sch 3 makes provision for the incorporation of requirements that the child, 'submit to such treatment as may be specified' in respect of their mental or physical condition.[101] Such treatment may be as a residential patient.[102] Paragraph 5 is subject to the important proviso that a requirement under this paragraph can only be included in an order if the child consents to its inclusion, 'where the child has sufficient understanding to make an informed decision'.[103] Note also that in the case of treatment of mental health difficulties, a requirement can only be included if the child's condition is not such as would warrant their detention pursuant to a hospital order under Part III of the Mental Health Act 1983.[104]

## Duration, extension and discharge of supervision orders

**25.75** The primary provision governing the duration of a supervision order is para 6 of Sch 3 of the CA 1989, which provides as follows:

'(1) Subject to sub-paragraph (2) and section 91, a supervision order shall cease to have effect at the end of the period of one year beginning with the date on which it was made.

(2) A supervision order shall also cease to have effect if an event mentioned in section 25(1)(a) or (b) of the Child Abduction and Custody Act 1985 (termination of existing orders) occurs with respect to the child.

(3) Where the supervisor applies to the court to extend, or further extend, a supervision order the court may extend the order for such period as it may specify.

(4) A supervision order may not be extended so as to run beyond the end of the period of three years beginning with the date on which it was made.'

**25.76** (Section 91(3) provides that the making of a care order in respect of a child who is the subject of a supervision order discharges that order. Section 91(13) provides that a supervision order is one of those orders that shall

---

[99] Paragraph 4(2)(c).
[100] Paragraph 4(3).
[101] Paragraphs 5(1) and 5(3) respectively.
[102] See para 5(2)(c) in relation to the child's, 'mental condition' and para 5(4)(c) in relation to the child's, 'physical condition'. These provisions provide an unusual instance within the scheme of the public law orders under the CA 1989 of a court (as opposed to the responsible local authority) having the power to determine a child's place of residence, albeit for limited and specific purposes.
[103] Paragraph 5(5)(a).
[104] There is no lower limit on the age of persons who can be made the subject of such orders under the 1983 Act: the writer is grateful to Michael Ball, Tribunal Judge, for elucidating this point.

cease to have effect when the child reaches the age of 18 years, if it would otherwise still be in force at that time. The Child Abduction and Custody Act 1985 gives effect to the Convention on the Civil Aspects of International Child Abduction which was signed at The Hague on 25th October 1980: s 25(1) of the 1985 Act provides for certain orders to cease to have effect on the making of specified orders under that Act and subs (2) applies this to supervision orders.)

**25.77** This paragraph has caused a surprising amount of difficulty. Sir Matthew Thorpe, sitting as a judge of the Family Division, described para 6(1) as containing, 'an obvious ambiguity',[105] and as a Lord Justice sitting in the Court of Appeal he observed that the paragraph as a whole displayed a, 'lack of comprehensive clarity'.[106]

**25.78** The, 'obvious ambiguity' His Lordship had to consider in *M v Warwickshire County Council* was that of whether para 6(1) required an order to be for a period of one year (as the justices deciding the case concluded it did) or whether it could be for a shorter period (all parties, including the Children's Guardian, considering that an order for 6 months only was appropriate to meet the children's welfare needs). In resolving this ambiguity His Lordship took the approach that:[107]

> 'It seems to me very important that in construing the Act the court should, wherever possible, favour construction that is likely to make for practical advantage. It is obviously advantageous to those who have the management of difficult cases, such as this, that there should be a flexible range of powers. This case well illustrates the advantages of and need for a discretion that is not confined to a choice between 12 months or no supervision order at all.'

**25.79** He went on to conclude that nothing in the paragraph precluded the making of an order for less than one year. There was accordingly jurisdiction to do so, which the justices should have exercised on the merits of the application before them.

**25.80** *T (A Child) v Wakefield Metropolitan District Council* dealt with the converse issue of whether it was permissible within the terms of the paragraph to make an order that that would immediately be extended to the full three years allowed by para 6(4). In this case a supervision order was said to be required to assist in protecting the child from the risk of harm presented a relative of mother's who had a substantial criminal record for sexual offences. The trial judge accepted an argument that the need for supervision would extend beyond one year and held that there was:[108]

---

[105] *M v Warwickshire County Council* [1994] 2 FLR 593 at 595
[106] *T (A Child) v Wakefield Metropolitan District Council* [2008] EWCA Civ 199 at para 9: at the request of the Court counsel in this case researched the legislative history of the paragraph and found that there was no discussion of the duration of supervision orders in the House of Commons debates on the Children Bill, see paras 24–29.
[107] At p 595.
[108] Quoted by Thorpe LJ at para 5 of his judgment.

'... no barrier, even at the stage of the first hearing of an application, to making an order which extends, and is to be seen as an extension, from the regular twelve-month order for up to three years. That seems to me to be the constructive interpretation, in other words, the purposeful or purposive interpretation, of the statute because in this case where, even at this stage, the court can clearly see that the welfare of the child requires the making of what I might call a longer-term order it saves everybody the anxiety and the expense, often the public expense, of an application in twelve months down the line.'

**25.81** On appeal Thorpe LJ (with whom Arden and Hughes LJJ agreed) described counsel's argument in support of this approach as:[109]

'... an impermissible circumvention of the plain language of paragraph 6(1). The artificiality of an almost immediate application for the extension of the basic order is self evident. The outcome would be the frustration of the clear legislative intention to reform the pre-existing law which had expressly granted jurisdiction to impose a supervision order of three year duration.'

**25.82** Accordingly, it was held that the requirement for the initial supervision order to be for no more than one year could not be avoided in the way that the judge had sought to do so. His Lordship, however, recognised that there remained a lack of clarity in the schedule as to how the issue of extending a supervision order should be approached, a lacuna that was particularly surprising given that para 15(3) of the Schedule did make specific provision for applications to extend the duration of education supervision orders. In the light of this he gave the following guidance as to applications to extend the duration of supervision orders:

'20. I would fill the void in paragraph 6 by suggesting a like practice[110] in relation to supervision orders. Clearly before any extension is sought the need for and the acceptance of extension will be canvassed in correspondence. That exploration will reveal whether the extension is consensual and, if not, the extent of the dispute. The issue of any necessary application should not be delayed so as to imperil the local authority's imperative need for a determination before the expiration of the current order. I say imperative because once the order has expired the applicant would be compelled to prove and the court to determine the Section 31 threshold since the application would have become not an application for extension but an application for a new order.

21. In the great majority of cases the listing and determination of an extension application will not much burden the court. The determination will be discretionary and the factors relevant to the exercise of that discretion are unlikely to be either extensive or complex.

22. In summary I would doubt the need for any application to extend a supervision order of twelve months duration before the last quarter of its first life. How well within that quarter the application should sensibly be issued depends upon the

---

[109] Paragraph 18.
[110] i.e. to that applied to education supervision orders by para 15(3) of the Schedule.

facts of each case, that is to say the extent of the issues raised by the application, and the ascertainable capacity of the relevant court.'

**25.83** As noted by His Lordship, the extension of an existing supervision order does not require the court to be satisfied that 'threshold' is established. This was decided by the Court of Appeal in the case of *Re A (Supervision Order: Extension)*[111] in which it was held that an application to extend the duration of a supervision order was not an, 'application for a supervision order' with the terms of s 31 of the CA 1989. Accordingly, it was necessary to look at the terms of Sch 6 to ascertain the requirements for an extension to a supervision order and the approach to such an application. As Hoffman LJ (as he then was) put it the result of doing so led to the conclusion that:

> 'Paragraph 6(3) does not say that the power to extend a supervision order cannot be exercised unless the threshold conditions in s 31(2) are satisfied. Nor is there any reason to imply such a requirement. The principles to be applied are simply those stated in s 1 of the Act: the paramountcy of the interests of the child, the need to avoid delay, the welfare checklist applicable to all Part IV applications and the presumption against judicial intervention.'

**25.84** The conclusion that the requirements of s 31 were not to be imported into an application to extend a supervision order had the further, 'technical but important'[112] consequence that the court did not, on an application to extend the duration of a supervision order, have jurisdiction under s 31(5) to make a care order, as the judge below had done.[113]

**25.85** The court has a general power under s 39(2) of the CA 1989 to vary or discharge a supervision order on the application of:

'(a) any person who has parental responsibility for the child;
(b) the child himself; or
(c) the supervisor.'

**25.86** As noted above, s 35(1(c) imposes a duty on the supervisor to consider whether or not to apply for the order to be varied or discharged where they consider that it is not wholly complied with or may no longer be necessary.

**25.87** In addition, s 39(3) provides that:

> 'On the application of a person who is not entitled to apply for the order to be discharged, but who is a person with whom the child is living, a supervision order may be varied by the court in so far as it imposes a requirement which affects that person.'

The welfare checklist applies to an application to vary or discharge a supervision order.[114]

---

[111] [1995] 1 FLR 335
[112] Per Butler-Sloss LJ at p 338.
[113] See judgments of Butler-Sloss LJ at p 338 and Hoffman LJ at p 339.
[114] Section 1(4) of the CA 1989.

**25.88** When an application to discharge a supervision order has been made, no further such application may be made without leave of the court unless 6 months has elapsed between the disposal of that application and the making of a further application.[115]

**25.89** Applications to extend, vary or discharge supervision orders are rare. In the calendar year 2016, for example, such applications were made in respect of orders involving only 84 children and orders made on such applications affected only 51 children.[116] However, the published statistics do not identify cases where an application is made for a care order when a supervision order is already in place: if a care order is made this automatically discharges any existing supervision order.[117]

---

[115] Section 91(15) of the CA 1989.
[116] Ministry of Justice: Family Courts Statistics Quarterly, England and Wales April to June 2017, Tables 3 and 4.
[117] See s 91(3).

# CHAPTER 26

# PRIVATE LAW ORDERS IN THE CONTEXT OF CARE PROCEEDINGS (PART 1)

## GENERAL PRINCIPLES AND S 8 ORDERS: INTRODUCTION

### Alternative orders in public law proceedings

**26.1** When considering an application for a care or supervision order under Part IV of the Children Act 1989 the court's power is not limited to making, or not making, one of those, 'public law' orders. It also has powers, derived from Part II of the Act, to make child arrangements orders, prohibited steps orders or specific issue orders under s 8 of the Act[1] or special guardianship orders under s 14A of the Act.[2] The nature of these orders, the circumstances in which the court has power to make them and in which it may consider using these powers are considered here and in the following chapter.

**26.2** A point to note at the outset is that the court's exercise of its powers to make alternative orders is not dependent on a formal, written, application for such orders being made.[3] The court has wide powers to make such orders if it considers that they are required and may use this power at the urging of a party to the proceedings or entirely of its own motion. This flexibility is particularly useful when a court takes the view that the level of interference in family life involved in the making of a care order is not justified but that some degree of legal structure for the child's life[4] is required to secure the child's welfare. A typical, 'package' of orders in such a case would be for there to be a child arrangements order providing for the child to live with one parent whilst their relationship with the other parent, or other significant adults in their lives, is secured by a child arrangements order setting out contact arrangements. In other circumstances, the court may appoint a relative (often, a grandparent) to

---

[1] These orders are referred to collectively below, and within the Children Act 1989, as 'section 8 orders': see s 8(2).
[2] Section 14A–14F were inserted by the Adoption and Children Act 2002.
[3] For the procedure for making a formal application, see below.
[4] Over and above the structure that flows from the holding of parental responsibility by child's parents, or others with parental responsibility in accordance with the 1989 Act: see s 3 for the meaning of 'parental responsibility' and ss 2, 4, 4ZA, 4A and 5 for the circumstances in which a person can come to hold parental responsibility for a child.

act as the child's special guardian and to be their main carer whilst a child arrangements order makes provision for contact between the child and their parents.

## TWO FUNDAMENTAL DISTINCTIONS

**26.3** Section 8 orders and special guardianship orders differ from care orders and supervision orders in two fundamental respects, one relating the court's jurisdiction to make orders and the other to the effect of the orders.

### *Jurisdiction*

**26.4** As discussed in detail elsewhere in this work,[5] the court only has jurisdiction to make a care order or a supervision order if it is satisfied that:[6]

'(a) that the child concerned is suffering, or is likely to suffer, significant harm; and
(b) that the harm, or likelihood of harm, is attributable to –
  (i) the care given to the child, or likely to be given to him if the order were not made, not being what it would be reasonable to expect a parent to give to him; or
  (ii) the child's being beyond parental control.'

**26.5** This requirement to be satisfied that this, 'threshold' for making orders is crossed does not apply when the court is considering making s 8 or special guardianship orders. The test for making such orders is simply one of whether the child's welfare requires the making of the order, having regard to the terms of s 1 of the 1989 Act and all the circumstances of the case. It is accordingly unnecessary for the court to consider expressly whether findings can be made as required by s 31(2) when deciding to make such orders.

**26.6** The only circumstance in which it is necessary for a court to be satisfied that threshold is established before making a s 8 order or special guardianship order is when it is proposed that a supervision order be made to provide support to the child's placement. Supervision orders are considered in detail elsewhere in this work.[7]

**26.7** Although there is no requirement for threshold to be made out if a care or supervision order is not to be made, there is nothing in the legislation or reported case law to prevent a court considering threshold issues and making findings as to threshold in the course of its decision-making process. This is likely to be an essential element of the court's overall consideration of the case where it has to weigh competing arguments for the making of, one the one hand, a care order or supervision order and, on the other, a s 8 order or special guardianship order. In such cases the normal approach of the court will be to

---

[5] See chapter 7.
[6] Section 31(2) of the 1989 Act.
[7] See chapter 25.

consider whether threshold is established on the basis of an admitted or found factual background and, if it is found to be, to go on the carry out the 'balancing exercise' of weighing the pros and cons of the available orders.[8]

**26.8** In some cases, a court will wish to include a finding that the threshold is met, and of the factual basis for this finding, even where no s 31 order is actively sought, on the basis that this provides a 'base-line' should further proceedings be necessary.[9]

## Effect of orders

**26.9** The essence of s 8 orders and, to a much greater extent, special guardianship orders, is to regulate the way in which parental responsibility is exercised by those who hold it. However, these orders do not provide for the sharing of parental responsibility by a state agency as is the case when a care order[10] is made, still less for a state agency to be able to exercise, 'overriding' parental responsibility to the exclusion of others holding it.[11] This restriction on the power of the state to intervene in family life is crucially important and is follows inevitably from the court's decision that either threshold is not established or that the welfare of the child does not require the making of a care order.[12]

**26.10** Never the less, it would be naive to ignore (and wrong to disregard when giving advice to parents and others) the extent to which state involvement with a family may continue after the making of a s 8 or a special guardianship order. Such an order may well be accompanied by a supervision order under s 31 or a family assistance order under s 16 of the Children Act 1989. Furthermore, following the conclusion of proceedings a child will very often continue to be, 'in need' for the purposes of s 17 of the Act and, therefore, the local authority will have a continuing duty to provide services. If a special guardianship order is made, the local authority has specific duties to assess the need for support and provide services.[13] Whilst none of these provisions are supported by the powers of compulsion given by a care order, a failure to follow advice or to accept services that are offered can often result in the local authority re-considering the question of the need for it to share parental

---

[8] Re B-S (Adoption: Application of s 47(5)) [2014] 1 FLR 1035; see also Re W [2016] EWCA Civ 793.
[9] For a recent piece of research on the prevalence of further public law proceedings following the making of supervision orders and special guardianship orders, see Harwin and Alrouh 'Supervision Orders and Special Guardianship: how risky are they? Findings from the national study of supervision orders and special guardianship' [2017] Fam Law 513.
[10] But not a supervision order.
[11] See s 33 of the 1989 Act, discussed in detail in chapter 23.
[12] 'The threshold is designed to restrict compulsory intervention to cases which genuinely warrant it, while enabling the court to make the order which will best reflect the child's welfare once the threshold has been crossed.' per Baroness Hale of Richmond in Re J (Care Proceedings: Possible Perpetrators) [2013] 1 FLR 1373, para [2].
[13] Section 14F of the Act, considered in more detail in the following chapter.

responsibility for a child to ensure its needs are met and its welfare protected. This re-consideration may well lead the local authority to return the matter to court and to seek a care order.

## SECTION 8 ORDERS

## The court's power to make s 8 orders within care proceedings

**26.11** The court's power to make s 8 orders is set out in s 10 of the Act. Section 10(1) provides as follows:

> 'in any family proceedings in which a question arises with respect to the welfare of any child, the court may make a section 8 order with respect to the child if -
>
> (a) an application has been made by a person who -
>   (i) is entitled to apply for a section 8 order in respect to the child; or
>   (ii) has obtained the leave of the court to make the application; or
> (b) the court considers that the order should be made even though no such application has bene made.'

**26.12** For the purposes of the 1989 Act, 'family proceedings' include applications for care or supervision orders under Part IV of the Act.[14] The court accordingly has power to make s 8 orders when considering such applications and it can do so at an interim stage as well as when making its final determination.

**26.13** The procedure for making applications for private law orders is set out in Family Procedure Rules 2010, Pt 5 and Practice Direction 5A (form of application) and Pt 12, Chapters 1 and 4, and Practice Direction 12B (Child Arrangements Programme). In the event that an application for a s 8 order is before the court when proceedings for a care or supervision order are commenced in relation to the same child[15] or is made in respect of a child who is the subject of a current application for such an order, the court will invariably consider at an early stage the use of its general case management powers to consolidate the two sets of proceedings, to direct that they be heard on the same occasion or to stay the s 8 order application pending determination of the care or supervision order application or otherwise.[16]

---

[14] See section 8(3)(b) and 8(4)(a).
[15] For the circumstances in which a court dealing with an application for a section 8 order may direct that consideration be given to commencing proceedings for a care or supervision order, and in some circumstances can make such an order, see sections 37 and 38(1)(b) of the 1989 Act: these are considered in detail in chapter 13 of this work.
[16] For these powers, see Family Procedure Rules 2010, r 4.1(3)(h), (i) and (g) respectively. The decision as to which of these orders should be made in respect of the two sets of proceedings is highly fact specific.

## Who can apply for s 8 orders within care proceedings?

**26.14** The persons entitled to apply for s 8 orders are set in s 10 of the Act.[17] This provision applies whether or not the application is to be made as part of current care proceedings.

**26.15** Section 10 goes into some detail in defining various classes of persons entitled to apply but for practical purposes the most important of these are the child's parents, other persons holding parental responsibility for the child and persons with whom the child has lived either under a child arrangements order or, in the absence of an order, in the circumstances and for the periods set out in the section. Any other person may make an application only if the leave of the court has been obtained.

## APPLICATIONS FOR LEAVE TO APPLY

**26.16** Section 9(10) provides that when deciding whether or not to grant leave to apply the court should, 'have particular regard' to:

'(a) the nature of the proposed application for a section 8 order;
(b) the applicant's connection with the child;
(c) any risk there might be of that proposed application disrupting the child's life to such an extent that he would be harmed by it;
(d) where the child is being looked after by a local authority -
　(i) the authority's plans for the child's future; and
　(ii) the wishes and feelings of the child's parents.'

**26.17** This subsection has given rise to a substantial body of judicial comment over the years: a useful review appears in the judgment of Black LJ in the case of *Re B (A Child)*.[18] The effect of these authorities was succinctly stated by Ryder J in *KS v Neath Port Talbot Borough Council*[19] in the following terms:

'[16] The principles to be applied to an application such as that brought by the grandmother are well known and can be summarised quite quickly. The judge had to apply section 10(9) of the Children Act 1989 and additionally should have considered whether the grandmother had an arguable case (see, for example, *Re B (A Child)* [2012] EWCA Civ 737 per Black LJ at [37] and *Re J (Leave to issue an application for a residence order)* [2002] EWCA Civ 1364 at [17] and [18]. The overriding objective in rule 1 of the Family Procedure Rules 2010 [FPR 2010] applied which engaged the active case management principles to be found in r 1.2 FPR 2010 ...'

**26.18** In *KS v Neath Port Talbot Borough Council* the Court of Appeal set aside a judge's decision to defer consideration of a grandmother's application to

---

[17] See s 10(4), (5), (5A), (5B), (5C), (6), (7), (7A), (7B) and (8).
[18] [2012] EWCA Civ 737: see at paras 34 to 52. One point to note from Her Ladyship's review is that the case law is consistent in saying that the court's approach to an application to become a party to care proceedings should the same whether or not it is accompanied by a specific application to make a section 8 application: see at paras 35 and 37.
[19] [2014] EWCA Civ 941.

be joined in care proceedings and for leave to apply for a residence order to the end of the final hearing, when it was refused (the grandmother was allowed to sit in court throughout the hearing and gave evidence). The unanimous opinion of the court was that her application had not been given proper consideration. Ryder LJ explains the concerns of the court in the following terms:

> '[18] The paternal grandmother submits and I agree that the case management decision that the judge made was plainly wrong because it was procedurally unfair. If, by his case management decision, it was the judge's intention to exclude the grandparents from the care of the child, then he did not have regard to evidence relating to the section 10(9) factors or to the potential merits of her case which he would have found in the content of the assessment to which I have referred. His reasons lacked sufficient or any analysis. Case management decisions that have the character of deciding a substantive issue must be treated with particular care: hence the nature and extent of the enquiry that is made necessary by section 10(9) of the Act and its associated case law.
>
> [19] The purpose of section 10(9) of the 1989 Act and the case law that supports it is defeated if there is no analysis of the benefits and detriments inherent in the application and the arguability of the case. The section provides a framework for decisions of this kind to be made so that there is an appropriate balance between case management principles and the substantive issues in the proceedings. Furthermore, the lack of attention to detail and in particular the lack of analysis of what had been happening during the proceedings in particular as between the local authority and the grandmother and the child, including the timetable for the child and for the proceedings, deprived the decision of the character of individual and collective proportionality that application of the overriding objective would have provided. In simple terms, the decision was too superficial and un-reasoned to stand scrutiny.'

**26.19** These observations are important. In very many cases it is, sadly, clear that children cannot remain in the care of their birth parents and the only options for their future are to be placed with other family members, most commonly grandparents, or adoption. Ryder LJ's comments are a reminder of the importance of court's giving proper consideration to family members who seek to take an active role in proceedings and to argue for placement within the family, even if that option has been discounted by the local authority.

## THE ORDERS AVAILABLE UNDER S 8

**26.20** Section 8 of the Children Act 1989 (as amended by Children and Families Act 2014) provides for three different orders that can be made in respect of a child: a 'child arrangements order', a 'prohibited steps order' and a 'specific issue order'. These are defined in s 8(1) in the following terms:

> '(1) In this Act –
>
> > 'child arrangements order' means an order regulating arrangements relating to any of the following –
> > > (a) with whom a child is to live, spend time or otherwise have contact, and

(b) when a child is to live, spend time or otherwise have contact with any person;

'a prohibited steps order' means an order that no step which could be taken by a parent in meeting his parental responsibility for a child, and which is of a kind specified in the order, shall be taken by any person without the consent of the court; and

'a specific issue order' means an order giving directions for the purpose of determining a specific question which has arisen, or which may arise, in connection with any aspect of parental responsibility for a child.

(2) In this Act 'a section 8 order' means any of the orders mentioned in subsection (1) and any order varying or discharging such an order.'

**26.21** 'Child arrangements orders' were introduced by the Children and Families Act 2014, s 12, as a more flexible alternative to the 'residence'[20] and 'contact'[21] orders provided for by the s 8(1) of the 1989 Act as originally enacted.[22] This change in the law was particularly intended to recognise and reinforce the parity in status of parents who continue to share parental responsibility although they are no longer able to parent their children jointly in a shared household.[23]

**26.22** The various s 8 orders are not mutually exclusive. The court can, and very often will, use a combination of orders to provide the necessary legal structure to meet a child's needs and can do so on the same or separate occasions. Equally, s 8 orders can be varied or discharged as necessary either on a subsequent application to do so or the court's own motion.[24]

**26.23** Sections 9, 10, 11, 12 and 13 make further provision in relation to s 8 orders and these should be borne in mind when the making of such an order is being considered. Note in particular that s 11(7) allows the court to attach directions and/or conditions to an order and to provide for the order to have effect for a specified period.

**26.24** In the context of care proceedings, s 11(7)(c) is particularly useful. This provides that a s 8 order may:

---

[20] '... an order settling the arrangements to be made as to with whom a child is to live'.
[21] '... an order requiring the person with whom a child lives, or is to live, to visit or stay with the person named in the order, or for that person and the child otherwise to have contact with each other'.
[22] In common usage in the courts 'contact orders' live on as shorthand for child arrangements orders that provide for a child to have contact with a person who is not their main carer. Child arrangements orders that settle where a child is to live tend to be referred to by way of slightly clunky circumlocutions such as, 'a child arrangements order in terms that the child shall live with X' or a, 'a 'live with' child arrangements order'.
[23] See, for example, the comments of Ryder LJ in Re K (Children) [2015] 1 FLR 95. Older readers may recall that one of the reasons for the introduction of 'residence' and 'contact' orders by the 1989 Act was to move away from the perceived discrimination in the status of separated parents between those who had, 'custody' of their children and those who were merely allowed, 'access' to them, in accordance with the terminology of pre-1989 legislation.
[24] See below.

'be made to have effect for a specified period or contain provisions which are to have effect for a specified period.'

**26.25** A child arrangements order providing for the child to live with a named person pending final determination of the care proceedings is often used when a child is placed in the care of a family member whilst the assessments that the court requires in order to make long term decisions as to the child's future are carried out. This provides a legal structure for this placement, allows the carer to exercise parental responsibility (see below) and should simplify the process of obtaining relevant benefits[25] and other support for the child's carer.

## PARENTAL RESPONSIBILITY AND S 8 ORDERS

**26.26** Section 12 of the Act sets out the consequences for parental responsibility of the granting of child arrangements order. These are as follows -

- Section 12(1) requires that on the making of a child arrangements order in terms that the child live with a father, or woman who is a parent by virtue of the Human Fertilisation and Embryology Act 2008,[26] the court must also make a parental responsibility order[27] in favour of them if they would not otherwise have parental responsibility. A parental responsibility order made in these circumstances may not be brought to an end[28] whilst the relevant, 'live with' child arrangements order remains in force.[29]

- In the case of a child arrangements order that only provides for a father or second female parent to spend time with otherwise have contact with the child, s 12(1A) provides that the court, 'must decide whether it would be appropriate' for that person to have parental responsibility and, if it would be appropriate, make an order.[30]

---

[25] For example, s 141 of the Social Security Contributions and Benefits Act 1992 (as amended) provides for payment of Child Benefit to a person, 'responsible for' a child and s 143(1)(a) provides that a person is treated as 'responsible' for a child if the child is, 'living with' them. Whilst there is nothing in the 1992 Act (as amended) to suggest that a child arrangements order is required to establish that a child is, 'living with' the benefit claimant for the purposes of these sections, anecdotal experience is that Benefits Agency staff are reluctant to entertain claims for Child Benefit by a non-parent unless an order can be produced (see Sch 10 of the 1992 Act for the rules as to priority between claimants for Child Benefit).

[26] See ss 43–47 of the Human Fertilisation and Embryology Act 2008 for the circumstances in which a woman can be treated as the, 'parent' of another woman's child in accordance with the provisions of that Act. In the heading to s 4ZA a woman so treated is described as a, 'second female parent'.

[27] Under s 4 or s 4ZA of the Act as applicable.

[28] For the court's powers to terminate parental responsibility vested by an order see ss 4(2A) and 4ZA(5).

[29] Section 12(4).

[30] This important extension of the circumstances in which the court is obliged to consider granting parental responsibility to a person with whom the child is not to reside was introduced by the Children and Families Act 2014, s 12(4) and Sch 2, para 21. Before 2014 the court was obliged to make a parental responsibility order when making a residence order in favour of a parent who would otherwise not have parental responsibility but had no power to do so when only making a contact order.

- Section 12(2) of the Act has effect when a child arrangements order is made providing that the child live with a person who is neither a parent nor a guardian[31]. In such a case that person, '... shall have parental responsibility for the child while the order remains in force so far as providing for the child to live with that person'. In such cases, no separate parental responsibility order is made and a person's holding of parental responsibility comes to an end automatically when the child arrangements order providing for the child to live with that person ceases to have effect. This is a crucial provision within the Act's overall scheme as it provides the mechanism whereby a person who cares for a child, but is neither a parent nor guardian, can have, 'all the rights, duties, powers, responsibilities and authority which by law a parent of a child has in relation to the child'[32] whilst they are acting as the child's primary carer.

- When a child arrangements order provides that a person who is neither a parent nor a guardian should have contact with a child, s 12(2A) provides that the court, 'may provide' for that person to have parental responsibility whilst the order remains in effect but, in contrast to the position when to court makes orders for parents or guardians to have contact, there is no requirement that the court consider doing so.[33]

**26.27** The fact that a person acquires parental responsibility in accordance with one of these provisions does not remove the parental responsibility of any other person who already holds it[34] nor does it of itself impinge on the general right of each person with parental responsibility to act alone in meeting that responsibility without reference to others who do so.[35] If it is considered necessary to regulate the way in which a person exercises their parental responsibility for a child generally or in a particular instance prohibited steps or specific issue orders may be made. In cases where a child's welfare makes it desirable that a person or persons holding parental responsibility be able to exercise it in all circumstances[36] to the exclusion of others who do so, a special guardianship order may be made rather than a child arrangements order: this

---

[31] ie a guardian appointed in accordance with s 5 of the Act, most commonly a testamentary guardian appointed to act as a child's guardian following the death of a parent, guardian or special guardian.

[32] This being the definition of, 'parental responsibility' set out in s 3(1) of the Act.

[33] Orders under this sub-section granting parental responsibility to a non-parent who only has contact with a child are not often encountered in practice. However, a person without parental responsibility who has care of a child in accordance with a child arrangements order for contact (or indeed in any other circumstances) can in any event, '... do what is reasonable in all the circumstances of the case for the purposes of safeguarding or promoting the child's welfare': see s 3(5) of the 1989 Act.

[34] Section 3(6) of the Act.

[35] Section 3(7). Note that this power to act alone is subject to any enactment that requires the consent of more than one person in a matter affecting the child (important examples are the prohibition on changing a child's surname or removing them from the United Kingdom with the consent of every person with parental responsibility, or leave of the court: s 13(1) of the 1989 Act) and to the general prohibition on acting a way that would be incompatible with an order made under the 1989 Act: s 2(8).

[36] Subject to statutory restrictions or contrary orders.

order are discussed in the following chapter. Note, however, that a child's parent cannot be appointed as their special guardian.[37]

## Making and duration of s 8 orders: considerations as to the age of the child

**26.28** Section 8 orders are expressed to be made in respect of a, 'child' and accordingly can be made until the child attains the age of 18 years.[38] For the same reason, once made an order will continue in force until the child attains that age, unless the court has made an order under s 11(7)(c) of the Act specifying a shorter period for which the order is to have effect.

**26.29** However, s 9 of the Act places important restrictions on the making of, and continuing effect of, s 8 orders in relation to older children. Section (7) provides that:

'No court shall make any section 8 order, other than one varying or discharging such an order, with respect to a child who has reached the age of sixteen unless it is satisfied that the circumstances of the case are exceptional.'

**26.30** Furthermore, s 9(6) of the Act provides that:

'No court shall make a section 8 order which is to have effect for a period which will end after the child has reached the age of sixteen unless it is satisfied that the circumstances of the case are exceptional.'

**26.31** The Act provides no guidance as to what circumstances should be regarded as, 'exceptional' for the purposes of s 9(6) and (7). One commonly encountered example would be where a child's special needs make it desirable for aspects of their care to continue to be regulated by s 8 orders despite them having reached the age of 16. (Subsections (6A) and (6B) of the Act, introduced by the Children and Families Act 2014 exempt from this prohibition child arrangements orders that relate only to with whom a child is to live and/or when the child should live with that person.)

**26.32** These restrictions apply equally to s 8 orders that are being considered in the course of proceedings in which care or supervision orders are sought. It should also be borne in mind that in such proceedings the child who may be made subject to the order will be a party to proceedings, whether through their guardian or on their own behalf as a 'competent' child. The court will inevitably give considerable weight to the views of older children when considering making any s 8 order even when their age means that the statutory restrictions in s 9(6) and (7) are not yet relevant.

---

[37] Section 14A(2)(b) of the 1989 Act.
[38] See definition of, 'child' in s 105(1) of the 1989 Act. The age of eighteen is attained, as are other ages referred to in the 1989 Act, upon the, 'commencement of the relevant anniversary of the date of his birth': see s 9(1) of the Family Law Reform Act 1969.

## Variation and discharge of s 8 orders

**26.33** As is noted above, s 8(2) of the 1989 Act includes within the definition of, 'a section 8 order' any order to vary or discharge one of the orders provided for by s 8(1). The rules as to the persons entitled to apply for variation or discharge are the same as for applications for substantive orders save that a person who would not otherwise be entitled to apply may do so if the order in question was made on their application[39] or, in the case of a child arrangements order regulating contact, if they are named in the order as a person with whom the child is to have contact.[40] Other applicants for variation or discharge of orders would require leave before proceeding with the application.

**26.34** On an application to vary or discharge an order, the welfare principle set out in s 1 of the Act applies and the court is directed by s 1(4) of the Act to have regard to the checklist set out in s 1(3). Whilst there is no statutory requirement for an applicant to establish a change in circumstances before an order varying or discharging a previous order can be made a court will almost invariably want to consider whether there has been any change before varying or discharging an order as part of its consideration of whether making a variation or discharge order is, 'better for the child than making no order at all'.[41] Furthermore, checklist in s 1(3) requires the court to consider the effect on the child of, 'any change in his circumstances'.

**26.35** When making an order varying or discharging an existing s 8 order, the court has the full range of its powers under s 8. This includes its power under s 11(7) to give directions or impose conditions and to specify the period during which an order is to have effect.

---

[39] Section 10(6)(a).
[40] Section 10(6)(b).
[41] Section 1(5).

# CHAPTER 27

# PRIVATE LAW ORDERS IN THE CONTEXT OF CARE PROCEEDINGS (PART 2): SPECIAL GUARDIANSHIP ORDERS IN CARE PROCEEDINGS

## INTRODUCTION

### The 2000 White Paper: Adoption: a new approach[1]

**27.1** Special Guardianship Orders have their origin in the review of adoption law and practice that led to the 2000 White Paper *Adoption: A New Approach* and, in due course, to the Adoption and Children Act 2002. The White Paper's emphasis throughout was on the need to place children who cannot be cared for by their parents in permanent alternative families, and to do so with the least possible delay. Whilst it recognised that there are, 'many options suitable to children's needs' its main premise was that, 'adoption can work well' and that there was, 'scope to increase use of adoption'.[2] Although the White Paper emphasised that the welfare of each individual child remains the paramount consideration in making plans for their future, its overall thrust can be seen as pointing to adoption as the preferred, and indeed optimal, route to permanent placement in any case where this is achievable.

**27.2** However, the White Paper also recognised that the, 'first duty' of social services departments responsible for children who could not remain with their parents was to seek a home for them within their extended family.[3] Whilst such a placement could, and still can, be secured by the adoption of such children by the family members with whom they live[4] there can be difficulties with this course.[5] Other factors that may make adoption undesirable even if the child in question is not placed with family members. The White Paper acknowledged these issues by saying that:[6]

---

[1] CM 5017: referred to below as 'the White Paper'.
[2] All quotations in this sentence are from the Forward to the White Paper by the then Prime Minister, Rt. Hon. Tony Blair MP.
[3] Paragraph 5.4 of the White Paper.
[4] For the approach to be taken to proposed adoption by family members, following the decisions of the Supreme Court in *Re B (Care Proceedings: Appeal)* [2013] 2 FLR 1075 and the Court of Appeal in *Re B-S (Adoption: Application of s 47(5))* [2014] 1 FLR 1035, see observations of McFarlane LJ in *Re P (Step-Parent Adoption)* [2014] EWCA Civ 1174 and Theis J in *Medway Council v JL, AJ and X* [2016] EWFC 78 (Fam).
[5] 'A particular concern is that an adoption order has, as a matter of law, the effect of making the

'Adoption is not always appropriate for children who cannot return to their birth parents. Some older children do not wish to be legally separated from their birth families. Adoption may not be best for some children being cared for on a permanent basis by members of their wider birth family. Some minority ethnic communities have religious and cultural difficulties with adoption as it is set out in law. Unaccompanied asylum-seeking children may also need secure, permanent homes, but have strong attachments to their families abroad. All these children deserve the same chance as any other to enjoy the benefits of a legally secure, stable permanent placement that promotes a supportive, lifelong relationship with their carers, where the court decides that is in their best interests.'

**27.3** For these reasons:[7]

'In order to meet the needs of these children where adoption is not appropriate, and to modernise the law so it reflects the religious and cultural diversity of our country today, the Government believes there is a case to develop a new legislative option to provide permanence short of the legal separation involved in adoption.'

The, 'new legislative option' was to be the introduction of the special guardianship order.

## The Adoption and Children Act 2002 and its amendments to the Children Act 1989

**27.4** The Adoption and Children Act 2002 was a substantial piece of legislation[8] that gave effect to the proposals of the White Paper in relation to all aspects of adoption law and practice.

**27.5** Section 115(1) of the 2002 Act inserted a new group of sections, ss 14A–14G, into the Children Act 1989. Headed 'Special Guardianship', these sections form a self-contained legislative code in respect of these new orders.[9] These sections have since been amended, most notably to reflect the Children and Families Act 2014's replacement of, 'residence' and, 'contact' orders with 'child arrangements orders' in s 8 of the 1989 Act.[10]

---

adopted child the child of the adopters for all purposes. Accordingly, where a child is adopted by a member of his wider family, the familial relationships are inevitably changed. This is frequently referred to as the "skewing" or "distorting" effect of adoption, and is a factor which the court must take into account when considering whether or not to make an adoption order in such a case. This is not least because the checklist under section 1 of the 2002 Act requires it to do so: – see section 1(4)(f) ("the relationship which the child has with relatives."). However, the weight to be given to this factor will inevitably depend on the facts of the particular case, and it will be only one factor in the overall welfare equation.' per Wall LJ in *Re S (Adoption Order or Special Guardianship Order)* [2007] 1 FLR 819, at para [51].

[6] Paragraph 5.8 of the White Paper.
[7] Paragraph 5.9 of the White Paper.
[8] It contained 150 sections and had 6 schedules.
[9] For detailed judicial discussion of the background to and structure of this part of the 2002 Act, see the comments of Wall LJ when giving the judgment of the Court of Appeal in the case of *Re S (Adoption Order or Special Guardianship Order)* [2007] 1 FLR 819 at paras [10]–[76].
[10] Note that s 14G, 'Special guardianship support services: representations', was repealed in its entirety by the Health and Social Care (Community Health and Standards) Act 2003.

## Special guardianship: basic points

**27.6** Section 14A(1) of the Act defines a, 'special guardianship order' as, 'an order appointing one or more individuals to be a child's "special guardian" (or special guardians)'. Any person can be appointed a special guardian provided they are aged 18 years or over and are not a parent of the child in question.[11] The most commonly encountered proposed special guardians are members of the child's family (grandparents, aunts and uncles or adult siblings often come forward) or friends of the family but where a child has been in local authority foster care and their foster carers wish to offer them a permanent home, special guardianship will often be the suggested legal framework for this plan.

**27.7** The court has power to make a special guardianship against the wishes of the parties to the case. This can involve imposing the order on an unwilling party. The issue is what order will best serve the welfare interests of the child.[12]

**27.8** The welfare principle set out in s 1(1) of the 1989 Act applies when the court is considering making a special guardianship order. The court is specifically directed to have regard to the checklist in s 1(3) of the Act when considering whether to make, vary or discharge a special guardianship order.[13]

**27.9** Once made, a special guardianship order continues in force until the child reaches the age of eighteen years, unless brought to an end earlier.[14] The court has power to discharge a special guardianship order,[15] the nature and use of this power is discussed in detail below.

**27.10** The Act provides[16] that a special guardianship order or an order varying a special guardianship order can contain provisions which are to have effect for a specified period. The court also has the same general power to incorporate directions, conditions and supplementary or consequential provisions as it does in respect of s 8 orders.[17]

---

[11] Section 14A(2).
[12] See judgment of Wall LJ in *Re S (Adoption Order or Special Guardianship Order)* (above) at paras [73]–[77]. In this case, the issue was whether a child should be placed with their foster carer under the auspices of an adoption, as the foster carer wished, or as their special guardian, as was ultimately ordered by the trial judge in a decision approved by the Court of Appeal.
[13] Section 1(4)(b).
[14] Section 91(13).
[15] Section 14D.
[16] Section 14E(4).
[17] Section 14E(5) applies s 11(7), apart from s 11(7)(c) (the subject matter of this paragraph is dealt with by section 14E(4)), to special guardianship orders.

## Special guardianship orders in public law proceedings: some statistics[18]

**27.11** In recent years, there has been a steady and significant increase in the use of special guardianship orders within public law proceedings. In 2011, such orders were made in respect of 2,975 children whilst the equivalent figure for 2016 was 5,631 children.[19] By way of comparison, care orders were made in respect of 10,944 children in 2011 and 13,953 children in 2016.[20] Adoption orders were made affecting 4,709 children in 2011 and 5,829 children in 2016.[21]

**27.12** It is interesting to note that whereas the years 2011 to 2016 show an almost completely consistent pattern of a yearly increase in the number of children affected by special guardianship orders made in public law proceedings[22] the equivalent figures for both care orders and adoption orders have fallen away somewhat since the peak years of 2013 and 2014 respectively.[23] This may reflect an increased emphasis on the need to give proper consideration to the possibility of children being cared for within their wider family or social circle rather than committing them to local authority care or to live with a permanent alternative family by way of adoption.

# SPECIAL GUARDIANSHIP ORDERS: NATURE AND EFFECT

## The key concept: special guardianship and parental responsibility

**27.13** The defining feature of special guardianship orders is the effect that the making of such an order has on parental responsibility for the child concerned.

**27.14** Section 14C(1) of the 1989 Act provides as follows:

> 'The effect of a special guardianship order is that while the order remains in force –
>
> > (a) a special guardian appointed by the order has parental responsibility for the child in respect of whom it is made; and

---

[18] All statistics in this paragraph are drawn from the *Family Court Statistics Quarterly: April to June 2017*: Ministry of Justice.
[19] Table 4. This table also records the number of children in respect of whom special guardianship orders are made in private law proceedings: 1,806 were affected by orders that were made in such proceedings in 2016. Typically, 70 to 75 percent of all children made the subject of special guardianship orders each year are the subject of orders made in public law proceedings: Table 4.
[20] Table 4.
[21] Table 19.
[22] There was a small fall between 2013 and 2014: Table 4.
[23] Tables 4 and 19. There was, however, a significant increase in the number of children affected by care orders between 2015 and 2016 and this trend continued in the first two quarters of 2017: Table 4.

(b) subject to any other order in force with respect to the child under this Act, a special guardian is entitled to exercise parental responsibility to the exclusion of any other person with parental responsibility for the child (apart from another special guardian).'

**27.15** Whereas the making of an adoption order, '... operates to extinguish ... the parental responsibility which any person other than the adopter or adopters has for the adopted child immediately before the making of that order'[24] the appointment of a special guardian or special guardians does not remove the parental responsibility of other persons who hold it. However, it does confer on the special guardian, '... exclusivity in the exercise of parental responsibility'[25] to the extent that the parental responsibility of birth parents (and others) is, '... effectively and largely neutered ...'.[26]

**27.16** It is this vesting of overriding parental responsibility in the child's carers that can make the making of a special guardianship order an attractive option in cases where a child cannot continue to be cared for by their birth parents but can be offered a home by other family members or members of the family's wider social network. It will enable carers to take and implement most decisions necessary in caring for a child[27] without reference to birth parents (whose parenting will almost invariably have been found to be deficient if a special guardianship order has been made in care proceedings) or to others holding parental responsibility. However, it does not sever the legal tie between birth parent and child, preserves ties with the child's wider family, community and culture,[28] allows the birth parents access as of right to the court in the event of most disputes in relation to the child[29] and, subject to the individual circumstances of the case, is likely to be compatible with a higher level of contact between birth parent and child than would be the case were the child to be placed in long term local authority foster care or adopted.

---

[24] Adoption and Children Act 2002, s 46(1)(a).
[25] The expression is that of Wall LJ giving the judgment of the Court of Appeal in the case of *Birmingham City Council v R* [2007] 1 FLR 564 at para [78].
[26] Per Wall LJ in *Re S (Adoption Order or Special Guardianship Order)* (above) at para [67].
[27] Exceptions to the principle that special guardians can act without reference to others holding parental responsibility are set out in s 14C. These exceptions are:
(i) where doing so would be contrary to any, 'enactment or rule of law' requiring the consent of more than one person holding parental responsibility: s 14C(2)(a)
(ii) acting in relation to any rights that a parent has in relation to adoption or placement for adoption: s 14C(2)(b)
(iii) causing the child to be known by a new surname without the written consent of all persons holding parental responsibility: s 14C(3)(a)
(iv) removing the child from the jurisdiction for more than three months without the written consent of all persons holding parental responsibility: s 14C(3)(a) and s 14C(4).
[28] As an example of a case where this was a particularly important factor in the court's decision between appointing a child's carer (a local authority foster carer) as his special guardian or making an adoption order in their favour, see the decision of Russell J in *Re F (Special Guardianship Order: Contact with birth family)* [2016] 1 FLR 593.
[29] For restrictions on applications by birth parents and others, see s 10(7A) and (7B) and s 14D, all discussed below.

## The position of birth parents

**27.17** Although the making of a special guardianship order enables the special guardian to exercise parental responsibility without reference to birth parents (or other holders of parental responsibility) it remains possible for birth parents to seek orders under s 8 of the Act to regulate the way in which that parental responsibility is exercised and in respect of contact issues. This is because as, 'parents' they fall within the class of persons entitled to make any s 8 order[30] and this remains the case even if a special guardianship order is made.[31] There are, however, two important types of application in respect of which a birth parent (or other person who would otherwise be entitled to apply) requires leave of the court to make an application. These are, firstly, child arrangements orders that relate to the issue of with whom the child is to live and, secondly, applications to vary or discharge the special guardianship order itself. These requirements are discussed below in the context of the general issue of applications in respect of children who the subject of special guardianship orders.

**27.18** The continued right of parents to make applications, save in the two instances in respect of which leave is required, was described as, 'an anomaly' by Wall LJ, giving the judgment of the Court of Appeal in the case of *Re S (Adoption Order or Special Guardianship Order)*.[32] He also said:[33]

> 'The absence of a general requirement for leave may seem surprising. Special guardianship orders are designed to produce finality, and there is, accordingly, logic in the proposition that a parent requires the leave of the court to reopen the issue of the order itself or of the child's residence. But, if so, one might expect similar considerations to apply to other forms of order under section 8. An essential component of the advantages produced by an adoption order for both adopters and children is that they are in most cases then free from the threat of future litigation. If the same protection is not available in respect of special guardianship orders, this may be a substantial derogation from the security provided.'

---

[30] See s 10(4)(a) of the 1989 Act: for other persons who are also entitled to make applications for any s 8 order or for child arrangements orders only, and would continue to be entitled to do so if a special guardianship order is made, see s 10(4)(b) and (5).
[31] This is in sharp distinction to the position if an adoption order is made. In such a case the adopted child is, '... to be treated in law as the child of the adopter or adopters': see s 67(1) of the Adoption and Children Act 2002.
[32] Above, at para [68].
[33] At para [65].

**27.19** His Lordship went on to say that the court may invoke s 91(14) of the Act[34] to place a, 'a filter' on further applications by parents. He also commented that:[35]

> 'In any event, anomalous or not, it is plain to us that the statutory scheme for making special guardianship orders was designed generally to allow unfettered access to the court thereafter by parents in relation to all section 8 orders apart from residence. In this respect it must be accepted that special guardianship does not always provide the same permanency of protection as adoption. In our judgment, this is a factor, which in a finely balanced case, could well tip the scales in favour of adoption.'

**27.20** Although His Lordship's comments remain very much on point when the court is considering the relevant merits of placement of a child under a special guardianship order or an adoption order, it is worth noting that this, 'anomaly' does not arise in those cases, commonly encountered in practice when the court is concerned with older children, where the alternatives are placement with a family member as the child's special guardian or with local authority foster carers under a care order. In the latter case, parents remain entitled to apply for an order in respect of contact[36] or to discharge the care order[37] and leave is only required if a similar application has been disposed of within the previous 6 months.[38]

## Applications in relation to children who are the subject of special guardianship orders

### Applications for child arrangements orders

**27.21** Sections 10(7A) and 10(7B) of the Children Act, inserted by the 2002 Act and amended by the Children and Families Act 2014, provide as follows:

> '(7A) If a special guardianship order is in force with respect to a child, an application for a child arrangements order to which subsection (7B) applies may only be made with respect to him, if apart from this subsection the leave of the court is not required, with such leave.
>
> '(7B) This subsection applies to a child arrangements order if the arrangements regulated by the order consist of, or include, arrangements which relate to either or both of the following –
>
>     (a)    with whom the child concerned is to live, and
>     (b)    when the child is to live with any person.'

---

[34] Which provides that -
'On disposing of any application for an order under this Act, the court may (whether or not it makes any other order in response to the application) order that no application for an order under this Act of any specified kind may be made in respect to the child concerned by any person named in the order without leave of the court.'
[35] At para [68].
[36] Section 33(2) of the 1989 Act.
[37] Section 39(1)(a).
[38] Sections 91(15) and 91(16) respectively.

**27.22** Applications for leave made in compliance with this requirement fall to be decided in the same way as other applications for leave to apply for s 8 orders. The court has to have regard to the matters set out in s 10(9) of the 1989 Act:[39] this subsection and the case law on applications for leave to apply are discussed in more detail in the preceding chapter.

*Applications for other section 8 orders*

**27.23** In respect of other s 8 applications, ie for child arrangements orders that relate to contact only and not to the issue of with whom the child is to live, for prohibited steps orders and for specific issue orders, the general provisions as to persons entitled to make applications as of right or with leave of the court apply. These are set out in s 10 of the Act.

*Applications to vary or discharge special guardianship orders*

**27.24** Section 14D(1) of the 1989 Act provides that the court may vary or discharge a special guardianship order on the application of:

'(a)  the special guardian (or any of them, if there are more than one);
(b)  any parent or guardian of the child concerned;
(c)  any individual who is named in a child arrangements order as a person with whom the child is to live;[40]
(d)  any individual not falling within any of paragraphs (a) to (c) who has, or immediately before the making of the special guardianship order had, parental responsibility for the child;
(e)  the child himself; or
(f)  a local authority designated in a care order with respect to the child.[41]'

**27.25** Section 14D(3) provides that:

'The following must obtain the leave of the court before making an application under subsection (1) –

(a)  the child;
(b)  any parent or guardian of his;
(c)  any step-parent of his who has acquired, and has not lost, parental responsibility for him by virtue of section 4A;
(d)  any individual falling within subsection (1)(d) who immediately before the making of the special guardianship order had, but no longer has, parental responsibility for him.'

**27.26** Leave may only be granted to a person falling with within s 14D(3)(b), (c) or (d) if the court is satisfied that there has been, '... a significant change in

---

[39]  Or s 10(8) where the applicant for leave is the child concerned.
[40]  Note that the making of such a child arrangements order does not of itself discharge a special guardianship order in respect of the child concerned.
[41]  The making of a care order in respect of a child does not discharge a special guardianship order in relation to that child but the designated local authority has the power to determine the extent to which a special guardian can meet their parental responsibility for the child: s 33(3)(b)(i) of the 1989 Act. However, the making of a special guardianship order does discharge any care order (interim or final) in relation to the child concerned: s 91(5A) of the Act.

circumstances since the making of the special guardianship order'.[42] In the case of *Re G (A Child) (Special Guardianship Order)*[43] Wilson LJ, as he then was, considered[44] the approach to be taken to applications for leave and, in particular, to the issue of a change in circumstances. He considered the case law on applications for leave to apply to revoke a placement order under s 24(2) and 24(3) of the Adoption and Children Act 2002 and held that, despite the difference in the language used in the sections (s 24 does not use the qualifier, 'significant'), applications for leave to apply to discharge a special guardianship order should be approached in the same way. Referring to the guidance of the Court of Appeal in *M v Warwickshire County Council*[45] he said:[46]

> '... this court interpreted s.24(3) of the Act of 2002 as meaning that a change in circumstances since the order was made was a necessary, but not a sufficient, condition of leave to apply for revocation of a placement order; that, as explained at [29], the establishment of a change in circumstances gave rise to a discretion whether to grant leave, in the exercise of which the welfare of the child and the prospect of success of the proposed substantive application should both be weighed; and that, while the two considerations were linked and would often be consonant, it might be dangerous to subsume the one into the other.'

**27.27** He commended this approach when considering applications for leave to apply under s 14D of the Act. He specifically commented that he could see no ground for considering that the court was required to weigh the factors set out in s 10(9) of the Act when considering an application for leave to apply under s 14D.[47]

# MAKING SPECIAL GUARDIANSHIP ORDERS WITHIN CARE PROCEEDINGS

## The power to make orders: the statutory basics

**27.28** Section 14A of the Act sets out the circumstances in which the court may make a special guardianship order. These provisions apply whether or not consideration of making such an order arises within care proceedings or in other proceedings.

**27.29** The relevant parts of s 14A read as follows:

'(3) The court may make a special guardianship order with respect to any child on the application of an individual who –

    (a)    is entitled to make such an application with respect to the child; or
    (b)    has obtained the leave of the court to make the application,

---

[42] See s 14D(5): s 14D(4) provides that the child can only be granted leave if the court is satisfied they have, 'sufficient understanding' to make the application.
[43] [2010] 2 FLR 696, CA.
[44] In the absence of adversarial argument as the appeal was conceded.
[45] [2008] 1 FLR 1093.
[46] Paragraph [13].
[47] Paragraph [11].

or on the joint application of more than one such individual.

(4) Section 9(3)[48] applies in relation to an application for leave to apply for a special guardianship order as it applies in relation to an application for leave to apply for a section 8 order.

(5) The individuals who are entitled to apply for a special guardianship order with respect to a child are –

- (a) any guardian of the child;
- (b) any individual who is named in a child arrangements order as a person with whom the child is to live;
- (c) any individual listed in subsection (5)(b) or (c) of section 10 (as read with subsection (10) of that section);
- (d) a local authority foster parent with whom the child has lived for a period of at least one year immediately preceding the application;
- (e) a relative with whom the child has lived for a period of at least one year immediately preceding the application.

(6) The court may also make a special guardianship order with respect to a child in any family proceedings in which a question arises with respect to the welfare of the child if –

- (a) an application for the order has been made by an individual who falls within subsection (3)(a) or (b) (or more than one such individual jointly); or
- (b) the court considers that a special guardianship order should be made even though no such application has been made.

(7) No individual may make an application under subsection (3) or (6)(a) unless, before the beginning of the period of three months ending with the date of the application, he has given written notice of his intention to make the application –

- (a) if the child in question is being looked after by a local authority, to that local authority, or
- (b) otherwise, to the local authority in whose area the individual is ordinarily resident.

(8) On receipt of such a notice, the local authority must investigate the matter and prepare a report for the court dealing with –

- (a) the suitability of the applicant to be a special guardian;
- (b) such matters (if any) as may be prescribed by the Secretary of State; and
- (c) any other matter which the local authority consider to be relevant.

(9) The court may itself ask a local authority to conduct such an investigation and prepare such a report, and the local authority must do so.

(10) The local authority may make such arrangements as they see fit for any person to act on their behalf in connection with conducting an investigation or preparing a report referred to in subsection (8) or (9).

---

[48] This subsection restricts the making applications for leave to apply for a section 8 order by local authority foster carers for the child concerned. One of the circumstances in which such an application can be made is if the local authority consent and it is unusual (but not unknown) for foster carers to seek a special guardianship order without the prior approval and active cooperation of the local authority that placed the child with them.

(11) The court may not make a special guardianship order unless it has received a report dealing with the matters referred to in subsection (8).

(12) Subsections (8) and (9) of section 10[49] apply in relation to special guardianship orders as they apply in relation to section 8 orders.

(13) This section is subject to section 29(5) and (6)[50] of the Adoption and Children Act 2002.'

**27.30** The following points should be noted:

- Subsection (3) provides for both free-standing applications and ones made when an issue of the making of a special guardianship order arises in care proceedings.
- Subsection (6)(b) allows for the making of an order although no application has been made. This route to the making of an order is very commonly encountered in practice but presents potential difficulties: see the observations of Ryder and McCombe LJJ in the Court of Appeal case of *Re H (A Child) (Analysis of Realistic Options and SGOS)*[51] discussed below.
- The court has no jurisdiction to dispense with or vary the requirement in subs (7) that an applicant for a special guardianship order must have previously given three months' notice of their intention to apply for that order. If such notice has not been given, no application can be made and an order can only be made in the exercise of the court's power under subs (6)(b).
- Most importantly, the court has no jurisdiction at all to make a special guardianship order in the absence of a report in accordance with subs (8).[52]

## Case management when the issue of the making of a special guardianship order arises within care proceedings

**27.31** In any proceedings in which, 'any question of making, varying or discharging a special guardianship order arises' the court has a duty to draw up a timetable to ensure the determination of the question without delay and give directions for the purpose of ensuring, 'so far as is reasonably practicable' that

---

[49] These are the provisions that govern the grant of leave to apply for section 8 orders and are discussed in detail in the preceding chapter.
[50] These subsections govern the making of special guardianship orders when a placement order is in force
[51] [2016] 1 FLR 286.
[52] See, for example, comments of Wall LJ in *Re S (Adoption Order or Special Guardianship Order (No 2)* [2007] 1 FLR 855 at paras [10], [11] and [12]). His Lordship went on to say that, 'the court can properly adopt a pragmatic approach to the report' when the necessary information as before the court in a different form (para [14]). Note, however, the dangers of an unduly relaxed approach to the requirements of subs (8) identified by the Court of Appeal in the case of *Re H (A Child) (Analysis of Realistic Options and SGOS)* (above), discussed in detail below.

the timetable is adhered to'.[53] Whilst this reflects the court's general duty in carrying out active case management[54] it is a particularly important exercise in cases where a special guardianship order may be the outcome as the need to carry out the required assessments of alternative carers is a frequent source of delay in concluding these cases.

**27.32** The Family Procedure Rules 2010 envisage, and indeed require, the earliest possible identification of potential special guardians. Practice Direction 12A – Care, Supervision and Other Part 4 Proceedings: Guide to Case Management requires the court to give on issue of an application, 'standard directions', that include a direction for the filing and service of a, 'Parents' Response' and this document is required, inter alia, to set out 'the parents' placement proposals including the identity and whereabouts of all relatives and friends they propose be considered by the court'.[55] Whilst it is not always possible to identify all such relatives and friends at this very early stage, the court will invariably expect it to be done as soon as possible, whether by a formal document filed with the court or by giving notice direct to the local authority. Whilst, in the writer's experience, courts are always reluctant to refuse to consider a potential carer a balance has to be struck between looking at all possible placement options and the need to avoid delay both generally[56] and by reference to the court's duty to manage the case so that it is concluded within 26 weeks.[57]

**27.33** Once an alternative carer is identified the court will generally direct the carrying out of a, 'viability assessment'[58] if the local authority does not already have this in hand. If that assessment is positive, and the person concerned remains willing to be considered as a carer for the child, the court will give directions for the carrying out of a full assessment in accordance with s 14A(8). The Schedule to the Special Guardianship Regulations 2005[59] sets out the prescribed information in accordance with s 14(8)(c).

**27.34** The local authority will also be expected to carry out an assessment of the support services that will be required, and will be provided, and to provide a, 'Special Guardianship Support Plan': see s 14F of the Act and the 2005 Regulations. Support for the special guardian may include financial support if the circumstances are as set out in reg 6 of the 2005 Regulations, the most important such circumstance is, 'where the local authority consider that it is necessary to ensure that the special guardian or prospective special guardian

---

[53] Section 14E(1).
[54] See Family Procedure Rules 2010, r 1.4(a).
[55] Practice Direction 12A, para 7.1.
[56] See s 1(2) of the 1989 Act.
[57] Section 32(1)(a)(ii) of the 1989 Act.
[58] 'Viability assessment' is not a term of art defined in legislation but is helpfully described on the website of one independent social work agency as, '. . . a concise assessment designed to gather all the necessary information, in a short time-frame to determine the suitability of the adult as an alternative carer and the feasibility of further assessment': Avocetisw.co.uk accessed 25 September 2017.
[59] Set out in Appendix 6 below.

can look after the child'.⁶⁰ The correct approach to calculating the level of financial support has been considered by the Administrative Court in a number of cases, see for example *R (TT) v London Borough of Merton*.⁶¹

**27.35** The question of which local authority is responsible for providing support services was considered by Hedley J (giving the judgment of the Court of Appeal) in the case of *Suffolk County Council v Nottinghamshire County Council*.⁶² The, very common, factual nexus here was that a child had been removed from parents living in Nottinghamshire in the course of proceedings taken by that County Council and was now being placed under a special guardianship order with alternative carers who lived in Suffolk. Having reviewed the terms of s 14F and relevant authorities His Lordship concluded:⁶³

> 'The key question in determining which local authority is responsible is whether or not the child is "looked after" by an authority; if yes, then that is the responsible authority but, if no, then the responsible authority is the one in whose area the child is living. By s 22(1) of the Act a child who is looked after is either (a) in the care of a local authority or (b) is provided with accommodation by that authority. A child is in the care of the local authority if the child is subject to a care order whether final or interim – s 105(1). A child is provided with accommodation if he comes within either s 23(2) or 23(6) of the Act. Crucially, however, the child ceases to be a looked after child if parental responsibility is vested in another by the making, for example, of a residence order or special guardianship order.'

However, he went on to draw attention to the powers of local authorities to cooperate in carrying out their functions and to reach agreement as to how they should do so.⁶⁴

## Case management guidance from Ryder LJ

**27.36** The case management required when a court is asked to consider making a special guardianship order was the subject of the judgments of Ryder and McCombe LJJ (sitting with Longmore LJ) in the case of *Re H (A Child)(Analysis of Realistic Options and SGOS)*.⁶⁵ As is so often the case when the Court of Appeal gives guidance on case management issues, it was prompted to do so by spectacular failings in the way in which the case before it had proceeded in the courts below.⁶⁶

**27.37** In *Re H* there were longstanding concerns about the family and there had previously been a supervision order. Further concerns arose and

---

⁶⁰ Regulation 6(2)(a).
⁶¹ [2010] EWHC 2055 (Admin).
⁶² [2013] 2 FLR 106.
⁶³ Paragraph [18].
⁶⁴ Paragraph [19].
⁶⁵ Above.
⁶⁶ 'At first sight of the papers one could be forgiven for wondering what compliance there had been with the rules in the preparation there had been for the final hearing.' Per Ryder LJ at para [25].

proceedings were commenced, at this time the parents remained in a relationship and the child lived with both of them. Following the breakdown of the parents' relationship and other difficulties the child moved to the care of the father. By the time of the Issues Resolution Hearing an associate of the mother's ('A') had come forward as a prospective special guardian but there was a failure, in the strongly expressed view of the Court of Appeal, to identify and properly case manage what had become the main issue; that of whether placement with father or with 'A' best met the child's needs. At the final hearing the local authority supported a special guardianship order to 'A' but failed to provide an amended care plan until the eve of the final hearing and generally there was a comprehensive failure to prepare the case in a way that would allow a fair and proper decision between the two placement options. The special guardianship order was made. Father's appeal was allowed and the case remitted for a re-hearing.

**27.38** Ryder LJ had this to say about the flawed procedural aspects of the final hearing and what should have been done:

'[26] What was happening was that the local authority were seeking to persuade the court to make a SGO. Although the court has power to make such an order of its own motion in accordance with section 14A(6)(b) CA 1989, that should not be the default position. Such a process can, as it nearly did in this case, give rise to procedural irregularity for lack of notice. The special guardian or the local authority on her behalf should have made the application. The important procedural hurdle of the satisfaction of the test in section 10(9) CA 1989 would then have been addressed. It is only where parties agree that an application for a SGO should be dispensed with that the section 14A(6)(b) CA 1989 power can be exercised without good reason. In any other case, the use by the court of this power must be reasoned. The parties in this case did not agree and the use of the power was assumed not reasoned.

[27] In accordance with section 14A(8) CA 1989 the local authority must prepare an SGO report and by section 14A(11) the court cannot make a SGO without such a report. The statutory purpose is a very real protection. The contents of such a report are set out in a regulatory scheme which is to be found in the schedule to the Special Guardianship Regulations 2005, which is designed to ensure that necessary questions are addressed before controlling parental responsibility for a child is vested in a person other than a local authority. Such a report was never directed to be prepared in this case because no SGO application was ever made.

[28] In her judgment the judge accepts that a report, a support plan and an addendum report which she identifies are sufficient for the statutory purpose. It is only because there is a concession before this court that the content of an earlier 'connected person's assessment' of A fulfil those requirements that this court has not moved on to question whether the assessment was sufficient for its purpose. During case management, the court should have addressed the question directly. On identifying that one of the realistic options that the court was being asked to consider was special guardianship, it should have made directions in the prospective application including for the SGO report and any relevant evidence. If a report which is being or has been prepared is to be deemed to satisfy the regulatory and statutory requirements, then the case management judge should say

so: allowing anyone who disagrees to be heard given the statutory importance that is attached to the report. In other words, the assertion must be scrutinised. By section 14C(1) CA 1989 the holder of a SGO shares parental responsibility with the parents of a child but has the right to override the responsibilities of the parents. Such an order is a significant step in a child's life that is intended to have long term consequences and the protections that surround it should be respected.'

**27.39** The Court of Appeal was also critical of the way in which the trial judge had dealt with both father's case that he could meet the child's needs and the asserted capability of the proposed special guardian to do so. This again emphasises the care that is needed in making such far reaching orders.

## The court's duty to consider ancillary matters

**27.40** Section 14B(1) of the Act sets out a number matters that the court is required to consider before making a special guardianship order. The most important of these are that the court is required, before making a special guardianship order, to consider whether, if the order is made, a child arrangements order containing contact provisions should also be made.[67]

**27.41** The sort of issues that may lead a court to exercise this power in relation to contact are well illustrated by the decision of Russell J in the case of *Re F (Special Guardianship Order)*.[68] In this case, a special guardianship order was made in favour of the child's existing foster carer but Her Ladyship considered that a contact order should also be made both to ensure continuing contact with a family member who had a positive role in the child's life and also to ensure that his parents (who had been found to be culpable[69] in respect of very serious injuries to the child) had only indirect contact. In making this order she said:[70]

> 'I intend to make a contact order to emphasise the importance of the role of contact in the life and development of this child. It is too important, too significant a part of the plan for [the child's] future welfare to be left to chance or depend on the goodwill of the adults involved. It is a necessary order as the continuation and the progression of contact form part of the basis of this court's decision and a contact order reflects the imperative need for contact to take place. In addition, it will deal with the parents' contact and will provide support for [the special guardian] as any application for contact by either parent will be in the face of an existing order regarding their contact.'

**27.42** The court is also directed to consider whether any existing s 8 order in respect of the child should be varied or discharged.[71]

---

[67] Section 14B(1)(a).
[68] [2016] 1 FLR 593.
[69] Father by perpetrating and mother by failing to protect.
[70] Paragraph 52.
[71] Sections 14B(1)(b).

**27.43** Section 14B(2) gives the court power, on making a special guardianship order, to also give leave for the child to be known by a new surname or to give leave from the child to be removed from the jurisdiction, either generally or for a specific purposes.[72]

## THE DECISION TO MAKE A SPECIAL GUARDIANSHIP ORDER: WELFARE CONSIDERATIONS

### The statutory provisions

**27.44** As is in all matters relating to the upbringing of a child, the welfare of the child is the court's paramount consideration when it is considering the making of a special guardianship order.[73] The court is directed to have particular regard to the, 'welfare checklist' set out in s 1(3) of the 1989 Act.[74] These provisions apply equally when the court is considering varying or discharging a special guardianship order.

**27.45** In case where the making of a special guardianship order is one of several proposed disposals, it is necessary, as in all cases where the court has to evaluate alternative proposals for a child's future, to carry out an, 'holistic' analysis, guided by the statutory checklist, of the pros and cons of each proposal. This exercise is inevitably highly fact specific.

**27.46** As by its nature a special guardianship order interferes with existing family relationships, the court will need to bear in mind Art 8 of the European Convention for the Protection of Human Rights and Fundamental Freedoms. It will need to be satisfied that, 'its order is a proportionate response to the problem, having regard to the interference with family life which is involved'.[75]

### Special guardianship order or placement for adoption? 'The core, long-term welfare decision'[76]

**27.47** Particular issues arise when the options before the court include, or are limited to, making a special guardianship order in favour of a member of the child's family (or other connected person) and the making of a placement order, under s 21 of the Adoption and Children Act 2002, to facilitate the child being adopted by alternative carers outside their family. In such a case, the court has not only to consider the checklist in s 1(3) of the Children Act 1989 when deciding if it should make a special guardianship order or a care order but also,

---

[72] Sections 14B(3)(a) and (b) respectively.
[73] Section 1(1)(a) of the 1989 Act.
[74] Section 1(4)(b).
[75] Per Wall LJ in *Re S (Adoption or Special Guardianship Order)* (above) at para [49].
[76] Per McFarlane LJ in *Re C (Appeal from Care and Placement Orders)* [2014] 2 FLR 131 at para [33].

when considering whether to make a placement order, the extended checklist set out in s 1(4) of the Adoption and Children Act 2002.[77]

**27.48** The implications of the need to consider both statutes were considered by McFarlane LJ in the case of *Re C (Appeal from Care and Placement Orders)*.[78] In this case, the trial judge was faced with a choice between making a special guardianship order in favour of a grandparent of the child or making care and placement orders. He made the latter orders but his judgment was criticised for being, 'linear' and failing to carry out a, 'proper holistic evaluation of the central welfare question'.[79] Although McFarlane LJ was critical of the, 'unhelpful' structure of the judgment below[80] he ultimately concluded that the judge did, 'have the relevant long term factors in mind' and did, 'engage sufficiently with the core, long term welfare decision in this case'.[81]

**27.49** His Lordship had this to say about structure of decision making with reference to the checklists in the 1989 and 2002 Acts:[82]

> 'The CA 1989 welfare checklist must, by reason of s 1(4)(b) of the CA 1989, be used when the court is considering making a care order under s 31. A linear judgment, which unnecessarily compartmentalises the decision making into discrete and separate stages ("care order" and only then "adoption"), with the 1989 Act provisions alone being used to approve a plan for adoption, in some cases may prevent the evaluation of what is ultimately the one issue in the case, the choice between family placement or adoption, as a whole and for that evaluation to be undertaken with the tailor-made, adoption focused, welfare checklist in s 1 of the ACA 2002 at the forefront of the judicial mind.'

**27.50** This approach is, of course, reflective of all the recent case law[83] emphasising the need for proper, 'holistic' consideration of all options for a child, with their relevant pros and cons, and the converse need to avoid a 'linear' approach that can result in the court approving an adoption plan simply by a process of elimination.

## A presumption in favour of special guardianship order as, 'the least interventionist option'?

**27.51** The argument is sometimes advanced that the court is constrained to prefer the making of a special guardianship order to a plan for adoption

---

[77] See s 1(7)(a) of the 2002 Act.
[78] [2014] 2 FLR 131.
[79] The phrase is that of McFarlane LJ at para [29].
[80] See, for example, at paras [28] and [32]; see also comments of Floyd LJ at para [34]. Guidance as to the structure of judgments where the court had to choose between options for a child's future care was given by the Court of Appeal in the case of *Re G (Care Proceedings: Welfare Evaluation)* [2014] 1 FLR 670.
[81] Quotations from paras [32] and [33] respectively.
[82] Paragraph [31].
[83] The best known such case being, of course, *Re B-S (Adoption: Application of s 47(5))* [2014] 1 FLR 1035.

because it is, by its nature, a 'less interventionist' order. Although unarguable as a description of the legal effect of the orders, this line of reasoning runs the risk of diverting attention from the overall welfare analysis that the court is obliged to undertake.

**27.52** This is made clear by dicta of Wall LJ in two cases (one of them already drawn on extensively in this chapter) decided by then Court of Appeal on the same day, 6 February 2007:

*Re S (Adoption Order or Special Guardianship Order)*[84]

'Certain other points arise from the statutory scheme:-

(i) The carefully constructed statutory regime (notice to the local authority, leave requirements in certain cases, the role of the court, and the report from the local authority – even where the order is made by the court of its own motion) demonstrates the care which is required before making a special guardianship order, and that it is only appropriate if, in the particular circumstances of the particular case, it is best fitted to meet the needs of the child or children concerned.

(ii) There is nothing in the statutory provisions themselves which limits the making of a special guardianship order or an adoption order to any given set of circumstances. The statute itself is silent on the circumstances in which a special guardianship order is likely to be appropriate, and there is no presumption contained within the statute that a special guardianship order is preferable to an adoption order in any particular category of case. Each case must be decided on its particular facts; and each case will involve the careful application of a judicial discretion to those facts.

(iii) The key question which the court will be obliged to ask itself in every case in which the question of adoption as opposed to special guardianship arises will be: which order will better serve the welfare of this particular child?'[85]

*Re M-J (Adoption Order or Special Guardianship Order)*[86]

[17] ... Whilst special guardianship orders may well have been designed to encompass, and in many cases are suitable for, long term familial placements, we do not think it helpful to approach any given case on the basis that one option is "the preferred option" unless there are cogent reasons against it. The proper formulation for the approach is, we think, that stated by this court in paragraphs 47 to 49 of the judgment in *Re S*. Each case, as the recorder recognised, depends on the order which in all the circumstances of the case best meets the welfare needs of the child or children concerned. The recorder in due course appropriately applied this test. We do not think, however, that it was either appropriate or necessary for her to set up what would be in danger of becoming a presumption which then had to be rebutted ...

---

[84] [2007] 1 FLR 819.
[85] At para [47].
[86] [2007] 1 FLR 691.

[19] Again, with respect to the recorder, we think it goes too far to say that it is "incumbent" on the court to adopt "the least interventionist option". It is true that section 1(5) of the 1989 Act (the terms of which we have set out in paragraph 26 of the judgment in *Re S*) requires the court to make an order under the Act only if it considers that doing so would be better for the child than making no order at all. However, in the instant case, an order is manifestly necessary. Indeed, MJ is already subject to a care order. The recorder was right to consider whether the order was a "proportionate" response to the child's needs. In that context, it may be material for the court to be required to consider which order is less "interventionist". However, in so far as any such consideration is allowed to derogate from the welfare principle, it is plainly unacceptable. The danger of the recorder's formulation is that because a special guardianship order is less "interventionist" than an adoption order, that is the order which the court will feel constrained to make. That would be wrong as a matter of law, because it would be a clear derogation from the paramountcy of the welfare principle. It is also not the decision which the recorder ultimately reached.'

**27.53** The observations made in these cases are, it is suggested, entirely consistent with subsequent case law. In particular, they are a clear statement of the frequently emphasised need to avoid preconceptions and to ensure that the decision in each case is based on a clear welfare analysis, shaped by the relevant checklists and based on the facts of the individual case, of what is best for the particular child the court whose future is to be determined.

# CHAPTER 28

# ADOPTION: GENERAL CONSIDERATIONS

## THE PROCESS OF ADOPTION

**28.1** An adoption order is an order that results in a child ceasing to be a member of their birth family and becoming a member of a new, adoptive family. The Adoption and Children Act 2002 ('ACA 2002') governs all of the legal issues pertaining to adoption, including the procedural issues, orders that must be in place and the welfare determination that the court must make.

### What is adoption?

**28.2** Section 46(1) of the ACA 2002 defines an adoption order as follows:

> 'An adoption order is an order made by the court on an application under section 50 or 51 giving parental responsibility for a child to the adopters or adopter.'

**28.3** On the making of an adoption order, parental responsibility is removed from the birth parents and is invested in the adoptive parents by virtue of s 46(2) of the ACA 2002. Section 46(2) stipulates:

> 'The making of an adoption order operates to extinguish –
>
> (a) the parental responsibility which any person other than the adopters or adopter has for the adopted child immediately before the making of the order,
>
> (b) any order under the 1989 Act or the Children (Northern Ireland) Order 1995 (S.I. 1995/755 (N.I. 2)),
>
> (c) any order under the Children (Scotland) Act 1995 (c. 36) other than an excepted order, and
>
> (d) any duty arising by virtue of an agreement or an order of a court to make payments, so far as the payments are in respect of the adopted child's maintenance or upbringing for any period after the making of the adoption order.'

**28.4** Every child has a fundamental right to belong to a family. This principle is reflected clearly in the United Nations Convention on the Rights of the Child, ratified by the UK in 1991. Therefore, where it is not possible for a child to live with their birth parents for whatever reason, the state steps in to ensure that they have the opportunity to become part of a family. It must not be forgotten however, that removing a child from their birth family and severing all of their legal and practical ties with them will have a profound impact upon the child and their family, and is the most significant intervention in family life that the state can achieve.

**28.5** A number of steps must first be taken before an adoption order is made. The court must take great care when considering the preliminary steps given the huge impact of adoption upon the subject child.

## Adoption with an international element

**28.6** Adoption with an international element is a very complex and fast changing area of law which is outside the scope of this book. However, in outline, the ACA 2002 makes provision for the adoption of a child who is habitually resident in another country. If the country in which the child is habitually resident is a signatory to The Hague Convention on Intercountry Adoption, this will qualify as an adoption pursuant to a convention order.[1] If a country is not a signatory of the Convention, it may still constitute a valid 'overseas adoption' in accordance with s 87 of the ACA 2002.

# THE ADOPTION AND CHILDREN ACT 2002

**28.7** The ACA 2002 came into force came in December 2005, replacing the Adoption Act 1976 and amending the Children Act 1989 ('CA 1989'). The ACA 2002 modernised the law governing adoption in the UK and incorporates provisions for international adoptions. Amongst other changes to the system, the ACA 2002 widened the pool of people that can be considered by the adoption agency as prospective adoptive parents.

**28.8** The ACA 2002 contains a clear welfare checklist which must be applied by the court and adoption agencies when considering whether the plan for a child should be adoption, whether a placement order should be made, and whether an adoption order should be made.[2] The ACA 2002 welfare checklist, encapsulated in s 1(4) of the ACA 2002 builds on the welfare checklist contained in the CA 1989 (see chapter 2) and extends the consideration of a child's welfare throughout their life, not just during their minority.

**28.9** The ACA 2002 applies whenever a court or adoption agency must come to a decision relating to the adoption of a child.[3] The paramount consideration of the court and the adoption agency must be the welfare of the child throughout their life, in accordance with s 1(2) of the ACA 2002, and this must be the guiding principle when decisions are made in relation to the child in question.

---

[1] ACA 2002, s 67.
[2] ACA 2002, s 1(1).
[3] ACA 2002, s 1(1).

**28.10** Section 1(3) of the ACA 2002 mirrors the 'no delay principle' contained in the CA 1989[4] and this again applies to not only the court but to the adoption agency also.

**28.11** Unlike the vast majority of jurisdictions, the UK enables children to be placed for adoption without the consent of their parents. The issue of consent is considered more closely in chapter 29, but this ability to make an adoption order after dispensing with a parents' consent emphasises the need for the court to consider any application under the ACA 2002 very carefully.

**28.12** The meaning of 'coming to a decision relating to the adoption of a child' is specified in s 1(7) of the ACA 2002.

## The welfare checklist under the ACA 2002

**28.13** The welfare checklist contained at s 1(4) of the ACA 2002 requires that the court and the adoption agency must consider, amongst other things:

'(a) the child's ascertainable wishes and feelings regarding the decision (considered in the light of the child's age and understanding),
(b) the child's particular needs,
(c) the likely effect on the child (throughout his life) of having ceased to be a member of the original family and become an adopted person,
(d) the child's age, sex, background and any of the child's characteristics which the court or agency considers relevant,
(e) any harm (within the meaning of the Children Act 1989 (c. 41)) which the child has suffered or is at risk of suffering,
(f) the relationship which the child has with relatives, and with any other person in relation to whom the court or agency considers the relationship to be relevant, including –
  (i) the likelihood of any such relationship continuing and the value to the child of its doing so,
  (ii) the ability and willingness of any of the child's relatives, or of any such person, to provide the child with a secure environment in which the child can develop, and otherwise to meet the child's needs,
  (iii) the wishes and feelings of any of the child's relatives, or of any such person, regarding the child.'

**28.14** In *YC v United Kingdom*[5] the European Court of Human Rights considered where a child's best interests lay when the court is considering an adoption order. It was held that two considerations should be borne in mind: first, that it is in the child's best interest that ties with their birth family are maintained, except in cases where the family has proved particularly unfit. Second, it is in the child's best interests to ensure their development in a safe and secure environment.

---

[4] See chapter 2.
[5] *YC v United Kingdom* (Application No 4547/10) [2012] 2 FLR 332.

**28.15** Section 1(4)(c) of the ACA 2002 requires the court to have regard to the likely effect on the child throughout their life, of ceasing to be a member of their original family throughout their life and becoming an adopted child. This consideration is part of the balancing exercise for the court and the adoption agency, and careful thought must be given to the impact upon the child and their identity if ties are severed with their birth family versus, any harm they may suffer if they remain part of their birth family. This includes being cared for by their birth family, being placed in long-term foster care, or being cared for under any lesser order such as a child arrangements or special guardianship order.

**28.16** The paramountcy of welfare is clear and must be specifically considered when determining what orders (if any) the court should make in relation to the arrangements for the children it is concerned with.

**28.17** The court must demonstrate that the checklist elements are at the forefront of its mind when making final orders. The judge does not need to address each element of the checklist in the judgment provided, but they must make it clear that they have considered the elements,[6] and that the court's approach is compatible with the law.[7]

**28.18** The Senior President of the Tribunals, Lord Justice Vos, addressed the issue of how thoroughly a judge is required to address the welfare checklist in judgments in the matter of *P (A child)* [2016]:[8]

> 'We are entitled to assume that a judge of the experience of Judge Ansell knew how to perform the welfare review, and knew which matters he should take into account, unless he has demonstrated the contrary. There was no need for him laboriously to rehearse each item of the checklist as if a pilot conducting his pre-flight checks (see Staughton LJ in *H v H (Residence Order: leave to remove from the jurisdiction)* [1995] 1 FLR 529), even if, in a difficult or finely balanced case, it is a great help to address each of the factors in the list, along with any others which may be relevant, so as to ensure that no particular feature of the case is given more weight than it should properly bear.'

**28.19** The checklist serves as a balancing exercise for the court when considering the range of potential outcomes available, and whether any order should be made.[9] However, the court is not bound to solely consider the issues raised by the parties and may highlight other issues it considers relevant. Importantly, no one element of the checklist is more important than another. The overriding concern when considering an application for either a placement or adoption order will inevitably be the impact of the order throughout the life of the child, not just their majority.

---

[6] *P (A Child)* [2016] EWCA Civ 3.
[7] *Re E (Adoption Order: Proportionality of Outcome to Circumstances)* [2014] 2 FLR 514.
[8] *P (A Child)* [2016] EWCA Civ 3 at [48].
[9] *B v B (Residence Order: Reasons for decision)* [1997] 2 FLR 602.

## Requirements for making an adoption order

**28.20** Section 47 of the ACA 2002 outlines the circumstances in which an adoption order can be made. Pursuant to s 47, an adoption order may not be made unless one of the following three conditions is met (subject to s 52 of the ACA 2002):[10]

'The first condition is that, in the case of each parent or guardian of the child, the court is satisfied –

(a) that the parent or guardian consents to the making of the adoption order,
(b) that the parent or guardian has consented under section 20 (and has not withdrawn the consent) and does not oppose the making of the adoption order, or
(c) that the parent's or guardian's consent should be dispensed with.'[11]

**28.21** The issue of parental consent, s 52 of the ACA 2002 and the opposition to the making of an adoption order is dealt with below.

**28.22** Section 47(4) ACA 2002 sets out the second condition as follows:

'(a) the child has been placed for adoption by an adoption agency with the prospective adopters in whose favour the order is proposed to be made,
(b) either –
　(i) the child was placed for adoption with the consent of each parent or guardian and the consent of the mother was given when the child was at least six weeks old, or
　(ii) the child was placed for adoption under a placement order, and
(c) no parent or guardian opposes the making of the adoption order.'

**28.23** The third condition relates to Scotland and Northern Ireland, not England and Wales, and requires that the child is free for adoption under the necessary statutory provisions.

## Opposing an adoption order

**28.24** Sections 47(3) and (5) of the ACA 2002 are clear that an application to oppose an adoption order under the two conditions set out in s 47(2) and (4) of the ACA 2002 can only be made with the leave of the court. Section 47(7) is clear that:[12]

'The court cannot give leave under subsection (3) or (5) unless satisfied that there has been a change in circumstances since the consent of the parent or guardian was given or, as the case may be, the placement order was made.'

**28.25** Clearly in a situation where a parent gives consent to a child being made the subject of an adoption order, care must be taken as to how this consent is given. Notably, in accordance with s 47(4)(b)(i) of the ACA 2002, the child must be over 6 weeks old before any parental consent can be accepted. If a

---

[10] ACA 2002, s 47(1).
[11] ACA 2002, s 47(2).
[12] ACA 2002, s 47(7).

child has been placed for adoption and an order is applied for but the parent no longer consents, leave of the court will only be given in the event that there has been a change of circumstances following the consent given initially.

**28.26** If a placement order has been made and the parent wishes to oppose the adoption order, again, leave will only be given under s 47(5) of the ACA 2002.

**28.27** An adoption order can be made without the consent of the parent if the court determines that the consent should be dispensed with.[13]

## 'Change of circumstances' and the considerations for granting leave to oppose an adoption application

**28.28** Applications for leave to oppose an adoption order under ss 47(3) and (5) are subject to the considerations set out in s 1 of the ACA 2002, the welfare checklist. Section 1(7)(b) specifically states that s 1 applies when:

> 'Coming to a decision about granting leave in respect of any action (other than the initiation of proceedings in any court) which may be taken by an adoption agency or individual under this Act.'

**28.29** Under s 1(2), the paramount consideration of the court must be the child's welfare, throughout their life, and the court must have regard to the matters set out in the welfare checklist contained in s 1(4) of the ACA 2002.

**28.30** In *Re P (Adoption: Leave Provisions)*, Wall LJ considered what may amount to a change in circumstances for the purposes of s 47(7):[14]

> 'There has been a change in circumstances within s 47(7), then the door to the exercise of a judicial discretion to permit the parents to defend the adoption proceedings is open, and the decision whether or not to grant leave is governed by s.1 of the 2002 Act. In other words, "the paramount consideration of the court must be the child's welfare throughout his life".'

**28.31** This approach was confirmed by the Court of Appeal in *Re B-S (Adoption: Application of S 47(5))*. *Re B-S* will be a very familiar case for care practitioners because of the discussions it contains on the considerations of the court when the local authority has a care plan for adoption and makes a placement order application. This case was, in fact, an application to oppose an adoption order and considered the procedure for leave very carefully. Sir James Munby P made one qualification to the words of Wall J, that:[15]

> 'The exercise at the second stage is more appropriately described as one of judicial evaluation rather than one involving mere discretion.'

---

[13] ACA 2002, s 47(2)(c).
[14] *Re P (Adoption: Leave Provisions)* [2007] EWCA Civ 616 at [26].
[15] *Re B-S (Adoption: Application of S 47(5))* [2013] EWCA Civ 1146 at [72].

**28.32** In essence therefore, the first stage considers whether there has been a change of circumstances and if so, the second stage then considers the application it light of the welfare of the child throughout their life.

**28.33** When considering the first stage of the test, the question necessarily arises as to when a change in circumstances would 'open the door' to the court's consideration of the second stage. In *Re P* Wall J states that:[16]

> '... the change in circumstances since the placement order was made must, self evidently and as a matter of statutory construction, relate to the grant of leave. It must equally be of a nature and degree sufficient, on the facts of the particular case, to open the door to the exercise of the judicial discretion to permit the parents to defend the adoption proceedings ... self evidently, a change in circumstances can embrace a wide range of different factual situations. S.47(7) of the 2002 Act does not relate a change to the circumstances of the parents. The only limiting factor is that it must be a change in circumstances "since the placement order was made".'

**28.34** In relation to the second stage, the leading authority is remains the Court of Appeal's decision in *Re B-S*. The President provides clear guidance as to the court's approach in an application for leave to oppose an adoption order:

> 'In relation to the second question – If there has been a change in circumstances, should leave to oppose be given? – the court will, of course, need to consider all the circumstances. The court will in particular have to consider two inter-related questions: one, the parent's ultimate prospect of success if given leave to oppose; the other, the impact on the child if the parent is, or is not, given leave to oppose, always remembering, of course, that at this stage the child's welfare is paramount. In relation to the evaluation, the weighing and balancing, of these factors we make the following points:
>
> (i) Prospect of success here relates to the prospect of resisting making of an adoption order, not, we emphasise, the prospect of ultimately having the child restored to the parent's care.
>
> (ii) For purposes of exposition and analysis we treat as two separate issues the questions of whether there has been a change in circumstances and whether the parent has solid grounds for seeking leave. Almost invariably, however, they will be intertwined; in many cases the one may very well follow from the other.
>
> (iii) Once he or she has got to the point of concluding that there has been a change of circumstances and that the parent has solid grounds for seeking leave, the judge must consider very carefully indeed whether the child's welfare really does necessitate the refusal of leave. The judge must keep at the forefront of his mind the teaching of *Re B (Care Proceedings: Appeal)* [2013] UKSC 33, in particular that adoption is the "last resort" and only permissible if "nothing else will do" and that, as Lord Neuberger emphasised, the child's interests include being brought up by the parents or wider family unless the overriding requirements of the child's welfare make that not possible. That said, the child's welfare is paramount.

---

[16] *Re P (Adoption: Leave Provisions)* [2007] EWCA Civ 616 at [30]–[31].

(iv) At this, as at all other stages in the adoption process, the judicial evaluation of the child's welfare must take into account all the negatives and the positives, all the pros and cons, of each of the two options, that is, either giving or refusing the parent leave to oppose. Here again, as elsewhere, the use of Thorpe LJ's "balance sheet" is to be encouraged.

(v) This close focus on the circumstances requires that the court has proper evidence. But this does not mean that judges will always need to hear oral evidence and cross-examination before coming to a conclusion. Sometimes, though we suspect not very often, the judge will be assisted by oral evidence. Typically, however, an application for leave under s 47(5) can fairly and should appropriately be dealt with on the basis of written evidence and submissions: see *Re P* paras [53]–[54].

(vi) As a general proposition, the greater the change in circumstances (assuming, of course, that the change is positive) and the more solid the parent's grounds for seeking leave to oppose, the more cogent and compelling the arguments based on the child's welfare must be if leave to oppose is to be refused.

(vii) The mere fact that the child has been placed with prospective adopters cannot be determinative, nor can the mere passage of time. On the other hand, the older the child and the longer the child has been placed the greater the adverse impacts of disturbing the arrangements are likely to be.

(viii) The judge must always bear in mind that what is paramount in every adoption case is the welfare of the child "throughout his life". Given modern expectation of life, this means that, with a young child, one is looking far ahead into a very distant future – upwards of eighty or even ninety years. Against this perspective, judges must be careful not to attach undue weight to the short term consequences for the child if leave to oppose is given. In this as in other contexts, judges should be guided by what Sir Thomas Bingham MR said in *Re O (Contact: Imposition of Conditions)* [1995] 2 FLR 124, 129, that: "the court should take a medium-term and long-term view of the child's development and not accord excessive weight to what appear likely to be short-term or transient problems". That was said in the context of contact but it has a much wider resonance: *Re G (Education: Religious Upbringing)* [2012] EWCA Civ 1233, [2013] 1 FLR 677, para [26].

(ix) Almost invariably the judge will be pressed with the argument that leave to oppose should be refused, amongst other reasons, because of the adverse impact on the prospective adopters, and thus on the child, of their having to pursue a contested adoption application. We do not seek to trivialise an argument which may in some cases have considerable force, particularly perhaps in a case where the child is old enough to have some awareness of what is going on. But judges must be careful not to attach undue weight to the argument. After all, what from the perspective of the proposed adopters was the smoothness of the process which they no doubt anticipated when issuing their application with the assurance of a placement order, will already have been disturbed by the unwelcome making of the application for leave to oppose. And the disruptive effects of an order giving a parent leave to oppose can be minimised by firm judicial case management before the hearing of the application for leave. If appropriate directions are given, in particular in relation to the expert and other evidence to be adduced on behalf of the parent, as soon as the application for leave is issued and before the question of leave has been determined, it ought to be possible to direct either that the application for leave is to be listed with the substantive adoption application to follow immediately, whether or not leave is given, or, if that is not feasible, to direct that the substantive application is to be listed, whether or not leave has been given, very shortly after the leave hearing.

(x) We urge judges always to bear in mind the wise and humane words of Wall LJ in Re P, para [32]. We have already quoted them but they bear repetition: "the test should not be set too high, because ... parents ... should not be discouraged either from bettering themselves or from seeking to prevent the adoption of their child by the imposition of a test which is unachievable".'

**28.35** It has been confirmed in *The Prospective Adopters v IA and Croyden LBC*,[17] that a change in circumstances can include a change or clarification of law.

## CONTACT WITH A CHILD PURSUANT TO AN ADOPTION ORDER

**28.36** Prior to a placement order being made, the court must consider what provisions for contact have been proposed by the adoption agency applying for the order in accordance with s 27(4) of the ACA 2002. These proposals should include contact following the adoption order being made.

**28.37** Under this section, the parties have the opportunity to comment on the proposed arrangements. The adoption agency must take into consideration the wishes of the parents, along with the advice of the adoption panel[18] and the best interests of the child before making a decision as to their contact proposals.[19] The adoption agency may suggest direct, face-to-face contact, or indirect contact by way of letters and cards.

**28.38** Any application for contact between a child and their parents will need to be made under s 26 of the ACA 2002, not the CA 1989.

**28.39** Section 26(2) ACA 2002 provides that:

'While an adoption agency is so authorised or a child is placed for adoption –

(a) no application may be made for any provision for contact under that Act, but
(b) the court may make an order under this section requiring the person with whom the child lives, or is to live, to allow the child to visit or stay with the person named in the order, or for the person named in the order and the child otherwise to have contact with each other.'

**28.40** Whilst a placement order is in force, the following people listed in s 26(3), are entitled to make an application for contact:

'An application for an order under this section may be made by –

---

[17] [2014] 2 FLR 1158.
[18] The adoption panel is an internal panel within the adoption agency established in accordance with reg 3 of the Adoption Agency Regulations 2005.
[19] Adoption Agency Regulations 2005, reg 46

(a) the child or the agency,
(b) any parent, guardian or relative,
(c) any person in whose favour there was provision for contact under the 1989 Act which ceased to have effect by virtue of subsection (1),
(d) if a residence order was in force immediately before the adoption agency was authorised to place the child for adoption or (as the case may be) placed the child for adoption at a time when he was less than six weeks old, the person in whose favour the order was made,
(e) if a person had care of the child immediately before that time by virtue of an order made in the exercise of the High Court's inherent jurisdiction with respect to children, that person,
(f) any person who has obtained the court's leave to make the application.'

**28.41** When considering post-adoption contact orders, Wall LJ in *Re P (Placement Orders: Parental Consent)*, stated that the courts were only likely to make a contact order where the circumstances could be termed 'highly exceptional'.[20] He reaffirmed this position in the subsequent case of *Re C*:[21]

'the purpose of adoption is for the child to develop in a quite different family [...] and the purpose of contact is [...] for identity purposes, not to develop a relationship between the natural parent and the child who is adopted.'

**28.42** Applications can still be made under s 8 of the CA 1989 for contact. This will involve the consideration of the welfare checklist contained within the CA 1989, ie the best interest of the child throughout the child's minority, as opposed to throughout the child's life.

**28.43** Any application made under s 26 of the ACA 2002 must be decided in accordance with the provisions set out in s 1 of the ACA 2002, namely the provisions of the paramountcy of the child's best interests, the no delay principle and the welfare checklist discussed above.

**28.44** Once an adoption order has been made, the parents will no longer have any legal relationship with the child and therefore will not be a category of person who is entitled to apply for a s 8 order.[22]

---

[20] *Re P (Placement Orders: Parental Consent)* [2008] EWCA Civ 535.
[21] *Re C (Contact)* [2008] 1 FLR 1151.
[22] CA 1989, s 10.

# CHAPTER 29

# ADOPTION: PARENTAL CONSENT AND PLACEMENT ORDERS

## PLACEMENT ORDER

**29.1** An adoption agency may only place a child for adoption if each parent or guardian consents to the placement,[1] or if the court has made a placement order authorising the local authority to place the child for adoption.[2]

**29.2** An adoption agency is defined for the purposes of the Adoption and Children Act 2002 ('ACA 2002') as 'a local authority or registered adoption society may be referred to as an adoption agency'.[3]

**29.3** Section 21(1) of the ACA 2002 defines a placement order as follows:

'A placement order is an order made by the court authorising a local authority to place a child for adoption with any prospective adopters who may be chosen by the authority.'

**29.4** Section 21(2) of the ACA 2002 provides that the court can only make a placement order if:

'(a) the child is subject to a care order,
(b) the court is satisfied that the conditions in section 31(2) of the 1989 Act (conditions for making a care order) are met, or
(c) the child has no parent or guardian.'

**29.5** Section 21(3) of the ACA 2002 continues:

'The court may only make a placement order if, in the case of each parent or guardian of the child, the court is satisfied –

(a) that the parent or guardian has consented to the child being placed for adoption with any prospective adopters who may be chosen by the local authority and has not withdrawn the consent, or
(b) that the parent's or guardian's consent should be dispensed with.

This subsection is subject to section 52 (parental etc. consent).'

**29.6** Previous chapters consider the process of making a care order with a care plan for adoption. In such circumstances, the local authority must apply

---

[1] ACA 2002, s 19.
[2] ACA 2002, s 21.
[3] ACA 2002, s 2(1).

separately for a placement order. Although this is a standalone application, separate from any a care order application, the two applications can be consolidated and usually are. The process of making a placement order application is considered later in this chapter.

## Adoption and Children Act 2002

**29.7** The ACA 2002 came into force in December 2005, replacing the Adoption Act 1976 and amending the Children Act 1989. The ACA 2002 modernised the law governing adoption in the UK and incorporates provisions for international adoptions. Amongst other changes to the system, the ACA 2002 widened the pool of people that can be considered by the adoption agency as prospective adoptive parents.

**29.8** The ACA 2002 contains a clear welfare checklist which must be applied by the court and adoption agencies when considering whether the plan for a child should be adoption, whether a placement order should be made, and whether an adoption order should be made.[4]

**29.9** Sections 1(2) and (3) reflects the Children Act 1989 ('CA 1989') in terms of the welfare of the child being the paramount consideration of the court and the no delay principle, discussed in chapter 2.

**29.10** Section 1(2) and (3) ACA 2002 specify that:

'(2) The paramount consideration of the court or adoption agency must be the child's welfare, throughout his life.

(3) The court or adoption agency must at all times bear in mind that, in general, any delay in coming to the decision is likely to prejudice the child's welfare.'

**29.11** Further, s 1(6) provides:

'The court or adoption agency must always consider the whole range of powers available to it in the child's case (whether under this Act or the Children Act 1989); and the court must not make any order under this Act unless it considers that making the order would be better for the child than not doing so.'

**29.12** Section 1(7) identifies the meaning of 'coming to a decision relating to the adoption of a child' in the context of the ACA 2002:

'In this section, "coming to a decision relating to the adoption of a child", in relation to a court, includes –

(a) coming to a decision in any proceedings where the orders that might be made by the court include an adoption order (or the revocation of such an order), a placement order (or the revocation of such an order) or an order under section 26 (or the revocation or variation of such an order),

---

[4] ACA 2002, s 1(1).

(b) coming to a decision about granting leave in respect of any action (other than the initiation of proceedings in any court) which may be taken by an adoption agency or individual under this Act,

but does not include coming to a decision about granting leave in any other circumstances.'

Discussion of applications for leave to apply to oppose an adoption order can be found in chapter 28.

## *Welfare checklist under the ACA 2002*

**29.13** The ACA 2002 welfare checklist, encapsulated in s 1(4) builds on the welfare checklist contained in the CA 1989 (see chapter 2) and extends the consideration of a child's welfare throughout their life, not just during their minority.

**29.14** The welfare checklist contained at s 1(4) requires that the court and the adoption agency must consider, amongst other things:

'(a) the child's ascertainable wishes and feelings regarding the decision (considered in the light of the child's age and understanding),
(b) the child's particular needs,
(c) the likely effect on the child (throughout his life) of having ceased to be a member of the original family and become an adopted person,
(d) the child's age, sex, background and any of the child's characteristics which the court or agency considers relevant,
(e) any harm (within the meaning of the Children Act 1989 (c. 41)) which the child has suffered or is at risk of suffering,
(f) the relationship which the child has with relatives, and with any other person in relation to whom the court or agency considers the relationship to be relevant, including –
  (i) the likelihood of any such relationship continuing and the value to the child of its doing so,
  (ii) the ability and willingness of any of the child's relatives, or of any such person, to provide the child with a secure environment in which the child can develop, and otherwise to meet the child's needs,
  (iii) the wishes and feelings of any of the child's relatives, or of any such person, regarding the child.'

**29.15** In *YC v United Kingdom*[5] the European Court of Human Rights considered where a child's best interests lay when the court is considering an adoption order. It was held that two considerations should be borne in mind: first, that it is in the child's best interest that ties with their birth family are maintained, except in cases where the family has proved particularly unfit. Second, it is in the child's best interests to ensure their development in a safe and secure environment.

---

[5] *YC v United Kingdom* (Application No 4547/10) [2012] 2 FLR 332.

**29.16** Section 1(4)(c) of the ACA 2002 requires the court to have regard to the likely effect on the child throughout their life, of ceasing to be a member of their original family throughout their life and becoming an adopted child. This consideration is part of the balancing exercise for the court and the adoption agency, and careful thought must be given to the impact upon the child and their identity if ties are severed with their birth family versus, any harm they may suffer if they remain part of their birth family. This includes being cared for by their birth family, being placed in long-term foster care, or being cared for under any lesser order such as a child arrangements or special guardianship order.

**29.17** The paramountcy of welfare is clear and must be specifically considered when determining what orders (if any) the court should make in relation to the arrangements for the children it is concerned with.

**29.18** The court must demonstrate that the checklist elements are at the forefront of its mind when making final orders. The judge does not need to address each element of the checklist in the judgment provided, but they must make it clear that they have considered the elements,[6] and that the court's approach is compatible with the law.[7]

**29.19** The Senior President of the Tribunals, Lord Justice Vos, addressed the issue of how thoroughly a judge is required to address the welfare checklist in judgments in the matter of *P (A child)* [2016]:[8]

> 'We are entitled to assume that a judge of the experience of Judge Ansell knew how to perform the welfare review, and knew which matters he should take into account, unless he has demonstrated the contrary. There was no need for him laboriously to rehearse each item of the checklist as if a pilot conducting his pre-flight checks (see Staughton LJ in *H v H (Residence Order: leave to remove from the jurisdiction)* [1995] 1 FLR 529), even if, in a difficult or finely balanced case, it is a great help to address each of the factors in the list, along with any others which may be relevant, so as to ensure that no particular feature of the case is given more weight than it should properly bear.'

**29.20** The checklist serves as a balancing exercise for the court when considering the range of potential outcomes available, and whether any order should be made.[9] However, the court is not bound to solely consider the issues raised by the parties and may highlight other issues it considers relevant. Importantly, no one element of the checklist is more important than another. The overriding concern when considering an application for either a placement or adoption order will inevitably be the impact of the order throughout the life of the child, not just their majority.

---

[6] *P (A Child)* [2016] EWCA Civ 3.
[7] *Re E (Adoption Order: Proportionality of Outcome to Circumstances)* [2014] 2 FLR 514.
[8] *P (A Child)* [2016] EWCA Civ 3 at [48].
[9] *B v B (Residence Order: Reasons for decision)* [1997] 2 FLR 602.

## EFFECT OF A PLACEMENT ORDER

**29.21** A placement order enables the adoption agency[10] to place a child for adoption with any prospective adopters who may be chosen by the authority. Placement orders cannot be made specifying placement with a specific prospective adopter.

**29.22** Section 21(4) specifies that:

'A placement order continues in force until –

(a) it is revoked under section 24,
(b) an adoption order is made in respect of the child, or
(c) the child marries or attains the age of 18 years.'

## Parental responsibility under a placement order

**29.23** Section 25 of the ACA 2002 sets out the impact of a placement order upon parental responsibility, both before and after placement with prospective adopters. Section 25 states:

'(1) This section applies while –

(a) a child is placed for adoption under section 19[11] or an adoption agency is authorised to place a child for adoption under that section, or
(b) a placement order is in force in respect of a child.

(2) Parental responsibility for the child is given to the agency concerned.

(3) While the child is placed with prospective adopters, parental responsibility is given to them.

(4) The agency may determine that the parental responsibility of any parent or guardian, or of prospective adopters, is to be restricted to the extent specified in the determination.'

**29.24** In the same way as the local authority can make decisions against the parents' wishes under a care order, the adoption agency can make the decisions for the child contrary to their birth parents' wishes under a placement order.

## Contact to a child subject to a placement order

**29.25** Prior to making a placement order, the court must consider what provisions for contact are proposed by the adoption agency applying for the order in accordance with s 27(4) of the ACA 2002. Under this section, the parties have the opportunity to comment on the proposed arrangements. The adoption agency must take into consideration the wishes of the parents, along

---

[10] ACA 2002, s 2(1): 'a local authority or registered adoption society may be referred to as an adoption agency'.
[11] Placed for adoption with parental consent.

with the advice of the adoption panel[12] and the best interests of the child before making a decision as to their contact proposals.[13]

**29.26** Any application for contact between a child and their parents will need to be made under s 26 of the ACA 2002, not the CA 1989.

**29.27** Section 26(2) of the ACA 202 provides that:

'While an adoption agency is so authorised or a child is placed for adoption –

(a) no application may be made for any provision for contact under that Act, but

(b) the court may make an order under this section requiring the person with whom the child lives, or is to live, to allow the child to visit or stay with the person named in the order, or for the person named in the order and the child otherwise to have contact with each other.'

**29.28** Whilst a placement order is in force, the following people listed in s 26(3), are entitled to make an application for contact:

'An application for an order under this section may be made by –

(a) the child or the agency,
(b) any parent, guardian or relative,
(c) any person in whose favour there was provision for contact under the 1989 Act which ceased to have effect by virtue of subsection (1),
(d) if a residence order was in force immediately before the adoption agency was authorised to place the child for adoption or (as the case may be) placed the child for adoption at a time when he was less than six weeks old, the person in whose favour the order was made,
(e) if a person had care of the child immediately before that time by virtue of an order made in the exercise of the High Court's inherent jurisdiction with respect to children, that person,
(f) any person who has obtained the court's leave to make the application.'

**29.29** When considering post-adoption contact orders, Wall LJ in *Re P (Placement Orders: Parental Consent)*, stated that the courts were only likely to make a contact order where the circumstances could be termed 'highly exceptional'.[14] He reaffirmed this position in the subsequent case of *Re C*:[15]

'the purpose of adoption is for the child to develop in a quite different family [...] and the purpose of contact is [...] for identity purposes, not to develop a relationship between the natural parent and the child who is adopted.'

---

[12] The adoption panel is an internal panel within the adoption agency established in accordance with reg 3 of the Adoption Agency Regulations 2005 (SI 2005/389).
[13] Adoption Agency Regulations 2005, reg 46.
[14] *Re P (Placement Orders: Parental Consent)* [2008] EWCA Civ 535.
[15] *Re C (Contact)* [2008] 1 FLR 1151.

**29.30** Applications can still be made under s 8 of the CA 1989 for contact. This will involve the consideration of the welfare checklist contained within the CA 1989, ie the best interest of the child throughout the child's minority, as opposed to throughout the child's life.

**29.31** Any application made under s 26 of the ACA 2002 must be decided in accordance with the provisions set out in s 1 of the ACA 2002, namely the provisions of the paramountcy of the child's best interests, the no delay principle and the welfare checklist discussed above.

## Effect on any other orders in place at the point at which a placement order is made

**29.32** Once a placement order is made, under s 29 of the ACA 2002 any private law orders, supervision or care orders made under the CA 1989 will cease to have effect.

## PROCESS OF APPLICATION

**29.33** A placement order application is made pursuant to Part 14 of the Family Procedure Rules 2010 ('FPR 2010'). The parties to a placement order are set out in r 14.3 of the FPR 2010.

### When an application can be made

**29.34** If the application is made during the course of care proceedings, the two applications should be consolidated, the child made a party to the placement order proceedings and a guardian appointed. If the local authority's care plan is for adoption, they must make their application within the proceedings in order to ensure that the adoption plan is possible. If no placement order application has been made during the course of care proceedings with a plan for adoption, the local authority cannot place a child for adoption without the parents' consent in accordance with s 19 of the ACA 2002.

**29.35** Section 22(1) of the ACA 2002 specifies when a local authority must apply to the court for a placement order:

'A local authority must apply to the court for a placement order in respect of a child if –

(a) the child is placed for adoption by them or is being provided with accommodation by them,
(b) no adoption agency is authorised to place the child for adoption,
(c) the child has no parent or guardian or the authority consider that the conditions in section 31(2) of the 1989 Act are met, and
(d) the authority are satisfied that the child ought to be placed for adoption.'

**29.36** An application for a placement order constitutes specified proceedings in accordance with s 41 of the CA 1989 and as such there is a presumption that a guardian will be appointed for the child. The child is an automatic respondent to any application for a placement order.

## Case management

**29.37** Rule 14.6 of the FPR 2010 provides a list of tasks that the court office must complete once an application is made for a placement order. Rule 14.7 provides that unless the court directs otherwise, the first directions hearing must be within 4 weeks of the date the application was issued.

**29.38** At the first directions hearing the court will:

'(a) fix a timetable for the proceedings including a timetable for the filing of –
- (i) any report relating to the suitability of the applicants to adopt a child;
- (ii) any report from the local authority;
- (iii) any report from a children's guardian, reporting officer or children and family reporter;
- (iv) if a statement of facts has been filed, any amended statement of facts;
- (v) any other evidence, and
- (vi) give directions relating to the reports and other evidence;

(b) consider whether the child or any other person should be a party to the proceedings and, if so, give directions in accordance with rule 14.3(2) or (3) joining that child or person as a party;

(c) give directions relating to the appointment of a litigation friend for any protected party or child who is a party to, but not the subject of, proceedings unless a litigation friend has already been appointed;

(d) consider in accordance with rule 29.17 whether the case needs to be transferred to another court and, if so, give directions to transfer the proceedings to another court;

(e) give directions about –
- (i) tracing parents or any other person the court considers to be relevant to the proceedings;
- (ii) service of documents;
- (iii) subject to paragraph (2), disclosure as soon as possible of information and evidence to the parties; and
- (iv) the final hearing.'

**29.39** If the application has been made within the care proceedings, directions will be made for the child to be joined as a party, the guardian to be appointed and for the parents and the guardian to respond to the application in their final evidence. It is usually the case that the final analysis and recommendation from the guardian will be a composite report incorporating consideration of the placement order application, together with the original care order application.

## WELFARE TEST

**29.40** When the court considers making a placement order, it must consider the welfare checklist contained in s 1(4) of the ACA 2002.

**29.41** It is important to remember that s 1(6) ACA02 specifies that:

> 'The court or adoption agency must always consider the whole range of powers available to it in the child's case (whether under this Act or the Children Act 1989); and the court must not make any order under this Act unless it considers that making the order would be better for the child than not doing so.'

**29.42** In *Re B-S (Children)*, the President provided a clear outline for courts when considering a care plan for adoption. This case followed the Supreme Court's decision in *Re B (A Child)* and highlighted the Court of Appeal's concern as to how matters involving adoption had been dealt with following four cases being referred to the Court of Appeal within the last ten days of July 2013.

**29.43** The President emphasised the remarks of Baroness Hale in *Re B*:[16]

> 'The language used in *Re B* is striking. Different words and phrases are used, but the message is clear. Orders contemplating non-consensual adoption – care orders with a plan for adoption, placement orders and adoption orders – are "a very extreme thing, a last resort", only to be made where "nothing else will do", where "no other course [is] possible in [the child's] interests", they are "the most extreme option", a "last resort – when all else fails", to be made "only in exceptional circumstances and where motivated by overriding requirements pertaining to the child's welfare, in short, where nothing else will do": see *Re B* paras 74, 76, 77, 82, 104, 130, 135, 145, 198, 215.'

**29.44** He continued, highlighting the considerations of McFarlane J in *Re G*:[17]

> 'A process which acknowledges that long-term public care, and in particular adoption contrary to the will of a parent, is "the most draconian option", yet does not engage with the very detail of that option which renders it "draconian" cannot be a full or effective process of evaluation.'

**29.45** The term 'nothing else will do' should not be considered in isolation. McFarlane LJ in *Re W (A Child)* said:[18]

> 'The phrase is meaningless, and potentially dangerous, if it is applied as some freestanding, shortcut test divorced from, or even in place of, an overall evaluation of the child's welfare. Used properly, as Baroness Hale explained, the phrase "nothing else will do" is no more, nor less, than a useful distillation of the

---

[16] *Re BS (Children)* [2013] EWCA Civ 1146 at [22].
[17] *Re BS (Children)* [2013] EWCA Civ 1146 at [41].
[18] *Re W (A Child)* [2016] EWCA Civ 793 at [68].

proportionality and necessity test as embodied in the ECHR and reflected in the need to afford paramount consideration to the welfare of the child throughout her lifetime.'

**29.46** It is clear then, that the court must consider all other possibilities before proposing adoption, in order to ensure that no lesser order that will preserve family ties, is available.

## PARENTAL CONSENT

**29.47** In accordance with s 21(3) of the ACA 2002:

> 'The court may only make a placement order if, in the case of each parent or guardian of the child, the court is satisfied –
> 
> (a) that the parent or guardian has consented to the child being placed for adoption with any prospective adopters who may be chosen by the local authority and has not withdrawn the consent, or
> (b) that the parent's or guardian's consent should be dispensed with.
> 
> This subsection is subject to section 52 (parental etc. consent).'

### *Dispensing with the consent of a parent*

**29.48** If the court must determine whether a parent's consent to a placement order should be dispensed with, the court must undertake a two-stage test. First, the court must consider whether adoption is in the child's best interests; and if so, whether it is necessary to dispense with a parent's consent to enable the order to be made.

**29.49** The first part of the test which considers whether adoption is in the best interest of the child, is discussed above. The second part must be considered in light of the welfare checklist at s 1(4) of the ACA 2002, the child's welfare throughout their life.

**29.50** Wall LJ in *Re P (A Child)*, summarised the task faced by the court when considering whether to dispense with a parent's consent to the placement of a child for adoption. He said:[19]

> 'In the first place, section 1(2) of the 2002 Act, in contrast to section 1(1) of the 1989 Act, requires a judge considering dispensing with parental consent in accordance with section 52(1)(b) to focus on the child's welfare "throughout his life". This emphasises that adoption, unlike other forms of order made under the 1989 Act, is something with lifelong implications. In other words, a judge exercising his powers under section 52(1)(b) has to be satisfied that the child's welfare now, throughout the rest of his childhood, into adulthood and indeed throughout his life, requires that he or she be adopted. Secondly, and reinforcing this point, it is important to bear in mind the more extensive "welfare checklist" to be found in section 1(4) of the 2002 Act as compared with the "welfare checklist"

---

[19] *Re P (A Child)* [2008] EWCA Civ 535 at [128].

in section 1(3) of the 1989 Act; in particular, the provisions of section 1(4)(c) – which specifically directs attention to the consequences for the child "throughout his life" – and section 1(4)(f). This all feeds into the ultimate question under section 52(1)(b): does the child's welfare throughout his life require adoption as opposed to something short of adoption?'

**29.51** The test as to whether adoption is in the best interest of the child, is discussed above. However, test as to whether it is in the child's best interest that the parents' consent is dispensed with is considered in light of the welfare checklist at s 1(4) ACA 2002, the child's interest throughout their life.

# CHAPTER 30

# APPEALS

## GENERAL PRINCIPLES

**30.1** The procedure for an application to appeal a decision of a lower court is contained in FPR 2010, Pt 30. Rule 30.12 provides:

'(1) Every appeal will be limited to a review of the decision of the lower court unless –

(a) an enactment or practice direction makes different provision for a particular category of appeal; or
(b) the court considers that in the circumstances of an individual appeal it would be in the interests of justice to hold a re-hearing.

(2) Unless it orders otherwise, the appeal court will not receive –

(a) oral evidence; or
(b) evidence which was not before the lower court.

(3) The appeal court will allow an appeal where the decision of the lower court was –

(a) wrong; or
(b) unjust because of a serious procedural or other irregularity in the proceedings in the lower court.

(4) The appeal court may draw any inference of fact which it considers justified on the evidence.

(5) At the hearing of the appeal a party may not rely on a matter not contained in that party's appeal notice unless the appeal court gives permission.'

Civil Procedure Rules 1998 ('CPR 1998') Pt 52 also deals with the procedure for appeals and there are mirror provisions in CPR 1998, r 52.21.

**30.2** The decision for an appeal court is whether the decision made was wrong on the basis of the information and evidence that the lower court had before it when making the decision. The court is able to direct that further evidence is heard and this is discussed below.

## Which court?

**30.3** FPR 2010, PD30A provides a helpful table outlining whether permission is need to appeal and to what court an appeal should be made.

| Decision of judge sitting in the family court | Permission generally required (subject to exception in rules of court, for example, no permission required to appeal against a committal order) | Appeal to |
| --- | --- | --- |
| 1. A bench of – two or three lay magistrates; or a lay justice | No | a judge of circuit judge level sitting in the family court; a judge of High Court judge level sitting in the family court where a Designated Family Judge or a judge of High Court Judge level considers that the appeal would raise an important point of principle or practice. (NB a judge of High Court judge level may hear the appeal in interests of effective and efficient use of local judicial resource and the resource of the High Court bench) |
| 2. A judge of district judge level (except the Senior District Judge of the Family Division or a District Judge (PRFD) in proceedings for a financial remedy) | Yes | As above |
| 3. District Judge (PRFD) in proceedings for financial remedy | Yes | Judge of High Court judge level sitting in the family court |
| 4. Senior District Judge of the Family Division in proceedings for financial remedy | Yes | Judge of High Court judge level sitting in the family court |
| 4A. Circuit judge or Recorder, except where para 5 of this table applies. | Yes | High Court Judge (sitting in the High Court) |

| Decision of judge sitting in the family court | Permission generally required (subject to exception in rules of court, for example, no permission required to appeal against a committal order) | Appeal to |
|---|---|---|
| 5. Circuit judge or Recorder, where the appeal is from:<br>(a) a decision or order in proceedings under—<br>(i) Part 4 or 5 of, or para 19(1) of Sch 2 to, the Children Act 1989; or<br>(ii) the Adoption and Children Act 2002;<br>(b) a decision or order in exercise of the court's jurisdiction in relation to contempt of court, where that decision or order was made in, or in connection with, proceedings of a type referred to in sub-para (a); or<br>(c) a decision or order made on appeal to the family court. | Yes | Court of Appeal |
| 6. Costs Judge | Yes | Judge of High Court judge level sitting in the family court |
| 7. Judge of High Court judge level | Yes | Court of Appeal |
| 8. Any other judge of the family court not referred to in paragraphs 1 to 7 of | Yes | Court of Appeal |

**30.4** There are further provisions in PD30A for appeals that are to go before the family court rather than the Court of Appeal, such appeals being heard by a High Court Judge as set out below;

| Decision of judge | Permission generally required (subject to exception in rules of court, for example, no permission required to appeal against a committal order) | Appeal to |
|---|---|---|
| 1. District Judge of the High Court; or a deputy district judge appointed under s 102 of the Senior Courts Act 1981 | Yes | High Court Judge |

| Decision of judge | Permission generally required (subject to exception in rules of court, for example, no permission required to appeal against a committal order) | Appeal to |
| --- | --- | --- |
| 2. The Senior District Judge of the Family Division; District Judge of the PRFD; or a person appointed to act as deputy for a District Judge of the PRFD or to act as a temporary additional officer for such office | Yes | High Court Judge |
| 3. Costs judge; or a person appointed to act as deputy for a costs judge who is a taxing master of the senior courts or to act as a temporary additional officer for such office | Yes | High Court Judge |
| 4. Judge of the High Court (including a person acting as a judge of the High Court in accordance with s 9(1) or s 9(4) of the Senior Courts Act 1981) | Yes | Court of Appeal |

**30.5** It is possible for a judge to transfer the appeal to the Court of Appeal in the event that it is felt that the appeal raises an important point of practice or if there is another compelling reason.

## PROCEDURE

**30.6** There are several steps that must be taken in the event that it is felt that a decision of a court should be appealed. When a decision is made by the court a judgment will be handed down, either orally on an extempore basis (immediately), or on a reserved basis where the court hands down the decision and reasons following a period of consideration. The judgment is essential as it must give the reasons for the decision made and the evidence that was read and heard in order to reach the decision. A transcript of this judgment will be needed when applying to appeal a decision so that the appeal court will be able to consider the reasoning of the judge when looking at the decision itself.

**30.7** Unless directed otherwise, an appeal does not operate as a stay of any order or decision made by a lower court, see below.[1]

---

[1] FPR 2010, r 30.8.

## Clarification

**30.8** In the event that it is felt that the judgment is deficient it is essential that the judge is asked for clarification. In *Re A and L (Fact-finding Hearing Extempore Judgment)*[2] Munby LJ, as he then was, outlined:[3]

> 'First, it is the responsibility of the advocate, whether or not invited to do so by the judge, to raise with the judge and draw to his attention any material omission in the judgment, any genuine query or ambiguity which arises on the judgment, and any perceived lack of reasons or other perceived deficiency in the judge's reasoning process.
>
> Second, and whether or not the advocates have raised the point with the judge, where permission is sought from the trial judge to appeal on the ground of lack of reasons, the judge should consider whether his judgment is defective for lack of reasons and, if he concludes that it is, he should set out to remedy the defect by the provision of additional reasons.'

**30.9** If neither clarification has been sort or the judge has not sought to consider the judgment, Munby LJ provided:[4]

> '... the court can either proceed to deal with the appeal on the basis of the judgment as it was, or remit the case to the trial judge for additional reasons or clarification to be provided, usually with an indication of the distinct areas where clarification is required.'

**30.10** If a party's advocate is of the view that there is a material omission from the judgment or written reasons, the advocate should give the lower court the opportunity to consider whether there is an omission.[5]

**30.11** If a judgment was reserved to be delivered at a later time, but the judge gives an indication of the decision, the judge is entitled to change their mind about the value of some of the evidence before delivering the judgment.[6] This re-evaluation of the evidence must be dealt with in the judgment.

## Permission to appeal

**30.12** Other than a decision made by lay magistrates or a lay justice, permission should be sought by way of oral application at the hearing at which the decision has been made for permission to appeal.[7] Where the lower court refuses an application for permission, an application can then be made in an appeal notice.[8]

---

[2] *Re A and L (Fact-finding Hearing Extempore Judgment)* [2012] 1 FLR 1243, CA.
[3] *Re A and L (Fact-finding Hearing Extempore Judgment)* [2012] 1 FLR 1243, CA at [16], [17].
[4] *Re A and L (Fact-finding Hearing Extempore Judgment)* [2012] 1 FLR 1243, CA at [18].
[5] FPR 2010, PD30A, para 4.6.
[6] *Re R (Care Proceedings: Appeal)* [2013] 1 FLR 467, CA.
[7] FPR 2010, PD30A, para 2.2.
[8] FPR 2010, r 30.3(3).

**30.13** Where an application is made for permission to appeal the lower court must consider whether there is a material omission from the judgment. If the application for permission is made to the appeal court, the appeal court must consider whether there is a material omission and if so it may remit the matter back to the lower court for this to be addressed.[9] The normal procedure is for remittal to the lower court with a list of questions.[10]

**30.14** If the application for permission to appeal is not made at the hearing at which the judgment was given, handed down or at a subsequent hearing listed for the purposes of the consideration of the judgment, the lower court no longer has jurisdiction to grant the permission. After this time an application will have to be made to the Court of Appeal.[11]

**30.15** In accordance with FPR 2010, r 39.3(7), permission to appeal may only be given where:

> '(a) the court considers that the appeal would have a real prospect of success; or
> (b) there is some other compelling reason why the appeal should be heard.'

**30.16** If an application is made to the Court of Appeal, it is usual for this application to be considered on paper. If this application is refused, it is then possible for the applicant to request an oral hearing. The respondent need not attend the oral hearing for permission to appeal and, if refused, the application cannot be renewed.

## Time limitation

**30.17** There are strict time limitations in place governing the time by which an appellant can make an application to appeal a decision of the court.

**30.18** FPR 2010, r 30.4(2) provides:

> '(2) Subject to paragraph (3), the appellant must file the appellant's notice at the appeal court within –
> (a) such period as may be directed by the lower court (which may be longer or shorter than the period referred to in sub-paragraph (b)); or
> (b) where the court makes no such direction, 21 days after the date of the decision of the lower court against which the appellant wishes to appeal.'

**30.19** Paragraph 3 provides:

> '(3) Where the appeal is against –
> (a) a case management decision; or
> (b) an order under section 38(1) of the 1989 Act,
>
> the appellant must file the appellant's notice within 7 days beginning with the date

---

[9] FPR 2010, PD30A, paras 4.7–4.9.
[10] Re A and L (Children) [2012] 1 FLR 134, CA.
[11] Monroe v Hopkins [2017] EWHC 645 (QB).

of the decision of the lower court.'

**30.20** If the court has provided its decision but reserves the reasons for its judgment until a later date, it should fix a period for filing the appellant's notice to take the delay into account.[12]

**30.21** If the time has passed, it is still possible to file an appellant's notice, but an application must be made to do so 'out of time'. FPR 2010, r 30.7 provides:

'(1) An application to vary the time limit for filing an appeal notice must be made to the appeal court.

(2) The parties may not agree to extend any date or time limit set by –

(a) these rules;
(b) Practice Direction 30A; or
(c) an order of the appeal court or the lower court.

(Rule 4.1(3)(a) provides that the court may extend or shorten the time for compliance with a rule, practice direction or court order (even if an application for extension is made after the time for compliance has expired).)

(Rule 4.1(3)(c) provides that the court may adjourn or bring forward a hearing.)'

**30.22** An application for an extension of time must be made in the appellant's notice with reasons given for the delay. When considering an application to allow an appeal out of time, the court will consider the merits of the proposed appeal, especially when the grounds for appeal appear either very strong or very weak.[13]

**30.23** The respondent to an application for an extension of time has the right to be heard on this application. However, if it is found that a respondent has unreasonably opposed the extension of time, they are at risk of being ordered to pay the costs of the applicant.[14]

# Application

## Grounds of appeal

**30.24** It is not possible for a decision of the court to be appealed simply because it is not the decision that was wanted. As set out above, the grounds of appeal are set out in FPR 2010, r 30.12(3) and CPR 1998, r 52.21:

'The appeal court will allow an appeal where the decision of the lower court was –

(a) wrong; or
(b) unjust because of a serious procedural or other irregularity in the proceedings in the lower court.'

---

[12] FPR 2010, PD30A, para 5.37.
[13] *Re H (Children) (Application to Extend Time: Merits of Proposed Appeal)* [2016] 1 FLR 952.
[14] FPR 2010, PD30A, paras 5.4–5.6.

**30.25** The decision for an appeal court is whether the decision made was wrong on the basis of the information and evidence that the lower court had before it when making the decision.

**30.26** The court hearing the appeal will not consider evidence that was not available before the lower court unless it directs otherwise.[15] The court will also not consider any matter that isn't contained in that party's appeal notice unless the appeal court gives permission.[16]

## Appellants notice

**30.27** FPR 2010, PD30A, para 5.1 provides:

> 'An appellant's notice must be filed and served in all cases. Where an application for permission to appeal is made to the appeal court it must be applied for in the appellant's notice.'

**30.28** The appellant's notice must be completed on form N161 unless the appeal is to the Family Division of the High Court.[17] If an appeal is to the Family Division of the High Court it must be completed on form FP161.

**30.29** The grounds for appeal provided in the notice are of the upmost importance as it is not possible for the court to consider any matters that are not contained in the appeal notice. When preparing the grounds, the circumstances upon which an appeal will be allowed should form the basis of the information contained in the grounds. FPR 2010, PD30A, para 3.2 provides:

> 'The grounds of appeal should –
> 
> (a) set out clearly the reasons why rule 30.12 (3)(a) or (b) is said to apply; and
> (b) specify in respect of each ground, whether the ground raises an appeal on a point of law or is an appeal against a finding of fact.'

**30.30** As set out above, r 30.12 provides:

> '(3) The appeal court will allow an appeal where the decision of the lower court was –
> 
> (a) wrong; or
> (b) unjust because of a serious procedural or other irregularity in the proceedings in the lower court.'

**30.31** Along with the appellant's notice, the following documents must be filed with an appeal bundle where an appeal is made to the family court:[18]

- one copy of the appellant's notice for each of the respondents;

---

[15] FPR 2010, r 30.12(2).
[16] FPR 2010, r 30.12(5).
[17] FPR 2010, PD5A.
[18] FPR 2010, PD30A, para 5.8.

- one copy of the appellant's skeleton argument for each of the respondents;
- any witness statements or affidavits in support of any application included in the appellant's notice.

**30.32** The appeal bundle in the family court must contain:[19]

- a sealed or stamped copy of the appellant's notice;
- a sealed or stamped copy of the order being appealed, or a copy of the notice of the making of an order;
- a copy of any order giving or refusing permission to appeal, together with a copy of the court's reasons for allowing or refusing permission to appeal;
- any affidavit or witness statement filed in support of any application included in the appellant's notice;
- where the appeal is against a consent order, a statement setting out the change in circumstances since the order was agreed or other circumstances justifying a review or re-hearing;
- a copy of the appellant's skeleton argument;
- a transcript or note of judgment or, in a magistrates' court, written reasons for the court's decision (see para 5.23), and in cases where permission to appeal was given by the lower court or is not required those parts of any transcript of evidence which are directly relevant to any question at issue on the appeal;
- the application form;
- any application notice (or case management documentation) relevant to the subject of the appeal;
- any other documents which the appellant reasonably considers necessary to enable the appeal court to reach its decision on the hearing of the application or appeal; and
- such other documents as the court may direct.

**30.33** In accordance with FPR 2010, PD30A, para 5.10, only documents directly relevant to the appeal can be included in the appeal bundle. Any document that is not relevant must be left out of the bundle.

**30.34** Where to appeal is to the High Court the appellant must file the following documents, in the sequence set out below, in the appeal bundle:[20]

- a sealed or stamped copy of the appellant's notice (including the grounds of appeal);
- a sealed or stamped copy of the order being appealed (or a copy of the notice of the making of an order);
- a transcript or note of the judgment (see also paras 5.23 and 5.24);

---

[19] FPR 2010, PD30A, para 5.9.
[20] FPR 2010, PD30A, para 5.10A.

- copies of any documents specifically referred to in the judgment;
- a copy of the appellant's skeleton argument (see also paras 5.14 and 5.15).

**30.35** No further documents other than the above may be filed without an order of the High Court. In addition to the appeal bundle the appellant must file in duplicate:

- One copy of the appellant's notice for each of the respondents.
- One copy of the appellant's skeleton argument for each of the respondents.

## Skeleton argument

**30.36** The appellant's notice must be accompanied by a skeleton argument.[21] The skeleton argument may be included in the body of the appellant's notice or as a standalone document. If it is impracticable for the appellant's skeleton argument to be filed with the notice it must be filed and served within 14 days of the filing of the notice.[22] If the appeal is in relation to case management and the skeleton argument is not filed with the appellant's notice, it must be filed as soon as practicable but in any event not less than 3 days before the hearing of the appeal.[23]

**30.37** FPR 2010, PD30A provides clearly what must be included in a skeleton argument that is to be provided with the appellant's notice:

> '5.16 A skeleton argument must contain a numbered list of the points which the party wishes to make. These should both define and confine the areas of controversy. Each point should be stated as concisely as the nature of the case allows.
>
> 5.17 A numbered point must be followed by a reference to any document on which the party wishes to rely.
>
> 5.18 A skeleton argument must state, in respect of each authority cited –
>
> (a) the proposition of law that the authority demonstrates; and
> (b) the parts of the authority (identified by page or paragraph references) that support the proposition.
>
> 5.19 If more than one authority is cited in support of a given proposition, the skeleton argument must briefly state the reason for taking that course.
>
> 5.20 The statement referred to in paragraph 5.19 should not materially add to the length of the skeleton argument but should be sufficient to demonstrate, in the context of the argument –
>
> (a) the relevance of the authority or authorities to that argument; and
> (b) that the citation is necessary for a proper presentation of that argument.'

---

[21] In accordance with FPR 2010, PD30A, para 5.13.
[22] FPR 2010, PD30A, para 5.14.
[23] FPR 2010, PD30A, para 5.14A.

**30.38** It is important to remember that if a skeleton argument does not comply with the requirements set out above, or was not filed in time, the cost of the preparation of the document cannot be claimed when the costs are assessed at the end of the appeal.[24]

**30.39** In addition to all of the above, the appellant must consider what further information would assist the appeal court and prepare, for example, a list of persons who feature in the case, a chronology or glossary of terms.[25] It is likely that a chronology will be required in most appeal cases.

**30.40** If the appellant is a litigant in person, it is not necessary for them to file a skeleton argument, but they should be encouraged to do so.[26]

## Respondent's notice

**30.41** A respondent who wishes to appeal, or who wishes to ask the appeal court to uphold the order of the lower court for reasons different from or additional to those given by the lower court, must file a respondent's notice.[27] If a respondent does not file a notice they will not be entitled to rely on any other reasons than those relied upon by the lower court.

**30.42** The time limits for filing a respondent's notice are set out in FPR 2010, r 30.5(4) and (5), the time limit being within 14 days of notification of the permission to appeal being granted, or if no permission is required, within 14 days of notification of the appeal.[28] The court may also direct an alternative date for the filing of the notice.

**30.43** Where an extension of time is required the extension must be requested in the respondent's notice and the reasons why the respondent failed to act within the specified time must be included.[29]

**30.44** The respondent must file a skeleton argument for the court in all cases where the respondent proposes to address arguments to the court. As with the appellant's skeleton argument, it may be included within a respondent's notice or as a standalone document.[30] If a skeleton argument is not filed with the notice, it must be filed within 14 days of the filing of the notice.

**30.45** In appeals against case management decisions, where the respondent's skeleton argument cannot accompany the respondent's notice, or a respondent does not file a respondent's notice but files a skeleton argument, the skeleton

---

[24] FPR 2010, PD30A, para 5.21.
[25] FPR 2010, PD30A, para 5.22.
[26] FPR 2010, PD30A para 5.15.
[27] FPR 2010, r 30.5(2) and PD30A, para 7.2.
[28] FPR 2010, r 30.5(5).
[29] FPR 2010, PD30A, para 7.6.
[30] FPR 2010, PD30A, para 7.7.

argument must be filed as soon as practicable or as directed by the court, but in any event not less than 3 days before the hearing of the appeal.[31]

**30.46** Again as for the appellant, if the respondent is not represented they are not required to file a skeleton argument but are encouraged to do so in order to assist the court.

**30.47** In accordance with FPR 2010, PD30A, para 7.12, a respondent's skeleton argument must conform to the directions at paras 5.16–5.22, set out above, with any necessary modifications. It should, where appropriate, answer the arguments set out in the appellant's skeleton argument.

**30.48** The respondent must file the following documents with the respondent's notice in every case:

- two additional copies of the respondent's notice for the appeal court; and
- one copy each for the appellant, any other respondents and any persons referred to in para 5.39.[32]

**30.49** The respondent may file a skeleton argument with the respondent's notice and:

- where doing so must file two copies; and
- where not doing so must comply with para 7.8.[33]

**30.50** If the respondent considers documents in addition to those filed by the appellant to be necessary to enable the appeal court to reach its decision on the appeal and wishes to rely on those documents, any amendments to the appeal bundle should be agreed with the appellant if possible.[34] It is only if the representatives are unable to agree the bundle that the respondent prepares a supplemental bundle.

**30.51** In accordance with FPR 2010, PD30A, para 7.19 the respondent must serve:

- the respondent's notice;
- the skeleton argument (if any); and
- the supplemental bundle (if any), on
- the appellant; and
- any other respondent;

---

[31] FPR 2010, PD30A, para 7.9A.
[32] FPR 2010, PD30A, para 7.14.
[33] FPR 2010, PD30A, para 7.15.
[34] FPR 2010, PD30A, para 7.16.

## Orders pending an appeal

**30.52** Unless directed otherwise, an appeal does not operate as a stay of any order or decision made by a lower court.[35]

**30.53** Section 40 CA 1989 gives the court the power to make an order pending an appeal. There are a number of scenarios that the court may face and s 40 provides for orders that the court may make in such circumstances:

'(1) Where –

    (a)    a court dismisses an application for a care order; and

    (b)    at the time when the court dismisses the application, the child concerned is the subject of an interim care order,

the court may make a care order with respect to the child to have effect subject to such directions (if any) as the court may see fit to include in the order.

(2) Where –

    (a)    a court dismisses an application for a care order, or an application for a supervision order; and

    (b)    at the time when the court dismisses the application, the child concerned is the subject of an interim supervision order,

the court may make a supervision order with respect to the child to have effect subject to such directions (if any) as the court may see fit to include in the order.

(3) Where a court grants an application to discharge a care order or supervision order, it may order that –

    (a)    its decision is not to have effect; or

    (b)    the care order, or supervision order, is to continue to have effect but subject to such directions as the court sees fit to include in the order.'

**30.54** If the court makes any orders in accordance with the above provisions, the orders shall have effect for the period of time specified in the court order. This period of time must not exceed the appeal period.[36] Section 40(6) CA 1989 provides that the 'appeal period' means the period between the making of the decision and the determination of the appeal. This also includes the period during which an appeal may be made against the decision.

**30.55** In the event that the lower court refused to make a care order pending the appeal, the appeal court has no power to make the care order.[37]

**30.56** The lower court has the power to grant a stay and any application should be made to that court. Where an application is made to stay the operation of an interim care order, that would result in a child being removed

---

[35] FPR 2010, r 30.8.
[36] CA 1989, s 40(4).
[37] *Croydon London Borough Council v A (No 2)* [1992] 2 FLR 348.

from the care of the parents, the court making the order should allow a short and reasonable stay if there is no immediate danger.[38]

---

[38] *Re T (Interim Care Order: Removal of Children Where No Immediate Emergency)* [2016] 1 FLR 347.

# APPENDIX 1

# CHILDREN ACT 1989

## PART I
## INTRODUCTORY

**1 Welfare of the child**

(1) When a court determines any question with respect to –

(a) the upbringing of a child; or
(b) the administration of a child's property or the application of any income arising from it,

the child's welfare shall be the court's paramount consideration.

(2) In any proceedings in which any question with respect to the upbringing of a child arises, the court shall have regard to the general principle that any delay in determining the question is likely to prejudice the welfare of the child.

(2A) A court, in the circumstances mentioned in subsection (4)(a) or (7), is as respects each parent within subsection (6)(a) to presume, unless the contrary is shown, that involvement of that parent in the life of the child concerned will further the child's welfare.

(2B) In subsection (2A) 'involvement' means involvement of some kind, either direct or indirect, but not any particular division of a child's time.

(3) In the circumstances mentioned in subsection (4), a court shall have regard in particular to –

(a) the ascertainable wishes and feelings of the child concerned (considered in the light of his age and understanding);
(b) his physical, emotional and educational needs;
(c) the likely effect on him of any change in his circumstances;
(d) his age, sex, background and any characteristics of his which the court considers relevant;
(e) any harm which he has suffered or is at risk of suffering;
(f) how capable each of his parents, and any other person in relation to whom the court considers the question to be relevant, is of meeting his needs;
(g) the range of powers available to the court under this Act in the proceedings in question.

(4) The circumstances are that –

(a) the court is considering whether to make, vary or discharge a section 8 order, and the making, variation or discharge of the order is opposed by any party to the proceedings; or
(b) the court is considering whether to make, vary or discharge a special guardianship order or an order under Part IV.

(5) Where a court is considering whether or not to make one or more orders under this Act with respect to a child, it shall not make the order or any of the orders unless it considers that doing so would be better for the child than making no order at all.

(6) In subsection (2A) 'parent' means parent of the child concerned; and, for the purposes of that subsection, a parent of the child concerned –

(a) is within this paragraph if that parent can be involved in the child's life in a way that does not put the child at risk of suffering harm; and
(b) is to be treated as being within paragraph (a) unless there is some evidence before the court in the particular proceedings to suggest that involvement of that parent in the child's life would put the child at risk of suffering harm whatever the form of the involvement.

(7) The circumstances referred to are that the court is considering whether to make an order under section 4(1)(c) or (2A) or 4ZA(1)(c) or (5) (parental responsibility of parent other than mother).

**Amendments**—Adoption and Children Act 2002, s 115; Children and Families Act 2014, s 11.

\* \* \*

## PART II
## ORDERS WITH RESPECT TO CHILDREN IN FAMILY PROCEEDINGS

*General*

### 8 Child arrangements orders and other orders with respect to children

(1) In this Act –

'child arrangements order' means an order regulating arrangements relating to any of the following –
   (a) with whom a child is to live, spend time or otherwise have contact, and
   (b) when a child is to live, spend time or otherwise have contact with any person;

…

'a prohibited steps order' means an order that no step which could be taken by a parent in meeting his parental responsibility for a child, and which is of a kind specified in the order, shall be taken by any person without the consent of the court;

… and

'a specific issue order' means an order giving directions for the purpose of determining a specific question which has arisen, or which may arise, in connection with any aspect of parental responsibility for a child.

(2) In this Act 'a section 8 order' means any of the orders mentioned in subsection (1) and any order varying or discharging such an order.

(3) For the purposes of this Act 'family proceedings' means any proceedings –

(a) under the inherent jurisdiction of the High Court in relation to children; and
(b) under the enactments mentioned in subsection (4),

but does not include proceedings on an application for leave under section 100(3).

(4) The enactments are –

(a) Parts I, II and IV of this Act;
(b) the Matrimonial Causes Act 1973;
(ba) Schedule 5 to the Civil Partnership Act 2004;
(c) (*repealed*)
(d) the Adoption Act and Children Act 2002;
(e) the Domestic Proceedings and Magistrates' Courts Act 1978;
(ea) Schedule 6 to the Civil Partnership Act 2004;
(f) (*repealed*)
(g) Part III of the Matrimonial and Family Proceedings Act 1984;
(h) the Family Law Act 1996.
(i) sections 11 and 12 of the Crime and Disorder Act 1998.

Amendments—Family Law Act 1996, s 66(1), (3), Sch 8, para 60(1), Sch 10; Crime and Disorder Act 1998, s 119, Sch 8, para 68; Adoption and Children 2002, Sch 3, para 55; Civil Partnership Act 2004, s 261(1), Sch 27, para 129(1)–(3); Children and Families 2014, ss 9, 12, Sch 2.

## 9 Restrictions on making section 8 orders

(1) No court shall make any section 8 order, other than a child arrangements order to which subsection (6B) applies, with respect to a child who is in the care of a local authority.

(2) No application may be made by a local authority for a child arrangements order and no court shall make such an order in favour of a local authority.

(3) A person who is, or was at any time within the last six months, a local authority foster parent of a child may not apply for leave to apply for a section 8 order with respect to the child unless –

(a) he has the consent of the authority;
(b) he is a relative of the child; or
(c) the child has lived with him for at least one year preceding the application.

(4) (*repealed*)

(5) No court shall exercise its powers to make a specific issue order or prohibited steps order –

(a) with a view to achieving a result which could be achieved by making a child arrangements order or an order under section 51A of the Adoption and Children Act 2002 (post-adoption contact); or
(b) in any way which is denied to the High Court (by section 100(2)) in the exercise of its inherent jurisdiction with respect to children.

(6) No court shall make a section 8 order which is to have effect for a period which will end after the child has reached the age of sixteen unless it is satisfied that the circumstances of the case are exceptional.

(6A) Subsection (6) does not apply to a child arrangements order to which subsection (6B) applies.

(6B) This subsection applies to a child arrangements order if the arrangements regulated by the order relate only to either or both of the following –

(a) with whom the child concerned is to live, and
(b) when the child is to live with any person.

(7) No court shall make any section 8 order, other than one varying or discharging such an order, with respect to a child who has reached the age of sixteen unless it is satisfied that the circumstances of the case are exceptional.

**Amendments**— Adoption and Children 2002, ss 113, 114(2); Children and Young Persons Act 2008, s 37(1); Children and Families 2014, ss 9, 12, Sch 2.

## 10 Power of court to make section 8 orders

(1) In any family proceedings in which a question arises with respect to the welfare of any child, the court may make a section 8 order with respect to the child if –

(a) an application for the order has been made by a person who –
   (i) is entitled to apply for a section 8 order with respect to the child; or
   (ii) has obtained the leave of the court to make the application; or
(b) the court considers that the order should be made even though no such application has been made.

(2) The court may also make a section 8 order with respect to any child on the application of a person who –

(a) is entitled to apply for a section 8 order with respect to the child; or
(b) has obtained the leave of the court to make the application.

(3) This section is subject to the restrictions imposed by section 9.

(4) The following persons are entitled to apply to the court for any section 8 order with respect to a child –

(a) any parent, guardian or special guardian of the child;
(aa any person who by virtue of section 4A has parental responsibility for the child;
(b) any person who is named, in a child arrangements order that is in force with respect to the child, as a person with whom the child is to live.

(5) The following persons are entitled to apply for a child arrangements order with respect to a child –

- (a) any party to a marriage (whether or not subsisting) in relation to whom the child is a child of the family;
- (aa) any civil partner in a civil partnership (whether or not subsisting) in relation to whom the child is a child of the family;
- (b) any person with whom the child has lived for a period of at least three years;
- (c) any person –
    - (i) in any case where a child arrangements order in force with respect to the child regulates arrangements relating to with whom the child is to live or when the child is to live with any person, has the consent of each of the persons named in the order as a person with whom the child is to live;
    - (ii) in any case where the child is in the care of a local authority, has the consent of that authority; or
    - (iii) in any other case, has the consent of each of those (if any) who have parental responsibility for the child;
- (d) any person who has parental responsibility for the child by virtue of provision made under section 12(2A).

(5A) A local authority foster parent is entitled to apply for a child arrangements order to which subsection (5C) applies with respect to a child if the child has lived with him for a period of at least one year immediately preceding the application.

(5B) A relative of a child is entitled to apply for a child arrangements order to which subsection (5C) applies with respect to the child if the child has lived with the relative for a period of at least one year immediately preceding the application.

(5C) This subsection applies to a child arrangements order if the arrangements regulated by the order relate only to either or both of the following–

- (a) with whom the child concerned is to live, and
- (b) when the child is to live with any person.

(6) A person who would not otherwise be entitled (under the previous provisions of this section) to apply for the variation or discharge of a section 8 order shall be entitled to do so if –

- (a) the order was made on his application; or
- (b) in the case of a child arrangements order, he is named in provisions of the order regulating arrangements relating to –
    - (i) with whom the child concerned is to spend time or otherwise have contact, or
    - (ii) when the child is to spend time or otherwise have contact with any person.

(7) Any person who falls within a category of person prescribed by rules of court is entitled to apply for any such section 8 order as may be prescribed in relation to that category of person.

(7A) If a special guardianship order is in force with respect to a child, an application for a child arrangements order to which subsection (7B) applies may only be made with respect to him, if apart from this subsection the leave of the court is not required, with such leave.

(7B) This subsection applies to a child arrangements order if the arrangements regulated by the order consist of, or include, arrangements which relate to either or both of the following –

(a) with whom the child concerned is to live, and
(b) when the child is to live with any person.

(8) Where the person applying for leave to make an application for a section 8 order is the child concerned, the court may only grant leave if it is satisfied that he has sufficient understanding to make the proposed application for the section 8 order.

(9) Where the person applying for leave to make an application for a section 8 order is not the child concerned, the court shall, in deciding whether or not to grant leave, have particular regard to –

(a) the nature of the proposed application for the section 8 order;
(b) the applicant's connection with the child;
(c) any risk there might be of that proposed application disrupting the child's life to such an extent that he would be harmed by it; and
(d) where the child is being looked after by a local authority –
   (i) the authority's plans for the child's future; and
   (ii) the wishes and feelings of the child's parents.

(10) The period of three years mentioned in subsection (5)(b) need not be continuous but must not have begun more than five years before, or ended more than three months before, the making of the application.

**Amendments**—Adoption and Children 2002, s 139(1), Sch 3, paras 54, 56; Civil Partnership Act 2004 2004, s 77; Children and Young Persons Act 2008, s 36; Children and Families 2014, s 12, Sch 2.

## 14A Special guardianship orders

(1) A 'special guardianship order' is an order appointing one or more individuals to be a child's 'special guardian' (or special guardians).

(2) A special guardian –

(a) must be aged eighteen or over; and
(b) must not be a parent of the child in question,

and subsections (3) to (6) are to be read in that light.

(3) The court may make a special guardianship order with respect to any child on the application of an individual who –

(a) is entitled to make such an application with respect to the child; or
(b) has obtained the leave of the court to make the application,

or on the joint application of more than one such individual.

(4) Section 9(3) applies in relation to an application for leave to apply for a special guardianship order as it applies in relation to an application for leave to apply for a section 8 order.

(5) The individuals who are entitled to apply for a special guardianship order with respect to a child are –

- (a) any guardian of the child;
- (b) any individual who is named in a child arrangements order as a person with whom the child is to live;
- (c) any individual listed in subsection (5)(b) or (c) of section 10 (as read with subsection (10) of that section);
- (d) a local authority foster parent with whom the child has lived for a period of at least one year immediately preceding the application;
- (e) a relative with whom the child has lived for a period of at least one year immediately preceding the application.

(6) The court may also make a special guardianship order with respect to a child in any family proceedings in which a question arises with respect to the welfare of the child if –

- (a) an application for the order has been made by an individual who falls within subsection (3)(a) or (b) (or more than one such individual jointly); or
- (b) the court considers that a special guardianship order should be made even though no such application has been made.

(7) No individual may make an application under subsection (3) or (6)(a) unless, before the beginning of the period of three months ending with the date of the application, he has given written notice of his intention to make the application –

- (a) if the child in question is being looked after by a local authority, to that local authority, or
- (b) otherwise, to the local authority in whose area the individual is ordinarily resident.

(8) On receipt of such a notice, the local authority must investigate the matter and prepare a report for the court dealing with –

- (a) the suitability of the applicant to be a special guardian;
- (b) such matters (if any) as may be prescribed by the Secretary of State; and
- (c) any other matter which the local authority consider to be relevant.

(9) The court may itself ask a local authority to conduct such an investigation and prepare such a report, and the local authority must do so.

(10) The local authority may make such arrangements as they see fit for any person to act on their behalf in connection with conducting an investigation or preparing a report referred to in subsection (8) or (9).

(11) The court may not make a special guardianship order unless it has received a report dealing with the matters referred to in subsection (8).

(12) Subsections (8) and (9) of section 10 apply in relation to special guardianship orders as they apply in relation to section 8 orders.

(13) This section is subject to section 29(5) and (6) of the Adoption and Children Act 2002.

**Amendments**—Inserted by Adoption and Children 2002, s 115. Amended by Children and Young Persons Act 2008, s 38; Children and Families 2014, s 12, Sch 2.

## 14B Special guardianship orders: making

(1) Before making a special guardianship order, the court must consider whether, if the order were made –

(a) a child arrangements order containing contact provision should also be made with respect to the child,
(b) any section 8 order in force with respect to the child should be varied or discharged,
(c) where provision contained in a child arrangements order made with respect to the child is not discharged, any enforcement order relating to that provision should be revoked, and
(d) where an activity direction has been made –
  (i) in proceedings for the making, variation or discharge of a child arrangements order with respect to the child, or
  (ii) in other proceedings that relate to such an order,
  that direction should be discharged.

(1A) In subsection (1) 'contact provision' means provision which regulates arrangements relating to –

(a) with whom a child is to spend time or otherwise have contact, or
(b) when a child is to spend time or otherwise have contact with any person;

but in paragraphs (a) and (b) a reference to spending time or otherwise having contact with a person is to doing that otherwise than as a result of living with the person.

(2) On making a special guardianship order, the court may also –

(a) give leave for the child to be known by a new surname;
(b) grant the leave required by section 14C(3)(b), either generally or for specified purposes.

**Amendments**—Inserted by Adoption and Children 2002, s 115. Amended by Children and Adoption Act 2006, s 15, Sch 2, paras 7, 8, Sch 3; Children and Families 2014, s 12, Sch 2.

### 14C Special guardianship orders: effect

(1) The effect of a special guardianship order is that while the order remains in force –

 (a) a special guardian appointed by the order has parental responsibility for the child in respect of whom it is made; and
 (b) subject to any other order in force with respect to the child under this Act, a special guardian is entitled to exercise parental responsibility to the exclusion of any other person with parental responsibility for the child (apart from another special guardian).

(2) Subsection (1) does not affect –

 (a) the operation of any enactment or rule of law which requires the consent of more than one person with parental responsibility in a matter affecting the child; or
 (b) any rights which a parent of the child has in relation to the child's adoption or placement for adoption.

(3) While a special guardianship order is in force with respect to a child, no person may –

 (a) cause the child to be known by a new surname; or
 (b) remove him from the United Kingdom,

without either the written consent of every person who has parental responsibility for the child or the leave of the court.

(4) Subsection (3)(b) does not prevent the removal of a child, for a period of less than three months, by a special guardian of his.

(5) If the child with respect to whom a special guardianship order is in force dies, his special guardian must take reasonable steps to give notice of that fact to –

 (a) each parent of the child with parental responsibility; and
 (b) each guardian of the child,

but if the child has more than one special guardian, and one of them has taken such steps in relation to a particular parent or guardian, any other special guardian need not do so as respects that parent or guardian.

(6) This section is subject to section 29(7) of the Adoption and Children Act 2002.

Amendments—Inserted by Adoption and Children 2002, s 115.

### 14D Special guardianship orders: variation and discharge

(1) The court may vary or discharge a special guardianship order on the application of –

 (a) the special guardian (or any of them, if there are more than one);
 (b) any parent or guardian of the child concerned;

(c) any individual who is named in a child arrangements order as a person with whom the child is to live;
(d) any individual not falling within any of paragraphs (a) to (c) who has, or immediately before the making of the special guardianship order had, parental responsibility for the child;
(e) the child himself; or
(f) a local authority designated in a care order with respect to the child.

(2) In any family proceedings in which a question arises with respect to the welfare of a child with respect to whom a special guardianship order is in force, the court may also vary or discharge the special guardianship order if it considers that the order should be varied or discharged, even though no application has been made under subsection (1).

(3) The following must obtain the leave of the court before making an application under subsection (1) –

(a) the child;
(b) any parent or guardian of his;
(c) any step-parent of his who has acquired, and has not lost, parental responsibility for him by virtue of section 4A;
(d) any individual falling within subsection (1)(d) who immediately before the making of the special guardianship order had, but no longer has, parental responsibility for him.

(4) Where the person applying for leave to make an application under subsection (1) is the child, the court may only grant leave if it is satisfied that he has sufficient understanding to make the proposed application under subsection (1).

(5) The court may not grant leave to a person falling within subsection (3)(b)(c) or (d) unless it is satisfied that there has been a significant change in circumstances since the making of the special guardianship order.

**Amendments**—Inserted by Adoption and Children 2002, s 115. Amended by Children and Families 2014, s 12, Sch 2.

## 14E Special guardianship orders: supplementary

(1) In proceedings in which any question of making, varying or discharging a special guardianship order arises, the court shall (in the light of any provision in rules of court that is of the kind mentioned in section 11(2)(a) or (b)) –

(a) draw up a timetable with a view to determining the question without delay; and
(b) give such directions as it considers appropriate for the purpose of ensuring, so far as is reasonably practicable, that the timetable is adhered to.

(2) Subsection (1) applies also in relation to proceedings in which any other question with respect to a special guardianship order arises.

(3) The power to make rules in subsection (2) of section 11 applies for the purposes of this section as it applies for the purposes of that.

(4) A special guardianship order, or an order varying one, may contain provisions which are to have effect for a specified period.

(5) Section 11(7) (apart from paragraph (c)) applies in relation to special guardianship orders and orders varying them as it applies in relation to section 8 orders.

**Amendments**—Inserted by Adoption and Children 2002, s 115. Amended by Children and Families 2014, s 13.

### 14F Special guardianship support services

(1) Each local authority must make arrangements for the provision within their area of special guardianship support services, which means –

- (a) counselling, advice and information; and
- (b) such other services as are prescribed,

in relation to special guardianship.

(2) The power to make regulations under subsection (1)(b) is to be exercised so as to secure that local authorities provide financial support.

(3) At the request of any of the following persons –

- (a) a child with respect to whom a special guardianship order is in force;
- (b) a special guardian;
- (c) a parent;
- (d) any other person who falls within a prescribed description,

a local authority may carry out an assessment of that person's needs for special guardianship support services (but, if the Secretary of State so provides in regulations, they must do so if he is a person of a prescribed description, or if his case falls within a prescribed description, or if both he and his case fall within prescribed descriptions).

(4) A local authority may, at the request of any other person, carry out an assessment of that person's needs for special guardianship support services.

(5) Where, as a result of an assessment, a local authority decide that a person has needs for special guardianship support services, they must then decide whether to provide any such services to that person.

(6) If –

- (a) a local authority decide to provide any special guardianship support services to a person, and
- (b) the circumstances fall within a prescribed description,

the local authority must prepare a plan in accordance with which special guardianship support services are to be provided to him, and keep the plan under review.

(7) The Secretary of State may by regulations make provision about assessments, preparing and reviewing plans, the provision of special guardianship support services in accordance with plans and reviewing the provision of special guardianship support services.

(8) The regulations may in particular make provision –

- (a) about the type of assessment which is to be carried out, or the way in which an assessment is to be carried out;
- (b) about the way in which a plan is to be prepared;
- (c) about the way in which, and the time at which, a plan or the provision of special guardianship support services is to be reviewed;
- (d) about the considerations to which a local authority are to have regard in carrying out an assessment or review or preparing a plan;
- (e) as to the circumstances in which a local authority may provide special guardianship support services subject to conditions (including conditions as to payment for the support or the repayment of financial support);
- (f) s to the consequences of conditions imposed by virtue of paragraph (e) not being met (including the recovery of any financial support provided);
- (g) as to the circumstances in which this section may apply to a local authority in respect of persons who are outside that local authority's area;
- (h) as to the circumstances in which a local authority may recover from another local authority the expenses of providing special guardianship support services to any person.

(9) A local authority may provide special guardianship support services (or any part of them) by securing their provision by –

- (a) another local authority; or
- (b) a person within a description prescribed in regulations of persons who may provide special guardianship support services,

and may also arrange with any such authority or person for that other authority or that person to carry out the local authority's functions in relation to assessments under this section.

(10) A local authority may carry out an assessment of the needs of any person for the purposes of this section at the same time as an assessment of his needs is made under any other provision of this Act or under any other enactment.

(11) Section 27 (co-operation between authorities) applies in relation to the exercise of functions of a local authority in England under this section as it applies in relation to the exercise of functions of a local authority in England under Part 3 and see sections 164 and 164A of the Social Services and Well-being (Wales) Act 2014 for provision about co-operation between local authorities in Wales and other bodies.

**Amendments**—Inserted by Adoption and Children 2002, s 115. Amended by SI 2016/413.

\* \* \*

## PART III
## SUPPORT FOR CHILDREN AND FAMILIES PROVIDED BY LOCAL AUTHORITIES IN ENGLAND

*Provision of accommodation for children*

### 20 Provision of accommodation for children: general

(1) Every local authority shall provide accommodation for any child in need within their area who appears to them to require accommodation as a result of –

(a) there being no person who has parental responsibility for him;
(b) his being lost or having been abandoned; or
(c) the person who has been caring for him being prevented (whether or not permanently, and for whatever reason) from providing him with suitable accommodation or care.

(2) Where a local authority provide accommodation under subsection (1) for a child who is ordinarily resident in the area of another local authority, that other local authority may take over the provision of accommodation for the child within –

(a) three months of being notified in writing that the child is being provided with accommodation; or
(b) such other longer period as may be prescribed in regulations made by the Secretary of State.

(2A) Where a local authority in Wales provide accommodation under section 76(1) of the Social Services and Well-being (Wales) Act 2014 (accommodation for children without parents or who are lost or abandoned etc) for a child who is ordinarily resident in the area of a local authority in England, that local authority in England may take over the provision of accommodation for the child within –

(a) three months of being notified in writing that the child is being provided with accommodation; or
(b) such other longer period as may be prescribed in regulations made by the Secretary of State.

(3) Every local authority shall provide accommodation for any child in need within their area who has reached the age of sixteen and whose welfare the authority consider is likely to be seriously prejudiced if they do not provide him with accommodation.

(4) A local authority may provide accommodation for any child within their area (even though a person who has parental responsibility for him is able to provide him with accommodation) if they consider that to do so would safeguard or promote the child's welfare.

(5) A local authority may provide accommodation for any person who has reached the age of sixteen but is under twenty-one in any community home which takes children who have reached the age of sixteen if they consider that to do so would safeguard or promote his welfare.

(6) Before providing accommodation under this section, a local authority shall, so far as is reasonably practicable and consistent with the child's welfare –

(a) ascertain the child's wishes and feelings regarding the provision of accommodation; and
(b) give due consideration (having regard to his age and understanding) to such wishes and feelings of the child as they have been able to ascertain.

(7) A local authority may not provide accommodation under this section for any child if any person who –

(a) has parental responsibility for him; and
(b) is willing and able to –
  (i) provide accommodation for him; or
  (ii) arrange for accommodation to be provided for him,

objects.

(8) Any person who has parental responsibility for a child may at any time remove the child from accommodation provided by or on behalf of the local authority under this section.

(9) Subsections (7) and (8) do not apply while any person –

(a) who is named in a child arrangements order as a person with whom the child is to live;
(aa) who is a special guardian of the child; or
(b) who has care of the child by virtue of an order made in the exercise of the High Court's inherent jurisdiction with respect to children,

agrees to the child being looked after in accommodation provided by or on behalf of the local authority.

(10) Where there is more than one such person as is mentioned in subsection (9), all of them must agree.

(11) Subsections (7) and (8) do not apply where a child who has reached the age of sixteen agrees to being provided with accommodation under this section.

**Amendments**—Adoption and Children 2002, s 139(1), (3), Sch 3, paras 54, 59, Sch 5; Children Act 2004, s 53; Children and Families 2014, s 12, Sch 2; SI 2016/413.

## 21 Provision for accommodation for children in police protection or detention or on remand, etc

(1) Every local authority shall make provision for the reception and accommodation of children who are removed or kept away from home under Part V.

(2) Every local authority shall receive, and provide accommodation for, children –

(a) in police protection whom they are requested to receive under section 46(3)(f);

(b) whom they are requested to receive under section 38(6) of the Police and Criminal Evidence Act 1984;
(c) who are –
  (i) *(repealed)*
  (ia) remanded to accommodation provided by or on behalf of a local authority by virtue of paragraph 4 of Schedule 1 or paragraph 6 of Schedule 8 to the Powers of Criminal Courts (Sentencing) Act 2000 (breach etc of referral orders and reparation orders);
  (ii) remanded to accommodation provided by or on behalf of a local authority by virtue of paragraph 21 of Schedule 2 to the Criminal Justice and Immigration Act 2008 (breach etc of youth rehabilitation orders);
  (iia) remanded to accommodation provided by or on behalf of a local authority by virtue of paragraph 10 of the Schedule to the Street Offences Act 1959 (breach of orders under section 1(2A) of that Act);
  (iii) the subject of a youth rehabilitation order imposing a local authority residence requirement or a youth rehabilitation order with fostering,

and with respect to whom they are the designated authority.

(2A) In subsection (2)(c)(iii), the following terms have the same meanings as in Part 1 of the Criminal Justice and Immigration Act 2008 (see section 7 of that Act) –

'local authority residence requirement';
'youth rehabilitation order';
'youth rehabilitation order with fostering'.

(3) Where a child has been –

(a) removed under Part V; or
(b) detained under section 38 of the Police and Criminal Evidence Act 1984,

and he is not being provided with accommodation by a local authority or by a local authority in Wales or in a hospital vested in the Secretary of State or the Welsh Ministers , or otherwise made available pursuant to arrangements made by the Secretary of State, the National Health Service Commissioning Board or a clinical commissioning group under the National Health Service Act 2006 or a Local Health Board , any reasonable expenses of accommodating him shall be recoverable from the local authority, or local authority in Wales, in whose area he is ordinarily resident.

**Amendments**—Courts and Legal Services Act 1990, s 116, Sch 16, para 11; National Health Service and Community Care Act 1990, s 66(1), Sch 9, para 36; Health Authorities Act 1995, s 2, Sch 1, para 118; SI 2000/90; Powers of Criminal Courts (Sentencing) Act 2000, s 165, Sch 9, para 126; Anti-social Behaviour Act 2003, s 88, Sch 2, para 5; SI 2007/961; Children and Young Persons Act 2008, s 39, Sch 3, paras 1, 5; Criminal Justice and Immigration Act 2008, ss 6(2), 6(3), 149, Sch 4, paras 34 and 105, Sch 28, Pt 1; Policing and Crime Act 2009, s 112, Sch 7, para 21; Legal Aid, Sentencing and Punishment of Offenders Act 2012, s 105, Sch 12, para 24 (subject to savings in certain cases); Health and Social Care Act 2012, s 55(2), Sch 5, para 48; SI 2016/413.

## *Duties of local authorities in relation to children looked after by them*

### 22 General duty of local authority in relation to children looked after by them

(1) In this section, any reference to a child who is looked after by a local authority is a reference to a child who is –

  (a)  in their care; or
  (b)  provided with accommodation by the authority in the exercise of any functions (in particular those under this Act) which are social services functions within the meaning of the Local Authority Social Services Act 1970, apart from functions under sections 17, 23B and 24B.

(2) In subsection (1) 'accommodation' means accommodation which is provided for a continuous period of more than 24 hours.

(3) It shall be the duty of a local authority looking after any child –

  (a)  to safeguard and promote his welfare; and
  (b)  to make such use of services available for children cared for by their own parents as appears to the authority reasonable in his case.

(3A) The duty of a local authority under subsection (3)(a) to safeguard and promote the welfare of a child looked after by them includes in particular a duty to promote the child's educational achievement.

(3B) A local authority must appoint at least one person for the purpose of discharging the duty imposed by virtue of subsection (3A).

(3C) A person appointed by a local authority under subsection (3B) must be an officer employed by that authority or another local authority.

(4) Before making any decision with respect to a child whom they are looking after, or proposing to look after, a local authority shall, so far as is reasonably practicable, ascertain the wishes and feelings of –

  (a)  the child;
  (b)  his parents;
  (c)  any person who is not a parent of his but who has parental responsibility for him; and
  (d)  any other person whose wishes and feelings the authority consider to be relevant,

regarding the matter to be decided.

(5) In making any such decision a local authority shall give due consideration –

  (a)  having regard to his age and understanding, to such wishes and feelings of the child as they have been able to ascertain;
  (b)  to such wishes and feelings of any person mentioned in subsection (4)(*b*) to (*d*) as they have been able to ascertain; and

(c) to the child's religious persuasion, racial origin and cultural and linguistic background.

(6) If it appears to a local authority that it is necessary, for the purpose of protecting members of the public from serious injury, to exercise their powers with respect to a child whom they are looking after in a manner which may not be consistent with their duties under this section, they may do so.

(7) If the Secretary of State considers it necessary, for the purpose of protecting members of the public from serious injury, to give directions to a local authority with respect to the exercise of their powers with respect to a child whom they are looking after, the Secretary of State may give such directions to the authority.

(8) Where any such directions are given to an authority they shall comply with them even though doing so is inconsistent with their duties under this section.

Amendments—Children (Leaving Care) Act 2000, s 2(1), (2); Local Government Act 2000, s 107(1), Sch 5, para 19; Adoption and Children 2002, s 116(2); Children Act 2004, s 52; Children and Young Persons Act 2008, s 39, Sch 3, paras 1, 6; Children and Families 2014, s 99; SI 2016/413.

## 22A Provision of accommodation for children in care

When a child is in the care of a local authority, it is their duty to provide the child with accommodation.

Amendments—Inserted by Children and Young Persons Act 2008, s 8(1).

## 22B Maintenance of looked after children

It is the duty of a local authority to maintain a child they are looking after in other respects apart from the provision of accommodation.

Amendments—Inserted by Children and Young Persons Act 2008, s 8(1).

## 22C Ways in which looked after children are to be accommodated and maintained

(1) This section applies where a local authority are looking after a child ('C').

(2) The local authority must make arrangements for C to live with a person who falls within subsection (3) (but subject to subsection (4)).

(3) A person ('P') falls within this subsection if –

(a) P is a parent of C;
(b) P is not a parent of C but has parental responsibility for C; or
(c) in a case where C is in the care of the local authority and there was a child arrangements order in force with respect to C immediately before the care order was made, P was a person named in the child arrangements order as a person with whom C was to live.

(4) Subsection (2) does not require the local authority to make arrangements of the kind mentioned in that subsection if doing so –

(a) would not be consistent with C's welfare; or
(b) would not be reasonably practicable.

(5) If the local authority are unable to make arrangements under subsection (2), they must place C in the placement which is, in their opinion, the most appropriate placement available.

(6) In subsection (5) 'placement' means –

(a) placement with an individual who is a relative, friend or other person connected with C and who is also a local authority foster parent;
(b) placement with a local authority foster parent who does not fall within paragraph (a);
(c) placement in a children's home in respect of which a person is registered under Part 2 of the Care Standards Act 2000; or
(d) subject to section 22D, placement in accordance with other arrangements which comply with any regulations made for the purposes of this section.

(7) In determining the most appropriate placement for C, the local authority must, subject to subsection (9B) and the other provisions of this Part (in particular, to their duties under section 22) –

(a) give preference to a placement falling within paragraph (a) of subsection (6) over placements falling within the other paragraphs of that subsection;
(b) comply, so far as is reasonably practicable in all the circumstances of C's case, with the requirements of subsection (8); and
(c) comply with subsection (9) unless that is not reasonably practicable.

(8) The local authority must ensure that the placement is such that –

(a) it allows C to live near C's home;
(b) it does not disrupt C's education or training;
(c) if C has a sibling for whom the local authority are also providing accommodation, it enables C and the sibling to live together;
(d) if C is disabled, the accommodation provided is suitable to C's particular needs.

(9) The placement must be such that C is provided with accommodation within the local authority's area.

(9A) Subsection (9B) applies (subject to subsection (9C)) where the local authority –

(a) are considering adoption for C, or
(b) are satisfied that C ought to be placed for adoption but are not authorised under section 19 of the Adoption and Children Act 2002 (placement with parental consent) or by virtue of section 21 of that Act (placement orders) to place C for adoption.

(9B) Where this subsection applies –

(a) subsections (7) to (9) do not apply to the local authority,

(b) the local authority must consider placing C with an individual within subsection (6)(a), and
(c) where the local authority decide that a placement with such an individual is not the most appropriate placement for C, the local authority must consider placing C with a local authority foster parent who has been approved as a prospective adopter.

(9C) Subsection (9B) does not apply where the local authority have applied for a placement order under section 21 of the Adoption and Children Act 2002 in respect of C and the application has been refused.

(10) The local authority may determine –

(a) the terms of any arrangements they make under subsection (2) in relation to C (including terms as to payment); and
(b) the terms on which they place C with a local authority foster parent (including terms as to payment but subject to any order made under section 49 of the Children Act 2004).

(11) The Secretary of State may make regulations for, and in connection with, the purposes of this section.

(12) For the meaning of 'local authority foster parent' see section 105(1).

**Amendments**—Inserted by Children and Young Persons Act 2008, s 8(1). Amended by Children and Families 2014, ss 2, 12, Sch 2; SI 2016/413.

## 22D Review of child's case before making alternative arrangements for accommodation

(1) Where a local authority are providing accommodation for a child ('C') other than by arrangements under section 22C(6)(d), they must not make such arrangements for C unless they have decided to do so in consequence of a review of C's case carried out in accordance with regulations made under section 26.

(2) But subsection (1) does not prevent a local authority making arrangements for C under section 22C(6)(d) if they are satisfied that in order to safeguard C's welfare it is necessary –

(a) to make such arrangements; and
(b) to do so as a matter of urgency.

**Amendments**—Inserted by Children and Young Persons Act 2008, s 8(1).

## 22E Children's homes provided by Secretary of State or Welsh Ministers

Where a local authority place a child they are looking after in a children's home provided, equipped and maintained by the Secretary of State or the Welsh Ministers under section 82(5), they must do so on such terms as the Secretary of State or the Welsh Ministers (as the case may be) may from time to time determine.

**Amendments**—Inserted by Children and Young Persons Act 2008, s 8(1). Substituted by SI 2016/413.

## 22F Regulations as to children looked after by local authorities

Part 2 of Schedule 2 has effect for the purposes of making further provision as to children looked after by local authorities and in particular as to the regulations which may be made under section 22C(11).

**Amendments**—Inserted by Children and Young Persons Act 2008, s 8(1).

## 22G General duty of local authority to secure sufficient accommodation for looked after children

(1) It is the general duty of a local authority to take steps that secure, so far as reasonably practicable, the outcome in subsection (2).

(2) The outcome is that the local authority are able to provide the children mentioned in subsection (3) with accommodation that –

   (a) is within the authority's area; and
   (b) meets the needs of those children.

(3) The children referred to in subsection (2) are those –

   (a) that the local authority are looking after,
   (b) in respect of whom the authority are unable to make arrangements under section 22C(2), and
   (c) whose circumstances are such that it would be consistent with their welfare for them to be provided with accommodation that is in the authority's area.

(4) In taking steps to secure the outcome in subsection (2), the local authority must have regard to the benefit of having –

   (a) a number of accommodation providers in their area that is, in their opinion, sufficient to secure that outcome; and
   (b) a range of accommodation in their area capable of meeting different needs that is, in their opinion, sufficient to secure that outcome.

(5) In this section 'accommodation providers' means –

   local authority foster parents; and
   children's homes in respect of which a person is registered under Part 2 of the Care Standards Act 2000.

**Amendments**—Inserted by Children and Young Persons Act 2008, s 9.

## PART IV
## CARE AND SUPERVISION

*General*

### 31 Care and supervision orders

(1) On the application of any local authority or authorised person, the court may make an order –

(a) placing the child with respect to whom the application is made in the care of a designated local authority; or

(b) putting him under the supervision of a designated local authority.

(2) A court may only make a care order or supervision order if it is satisfied –

(a) that the child concerned is suffering, or is likely to suffer, significant harm; and

(b) that the harm, or likelihood of harm, is attributable to –

   (i) the care given to the child, or likely to be given to him if the order were not made, not being what it would be reasonable to expect a parent to give to him; or

   (ii) the child's being beyond parental control.

(3) No care order or supervision order may be made with respect to a child who has reached the age of seventeen (or sixteen, in the case of a child who is married).

(3A) A court deciding whether to make a care order –

(a) is required to consider the permanence provisions of the section 31A plan for the child concerned, but

(b) is not required to consider the remainder of the section 31A plan, subject to section 34(11).

(3B) For the purposes of subsection (3A), the permanence provisions of a section 31A plan are –

(a) such of the plan's provisions setting out the long-term plan for the upbringing of the child concerned as provide for any of the following –

   (i) the child to live with any parent of the child's or with any other member of, or any friend of, the child's family;

   (ii) adoption;

   (iii) long-term care not within sub-paragraph (i) or (ii);

(b) such of the plan's provisions as set out any of the following –

   (i) the impact on the child concerned of any harm that he or she suffered or was likely to suffer;

   (ii) the current and future needs of the child (including needs arising out of that impact);

   (iii) the way in which the long-term plan for the upbringing of the child would meet those current and future needs.

(3C) The Secretary of State may by regulations amend this section for the purpose of altering what for the purposes of subsection (3A) are the permanence provisions of a section 31A plan.

(4) An application under this section may be made on its own or in any other family proceedings.

(5) The court may –
- (a) on an application for a care order, make a supervision order;
- (b) on an application for a supervision order, make a care order.

(6) Where an authorised person proposes to make an application under this section he shall –
- (a) if it is reasonably practicable to do so; and
- (b) before making the application,

consult the local authority appearing to him to be the authority in whose area the child concerned is ordinarily resident.

(7) An application made by an authorised person shall not be entertained by the court if, at the time when it is made, the child concerned is –
- (a) the subject of an earlier application for a care order, or supervision order, which has not been disposed of; or
- (b) subject to –
  - (i) a care order or supervision order;
  - (ii) a youth rehabilitation order within the meaning of Part 1 of the Criminal Justice and Immigration Act 2008; or
  - (iii) a supervision requirement within the meaning of Part II of the Children (Scotland) Act 1995.

(8) The local authority designated in a care order must be –
- (a) the authority within whose area the child is ordinarily resident; or
- (b) where the child does not reside in the area of a local authority, the authority within whose area any circumstances arose in consequence of which the order is being made.

(9) In this section –

'authorised person' means –
- (a) the National Society for the Prevention of Cruelty to Children and any of its officers; and
- (b) any person authorised by order of the Secretary of State to bring proceedings under this section and any officer of a body which is so authorised;

'harm' means ill-treatment or the impairment of health or development including, for example, impairment suffered from seeing or hearing the ill-treatment of another;

'development' means physical, intellectual, emotional, social or behavioural development;

'health' means physical or mental health; and

'ill-treatment' includes sexual abuse and forms of ill-treatment which are not physical.

(10) Where the question of whether harm suffered by a child is significant turns on the child's health or development, his health or development shall be compared with that which could reasonably be expected of a similar child.

(11) In this Act –

'a care order' means (subject to section 105(1)) an order under subsection (1)(a) and (except where express provision to the contrary is made) includes an interim care order made under section 38; and

'a supervision order' means an order under subsection (1)(b) and (except where express provision to the contrary is made) includes an interim supervision order made under section 38.

Amendments—Children (Scotland) Act 1995, s 105(4), Sch 4, para 48(1),(2); CJCSA 2000 ss 74, 75, Sch 7, paras 87, 90; Powers of Criminal Courts (Sentencing) Act 2000, s 165, Sch 9, para 127; Adoption and Children 2002, ss 120, 121; Criminal Justice and Immigration Act 2008, ss 6(2), 149, Sch 4, para 35; Children and Families 2014, s 15; Children and Social Work Act 2017, s 8.

## 31A Care orders: care plans

(1) Where an application is made on which a care order might be made with respect to a child, the appropriate local authority must, within such time as the court may direct, prepare a plan ('a care plan') for the future care of the child.

(2) While the application is pending, the authority must keep any care plan prepared by them under review and, if they are of the opinion some change is required, revise the plan, or make a new plan, accordingly.

(3) A care plan must give any prescribed information and do so in the prescribed manner.

(4) For the purposes of this section, the appropriate local authority, in relation to a child in respect of whom a care order might be made, is the local authority proposed to be designated in the order.

(5) In section 31(3A) and this section, references to a care order do not include an interim care order.

(6) A plan prepared, or treated as prepared, under this section is referred to in this Act as a 'section 31A plan'.

Amendments—Inserted by Adoption and Children 2002, s 121.

Modifications—Section 31A is modified for certain purposes by SI 2010/1898, reg 5(3).

## 32 Period within which application for order under this Part must be disposed of

(1) A court in which an application for an order under this Part is proceeding shall (in the light of any provision in rules of court that is of the kind mentioned in subsection (2)(a) or (b)) –

(a) draw up a timetable with a view to disposing of the application –

(i) without delay, and
(ii) in any event within twenty-six weeks beginning with the day on which the application was issued; and
(b) give such directions as it considers appropriate for the purpose of ensuring, so far as is reasonably practicable, that that timetable is adhered to.

(2) Rules of court may –

(a) specify periods within which specified steps must be taken in relation to such proceedings; and
(b) make other provision with respect to such proceedings for the purpose of ensuring, so far as is reasonably practicable, that they are disposed of without delay.

(3) A court, when drawing up a timetable under subsection (1)(a), must in particular have regard to –

(a) the impact which the timetable would have on the welfare of the child to whom the application relates; and
(b) the impact which the timetable would have on the conduct of the proceedings.

(4) A court, when revising a timetable drawn up under subsection (1)(a) or when making any decision which may give rise to a need to revise such a timetable (which does not include a decision under subsection (5)), must in particular have regard to –

(a) the impact which any revision would have on the welfare of the child to whom the application relates; and
(b) the impact which any revision would have on the duration and conduct of the proceedings.

(5) A court in which an application under this Part is proceeding may extend the period that is for the time being allowed under subsection (1)(a)(ii) in the case of the application, but may do so only if the court considers that the extension is necessary to enable the court to resolve the proceedings justly.

(6) When deciding whether to grant an extension under subsection (5), a court must in particular have regard to –

(a) the impact which any ensuing timetable revision would have on the welfare of the child to whom the application relates, and
(b) the impact which any ensuing timetable revision would have on the duration and conduct of the proceedings;

and here 'ensuing timetable revision' means any revision, of the timetable under subsection (1)(a) for the proceedings, which the court considers may ensue from the extension.

(7) When deciding whether to grant an extension under subsection (5), a court is to take account of the following guidance: extensions are not to be granted routinely and are to be seen as requiring specific justification.

(8) Each separate extension under subsection (5) is to end no more than eight weeks after the later of –

(a) the end of the period being extended; and
(b) the end of the day on which the extension is granted.

(9) The Lord Chancellor may by regulations amend subsection (1)(a)(ii), or the opening words of subsection (8), for the purpose of varying the period for the time being specified in that provision.

(10) Rules of court may provide that a court –

(a) when deciding whether to exercise the power under subsection (5), or
(b) when deciding how to exercise that power,

must, or may or may not, have regard to matters specified in the rules, or must take account of any guidance set out in the rules.

Amendments—Children and Families 2014, s 14.

## *Care Orders*

### 33 Effect of care order

(1) Where a care order is made with respect to a child it shall be the duty of the local authority designated by the order to receive the child into their care and to keep him in their care while the order remains in force.

(2) Where –

(a) a care order has been made with respect to a child on the application of an authorised person; but
(b) the local authority designated by the order was not informed that that person proposed to make the application,

the child may be kept in the care of that person until received into the care of the authority.

(3) While a care order is in force with respect to a child, the local authority designated by the order shall –

(a) have parental responsibility for the child; and
(b) have the power (subject to the following provisions of this section) to determine the extent to which
   (i) a parent, guardian or special guardian of the child; or
   (ii) a person who by virtue of section 4A has parental responsibility for the child
   may meet his parental responsibility for him.

(4) The authority may not exercise the power in subsection (3)(b) unless they are satisfied that it is necessary to do so in order to safeguard or promote the child's welfare.

(5) Nothing in subsection (3)(b) shall prevent a person mentioned in that provision who has care of the child from doing what is reasonable in all the circumstances of the case for the purpose of safeguarding or promoting his welfare.

(6) While a care order is in force with respect to a child, the local authority designated by the order shall not –

(a) cause the child to be brought up in any religious persuasion other than that in which he would have been brought up if the order had not been made; or
(b) have the right –
  (i) *(repealed)*
  (ii) to agree or refuse to agree to the making of an adoption order, or an order under section 84 of the Adoption and Children Act 2002, with respect to the child; or
  (iii) to appoint a guardian for the child.

(7) While a care order is in force with respect to a child, no person may –

(a) cause the child to be known by a new surname; or
(b) remove him from the United Kingdom,

without either the written consent of every person who has parental responsibility for the child or the leave of the court.

(8) Subsection (7)(b) does not –

(a) prevent the removal of such a child, for a period of less than one month, by the authority in whose care he is; or
(b) apply to arrangements for such a child to live outside England and Wales (which are governed by paragraph 19 of Schedule 2 in England, and section 124 of the Social Services and Well-being (Wales) Act 2014 in Wales).

(9) The power in subsection (3)(b) is subject (in addition to being subject to the provisions of this section) to any right, duty, power, responsibility or authority which a person mentioned in that provision has in relation to the child and his property by virtue of any other enactment.

**Amendments**—Adoption and Children 2002, s 139(1), Sch 3, paras 54, 63, Sch 5; SI 2016/413.

## 34 Parental contact etc with children in care

(1) Where a child is in the care of a local authority, the authority shall (subject to the provisions of this section and their duty under section 22(3)(a) or, where the local authority is in Wales, under section 78(1)(a) of the Social Services and Well-being (Wales) Act 2014) allow the child reasonable contact with –

(a) his parents;
(b) any guardian or special guardian of his;
(ba) any person who by virtue of section 4A has parental responsibility for him;

(c) where there was a child arrangements order in force with respect to the child immediately before the care order was made, any person named in the child arrangements order as a person with whom the child was to live; and
(d) where, immediately before the care order was made, a person had care of the child by virtue of an order made in the exercise of the High Court's inherent jurisdiction with respect to children, that person.

(2) On an application made by the authority or the child, the court may make such order as it considers appropriate with respect to the contact which is to be allowed between the child and any named person.

(3) On an application made by –

(a) any person mentioned in paragraph (a) to (d) of subsection (1); or
(b) any person who has obtained the leave of the court to make the application,

the court may make such order as it considers appropriate with respect to the contact which is to be allowed between the child and that person.

(4) On an application made by the authority or the child, the court may make an order authorising the authority to refuse to allow contact between the child and any person who is mentioned in paragraphs (a) to (d) of subsection (1) and named in the order.

(5) When making a care order with respect to a child, or in any family proceedings in connection with a child who is in the care of a local authority, the court may make an order under this section, even though no application for such an order has been made with respect to the child, if it considers that the order should be made.

(6) An authority may refuse to allow the contact that would otherwise be required by virtue of subsection (1) or an order under this section if –

(a) they are satisfied that it is necessary to do so in order to safeguard or promote the child's welfare; and
(b) the refusal –
  (i) is decided upon as a matter of urgency; and
  (ii) does not last for more than seven days.

(6A) Where (by virtue of an order under this section, or because subsection (6) applies) a local authority in England are authorised to refuse to allow contact between the child and a person mentioned in any of paragraphs (a) to (c) of paragraph 15(1) of Schedule 2, paragraph 15(1) of that Schedule does not require the authority to endeavour to promote contact between the child and that person.

(6B) Where (by virtue of an order under this section, or because subsection (6) applies) a local authority in Wales is authorised to refuse contact between the child and a person mentioned in any of paragraphs (a) to (c) of section 95(1) of the Social Services and Wellbeing (Wales) Act 2014, section 95(1) of that Act does not require the authority to promote contact between the child and that person.

(7) An order under this section may impose such conditions as the court considers appropriate.

(8) The Secretary of State may by regulations make provision as to –
- (za) what a local authority in England must have regard to in considering whether contact between a child and a person mentioned in any of paragraphs (a) to (d) of subsection (1) is consistent with safeguarding and promoting the child's welfare;
- (a) the steps to be taken by a local authority who have exercised their power under subsection (6);
- (b) the circumstances in which, and conditions subject to which, the terms of any order under this section may be departed from by agreement between the local authority and the person in relation to whom the order is made;
- (c) notification by a local authority of any variation or suspension of arrangements made (otherwise than under an order under this section) with a view to affording any person contact with a child to whom this section applies.

(9) The court may vary or discharge any order made under this section on the application of the authority, the child concerned or the person named in the order.

(10) An order under this section may be made either at the same time as the care order itself or later.

(11) Before making, varying or discharging an order under this section or making a care order with respect to any child the court shall –
- (a) consider the arrangements which the authority have made, or propose to make, for affording any person contact with a child to whom this section applies; and
- (b) invite the parties to the proceedings to comment on those arrangements.

**Amendments**—Adoption and Children 2002, s 139(1), Sch 3, paras 54, 64; Children and Families 2014, ss 8, 12, Sch 2; SI 2016/413.

## Supervision orders

### 35 Supervision orders

(1) While a supervision order is in force it shall be the duty of the supervisor –
- (a) to advise, assist and befriend the supervised child;
- (b) to take such steps as are reasonably necessary to give effect to the order; and
- (c) where –
  - (i) the order is not wholly complied with; or

(ii) the supervisor considers that the order may no longer be necessary,

to consider whether or not to apply to the court for its variation or discharge.

(2) Parts I and II of Schedule 3 make further provision with respect to supervision orders.

### 36 Education supervision orders

(1) On the application of any local authority, the court may make an order putting the child with respect to whom the application is made under the supervision of a designated local authority.

(2) In this Act 'an education supervision order' means an order under subsection (1).

(3) A court may only make an education supervision order if it is satisfied that the child concerned is of compulsory school age and is not being properly educated.

(4) For the purposes of this section, a child is being properly educated only if he is receiving efficient full-time education suitable to his age, ability and aptitude and any special educational needs he may have.

(5) Where a child is –

(a) the subject of a school attendance order which is in force under section 437 of the Education Act 1996 and which has not been complied with; or
(b) is not attending regularly within the meaning of section 444 of that Act –
  (i) a school at which he is a registered pupil,
  (ii) any place at which education is provided for him in the circumstances mentioned in subsection (1) of section 444ZA of that Act, or
  (iii) any place which he is required to attend in the circumstances mentioned in subsection (2) of that section,
then, unless it is proved that he is being properly educated, it shall be assumed that he is not.

(6) An education supervision order may not be made with respect to a child who is in the care of a local authority.

(7) The local authority designated in an education supervision order must be –

(a) the authority within whose area the child concerned is living or will live; or
(b) where –
  (i) the child is a registered pupil at a school; and
  (ii) the authority mentioned in paragraph (a) and the authority within whose area the school is situated agree,
the latter authority.

(8) Where a local authority propose to make an application for an education supervision order they shall, before making the application, consult the appropriate local authority if different.

(9) The appropriate local authority is –

(a) in the case of a child who is being provided with accommodation by, or on behalf of, a local authority, that authority; and
(b) in any other case, the local authority within whose area the child concerned lives, or will live.

(10) Part III of Schedule 3 makes further provision with respect to education supervision orders.

**Amendments**—Education Act 1993, s 307(1),(3), Sch 19, para 149, Sch 21, Pt II; Education Act 1996, s 582(1), Sch 37, Pt I, para 85; Education Act 2005, s 117, Sch 18, para 1; SI 2010/1158.

## Powers of Court

### 37 Powers of court in certain family proceedings

(1) Where, in any family proceedings in which a question arises with respect to the welfare of any child, it appears to the court that it may be appropriate for a care or supervision order to be made with respect to him, the court may direct the appropriate authority to undertake an investigation of the child's circumstances.

(2) Where the court gives a direction under this section the local authority concerned shall, when undertaking the investigation, consider whether they should –

(a) apply for a care order or for a supervision order with respect to the child;
(b) provide services or assistance for the child or his family; or
(c) take any other action with respect to the child.

(3) Where a local authority undertake an investigation under this section, and decide not to apply for a care order or supervision order with respect to the child concerned, they shall inform the court of –

(a) their reasons for so deciding;
(b) any service or assistance which they have provided, or to intend to provide, for the child and his family; and
(c) any other action which they have taken, or propose to take, with respect to the child.

(4) The information shall be given to the court before the end of the period of eight weeks beginning with the date of the direction, unless the court otherwise directs.

(5) The local authority named in a direction under subsection (1) must be –

(a) the authority in whose area the child is ordinarily resident; or

(b) where the child is not ordinarily resident in the area of a local authority, the authority within whose area any circumstances arose in consequence of which the direction is being given.

(6) If, on the conclusion of any investigation or review under this section, the authority decide not to apply for a care order or supervision order with respect to the child –

(a) they shall consider whether it would be appropriate to review the case at a later date; and
(b) if they decide that it would be, they shall determine the date on which that review is to begin.

Amendments—Courts and Legal Services Act 1990, s 116, Sch 16, para 16.

## 38 Interim orders

(1) Where –

(a) in any proceedings on an application for a care order or supervision order, the proceedings are adjourned; or
(b) the court gives a direction under section 37(1).

the court may make an interim care order or an interim supervision order with respect to the child concerned.

(2) A court shall not make an interim care order or interim supervision order under this section unless it is satisfied that there are reasonable grounds for believing that circumstances with respect to the child are as mentioned in section 31(2).

(3) Where, in any proceedings on an application for a care order or supervision order, a court makes a child arrangements order with respect to the living arrangements of the child concerned, it shall also make an interim supervision order with respect to him unless satisfied that his welfare will be satisfactorily safeguarded without an interim order being made.

(3A) For the purposes of subsection (3), a child arrangements order is one made with respect to the living arrangements of the child concerned if the arrangements regulated by the order consist of, or include, arrangements which relate to either or both of the following –

(a) with whom the child is to live, and
(b) when the child is to live with any person.

(4) An interim order made under or by virtue of this section shall have effect for such period as may be specified in the order, but shall in any event cease to have effect on whichever of the following events first occurs –

(a), (b) *(repealed)*
(c) in a case which falls within subsection (1)(a), the disposal of the application;

(d) in a case which falls within subsection (1)(b), the disposal of an application for a care order or a supervision order made by the authority with respect to the child;
(da) in a case which falls within subsection (1)(b) and in which –
  (i) no direction has been given under section 37(4), and
  (ii) no application for a care order or supervision order has been made with respect to the child, the expiry of the period of eight weeks beginning with the date on which the order is made;
(e) in a case which falls within subsection (1)(b) and in which –
  (i) the court has given a direction under section 37(4), but
  (ii) no application for a care order or supervision order has been made with respect to the child,
  the expiry of the period fixed by that direction.

(5) (*repealed*)

(6) Where the court makes an interim care order, or interim supervision order, it may give such directions (if any) as it considers appropriate with regard to the medical or psychiatric examination or other assessment of the child; but if the child is of sufficient understanding to make an informed decision he may refuse to submit to the examination or other assessment.

(7) A direction under subsection (6) may be to the effect that there is to be –

(a) no such examination or assessment; or
(b) no such examination or assessment unless the court directs otherwise.

(7A) A direction under subsection (6) to the effect that there is to be a medical or psychiatric examination or other assessment of the child may be given only if the court is of the opinion that the examination or other assessment is necessary to assist the court to resolve the proceedings justly.

(7B) When deciding whether to give a direction under subsection (6) to that effect the court is to have regard in particular to –

(a) any impact which any examination or other assessment would be likely to have on the welfare of the child, and any other impact which giving the direction would be likely to have on the welfare of the child,
(b) the issues with which the examination or other assessment would assist the court,
(c) the questions which the examination or other assessment would enable the court to answer,
(d) the evidence otherwise available,
(e) the impact which the direction would be likely to have on the timetable, duration and conduct of the proceedings,
(f) the cost of the examination or other assessment, and
(g) any matters prescribed by Family Procedure Rules.

(8) A direction under subsection (6) may be –

(a) given when the interim order is made or at any time while it is in force; and

(b) varied at any time on the application of any person falling within any class of person prescribed by rules of court for the purposes of this subsection.

(9) Paragraphs 4 and 5 of Schedule 3 shall not apply in relation to an interim supervision order.

(10) Where a court makes an order under or by virtue of this section it shall, in determining the period for which the order is to be in force, consider whether any party who was, or might have been, opposed to the making of the order was in a position to argue his case against the order in full.

Amendments—Children and Families 2014, ss 12, 13, Sch 2.

Modifications—Section 38 is modified for certain purposes by SI 2010/1898, reg 5(2).

## 38A Power to include exclusion requirement in interim care order

(1) Where –

(a) on being satisfied that there are reasonable grounds for believing that the circumstances with respect to a child are as mentioned in section 31(2)(a) and (b)(i), the court makes an interim care order with respect to a child, and
(b) the conditions mentioned in subsection (2) are satisfied,

the court may include an exclusion requirement in the interim care order.

(2) The conditions are –

(a) that there is reasonable cause to believe that, if a person ('the relevant person') is excluded from a dwelling-house in which the child lives, the child will cease to suffer, or cease to be likely to suffer, significant harm, and
(b) that another person living in the dwelling-house (whether a parent of the child or some other person) –
 (i) is able and willing to give to the child the care which it would be reasonable to expect a parent to give him, and
 (ii) consents to the inclusion of the exclusion requirement.

(3) For the purposes of this section an exclusion requirement is any one or more of the following –

(a) a provision requiring the relevant person to leave a dwelling-house in which he is living with the child,
(b) a provision prohibiting the relevant person from entering a dwelling-house in which the child lives, and
(c) a provision excluding the relevant person from a defined area in which a dwelling-house in which the child lives is situated.

(4) The court may provide that the exclusion requirement is to have effect for a shorter period than the other provisions of the interim care order.

(5) Where the court makes an interim care order containing an exclusion requirement, the court may attach a power of arrest to the exclusion requirement.

(6) Where the court attaches a power of arrest to an exclusion requirement of an interim care order, it may provide that the power of arrest is to have effect for a shorter period than the exclusion requirement.

(7) Any period specified for the purposes of subsection (4) or (6) may be extended by the court (on one or more occasions) on an application to vary or discharge the interim care order.

(8) Where a power of arrest is attached to an exclusion requirement of an interim care order by virtue of subsection (5), a constable may arrest without warrant any person whom he has reasonable cause to believe to be in breach of the requirement.

(9) Sections 47(7), (11) and (12) and 48 of, and Schedule 5 to, the Family Law Act 1996 shall have effect in relation to a person arrested under subsection (8) of this section as they have effect in relation to a person arrested under section 47(6) of that Act.

(10) If, while an interim care order containing an exclusion requirement is in force, the local authority have removed the child from the dwelling-house from which the relevant person is excluded to other accommodation for a continuous period of more than 24 hours, the interim care order shall cease to have effect in so far as it imposes the exclusion requirement.

Amendments—Inserted by FLA 1996, s 52, Sch 6, para 1.

## 38B Undertakings relating to interim care orders

(1) In any case where the court has power to include an exclusion requirement in an interim care order, the court may accept an undertaking from the relevant person.

(2) No power of arrest may be attached to any undertaking given under subsection (1).

(3) An undertaking given to a court under subsection (1) –

    (a)    shall be enforceable as if it were an order of the court, and
    (b)    shall cease to have effect if, while it is in force, the local authority have removed the child from the dwelling-house from which the relevant person is excluded to other accommodation for a continuous period of more than 24 hours.

(4) This section has effect without prejudice to the powers of the High Court and family court apart from this section.

(5) In this section 'exclusion requirement' and 'relevant person' have the same meaning as in section 38A.

Amendments—Inserted by FLA 1996, s 52, Sch 6, para 1; CCA 2013, s 17, Sch 11.

## 39 Discharge and variation etc of care orders and supervision orders

(1) A care order may be discharged by the court on the application of –

(a) any person who has parental responsibility for the child;
(b) the child himself; or
(c) the local authority designated by the order.

(2) A supervision order may be varied or discharged by the court on the application of –

(a) any person who has parental responsibility for the child;
(b) the child himself; or
(c) the supervisor.

(3) On the application of a person who is not entitled to apply for the order to be discharged, but who is a person with whom the child is living, a supervision order may be varied by the court in so far as it imposes a requirement which affects that person.

(3A) On the application of a person who is not entitled to apply for the order to be discharged, but who is a person to whom an exclusion requirement contained in the order applies, an interim care order may be varied or discharged by the court in so far as it imposes the exclusion requirement.

(3B) Where a power of arrest has been attached to an exclusion requirement of an interim care order, the court may, on the application of any person entitled to apply for the discharge of the order so far as it imposes the exclusion requirement, vary or discharge the order in so far as it confers a power of arrest (whether or not any application has been made to vary or discharge any other provision of the order).

(4) Where a care order is in force with respect to a child the court may, on the application of any person entitled to apply for the order to be discharged, substitute a supervision order for the care order.

(5) When a court is considering whether to substitute one order for another under subsection (4) any provision of this Act which would otherwise require section 31(2) to be satisfied at the time when the proposed order is substituted or made shall be disregarded.

Amendments—Family Law Act 1996, s 52, Sch 6, para 2.

## 40 Orders pending appeals in cases about care or supervision orders

(1) Where –

(a) a court dismisses an application for a care order; and
(b) at the time when the court dismisses the application, the child concerned is the subject of an interim care order,

the court may make a care order with respect to the child to have effect subject to such directions (if any) as the court may see fit to include in the order.

(2) Where –

(a) a court dismisses an application for a care order, or an application for a supervision order; and
(b) at the time when the court dismisses the application, the child concerned is the subject of an interim supervision order,

the court may make a supervision order with respect to the child to have effect subject to such directions (if any) as the court sees fit to include in the order.

(3) Where a court grants an application to discharge a care order or supervision order, it may order that –

(a) its decision is not to have effect; or
(b) the care order, or supervision order, is to continue to have effect but subject to such directions as the court sees fit to include in the order.

(4) An order made under this section shall only have effect for such a period, not exceeding the appeal period, as may be specified in the order.

(5) Where –

(a) an appeal is made against any decision of a court under this section; or
(b) any application is made to the appellate court in connection with a proposed appeal against that decision,

the appellate court may extend the period for which the order in question is to have effect, but not so as to extend it beyond the end of the appeal period.

(6) In this section 'the appeal period' means –

(a) where an appeal is made against the decision in question, the period between the making of that decision and the determination of the appeal; and
(b) otherwise, the period during which an appeal may be made against the decision.

## Representation of Child

### 41 Representation of child and of his interests in certain proceedings

(1) For the purpose of any specified proceedings, the court shall appoint an officer of the Service or a Welsh family proceedings officer for the child concerned unless satisfied that it is not necessary to do so in order to safeguard his interests.

(2) The officer of the Service or a Welsh family proceedings officer shall –

(a) be appointed in accordance with rules of court; and
(b) be under a duty to safeguard the interests of the child in the manner prescribed by such rules.

(3) Where –

(a) the child concerned is not represented by a solicitor; and
(b) any of the conditions mentioned in subsection (4) is satisfied,

the court may appoint a solicitor to represent him.

(4) The conditions are that –
- (a) no officer of the Service or Welsh family proceedings officer has been appointed for the child;
- (b) the child has sufficient understanding to instruct a solicitor and wishes to do so;
- (c) it appears to the court that it would be in the child's best interests for him to be represented by a solicitor.

(5) Any solicitor appointed under or by virtue of this section shall be appointed, and shall represent the child, in accordance with rules of court.

(6) In this section 'specified proceedings' means any proceedings –
- (a) on an application for a care order or supervision order;
- (b) in which the court has given a direction under section 37(1) and has made, or is considering whether to make, an interim care order;
- (c) on an application for the discharge of a care order or the variation or discharge of a supervision order;
- (d) on an application under section 39(4);
- (e) in which the court is considering whether to make a child arrangements order with respect to the living arrangements of a child who is the subject of a care order;
- (f) with respect to contact between a child who is the subject of a care order and any other person;
- (g) under Part V;
- (h) on an appeal against –
  - (i) the making of, or refusal to make, a care order, supervision order or any order under section 34;
  - (ii) the making of, or refusal to make, a child arrangements order with respect to the living arrangements of a child who is the subject of a care order; or
  - (iii) the variation or discharge of, or refusal of an application to vary or discharge, an order of a kind mentioned in sub-paragraph (i) or (ii);
  - (iv) the refusal of an application under section 39(4);
  - (v) the making of, or refusal to make, an order under Part V;
- (hh) on an application for the making or revocation of a placement order (within the meaning of section 21 of the Adoption and Children Act 2002); or
- (i) which are specified for the time being, for the purposes of this section, by rules of court.

(6A) The proceedings which may be specified under subsection (6)(i) include (for example) proceedings for the making, varying or discharging of a section 8 order.

(6B) For the purposes of subsection (6), a child arrangements order is one made with respect to the living arrangements of a child if the arrangements regulated by the order consist of, or include, arrangements which relate to either or both of the following –

(a) with whom the child is to live, and
(b) when the child is to live with any person.

(7)–(9) (*repealed*)

(10) Rules of court may make this provision as to –

(a) the assistance which any officer of the Service or Welsh family proceedings officer may be required by the court to give to it;
(b) the consideration to be given by any officer of the Service or Welsh family proceedings officer, where an order of a specified kind has been made in the proceedings in question, as to whether to apply for the variation or discharge of the order;
(c) the participation of officers of the Service or Welsh family proceedings officers in reviews, of a kind specified in the rules, which are conducted by the court.

(11) Regardless of any enactment or rule of law which would otherwise prevent it from doing so, the court may take account of –

(a) any statement contained in a report made by an officer of the Service or a Welsh family proceedings officer who is appointed under this section for the purpose of the proceedings in question; and
(b) any evidence given in respect of the matters referred to in the report,

in so far as the statement or evidence is, in the opinion of the court, relevant to the question which the court is considering.

(12) (*repealed*)

**Amendments**—Courts and Legal Services Act 1990, s 116, Sch 16, para 17; CJCSA 2000, ss 74, 75, Sch 7, paras 87, 91, Sch 8; Adoption and Children 2002, s 122(1); CA 2004, s 40, Sch 3, paras 5, 9; Children and Families 2014, s 12, Sch 2.

## 42 Right of officer of the Service to have access to local authority records

(1) Where an officer of the Service or Welsh family proceedings officer has been appointed under section 41 he shall have the right at all reasonable times to examine and take copies of –

(a) any records of, or held by, a local authority or an authorised person which were compiled in connection with the making, or proposed making, by any person of any application under this Act with respect to the child concerned;
(b) any records of, or held by, a local authority which were compiled in connection with any functions which are social services functions within the meaning of the Local Authority Social Services Act 1970 or for the purposes of the Social Services and Well-being (Wales) Act 2014, so far as those records relate to that child; or
(c) any records of, or held by, an authorised person which were compiled in connection with the activities of that person, so far as those records relate to that child.

(2) Where an officer of the Service or Welsh family proceedings officer takes a copy of any record which he is entitled to examine under this section, that copy or any part of it shall be admissible as evidence of any matter referred to in any –

(a) report which he makes to the court in the proceedings in question; or
(b) evidence which he gives in those proceedings.

(3) Subsection (2) has effect regardless of any enactment or rule of law which would otherwise prevent the record in question being admissible in evidence.

(4) In this section 'authorised person' has the same meaning as in section 31.

Amendments—Courts and Legal Services Act 1990, ss 116, 125(7), Sch 16, para 18, Sch 20; Criminal Justice and Courts Services Act 2000 s 74, Sch 7, paras 87, 92; Local Government Act 2000, s 107(1), Sch 5, para 20; Children Act 2004, s 40, Sch 3, paras 5, 10; SI 2016/413.

## PART V
## PROTECTION OF CHILDREN

### 43 Child assessment orders

(1) On the application of a local authority or authorised person for an order to be made under this section with respect to a child, the court may make the order if, but only if, it is satisfied that –

(a) the applicant has reasonable cause to suspect that the child is suffering, or is likely to suffer, significant harm;
(b) an assessment of the state of the child's health or development, or of the way in which he has been treated, is required to enable the applicant to determine whether or not the child is suffering, or is likely to suffer, significant harm; and
(c) it is unlikely that such an assessment will be made, or be satisfactory, in the absence of an order under this section.

(2) In this Act 'a child assessment order' means an order under this section.

(3) A court may treat an application under this section as an application for an emergency protection order.

(4) No court shall make a child assessment order if it is satisfied –

(a) that there are grounds for making an emergency protection order with respect to the child; and
(b) that it ought to make such an order rather than a child assessment order.

(5) A child assessment order shall –

(a) specify a date by which the assessment is to begin; and
(b) have effect for such period, not exceeding 7 days beginning with that date, as may be specified in the order.

(6) Where a child assessment order is in force with respect to a child it shall be the duty of any person who is in a position to produce the child –

- (a) to produce him to such person as may be named in the order; and
- (b) to comply with such directions relating to the assessment of the child as the court thinks fit to specify in the order.

(7) A child assessment order authorises any person carrying out the assessment, or any part of the assessment, to do so in accordance with the terms of the order.

(8) Regardless of subsection (7), if the child is of sufficient understanding to make an informed decision he may refuse to submit to a medical or psychiatric examination or other assessment.

(9) The child may only be kept away from home –

- (a) in accordance with directions specified in the order;
- (b) if it is necessary for the purposes of the assessment; and
- (c) for such period or periods as may be specified in the order.

(10) Where the child is to be kept away from home, the order shall contain such directions as the court thinks fit with regard to the contact that he must be allowed to have with other persons while away from home.

(11) Any person making an application for a child assessment order shall take such steps as are reasonably practicable to ensure that notice of the application is given to –

- (a) the child's parents;
- (b) any person who is not a parent of his but who has parental responsibility for him;
- (c) any other person caring for the child;
- (d) any person named in a child arrangements order as a person with whom the child is to spend time or otherwise have contact;
- (e) any person who is allowed to have contact with the child by virtue of an order under section 34; and
- (f) the child,

before the hearing of the application.

(12) Rules of court may make provision as to the circumstances in which –

- (a) any of the persons mentioned in subsection (11); or
- (b) such other person as may be specified in the rules,
  may apply to the court for a child assessment order to be varied or discharged.
  (13) In this section 'authorised person' means a person who is an authorised person for the purposes of section 31.

Amendments—Children and Families 2014, s 12, Sch 2.

## 44 Orders for emergency protection of children

(1) Where any person ('the applicant') applies to the court for an order to be made under this section with respect to a child, the court may make the order if, but only if, it is satisfied that –

(a) there is reasonable cause to believe that the child is likely to suffer significant harm if –
  (i) he is not removed to accommodation provided by or on behalf of the applicant; or
  (ii) he does not remain in the place in which he is then being accommodated;
(b) in the case of an application made by the local authority –
  (i) enquiries are being made with respect to the child under section 47(1)(b); and
  (ii) those enquiries are being frustrated by access to the child being unreasonably refused to a person authorised to seek access and that the applicant has reasonable cause to believe that access to the child is required as a matter of urgency; or
(c) in the case of an application made by an authorised person –
  (i) the applicant has reasonable cause to suspect that a child is suffering, or is likely to suffer, significant harm;
  (ii) the applicant is making enquiries with respect to the child's welfare; and
  (iii) those enquiries are being frustrated by access to the child being unreasonably refused to a person authorised to seek access and the applicant has reasonable cause to believe that access to the child is required as a matter of urgency.

(2) In this section –

(a) 'authorised person' means a person who is an authorised person for the purposes of section 31; and
(b) 'a person authorised to seek access' means –
  (i) in the case of an application by a local authority, an officer of the local authority or a person authorised by the local authority to act on their behalf in connection with the enquiries; or
  (ii) in the case of an application by an authorised person, that person.

(3) Any person –

(a) seeking access to a child in connection with enquiries of a kind mentioned in subsection (1); and
(b) purporting to be a person authorised to do so,

shall, on being asked to do so, produce some duly authenticated document as evidence that he is such a person.

(4) While an order under this section ('an emergency protection order') is in force it –

(a) operates as a direction to any person who is in a position to do so to comply with any request to produce the child to the applicant;
(b) authorises –
  (i) the removal of the child at any time to accommodation provided by or on behalf of the applicant and his being kept there; or

(ii)  the prevention of the child's removal from any hospital, or other place, in which he was being accommodated immediately before the making of the order; and

(c)  gives the applicant parental responsibility for the child.

(5) Where an emergency protection order is in force with respect to a child, the applicant –

(a)  shall only exercise the power given by virtue of subsection (4)(b) in order to safeguard the welfare of the child;

(b)  shall take, and shall only take, such action in meeting his parental responsibility for the child as is reasonably required to safeguard or promote the welfare of the child (having regard in particular to the duration of the order); and

(c)  shall comply with the requirements of any regulations made by the Secretary of State for the purposes of this subsection.

(6) Where the court makes an emergency protection order, it may give such directions (if any) as it considers appropriate with respect to –

(a)  the contact which is, or is not, to be allowed between the child and any named person;

(b)  the medical or psychiatric examination or other assessment of the child.

(7) Where any direction is given under subsection (6)(b), the child may, if he is of sufficient understanding to make an informed decision, refuse to submit to the examination or other assessment.

(8) A direction under subsection (6)(a) may impose conditions and one under subsection (6)(b) may be to the effect that there is to be –

(a)  no such examination or assessment; or

(b)  no such examination or assessment unless the court directs otherwise.

(9) A direction under subsection (6) may be –

(a)  given when the emergency protection order is made or at any time while it is in force; and

(b)  varied at any time on the application of any person falling within any class of person prescribed by rules of court for the purposes of this subsection.

(10) Where an emergency protection order is in force with respect to a child and –

(a)  the applicant has exercised the power given by subsection (4)(b)(i) but it appears to him that it is safe for the child to be returned; or

(b)  the applicant has exercised the power given by subsection (4)(b)(ii) but it appears to him that it is safe for the child to be allowed to be removed from the place in question,

he shall return the child or (as the case may be) allow him to be removed.

(11) Where he is required by subsection (10) to return the child the applicant shall –

- (a) return him to the care of the person from whose care he was removed; or
- (b) if that is not reasonably practicable, return him to the care of –
  - (i) a parent of his;
  - (ii) any person who is not a parent of his but who has parental responsibility for him; or
  - (iii) such other person as the applicant (with the agreement of the court) considers appropriate.

(12) Where the applicant has been required by subsection (10) to return the child, or to allow him to be removed, he may again exercise his powers with respect to the child (at any time while the emergency protection order remains in force) if it appears to him that a change in the circumstances of the case makes it necessary for him to do so.

(13) Where an emergency protection order has been made with respect to a child, the applicant shall, subject to any direction given under subsection (6), allow the child reasonable contact with –

- (a) his parents;
- (b) any person who is not a parent of his but who has parental responsibility for him;
- (c) any person with whom he was living immediately before the making of the order;
- (d) any person named in a child arrangements order as a person with whom the child is to spend time or otherwise have contact;
- (e) any person who is allowed to have contact with the child by virtue of an order under section 34; and
- (f) any person acting on behalf of any of those persons.

(14) Wherever it is reasonably practicable to do so, an emergency protection order shall name the child; and where it does not name him it shall describe him as clearly as possible.

(15) A person shall be guilty of an offence if he intentionally obstructs any person exercising the power under subsection (4)(b) to remove, or prevent the removal of, a child.

(16) A person guilty of an offence under subsection (15) shall be liable on summary conviction to a fine not exceeding level 3 on the standard scale.

**Amendments**—Children and Families 2014, s 12, Sch 2.

## 44A Power to include exclusion requirement in emergency protection order

(1) Where –

- (a) on being satisfied as mentioned in section 44(1)(a), (b) or (c), the court makes an emergency protection order with respect to a child, and
- (b) the conditions mentioned in subsection (2) are satisfied,

the court may include an exclusion requirement in the emergency protection order.

(2) The conditions are –
- (a) that there is reasonable cause to believe that, if a person ('the relevant person') is excluded from a dwelling-house in which the child lives, then –
    - (i) in the case of an order made on the ground mentioned in section 44(1)(a), the child will not be likely to suffer significant harm, even though the child is not removed as mentioned in section 44(1)(a)(i) or does not remain as mentioned in section 44(1)(a)(ii), or
    - (ii) in the case of an order made on the ground mentioned in paragraph (b) or (c) of section 44(1), the enquiries referred to in that paragraph will cease to be frustrated, and
- (b) that another person living in the dwelling-house (whether a parent of the child or some other person) –
    - (i) is able and willing to give to the child the care which it would be reasonable to expect a parent to give him, and
    - (ii) consents to the inclusion of the exclusion requirement.

(3) For the purposes of this section an exclusion requirement is any one or more of the following –
- (a) a provision requiring the relevant person to leave a dwelling-house in which he is living with the child,
- (b) a provision prohibiting the relevant person from entering a dwelling-house in which the child lives, and
- (c) a provision excluding the relevant person from a defined area in which a dwelling-house in which the child lives is situated.

(4) The court may provide that the exclusion requirement is to have effect for a shorter period than the other provisions of the order.

(5) Where the court makes an emergency protection order containing an exclusion requirement, the court may attach a power of arrest to the exclusion requirement.

(6) Where the court attaches a power of arrest to an exclusion requirement of an emergency protection order, it may provide that the power of arrest is to have effect for a shorter period than the exclusion requirement.

(7) Any period specified for the purposes of subsection (4) or (6) may be extended by the court (on one or more occasions) on an application to vary or discharge the emergency protection order.

(8) Where a power of arrest is attached to an exclusion requirement of an emergency protection order by virtue of subsection (5), a constable may arrest without warrant any person whom he has reasonable cause to believe to be in breach of the requirement.

(9) Sections 47(7), (11) and (12) and 48 of, and Schedule 5 to, the Family Law Act 1996 shall have effect in relation to a person arrested under subsection (8) of this section as they have effect in relation to a person arrested under section 47(6) of that Act.

(10) If, while an emergency protection order containing an exclusion requirement is in force, the applicant has removed the child from the dwelling-house from which the relevant person is excluded to other accommodation for a continuous period of more than 24 hours, the order shall cease to have effect in so far as it imposes the exclusion requirement.

**Amendments**—Inserted by Family Law Act 1996, s 52, Sch 6, para 3.

### 44B Undertakings relating to emergency protection orders

(1) In any case where the court has power to include an exclusion requirement in an emergency protection order, the court may accept an undertaking from the relevant person.

(2) No power of arrest may be attached to any undertaking given under subsection (1).

(3) An undertaking given to a court under subsection (1) –

   (a)   shall be enforceable as if it were an order of the court, and
   (b)   shall cease to have effect if, while it is in force, the applicant has removed the child from the dwelling-house from which the relevant person is excluded to other accommodation for a continuous period of more than 24 hours.

(4) This section has effect without prejudice to the powers of the High Court and family court apart from this section.

(5) In this section 'exclusion requirement' and 'relevant person' have the same meaning as in section 44A.

**Amendments**—Inserted by Family Law Act 1996, s 52, Sch 6, para 3; Crime and Courts Act 2013, s 17, Sch 11.

### 45 Duration of emergency protection orders and other supplemental provisions

(1) An emergency protection order shall have effect for such period, not exceeding eight days, as may be specified in the order.

(2) Where –

   (a)   the court making an emergency protection order would, but for this subsection, specify a period of eight days as the period for which the order is to have effect; but
   (b)   the last of those eight days is a public holiday (that is to say, Christmas Day, Good Friday, a bank holiday or a Sunday),

the court may specify a period which ends at noon on the first later day which is not such a holiday.

(3) Where an emergency protection order is made on an application under section 46(7), the period of eight days mentioned in subsection (1) shall begin with the first day on which the child was taken into police protection under section 46.

(4) Any person who –

- (a) has parental responsibility for a child as the result of an emergency protection order; and
- (b) is entitled to apply for a care order with respect to the child,

may apply to the court for the period during which the emergency protection order is to have effect to be extended.

(5) On an application under subsection (4) the court may extend the period during which the order is to have effect by such period, not exceeding seven days, as it thinks fit, but may do so only if it has reasonable cause to believe that the child concerned is likely to suffer significant harm if the order is not extended.

(6) An emergency protection order may only be extended once.

(7) Regardless of any enactment or rule of law which would otherwise prevent it from doing so, a court hearing an application for, or with respect to, an emergency protection order may take account of –

- (a) any statement contained in any report made to the court in the course of, or in connection with, the hearing; or
- (b) any evidence given during the hearing,

which is, in the opinion of the court, relevant to the application.

(8) Any of the following may apply to the court for an emergency protection order to be discharged –

- (a) the child;
- (b) a parent of his;
- (c) any person who is not a parent of his but who has parental responsibility for him; or
- (d) any person with whom he was living immediately before the making of the order.

(8A) On the application of a person who is not entitled to apply for the order to be discharged, but who is a person to whom an exclusion requirement contained in the order applies, an emergency protection order may be varied or discharged by the court in so far as it imposes the exclusion requirement.

(8B) Where a power of arrest has been attached to an exclusion requirement of an emergency protection order, the court may, on the application of any person entitled to apply for the discharge of the order so far as it imposes the exclusion requirement, vary or discharge the order in so far as it confers a power of arrest (whether or not any application has been made to vary or discharge any other provision of the order).

(9) *(repealed)*

(10) No appeal may be made against –

(a) the making of, or refusal to make, an emergency protection order;
(b) the extension of, or refusal to extend, the period during which such an order is to have effect;
(c) the discharge of, or refusal to discharge, such an order; or
(d) the giving of, or refusal to give, any direction in connection with such an order.

(11) Subsection (8) does not apply –

(a) where the person who would otherwise be entitled to apply for the emergency protection order to be discharged –
  (i) was given notice (in accordance with rules of court) of the hearing at which the order was made; and
  (ii) was present at that hearing; or
(b) to any emergency protection order the effective period of which has been extended under subsection (5).

(12) A court making an emergency protection order may direct that the applicant may, in exercising any powers which he has by virtue of the order, be accompanied by a registered medical practitioner, registered nurse or registered midwife, if he so chooses.

(13) The reference in subsection (12) to a registered midwife is to such a midwife who is also registered in the Specialist Community Public Health Nurses' Part of the register maintained under article 5 of the Nursing and Midwifery Order 2001.

**Amendments**—Courts and Legal Services Act 1990, s 116, Sch 16, para 19; Family Law Act 1996, s 52, Sch 6, para 4; SI 2002/253; SI 2004/1771; Children and Young Persons Act 2008, s 30.

## 46 Removal and accommodation of children by police in cases of emergency

(1) Where a constable has reasonable cause to believe that a child would otherwise be likely to suffer significant harm, he may –

(a) remove the child to suitable accommodation and keep him there; or
(b) take such steps as are reasonable to ensure that the child's removal from any hospital, or other place, in which he is then being accommodated is prevented.

(2) For the purposes of this Act, a child with respect to whom a constable has exercised his powers under this section is referred to as having been taken into police protection.

(3) As soon as is reasonably practicable after taking a child into police protection, the constable concerned shall –

(a) inform the local authority within whose area the child was found of the steps that have been, and are proposed to be, taken with respect to the child under this section and the reasons for taking them;

(b) give details to the authority within whose area the child is ordinarily resident ('the appropriate authority') of the place at which the child is being accommodated;
(c) inform the child (if he appears capable of understanding) –
 (i) of the steps that have been taken with respect to him under this section and of the reasons for taking them; and;
 (ii) of the further steps that may be taken with respect to him under this section;
(d) take such steps as are reasonably practicable to discover the wishes and feelings of the child;
(e) secure that the case is inquired into by an officer designated for the purposes of this section by the chief officer of the police area concerned; and
(f) where the child was taken into police protection by being removed to accommodation which is not provided –
 (i) by or on behalf of a local authority; or
 (ii) as a refuge, in compliance with the requirements of section 51, secure that he is moved to accommodation which is so provided.

(4) As soon as is reasonably practicable after taking a child into police protection, the constable concerned shall take such steps as are reasonably practicable to inform –

(a) the child's parents;
(b) every person who is not a parent of his but who has parental responsibility for him; and
(c) any other person with whom the child was living immediately before being taken into police protection,

of the steps that he has taken under this section with respect to the child, the reasons for taking them and the further steps that may be taken with respect to him under this section.

(5) On completing any inquiry under subsection (3)(e), the officer conducting it shall release the child from police protection unless he considers that there is still reasonable cause for believing that the child would be likely to suffer significant harm if released.

(6) No child may be kept in police protection for more than 72 hours.

(7) While a child is being kept in police protection, the designated officer may apply on behalf of the appropriate authority for an emergency protection order to be made under section 44 with respect to the child.

(8) An application may be made under subsection (7) whether or not the authority know of it or agree to its being made.

(9) While a child is being kept in police protection –

(a) neither the constable concerned nor the designated officer shall have parental responsibility for him; but
(b) the designated officer shall do what is reasonable in all the circumstances of the case for the purpose of safeguarding or promoting

the child's welfare (having regard in particular to the length of the period during which the child will be so protected).

(10) Where a child has been taken into police protection, the designated officer shall allow –

(a) the child's parents;
(b) any person who is not a parent of the child but who has parental responsibility for him;
(c) any person with whom the child was living immediately before he was taken into police protection;
(d) any person named in a child arrangements order as a person with whom the child is to spend time or otherwise have contact;
(e) any person who is allowed to have contact with the child by virtue of an order under section 34; and
(f) any person acting on behalf of any of those persons,

to have such contact (if any) with the child as, in the opinion of the designated officer, is both reasonable and in the child's best interests.

(11) Where a child who has been taken into police protection is in accommodation provided by, or on behalf of, the appropriate authority, subsection (10) shall have effect as if it referred to the authority rather than to the designated officer.

Amendments—Children and Families 2014, s 12, Sch 2.

## 47 Local authority's duty to investigate

(1) Where a local authority –

(a) are informed that a child who lives, or is found, in their area –
  (i) is the subject of an emergency protection order; or
  (ii) is in police protection; or
  (iii) has contravened a ban imposed by a curfew notice within the meaning of Chapter I of Part I of the Crime and Disorder Act 1998; or
(b) have reasonable cause to suspect that a child who lives, or is found, in their area is suffering, or is likely to suffer, significant harm,

the authority shall make, or cause to be made, such enquiries as they consider necessary to enable them to decide whether they should take any action to safeguard or promote the child's welfare.

In the case of a child falling within paragraph (a)(iii) above, the enquiries shall be commenced as soon as practicable and, in any event, within 48 hours of the authority receiving the information.

(2) Where a local authority have obtained an emergency protection order with respect to a child, they shall make, or cause to be made, such enquiries as they consider necessary to enable them to decide what action they should take to safeguard or promote the child's welfare.

(3) The enquiries shall, in particular, be directed towards establishing –

(a) whether the authority should –
  (i) make any application to court under this Act;
  (ii) exercise any of their other powers under this Act;
  (iii) exercise any of their powers under section 11 of the Crime and Disorder Act 1998 (child safety orders); or
  (iv) (where the authority is a local authority in Wales) exercise any of their powers under the Social Services and Well-being (Wales) Act 2014;
  with respect to the child;
(b) whether, in the case of a child –
  (i) with respect to whom an emergency protection order has been made; and
  (ii) who is not in accommodation provided by or on behalf of the authority,
  it would be in the child's best interests (while an emergency protection order remains in force) for him to be in such accommodation; and
(c) whether, in the case of a child who has been taken into police protection, it would be in the child's best interests for the authority to ask for an application to be made under section 46(7).

(4) Where enquiries are being made under subsection (1) with respect to a child, the local authority concerned shall (with a view to enabling them to determine what action, if any, to take with respect to him) take such steps as are reasonably practicable –

(a) to obtain access to him; or
(b) to ensure that access to him is obtained, on their behalf, by a person authorised by them for the purpose,

unless they are satisfied that they already have sufficient information with respect to him.

(5) Where, as a result of any such enquiries, it appears to the authority that there are matters connected with the child's education which should be investigated, they shall consult the local authority (as defined in section 579(1) of the Education 1996), if different, specified in subsection (5ZA).

(5ZA) The local authority referred to in subsection (5) is –

(a) the local authority who –
  (i) maintain any school at which the child is a pupil, or
  (ii) make arrangements for the provision of education for the child otherwise than at school pursuant to section 19 of the Education Act 1996, or
(b) in a case where the child is a pupil at a school which is not maintained by a local authority, the local authority in whose area the school is situated.

(5A) For the purposes of making a determination under this section as to the action to be taken with respect to a child, a local authority shall, so far as is reasonably practicable and consistent with the child's welfare –

(a) ascertain the child's wishes and feelings regarding the action to be taken with respect to him; and
(b) give due consideration (having regard to his age and understanding) to such wishes and feelings of the child as they have been able to ascertain.

(6) Where, in the course of enquiries made under this section –

(a) any officer of the local authority concerned; or
(b) any person authorised by the authority to act on their behalf in connection with those enquiries –
   (i) is refused access to the child concerned; or
   (ii) is denied information as to his whereabouts,

the authority shall apply for an emergency protection order, a child assessment order, a care order or a supervision order with respect to the child unless they are satisfied that his welfare can be satisfactorily safeguarded without their doing so.

(7) If, on the conclusion of any enquiries or review made under this section, the authority decide not to apply for an emergency protection order, a care order, a child assessment order or a supervision order they shall –

(a) consider whether it would be appropriate to review the case at a later date; and
(b) if they decide that it would be, determine the date on which that review is to begin.

(8) Where, as a result of complying with this section, a local authority conclude that they should take action to safeguard or promote the child's welfare they shall take that action (so far as it is both within their power and reasonably practicable for them to do so).

(9) Where a local authority are conducting enquiries under this section, it shall be the duty of any person mentioned in subsection (11) to assist them with those enquiries (in particular by providing relevant information and advice) if called upon by the authority to do so.

(10) Subsection (9) does not oblige any person to assist a local authority where doing so would be unreasonable in all the circumstances of the case.

(11) The persons are –

(a) any local authority;
(b) *(repealed)*
(c) any local housing authority;
(ca) the National Health Service Commissioning Board;
(d) any clinical commissioning group, Local Health Board, Special Health Authority, National Health Service trust or NHS foundation trust; and
(e) any person authorised by the Secretary of State for the purposes of this section.

(12) Where a local authority are making enquiries under this section with respect to a child who appears to them to be ordinarily resident within the area

of another authority, they shall consult that other authority, who may undertake the necessary enquiries in their place.

**Amendments**—Courts and Legal Services Act 1990, s 116, Sch 16, para 20; Health Authorities Act 1995, s 2, Sch 1, para 118; Crime and Disorder Act 1998, ss 15(4), 119, Sch 8, para 69; SI 2000/90; Health and Social Care (Community Health and Standards) Act 2003, s 34, Sch 4, para 79; CA 2004, s 53; SI 2007/961; SI 2010/1158; Health and Social Care Act 2012, s 55(2), Sch 5, para 53; SI 2016/413.

## 48 Powers to assist in discovery of children who may be in need of emergency protection

(1) Where it appears to a court making an emergency protection order that adequate information as to the child's whereabouts –

- (a) is not available to the applicant for the order; but
- (b) is available to another person,

it may include in the order a provision requiring that other person to disclose, if asked to do so by the applicant, any information that he may have as to the child's whereabouts.

(2) No person shall be excused from complying with such a requirement on the ground that complying might incriminate him or his spouse or civil partner of an offence; but a statement of admission made in complying shall not be admissible in evidence against either of them in proceedings for any offence other than perjury.

(3) An emergency protection order may authorise the applicant to enter premises specified by the order and search for the child with respect to whom the order is made.

(4) Where the court is satisfied that there is reasonable cause to believe that there may be another child on those premises with respect to whom an emergency protection order ought to be made, it may make an order authorising the applicant to search for that other child on those premises.

(5) Where –

- (a) an order has been made under subsection (4);
- (b) the child concerned has been found on the premises; and
- (c) the applicant is satisfied that the grounds for making an emergency protection order exist with respect to him,

the order shall have effect as if it were an emergency protection order.

(6) Where an order has been made under subsection (4), the applicant shall notify the court of its effect.

(7) A person shall be guilty of an offence if he intentionally obstructs any person exercising the power of entry and search under subsection (3) or (4).

(8) A person guilty of an offence under subsection (7) shall be liable on summary conviction to a fine not exceeding level 3 on the standard scale.

(9) Where, on an application made by any person for a warrant under this section, it appears to the court –

(a) that a person attempting to exercise powers under an emergency protection order has been prevented from doing so by being refused entry to the premises concerned or access to the child concerned; or

(b) that any such person is likely to be so prevented from exercising any such powers,

it may issue a warrant authorising any constable to assist the person mentioned in paragraph (a) or (b) in the exercise of those powers, using reasonable force if necessary.

(10) Every warrant issued under this section shall be addressed to, and executed by, a constable who shall be accompanied by the person applying for the warrant if –

(a) that person so desires; and
(b) the court by whom the warrant is issued does not direct otherwise.

(11) A court granting an application for a warrant under this section may direct that the constable concerned may, in executing the warrant, be accompanied by a registered medical practitioner, registered nurse or registered midwife if he so chooses.

(11A) The reference in subsection (11) to a registered midwife is to such a midwife who is also registered in the Specialist Community Public Health Nurses' Part of the register maintained under article 5 of the Nursing and Midwifery Order 2001.

(12) An application for a warrant under this section shall be made in the manner and form prescribed by rules of court.

(13) Wherever it is reasonably practicable to do so, an order under subsection (4), an application for a warrant under this section and any such warrant shall name the child; and where it does not name him it shall describe him as clearly as possible.

**Amendments**—SI 2002/253; Civil Partnership Act 2004, s 261(1), Sch 27, para 130; SI 2004/1771.

## 49 Abduction of children in care etc

(1) A person shall be guilty of an offence if, knowingly and without lawful authority or reasonable excuse, he –

(a) takes a child to whom this section applies away from the responsible person;
(b) keeps such a child away from the responsible person; or
(c) induces, assists or incites such a child to run away or stay away from the responsible person.

(2) This section applies in relation to a child who is –

(a) in care;
(b) the subject of an emergency protection order; or

(c) in police protection,

and in this section 'the responsible person' means any person who for the time being has care of him by virtue of the care order, the emergency protection order, or section 46, as the case may be.

(3) A person guilty of an offence under this section shall be liable on summary conviction to imprisonment for a term not exceeding six months, or to a fine not exceeding level 5 on the standard scale, or to both.

## 50 Recovery of abducted children etc

(1) Where it appears to the court that there is reason to believe that a child to whom this section applies –

- (a) has been unlawfully taken away or is being unlawfully kept away from the responsible person;
- (b) has run away or is staying away from the responsible person; or
- (c) is missing,

the court may make an order under this section ('a recovery order').

(2) This section applies to the same children to whom section 49 applies and in this section 'the responsible person' has the same meaning as in section 49.

(3) A recovery order –

- (a) operates as a direction to any person who is in a position to do so to produce the child on request to any authorised person;
- (b) authorises the removal of the child by any authorised person;
- (c) requires any person who has information as to the child's whereabouts to disclose that information, if asked to do so, to a constable or an officer of the court;
- (d) authorises a constable to enter any premises specified in the order and search for the child, using reasonable force if necessary.

(4) The court may make a recovery order on the application of –

- (a) any person who has parental responsibility for the child by virtue of a care order or emergency protection order; or
- (b) where the child is in police protection, the designated officer.

(5) A recovery order shall name the child and –

- (a) any person who has parental responsibility for the child by virtue of a care order or emergency protection order; or
- (b) where the child is in police protection, the designated officer.

(6) Premises may only be specified under subsection (3)(d) if it appears to the court that there are reasonable grounds for believing the child to be on them.

(7) In this section –

'an authorised person' means –
- (a) any person specified by the court;
- (b) any constable;

(c) any person who is authorised –
  (i) after the recovery order is made; and
  (ii) by a person who has parental responsibility for the child by virtue of a care order or an emergency protection order,
to exercise any power under a recovery order; and

'the designated officer' means the officer designated for the purposes of section 46.

(8) Where a person is authorised as mentioned in subsection (7)(c) –
  (a) the authorisation shall identify the recovery order; and
  (b) any person claiming to be so authorised shall, if asked to do so, produce some duly authenticated document showing that he is so authorised.

(9) A person shall be guilty of an offence if he intentionally obstructs an authorised person exercising the power under subsection (3)(b) to remove a child.

(10) A person guilty of an offence under this section shall be liable on summary conviction to a fine not exceeding level 3 on the standard scale.

(11) No person shall be excused from complying with any request made under subsection (3)(c) on the ground that complying with it might incriminate him or his spouse or civil partner of an offence; but a statement or admission made in complying shall not be admissible in evidence against either of them in proceedings for an offence other than perjury.

(12)-(14) . . .

Amendments—Civil Partnership Act 2004, s 261(1), Sch 27, para 131.

## 51 Refuges for children at risk

(1) Where it is proposed to use a voluntary home or private children's home to provide a refuge for children who appear to be at risk of harm, the Secretary of State may issue a certificate under this section with respect to that home.

(2) Where a local authority or voluntary organisation arrange for a foster parent to provide such a refuge, the Secretary of State may issue a certificate under this section with respect to that foster parent.

(3) In subsection (2) 'foster parent' means a person who is, or who from time to time is, a local authority foster parent or a foster parent with whom children are placed by a voluntary organisation.

(4) The Secretary of State may by regulations –
  (a) make provision as to the manner in which certificates may be issued;
  (b) impose requirements which must be complied with while any certificate is in force; and
  (c) provide for the withdrawal of certificates in prescribed circumstances.

(5) Where a certificate is in force with respect to a home, none of the provisions mentioned in subsection (7) shall apply in relation to any person providing a refuge for any child in that home.

(6) Where a certificate is in force with respect to a foster parent, none of those provisions shall apply in relation to the provision by him of a refuge for any child in accordance with arrangements made by the local authority or voluntary organisation.

(7) The provisions are –

    (a)    section 49;
    (b)    sections 82 (recovery of certain fugitive children) and 83 (harbouring) of the Children (Scotland) Act 1995, so far as they apply in relation to anything done in England and Wales;
    (c)    section 32(3) of the Children and Young Persons Act 1969 (compelling, persuading, inciting or assisting any person to be absent from detention etc), so far as it applies in relation to anything done in England and Wales;
    (d)    section 2 of the Child Abduction Act 1984.

**Amendments**—Children (Scotland) Act 1995, s 105(4), Sch 4, para 48(1),(3); Care Standards Act 2000, s 116, Sch 4, para 14(1),(7).

**Modifications**—Section 51(7) is modified for certain purposes by SI 2013/1465, art 17, Sch 1, para 2.

## 52 Rules and regulations

(1) Without prejudice to section 93 or any other power to make such rules, rules of court may be made with respect to the procedure to be followed in connection with proceedings under this Part.

(2) The rules may in particular make provision –

    (a)    as to the form in which any application is to be made or direction is to be given;
    (b)    prescribing the persons who are to be notified of –
        (i)    the making, or extension, of an emergency protection order; or
        (ii)    the making of an application under section 45(4) or (8) or 46(7); and
    (c)    as to the content of any such notification and the manner in which, and person by whom, it is to be given.

(3) The Secretary of State may by regulations provide that, where –

    (a)    an emergency protection order has been made with respect to a child;
    (b)    the applicant for the order was not the local authority within whose area the child is ordinarily resident; and
    (c)    that local authority are of the opinion that it would be in the child's best interests for the applicant's responsibilities under the order to be transferred to them,

that authority shall (subject to their having complied with any requirements imposed by the regulations) be treated, for the purposes of this Act, as though they and not the original applicant had applied for, and been granted, the order.

(4) Regulations made under subsection (3) may, in particular, make provision as to –

- (a) the considerations to which the local authority shall have regard in forming an opinion as mentioned in subsection (3)(c); and
- (b) the time at which responsibility under any emergency protection order is to be treated as having been transferred to a local authority.

\* \* \* \*

## PART XII
## MISCELLANEOUS AND GENERAL

\* \* \* \*

*Effect and Duration of Orders etc*

### 91 Effect and duration of orders etc

(1) The making of a child arrangements order with respect to the living arrangements of a child who is the subject of a care order discharges the care order.

(1A) For the purposes of subsection (1), a child arrangements order is one made with respect to the living arrangements of a child if the arrangements regulated by the order consist of, or include, arrangements which relate to either or both of the following –

- (a) with whom the child is to live, and
- (b) when the child is to live with any person.

(2) The making of a care order with respect to a child who is the subject of any section 8 order discharges that order.

(2A) Where an activity direction has been made with respect to a child, the making of a care order with respect to the child discharges the direction.

(3) The making of a care order with respect to a child who is the subject of a supervision order discharges that other order.

(4) The making of a care order with respect to a child who is a ward of court brings that wardship to an end.

(5) The making of a care order with respect to a child who is the subject of a school attendance order made under section 437 of the Education Act 1996 discharges the school attendance order.

(5A) The making of a special guardianship order with respect to a child who is the subject of –

- (a) a care order; or
- (b) an order under section 34,

discharges that order.

(6) Where an emergency protection order is made with respect to a child who is in care, the care order shall have effect subject to the emergency protection order.

(7) Any order made under section 4(1), 4ZA(1), 4A(1) or 5(1) shall continue in force until the child reaches the age of eighteen, unless it is brought to an end earlier.

(8) Any –

    (a)    agreement under section 4, 4ZA or 4A; or
    (b)    appointment under section 5(3) or (4),

shall continue in force until the child reaches the age of eighteen, unless it is brought to an end earlier.

(9) An order under Schedule 1 has effect as specified in that Schedule.

(10) A section 8 order shall, if it would otherwise still be in force, cease to have effect when the child reaches the age of sixteen, unless it is to have effect beyond that age by virtue of section 9(6).

(10A) Subsection (10) does not apply to provision in a child arrangements order which regulates arrangements relating to –

    (a)    with whom a child is to live, or
    (b)    when a child is to live with any person.

(11) Where a section 8 order has effect with respect to a child who has reached the age of sixteen, it shall, if it would otherwise still be in force, cease to have effect when he reaches the age of eighteen.

(12) Any care order, other than an interim care order, shall continue in force until the child reaches the age of eighteen, unless it is brought to an end earlier.

(13) Any order made under any other provision of this Act in relation to a child shall, if it would otherwise still be in force, cease to have effect when he reaches the age of eighteen.

(14) On disposing of any application for an order under this Act, the court may (whether or not it makes any other order in response to the application) order that no application for an order under this Act of any specified kind may be made with respect to the child concerned by any person named in the order without leave of the court.

(15) Where an application ('the previous application') has been made for –

    (a)    the discharge of a care order;
    (b)    the discharge of a supervision order;
    (c)    the discharge of an education supervision order;
    (d)    the substitution of a supervision order for a care order; or
    (e)    a child assessment order,

no further application of a kind mentioned in paragraphs (a) to (e) may be made with respect to the child concerned, without leave of the court, unless the period between the disposal of the previous application and the making of the further application exceeds six months.

(16) Subsection (15) does not apply to applications made in relation to interim orders.

(17) Where –

(a) a person has made an application for an order under section 34;
(b) the application has been refused; and
(c) a period of less than six months has elapsed since the refusal,

that person may not make a further application for such an order with respect to the same child, unless he has obtained the leave of the court.

**Amendments**—Education Act 1996, s 582(1), Sch 37, Pt I, para 90; Adoption and Children 2002, ss 114(5), 139(1), Sch 3, paras 54 and 68; Children and Adoption 2006, s 15(1), Sch 2, paras 7, 9; Children and Young Persons Act 2008, s 37(3); Human Fertilisation and Embryology Act 2008, s 56, Sch 6, para 31; Children and Families 2014, s 12, Sch 2.

\* \* \* \*

## 98 Self-incrimination

(1) In any proceedings in which a court is hearing an application for an order under Part IV or V, no person shall be excused from –

(a) giving evidence on any matter; or
(b) answering any question put to him in the course of his giving evidence,

on the ground that doing so might incriminate him or his spouse or civil partner of an offence.

(2) A statement or admission made in such proceedings shall not be admissible in evidence against the person making it or his spouse or civil partner in proceedings for an offence other than perjury.

**Amendments**—Civil Partnership Act 2004, s 261(1), Sch 27, para 132.

\* \* \* \*

## 100 Restrictions on use of wardship jurisdiction

(1) Section 7 of the Family Law Reform Act 1969 (which gives the High Court power to place a ward of court in the care, or under the supervision, of a local authority) shall cease to have effect.

(2) No court shall exercise the High Court's inherent jurisdiction with respect to children –

(a) so as to require a child to be placed in the care, or put under the supervision, of a local authority;
(b) so as to require a child to be accommodated by or on behalf of a local authority;

(c) so as to make a child who is the subject of a care order a ward of court; or
(d) for the purpose of conferring on any local authority power to determine any question which has arisen, or which may arise, in connection with any aspect of parental responsibility for a child.

(3) No application for any exercise of the court's inherent jurisdiction with respect to children may be made by a local authority unless the authority have obtained the leave of the court.

(4) The court may only grant leave if it is satisfied that –

(a) the result which the authority wish to achieve could not be achieved through the making of any order of a kind to which subsection (5) applies; and
(b) there is reasonable cause to believe that if the court's inherent jurisdiction is not exercised with respect to the child he is likely to suffer significant harm.

(5) This subsection applies to any order –

(a) made otherwise than in the exercise of the court's inherent jurisdiction; and
(b) which the local authority is entitled to apply for (assuming, in the case of any application which may only be made with leave, that leave is granted).

\*\*\*\*

## SCHEDULE 2
## SUPPORT FOR CHILDREN AND FAMILIES PROVIDED BY LOCAL AUTHORITIES IN ENGLAND

*Application to Local Authorities in England*

**A1**

(1) This Schedule applies only in relation to local authorities in England.

(2) Accordingly, unless the contrary intention appears, a reference in this Schedule to a local authority means a local authority in England.

Amendments—Provision (and heading) inserted by SI 2016/413.

## PART I
## PROVISION OF SERVICES FOR FAMILIES

**1 Identification of children in need and provision of information**

(1) Every local authority shall take reasonable steps to identify the extent to which there are children in need within their area.

(2) Every local authority shall –

(a) publish information –

(i) about services provided by them under sections 17, 18, 20, 23B to 23D, 24A and 24B; and
(ii) where they consider it appropriate, about the provision by others (including, in particular, voluntary organisations) of services which the authority have power to provide under those sections; and
(b) take such steps as are reasonably practicable to ensure that those who might benefit from the services receive the information relevant to them.

Amendments—Children (Leaving Care) Act 2000, s 7(4).

## 1A (*repealed*)

## 2 Maintenance of a register of disabled children

(1) Every local authority shall open and maintain a register of disabled children within their area.

(2) The register may be kept by means of a computer.

## 3 Assessment of children's needs

Where it appears to a local authority that a child within their area is in need, the authority may assess his needs for the purposes of this Act at the same time as any assessment of his needs is made under –

(a) the Chronically Sick and Disabled Persons Act 1970;
(b) Part IV of the Education Act 1996;
(ba) Part 3 of the Children and Families Act 2014;
(c) the Disabled Persons (Services, Consultation and Representation) Act 1986; or
(d) any other enactment.

Amendments—Education Act 1996, s 582(1), Sch 37, Pt I, para 92; Children and Families 2014, s 82, Sch 3.

## 4 Prevention of neglect and abuse

(1) Every local authority shall take reasonable steps, through the provision of services under Part III of this Act, to prevent children within their area suffering ill-treatment or neglect.

(2) Where a local authority believe that a child who is at any time within their area –

(a) is likely to suffer harm; but
(b) lives or proposes to live in the area of another local authority or in the area of a local authority in Wales

they shall inform that other local authority or the local authority in Wales, as the case may be.

(3) When informing that other local authority or the local authority in Wales they shall specify –

(a) the harm that they believe he is likely to suffer; and
(b) (if they can) where the child lives or proposes to live.

**Amendments**—SI 2016/413.

## 5 Provision of accommodation in order to protect child

(1) Where –

(a) it appears to a local authority that a child who is living on particular premises is suffering, or is likely to suffer, ill treatment at the hands of another person who is living on those premises; and
(b) that other person proposes to move from the premises,

the authority may assist that other person to obtain alternative accommodation.

(2) Assistance given under this paragraph may be in cash.

(3) Subsections (7) to (9) of section 17 shall apply in relation to assistance given under this paragraph as they apply in relation to assistance given under that section.

## 6 Provision for disabled children

(1) Every local authority shall provide services designed –

(a) to minimise the effect on disabled children within their area of their disabilities;
(b) to give such children the opportunity to lead lives which are as normal as possible; and
(c) to assist individuals who provide care for such children to continue to do so, or to do so more effectively, by giving them breaks from caring.

(2) The duty imposed by sub-paragraph (1)(c) shall be performed in accordance with regulations made by the Secretary of State.

**Amendments**—Children and Young Persons Act 2008, s 25; SI 2016/413.

## 7 Provision to reduce need for care proceedings etc

Every local authority shall take reasonable steps designed –

(a) to reduce the need to bring –
 (i) proceedings for care or supervision orders with respect to children within their area;
 (ii) criminal proceedings against such children;
 (iii) any family or other proceedings with respect to such children which might lead to them being placed in the authority's care; or
 (iv) proceedings under the inherent jurisdiction of the High Court with respect to children;

(b) to encourage children within their area not to commit criminal offences; and
(c) to avoid the need for children within their area to be placed in secure accommodation within the meaning given in section 25 and in section 119 of the Social Services and Well-being (Wales) Act 2014.

Amendments—SI 2016/413.

## 8 Provision for children living with their families

Every local authority shall make such provision as they consider appropriate for the following services to be available with respect to children in need within their area while they are living with their families –

(a) advice, guidance and counselling;
(b) occupational, social, cultural or recreational activities;
(c) home help (which may include laundry facilities);
(d) facilities for, or assistance with, travelling to and from home for the purpose of taking advantage of any other service provided under this Act or of any similar service;
(e) assistance to enable the child concerned and his family to have a holiday.

## 8A Provision for accommodated children

(1) Every local authority shall make provision for such services as they consider appropriate to be available with respect to accommodated children.

(2) 'Accommodated children' are those children in respect of whose accommodation the local authority have been notified under section 85 or 86 or under section 120 of the Social Services and Well-being (Wales) Act 2014 (assessment of children accommodated by health authorities and education authorities).

(3) The services shall be provided with a view to promoting contact between each accommodated child and that child's family.

(4) The services may, in particular, include –

(a) advice, guidance and counselling;
(b) services necessary to enable the child to visit, or to be visited by, members of the family;
(c) assistance to enable the child and members of the family to have a holiday together.

(5) Nothing in this paragraph affects the duty imposed by paragraph 10.

Amendments—Inserted by Children and Young Persons Act 2008, s 19. Amended by SI 2016/413.

## 9 Family centres

(1) Every local authority shall provide such family centres as they consider appropriate in relation to children within their area.

(2) 'Family centre' means a centre at which any of the persons mentioned in sub-paragraph (3) may –

- (a) attend for occupational, social, cultural or recreational activities;
- (b) attend for advice, guidance or counselling; or
- (c) be provided with accommodation while he is receiving advice, guidance or counselling.

(3) The persons are –

- (a) a child;
- (b) his parents;
- (c) any person who is not a parent of his but who has parental responsibility for him;
- (d) any other person who is looking after him.

## 10 Maintenance of the family home

Every local authority shall take such steps as are reasonably practicable, where any child within their area who is in need and whom they are not looking after is living apart from his family –

- (a) to enable him to live with his family; or
- (b) to promote contact between him and his family,

if, in their opinion, it is necessary to do so in order to safeguard or promote his welfare.

## 11 Duty to consider racial groups to which children in need belong

Every local authority shall, in making any arrangements –

- (a) for the provision of day care within their area; or
- (b) designed to encourage persons to act as local authority foster parents,

have regard to the different racial groups to which children within their area who are in need belong.

# PART II
# CHILDREN LOOKED AFTER BY LOCAL AUTHORITIES IN ENGLAND

Amendments—SI 2016/413.

## 12A Regulations as to conditions under which child in care is allowed to live with parent, etc

Regulations under section 22C may, in particular, impose requirements on a local authority as to –

- (a) the making of any decision by a local authority to allow a child in their care to live with any person falling within section 22C(3) (including requirements as to those who must be consulted before the decision is made and those who must be notified when it has been made);
- (b) the supervision or medical examination of the child concerned;

(c) the removal of the child, in such circumstances as may be prescribed, from the care of the person with whom the child has been allowed to live;
(d) the records to be kept by local authorities.

## 12B Regulations as to placements of a kind specified in section 22C(6)(d)

Regulations under section 22C as to placements of the kind specified in section 22C(6)(d) may, in particular, make provision as to –

(a) the persons to be notified of any proposed arrangements;
(b) the opportunities such persons are to have to make representations in relation to the arrangements proposed;
(c) the persons to be notified of any proposed changes in arrangements;
(d) the records to be kept by local authorities;
(e) the supervision by local authorities of any arrangements made.

## 12C Placements out of area

Regulations under section 22C may, in particular, impose requirements which a local authority must comply with –

(a) before a child looked after by them is provided with accommodation at a place outside the area of the authority; or
(b) if the child's welfare requires the immediate provision of such accommodation, within such period of the accommodation being provided as may be prescribed.

## 12D Avoidance of disruption in education

(1) Regulations under section 22C may, in particular, impose requirements which a local authority must comply with before making any decision concerning a child's placement if he is in the fourth key stage.

(2) A child is 'in the fourth key stage' if he is a pupil in the fourth key stage for the purposes of Part 6 or 7 of the Education 2002 (see section 82 and 103 of that Act).

## 12E Regulations as to placing of children with local authority foster parents

Regulations under section 22C may, in particular, make provision –

(a) with regard to the welfare of children placed with local authority foster parents;
(b) as to the arrangements to be made by local authorities in connection with the health and education of such children;
(c) as to the records to be kept by local authorities;
(d) for securing that where possible the local authority foster parent with whom a child is to be placed is –
 (i) of the same religious persuasion as the child; or
 (ii) gives an undertaking that the child will be brought up in that religious persuasion;

(e) for securing the children placed with local authority foster parents, and the premises in which they are accommodated, will be supervised and inspected by a local authority and that the children will be removed from those premises if their welfare appears to require it.

## 12F

(1) Regulations under section 22C may, in particular, also make provision –

  (a) for securing that a child is not placed with a local authority foster parent unless that person is for the time being approved as a local authority foster parent by such local authority as may be prescribed in regulations made by the Secretary of State;
  (b) establishing a procedure under which any person in respect of whom a qualifying determination has been made may apply to the Secretary of State for a review of that determination by a panel constituted by the Secretary of State.

(2) A determination is a qualifying determination if –

  (a) it relates to the issue of whether a person should be approved, or should continue to be approved, as a local authority foster parent; and
  (b) it is of a prescribed description.

(3) Regulations made by virtue of sub-paragraph (1)(b) may include provision as to –

  (a) the duties and powers of a panel;
  (b) the administration and procedures of a panel;
  (c) the appointment of members of a panel (including the number, or any limit on the number, of members who may be appointed and any conditions for appointment);
  (d) the payment of fees to members of a panel;
  (e) the duties of any person in connection with a review conducted under the regulations;
  (f) the monitoring of any such reviews.

(4) Regulations made by virtue of sub-paragraph (3)(e) may impose a duty to pay to the Secretary of State such sum as that national authority may determine; but such a duty may not be imposed upon a person who has applied for a review of a qualifying determination.

(5) The Secretary of State must secure that, taking one financial year with another, the aggregate of the sums which become payable to it under regulations made by virtue of subparagraph (4) does not exceed the cost to it of performing its independent review functions.

(6) The Secretary of State may make an arrangement with an organisation under which independent review functions are performed by the organisation on the national authority's behalf.

(7) If the Secretary of State makes such an arrangement with an organisation, the organisation is to perform its functions under the arrangement in accordance with any general or special directions given by that national authority.

(8) The arrangement may include provision for payments to be made to the organisation by the Secretary of State.

(9) Payments made by the Secretary of State in accordance with such provision shall be taken into account in determining (for the purpose of sub-paragraph (5)) the cost to that national authority of performing its independent review functions.

(10) Where the Welsh Ministers are the Secretary of State, sub-paragraphs (6) and (8) also apply as if references to an organisation included references to the Secretary of State.

(11) In this paragraph –

'financial year' means a period of twelve months ending with 31 March;
'independent review function' means a function conferred or imposed on a national authority by regulations made by virtue of sub-paragraph (1)(b);
'organisation' includes the Welsh Ministers, a public body and a private or voluntary organisation.

Amendments—SI 2016/413.

## 12G

Regulations under section 22C may, in particular, also make provision as to the circumstances in which local authorities may make arrangements for duties imposed on them by the regulations to be discharged on their behalf.

Amendments—Courts and Legal Services Act 1990, s 116, Sch 16, para 26; Children and Young Persons Act 2008, s 8(2), Sch 1, para 4.

## 15 Promotion and maintenance of contact between child and family

(1) Where a child is being looked after by a local authority, the authority shall, unless it is not reasonably practicable or consistent with his welfare, endeavour to promote contact between the child and –

- (a) his parents;
- (b) any person who is not a parent of his but who has parental responsibility for him; and
- (c) any relative, friend or other person connected with him.

(2) Where a child is being looked after by a local authority –

- (a) the authority shall take such steps as are reasonably practicable to secure that
    - (i) his parents; and
    - (ii) any person who is not a parent of his but who has parental responsibility for him,

are kept informed of where he is being accommodated; and
(b) every such person shall secure that the authority are kept informed of his or her address.

(3) Where a local authority ('the receiving authority') take over the provision of accommodation for a child from another local authority or a local authority in Wales ('the transferring authority') under section 20(2) –

(a) the receiving authority shall (where reasonably practicable) inform
   (i) the child's parents; and
   (ii) any person who is not a parent of his but who has parental responsibility for him;
(b) sub-paragraph (2)(a) shall apply to the transferring authority, as well as the receiving authority, until at least one such person has been informed of the change; and
(c) sub-paragraph (2)(b) shall not require any person to inform the receiving authority of his address until he has been so informed.

(4) Nothing in this paragraph requires a local authority to inform any person of the whereabouts of a child if –

(a) the child is in the care of the authority; and
(b) the authority has reasonable cause to believe that informing the person would prejudice the child's welfare.

(5) Any person who fails (without reasonable excuse) to comply with sub-paragraph (2)(b) shall be guilty of an offence and liable on summary conviction to a fine not exceeding level 2 on the standard scale.

(6) It shall be a defence in any proceedings under sub-paragraph (5) to prove that the defendant was residing at the same address as another person who was the child's parent or had parental responsibility for the child and had reasonable cause to believe that the other person had informed the appropriate authority that both of them were residing at that address.

Amendments—SI 2016/413.

**16 Visits to or by children: expenses**

(1) This paragraph applies where –

(a) a child is being looked after by a local authority; and
(b) the conditions mentioned in sub-paragraph (3) are satisfied.

(2) The authority may –

(a) make payments to –
   (i) a parent of the child;
   (ii) any person who is not a parent of his but who has parental responsibility for him; or
   (iii) any relative, friend or other person connected with him,
   in respect of travelling, subsistence or other expenses incurred by that person in visiting the child; or

(b) make payments to the child, or to any person on his behalf, in respect of travelling, subsistence or other expenses incurred by or on behalf of the child in his visiting –
    (i) a parent of his;
    (ii) any person who has parental responsibility for him; or
    (iii) any relative, friend or other person connected with him.

(3) The conditions are that –

(a) it appears to the authority that the visit in question could not otherwise be made without undue financial hardship; and
(b) the circumstances warrant the making of the payments.

17 (*repealed*)

## 18 Power to guarantee apprenticeship deeds etc

(1) While a child is being looked after by a local authority, or is a person qualifying for advice and assistance, the authority may undertake any obligation by way of guarantee under any deed of apprenticeship or articles of clerkship which he enters into.

(2) Where a local authority have undertaken any such obligation under any deed or articles they may at any time (whether or not they are still looking after the person concerned) undertake the like obligation under any supplemental deed or articles.

## 19 Arrangements to assist children to live abroad

(1) A local authority may only arrange for, or assist in arranging for, any child in their care to live outside England and Wales with the approval of the court.

(2) A local authority may, with the approval of every person who has parental responsibility for the child arrange for, or assist in arranging for, any other child looked after by them to live outside England and Wales.

(3) The court shall not give its approval under sub-paragraph (1) unless it is satisfied that –

(a) living outside England and Wales would be in the child's best interests;
(b) suitable arrangements have been, or will be, made for his reception and welfare in the country in which he will live;
(c) the child has consented to living in that country; and
(d) every person who has parental responsibility for the child has consented to his living in that country.

(4) Where the court is satisfied that the child does not have sufficient understanding to give or withhold his consent, it may disregard sub-paragraph (3)(c) and give its approval if the child is to live in the country concerned with a parent, guardian, special guardian or other suitable person.

(5) Where a person whose consent is required by sub-paragraph (3)(d) fails to give his consent, the court may disregard that provision and give its approval if it is satisfied that that person –

(a) cannot be found;
(b) is incapable of consenting; or
(c) is withholding his consent unreasonably.

(6) Section 85 of the Adoption and Children Act 2002 (which imposes restrictions on taking children out of the United Kingdom) shall not apply in the case of any child who is to live outside England and Wales with the approval of the court given under this paragraph.

(7) Where a court decides to give its approval under this paragraph it may order that its decision is not to have effect during the appeal period.

(8) In sub-paragraph (7) 'the appeal period' means –

(a) where an appeal is made against the decision, the period between the making of the decision and the determination of the appeal; and
(b) otherwise, the period during which an appeal may be made against the decision.

(9) This paragraph does not apply to a local authority placing a child for adoption with prospective adopters.

Amendments—Adoption and Children 2002, s 139(1), Sch 3, paras 54, 72.

## Preparation for ceasing to be looked after

### 19A

It is the duty of the local authority looking after a child to advise, assist and befriend him with a view to promoting his welfare when they have ceased to look after him.

Amendments—Inserted by Children (Leaving Care) Act 2000, s 1.

### 19B

(1) A local authority shall have the following additional functions in relation to an eligible child whom they are looking after.

(2) In sub-paragraph (1) 'eligible child' means, subject to sub-paragraph (3), a child who –

(a) is aged sixteen or seventeen; and
(b) has been looked after by a local authority or by a local authority in Wales for a prescribed period, or periods amounting in all to a prescribed period, which began after he reached a prescribed age and ended after he reached the age of sixteen.

(3) The Secretary of State may prescribe –

(a) additional categories of eligible children; and

(b) categories of children who are not to be eligible children despite falling within sub-paragraph (2).

(4) For each eligible child, the local authority shall carry out an assessment of his needs with a view to determining what advice, assistance and support it would be appropriate for them to provide him under this Act –

   (a) while they are still looking after him; and
   (b) after they cease to look after him,

and shall then prepare a pathway plan for him.

(5) The local authority shall keep the pathway plan under regular review.

(6) Any such review may be carried out at the same time as a review of the child's case carried out by virtue of section 26.

(7) The Secretary of State may by regulations make provision as to assessments for the purposes of sub-paragraph (4).

(8) The regulations may in particular provide for the matters set out in section 23B(6).

**Amendments**—Inserted by Children (Leaving Care) Act 2000, s 1. Amended by Children and Young Persons Act 2008, s 39, Sch 3, paras 1, 27; SI 2016/413.

## 19BA Preparation for ceasing to be looked after: staying put arrangements

(1) This paragraph applies in relation to an eligible child (within the meaning of paragraph 19B) who has been placed by a local authority with a local authority foster parent.

(2) When carrying out the assessment of the child's needs in accordance with paragraph 19B(4), the local authority must determine whether it would be appropriate to provide advice, assistance and support under this Act in order to facilitate a staying put arrangement, and with a view to maintaining such an arrangement, after the local authority cease to look after him or her.

(3) The local authority must provide advice, assistance and support under this Act in order to facilitate a staying put arrangement if –

   (a) the local authority determine under sub-paragraph (2) that it would be appropriate to do so, and
   (b) the eligible child and the local authority foster parent wish to make a staying put arrangement.

(4) In this paragraph, 'staying put arrangement' has the meaning given by section 23CZA.

**Amendments**—Inserted by Children and Families 2014, s 98. Amended by SI 2016/413.

## 19C Personal advisers

A local authority shall arrange for each child whom they are looking after who is an eligible child for the purposes of paragraph 19B to have a personal adviser.

**Amendments**—Inserted by Children (Leaving Care) Act 2000, s 1.

## 20 Death of children being looked after by local authorities

(1) If a child who is being looked after by a local authority dies, the authority –

(a) shall notify the Secretary of State and Her Majesty's Chief Inspector of Education, Children's Services and Skills;
(b) shall, so far as is reasonably practicable, notify the child's parents and every person who is not a parent of his but who has parental responsibility for him;
(c) may, with the consent (so far as it is reasonably practicable to obtain it) of every person who has parental responsibility for the child, arrange for the child's body to be buried or cremated; and
(d) may, if the conditions mentioned in sub-paragraph (2) are satisfied, make payments to any person who has parental responsibility for the child, or any relative, friend or other person connected with the child, in respect of travelling, subsistence or other expenses incurred by that person in attending the child's funeral.

(2) The conditions are that –

(a) it appears to the authority that the person concerned could not otherwise attend the child's funeral without undue financial hardship; and
(b) that the circumstances warrant the making of the payments.

(3) Sub-paragraph (1) does not authorise cremation where it does not accord with the practice of the child's religious persuasion.

(4) Where a local authority have exercised their power under sub-paragraph (1)(c) with respect to a child who was under sixteen when he died, they may recover from any parent of the child any expenses incurred by them.

(5) Any sums so recoverable shall, without prejudice to any other method of recovery, be recoverable summarily as a civil debt.

(6) Nothing in this paragraph affects any enactment regulating or authorising the burial, cremation or anatomical examination of the body of a deceased person.

**Amendments**—Health and Social Care (Community Health and Standards) Act 2003, s 147, Sch 9, para 10; Education and Inspection Act 2006, Sch 14, para 17; Children and Young Persons Act 2008, s 39, Sch 3, paras 1, 27; SI 2016/413.

## PART III
## CONTRIBUTIONS TOWARDS MAINTENANCE OF CHILDREN LOOKED AFTER BY LOCAL AUTHORITIES IN ENGLAND

**Amendments**—SI 2016/413.

## 21 Liability to contribute

(1) Where a local authority are looking after a child (other than in the cases mentioned in sub-paragraph (7)) they shall consider whether they should recover contributions towards the child's maintenance from any person liable to contribute ('a contributor').

(2) An authority may only recover contributions from a contributor if they consider it reasonable to do so.

(3) The persons liable to contribute are –

   (a) where the child is under sixteen, each of his parents;
   (b) where he has reached the age of sixteen, the child himself.

(4) A parent is not liable to contribute during any period when he is in receipt of universal credit (except in such circumstances as may be prescribed), income support under Part VII of the Social Security Contributions and Benefits Act 1992, of any element of child tax credit other than the family element, of working tax credit of an income-based jobseeker's allowance or of an income-related employment and support allowance.

(5) A person is not liable to contribute towards the maintenance of a child in the care of a local authority in respect of any period during which the child is living with, under arrangements made by the authority in accordance with section 22C, a parent of his.

(6) A contributor is not obliged to make any contribution towards a child's maintenance except as agreed or determined in accordance with this Part of this Schedule.

(7) The cases are where the child is looked after by a local authority under –

   (a) section 21;
   (b) an interim care order;
   (c) section 92 of the Powers of Criminal Courts (Sentencing) Act 2000.

**Amendments**—Disability Living Allowance and Disability Working Allowance Act 1991, s 7(2), Sch 3, para 15; Social Security (Consequential Provisions) Act 1992, s 4, Sch 2, para 108; Jobseekers Act 1995, s 41, Sch 2, para 19; Tax Credits Act 1999, s 1(2), Sch 1, paras 1, 6(d)(iii); Powers of Criminal Courts (Sentencing) Act 2000, s 165, Sch 9, para 130; Tax Credits Act 2002, s 47, Sch 3, paras 15, 20; Welfare Reform Act 2007, s 28(1), Sch 3, para 6(1),(6); Children and Young Persons Act 2008, s 8(3), Sch 1, para 5; Welfare Reform Act 2012, s 31, Sch 2, para 1.

## 22 Agreed contributions

(1) Contributions towards a child's maintenance may only be recovered if the local authority have served a notice ('a contribution notice') on the contributor specifying –

   (a) the weekly sum which they consider that he should contribute; and
   (b) arrangements for payment.

(2) The contribution notice must be in writing and dated.

(3) Arrangements for payment shall, in particular, include –

(a) the date on which liability to contribute begins (which must not be earlier than the date of the notice);
(b) the date on which liability under the notice will end (if the child has not before that date ceased to be looked after by the authority); and
(c) the date on which the first payment is to be made.

(4) The authority may specify in a contribution notice a weekly sum which is a standard contribution determined by them for all children looked after by them.

(5) The authority may not specify in a contribution notice a weekly sum greater than that which they consider –

(a) they would normally be prepared to pay if they had placed a similar child with local authority foster parents; and
(b) it is reasonably practicable for the contributor to pay (having regard to his means).

(6) An authority may at any time withdraw a contribution notice (without prejudice to their power to serve another).

(7) Where the authority and the contributor agree –

(a) the sum which the contributor is to contribute; and
(b) arrangements for payment,

(whether as specified in the contribution notice or otherwise) and the contributor notifies the authority in writing that he so agrees, the authority may recover summarily as a civil debt any contribution which is overdue and unpaid.

(8) A contributor may, by serving a notice in writing on the authority, withdraw his agreement in relation to any period of liability falling after the date of service of the notice.

(9) Sub-paragraph (7) is without prejudice to any other method of recovery.

**23 Contribution orders**

(1) Where a contributor has been served with a contribution notice and has –

(a) failed to reach any agreement with the local authority as mentioned in paragraph 22(7) within the period of one month beginning with the day on which the contribution notice was served; or
(b) served a notice under paragraph 22(8) withdrawing his agreement,

the authority may apply to the court for an order under this paragraph.

(2) On such an application the court may make an order ('a contribution order') requiring the contributor to contribute a weekly sum towards the child's maintenance in accordance with arrangements for payment specified by the court.

(3) A contribution order –

(a) shall not specify a weekly sum greater than that specified in the contribution notice; and
(b) shall be made with due regard to the contributor's means.

(4) A contribution order shall not –

(a) take effect before the date specified in the contribution notice; or
(b) have effect while the contributor is not liable to contribute (by virtue of paragraph 21); or
(c) remain in force after the child has ceased to be looked after by the authority who obtained the order.

(5) An authority may not apply to the court under sub-paragraph (1) in relation to a contribution notice which they have withdrawn.

(6) Where –

(a) a contribution order is in force;
(b) the authority serve another contribution notice; and
(c) the contributor and the authority reach an agreement under paragraph 22(7) in respect of that other contribution notice,

the effect of the agreement shall be to discharge the order from the date on which it is agreed that the agreement shall take effect.

(7) Where an agreement is reached under sub-paragraph (6) the authority shall notify the court –

(a) of the agreement; and
(b) of the date on which it took effect.

(8) A contribution order may be varied or revoked on the application of the contributor or the authority.

(9) In proceedings for the variation of a contribution order, the authority shall specify –

(a) the weekly sum which, having regard to paragraph 22, they propose that the contributor should contribute under the order as varied; and
(b) the proposed arrangements for payment.

(10) Where a contribution order is varied, the order –

(a) shall not specify a weekly sum greater than that specified by the authority in the proceedings for variation; and
(b) shall be made with due regard to the contributor's means.

(11) An appeal shall lie in accordance with rules of court from any order made under this paragraph.

## 24 Enforcement of contribution orders etc

(1) (*repealed*)

(2) Where a contributor has agreed, or has been ordered, to make contributions to a local authority, any other local authority within whose area the contributor is for the time being living may –

(a) at the request of the local authority who served the contribution notice; and
(b) subject to agreement as to any sum to be deducted in respect of services rendered,

collect from the contributor any contributions due on behalf of the authority who served the notice.

(3) In sub-paragraph (2) the reference to any other local authority includes a reference to –

(aa) a local authority in Wales;
(a) a local authority within the meaning of section 1(2) of the Social Work (Scotland) Act 1968; and
(b) a Health and Social Services Board established under Article 16 of the Health and Personal Social Services (Northern Ireland) Order 1972.

(4) The power to collect sums under sub-paragraph (2) includes the power to –

(a) receive and give a discharge for any contributions due; and
(b) (if necessary) enforce payment of any contributions,

even though those contributions may have fallen due at a time when the contributor was living elsewhere.

(5) Any contributions collected under sub-paragraph (2) shall be paid (subject to any agreed deduction) to the local authority who served the contribution notice.

(6) In any proceedings under this paragraph, a document which purports to be –

(a) a copy of an order made by a court under or by virtue of paragraph 23; and
(b) certified as a true copy by the designated officer for the court,

shall be evidence of the order.

(7) In any proceedings under this paragraph, a certificate which –

(a) purports to be signed by the clerk or some other duly authorised officer of the local authority who obtained the contribution order; and
(b) states that any sum due to the authority under the order is overdue and unpaid,

shall be evidence that the sum is overdue and unpaid.

**Amendments**—AJA 1999, s 90, Sch 13, para 162; Courts Act 2003, s 109(1), Sch 8, para 340; CCA 2013, s 17, Sch 11; SI 2016/413.

## 25 Regulations

The Secretary of State may make regulations –

(a) as to the considerations which a local authority must take into account in deciding –
  (i) whether it is reasonable to recover contributions; and
  (ii) what the arrangements for payment should be;
(b) as to the procedures they must follow in reaching agreements with –
  (i) contributors (under paragraphs 22 and 23); and
  (ii) any other local authority under paragraph 24(2).

Amendments—Children and Young Persons Act 2008, s 39, Sch 3, paras 1, 27; SI 2016/413.

## SCHEDULE 3
## SUPERVISION ORDERS

### PART I
### GENERAL

**1 Meaning of 'responsible person'**

In this Schedule, 'the responsible person', in relation to a supervised child, means –

(a) any person who has parental responsibility for the child; and
(b) any other person with whom the child is living.

**2 Power of supervisor to give directions to supervised child**

(1) A supervision order may require the supervised child to comply with any directions given from time to time by the supervisor which require him to do all or any of the following things –

(a) to live at a place or places specified in the directions for a period or periods so specified;
(b) to present himself to a person or persons specified in the directions at a place or places and on a day or days so specified;
(c) to participate in activities specified in the directions on a day or days so specified.

(2) It shall be for the supervisor to decide whether, and to what extent, he exercises his power to give directions and to decide the form of any directions which he gives.

(3) Sub-paragraph (1) does not confer on a supervisor power to give directions in respect of any medical or psychiatric examination or treatment (which are matters dealt with in paragraphs 4 and 5).

**3 Imposition of obligations on responsible person**

(1) With the consent of any responsible person, a supervision order may include a requirement –

(a) that he take all reasonable steps to ensure that the supervised child complies with any direction given by the supervisor under paragraph 2;
(b) that he take all reasonable steps to ensure that the supervised child complies with any requirement included in the order under paragraph 4 or 5;
(c) that he comply with any directions given by the supervisor requiring him to attend at a place specified in the directions for the purpose of taking part in activities so specified.

(2) A direction given under sub-paragraph (1)(c) may specify the time at which the responsible person is to attend and whether or not the supervised child is required to attend with him.

(3) A supervision order may require any person who is a responsible person in relation to the supervised child to keep the supervisor informed of his address, if it differs from the child's.

## 4 Psychiatric and medical examinations

(1) A supervision order may require the supervised child –

(a) to submit to a medical or psychiatric examination; or
(b) to submit to any such examination from time to time as directed by the supervisor.

(2) Any such examination shall be required to be conducted –

(a) by, or under the direction of, such registered medical practitioner as may be specified in the order;
(b) at a place specified in the order and at which the supervised child is to attend as a non-resident patient; or
(c) at –
 (i) a health service hospital; or
 (ii) in the case of a psychiatric examination, a hospital, independent hospital or care home,
 at which the supervised child is, or is to attend as, a resident patient.

(3) A requirement of a kind mentioned in sub-paragraph (2)(c) shall not be included unless the court is satisfied, on the evidence of a registered medical practitioner, that –

(a) the child may be suffering from a physical or mental condition that requires, and may be susceptible to, treatment; and
(b) a period as a resident patient is necessary if the examination is to be carried out properly.

(4) No court shall include a requirement under this paragraph in a supervision order unless it is satisfied that –

(a) where the child has sufficient understanding to make an informed decision, he consents to its inclusion; and
(b) satisfactory arrangements have been, or can be, made for the examination.

**Amendments**—Care Standards Act 2000, s 116, Sch 4, para 14(24).

## 5 Psychiatric and medical treatment

(1) Where a court which proposes to make or vary a supervision order is satisfied, on the evidence of a registered medical practitioner approved for the purposes of section 12 of the Mental Health Act 1983, that the mental condition of the supervised child –

(a) is such as requires, and may be susceptible to, treatment; but
(b) is not such as to warrant his detention in pursuance of a hospital order under Part III of that Act,

the court may include in the order a requirement that the supervised child shall, for a period specified in the order, submit to such treatment as is so specified.

(2) The treatment specified in accordance with sub-paragraph (1) must be –

(a) by, or under the direction of, such registered medical practitioner as may be specified in the order;
(b) as a non-resident patient at such a place as may be so specified; or
(c) as a resident patient in a hospital, independent hospital or care home.

(3) Where a court which proposes to make or vary a supervision order is satisfied, on the evidence of a registered medical practitioner, that the physical condition of the supervised child is such as requires, and may be susceptible to, treatment, the court may include in the order a requirement that the supervised child shall, for a period specified in the order, submit to such treatment as is so specified.

(4) The treatment specified in accordance with sub-paragraph (3) must be –

(a) by, or under the direction of, such registered medical practitioner as may be specified in the order;
(b) as a non-resident patient at such place as may be so specified; or
(c) as a resident patient in a health service hospital.

(5) No court shall include a requirement under this paragraph in a supervision order unless it is satisfied –

(a) where the child has sufficient understanding to make an informed decision, that he consents to its inclusion; and
(b) that satisfactory arrangements have been, or can be, made for the treatment.

(6) If a medical practitioner by whom or under whose direction a supervised person is being treated in pursuance of a requirement included in a supervision order by virtue of this paragraph is unwilling to continue to treat or direct the treatment of the supervised child or is of the opinion that –

(a) the treatment should be continued beyond the period specified in the order;
(b) the supervised child needs different treatment;
(c) he is not susceptible to treatment; or

(d) he does not require further treatment,

the practitioner shall make a report in writing to that effect to the supervisor.

(7) On receiving a report under this paragraph the supervisor shall refer it to the court, and on such a reference the court may make an order cancelling or varying the requirement.

Amendments—Care Standards Act 2000, s 116, Sch 4, para 14(24).

## PART II
## MISCELLANEOUS

### 6 Life of supervision order

(1) Subject to sub-paragraph (2) and section 91, a supervision order shall cease to have effect at the end of the period of one year beginning with the date on which it was made.

(2) A supervision order shall also cease to have effect if an event mentioned in section 25(1)(a) or (b) of the Child Abduction and Custody Act 1985 (termination of existing orders) occurs with respect to the child.

(3) Where the supervisor applies to the court to extend, or further extend, a supervision order the court may extend the order for such period as it may specify.

(4) A supervision order may not be extended so as to run beyond the end of the period of three years beginning with the date on which it was made.

### 7 (repealed)

### 8 Information to be given to supervisor etc

(1) A supervision order may require the supervised child –

  (a) to keep the supervisor informed of any change in his address; and
  (b) to allow the supervisor to visit him at the place where he is living.

(2) The responsible person in relation to any child with respect to whom a supervision order is made shall –

  (a) if asked by the supervisor, inform him of the child's address (if it is known to him); and
  (b) if he is living with the child, allow the supervisor reasonable contact with the child.

### 9 Selection of supervisor

(1) A supervision order shall not designate a local authority as the supervisor unless –

  (a) the authority agree; or
  (b) the supervised child lives or will live within their area.

(2)-(5) (*repealed*)

**Amendments**—Probation Service Act 1993, s 32, Sch 3, para 9; Criminal Justice and Courts Services Act 2000, ss 74, 75, Sch 7, paras 87, 96, Sch 8.

## 10 Effect of supervision order on earlier orders

The making of a supervision order with respect to any child brings to an end any earlier care or supervision order which –

(a) was made with respect to that child; and
(b) would otherwise continue in force.

## 11 Local authority functions and expenditure

(1) The Secretary of State may make regulations with respect to the exercise by a local authority of their functions where a child has been placed under their supervision by a supervision order.

(2) Where a supervision order requires compliance with directions given by virtue of this section, any expenditure incurred by the supervisor for the purposes of the directions shall be defrayed by the local authority designated in the order.

# PART III
# EDUCATION SUPERVISION ORDERS

## Effect of orders

## 12

(1) Where an education supervision order is in force with respect to a child, it shall be the duty of the supervisor –

(a) to advise, assist and befriend, and give directions to –
(i) the supervised child; and
(ii) his parents;
in such a way as will, in the opinion of the supervisor, secure that he is properly educated;
(b) where any such directions given to
(i) the supervised child; or
(ii) a parent of his,
have not been complied with, to consider what further steps to take in the exercise of the supervisor's powers under this Act.

(2) Before giving any directions under sub-paragraph (1) the supervisor shall, so far as is reasonably practicable, ascertain the wishes and feelings of –

(a) the child; and
(b) his parents;

including, in particular, their wishes as to the place at which the child should be educated.

(3) When settling the terms of any such directions, the supervisor shall give due consideration –
  (a) having regard to the child's age and understanding, to such wishes and feelings of his as the supervisor has been able to ascertain; and
  (b) to such wishes and feelings of the child's parents as he has been able to ascertain.

(4) Directions may be given under this paragraph at any time while the education supervision order is in force.

## 13

(1) Where an education supervision order is in force with respect to a child, the duties of the child's parents under sections 7 and 444 of the Education Act 1996 (duties to secure education of children and to secure regular attendance of registered pupils) shall be superseded by their duty to comply with any directions in force under the education supervision order.

(2) Where an education supervision order is made with respect to a child –
  (a) any school attendance order –
     (i) made under section 437 of the Education Act 1996 with respect to the child; and
     (ii) in force immediately before the making of the education supervision order,
    shall cease to have effect; and
  (b) while the education supervision order remains in force, the following provisions shall not apply with respect to the child –
     (i) section 437 of that Act (school attendance orders);
     (ii) section 9 of that Act (pupils to be educated in accordance with wishes of their parents);
     (iii) sections 411 and 423 of that Act (parental preference and appeals against admission decisions);
  (c) a youth rehabilitation order made under Part 1 of the Criminal Justice and Immigration Act 2008 with respect to the child, while the education supervision order is in force, may not include an education requirement (within the meaning of that Part);
  (d) any education requirement of a kind mentioned in paragraph (c), which was in force with respect to the child immediately before the making of the education supervision order, shall cease to have effect.

Amendments—Education Act 1996, s 582(1), Sch 37, Pt I, para 93; Powers of Criminal Courts (Sentencing) Act 2000, s 165, Sch 9, para 131; Criminal Justice and Immigration Act 2008, ss 6(2), 149, Sch 4, para 37.

## 14 Effect where child also subject to supervision order

(1) This paragraph applies where an education supervision order and a supervision order, or youth rehabilitation order (within the meaning of Part 1 of the Criminal Justice and Immigration Act 2008), are in force at the same time with respect to the same child.

(2) Any failure to comply with a direction given by the supervisor under the education supervision order shall be disregarded if it would not have been reasonably practicable to comply with it without failing to comply with a direction or instruction given under the other order.

**Amendments**—Powers of Criminal Courts (Sentencing) Act 2000, s 165, Sch 9, para 131; Criminal Justice and Immigration Act 2008, ss 6(2), 149, Sch 4, para 37.

## 15 Duration of orders

(1) An education supervision order shall have effect for a period of one year, beginning with the date on which it is made.

(2) An education supervision order shall not expire if, before it would otherwise have expired, the court has (on the application of the authority in whose favour the order was made) extended the period during which it is in force.

(3) Such an application may not be made earlier than three months before the date on which the order would otherwise expire.

(4) The period during which an education supervision order is in force may be extended under sub-paragraph (2) on more than one occasion.

(5) No one extension may be for a period of more than three years.

(6) An education supervision order shall cease to have effect on –

(a) the child's ceasing to be of compulsory school age; or
(b) the making of a care order with respect to the child;

and sub-paragraphs (1) to (4) are subject to this sub-paragraph.

## 16 Information to be given to supervisor etc

(1) An education supervision order may require the child –

(a) to keep the supervisor informed of any change in his address; and
(b) to allow the supervisor to visit him at the place where he is living.

(2) A person who is the parent of a child with respect to whom an education supervision order has been made shall –

(a) if asked by the supervisor, inform him of the child's address (if it is known to him); and
(b) if he is living with the child, allow the supervisor reasonable contact with the child.

## 17 Discharge of orders

(1) The court may discharge any education supervision order on the application of –

(a) the child concerned;
(b) a parent of his; or
(c) the local authority designated in the order.

(2) On discharging an education supervision order, the court may direct the local authority within whose area the child lives, or will live, to investigate the circumstances of the child.

## 18 Offences

(1) If a parent of a child with respect to whom an education supervision order is in force persistently fails to comply with a direction given under the order he shall be guilty of an offence.

(2) It shall be a defence for any person charged with such an offence to prove that –

  (a) he took all reasonable steps to ensure that the direction was complied with;
  (b) the direction was unreasonable; or
  (c) he had complied with –
    (i) a requirement included in a supervision order made with respect to the child; or
    (ii) directions given under such a requirement,

and that it was not reasonably practicable to comply both with the direction and with the requirement or directions mentioned in this paragraph.

(3) A person guilty of an offence under this paragraph shall be liable on summary conviction to a fine not exceeding level 3 on the standard scale.

## 19 Persistent failure of child to comply with directions

(1) Where a child with respect to whom an education supervision order is in force persistently fails to comply with any direction given under the order, the local authority designated in the order shall notify the appropriate local authority, if different.

(2) Where a local authority have been notified under sub-paragraph (1) they shall investigate the circumstances of the child.

(3) In this paragraph 'the appropriate local authority' has the same meaning as in section 36.

## 20 Miscellaneous

The Secretary of State may by regulations make provision modifying, or displacing, the provisions of any enactment about education in relation to any child with respect to whom an education supervision order is in force to such extent as appears to the Secretary of State to be necessary or expedient in consequence of the provision made by this Act with respect to such orders.

## 21 Interpretation

In this part of this Schedule 'parent' has the same meaning as in the Education Act 1996.

**Amendments**—Education Act 1996, s 582(1), Sch 37, para 93; SI 2010/1185.

# APPENDIX 2

# ADOPTION AND CHILDREN ACT 2002

## PART I
## ADOPTION

*Chapter 1*
*Introductory*

**1 Considerations applying to the exercise of powers**

(1) Subsections (2) to (4) apply whenever a court or adoption agency is coming to a decision relating to the adoption of a child.

(2) The paramount consideration of the court or adoption agency must be the child's welfare, throughout his life.

(3) The court or adoption agency must at all times bear in mind that, in general, any delay in coming to the decision is likely to prejudice the child's welfare.

(4) The court or adoption agency must have regard to the following matters (among others) –

- (a) the child's ascertainable wishes and feelings regarding the decision (considered in the light of the child's age and understanding),
- (b) the child's particular needs,
- (c) the likely effect on the child (throughout his life) of having ceased to be a member of the original family and become an adopted person,
- (d) the child's age, sex, background and any of the child's characteristics which the court or agency considers relevant,
- (e) any harm (within the meaning of the Children Act 1989) which the child has suffered or is at risk of suffering,
- (f) the relationship which the child has with relatives, with any person who is a prospective adopter with whom the child is placed, and with any other person in relation to whom the court or agency considers the relationship to be relevant, including –
  - (i) the likelihood of any such relationship continuing and the value to the child of its doing so,
  - (ii) the ability and willingness of any of the child's relatives, or of any such person, to provide the child with a secure environment in which the child can develop, and otherwise to meet the child's needs,
  - (iii) the wishes and feelings of any of the child's relatives, or of any such person, regarding the child.

(5) In placing a child for adoption, an adoption agency in Wales must give due consideration to the child's religious persuasion, racial origin and cultural and linguistic background.

(6) In coming to a decision relating to the adoption of a child, a court or adoption agency must always consider the whole range of powers available to it in the child's case (whether under this Act or the Children Act 1989); and the court must not make any order under this Act unless it considers that making the order would be better for the child than not doing so.

(7) In this section, 'coming to a decision relating to the adoption of a child', in relation to a court, includes –

(a) coming to a decision in any proceedings where the orders that might be made by the court include an adoption order (or the revocation of such an order), a placement order (or the revocation of such an order) or an order under section 26 or 51A (or the revocation or variation of such an order),
(b) coming to a decision about granting leave in respect of any action (other than the initiation of proceedings in any court) which may be taken by an adoption agency or individual under this Act,

but does not include coming to a decision about granting leave in any other circumstances.

(8) For the purposes of this section –

(a) references to relationships are not confined to legal relationships,
(b) references to a relative, in relation to a child, include the child's mother and father.

(9) In this section 'adoption agency in Wales' means an adoption agency that is –

(a) a local authority in Wales, or
(b) a registered adoption society whose principal office is in Wales.

**Amendments**—Children and Families Act 2014, ss 3, 9; Children and Social Work Act 2017, s 9.

\* \* \*

## Chapter 3
## Placement for Adoption and Adoption Orders; Placement of Children by Adoption Agency for Adoption

### 18 Placement for adoption by agencies

(1) An adoption agency may –

(a) place a child for adoption with prospective adopters, or
(b) where it has placed a child with any persons (whether under this Part or not), leave the child with them as prospective adopters,

but, except in the case of a child who is less than six weeks old, may only do so under section 19 or a placement order.

(2) An adoption agency may only place a child for adoption with prospective adopters if the agency is satisfied that the child ought to be placed for adoption.

(3) A child who is placed or authorised to be placed for adoption with prospective adopters by a local authority is looked after by the authority.

(4) If an application for an adoption order has been made by any persons in respect of a child and has not been disposed of –

(a) an adoption agency which placed the child with those persons may leave the child with them until the application is disposed of, but

(b) apart from that, the child may not be placed for adoption with any prospective adopters.

'Adoption order' includes a Scottish or Northern Irish adoption order.

(5) References in this Act (apart from this section) to an adoption agency placing a child for adoption –

(a) are to its placing a child for adoption with prospective adopters, and

(b) include, where it has placed a child with any persons (whether under this Act or not), leaving the child with them as prospective adopters;

and references in this Act (apart from this section) to a child who is placed for adoption by an adoption agency are to be interpreted accordingly.

(6) References in this Chapter to an adoption agency being, or not being, authorised to place a child for adoption are to the agency being or (as the case may be) not being authorised to do so under section 19 or a placement order.

(7) This section is subject to sections 30 to 35 (removal of children placed by adoption agencies).

## 19 Placing children with parental consent

(1) Where an adoption agency is satisfied that each parent or guardian of a child has consented to the child –

(a) being placed for adoption with prospective adopters identified in the consent, or

(b) being placed for adoption with any prospective adopters who may be chosen by the agency,

and has not withdrawn the consent, the agency is authorised to place the child for adoption accordingly.

(2) Consent to a child being placed for adoption with prospective adopters identified in the consent may be combined with consent to the child subsequently being placed for adoption with any prospective adopters who may be chosen by the agency in circumstances where the child is removed from or returned by the identified prospective adopters.

(3) Subsection (1) does not apply where –

(a) an application has been made on which a care order might be made and the application has not been disposed of, or

(b) a care order or placement order has been made after the consent was given.

(4) References in this Act to a child placed for adoption under this section include a child who was placed under this section with prospective adopters and continues to be placed with them, whether or not consent to the placement has been withdrawn.

(5) This section is subject to section 52 (parental etc consent).

## 20 Advance consent to adoption

(1) A parent or guardian of a child who consents to the child being placed for adoption by an adoption agency under section 19 may, at the same or any subsequent time, consent to the making of a future adoption order.

(2) Consent under this section –

(a) where the parent or guardian has consented to the child being placed for adoption with prospective adopters identified in the consent, may be consent to adoption by them, or
(b) may be consent to adoption by any prospective adopters who may be chosen by the agency.

(3) A person may withdraw any consent given under this section.

(4) A person who gives consent under this section may, at the same or any subsequent time, by notice given to the adoption agency –

(a) state that he does not wish to be informed of any application for an adoption order, or
(b) withdraw such a statement.

(5) A notice under subsection (4) has effect from the time when it is received by the adoption agency but has no effect if the person concerned has withdrawn his consent.

(6) This section is subject to section 52 (parental etc consent).

## 21 Placement orders

(1) A placement order is an order made by the court authorising a local authority to place a child for adoption with any prospective adopters who may be chosen by the authority.

(2) The court may not make a placement order in respect of a child unless –

(a) the child is subject to a care order,
(b) the court is satisfied that the conditions in section 31(2) of the 1989 Act (conditions for making a care order) are met, or
(c) the child has no parent or guardian.

(3) The court may only make a placement order if, in the case of each parent or guardian of the child, the court is satisfied –

(a) that the parent or guardian has consented to the child being placed for adoption with any prospective adopters who may be chosen by the local authority and has not withdrawn the consent, or

(b) that the parent's or guardian's consent should be dispensed with.

This subsection is subject to section 52 (parental etc consent).

(4) A placement order continues in force until –

(a) it is revoked under section 24,
(b) an adoption order is made in respect of the child, or
(c) the child marries, forms a civil partnership or attains the age of 18 years.

'Adoption order' includes a Scottish or Northern Irish adoption order.

Amendments—Civil Partnership Act 2004, s 79(1), (2).

## 22 Applications for placement orders

(1) A local authority must apply to the court for a placement order in respect of a child if –

(a) the child is placed for adoption by them or is being provided with accommodation by them,
(b) no adoption agency is authorised to place the child for adoption,
(c) the child has no parent or guardian or the authority consider that the conditions in section 31(2) of the 1989 Act are met, and
(d) the authority are satisfied that the child ought to be placed for adoption.

(2) If –

(a) an application has been made (and has not been disposed of) on which a care order might be made in respect of a child, or
(b) a child is subject to a care order and the appropriate local authority are not authorised to place the child for adoption,

the appropriate local authority must apply to the court for a placement order if they are satisfied that the child ought to be placed for adoption.

(3) If –

(a) a child is subject to a care order, and
(b) the appropriate local authority are authorised to place the child for adoption under section 19,

the authority may apply to the court for a placement order.

(4) If a local authority –

(a) are under a duty to apply to the court for a placement order in respect of a child, or
(b) have applied for a placement order in respect of a child and the application has not been disposed of,

the child is looked after by the authority.

(5) Subsections (1) to (3) do not apply in respect of a child –

(a) if any persons have given notice of intention to adopt, unless the period of four months beginning with the giving of the notice has expired without them applying for an adoption order or their application for such an order has been withdrawn or refused, or
(b) if an application for an adoption order has been made and has not been disposed of.

'Adoption order' includes a Scottish or Northern Irish adoption order.

(6) Where –

(a) an application for a placement order in respect of a child has been made and has not been disposed of, and
(b) no interim care order is in force,

the court may give any directions it considers appropriate for the medical or psychiatric examination or other assessment of the child; but a child who is of sufficient understanding to make an informed decision may refuse to submit to the examination or other assessment.

(7) The appropriate local authority –

(a) in relation to a care order, is the local authority in whose care the child is placed by the order, and
(b) in relation to an application on which a care order might be made, is the local authority which makes the application.

## 23 Varying placement orders

(1) The court may vary a placement order so as to substitute another local authority for the local authority authorised by the order to place the child for adoption.

(2) The variation may only be made on the joint application of both authorities.

## 24 Revoking placement orders

(1) The court may revoke a placement order on the application of any person.

(2) But an application may not be made by a person other than the child or the local authority authorised by the order to place the child for adoption unless –

(a) the court has given leave to apply, and
(b) the child is not placed for adoption by the authority.

(3) The court cannot give leave under subsection (2)(a) unless satisfied that there has been a change in circumstances since the order was made.

(4) If the court determines, on an application for an adoption order, not to make the order, it may revoke any placement order in respect of the child.

(5) Where –

(a) an application for the revocation of a placement order has been made and has not been disposed of, and
(b) the child is not placed for adoption by the authority,

the child may not without the court's leave be placed for adoption under the order.

## 25 Parental responsibility

(1) This section applies while –

(a) a child is placed for adoption under section 19 or an adoption agency is authorised to place a child for adoption under that section, or
(b) a placement order is in force in respect of a child.

(2) Parental responsibility for the child is given to the agency concerned.

(3) While the child is placed with prospective adopters, parental responsibility is given to them.

(4) The agency may determine that the parental responsibility of any parent or guardian, or of prospective adopters, is to be restricted to the extent specified in the determination.

## 26 Contact

(1) On an adoption agency being authorised to place a child for adoption, or placing a child for adoption who is less than six weeks old –

(a) any contact provision in a child arrangements order under section 8 of the 1989 Act ceases to have effect,
(b) any order under section 34 of that Act (parental etc contact with children in care) ceases to have effect, and
(c) any activity direction made in proceedings for the making, variation or discharge of a child arrangements order with respect to the child, or made in other proceedings that relate to such an order, is discharged.

(2) While an adoption agency is so authorised or a child is placed for adoption –

(a) no application may be made for –
    (i) a child arrangements order under section 8 of the 1989 Act containing contact provision, or
    (ii) an order under section 34 of that Act, but
(b) the court may make an order under this section requiring the person with whom the child lives, or is to live, to allow the child to visit or stay with the person named in the order, or for the person named in the order and the child otherwise to have contact with each other.

(3) An application for an order under this section may be made by –

(a) the child or the agency,
(b) any parent, guardian or relative,

(c) any person in whose favour there was provision which ceased to have effect by virtue of subsection (1)(a) or an order which ceased to have effect by virtue of subsection (1)(b),

(d) if a child arrangements order was in force immediately before the adoption agency was authorised to place the child for adoption or (as the case may be) placed the child for adoption at a time when he was less than six weeks old, any person named in the order as a person with whom the child was to live,

(e) if a person had care of the child immediately before that time by virtue of an order made in the exercise of the High Court's inherent jurisdiction with respect to children, that person,

(f) any person who has obtained the court's leave to make the application.

(4) When making a placement order, the court may on its own initiative make an order under this section.

(5) This section does not prevent an application for a contact order under section 8 of the 1989 Act being made where the application is to be heard together with an application for an adoption order in respect of the child.

(5A) In this section 'contact provision' means provision which regulates arrangements relating to –

(a) with whom a child is to spend time or otherwise have contact, or
(b) when a child is to spend time or otherwise have contact with any person;

but in paragraphs (a) and (b) a reference to spending time or otherwise having contact with a person is to doing that otherwise than as a result of living with the person.

(6) In this section 'activity direction' has the meaning given by section 11A of the 1989 Act.

## 27 Contact: supplementary

(1) An order under section 26 –

(a) has effect while the adoption agency is authorised to place the child for adoption or the child is placed for adoption, but
(b) may be varied or revoked by the court on an application by the child, the agency or a person named in the order.

(2) The agency may refuse to allow the contact that would otherwise be required by virtue of an order under that section if –

(a) it is satisfied that it is necessary to do so in order to safeguard or promote the child's welfare, and
(b) the refusal is decided upon as a matter of urgency and does not last for more than seven days.

(3) Regulations may make provision as to –

(a) the steps to be taken by an agency which has exercised its power under subsection (2),
(b) the circumstances in which, and conditions subject to which, the terms of any order under section 26 may be departed from by agreement between the agency and any person for whose contact with the child the order provides,
(c) notification by an agency of any variation or suspension of arrangements made (otherwise than under an order under that section) with a view to allowing any person contact with the child.

(4) Before making a placement order the court must –

(a) consider the arrangements which the adoption agency has made, or proposes to make, for allowing any person contact with the child, and
(b) invite the parties to the proceedings to comment on those arrangements.

(5) An order under section 26 may provide for contact on any conditions the court considers appropriate.

## 28 Further consequences of placement

(1) Where a child is placed for adoption under section 19 or an adoption agency is authorised to place a child for adoption under that section –

(a) a parent or guardian of the child may not apply for a child arrangements order regulating the child's living arrangements unless an application for an adoption order has been made and the parent or guardian has obtained the court's leave under subsection (3) or (5) of section 47,
(b) if an application has been made for an adoption order, a guardian of the child may not apply for a special guardianship order unless he has obtained the court's leave under subsection (3) or (5) of that section.

(2) Where –

(a) a child is placed for adoption under section 19 or an adoption agency is authorised to place a child for adoption under that section, or
(b) a placement order is in force in respect of a child,

then (whether or not the child is in England and Wales) a person may not do either of the following things, unless the court gives leave or each parent or guardian of the child gives written consent.

(3) Those things are –

(a) causing the child to be known by a new surname, or
(b) removing the child from the United Kingdom.

(4) Subsection (3) does not prevent the removal of a child from the United Kingdom for a period of less than one month by a person who provides the child's home.

(5) For the purposes of subsection (1)(a), a child arrangements order regulates a child's living arrangements if the arrangements regulated by the order consist of, or include, arrangements which relate to either or both of the following –

(a) with whom the child is to live, and
(b) when the child is to live with any person.

Amendments—Children and Families Act 2014, s 12, Sch 2.

## 29 Further consequences of placement orders

(1) Where a placement order is made in respect of a child and either –

(a) the child is subject to a care order, or
(b) the court at the same time makes a care order in respect of the child,

the care order does not have effect at any time when the placement order is in force.

(2) On the making of a placement order in respect of a child, any order mentioned in section 8(1) of the 1989 Act, and any supervision order in respect of the child, ceases to have effect.

(3) Where a placement order is in force –

(a) no prohibited steps order or specific issue order, and
(b) no supervision order or child assessment order,

may be made in respect of the child.

(4) Where a placement order is in force, a child arrangements order may be made with respect to the child's living arrangements only if –

(a) an application for an adoption order has been made in respect of the child, and
(b) the child arrangements order is applied for by a parent or guardian who has obtained the court's leave under subsection (3) or (5) of section 47 or by any other person who has obtained the court's leave under this subsection.

(4A) For the purposes of subsection (4), a child arrangements order is one made with respect to a child's living arrangements if the arrangements regulated by the order consist of, or include, arrangements which relate to either or both of the following –

(a) with whom the child is to live, and
(b) when the child is to live with any person.

(5) Where a placement order is in force, no special guardianship order may be made in respect of the child unless –

(a) an application has been made for an adoption order, and
(b) the person applying for the special guardianship order has obtained the court's leave under this subsection or, if he is a guardian of the child, has obtained the court's leave under section 47(5).

(6) Section 14A(7) of the 1989 Act applies in respect of an application for a special guardianship order for which leave has been given as mentioned in subsection (5)(b) with the omission of the words 'the beginning of the period of three months ending with'.

(7) Where a placement order is in force –

(a) section 14C(1)(b) of the 1989 Act (special guardianship: parental responsibility) has effect subject to any determination under section 25(4) of this Act,

(b) section 14C(3) and (4) of the 1989 Act (special guardianship: removal of child from UK etc) does not apply.

**Amendments**—Children and Families Act 2014, s 12, Sch 2.

## *Removal of Children Who Are or May Be Placed by Adoption Agencies*

### 30 General prohibitions on removal

(1) Where –

(a) a child is placed for adoption by an adoption agency under section 19, or

(b) a child is placed for adoption by an adoption agency and either the child is less than six weeks old or the agency has at no time been authorised to place the child for adoption,

a person (other than the agency) must not remove the child from the prospective adopters.

(2) Where –

(a) a child who is not for the time being placed for adoption is being provided with accommodation by a local authority, and

(b) the authority have applied to the court for a placement order and the application has not been disposed of,

only a person who has the court's leave (or the authority) may remove the child from the accommodation.

(3) Where subsection (2) does not apply, but –

(a) a child who is not for the time being placed for adoption is being provided with accommodation by an adoption agency, and

(b) the agency is authorised to place the child for adoption under section 19 or would be so authorised if any consent to placement under that section had not been withdrawn,

a person (other than the agency) must not remove the child from the accommodation.

(4) This section is subject to sections 31 to 33 but those sections do not apply if the child is subject to a care order.

(5) This group of sections (that is, this section and those sections) apply whether or not the child in question is in England and Wales.

(6) This group of sections does not affect the exercise by any local authority or other person of any power conferred by any enactment, other than section 20(8) of the 1989 Act or section 76(5) of the 2014 Act (removal of children from local authority accommodation).

(7) This group of sections does not prevent the removal of a child who is arrested.

(8) A person who removes a child in contravention of this section is guilty of an offence and liable on summary conviction to imprisonment for a term not exceeding three months, or a fine not exceeding level 5 on the standard scale, or both.

Amendments—SI 2016/413.

## 31 Recovery by parent etc where child not placed or is a baby

(1) Subsection (2) applies where –

(a) a child who is not for the time being placed for adoption is being provided with accommodation by an adoption agency, and
(b) the agency would be authorised to place the child for adoption under section 19 if consent to placement under that section had not been withdrawn.

(2) If any parent or guardian of the child informs the agency that he wishes the child to be returned to him, the agency must return the child to him within the period of seven days beginning with the request unless an application is, or has been, made for a placement order and the application has not been disposed of.

(3) Subsection (4) applies where –

(a) a child is placed for adoption by an adoption agency and either the child is less than six weeks old or the agency has at no time been authorised to place the child for adoption, and
(b) any parent or guardian of the child informs the agency that he wishes the child to be returned to him,

unless an application is, or has been, made for a placement order and the application has not been disposed of.

(4) The agency must give notice of the parent's or guardian's wish to the prospective adopters who must return the child to the agency within the period of seven days beginning with the day on which the notice is given.

(5) A prospective adopter who fails to comply with subsection (4) is guilty of an offence and liable on summary conviction to imprisonment for a term not exceeding three months, or a fine not exceeding level 5 on the standard scale, or both.

(6) As soon as a child is returned to an adoption agency under subsection (4), the agency must return the child to the parent or guardian in question.

## 32 Recovery by parent etc where child placed and consent withdrawn

(1) This section applies where –

(a) a child is placed for adoption by an adoption agency under section 19, and
(b) consent to placement under that section has been withdrawn,

unless an application is, or has been, made for a placement order and the application has not been disposed of.

(2) If a parent or guardian of the child informs the agency that he wishes the child to be returned to him –

(a) the agency must give notice of the parent's or guardian's wish to the prospective adopters, and
(b) the prospective adopters must return the child to the agency within the period of 14 days beginning with the day on which the notice is given.

(3) A prospective adopter who fails to comply with subsection (2)(b) is guilty of an offence and liable on summary conviction to imprisonment for a term not exceeding three months, or a fine not exceeding level 5 on the standard scale, or both.

(4) As soon as a child is returned to an adoption agency under this section, the agency must return the child to the parent or guardian in question.

(5) Where a notice under subsection (2) is given, but –

(a) before the notice was given, an application –
  (i) for an adoption order (including a Scottish or Northern Irish adoption order),
  (ii) for a special guardianship order,
  (iii) for a child arrangements order to which subsection (6) applies, or
  (iv) for permission to apply for an order within subparagraph (ii) or (iii),
  was made in respect of the child, and
(b) the application (and, in a case where permission is given on an application to apply for an order within paragraph (a)(ii) or (iii), the application for the order) has not been disposed of, the prospective adopters are not required by virtue of the notice to return the child to the agency unless the court so orders.

(6) A child arrangements order is one to which this subsection applies if it is an order regulating arrangements that consist of, or include, arrangements which relate to either or both of the following –

(a) with whom a child is to live, and
(b) when the child is to live with any person.

Amendments—Children and Families Act 2014, s 12, Sch 2.

## 33 Recovery by parent etc where child placed and placement order refused

(1) This section applies where –

(a) a child is placed for adoption by a local authority under section 19,
(b) the authority have applied for a placement order and the application has been refused, and
(c) any parent or guardian of the child informs the authority that he wishes the child to be returned to him.

(2) The prospective adopters must return the child to the authority on a date determined by the court.

(3) A prospective adopter who fails to comply with subsection (2) is guilty of an offence and liable on summary conviction to imprisonment for a term not exceeding three months, or a fine not exceeding level 5 on the standard scale, or both.

(4) As soon as a child is returned to the authority, they must return the child to the parent or guardian in question.

## 34 Placement orders: prohibition on removal

(1) Where a placement order in respect of a child –

(a) is in force, or
(b) has been revoked, but the child has not been returned by the prospective adopters or remains in any accommodation provided by the local authority,

a person (other than the local authority) may not remove the child from the prospective adopters or from accommodation provided by the authority.

(2) A person who removes a child in contravention of subsection (1) is guilty of an offence.

(3) Where a court revoking a placement order in respect of a child determines that the child is not to remain with any former prospective adopters with whom the child is placed, they must return the child to the local authority within the period determined by the court for the purpose; and a person who fails to do so is guilty of an offence.

(4) Where a court revoking a placement order in respect of a child determines that the child is to be returned to a parent or guardian, the local authority must return the child to the parent or guardian as soon as the child is returned to the authority or, where the child is in accommodation provided by the authority, at once.

(5) A person guilty of an offence under this section is liable on summary conviction to imprisonment for a term not exceeding three months, or a fine not exceeding level 5 on the standard scale, or both.

(6) This section does not affect the exercise by any local authority or other person of a power conferred by any enactment, other than section 20(8) of the 1989 Act or section 76(5) of the 2014 Act (removal of children from local authority accommodation).

(7) This section does not prevent the removal of a child who is arrested.

(8) This section applies whether or not the child in question is in England and Wales.

Amendments—SI 2016/413.

## 35 Return of child in other cases

(1) Where a child is placed for adoption by an adoption agency and the prospective adopters give notice to the agency of their wish to return the child, the agency must –

- (a) receive the child from the prospective adopters before the end of the period of seven days beginning with the giving of the notice, and
- (b) give notice to any parent or guardian of the child of the prospective adopters' wish to return the child.

(2) Where a child is placed for adoption by an adoption agency, and the agency –

- (a) is of the opinion that the child should not remain with the prospective adopters, and
- (b) gives notice to them of its opinion,

the prospective adopters must, not later than the end of the period of seven days beginning with the giving of the notice, return the child to the agency.

(3) If the agency gives notice under subsection (2)(b), it must give notice to any parent or guardian of the child of the obligation to return the child to the agency.

(4) A prospective adopter who fails to comply with subsection (2) is guilty of an offence and liable on summary conviction to imprisonment for a term not exceeding three months, or a fine not exceeding level 5 on the standard scale, or both.

(5) Where –

- (a) an adoption agency gives notice under subsection (2) in respect of a child,
- (b) before the notice was given, an application –
  - (i) for an adoption order (including a Scottish or Northern Irish adoption order),
  - (ii) for a special guardianship order,
  - (iii) for a child arrangements order to which subsection (5A) applies, or
  - (iv) for permission to apply for an order within subparagraph (ii) or (iii), was made in respect of the child, and
- (c) the application (and, in a case where permission is given on an application to apply for an order within paragraph (b)(ii) or (iii), the application for the order) has not been disposed of,

prospective adopters are not required by virtue of the notice to return the child to the agency unless the court so orders.

(5A) A child arrangements order is one to which this subsection applies if it is an order regulating arrangements that consist of, or include, arrangements which relate to either or both of the following –

(a) with whom a child is to live, and
(b) when a child is to live with any person.

(6) This section applies whether or not the child in question is in England and Wales.

**Amendments**—Children and Families Act 2014, s 12, Sch 12.

## Removal of Children in Non-Agency Cases

### 36 Restrictions on removal

(1) At any time when a child's home is with any persons ('the people concerned') with whom the child is not placed by an adoption agency, but the people concerned –

(a) have applied for an adoption order in respect of the child and the application has not been disposed of,
(b) have given notice of intention to adopt, or
(c) have applied for leave to apply for an adoption order under section 42(6) and the application has not been disposed of,

a person may remove the child only in accordance with the provisions of this group of sections (that is, this section and sections 37 to 40).

The reference to a child placed by an adoption agency includes a child placed by a Scottish or Northern Irish adoption agency.

(2) For the purposes of this group of sections, a notice of intention to adopt is to be disregarded if –

(a) the period of four months beginning with the giving of the notice has expired without the people concerned applying for an adoption order, or
(b) the notice is a second or subsequent notice of intention to adopt and was given during the period of five months beginning with the giving of the preceding notice.

(3) For the purposes of this group of sections, if the people concerned apply for leave to apply for an adoption order under section 42(6) and the leave is granted, the application for leave is not to be treated as disposed of until the period of three days beginning with the granting of the leave has expired.

(4) This section does not prevent the removal of a child who is arrested.

(5) Where a parent or guardian may remove a child from the people concerned in accordance with the provisions of this group of sections, the people concerned must at the request of the parent or guardian return the child to the parent or guardian at once.

(6) A person who –

(a) fails to comply with subsection (5), or
(b) removes a child in contravention of this section,

is guilty of an offence and liable on summary conviction to imprisonment for a term not exceeding three months, or a fine not exceeding level 5 on the standard scale, or both.

(7) This group of sections applies whether or not the child in question is in England and Wales.

## 37 Applicants for adoption

If section 36(1)(a) applies, the following persons may remove the child –

(a) a person who has the court's leave,
(b) a local authority or other person in the exercise of a power conferred by any enactment, other than section 20(8) of the 1989 Act or section 76(5) of the 2014 Act.

Amendments—SI 2016/413.

## 38 Local authority foster parents

(1) This section applies if the child's home is with local authority foster parents.

(2) If –

(a) the child has had his home with the foster parents at all times during the period of five years ending with the removal and the foster parents have given notice of intention to adopt, or
(b) an application has been made for leave under section 42(6) and has not been disposed of,

the following persons may remove the child.

(3) They are –

(a) a person who has the court's leave,
(b) a local authority or other person in the exercise of a power conferred by any enactment, other than section 20(8) of the 1989 Act or section 76(5) of the 2014 Act.

(4) If subsection (2) does not apply but –

(a) the child has had his home with the foster parents at all times during the period of one year ending with the removal, and
(b) the foster parents have given notice of intention to adopt,

the following persons may remove the child.

(5) They are –

(a) a person with parental responsibility for the child who is exercising the power in section 20(8) of the 1989 Act or section 76(5) of 2014 Act,
(b) a person who has the court's leave,

(c) a local authority or other person in the exercise of a power conferred by any enactment, other than section 20(8) of the 1989 Act or section 76(5) of 2014 Act.

Amendments—SI 2016/413.

### 39 Partners of parents

(1) This section applies if a child's home is with a partner of a parent and the partner has given notice of intention to adopt.

(2) If the child's home has been with the partner for not less than three years (whether continuous or not) during the period of five years ending with the removal, the following persons may remove the child –

- (a) a person who has the court's leave,
- (b) a local authority or other person in the exercise of a power conferred by any enactment, other than section 20(8) of the 1989 Act or section 76(5) of 2014 Act.

(3) If subsection (2) does not apply, the following persons may remove the child –

- (a) a parent or guardian,
- (b) a person who has the court's leave,
- (c) a local authority or other person in the exercise of a power conferred by any enactment, other than section 20(8) of the 1989 Act or section 76(5) of 2014 Act.

Amendments—SI 2016/413.

### 40 Other non-agency cases

(1) In any case where sections 37 to 39 do not apply but –

- (a) the people concerned have given notice of intention to adopt, or
- (b) the people concerned have applied for leave under section 42(6) and the application has not been disposed of,

the following persons may remove the child.

(2) They are –

- (a) a person who has the court's leave,
- (b) a local authority or other person in the exercise of a power conferred by any enactment, other than section 20(8) of the 1989 Act or section 76(5) of 2014 Act.

Amendments—SI 2016/413.

## Breach of Restrictions on Removal

### 41 Recovery orders

(1) This section applies where it appears to the court –

(a) that a child has been removed in contravention of any of the preceding provisions of this Chapter or that there are reasonable grounds for believing that a person intends to remove a child in contravention of those provisions, or

(b) that a person has failed to comply with section 31(4), 32(2), 33(2), 34(3) or 35(2).

(2) The court may, on the application of any person, by an order –

(a) direct any person who is in a position to do so to produce the child on request to any person mentioned in subsection (4),

(b) authorise the removal of the child by any person mentioned in that subsection,

(c) require any person who has information as to the child's whereabouts to disclose that information on request to any constable or officer of the court,

(d) authorise a constable to enter any premises specified in the order and search for the child, using reasonable force if necessary.

(3) Premises may only be specified under subsection (2)(d) if it appears to the court that there are reasonable grounds for believing the child to be on them.

(4) The persons referred to in subsection (2) are –

(a) any person named by the court,
(b) any constable,
(c) any person who, after the order is made under that subsection, is authorised to exercise any power under the order by an adoption agency which is authorised to place the child for adoption.

(5) A person who intentionally obstructs a person exercising a power of removal conferred by the order is guilty of an offence and liable on summary conviction to a fine not exceeding level 3 on the standard scale.

(6) A person must comply with a request to disclose information as required by the order even if the information sought might constitute evidence that he had committed an offence.

(7) But in criminal proceedings in which the person is charged with an offence (other than one mentioned in subsection (8)) –

(a) no evidence relating to the information provided may be adduced, and
(b) no question relating to the information may be asked,

by or on behalf of the prosecution, unless evidence relating to it is adduced, or a question relating to it is asked, in the proceedings by or on behalf of the person.

(8) The offences excluded from subsection (7) are –

(a) an offence under section 2 or 5 of the Perjury Act 1911 (false statements made on oath otherwise than in judicial proceedings or made otherwise than on oath),

(b) an offence under section 44(1) or (2) of the Criminal Law (Consolidation) (Scotland) Act 1995 (false statements made on oath or otherwise than on oath).

(9) An order under this section has effect in relation to Scotland as if it were an order made by the Court of Session which that court had jurisdiction to make.

## *Preliminaries to Adoption*

### 42 Child to live with adopters before application

(1) An application for an adoption order may not be made unless –

(a) if subsection (2) applies, the condition in that subsection is met,
(b) if that subsection does not apply, the condition in whichever is applicable of subsections (3) to (5) applies.

(2) If –

(a) the child was placed for adoption with the applicant or applicants by an adoption agency or in pursuance of an order of the High Court, or
(b) the applicant is a parent of the child,

the condition is that the child must have had his home with the applicant or, in the case of an application by a couple, with one or both of them at all times during the period of ten weeks preceding the application.

(3) If the applicant or one of the applicants is the partner of a parent of the child, the condition is that the child must have had his home with the applicant or, as the case may be, applicants at all times during the period of six months preceding the application.

(4) If the applicants are local authority foster parents, the condition is that the child must have had his home with the applicants at all times during the period of one year preceding the application.

(5) In any other case, the condition is that the child must have had his home with the applicant or, in the case of an application by a couple, with one or both of them for not less than three years (whether continuous or not) during the period of five years preceding the application.

(6) But subsections (4) and (5) do not prevent an application being made if the court gives leave to make it.

(7) An adoption order may not be made unless the court is satisfied that sufficient opportunities to see the child with the applicant or, in the case of an application by a couple, both of them together in the home environment have been given –

(a) where the child was placed for adoption with the applicant or applicants by an adoption agency, to that agency,
(b) in any other case, to the local authority within whose area the home is.

(8) In this section and sections 43 and 44(1) –

(a) references to an adoption agency include a Scottish or Northern Irish adoption agency,
(b) references to a child placed for adoption by an adoption agency are to be read accordingly.

## 43 Reports where child placed by agency

Where an application for an adoption order relates to a child placed for adoption by an adoption agency, the agency must –

(a) submit to the court a report on the suitability of the applicants and on any other matters relevant to the operation of section 1, and
(b) assist the court in any manner the court directs.

## 44 Notice of intention to adopt

(1) This section applies where persons (referred to in this section as 'proposed adopters') wish to adopt a child who is not placed for adoption with them by an adoption agency.

(2) An adoption order may not be made in respect of the child unless the proposed adopters have given notice to the appropriate local authority of their intention to apply for the adoption order (referred to in this Act as a 'notice of intention to adopt').

(3) The notice must be given not more than two years, or less than three months, before the date on which the application for the adoption order is made.

(4) Where –

(a) if a person were seeking to apply for an adoption order, subsection (4) or (5) of section 42 would apply, but
(b) the condition in the subsection in question is not met,

the person may not give notice of intention to adopt unless he has the court's leave to apply for an adoption order.

(5) On receipt of a notice of intention to adopt, the local authority must arrange for the investigation of the matter and submit to the court a report of the investigation.

(6) In particular, the investigation must, so far as practicable, include the suitability of the proposed adopters and any other matters relevant to the operation of section 1 in relation to the application.

(7) If a local authority receive a notice of intention to adopt in respect of a child whom they know was (immediately before the notice was given) looked after by another local authority, they must, not more than seven days after the receipt of the notice, inform the other local authority in writing that they have received the notice.

(8) Where –

(a) a local authority have placed a child with any persons otherwise than as prospective adopters, and
(b) the persons give notice of intention to adopt,

the authority are not to be treated as leaving the child with them as prospective adopters for the purposes of section 18(1)(b).

(9) In this section, references to the appropriate local authority, in relation to any proposed adopters, are –
(a) in prescribed cases, references to the prescribed local authority,
(b) in any other case, references to the local authority for the area in which, at the time of giving the notice of intention to adopt, they have their home,

and 'prescribed' means prescribed by regulations.

**45 Suitability of adopters**

(1) Regulations under section 9 may make provision as to the matters to be taken into account by an adoption agency in determining, or making any report in respect of, the suitability of any persons to adopt a child.

(2) In particular, the regulations may make provision for the purpose of securing that, in determining the suitability of a couple to adopt a child, proper regard is had to the need for stability and permanence in their relationship.

## *The Making of Adoption Orders*

**46 Adoption orders**

(1) An adoption order is an order made by the court on an application under section 50 or 51 giving parental responsibility for a child to the adopters or adopter.

(2) The making of an adoption order operates to extinguish –
(a) the parental responsibility which any person other than the adopters or adopter has for the adopted child immediately before the making of the order,
(b) any order under the 1989 Act or the Children (Northern Ireland) Order 1995 (SI 1995/755 (NI 2)),
(c) any order under the Children (Scotland) Act 1995 other than an excepted order, and
(d) any duty arising by virtue of an agreement or an order of a court to make payments, so far as the payments are in respect of the adopted child's maintenance or upbringing for any period after the making of the adoption order.

'Excepted order' means an order under section 9, 11(1)(d) or 13 of the Children (Scotland) Act 1995 or an exclusion order within the meaning of section 76(1) of that Act.

(3) An adoption order –

(a) does not affect parental responsibility so far as it relates to any period before the making of the order, and
(b) in the case of an order made on an application under section 51(2) by the partner of a parent of the adopted child, does not affect the parental responsibility of that parent or any duties of that parent within subsection (2)(d).

(4) Subsection (2)(d) does not apply to a duty arising by virtue of an agreement –

(a) which constitutes a trust, or
(b) which expressly provides that the duty is not to be extinguished by the making of an adoption order.

(5) An adoption order may be made even if the child to be adopted is already an adopted child.

(6) Before making an adoption order, the court must consider whether there should be arrangements for allowing any person contact with the child; and for that purpose the court must consider any existing or proposed arrangements and obtain any views of the parties to the proceedings.

## 47 Conditions for making adoption orders

(1) An adoption order may not be made if the child has a parent or guardian unless one of the following three conditions is met; but this section is subject to section 52 (parental etc consent).

(2) The first condition is that, in the case of each parent or guardian of the child, the court is satisfied –

(a) that the parent or guardian consents to the making of the adoption order,
(b) that the parent or guardian has consented under section 20 (and has not withdrawn the consent) and does not oppose the making of the adoption order, or
(c) that the parent's or guardian's consent should be dispensed with.

(3) A parent or guardian may not oppose the making of an adoption order under subsection (2)(b) without the court's leave.

(4) The second condition is that –

(a) the child has been placed for adoption by an adoption agency with the prospective adopters in whose favour the order is proposed to be made,
(b) either –
　(i) the child was placed for adoption with the consent of each parent or guardian and the consent of the mother was given when the child was at least six weeks old, or
　(ii) the child was placed for adoption under a placement order, and
(c) no parent or guardian opposes the making of the adoption order.

(5) A parent or guardian may not oppose the making of an adoption order under the second condition without the court's leave.

(6) The third condition is that the child –

(a) is the subject of a Scottish permanence order which includes provision granting authority for the child to be adopted, or
(b) is free for adoption by virtue of an order made under Article 17(1) or 18(1) of the Adoption (Northern Ireland) Order 1987 (SI 1987/2203).

(7) The court cannot give leave under subsection (3) or (5) unless satisfied that there has been a change in circumstances since the consent of the parent or guardian was given or, as the case may be, the placement order was made.

(8) An adoption order may not be made in relation to a person who is or has been married.

(8A) An adoption order may not be made in relation to a person who is or has been a civil partner.

(9) An adoption order may not be made in relation to a person who has attained the age of 19 years.

(10) In this section, 'Scottish permanence order' means a permanence order under section 80 of the Adoption and Children (Scotland) Act 2007 (including a deemed permanence order having effect by virtue of article 13(1), 14(2), 17(1) or 19(2) of the Adoption and Children (Scotland) Act 2007 (Commencement No 4, Transitional and Savings Provisions) Order 2009 (SSI 2009/267)).

**Amendments**—Civil Partnership Act 2002, s 79(1), (2); SI 2011/1740.

**Modification**—Section 47(6) modified for certain purposes (SI 2010/2469).

## 48 Restrictions on making adoption orders

(1) The court may not hear an application for an adoption order in relation to a child, where a previous application to which subsection (2) applies made in relation to the child by the same persons was refused by any court, unless it appears to the court that, because of a change in circumstances or for any other reason, it is proper to hear the application.

(2) This subsection applies to any application –

(a) for an adoption order or a Scottish or Northern Irish adoption order, or
(b) for an order for adoption made in the Isle of Man or any of the Channel Islands.

## 49 Applications for adoption

(1) An application for an adoption order may be made by –

(a) a couple, or
(b) one person,

but only if it is made under section 50 or 51 and one of the following conditions is met.

(2) The first condition is that at least one of the couple (in the case of an application under section 50) or the applicant (in the case of an application under section 51) is domiciled in a part of the British Islands.

(3) The second condition is that both of the couple (in the case of an application under section 50) or the applicant (in the case of an application under section 51) have been habitually resident in a part of the British Islands for a period of not less than one year ending with the date of the application.

(4) An application for an adoption order may only be made if the person to be adopted has not attained the age of 18 years on the date of the application.

(5) References in this Act to a child, in connection with any proceedings (whether or not concluded) for adoption, (such as 'child to be adopted' or 'adopted child') include a person who has attained the age of 18 years before the proceedings are concluded.

## 50 Adoption by couple

(1) An adoption order may be made on the application of a couple where both of them have attained the age of 21 years.

(2) An adoption order may be made on the application of a couple where –

- (a) one of the couple is the mother or the father of the person to be adopted and has attained the age of 18 years, and
- (b) the other has attained the age of 21 years.

## 51 Adoption by one person

(1) An adoption order may be made on the application of one person who has attained the age of 21 years and is not married or a civil partner.

(2) An adoption order may be made on the application of one person who has attained the age of 21 years if the court is satisfied that the person is the partner of a parent of the person to be adopted.

(3) An adoption order may be made on the application of one person who has attained the age of 21 years and is married if the court is satisfied that –

- (a) the person's spouse cannot be found,
- (b) the spouses have separated and are living apart, and the separation is likely to be permanent, or
- (c) the person's spouse is by reason of ill-health, whether physical or mental, incapable of making an application for an adoption order.

(3A) An adoption order may be made on the application of one person who has attained the age of 21 years and is a civil partner if the court is satisfied that –

- (a) the person's civil partner cannot be found,
- (b) the civil partners have separated and are living apart, and the separation is likely to be permanent, or
- (c) the person's civil partner is by reason of ill-health, whether physical or mental, incapable of making an application for an adoption order.

(4) An adoption order may not be made on an application under this section by the mother or the father of the person to be adopted unless the court is satisfied that –

- (a) the other natural parent is dead or cannot be found,
- (b) by virtue of the provisions specified in subsection (5), there is no other parent, or
- (c) there is some other reason justifying the child's being adopted by the applicant alone,

and, where the court makes an adoption order on such an application, the court must record that it is satisfied as to the fact mentioned in paragraph (a) or (b) or, in the case of paragraph (c), record the reason.

(5) The provisions referred to in subsection (4)(b) are –

- (a) section 28 of the Human Fertilisation and Embryology Act 1990 (disregarding subsections (5A) to (5I) of that section), or
- (b) sections 34 to 47 of the Human Fertilisation and Embryology Act 2008 (disregarding sections 39, 40 and 46 of that Act).

Amendments—Civil Partnership Act 2002, s 79(1), (4), (5); Human Fertilisation and Embryology (Deceased Fathers) Act 2003, s 2(1), Sch, para 18; Human Fertilisation and Embryology Act 2008, Sch 6, para 39.

## Post-Adoption Contact

### 51A Post-adoption contact

(1) This section applies where –

- (a) an adoption agency has placed or was authorised to place a child for adoption, and
- (b) the court is making or has made an adoption order in respect of the child.

(2) When making the adoption order or at any time afterwards, the court may make an order under this section –

- (a) requiring the person in whose favour the adoption order is or has been made to allow the child to visit or stay with the person named in the order under this section, or for the person named in that order and the child otherwise to have contact with each other, or
- (b) prohibiting the person named in the order under this section from having contact with the child.

(3) The following people may be named in an order under this section –

- (a) any person who (but for the child's adoption) would be related to the child by blood (including half-blood), marriage or civil partnership;
- (b) any former guardian of the child;
- (c) any person who had parental responsibility for the child immediately before the making of the adoption order;

- (d) any person who was entitled to make an application for an order under section 26 in respect of the child (contact with children placed or to be placed for adoption) by virtue of subsection (3)(c), (d) or (e) of that section;
- (e) any person with whom the child has lived for a period of at least one year.

(4) An application for an order under this section may be made by –

- (a) a person who has applied for the adoption order or in whose favour the adoption order is or has been made,
- (b) the child, or
- (c) any person who has obtained the court's leave to make the application.

(5) In deciding whether to grant leave under subsection (4)(c), the court must consider –

- (a) any risk there might be of the proposed application disrupting the child's life to such an extent that he or she would be harmed by it (within the meaning of the 1989 Act),
- (b) the applicant's connection with the child, and
- (c) any representations made to the court by –
  - (i) the child, or
  - (ii) a person who has applied for the adoption order or in whose favour the adoption order is or has been made.

(6) When making an adoption order, the court may on its own initiative make an order of the type mentioned in subsection (2)(b).

(7) The period of one year mentioned in subsection (3)(e) need not be continuous but must not have begun more than five years before the making of the application.

(8) Where this section applies, an order under section 8 of the 1989 Act may not make provision about contact between the child and any person who may be named in an order under this section.

**Amendments**—Inserted by Children and Families Act 2014, s 9.

## 51B Orders under section 51A: supplementary

(1) An order under section 51A –

- (a) may contain directions about how it is to be carried into effect,
- (b) may be made subject to any conditions the court thinks appropriate,
- (c) may be varied or revoked by the court on an application by the child, a person in whose favour the adoption order was made or a person named in the order, and
- (d) has effect until the child's 18th birthday, unless revoked.

(2) Subsection (3) applies to proceedings –

- (a) on an application for an adoption order in which –
  - (i) an application is made for an order under section 51A, or

(ii) the court indicates that it is considering making such an order on its own initiative;
(b) on an application for an order under section 51A;
(c) on an application for such an order to be varied or revoked.

(3) The court must (in the light of any rules made by virtue of subsection (4)) –

(a) draw up a timetable with a view to determining without delay whether to make, (or as the case may be) vary or revoke an order under section 51A, and
(b) give directions for the purpose of ensuring, so far as is reasonably practicable, that that timetable is adhered to.

(4) Rules of court may –

(a) specify periods within which specified steps must be taken in relation to proceedings to which subsection (3) applies, and
(b) make other provision with respect to such proceedings for the purpose of ensuring, so far as is reasonably practicable, that the court makes determinations about orders under section 51A without delay.

**Amendments**—Inserted by Children and Families Act 2014, s 9.

## Placement and Adoption: General

### 52 Parental etc consent

(1) The court cannot dispense with the consent of any parent or guardian of a child to the child being placed for adoption or to the making of an adoption order in respect of the child unless the court is satisfied that –

(a) the parent or guardian cannot be found or lacks capacity (within the meaning of the Mental Capacity Act 2005) to give consent, or
(b) the welfare of the child requires the consent to be dispensed with.

(2) The following provisions apply to references in this Chapter to any parent or guardian of a child giving or withdrawing –

(a) consent to the placement of a child for adoption, or
(b) consent to the making of an adoption order (including a future adoption order).

(3) Any consent given by the mother to the making of an adoption order is ineffective if it is given less than six weeks after the child's birth.

(4) The withdrawal of any consent to the placement of a child for adoption, or of any consent given under section 20, is ineffective if it is given after an application for an adoption order is made.

(5) 'Consent' means consent given unconditionally and with full understanding of what is involved; but a person may consent to adoption without knowing the identity of the persons in whose favour the order will be made.

(6) 'Parent' (except in subsections (9) and (10) below) means a parent having parental responsibility.

(7) Consent under section 19 or 20 must be given in the form prescribed by rules, and the rules may prescribe forms in which a person giving consent under any other provision of this Part may do so (if he wishes).

(8) Consent given under section 19 or 20 must be withdrawn –

(a) in the form prescribed by rules, or
(b) by notice given to the agency.

(9) Subsection (10) applies if –

(a) an agency has placed a child for adoption under section 19 in pursuance of consent given by a parent of the child, and
(b) at a later time, the other parent of the child acquires parental responsibility for the child.

(10) The other parent is to be treated as having at that time given consent in accordance with this section in the same terms as those in which the first parent gave consent.

Amendments—Mental Capacity Act 2005, s 67(1), Sch 6, para 45.

## 53 Modification of 1989 Act and 2014 Act in relation to adoption

(1) Where –

(a) a local authority are authorised to place a child for adoption, or
(b) a child who has been placed for adoption by a local authority is less than six weeks old,

regulations may provide for the following provisions to apply with modifications, or not to apply, in relation to the child.

(2) The provisions are –

(a) section 22(4)(b), (c) and (d) and (5)(b) of the 1989 Act (duty to ascertain wishes and feelings of certain persons);
(b) sections 6(4)(b) and 78(3)(a) of the 2014 Act (duty to ascertain wishes and feelings of certain persons);
(c) paragraphs 15 and 21 of Schedule 2 to the 1989 Act (promoting contact with parents and parents' obligations to contribute towards maintenance);
(d) section 95 of and paragraph 1 of Schedule 1 to the 2014 Act (promoting contact with parents and parents' obligations to contribute towards maintenance).

(3) Where a registered adoption society is authorised to place a child for adoption or a child who has been placed for adoption by a registered adoption society is less than six weeks old, regulations may provide –

(a) for section 61 of the 1989 Act to have effect in relation to the child whether or not he is accommodated by or on behalf of the society,
(b) for subsections (2)(b) to (d) and (3)(b) of that section (duty to ascertain wishes and feelings of certain persons) to apply with modifications, or not to apply, in relation to the child.

(4) Where a child's home is with persons who have given notice of intention to adopt, no contribution is payable (whether under a contribution order or otherwise) under Part 3 of Schedule 2 to the 1989 Act (contributions towards maintenance of children looked after by local authorities) or under Schedule 1 to the 2014 Act (contributions towards maintenance of looked after children) in respect of the period referred to in subsection (5).

(5) That period begins when the notice of intention to adopt is given and ends if –

(a) the period of four months beginning with the giving of the notice expires without the prospective adopters applying for an adoption order, or
(b) an application for such an order is withdrawn or refused.

(6) In this section, 'notice of intention to adopt' includes notice of intention to apply for a Scottish or Northern Irish adoption order.

Amendments—SI 2016/413.

## 54 Disclosing information during adoption process

Regulations under section 9 may require adoption agencies in prescribed circumstances to disclose in accordance with the regulations prescribed information to prospective adopters.

## 55 Revocation of adoptions on legitimation

(1) Where any child adopted by one natural parent as sole adoptive parent subsequently becomes a legitimated person on the marriage of the natural parents, the court by which the adoption order was made may, on the application of any of the parties concerned, revoke the order.

(2) (*repealed*)

Amendments—Courts Act 2003, s 109(1), Sch 8, para 412; Crime and Courts Act 2013, s 17, Sch 11.

## Chapter 4
## Status of Adopted Children

### 66 Meaning of adoption in Chapter 4

(1) In this Chapter 'adoption' means –

(a) adoption by an adoption order or a Scottish or Northern Irish adoption order,
(b) adoption by an order made in the Isle of Man or any of the Channel Islands,
(c) an adoption effected under the law of a Convention country outside the British Islands, and certified in pursuance of Article 23(1) of the Convention (referred to in this Act as a 'Convention adoption'),
(d) an overseas adoption, or

(e) an adoption recognised by the law of England and Wales and effected under the law of any other country;

and related expressions are to be interpreted accordingly.

(2) But references in this Chapter to adoption do not include an adoption effected before the day on which this Chapter comes into force (referred to in this Chapter as 'the appointed day').

(3) Any reference in an enactment to an adopted person within the meaning of this Chapter includes a reference to an adopted child within the meaning of Part 4 of the Adoption Act 1976.

## 67 Status conferred by adoption

(1) An adopted person is to be treated in law as if born as the child of the adopters or adopter.

(2) An adopted person is the legitimate child of the adopters or adopter and, if adopted by –

(a) a couple, or
(b) one of a couple under section 51(2),

is to be treated as the child of the relationship of the couple in question.

(3) An adopted person –

(a) if adopted by one of a couple under section 51(2), is to be treated in law as not being the child of any person other than the adopter and the other one of the couple, and
(b) in any other case, is to be treated in law, subject to subsection (4), as not being the child of any person other than the adopters or adopter;

but this subsection does not affect any reference in this Act to a person's natural parent or to any other natural relationship.

(4) In the case of a person adopted by one of the person's natural parents as sole adoptive parent, subsection (3)(b) has no effect as respects entitlement to property depending on relationship to that parent, or as respects anything else depending on that relationship.

(5) This section has effect from the date of the adoption.

(6) Subject to the provisions of this Chapter and Schedule 4, this section –

(a) applies for the interpretation of enactments or instruments passed or made before as well as after the adoption, and so applies subject to any contrary indication, and
(b) has effect as respects things done, or events occurring, on or after the adoption.

## 68 Adoptive relatives

(1) A relationship existing by virtue of section 67 may be referred to as an adoptive relationship, and –

(a) an adopter may be referred to as an adoptive parent or (as the case may be) as an adoptive father or adoptive mother,
(b) any other relative of any degree under an adoptive relationship may be referred to as an adoptive relative of that degree.

(2) Subsection (1) does not affect the interpretation of any reference, not qualified by the word 'adoptive', to a relationship.

(3) A reference (however expressed) to the adoptive mother and father of a child adopted by –

(a) a couple of the same sex, or
(b) a partner of the child's parent, where the couple are of the same sex,

is to be read as a reference to the child's adoptive parents.

## 69 Rules of interpretation for instruments concerning property

(1) The rules of interpretation contained in this section apply (subject to any contrary indication and to Schedule 4) to any instrument so far as it contains a disposition of property.

(2) In applying section 67(1) and (2) to a disposition which depends on the date of birth of a child or children of the adoptive parent or parents, the disposition is to be interpreted as if –

(a) the adopted person had been born on the date of adoption,
(b) two or more people adopted on the same date had been born on that date in the order of their actual births;

but this does not affect any reference to a person's age.

(3) Examples of phrases in wills on which subsection (2) can operate are –

1. Children of A 'living at my death or born afterwards'.
2. Children of A 'living at my death or born afterwards before any one of such children for the time being in existence attains a vested interest and who attain the age of 21 years'.
3. As in example 1 or 2, but referring to grandchildren of A instead of children of A.
4. A for life 'until he has a child', and then to his child or children.

*Note.* Subsection (2) will not affect the reference to the age of 21 years in example 2.

(4) Section 67(3) does not prejudice –

(a) any qualifying interest,
(b) any interest expectant (whether immediately or not) upon a qualifying interest, or
(c) any contingent interest (other than a contingent interest in remainder) which the adopted person has immediately before the adoption in the estate of a deceased parent, whether testate or intestate.

'Qualifying interest' means an interest vested in possession in the adopted person before the adoption.

(5) Where it is necessary to determine for the purposes of a disposition of property effected by an instrument whether a woman can have a child –

- (a) it must be presumed that once a woman has attained the age of 55 years she will not adopt a person after execution of the instrument, and
- (b) if she does so, then (in spite of section 67) that person is not to be treated as her child or (if she does so as one of a couple) as the child of the other one of the couple for the purposes of the instrument.

(6) In this section, 'instrument' includes a private Act settling property, but not any other enactment.

**Amendments**—Inheritance and Trustees' Powers Act 2014, s 4.

## 70 Dispositions depending on date of birth

(1) Where a disposition depends on the date of birth of a person who was born illegitimate and who is adopted by one of the natural parents as sole adoptive parent, section 69(2) does not affect entitlement by virtue of Part 3 of the Family Law Reform Act 1987 (dispositions of property).

(2) Subsection (1) applies for example where –

- (a) a testator dies in 2001 bequeathing a legacy to his eldest grandchild living at a specified time,
- (b) his unmarried daughter has a child in 2002 who is the first grandchild,
- (c) his married son has a child in 2003,
- (d) subsequently his unmarried daughter adopts her child as sole adoptive parent.

In that example the status of the daughter's child as the eldest grandchild of the testator is not affected by the events described in paragraphs (c) and (d).

## 71 Property devolving with peerages etc

(1) An adoption does not affect the descent of any peerage or dignity or title of honour.

(2) An adoption does not affect the devolution of any property limited (expressly or not) to devolve (as nearly as the law permits) along with any peerage or dignity or title of honour.

(3) Subsection (2) applies only if and so far as a contrary intention is not expressed in the instrument, and has effect subject to the terms of the instrument.

## 72 Protection of trustees and personal representatives

(1) A trustee or personal representative is not under a duty, by virtue of the law relating to trusts or the administration of estates, to enquire, before conveying

or distributing any property, whether any adoption has been effected or revoked if that fact could affect entitlement to the property.

(2) A trustee or personal representative is not liable to any person by reason of a conveyance or distribution of the property made without regard to any such fact if he has not received notice of the fact before the conveyance or distribution.

(3) This section does not prejudice the right of a person to follow the property, or any property representing it, into the hands of another person, other than a purchaser, who has received it.

## 73 Meaning of disposition

(1) This section applies for the purposes of this Chapter.

(2) A disposition includes the conferring of a power of appointment and any other disposition of an interest in or right over property; and in this subsection a power of appointment includes any discretionary power to transfer a beneficial interest in property without the furnishing of valuable consideration.

(3) This Chapter applies to an oral disposition as if contained in an instrument made when the disposition was made.

(4) The date of death of a testator is the date at which a will or codicil is to be regarded as made.

(5) The provisions of the law of intestate succession applicable to the estate of a deceased person are to be treated as if contained in an instrument executed by him (while of full capacity) immediately before his death.

## 74 Miscellaneous enactments

(1) Section 67 does not apply for the purposes of –

    (a)    section 1 of and Schedule 1 to the Marriage Act 1949 or Schedule 1 to the Civil Partnership Act 2004 (prohibited degrees of kindred and affinity),

    (b)    sections 64 and 65 of the Sexual Offences Act 2003 (sex with an adult relative).

(2) Section 67 does not apply for the purposes of any provision of –

    (a)    the British Nationality Act 1981,

    (b)    the Immigration Act 1971,

    (c)    any instrument having effect under an enactment within paragraph (a) or (b), or

    (d)    any other provision of the law for the time being in force which determines British citizenship, British overseas territories citizenship, the status of a British National (Overseas) or British Overseas citizenship.

**Amendments**—Sexual Offences Act 2003, s 139, Sch 6, para 47; Civil Partnership, s 79(1), (7).

**75 Pensions**

Section 67(3) does not affect entitlement to a pension which is payable to or for the benefit of a person and is in payment at the time of the person's adoption.

**76 Insurance**

(1) Where a child is adopted whose natural parent has effected an insurance with a friendly society or a collecting society or an industrial insurance company for the payment on the death of the child of money for funeral expenses, then –

(a) the rights and liabilities under the policy are by virtue of the adoption transferred to the adoptive parents, and
(b) for the purposes of the enactments relating to such societies and companies, the adoptive parents are to be treated as the person who took out the policy.

(2) Where the adoption is effected by an order made by virtue of section 51(2), the references in subsection (1) to the adoptive parents are to be read as references to the adopter and the other one of the couple.

# APPENDIX 3

# FAMILY PROCEDURE RULES 2010, SI 2010/2955, PART 12

### CHILDREN PROCEEDINGS EXCEPT PARENTAL ORDER PROCEEDINGS AND PROCEEDINGS FOR APPLICATIONS IN ADOPTION, PLACEMENT AND RELATED PROCEEDINGS

*Chapter 1*
*Interpretation and Application of this Part*

Amendments—SI 2012/3061.

### 12.1 Application of this Part

(1) The rules in this Part apply to –

- (a) emergency proceedings;
- (b) private law proceedings;
- (c) public law proceedings;
- (d) proceedings relating to the exercise of the court's inherent jurisdiction (other than applications for the court's permission to start such proceedings);
- (e) proceedings relating to child abduction and the recognition and enforcement of decisions relating to custody under the European Convention;
- (f) proceedings relating to the Council Regulation or the 1996 Hague Convention in respect of children; and
- (g) any other proceedings which may be referred to in a practice direction.

(Part 18 sets out the procedure for making an application for permission to bring proceedings.)

(Part 31 sets out the procedure for making applications for recognition and enforcement of judgments under the Council Regulation or the 1996 Hague Convention.)

(2) The rules in Chapter 7 of this Part also apply to family proceedings which are not within paragraph (1) but which otherwise relate wholly or mainly to the maintenance or upbringing of a minor.

### 12.2 Interpretation

In this Part –

'the 2006 Act' means the Childcare Act 2006;

'activity condition' has the meaning given to it by section 11C(2) of the 1989 Act;
'activity direction' has the meaning given to it by section 11A(3) of the 1989 Act;
'advocate' means a person exercising a right of audience as a representative of, or on behalf of, a party;
'care proceedings' means proceedings for a care order under section 31(1)(a) of the 1989 Act;
'Case Management Order' means an order in the form referred to in Practice Direction 12A;
'child assessment order' has the meaning assigned to it by section 43(2) of the 1989 Act;
...
'contribution order' has the meaning assigned to it by paragraph 23(2) of Schedule 2 to the 1989 Act;
'education supervision order' has the meaning assigned to it by section 36(2) of the 1989 Act;
'emergency proceedings' means proceedings for –
- (a) the disclosure of information as to the whereabouts of a child under section 33 of the 1986 Act;
- (b) an order authorising the taking charge of and delivery of a child under section 34 of the 1986 Act;
- (c) an emergency protection order;
- (d) an order under section 44(9)(b) of the 1989 Act varying a direction in an emergency protection order given under section 44(6) of that Act;
- (e) an order under section 45(5) of the 1989 Act extending the period during which an emergency protection order is to have effect;
- (f) an order under section 45(8) of the 1989 Act discharging an emergency protection order;
- (g) an order under section 45(8A) of the 1989 Act varying or discharging an emergency protection order in so far as it imposes an exclusion requirement on a person who is not entitled to apply for the order to be discharged;
- (h) an order under section 45(8B) of the 1989 Act varying or discharging an emergency protection order in so far as it confers a power of arrest attached to an exclusion requirement;
- (i) warrants under sections 48(9) and 102(1) of the 1989 Act and under section 79 of the 2006 Act; or
- (j) a recovery order under section 50 of the 1989 Act;

'emergency protection order' means an order under section 44 of the 1989 Act;
'enforcement order' has the meaning assigned to it by section 11J(2) of the 1989 Act;
'financial compensation order' means an order made under section 11O(2) of the 1989 Act;

'interim order' means an interim care order or an interim supervision order referred to in section 38(1) of the 1989 Act;

'Part 4 proceedings' means proceedings for –
- (a) a care order, or the discharge of such an order, under section 39(1) of the 1989 Act;
- (b) an order giving permission to change a child's surname or remove a child from the United Kingdom under section 33(7) of the 1989 Act;
- (c) a supervision order, the discharge or variation of such an order under section 39(2) of the 1989 Act, or the extension of such an order under paragraph 6(3) of Schedule 3 to that Act;
- (d) an order making provision regarding contact under section 34(2) to (4) of the 1989 Act or an order varying or discharging such an order under section 34(9) of that Act;
- (e) an education supervision order, the extension of an education supervision order under paragraph 15(2) of Schedule 3 to the 1989 Act, or the discharge of such an order under paragraph 17(1) of Schedule 3 to that Act;
- (f) an order varying directions made with an interim care order or interim supervision order under section 38(8)(b) of the 1989 Act;
- (g) an order under section 39(3) of the 1989 Act varying a supervision order in so far as it affects a person with whom the child is living but who is not entitled to apply for the order to be discharged;
- (h) an order under section 39(3A) of the 1989 Act varying or discharging an interim care order in so far as it imposes an exclusion requirement on a person who is not entitled to apply for the order to be discharged;
- (i) an order under section 39(3B) of the 1989 Act varying or discharging an interim care order in so far as it confers a power of arrest attached to an exclusion requirement; or
- (j) the substitution of a supervision order for a care order under section 39(4) of the 1989 Act;

'private law proceedings' means proceedings for –
- (a) a section 8 order except a child arrangements order to which section 9(6B) of the 1989 Act applies with respect to a child who is in the care of a local authority;
- (b) a parental responsibility order under sections 4(1)(c), 4ZA(1)(c) or 4A(1)(b) of the 1989 Act or an order terminating parental responsibility under sections 4(2A), 4ZA(5) or 4A(3) of that Act;
- (c) an order appointing a child's guardian under section 5(1) of the 1989 Act or an order terminating the appointment under section 6(7) of that Act;
- (d) an order giving permission to change a child's surname or remove a child from the United Kingdom under sections 13(1) or 14C(3) of the 1989 Act;
- (e) a special guardianship order except where that order relates to a child who is subject of a care order;

(f) an order varying or discharging such an order under section 14D of the 1989 Act;
(g) an enforcement order;
(h) a financial compensation order;
(i) an order under paragraph 9 of Schedule A1 to the 1989 Act following a breach of an enforcement order;
(j) an order under Part 2 of Schedule A1 to the 1989 Act revoking or amending an enforcement order; or
(k) an order that a warning notice be attached to a child arrangements order;

'public law proceedings' means Part 4 proceedings and proceedings for –
(a) a child arrangements order to which section 9(6B) of the 1989 Act applies with respect to a child who is in the care of a local authority;
(b) a special guardianship order relating to a child who is the subject of a care order;
(c) a secure accommodation order under section 25 of the 1989 Act;
(d)–(m) *(revoked)*
(n) a child assessment order, or the variation or discharge of such an order under section 43(12) of the 1989 Act;
(o) an order permitting the local authority to arrange for any child in its care to live outside England and Wales under paragraph 19(1) of Schedule 2 to the 1989 Act;
(p) a contribution order, or revocation of such an order under paragraph 23(8) of Schedule 2 to the 1989 Act;
(q) an appeal under paragraph 8(1) of Schedule 8 to the 1989 Act;

'special guardianship order' has the meaning assigned to it by section 14A(1) of the 1989 Act;

'supervision order' has the meaning assigned to it by section 31(11) of the 1989 Act;

'supervision proceedings' means proceedings for a supervision order under section 31(1)(b) of the 1989 Act;

'warning notice' means a notice attached to an order pursuant to section 8(2) of the Children and Adoption Act 2006.

(The 1980 Hague Convention, the 1996 Hague Convention, the Council Regulation, and the European Convention are defined in rule 2.3.)

Amendments—SI 2014/843.

## Chapter 2
## General Rules

### 12.3 Who the parties are

(1) In relation to the proceedings set out in column 1 of the following table, column 2 sets out who may make the application and column 3 sets out who the respondents to those proceedings will be.

| Proceedings for | Applicants | Respondents |
|---|---|---|
| A parental responsibility order (section 4(1)(c), 4ZA(1)(c), or section 4A(1)(b) of the 1989 Act). | The child's father; the step parent; or the child's parent (being a woman who is a parent by virtue of section 43 of the Human Fertilisation and Embryology Act 2008 and who is not a person to whom section 1(3) of the Family Law Reform Act 1987 applies) (sections 4(1)(c), 4ZA(1)(c) and 4A(1)(b) of the 1989 Act). | Every person whom the applicant believes to have parental responsibility for the child; where the child is the subject of a care order, every person whom the applicant believes to have had parental responsibility immediately prior to the making of the care order; in the case of an application to extend, vary or discharge an order, the parties to the proceedings leading to the order which it is sought to have extended, varied or discharged; in the case of specified proceedings, the child. |
| An order terminating a parental responsibility order or agreement (section 4(2A), 4ZA(5) or section 4A(3) of the 1989 Act). | Any person who has parental responsibility for the child; or with the court's permission, the child (section 4(3), 4ZA(6) and section 4A(3) of the 1989 Act). | As above. |
| An order appointing a guardian (section 5(1) of the 1989 Act). | An individual who wishes to be appointed as guardian (section 5(1) of the 1989 Act). | As above. |

| Proceedings for | Applicants | Respondents |
|---|---|---|
| An order terminating the appointment of a guardian (section 6(7) of the 1989 Act). | Any person who has parental responsibility for the child; or with the court's permission, the child (section 6(7) of the 1989 Act). | As above. |
| A section 8 order. | Any person who is entitled to apply for a section 8 order with respect to the child (section 10(4) to (7) of the 1989 Act); or with the court's permission, any person (section 10(2)(b) of the 1989 Act). | As above. |
| An enforcement order (section 11J of the 1989 Act). | A person who is, for the purposes of the child arrangements order, a person with whom the child concerned lives or is to live; any person whose contact with the child concerned is provided for in the child arrangements order; any individual subject to a condition under section 11(7)(b) of the 1989 Act or an activity condition imposed by a child arrangements order; or with the court's permission, the child (section 11J(5) of the 1989 Act). | The person the applicant alleges has failed to comply with the child arrangements order. |

| Proceedings for | Applicants | Respondents |
|---|---|---|
| A financial compensation order (section 110 of the 1989 Act). | Any person who is, for the purposes of the child arrangements order, a person with whom the child concerned lives or is to live; any person whose contact with the child concerned is provided for in the child arrangements order; any individual subject to a condition under section 11(7)(b) of the 1989 Act or an activity condition imposed by a child arrangements order; or with the court's permission, the child (section 110(6) of the 1989 Act). | The person the applicant alleges has failed to comply with the child arrangements order. |
| An order permitting the child's name to be changed or the removal of the child from the United Kingdom (section 13(1), 14C(3) or 33(7) of the 1989 Act). | Any person (section 13(1), 14C(3), 33(7) of the 1989 Act). | As for a parental responsibility order. |
| A special guardianship order (section 14A of the 1989 Act). | Any guardian of the child; any individual who is named in a child arrangements order as a person with whom the child is to live; | As above, and if a care order is in force with respect to the child, the child. |

| Proceedings for | Applicants | Respondents |
|---|---|---|
|  | any individual listed in subsection (5)(b) or (c) of section 10 (as read with subsection (10) of that section) of the 1989 Act; a local authority foster parent with whom the child has lived for a period of at least one year immediately preceding the application; or any person with the court's permission (section 14A(3) of the 1989 Act) (more than one such individual can apply jointly (section 14A(3) and (5) of that Act)). |  |
| Variation or discharge of a special guardianship order (section 14D of the 1989 Act). | The special guardian (or any of them, if there is more than one); any individual who is named in a child arrangements order as a person with whom the child is to live; the local authority designated in a care order with respect to the child; any individual within section 14D(1)(d) of the 1989 Act who has parental responsibility for the child; | As above. |

| Proceedings for | Applicants | Respondents |
|---|---|---|
|  | the child, any parent or guardian of the child and any step-parent of the child who has acquired, and has not lost, parental responsibility by virtue of section 4A of that Act with the court's permission; or any individual within section 14D(1)(d) of that Act who immediately before the making of the special guardianship order had, but no longer has, parental responsibility for the child with the court's permission. |  |

| Proceedings for | Applicants | Respondents |
|---|---|---|
| A secure accommodation order (section 25 of the 1989 Act). | The local authority which is looking after the child; or the Health Authority, Secretary of State, National Health Service Commissioning Board, clinical commissioning group, National Health Service Trust established under section 25 of the National Health Service Act 2006 or section 18(1) of the National Health Service (Wales) Act 2006, National Health Service Foundation Trust or any local authority providing or arranging accommodation for the child (unless the child is looked after by a local authority). | As above. |
| A care or supervision order (section 31 of the 1989 Act). | Any local authority; the National Society for the Prevention of Cruelty to Children and any of its officers (section 31(1) of the 1989 Act); or any authorised person. | As above. |
| An order varying directions made with an interim care or interim supervision order (section 38(8)(b) of the 1989 Act). | The parties to proceedings in which directions are given under section 38(6) of the 1989 Act; or any person named in such a direction. | As above. |

| Proceedings for | Applicants | Respondents |
| --- | --- | --- |
| An order discharging a care order (section 39(1) of the 1989 Act). | Any person who has parental responsibility for the child; the child; or the local authority designated by the order (section 39(1) of the 1989 Act). | As above. |
| An order varying or discharging an interim care order in so far as it imposes an exclusion requirement (section 39(3A) of the 1989 Act). | A person to whom the exclusion requirement in the interim care order applies who is not entitled to apply for the order to be discharged (section 39(3A) of the 1989 Act). | As above. |
| An order varying or discharging an interim care order in so far as it confers a power of arrest attached to an exclusion requirement (section 39(3B) of the 1989 Act). | Any person entitled to apply for the discharge of the interim care order in so far as it imposes the exclusion requirement (section 39(3B) of the 1989 Act). | As above. |
| An order substituting a supervision order for a care order (section 39(4) of the 1989 Act). | Any person entitled to apply for a care order to be discharged under section 39(1) (section 39(4) of the 1989 Act). | As above. |
| A child assessment order (section 43(1) of the 1989 Act). | Any local authority; the National Society for the Prevention of Cruelty to Children and any of its officers; or | As above. |

| Proceedings for | Applicants | Respondents |
|---|---|---|
| | any person authorised by order of the Secretary of State to bring the proceedings and any officer of a body who is so authorised (section 43(1) and (13) of the 1989 Act). | |
| An order varying or discharging a child assessment order (section 43(12) of the 1989 Act). | The applicant for an order that has been made under section 43(1) of the 1989 Act; or the persons referred to in section 43(11) of the 1989 Act (section 43(12) of that Act). | As above. |
| An emergency protection order (section 44(1) of the 1989 Act). | Any person (section 44(1) of the 1989 Act). | As for a parental responsibility order. |
| An order extending the period during which an emergency protection order is to have effect (section 45(4) of the 1989 Act). | Any person who – has parental responsibility for a child as the result of an emergency protection order; and is entitled to apply for a care order with respect to the child (section 45(4) of the 1989 Act). | As above. |
| An order discharging an emergency protection order (section 45(8) of the 1989 Act). | The child; a parent of the child; any person who is not a parent of the child but who has parental responsibility for the child; or | As above. |

| Proceedings for | Applicants | Respondents |
|---|---|---|
| | any person with whom the child was living before the making of the emergency protection order (section 45(8) of the 1989 Act). | |
| An order varying or discharging an emergency protection order in so far as it imposes the exclusion requirement (section 45(8A) of the 1989 Act). | A person to whom the exclusion requirement in the emergency protection order applies who is not entitled to apply for the emergency protection order to be discharged (section 45(8A) of the 1989 Act). | As above. |
| An order varying or discharging an emergency protection order in so far as it confers a power of arrest attached to an exclusion requirement (section 45(8B) of the 1989 Act). | Any person entitled to apply for the discharge of the emergency protection order in so far as it imposes the exclusion requirement (section 45(8B) of the 1989 Act). | As above. |
| An emergency protection order by the police (section 46(7) of the 1989 Act). | The officer designated officer for the purposes of section 46(3)(e) of the 1989 Act (section 46(7) of the 1989 Act). | As above. |

| Proceedings for | Applicants | Respondents |
|---|---|---|
| A warrant authorising a constable to assist in exercise of certain powers to search for children and inspect premises (section 48 of the 1989 Act). | Any person attempting to exercise powers under an emergency protection order who has been or is likely to be prevented from doing so by being refused entry to the premises concerned or refused access to the child concerned (section 48(9) of the 1989 Act). | As above. |
| A warrant authorising a constable to assist in exercise of certain powers to search for children and inspect premises (section 102 of the 1989 Act). | Any person attempting to exercise powers under the enactments mentioned in section 102(6) of the 1989 Act who has been or is likely to be prevented from doing so by being refused entry to the premises concerned or refused access to the child concerned (section 102(1) of that Act). | As above. |
| An order revoking an enforcement order (paragraph 4 of Schedule A1 to the 1989 Act). | The person subject to the enforcement order. | The person who was the applicant for the enforcement order; and where the child was a party to the proceedings in which the enforcement order was made, the child. |

| Proceedings for | Applicants | Respondents |
| --- | --- | --- |
| An order amending an enforcement order (paragraphs 5 to 7 of Schedule A1 to the 1989 Act). | The person subject to the enforcement order. | The person who was the applicant for the enforcement order. (Rule 12.33 makes provision about applications under paragraph 5 of Schedule A1 to the 1989 Act.) |
| An order following breach of an enforcement order (paragraph 9 of Schedule A1 to the 1989 Act). | Any person who is, for the purposes of the child arrangements order, the person with whom the child lives or is to live; any person whose contact with the child concerned is provided for in the child arrangements order; any individual subject to a condition under section 11(7)(b) of the 1989 Act or an activity condition imposed by a child arrangements order; or with the court's permission, the child (paragraph 9 of Schedule A1 to the 1989 Act). | The person the applicant alleges has failed to comply with the unpaid work requirement imposed by an enforcement order; and where the child was a party to the proceedings in which the enforcement order was made, the child. |
| An order permitting the local authority to arrange for any child in its care to live outside England and Wales (Schedule 2, paragraph 19(1), to the 1989 Act). | The local authority (Schedule 2, paragraph 19(1), to the 1989 Act). | As for a parental responsibility order. |

| Proceedings for | Applicants | Respondents |
|---|---|---|
| A contribution order (Schedule 2, paragraph 23(1), to the 1989 Act). | The local authority (Schedule 2, paragraph 23(1), to the 1989 Act). | As above and the contributor. |
| An order revoking a contribution order (Schedule 2, paragraph 23(8), to the 1989 Act). | The contributor; or the local authority. | As above. |
| An order relating to contact with the child in care and any named person (section 34(2) of the 1989 Act) or permitting the local authority to refuse contact (section 34(4) of that Act). | The local authority; or the child (section 34(2) or 34(4) of the 1989 Act). | As above; and the person whose contact with the child is the subject of the application. |
| An order relating to contact with the child in care (section 34(3) of the 1989 Act). | The child's parents; any guardian or special guardian of the child; any person who by virtue of section 4A of the 1989 Act has parental responsibility for the child; where there was a child arrangements order in force with respect to the child immediately before the care order was made, any person named in that order as a person with whom the child was to live; | As above; and the person whose contact with the child is the subject of the application. |

| Proceedings for | Applicants | Respondents |
|---|---|---|
| | a person who by virtue of an order made in the exercise of the High Court's inherent jurisdiction with respect to children had care of the child immediately before the care order was made (section 34(3)(a) of the 1989 Act); or with the court's permission, any person (section 34(3)(b) of that Act). | |
| An order varying or discharging an order for contact with a child in care under section 34 (section 34((9) of the 1989 Act). | The local authority; the child; or any person named in the order (section 34(9) of the 1989 Act). | As above; and the person whose contact with the child is the subject of the application. |
| An education supervision order (section 36 of the 1989 Act). | Any local authority (section 36(1) of the 1989 Act). | As above; and the child. |
| An order varying or discharging a supervision order (section 39(2) of the 1989 Act). | Any person who has parental responsibility for the child; the child; or the supervisor (section 39(2) of the 1989 Act). | As above; and the supervisor. |
| An order varying a supervision order in so far as it affects the person with whom the child is living (section 39(3) of the 1989 Act). | The person with whom the child is living who is not entitled to apply for the order to be discharged (section 39(3) of the 1989 Act). | As above; and the supervisor. |

| Proceedings for | Applicants | Respondents |
|---|---|---|
| An order varying a direction under section 44(6) of the 1989 Act in an emergency protection order (section 44(9)(b) of that Act). | The parties to the application for the emergency protection order in respect of which it is sought to vary the directions; the children's guardian; the local authority in whose area the child is ordinarily resident; or any person who is named in the directions. | As above, and the parties to the application for the order in respect of which it is sought to vary the directions; any person who was caring for the child prior to the making of the order; and any person named in a child arrangements order as a person with whom the child is to spend time or otherwise have contact and who is affected by the direction which it is sought to have varied. |
| A recovery order (section 50 of the 1989 Act). | Any person who has parental responsibility for the child by virtue of a care order or an emergency protection order; or where the child is in police protection the officer designated for the purposes of section 46(3)(e) of the 1989 Act (section 50(4) of the 1989 Act). | As above; and the person whom the applicant alleges to have effected or to have been or to be responsible for the taking or keeping of the child. |

| Proceedings for | Applicants | Respondents |
|---|---|---|
| An order discharging an education supervision order (Schedule 3, paragraph 17(1), to the 1989 Act). | The child concerned; a parent of the child; or the local authority concerned (Schedule 3, paragraph 17(1), to the 1989 Act). | As above; and the local authority concerned; and the child. |
| An order extending an education supervision order (Schedule 3, paragraph 15(2), to the 1989 Act). | The local authority in whose favour the education supervision order was made (Schedule 3, paragraph 15(2), to the 1989 Act). | As above; and the child. |
| An appeal under paragraph (8) of Schedule 8 to the 1989 Act. | A person aggrieved by the matters listed in paragraph 8(1) of Schedule 8 to the 1989 Act. | The appropriate local authority. |
| An order for the disclosure of information as to the whereabouts of a child under section 33 of the 1986 Act. | Any person with a legitimate interest in proceedings for an order under Part 1 of the 1986 Act; or a person who has registered an order made elsewhere in the United Kingdom or a specified dependent territory. | Any person alleged to have information as to the whereabouts of the child. |
| An order authorising the taking charge of and delivery of a child under section 34 of the 1986 Act. | The person to whom the child is to be given up under section 34(1) of the 1986 Act. | As above; and the person who is required to give up the child in accordance with section 34(1) of the 1986 Act. |

| Proceedings for | Applicants | Respondents |
|---|---|---|
| An order relating to the exercise of the court's inherent jurisdiction (including wardship proceedings). | A local authority (with the court's permission); any person with a genuine interest in or relation to the child; or the child (wardship proceedings only). | The parent or guardian of the child; any other person who has an interest in or relationship to the child; and the child (wardship proceedings only and with the court's permission as described at rule 12.37). |
| A warrant under section 79 of the 2006 Act authorising any constable to assist Her Majesty's Chief Inspector for Education, Children's Services and Skills in the exercise of powers conferred on him by section 77 of the 2006 Act. | Her Majesty's Chief Inspector for Education, Children's Services and Skills. | Any person preventing or likely to prevent Her Majesty's Chief Inspector for Education, Children's Services and Skills from exercising powers conferred on him by section 77 of the 2006 Act. |
| An order in respect of a child under the 1980 Hague Convention. | Any person, institution or body who claims that a child has been removed or retained in breach of rights of custody or claims that there has been a breach of rights of access in relation to the child. | The person alleged to have brought the child into the United Kingdom; the person with whom the child is alleged to be; any parent or guardian of the child who is within the United Kingdom and is not otherwise a party; any person in whose favour a decision relating to custody has been made if that person is not otherwise a party; and |

| Proceedings for | Applicants | Respondents |
|---|---|---|
| | | any other person who appears to the court to have sufficient interest in the welfare of the child. |
| An order concerning the recognition and enforcement of decisions relating to custody under the European Convention. | Any person who has a court order giving that person rights of custody in relation to the child. | As above. |
| An application for the High Court to request transfer of jurisdiction under Article 15 of the Council Regulation or Article 9 of the 1996 Hague Convention (rule 12.65). | Any person with sufficient interest in the welfare of the child and who would be entitled to make a proposed application in relation to that child, or who intends to seek the permission of the court to make such application if the transfer is agreed. | As directed by the court in accordance with rule 12.65. |
| An application under rule 12.71 for a declaration as to the existence, or extent, of parental responsibility under Article 16 of the 1996 Convention. | Any interested person including a person who holds, or claims to hold, parental responsibility for the child under the law of another State which subsists in accordance with Article 16 of the 1996 Hague Convention following the child becoming habitually resident in a territorial unit of the United Kingdom. | Every person whom the applicant believes to have parental responsibility for the child; any person whom the applicant believes to hold parental responsibility for the child under the law of another State which subsists in accordance with Article 16 of the 1996 Hague Convention following the child becoming habitually resident in a territorial unit of the United Kingdom; and |

| Proceedings for | Applicants | Respondents |
| --- | --- | --- |
| | | where the child is the subject of a care order, every person whom the applicant believes to have had parental responsibility immediately prior to the making of the care order |
| A warning notice. | The person who is, for the purposes of the child arrangements order, the person with whom the child concerned lives or is to live; the person whose contact with the child concerned is provided for in the child arrangements order; any individual subject to a condition under section 11(7)(b) of the 1989 Act or an activity condition imposed by the child arrangements order; or with the court's permission, the child. | Any person who was a party to the proceedings in which the child arrangements order was made. (Rule 12.33 makes provision about applications for warning notices). |

(2) The court will direct that a person with parental responsibility be made a party to proceedings where that person requests to be one.

(3) Subject to rule 16.2, the court may at any time direct that –

(a) any person or body be made a party to proceedings; or
(b) a party be removed.

(4) If the court makes a direction for the addition or removal of a party under this rule, it may give consequential directions about –

(a) the service of a copy of the application form or other relevant documents on the new party;

(b) the management of the proceedings.

(5) In this rule –

'a local authority foster parent' has the meaning assigned to it by section 23(3) of the 1989 Act; and

'care home', 'independent hospital', 'local authority' and 'clinical commissioning group' have the meanings assigned to them by section 105 of the 1989 Act.

(Part 16 contains the rules relating to the representation of children.)

Amendments—SI 2013/235; SI 2014/843.

### 12.4 Notice of proceedings to person with foreign parental responsibility

(1) This rule applies where a child is subject to proceedings to which this Part applies and –

(a) a person holds or is believed to hold parental responsibility for the child under the law of another State which subsists in accordance with Article 16 of the 1996 Hague Convention following the child becoming habitually resident in a territorial unit of the United Kingdom; and

(b) that person is not otherwise required to be joined as a respondent under rule 12.3.

(2) The applicant shall give notice of the proceedings to any person to whom the applicant believes paragraph (1) applies in any case in which a person whom the applicant believed to have parental responsibility under the 1989 Act would be a respondent to those proceedings in accordance with rule 12.3.

(3) The applicant and every respondent to the proceedings shall provide such details as they possess as to the identity and whereabouts of any person they believe to hold parental responsibility for the child in accordance with paragraph (1) to the court officer, upon making, or responding to the application as appropriate.

(4) Where the existence of a person who is believed to have parental responsibility for the child in accordance with paragraph (1) only becomes apparent to a party at a later date during the proceedings, that party must notify the court officer of those details at the earliest opportunity.

(5) Where a person to whom paragraph (1) applies receives notice of proceedings, that person may apply to the court to be joined as a party using the Part 18 procedure.

### 12.5 What the court will do when the application has been issued

(1) When proceedings other than public law proceedings have been issued the court will consider –

(a) setting a date for –
  (i) a directions appointment;

(ii) in private law proceedings, a First Hearing Dispute Resolution Appointment; or
(iii) *(revoked)*
(iv) the hearing of the application,
and if the court sets a date it will do so in accordance with rule 12.13 and Practice Direction 12B;
(b) giving any of the directions listed in rule 12.12 or, where Chapter 6, section 1 applies, rule 12.48; and
(c) doing anything else which is set out in Practice Direction 12B or any other practice direction.

(2) When Part 4 proceedings and in so far as practicable other public law proceedings have been issued the court will –

(a) set a date for the Case Management Hearing in accordance with Practice Direction 12A;
(b) set a date for the hearing of an application for an interim order if necessary;
(c) give any directions listed in rule 12.12; and
(d) do anything else which is set out in Practice Direction 12A.

(Practice Direction 12A sets out details relating to the Case Management Hearing. Practice Direction 12B supplementing this Part sets out details relating to the First Hearing Dispute Resolution Appointment.)

Amendments—SI 2014/843.

## 12.6 Children's guardian, solicitor and reports under section 7 of the 1989 Act

Within a day of the issue of Part 4 proceedings or the transfer of Part 4 Proceedings to the court and as soon as practicable after the issue of other proceedings or the transfer of the other proceedings to the court, the court will –

(a) in specified proceedings, appoint a children's guardian under rule 16.3(1) unless –
   (i) such an appointment has already been made by the court which made the transfer and is subsisting; or
   (ii) the court considers that such an appointment is not necessary to safeguard the interests of the child;
(b) where section 41(3) of the 1989 Act applies, consider whether a solicitor should be appointed to represent the child, and if so, appoint a solicitor accordingly;
(c) consider whether to ask an officer of the service or a Welsh family proceedings officer for advice relating to the welfare of the child;
(d) consider whether a report relating to the welfare of the child is required, and if so, request such a report in accordance with section 7 of the 1989 Act.

(Part 16 sets out the rules relating to representation of children.)

Amendments—SI 2014/843.

### 12.7 What a court officer will do

(1) As soon as practicable after the issue of proceedings the court officer will return to the applicant the copies of the application together with the forms referred to in Practice Direction 5A.

(2) As soon as practicable after the issue of proceedings or the transfer of proceedings to the court or at any other stage in the proceedings the court officer will –

  (a) give notice of any hearing set by the court to the applicant; and
  (b) do anything else set out in Practice Directions 12A or 12B or any other practice direction.

### 12.8 Service

(1) After the issue of proceedings under this Part, the documents specified in paragraph (5) must be served on the respondent or respondents.

(2) In section 8 private law proceedings, service under paragraph (1) will be effected by the court officer, unless –

  (a) the applicant requests to do so; or
  (b) the court directs the applicant to do so.

(3) In this Rule, 'section 8 private law proceedings' are proceedings for a section 8 order except proceedings for a child arrangements order to which section 9(6B) of the 1989 Act applies with respect to a child who is in the care of a local authority.

(4) In any other proceedings to which this Part applies, service under paragraph (1) must be effected by the applicant.

(5) The documents are –

  (a) the application together with the documents referred to in Practice Direction 12C; and
  (b) notice of any hearing set by the court.

(6) Service under this rule must be carried out in accordance with Practice Direction 12C.

(7) The general rules about service in Part 6 apply but are subject to this rule.

> (Practice Direction 12C (Service of Application in Children Proceedings) provides that in Part 4 proceedings (except proceedings for an interim order) the minimum number of days prior to the Case Management Hearing for service of the application and accompanying documents is 7 days. The Court has discretion to extend or shorten this time (see rule 4.1(3)(a)).

Amendments—SI 2014/843.

### 12.9–12.11 (revoked)

**12.12 Directions**

(1) This rule does not apply to proceedings under Chapter 6 of this Part.

(2) At any stage in the proceedings, the court may give directions about the conduct of the proceedings including –

- (a) the management of the case;
- (b) the timetable for steps to be taken between the giving of directions and the final hearing;
- (c) the joining of a child or other person as a party to the proceedings in accordance with rules 12.3(2) and (3);
- (d) the attendance of the child;
- (e) the appointment of a children's guardian or of a solicitor under section 41(3) of the 1989 Act;
- (f) the appointment of a litigation friend;
- (g) the service of documents;
- (h) the filing of evidence including experts' reports; and
- (i) the exercise by an officer of the Service, Welsh family proceedings officer or local authority officer of any duty referred to in rule 16.38(1).

(3) Paragraph (4) applies where –

- (a) an officer of the Service or a Welsh family proceedings officer has filed a report or a risk assessment as a result of exercising a duty referred to in rule 16.38(1)(a); or
- (b) a local authority officer has filed a report as a result of exercising a duty referred to in rule 16.38(1)(b).

(4) The court may –

- (a) give directions setting a date for a hearing at which that report or risk assessment will be considered; and
- (b) direct that the officer who prepared the report or risk assessment attend any such hearing.

(5) The court may exercise the powers in paragraphs (2) and (4) on an application or of its own initiative.

(6) Where the court proposes to exercise its powers of its own initiative the procedure set out in rule 4.3(2) to (6) applies.

(7) Directions of a court which are still in force immediately prior to the transfer of proceedings to another court will continue to apply following the transfer subject to –

- (a) any changes of terminology which are required to apply those directions to the court to which the proceedings are transferred; and
- (b) any variation or revocation of the direction.

(8) The court or court officer will –

- (a) take a note of the giving, variation or revocation of a direction under this rule; and (b)　as soon as practicable serve a copy of the note on every party.

(Rule 12.48 provides for directions in proceedings under the 1980 Hague Convention and the European Convention.)

### 12.13 Setting dates for hearings and setting or confirming the timetable and date for the final hearing

(1) At the –

- (a)　transfer to a court of proceedings;
- (b)　postponement or adjournment of any hearing; or
- (c)　conclusion of any hearing at which the proceedings are not finally determined,

the court will set a date for the proceedings to come before the court again for the purposes of giving directions or for such other purposes as the court directs.

(2) At any hearing the court may –

- (a)　confirm a date for the final hearing or the week within which the final hearing is to begin (where a date or period for the final hearing has already been set);
- (b)　set a timetable for the final hearing unless a timetable has already been fixed, or the court considers that it would be inappropriate to do so; or
- (c)　set a date for the final hearing or a period within which the final hearing of the application is to take place.

(3) The court officer will notify the parties of –

- (a)　the date of a hearing fixed in accordance with paragraph (1);
- (b)　the timetable for the final hearing; and
- (c)　the date of the final hearing or the period in which it will take place.

(4) Where the date referred to in paragraph (1) is set at the transfer of proceedings, the date will be as soon as possible after the transfer.

(5) The requirement in paragraph (1) to set a date for the proceedings to come before the court again is satisfied by the court setting or confirming a date for the final hearing.

### 12.14 Attendance at hearings

(1) This rule does not apply to proceedings under Chapter 6 of this Part except for proceedings for a declaration under rule 12.71.

(2) Unless the court directs otherwise and subject to paragraph (3), the persons who must attend a hearing are –

- (a)　any party to the proceedings;
- (b)　any litigation friend for any party or legal representative instructed to act on that party's behalf; and
- (c)　any other person directed by the court or required by Practice Directions 12A or 12B or any other practice direction to attend.

(3) Proceedings or any part of them will take place in the absence of a child who is a party to the proceedings if –

(a) the court considers it in the interests of the child, having regard to the matters to be discussed or the evidence likely to be given; and
(b) the child is represented by a children's guardian or solicitor.

(4) When considering the interests of the child under paragraph (3) the court will give –

(a) the children's guardian;
(b) the solicitor for the child; and
(c) the child, if of sufficient understanding,

an opportunity to make representations.

(5) Subject to paragraph (6), where at the time and place appointed for a hearing, the applicant appears but one or more of the respondents do not, the court may proceed with the hearing.

(6) The court will not begin to hear an application in the absence of a respondent unless the court is satisfied that –

(a) the respondent received reasonable notice of the date of the hearing; or
(b) the circumstances of the case justify proceeding with the hearing.

(7) Where, at the time and place appointed for a hearing one or more of the respondents appear but the applicant does not, the court may –

(a) refuse the application; or
(b) if sufficient evidence has previously been received, proceed in the absence of the applicant.

(8) Where at the time and place appointed for a hearing neither the applicant nor any respondent appears, the court may refuse the application.

(9) Paragraphs (5) to (8) do not apply to a hearing where the court –

(a) is considering –
    (i) whether to make a contact activity direction or to attach an activity condition to a child arrangements order; or
    (ii) an application for a financial compensation order, an enforcement order or an order under paragraph 9 of Schedule A1 to the 1989 Act following a breach of an enforcement order; and
(b) has yet to obtain sufficient evidence from, or in relation to, the person who may be the subject of the direction, condition or order to enable it to determine the matter.

(10) Nothing in this rule affects the provisions of Article 18 of the Council Regulation in cases to which that provision applies.

(The Council Regulation makes provision in Article 18 for the court to stay proceedings where the respondent is habitually resident in another Member State of the European Union and has not been adequately served with the proceedings as required by that provision.)

**Amendments**—SI 2014/843.

## 12.15 Steps taken by the parties

If –

(a) the parties or any children's guardian agree proposals for the management of the proceedings (including a proposed date for the final hearing or a period within which the final hearing is to take place); and

(b) the court considers that the proposals are suitable,

it may approve them without a hearing and give directions in the terms proposed.

> (Practice Direction 12A gives guidance as to the application of this rule to Part 4 proceedings in the light of the period that is for the time being allowed under section 32(1)(a)(ii) of the 1989 Act)

**Amendments**—SI 2014/843.

## 12.16 Applications without notice

(1) This rule applies to –

(a) proceedings for a section 8 order;
(b) emergency proceedings; and
(c) proceedings relating to the exercise of the court's inherent jurisdiction (other than an application for the court's permission to start such proceedings and proceedings for collection, location and passport orders where Chapter 6 applies).

(2) An application in proceedings referred to in paragraph (1) may be made without notice in which case the applicant must file the application –

(a) where the application is made by telephone, the next business day after the making of the application; or
(b) in any other case, at the time when the application is made.

(3) *(revoked)*

(4) Where –

(a) a section 8 order;
(b) an emergency protection order;
(c) an order for the disclosure of information as to the whereabouts of a child under section 33 of the 1986 Act; or
(d) an order authorising the taking charge of and delivery of a child under section 34 of the 1986 Act,

is made without notice, the applicant must serve a copy of the application on each respondent within 48 hours after the order is made.

(5) Within 48 hours after the making of an order without notice, the applicant must serve a copy of the order on –

(a) the parties, unless the court directs otherwise;

(b) any person who has actual care of the child or who had such care immediately prior to the making of the order; and
(c) in the case of an emergency protection order and a recovery order, the local authority in whose area the child lives or is found.

(6) Where the court refuses to make an order on an application without notice it may direct that the application is made on notice in which case the application will proceed in accordance with rules 12.3 to 12.15.

(7) Where the hearing takes place outside the hours during which the court office is normally open, the court or court officer will take a note of the proceedings.

(Practice Direction 12E (Urgent Business) provides further details of the procedure for out of hours applications. See also Practice Direction 12D (Inherent Jurisdiction (including Wardship Proceedings).)

(Rule 12.47 provides for without-notice applications in proceedings under Chapter 6, section 1 of this Part, (proceedings under the 1980 Hague Convention and the European Convention).)

Amendments—SI 2013/3204.

### 12.17 Investigation under section 37 of the 1989 Act

(1) This rule applies where a direction is given to an appropriate authority by the court under section 37(1) of the 1989 Act.

(2) On giving the direction the court may adjourn the proceedings.

(3) As soon as practicable after the direction is given the court will record the direction.

(4) As soon as practicable after the direction is given the court officer will –

(a) serve the direction on –
   (i) the parties to the proceedings in which the direction is given; and
   (ii) the appropriate authority where it is not a party;
(b) serve any documentary evidence directed by the court on the appropriate authority.

(5) Where a local authority informs the court of any of the matters set out in section 37(3)(a) to (c) of the 1989 Act it will do so in writing.

(6) Unless the court directs otherwise, the court officer will serve a copy of any report to the court under section 37 of the 1989 Act on the parties.

(Section 37 of the 1989 Act refers to the appropriate authority and section 37(5) of that Act sets out which authority should be named in a particular case.)

### 12.18 Disclosure of a report under section 14A(8) or (9) of the 1989 Act

(1) In proceedings for a special guardianship order, the local authority must file the report under section 14A(8) or (9) of the 1989 Act within the timetable fixed by the court.

(2) The court will consider whether to give a direction that the report under section 14A(8) or (9) of the 1989 Act be disclosed to each party to the proceedings.

(3) Before giving a direction for the report to be disclosed, the court must consider whether any information should be deleted from the report.

(4) The court may direct that the report must not be disclosed to a party.

(5) The court officer must serve a copy of the report in accordance with any direction under paragraph (2).

(6) In paragraph (3), information includes information which a party has declined to reveal under rule 29.1(1).

## 12.19 Additional evidence

(1) This rule applies to proceedings for a section 8 order or a special guardianship order.

(2) Unless the court directs otherwise, a party must not –

(a) file or serve any document other than in accordance with these rules or any practice direction;
(b) in completing a form prescribed by these rules or any practice direction, give information or make a statement which is not required or authorised by that form; or
(c) file or serve at a hearing –
　(i) any witness statement of the substance of the oral evidence which the party intends to adduce; or
　(ii) any copy of any document (including any experts' report) which the party intends to rely on.

(3) Where a party fails to comply with the requirements of this rule in relation to any witness statement or other document, the party cannot seek to rely on that statement or other document unless the court directs otherwise.

## 12.20 *(revoked)*

## 12.21 Hearings

(1) The court may give directions about the order of speeches and the evidence at a hearing.

(2) Subject to any directions given under paragraph (1), the parties and the children's guardian must adduce their evidence at a hearing in the following order –

(a) the applicant;
(b) any party with parental responsibility for the child;
(c) other respondents;
(d) the children's guardian;
(e) the child, if the child is a party to proceedings and there is no children's guardian.

## Chapter 3
## Special Provisions About Public Law Proceedings

### 12.22 Timetable for the proceedings

In public law proceedings other than Part 4 proceedings, in so far as practicable the court will draw up the timetable for the proceedings or revise that timetable with a view to disposing of the application without delay and in any event within 26 weeks beginning with the date on which the application is issued.

> (In relation to Part 4 proceedings, section 32(1)(a) of the 1989 Act requires the court to draw up a timetable with a view to disposing of the application without delay and in any event within 26 weeks beginning with the day on which the application is issued.)

**Amendments**—Substituted by SI 2014/843.

### 12.23 Application of rules 12.24 to 12.26C

Rules 12.24 to 12.26C apply to Part 4 proceedings and in so far as practicable other public law proceedings.

**Amendments**—SI 2014/843.

### 12.24 Directions

The court will direct the parties to –

(a) monitor compliance with the court's directions; and
(b) tell the court or court officer about –
   (i) any failure to comply with a direction of the court; and
   (ii) any other delay in the proceedings.

### 12.25 The Case Management Hearing and the Issues Resolution Hearing

(1) The court will conduct the Case Management Hearing with the objective of –

(a) confirming the level of judge to which the proceedings have been allocated;
(b) drawing up a timetable for the proceedings including the time within which the proceedings are to be resolved;
(c) identifying the issues; and
(d) giving directions in accordance with rule 12.12 and Practice Direction 12A to manage the proceedings.

(2) The court may hold a further Case Management Hearing only where this hearing is necessary to fulfil the objectives of the Case Management Hearing set out in paragraph (1).

(3) The court will conduct the Issues Resolution Hearing with the objective of –

(a) identifying the remaining issues in the proceedings;
(b) as far as possible resolving or narrowing those issues; and

(c) giving directions to manage the proceedings to the final hearing in accordance with rule 12.12 and Practice Direction 12A.

(4) Where it is possible for all the issues in the proceedings to be resolved at the Issues Resolution Hearing, the court may treat the Issues Resolution Hearing as a final hearing and make orders disposing of the proceedings.

(5) The court may set a date for the Case Management Hearing, a further Case Management Hearing and the Issues Resolution Hearing at the times referred to in Practice Direction 12A.

(6) The matters which the court will consider at the hearings referred to in this rule are set out in Practice Direction 12A.

(Rule 25.6 (experts: when to apply for the court's permission) provides that unless the court directs otherwise, parties must apply for the court's permission as mentioned in section 13(1), (3) and (5) of the 2014 Act as soon as possible and in Part 4 proceedings and in so far as practicable other public law proceedings no later than the Case Management Hearing.)

Amendments—Substituted by SI 2014/843.

### 12.26 Discussion between advocates

(1) When setting a date for the Case Management Hearing or the Issues Resolution Hearing the court will direct a discussion between the parties' advocates to –

(a) discuss the provisions of a draft of the Case Management Order; and
(b) consider any other matter set out in Practice Direction 12A.

(2) Where there is a litigant in person the court will give directions about how that person may take part in the discussions between the parties' advocates.

(3) Unless the court directs otherwise –

(a) any discussion between advocates must take place no later than 2 days before the Case Management Hearing; and
(b) a draft of the Case Management Order must be filed with the court no later than 11a.m. on the day before the Case Management Hearing.

(4) Unless the court directs otherwise –

(a) any discussion between advocates must take place no later than 7 days before the Issues Resolution Hearing; and
(b) a draft of the Case Management Order must be filed with the court no later than 11a.m. on the day before the Issues Resolution Hearing.

(5) For the purposes of this rule 'advocate' includes a litigant in person.

Amendments—Substituted by SI 2014/843.

### 12.26A Application for extension of the time limit for disposing of the application

(1) An application requesting the court to grant an extension must state –

(a) the reasons for the request;
(b) the period of extension being requested; and
(c) a short explanation of –
   (i) why it is necessary for the request to be granted to enable the court to resolve the proceedings justly;
   (ii) the impact which any ensuing timetable revision would have on the welfare of the child to whom the application relates;
   (iii) the impact which any ensuing timetable revision would have on the duration and conduct of the proceedings; and
   (iv) the reasons for the grant or refusal of any previous request for extension.

(2) Part 18 applies to an application requesting the grant of an extension.
(3) In this rule

'ensuing timetable revision' has the meaning given to it by section 32(6) of the 1989 Act;

'extension' means an extension of the period for the time being allowed under section 32(1)(a)(ii) of the 1989 Act which is to end no more than 8 weeks after the later of the times referred to in section 32(8) of that Act.

Amendments—Inserted by SI 2014/843.

### 12.26B Disapplication of rule 4.1(3)(a) court's power to extend or shorten the time for compliance with a rule

Rule 4.1(3)(a) does not apply to any period that is for the time being allowed under section 32(1)(a)(ii) of the 1989 Act.

Amendments—Inserted by SI 2014/843.

### 12.26C Extension of time limit: reasons for court's decision

(1) When refusing or granting an extension of the period that is for the time being allowed under section 32(1)(a)(ii) in the case of the application, the court will announce its decision and –

(a) the reasons for that decision; and
(b) where an extension is granted or refused, a short explanation of the impact which the decision would have on the welfare of the child.

(2) The court office will supply a copy of the order granting or refusing the extension including the reasons for the court's decision and the period of any extension and short explanation given under paragraph (1)(b) to –

(a) the parties; and
(b) any person who has actual care of the child who is the subject of the proceedings.

Amendments—Inserted by SI 2014/843.

## 12.27 Matters prescribed for the purposes of the Act

(1) Proceedings for an order under any of the following provisions of the 1989 Act –

   (a)  a secure accommodation order under section 25;
   (b)  an order giving permission to change a child's surname or remove a child from the United Kingdom under section 33(7);
   (c)  an order permitting the local authority to arrange for any child in its care to live outside England and Wales under paragraph 19(1) of Schedule 2;
   (d)  the extension or further extension of a supervision order under paragraph 6(3) of Schedule 3;
   (e)  appeals against the determination of proceedings of a kind set out in sub-paragraphs (a) to (d);

are specified for the purposes of section 41 of that Act in accordance with section 41(6)(i) of that Act.

(2) The persons listed as applicants in the table set out in rule 12.3 to proceedings for the variation of directions made with interim care or interim supervision orders under section 38(8) of the 1989 Act are the prescribed class of persons for the purposes of that section.

(3) The persons listed as applicants in the table set out in rule 12.3 to proceedings for the variation of a direction made under section 44(6) of the 1989 Act in an emergency protection order are the prescribed class of persons for the purposes of section 44(9) of that Act.

## 12.28 Exclusion requirements: interim care orders and emergency protection orders

(1) This rule applies where the court includes an exclusion requirement in an interim care order or an emergency protection order.

(2) The applicant for an interim care order or emergency protection order must –

   (a)  prepare a separate statement of the evidence in support of the application for an exclusion requirement;
   (b)  serve the statement personally on the relevant person with a copy of the order containing the exclusion requirement (and of any power of arrest which is attached to it);
   (c)  inform the relevant person of that person's right to apply to vary or discharge the exclusion requirement.

(3) Where a power of arrest is attached to an exclusion requirement in an interim care order or an emergency protection order, the applicant will deliver –

   (a)  a copy of the order; and
   (b)  a statement showing that the relevant person has been served with the order or informed of its terms (whether by being present when the order was made or by telephone or otherwise),

to the officer for the time being in charge of the police station for the area in which the dwelling-house in which the child lives is situated (or such other police station as the court may specify).

(4) Rules 10.6(2) and 10.10 to 10.17 will apply, with the necessary modifications, for the service, variation, discharge and enforcement of any exclusion requirement to which a power of arrest is attached as they apply to an order made on an application under Part 4 of the 1996 Act.

(5) The relevant person must serve the parties to the proceedings with any application which that person makes for the variation or discharge of the exclusion requirement.

(6) Where an exclusion requirement ceases to have effect whether –

- (a) as a result of the removal of a child under section 38A(10) or 44A(10) of the 1989 Act;
- (b) because of the discharge of the interim care order or emergency protection order; or
- (c) otherwise,

the applicant must inform –
- (i) the relevant person;
- (ii) the parties to the proceedings;
- (iii) any officer to whom a copy of the order was delivered under paragraph (3); and
- (iv) (where necessary) the court.

(7) Where the court includes an exclusion requirement in an interim care order or an emergency protection order of its own motion, paragraph (2) will apply with the omission of any reference to the statement of the evidence.

(8) In this rule, 'the relevant person' has the meaning assigned to it by sections 38A(2) and 44A(2) of the 1989 Act.

## 12.29 Notification of consent

(1) Consent for the purposes of the following provisions of the 1989 Act –

- (a) section 16(3);
- (b) section 38A(2)(b)(ii) or 44A(2)(b)(ii); or
- (c) paragraph 19(3)(c) or (d) of Schedule 2,

must be given either –
- (i) orally to the court; or
- (ii) in writing to the court signed by the person giving consent.

(2) Any written consent for the purposes of section 38A(2) or 44A(2) of the 1989 Act must include a statement that the person giving consent –

- (a) is able and willing to give to the child the care which it would be reasonable to expect a parent to give; and
- (b) understands that the giving of consent could lead to the exclusion of the relevant person from the dwelling-house in which the child lives.

## 12.30 Proceedings for secure accommodation orders: copies of reports

In proceedings under section 25 of the 1989 Act, the court will, if practicable, arrange for copies of all written reports filed in the case to be made available before the hearing to –

(a) the applicant;
(b) the parent or guardian of the child to whom the application relates;
(c) any legal representative of the child;
(d) the children's guardian; and
(e) the child, unless the court directs otherwise,

and copies of the reports may, if the court considers it desirable, be shown to any person who is entitled to notice of any hearing in accordance with Practice Direction 12C.

\*\*\*\*

# Chapter 5
## Special Provisions about Inherent Jurisdiction Proceedings

### 12.36 Where to start proceedings

(1) An application for proceedings under the Inherent Jurisdiction of the court must be started in the High Court.

(2) Wardship proceedings, except applications for an order that a child be made or cease to be a ward of court, may be transferred to the family court unless the issues of fact or law make them more suitable for hearing in the High Court.

(The question of suitability for hearing in the High Court is explained in Practice Direction 12D (Inherent Jurisdiction (including Wardship Proceedings)).)

Amendments—SI 2013/3204.

### 12.37 Child as respondent to wardship proceedings

(1) A child who is the subject of wardship proceedings must not be made a respondent to those proceedings unless the court gives permission following an application under paragraph (2).

(2) Where nobody other than the child would be a suitable respondent to wardship proceedings, the applicant may apply without notice for permission to make the wardship application –

(a) without notice; or
(b) with the child as the respondent.

### 12.38 Registration requirements

The court officer will send a copy of every application for a child to be made a ward of court to the principal registry for recording in the register of wards.

## 12.39 Notice of child's whereabouts

(1) Every respondent, other than a child, must file with the acknowledgment of service a notice stating –

    (a)    the respondent's address; and
    (b)    either –
        (i)    the whereabouts of the child; or
        (ii)    that the respondent is unaware of the child's whereabouts if that is the case.

(2) Unless the court directs otherwise, the respondent must serve a copy of that notice on the applicant.

(3) Every respondent other than a child must immediately notify the court in writing of –

    (a)    any subsequent changes of address; or
    (b)    any change in the child's whereabouts,

and, unless the court directs otherwise, serve a copy of that notice on the applicant.

(4) In this rule a reference to the whereabouts of a child is a reference to –

    (a)    the address at which the child is living;
    (b)    the person with whom the child is living; and
    (c)    any other information relevant to where the child may be found.

## 12.40 Enforcement of orders in wardship proceedings

The High Court may secure compliance with any direction relating to a ward of court by an order addressed to the tipstaff.

    (The role of the tipstaff is explained in Practice Direction 12D (Inherent Jurisdiction (including Wardship Proceedings)).)

## 12.41 Child ceasing to be ward of court

(1) A child who, by virtue of section 41(2) of the Senior Courts Act 1981, automatically becomes a ward of court on the making of a wardship application will cease to be a ward on the determination of the application unless the court orders that the child be made a ward of court.

(2) Nothing in paragraph (1) affects the power of the court under section 41(3) of the Senior Courts Act 1981 to order that any child cease to be a ward of court.

## 12.42 Adoption of a child who is a ward of court

An application for permission –

    (a)    to start proceedings to adopt a child who is a ward of court;
    (b)    to place such a child for adoption with parental consent; or
    (c)    to start proceedings for a placement order in relation to such a child,

may be made without notice in accordance with Part 18.

**12.42A Application for a writ of habeas corpus for release in relation to a minor**

(1) Part 87 of the CPR applies in respect of an application for a writ of habeas corpus for release in relation to a minor –

    (a)    as if –
        (i)    for rule 87.2(1)(a) of the CPR there were substituted –

            '(a)    an application notice; and'; and
        (ii)    for rule 87.2(4) of the CPR there were substituted –
            '(4) The application notice must be filed in the Family Division of the High Court.'; and

    (b)    subject to any additional necessary modifications.

(2) Rules 12.5 to 12.8, 12.12 to 12.16, 12.21 and 12.39 do not apply to an application to which this rule applies.

(The term 'application notice' is defined in rule 2.3(1).)

Amendments—Inserted by SI 2014/3296.

\* \* \* \*

## Chapter 7
## *Communication of Information: Children Proceedings*

Amendments—SI 2012/3061.

**12.72 Interpretation**

In this Chapter 'independent reviewing officer' means a person appointed in respect of a child in accordance with regulation 2A of the Review of Children's Cases Regulations 1991, or regulation 3 of the Review of Children's Cases (Wales) Regulations 2007.

Amendments—SI 2012/679.

**12.73 Communication of information: general**

(1) For the purposes of the law relating to contempt of court, information relating to proceedings held in private (whether or not contained in a document filed with the court) may be communicated –

    (a)    where the communication is to –
        (i)    a party;
        (ii)    the legal representative of a party;
        (iii)    a professional legal adviser;
        (iv)    an officer of the service or a Welsh family proceedings officer;
        (v)    the welfare officer;

(vi) the Director of Legal Aid Casework (within the meaning of section 4 of the Legal Aid, Sentencing and Punishment of Offenders Act 2012);
(vii) an expert whose instruction by a party has been authorised by the court for the purposes of the proceedings;
(viii) a professional acting in furtherance of the protection of children;
(ix) an independent reviewing officer appointed in respect of a child who is, or has been, subject to proceedings to which this rule applies;

(b) where the court gives permission; or
(c) subject to any direction of the court, in accordance with rule 12.75 and Practice Direction 12G.

(2) Nothing in this Chapter permits the communication to the public at large, or any section of the public, of any information relating to the proceedings.

(3) Nothing in rule 12.75 and Practice Direction 12G permits the disclosure of an unapproved draft judgment handed down by any court.

Amendments—SI 2013/534, subject to savings.

## 12.74 (revoked)

## 12.75 Communication of information for purposes connected with the proceedings

(1) A party or the legal representative of a party, on behalf of and upon the instructions of that party, may communicate information relating to the proceedings to any person where necessary to enable that party –

(a) by confidential discussion, to obtain support, advice or assistance in the conduct of the proceedings;
(b) to attend a mediation information and assessment meeting, or to engage in mediation or other forms of non-court dispute resolution;
(c) to make and pursue a complaint against a person or body concerned in the proceedings; or
(d) to make and pursue a complaint regarding the law, policy or procedure relating to a category of proceedings to which this Part applies.

(2) Where information is communicated to any person in accordance with paragraph (1)(a) of this rule, no further communication by that person is permitted.

(3) When information relating to the proceedings is communicated to any person in accordance with paragraphs (1)(b), (c) or (d) of this rule –

(a) the recipient may communicate that information to a further recipient, provided that –
    (i) the party who initially communicated the information consents to that further communication; and

(ii) the further communication is made only for the purpose or purposes for which the party made the initial communication; and
(b) the information may be successively communicated to and by further recipients on as many occasions as may be necessary to fulfil the purpose for which the information was initially communicated, provided that on each such occasion the conditions in sub-paragraph (a) are met.

Amendments—SI 2014/843.

## PRACTICE DIRECTION 12A - CARE, SUPERVISION AND OTHER PART 4 PROCEEDINGS: GUIDE TO CASE MANAGEMENT

This Practice Direction supplements FPR Part 12

### 1 The key stages of the court process

1.1 The Public Law Outline set out in the Table below contains an outline of -

(1) the order of the different stages of the process;
(2) the matters to be considered at the main case management hearings;
(3) the latest timescales within which the main stages of the process should take place in order to resolve the proceedings within 26 weeks.

1.2 In the Public Law Outline -

(1) 'CMH' means the Case Management Hearing;
(2) 'FCMH' means Further Case Management Hearing;
(3) 'ICO' means interim care order;
(4) 'IRH' means the Issues Resolution Hearing;
(5) 'LA' means the Local Authority which is applying for a care or supervision order or a final order in other Part 4 proceedings;
(6) 'OS' means the Official Solicitor.

1.3 In applying the provisions of FPR Part 12 and the Public Law Outline the court and the parties must also have regard to -

(1) all other relevant rules and Practice Directions and in particular -
 - FPR Part 1 (Overriding Objective);
 - FPR Part 4 (General Case Management Powers);
 - FPR Part 15 (Representation of Protected Parties) and Practice Direction 15B (Adults Who May Be Protected Parties and Children Who May Become Protected Parties in Family Proceedings);
 - FPR Part 18 (Procedure for Other Applications in Proceedings);
 - FPR Part 22 (Evidence);
 - FPR Part 24 (Witnesses, depositions generally and taking of evidence in Member States of the European Union);
 - FPR Part 25 (Experts) and the Experts Practice Directions;
 - FPR 27.6 and Practice Direction 27A (Court Bundles);

- FPR 30 (Appeals) and Practice Direction 30A (Appeals);
(2) the Allocation Rules;
(3) the Justices' Clerks Rules;
(4) President's Guidance issued from time to time on
    - Distribution of business of the family court;
    - Judicial continuity and deployment;
    - Prescribed templates and orders;
(5) International instruments
    - The Council Regulation (EC) No 2201/2003 (Brussels 2 revised);
    - The 1996 Hague Convention;
(6) Guidance relating to protected parties and others with a disability -
    - Protected Parties in Family Proceedings: Checklist For the Appointment of a Litigation Friend (including the Official Solicitor) (published in Family Law (January 2014);
    - The Mental Capacity Act 2005 (Transfer of Proceedings) Order 2007 SI 2007/1899, relating to young people over 16 where they are likely to lack decision-making capacity at age 18.

**Public Law Outline**

| PRE-PROCEEDINGS ||
|---|---|
| PRE-PROCEEDINGS CHECKLIST ||
| <u>Annex Documents</u> are the documents specified in the Annex to the Application Form which are to be attached to that form and filed with the court:<br><br>o Social Work Chronology<br><br>o Social Work Statement and Genogram<br><br>o The current assessments relating to the child and/or the family and friends of the child to which the Social Work Statement refers and on which the LA relies<br><br>o Care Plan<br>o Index of Checklist Documents | <u>Checklist documents</u> (already existing on the LA's files) are -<br>(a) Evidential documents including -<br><br>o Previous court orders including foreign orders and judgments/reasons<br><br>o Any assessment materials relevant to the key issues including capacity to litigate, section 7 and 37 reports<br><br>o Single, joint or inter-agency materials (e.g., health and education/Home Office and Immigration Tribunal documents);<br>(b) Decision-making records including -<br><br>o Records of key discussions with the family |

|  |  |
|---|---|
|  | o Key LA minutes and records for the child |
|  | o Pre-existing care plans (e.g., child in need plan, looked after child plan and child protection plan) |
|  | o Letters Before Proceedings |
|  | Only Checklist documents in *(a) are to be served* with the application form |
|  | Checklist Documents in *(b) are to be disclosed on request* by any party |
|  | Checklist documents are *not* to be - |
|  | o filed with the court unless the court directs otherwise; and |
|  | o older than 2 years before the date of issue of the proceedings unless reliance is placed on the same in the LA's evidence |

| STAGE 1 – ISSUE AND ALLOCATION |
|---|
| DAY 1 AND DAY 2 (see interpretation section) |
| On Day 1 (Day of issue):<br>o The LA files the Application Form and Annex Documents and sends copies to Cafcass/CAFCASS Cymru<br>o The LA notifies the court of the need for an urgent preliminary case management hearing or an urgent contested ICO hearing where this is known or expected<br>Court officer issues application<br>Within a day of issue (Day 2):<br>o Court considers jurisdiction in a case with an international element<br>o Court considers initial allocation to specified level of judge, in accordance with the Allocation Rules and any President's Guidance on the distribution of business<br>o LA serves the Application Form, Annex Documents and evidential Checklist Documents on the parties together with the notice of date and time of CMH and any urgent hearing<br>o Court gives standard directions on Issue and Allocation including: |

- Checking compliance with Pre-Proceedings Checklist including service of any missing Annex Documents
- Appointing Children's Guardian (to be allocated by Cafcass/CAFCASS Cymru)
- Appointing solicitor for the child only if necessary
- Appointing (if the person to be appointed consents) a litigation friend for any protected party or any non-subject child who is a party, including the OS where appropriate
- Identifying whether a request has been made or should be made to a Central Authority or other competent authority in a foreign state or a consular authority in England and Wales in a case with an international element
- Filing and service of a LA Case Summary
- Filing and service of a Case Analysis by the Children's Guardian
- Filing and Serving the Parents' Response
- Sending a request for disclosure to, e.g., the police or health service body
- Filing and serving an application for permission relating to experts under Part 25 on a date prior to the advocates meeting for the CMH
- Directing the solicitor for the child to arrange an advocates' meeting no later than 2 business days before the CMH
- Listing the CMH

o Court considers any request for an urgent preliminary case management hearing or an urgent contested ICO hearing and where necessary lists the hearing and gives additional directions.

o Court officer sends copy Notice of Hearing of the CMH and any urgent hearing by email to Cafcass/ CAFCASS Cymru.

| STAGE 2 – CASE MANAGEMENT HEARING | |
|---|---|
| ADVOCATES' MEETING<br><br>(including any litigants in person) | CASE MANAGEMENT HEARING |
| No later than 2 business days before CMH (or FCMH if it is necessary) | CMH: Not before day 12 and not later than day 18<br><br>A FCMH is to be held only if necessary, it is to be listed as soon as possible and in any event no later than day 25 |

| | |
|---|---|
| o Consider information on the Application Form and Annex documents, the LA Case Summary, and the Case Analysis | o Court gives detailed case management directions, including: |
| o Identify the parties' positions to be recited in the draft Case Management Order | - Considering jurisdiction in a case with an international element; |
| o Identify the parties' positions about jurisdiction, in particular arising out of any international element | - Confirming allocation |
| o If necessary, identify proposed experts and draft questions in accordance with Part 25 and the Experts Practice Directions | - Drawing up the timetable for the child and the timetable for the proceedings and considering if an extension is necessary |
| o Identify any disclosure that in the advocates' views is necessary | - Identifying additional parties, intervenors and representation (including confirming that Cafcass/CAFCASS Cymru have allocated a Children's Guardian and that a litigation friend is appointed for any protected party or non-subject child) |
| o Immediately notify the court of the need for a contested ICO hearing and any issue about allocation | |
| o LA advocate to file a draft Case Management Order in prescribed form with court by 11a.m. on the business day before the CMH and/or FCMH | - Giving directions for the determination of any disputed issue about litigation capacity |
| | - Identifying the key issues |
| | - Identifying the evidence necessary to enable the court to resolve the key issues |
| | - Deciding whether there is a real issue about threshold to be resolved |
| | - Determining any application made under Part 25 and otherwise ensuring compliance with Part 25 where it is necessary for expert(s) to be instructed |

|  |  |
|---|---|
|  | - Identifying any necessary disclosure and if appropriate giving directions |
|  | - Giving directions for any concurrent or proposed placement order proceedings |
|  | - Ensuring compliance with the court's directions |
|  | - If a FCMH is necessary, directing an advocates' meeting and Case Analysis if required |
|  | - Directing filing of any threshold agreement, final evidence and Care Plan and responses to those documents for the IRH |
|  | - Directing a Case Analysis for the IRH |
|  | - Directing an advocates' meeting for the IRH |
|  | - Listing (any FCMH) IRH, Final Hearing (including early Final Hearing), as appropriate |
|  | - Giving directions for special measures and/or interpreters and intermediaries |
|  | - Issuing the Case Management Order |

| STAGE 3 – ISSUES RESOLUTION HEARING ||
|---|---|
| ADVOCATES' MEETING (including any litigants in person) | IRH |
| No later than 7 business days before the IRH | As directed by the court, in accordance with the timetable for the proceedings |
| o Review evidence and the positions of the parties<br>o Identify the advocates' views of - | o Court identifies the key issue(s) (if any) to be determined and the extent to which those issues can be resolved or narrowed at the IRH |

| | |
|---|---|
| - the remaining key issues and how the issues may be resolved or narrowed at the IRH including by the making of final orders<br>- the further evidence which is required to be heard to enable the key issues to be resolved or narrowed at the IRH<br>- the evidence that is relevant and the witnesses that are required at the final hearing<br>- the need for a contested hearing and/or time for oral evidence to be given at the IRH<br>o LA advocate to -<br><br>- notify the court immediately of the outcome of the discussion at the meeting<br>- file a draft Case Management Order with the court by 11a.m. on the business day before the IRH | o Court considers whether the IRH can be used as a final hearing<br>o Court resolves or narrows the issues by hearing evidence<br><br>o Court identifies the evidence to be heard on the issues which remain to be resolved at the final hearing<br><br>o Court gives final case management directions including:<br><br>- Any extension of the timetable for the proceedings which is necessary<br><br>- Filing of the threshold agreement or a statement of facts/issues remaining to be determined<br>- Filing of:<br>   o Final evidence and Care Plan<br><br>   o Case Analysis for Final Hearing (if required)<br>   o Witness templates<br><br>   o Skeleton arguments<br>- Judicial reading list/reading time, including time estimate and an estimate for judgment writing time<br>- Ensuring Compliance with PD27A (the Bundles Practice Direction)<br>- Listing the Final Hearing<br>o Court issues Case Management Order |

## 2 Flexible powers of the court

2.1 Attention is drawn to the flexible powers of the court either following the issue of the application or at any other stage in the proceedings.

2.2 The court may give directions without a hearing including setting a date for the Final Hearing or a period within which the Final Hearing will take place. The steps, which the court will ordinarily take at the various stages of the proceedings provided for in the Public Law Outline, may be taken by the court at another stage in the proceedings if the circumstances of the case merit this approach.

2.3 The flexible powers of the court include the ability for the court to cancel or repeat a particular hearing. For example, if the issue on which the case turns can with reasonable practicability be crystallised and resolved by taking evidence at an IRH then such a flexible approach must be taken in accordance with the overriding objective and to secure compliance with section 1(2) of the 1989 Act and resolving the proceedings within 26 weeks or the period for the time being specified by the court.

2.4 Where a party has requested an urgent hearing a) to enable the court to give immediate directions or orders to facilitate any case management issue which is to be considered at the CMH, or b) to decide whether an ICO is necessary, the court may list such a hearing at any appropriate time before the CMH and give directions for that hearing. It is anticipated that an urgent preliminary case management hearing will only be necessary to consider issues such as jurisdiction, parentage, party status, capacity to litigate, disclosure and whether there is, or should be, a request to a Central Authority or other competent authority in a foreign state or consular authority in England and Wales in an international case. It is not intended that any urgent hearing will delay the CMH.

2.5 Where it is anticipated that oral evidence may be required at the CMH, FCMH or IRH, the court must be notified in accordance with Stages 2 and 3 of the Public Law Outline well in advance and directions sought for the conduct of the hearing.

2.6 It is expected that full case management will take place at the CMH. It follows that the parties must be prepared to deal with all relevant case management issues, as identified in Stage 2 of the Public Law Outline. A FCMH should only be directed where necessary and must not be regarded as a routine step in proceedings.

## 3 Compliance with pre-proceedings checklist

3.1 It is recognised that in a small minority of cases the circumstances are such that the safety and welfare of the child may be jeopardised if the start of proceedings is delayed until all of the documents appropriate to the case and referred to in the Pre-proceedings Checklist are available. The safety and welfare of the child should never be put in jeopardy by delaying issuing proceedings whether because of lack of documentation or otherwise. (Nothing in this Practice Direction affects an application for an emergency protection order under section 44 of the 1989 Act). Also, where an application for an interim order is urgent, then the hearing of that application is NOT expected to be postponed until the Case Management Hearing. The Case Management Hearing is still to be held not before day 12 and not later than day 18 in accordance with the Public Law Outline and guidance in this Practice Direction. If an urgent preliminary Case Management Hearing or an urgent contested ICO hearing is held before the CMH, the court should not dispense with the CMH unless all of the parties have been sufficiently prepared and the court has been able to deal with all case management issues which would have come before it at the CMH.

3.2 The court recognises that preparation may need to be varied to suit the circumstances of the case. In cases where any of the Annex Documents required to be attached to the Application Form are not available at the time of issue of the application, the court will consider making directions on issue about when any missing documentation is to be filed. The expectation is that there must be a good reason why one or more of the documents are not available. Further directions relating to any missing documentation will also be made at the Case Management Hearing.

### 4 Allocation

4.1 The court considers the allocation of proceedings in accordance with the Allocation Rules and any Guidance issued by the President on distribution of business of the family court. The justices' clerk or assistant justices' clerk (with responsibility for gatekeeping and allocation of proceedings) will discuss initial allocation with a district judge (with responsibility for allocation and gatekeeping of proceedings) as provided for in any Guidance issued by the President on distribution of business of the family court. The expectation is that, wherever possible, any question relating to allocation of the proceedings will be considered at the CMH.

### 5 The timetable for the child and the timetable for proceedings

5.1 The timetable for the proceedings:

(1) The court will draw up a timetable for the proceedings with a view to disposing of the application -
  (a) without delay; and
  (b) in any event within 26 weeks beginning with the day on which the application was issued in accordance with section 32(1)(a)(ii) of the Children Act 1989.
(2) The court, when drawing up or revising a timetable under paragraph (1), will in particular have regard to -
  (a) the impact which the timetable or any revised timetable would have on the welfare of the child to whom the application relates; and
  (b) the impact which the timetable or any revised timetable would have on the duration and conduct of the proceedings.

5.2 The impact which the timetable for the proceedings, any revision or extension of that timetable would have on the welfare of the child to whom the application relates are matters to which the court is to have particular regard. The court will use the Timetable for the Child to assess the impact of these matters on the welfare of the child and to draw up and revise the timetable for the proceedings.

5.3 The 'Timetable for the Child' is the timetable set by the court which takes into account dates which are important to the child's welfare and development.

5.4 The timetable for the proceedings is set having particular regard to the Timetable for the Child and the Timetable for the Child needs to be reviewed regularly. Where adjustments are made to the Timetable for the Child, the timetable for the proceedings will have to be reviewed consistently with resolving the proceedings within 26 weeks or the period for the time being specified by the court.

5.5 Examples of the dates the court will record and take into account when setting the Timetable for the Child are the dates of -

(1) any formal review by the Local Authority of the case of a looked after child (within the meaning of section 22(1) of the 1989 Act);
(2) any significant educational steps, including the child taking up a place at a new school and, where applicable, any review by the Local Authority of a statement of the child's special educational needs;
(3) any health care steps, including assessment by a paediatrician or other specialist;
(4) any review of Local Authority plans for the child, including any plans for permanence through adoption, Special Guardianship or placement with parents or relatives;
(5) any change or proposed change of the child's placement;
(6) any significant change in the child's social or family circumstances; or
(7) any timetable for the determination of an issue in a case with an international element.

5.6 To identify the Timetable for the Child, the applicant is required to provide the information needed about the significant steps in the child's life in the Application Form and the Social Work Statement and to update this information regularly taking into account information received from others involved in the child's life such as the parties, members of the child's family, the person who is caring for the child, the children's guardian, the Independent Reviewing Officer , the child's key social worker and any Central Authority or competent authority in a foreign state or a consular authority in England and Wales in a case with an international element.

5.7 Where more than one child is the subject of the proceedings, the court should consider and will set a Timetable for the Child for each child. The children may not all have the same timetable, and the court will consider the appropriate progress of the proceedings in relation to each child.

5.8 Where there are parallel care proceedings and criminal proceedings against a person connected with the child for a serious offence against the child, linked directions hearings should where practicable take place as the case progresses. The timing of the proceedings in a linked care and criminal case should appear in the Timetable for the Child. The time limit of resolving the proceedings within 26 weeks applies unless a longer timetable has been set by the court in order to resolve the proceedings justly in accordance with section 32(1)(a)(ii) and (5) of the 1989 Act. Early disclosure and listing of hearings is necessary in proceedings in a linked care and criminal case.

### 6 Extensions to the timetable for proceedings

6.1 The court is required to draw up a timetable for proceedings with a view to disposing of the application without delay and in any event within 26 weeks. If proceedings can be resolved earlier, then they should be. A standard timetable and process is expected to be followed in respect of the giving of standard directions on issue and allocation and other matters which should be carried out by the court on issue, including setting and giving directions for the Case Management Hearing.

6.2 Having regard to the circumstances of the particular case, the court may consider that it is necessary to extend the time by which the proceedings are to be resolved beyond 26 weeks to enable the court to resolve the proceedings justly (see section 32 (5) of the 1989 Act). When making this decision, the court is to take account of the guidance that extensions are not to be granted routinely and are to be seen as requiring specific justification (see section 32(7) of the 1989 Act). The decision and reason(s) for extending a case should be recorded in writing (in the Case Management Order) and orally stated in court, so that all parties are aware of the reasons for delay in the case (see FPR 12.26C). The Case Management Order must contain a record of this information, as well as the impact of the court's decision on the welfare of the child.

6.3 The court may extend the period within which proceedings are intended to be resolved on its own initiative or on application. Applications for an extension should, wherever possible, only be made so that they are considered at any hearing for which a date has been fixed or for which a date is about to be fixed. Where a date for a hearing has been fixed, a party who wishes to make an application at that hearing but does not have sufficient time to file an application notice should as soon as possible inform the court (if possible in writing) and, if possible, the other parties of the nature of the application and the reason for it. The party should then make the application orally at the hearing.

6.4 If the court agrees an extension is necessary, an initial extension to the time limit may be granted for up to eight weeks (or less if directed) in order to resolve the case justly (see section 32(8) of the 1989 Act). If more time is necessary, in order to resolve the proceedings justly, a further extension of up to eight weeks may be agreed by the court. There is no limit on the number of extensions that may be granted in a particular case.

6.5 If the court considers that the timetable for the proceedings will require an extension beyond the next eight week period in order to resolve the proceedings justly, the Case Management Order should -

(1) state the reason(s) why it is necessary to have a further extension;
(2) fix the date of the next effective hearing (which might be in a period shorter than a further eight weeks); and
(3) indicate whether it is appropriate for the next application for an extension of the timetable to be considered on paper.

6.6 The expectation is that, subject to paragraph 6.5, extensions should be considered at a hearing and that a court will not approve proposals for the management of a case under FPR 12.15 where the consequence of those proposals is that the case is unlikely to be resolved within 26 weeks or other period for the time being allowed for resolution of the proceedings. In accordance with FPR 4.1(3)(e), the court may hold a hearing and receive evidence by telephone or by using any other method of direct oral communication. When deciding whether to extend the timetable, the court must have regard to the impact of any ensuing timetable revision on the welfare of the child (see section 32(6) of the 1989 Act).

## 7 Interpretation

7.1 In this Practice Direction -

'Allocation Rules' mean any rules relating to composition of the court and distribution of business made under section 31D of the Matrimonial and Family Proceedings Act 1984;

'Care Plan' is a separate document from the evidence that is filed by the local authority. It is a 'section 31A plan' referred to in section 31A of the 1989 Act which complies with guidance as to content issued by the Secretary of State;

'Case Analysis' means a written or, if there is insufficient time for a written, an oral outline of the case from the perspective of the child's guardian or Welsh family proceedings officer for the CMH or FCMH (where one is necessary) and IRH or as otherwise directed by the court, incorporating an analysis of the key issues that need to be resolved in the case including -

(a) a threshold analysis;
(b) a case management analysis, including an analysis of the timetable for the proceedings, an analysis of the Timetable for the Child and the evidence which any party proposes is necessary to resolve the issues;
(c) a parenting capability analysis;
(d) a child impact analysis, including an analysis of the ascertainable wishes and feelings of the child and the impact on the welfare of the child of any application to adjourn a hearing or extend the timetable for the proceedings;

(e) an early permanence analysis including an analysis of the proposed placements and contact framework; by reference to a welfare and proportionality analysis;

(f) whether and if so what communication it is proposed there should be during the proceedings with the child by the court;

'Case Management Order' is the prescribed form of order referred to in any Guidance issued by the President from time to time on prescribed templates and orders;

'Day' means 'business day'. 'Day 1' is the day of issue and 'Day 2' is the next business day following the day of issue of proceedings. 'Day 12', 'Day 18' and 'Day 25' are respectively the 11th, 17th and the 24th business days after the day of issue of proceedings (Day 1). '26 weeks' means 26 calendar weeks beginning on the day of issue of proceedings (Day 1);

'Experts Practice Directions' mean -

(a) Practice Direction 25A (Experts – Emergencies and Pre Proceedings Instructions);

(b) Practice Direction 25B (The Duties of An Expert, The Expert's Report and Arrangements For An Expert To Attend Court);

(c) Practice Direction 25C (Children's Proceedings – The Use Of Single Joint Experts and The Process Leading to An Expert Being Instructed or Expert Evidence Being Put Before the Court);

(d) Practice Direction 25E (Discussions Between Experts in Family Proceedings);

'Genogram' means a family tree, setting out in diagrammatic form the child's family and extended family members and their relationship with the child;

'Index of Checklist Documents' means a list of Checklist Documents referred to in the Public Law Outline Pre-Proceedings Checklist which is divided into two parts with Part A being the documents referred to in column 2, paragraph (a) of the Pre- Proceedings Checklist and Part B being those referred to in column 2, paragraph (b) of the Pre-proceedings Checklist;

'International instruments'

'the Council Regulation (EC) No 2201/2003 (Brussels 2 revised)' means Council Regulation (EC) No 2201/2003 of 27 November 2003 on jurisdiction and the recognition and enforcement of judgments in matrimonial matters and in matters of parental responsibility;

'The 1996 Hague Convention' means the Convention on Jurisdiction, Applicable Law, Recognition, Enforcement and Co-operation in Respect of Parental Responsibility and Measures for the Protection of Children;

'Justices' Clerks Rules' means any rules made under section 310 of the Matrimonial and Family Proceedings Act 1984 enabling functions of the family court or judge of that court to be carried out by a justices' clerk or assistant to a justices' clerk;

'Letter Before Proceedings' means any letter from the Local Authority containing written notification to the parents and others with parental responsibility for the child of the Local Authority's likely intention to apply to court for a care or supervision order and any related subsequent correspondence confirming the Local Authority's position;

'Local Authority Case Summary' means a document prepared by the Local Authority legal representative for each case management hearing in the form referred to in any Guidance issued by the President from time to time on prescribed templates and orders;

'Parents' Response' means a document from either or both of the parents containing

(a) in no more than two pages, the parents' response to the Threshold Statement, and

(b) the parents' placement proposals including the identity and whereabouts of all relatives and friends they propose be considered by the court;

(c) Information which may be relevant to a person's capacity to litigate including information about any referrals to mental health services and adult services;

'Section 7 report' means any report under section 7 of the 1989 Act;

'Section 37 report' means any report by the Local Authority to the court as a result of a direction under section 37 of the 1989 Act;

'Social Work Chronology' means a schedule containing -

(a) a succinct summary of the length of involvement of the local authority with the family and in particular with the child;

(b) a succinct summary of the significant dates and events in the child's life in chronological order – i.e. a running record up to the issue of the proceedings; providing such information under the following headings -

(i) serial number;
(ii) date;
(iii) event-detail;
(iv) witness or document reference (where applicable);

'Social Work Statement' means a statement prepared by the Local Authority limited to the following evidence -

Summary
(a) The order sought;
(b) Succinct summary of reasons with reference as appropriate to the Welfare Checklist;

Family
(c) Family members and relationships especially the primary carers and significant adults/other children;
(d) Genogram;

Threshold
(e) Precipitating events;
(f) Background circumstances;
  (i) summary of children's services involvement cross-referenced to the chronology;
  (ii) previous court orders and emergency steps;
  (iii) previous assessments;

(g) Summary of significant harm and or likelihood of significant harm which the LA will seek to establish by evidence or concession;

Parenting capability
(h) Assessment of child's needs;
(i) Assessment of parental capability to meet needs;
(j) Analysis of why there is a gap between parental capability and the child's needs;
(k) Assessment of other significant adults who may be carers;

Child impact
(l) Wishes and feelings of the child(ren);
(m) Timetable for the Child;
(n) Delay and timetable for the proceedings;

Permanence and contact
(o) Parallel planning;
(p) Realistic placement options by reference to a welfare and proportionality analysis;
(q) Contact framework;

Case Management
(r) Evidence and assessments necessary and outstanding;
(s) Any information about any person's litigation capacity, mental health issues, disabilities or vulnerabilities that is relevant to their capability to participate in the proceedings; and
(t) Case management proposals.

'Standard Directions on Issue and Allocation' means directions given by the court on issue and upon allocation in the prescribed form referred to in any Guidance issued by the President from time to time on prescribed templates and orders;

'Threshold Statement' means a written outline by the legal representative of the LA in the application form of the facts which the LA will seek to establish by evidence or concession to satisfy the threshold criteria under s 31(2) of the 1989 Act limited to no more than 2 pages;

'Welfare Checklist' means the list of matters which is set out in section 1(3) of the 1989 Act and to which the court is to have particular regard in accordance with section (1)(3) and (4).

## PRACTICE DIRECTION 12C –
### SERVICE OF APPLICATION IN CERTAIN PROCEEDINGS

This Practice Direction supplements FPR Part 12 (Children Proceedings except Parental Order Proceedings and Proceedings for Applications in Adoption, Placement and Related Proceedings), rule 12.8 (Service of the application)

#### Persons who receive copy of application form

1.1 In relation to the proceedings in column 1 of the following table, column 2 sets out the documentation which persons listed in column 3 are to receive –

| Proceedings | Documentation | Who receives a copy of the documentation |
|---|---|---|
| 1 Private law proceedings; public law proceedings; emergency proceedings (except those proceedings referred to in entries 2 and 3 of the Table below); proceedings for a declaration under rule 12.71 as to the existence, or extent, of parental responsibility under Article 16 of the 1996 Hague Convention; an order relating to the exercise of the court's inherent jurisdiction (including wardship proceedings). | Application form (including any supplementary forms); Form C6 (Notice of proceedings); and in private law proceedings, the form of answer. | All the respondents to the application. |
| 2 An enforcement order (section 11J of the 1989 Act); a financial compensation order (section 11O of the 1989 Act). | As above | All the respondents to the application; and where the child was a party to the proceedings in which the child arrangements order was made – (a) the person who was the children's guardian or litigation friend in those proceedings; or (b) where there was no children's guardian or litigation friend, the person who was the legal representative of the child in those proceedings. |

| Proceedings | Documentation | Who receives a copy of the documentation |
|---|---|---|
| 3 A care or a supervision order (section 31 of the 1989 Act) and other Part 4 proceedings. | As above and such of the documents specified in the Annex to Form C110A as are available. | All the respondents to the application; and Cafcass or CAFCASS Cymru. |
| 4 Proceedings for an order for the return of a child under the 1980 Hague Convention or registration of an order under the European Convention. | As above and the documents referred to in part 2 of the Practice Direction 12F (International Child Abduction). | All the respondents to the application. |

(Rule 12.3 sets out who the parties to the proceedings are.)

1.2 When filing the documents referred to in column 2 of the Table in paragraph 1.1, the applicant must also file sufficient copies for one to be served on each respondent and, except for Part 4 proceedings, Cafcass or CAFCASS Cymru. In relation to Part 4 proceedings, the applicant need not file a copy of the documents for Cafcass or CAFCASS Cymru as it is the applicant who sends copies of these documents to Cafcass or CAFCASS Cymru in accordance with Practice Direction 12A.

1.3 Where the application for an order in proceedings referred to in column 1 of the Table in paragraph 1.1 is made in respect of more than one child all the children must be included in the same application form.

1.4 Form C6A (notice to non-parties) must be served on the persons referred to in the Table in paragraph 3.1 at the same time as serving the documents in column 2 of the Table in paragraph 1.1.

### Time for serving application

2.1 In relation to the proceedings in column 1 of the following table, column 2 sets out the time period within which the application and accompanying documents must be served on each respondent –

| Proceedings | Minimum number of days prior to hearing or directions appointment for service |
|---|---|
| 1 Private law proceedings; and proceedings for – | 14 days. |

| Proceedings | Minimum number of days prior to hearing or directions appointment for service |
|---|---|
| an order relating to the exercise of the court's inherent jurisdiction (including wardship proceedings); a declaration under rule 12.71 as to the existence, or extent, of parental responsibility under Article 16 of the 1996 Hague Convention. | |
| 2 Public law proceedings except proceedings for an interim care order, an interim supervision order or other proceedings referred to in Box 3 below. | 7 days. |
| 3 Proceedings for – an interim care order, or the discharge of such an order under section 39(1) of the 1989 Act; an interim supervision order under section 38(1) of the 1989 Act, the discharge or variation of such an order under section 39(2) of the 1989 Act, or the extension or further extension of such an order under paragraph 6(3) of Schedule 3 to that Act; an order varying directions made with an interim care order or interim supervision order under section 38(8)(b) of the 1989 Act; an order under section 39(3) of the 1989 Act varying an interim supervision order in so far as it affects a person with whom the child is living but who is not entitled to apply for the order to be discharged; an order under section 39(3A) of the 1989 Act varying or discharging an interim care order in so far as it imposes an exclusion requirement on a person who is not entitled to apply for the order to be discharged; | 3 days. |

| Proceedings | Minimum number of days prior to hearing or directions appointment for service |
|---|---|
| an order under section 39(3B) of the 1989 Act varying or discharging an interim care order in so far as it confers a power of arrest attached to an exclusion requirement. | |
| 4 Proceedings for an order for the return of a child under the 1980 Hague Convention or registration of an order under the European Convention. | 4 days. |
| 5 Emergency proceedings. | 1 day. |

2.2 The court may extend or shorten the time period referred to in column 2 of the table in paragraph 2.1 (see rule 4.1(3)(a)).

2.3 Where the application is to be served on a child, rule 6.33 provides that, in addition to the persons to be served in accordance with rules 6.28 and 6.32, the application must also be served on the persons or bodies listed in rule 6.33(3) unless the court orders otherwise.

**Persons who receive a copy of Form C6A (Notice to Non-Parties)**

3.1 In relation to each type of proceedings in column 1 of the following table, the persons listed in column 2 are to receive a copy of Form C6A (Notice of Proceedings/Hearing/Directions Appointment to Non-Parties) –

| Proceedings | Persons to whom notice is to be given |
|---|---|
| 1 All applications. | Subject to separate entries below: local authority providing accommodation for the child; persons who are caring for the child at the time when the proceedings are commenced; and in the case of proceedings brought in respect of a child who is alleged to be staying in a refuge which is certified under section 51(1) or (2) of the 1989 Act, the person who is providing the refuge. |

| Proceedings | Persons to whom notice is to be given |
|---|---|
| 2 An order appointing a guardian (section 5(1) of the 1989 Act). | As for all applications; and the father or parent (being a woman who is a parent by virtue of section 43 of the Human Fertilisation and Embryology Act 2008) of the child if that person does not have parental responsibility. |
| 3 A section 8 order (section 8 of the 1989 Act). | As for all applications; and, every person whom the applicant believes – <br> (i) to be named in a court order with respect to the same child, which has not ceased to have effect; <br> (ii) to be party to pending proceedings in respect of the same child; or <br> (iii) to be a person with whom the child has lived for at least 3 years prior to the application, <br> unless, in a case to which (i) or (ii) applies, the applicant believes that the court order or pending proceedings are not relevant to the application. |
| 4 A special guardianship order (section 14A of the 1989 Act); <br><br> variation or discharge of a special guardianship order (section 14D of the 1989 Act). | As for all applications; and every person whom the applicant believes – <br> (i) to be named in a court order with respect to the same child, which has not ceased to have effect; <br> (ii) to be party to pending proceedings in respect of the same child; or <br> (iii) to be a person with whom the child has lived for at least 3 years prior to the application, |

| Proceedings | Persons to whom notice is to be given |
|---|---|
| | unless, in a case to which (i) or (ii) applies, the applicant believes that the court order or pending proceedings are not relevant to the application; |
| | if the child is not being accommodated by the local authority, the local authority in whose area the applicant is ordinarily resident; and |
| | in the case of an application under section 14D of the 1989 Act, the local authority that prepared the report under section 14A(8) or (9) in the proceedings leading to the order which it is sought to have varied or discharged, if different from any local authority that will otherwise be notified. |
| 5 An order permitting the local authority to arrange for any child in its care to live outside England and Wales (Schedule 2, paragraph 19(1) of the 1989 Act). | As for all applications; and the parties to the proceedings leading to the care order. |
| 6 A care or supervision order (section 31 of the 1989 Act). | As for all applications; and every person whom the applicant believes to be a party to pending relevant proceedings in respect of the same child; and every person whom the applicant believes to be a parent without parental responsibility for the child. |
| 7 A child assessment order (section 43(1) of the 1989 Act). | As for all applications; and every person whom the applicant believes to be a parent of the child; every person whom the applicant believes to be caring for the child; |

| Proceedings | Persons to whom notice is to be given |
|---|---|
|  | every person in whose favour a child arrangements order is in force with respect to the child; and<br>every person who is allowed to have contact with the child by virtue of an order under section 34 of the 1989 Act. |
| 8 An order varying or discharging a child assessment order (section 43(12) of the 1989 Act). | The persons referred to in section 43(11)(a) to (e) of the 1989 Act who were not party to the application for the order which it is sought to have varied or discharged. |
| 9 An emergency protection order (section 44(1) of the 1989 Act). | As for all applications above; and<br>every person whom the applicant believes to be a parent of the child. |
| 10 An order varying a direction under section 44(6) in an emergency protection order (section 44(9)(b) of the 1989 Act). | As for all applications; and<br>the local authority in whose area the child is living; and<br>any person whom the applicant believes to be affected by the direction which it is sought to have varied. |
| 11 A warrant authorising a constable to assist in the exercise of certain powers to search for children and inspect premises (section 102 of the 1989 Act). | The person referred to in section 102(1) of the 1989 Act; and<br>any person preventing or likely to prevent such a person from exercising powers under enactments mentioned in subsection (6) of that section. |
| 12 An enforcement order (section 11J of the 1989 Act);<br>a financial compensation order (section 11O of the 1989 Act). | Any officer of the Service or Welsh family proceedings officer who is monitoring compliance with a child arrangements order (in accordance with section 11H(2) of the 1989 Act). |

| Proceedings | Persons to whom notice is to be given |
|---|---|
| 13 An order revoking or amending an enforcement order (Schedule A1, paragraphs 4 to 7 of the 1989 Act) (rule 12.33 makes provision regarding applications under Schedule A1, paragraph 5 of the 1989 Act); an order following a breach of an enforcement order (Schedule A1, paragraph 9 of the 1989 Act). | Any officer of the Service or Welsh family proceedings officer who is monitoring compliance with the enforcement order (in accordance with section 11M(1) of the 1989 Act); the responsible officer (as defined in section 197 of the Criminal Justice Act 2003, as modified by Schedule A1 to the 1989 Act). |
| 14 A declaration under rule 12.71 as to the existence, or extent, of parental responsibility under Article 16 of the 1996 Hague Convention. | A person who the applicant believes is a parent of the child. |

## PRACTICE DIRECTION 12E – URGENT BUSINESS

This Practice Direction supplements FPR Part 12

### Introduction

1.1 This Practice Direction describes the procedure to be followed in respect of urgent and out of hours cases in the Family Division of the High Court. For the avoidance of doubt, it does not relate to cases in respect of adults.

1.2 Urgent or out of hours applications, particularly those which have become urgent because they have not been pursued sufficiently promptly, should be avoided. A judge who has concerns that the urgent or out of hours facilities may have been abused may require a representative of the applicant to attend at a subsequent directions hearing to provide an explanation.

1.3 Urgent applications should whenever possible be made within court hours. The earliest possible liaison is required with the Clerk of the Rules who will attempt to accommodate genuinely urgent applications (at least for initial directions) in the Family Division applications court, from which the matter may be referred to another judge.

1.4 When it is not possible to apply within court hours, contact should be made with the security office at the Royal Courts of Justice (020 7947 6000 or 020 7947 6260) who will refer the matter to the urgent business officer. The urgent business officer can contact the duty judge. The judge may agree to hold a hearing, either convened at court or elsewhere, or by telephone.

1.5 When the hearing is to take place by telephone it should, unless not practicable, be by tape-recorded conference call arranged (and paid for in the first instance) by the applicant's solicitors. Solicitors acting for potential applicants should consider having standing arrangements with their telephone service providers under which such conference calls can be arranged. All parties (especially the judge) should be informed that the call is being recorded by the service provider. The applicant's solicitors should order a transcript of the hearing from the service provider. Otherwise the applicant's legal representative should prepare a note for approval by the judge.

### General Issues

2.1 Parents, carers or other necessary respondents should whenever possible be given the opportunity to have independent legal advice or at least to have access to support or counselling.

2.2 In suitable cases, application may be made for directions providing for anonymity of the parties and others involved in the matter in any order or subsequent listing of the case. Exceptionally, a reporting restriction order may be sought.

2.3 Either the Official Solicitor or Cafcass, or CAFCASS Cymru, as the case may be, may be invited by the court to be appointed as advocate to the court.

### Medical treatment and press injunction cases

3.1 It may be desirable for a child who is the subject of such proceedings to be made a party and represented through a children's guardian (usually an officer of Cafcass or a Welsh Family Proceedings Officer). Cafcass and CAFCASS Cymru stand ready to arrange for an officer to accept appointment as a children's guardian. They should be contacted at the earliest opportunity where an urgent application is envisaged. For urgent out of hours applications, the urgent business officer will contact a representative of Cafcass. CAFCASS Cymru is not able to deal with cases that arise out of office hours and those cases should be referred to Cafcass who will deal with the matter on behalf of CAFCASS Cymru until the next working day. A child of sufficient understanding to instruct his or her own solicitor should be made a party and given notice of any application.

3.2 Interim declarations/orders under the wardship jurisdiction or Children Act 1989 may be made on application either by an NHS trust, a local authority, an interested adult (where necessary with the leave of the court) or by the child if he or she has sufficient understanding to make the application.

### Consultation with Cafcass, CAFCASS Cymru and Official Solicitor

4.1 Cafcass, CAFCASS Cymru and members of the Official Solicitor's legal staff are prepared to discuss cases before proceedings are issued. In all cases in which the urgent and out of hours procedures are to be used it would be helpful if the Official Solicitor, Cafcass or CAFCASS Cymru have had some advance notice of the application and its circumstances.

4.2 Enquiries about children cases should be directed to the High Court Team Duty Manager at Cafcass National Office, 3rd Floor, 21 Bloomsbury Street,

London, WC1B 3HF. DX: Cafcass DX 310101 Bloomsbury 11. Telephone 01753 235273 (Cafcass High Court Team) or 01753 235295 (Cafcass Legal Duty Lawyer). Email HighCourtGM@Cafcass.gsi.gov.uk (office hours only). Enquiries should be marked 'FAO High Court Team' or 'FAO HCT'.

4.3 Enquiries about children cases in Wales should be directed to:

Social Care Team
Legal Services
Welsh Assembly Government
Cathays Park
Cardiff
CF10 3NQ
telephone 02920 370888,
fax 0872 437 7306.

4.4 Medical and welfare cases relating to an adult lacking capacity in relation to their medical treatment or welfare are brought in the Court of Protection. Enquiries about adult medical and welfare cases should be addressed to the Court of Protection Healthcare and Welfare Team, Office of the Official Solicitor, Victory House, 30-34 Kingsway, London, WC2B 6EX, telephone 020 3681 2751, fax 020 3681 2762, email enquiries@offsol.gsi.gov.uk.

Reference should also be made to Practice Direction E, accompanying Part 9 of the Court of Protection Rules 2007, and to Practice Direction B accompanying Part 10 of those Rules. Information for parties and practitioners is available on the website of the Ministry of Justice www.justice.gov.uk and general information for members of the public is available on www.direct.gov.uk.

## PRACTICE DIRECTION 12G – COMMUNICATION OF INFORMATION

This Practice Direction supplements FPR Part 12, Chapter 7

1.1 Chapter 7 deals with the communication of information (whether or not contained in a document filed with the court) relating to proceedings which relate to children.

1.2 Subject to any direction of the court, information may be communicated for the purposes of the law relating to contempt in accordance with paragraphs 2.1, 3.1 or 4.1.

### Communication of information by a party etc for other purposes

2.1 A person specified in the first column of the following table may communicate to a person listed in the second column such information as is specified in the third column for the purpose or purposes specified in the fourth column –

| | | | |
|---|---|---|---|
| A party | A lay adviser, a McKenzie Friend, or a person arranging or providing pro bono legal services | Any information relating to the proceedings | To enable the party to obtain advice or assistance in relation to the proceedings |
| A party | A health care professional or a person or body providing counselling services for children or families | | To enable the party or any child of the party to obtain health care or counselling |
| A party | The Secretary of State, a McKenzie Friend, a lay adviser or the First-tier Tribunal dealing with an appeal made under section 20 of the Child Support Act 1991 | | For the purposes of making or responding to an appeal under section 20 of the Child Support Act 1991 or the determination of such an appeal |

| | | | |
|---|---|---|---|
| A party or other person lawfully in receipt of information | The Secretary of State, a McKenzie Friend, a lay adviser or the Upper Tier Tribunal dealing with an appeal under section 24 of the Child Support Act 1991 in respect of a decision of the First-tier Tribunal that was made under section 20 of that Act | | For a purpose connected with an appeal under section 24 of the Child Support Act 1991 in respect of a decision of the First-tier Tribunal that was made under section 20 of that Act |
| A party | An adoption panel | | To enable the adoption panel to discharge its functions as appropriate |
| A party | A local authority's medical adviser appointed under the Adoption Agencies Regulations 2005 or the Adoption Agencies (Wales) Regulations 2005 | | To enable the medical adviser to discharge his or her functions as appropriate |
| A party | The European Court of Human Rights | | For the purpose of making an application to the European Court of Human Rights |

| | | | |
|---|---|---|---|
| A party or any person lawfully in receipt of information | The Children's Commissioner or the Children's Commissioner for Wales | | To refer an issue affecting the interests of children to the Children's Commissioner or the Children's Commissioner for Wales |
| A party, any person lawfully in receipt of information or a proper officer | A person or body conducting an approved research project | | For the purpose of an approved research project |
| A legal representative or a professional legal adviser | A person or body responsible for investigating or determining complaints in relation to legal representatives or professional legal advisers | | For the purposes of the investigation or determination of a complaint in relation to a legal representative or a professional legal adviser |
| A legal representative or a professional legal adviser | A professional indemnity insurer | | To enable the professional indemnity insurer to be notified of a claim or complaint, or potential claim or complaint, in relation to the legal representative or a professional legal adviser, and the legal representative or professional legal adviser to obtain advice in respect of that claim or complaint |

| | | | |
|---|---|---|---|
| A legal representative or a professional legal adviser | A person or body assessing quality assurance systems | | To enable the legal representative or professional legal adviser to obtain a quality assurance assessment |
| A legal representative or a professional legal adviser | An accreditation body | Any information relating to the proceedings providing that it does not, or is not likely to, identify any person involved in the proceedings | To enable the legal representative or professional legal adviser to obtain accreditation |
| A party | A police officer | The text or summary of the whole or part of a judgment given in the proceedings | For the purpose of a criminal investigation |
| A party or any person lawfully in receipt of information | A member of the Crown Prosecution Service | | To enable the Crown Prosecution Service to discharge its functions under any enactment |

**Communication for the effective functioning of Cafcass and CAFCASS Cymru**

3.1 An officer of the Service or a Welsh family proceedings officer, as appropriate, may communicate to a person listed in the second column such information as is specified in the third column for the purpose or purposes specified in the fourth column –

| | | | |
|---|---|---|---|
| A Welsh family proceedings officer | A person or body exercising statutory functions relating to inspection of CAFCASS Cymru | Any information relating to the proceedings which is required by the person or body responsible for the inspection | For the purpose of an inspection of CAFCASS Cymru by a body or person appointed by the Welsh Ministers |
| An officer of the Service or a Welsh family proceedings officer | The Health and Care Professions Council or the Care Council for Wales | Any information relating to the proceedings providing that it does not, or is not likely to, identify any person involved in the proceedings | For the purpose of initial and continuing accreditation as a social worker of a person providing services to Cafcass or CAFCASS Cymru in accordance with section 13(2) of the Criminal Justice and Courts Services Act 2000 or section 36 of the Children Act 2004 as the case may be |
| An officer of the Service or a Welsh family proceedings officer | A person or body providing services relating to professional development or training to Cafcass or CAFCASS Cymru | Any information relating to the proceedings providing that it does not, or is not likely to, identify any person involved in the proceedings without that person's consent | To enable the person or body to provide the services, where the services cannot be effectively provided without such disclosure |

| | | | |
|---|---|---|---|
| An officer of the Service or a Welsh family proceedings officer | A person employed by or contracted to Cafcass or CAFCASS Cymru for the purposes of carrying out the functions referred to in column 4 of this row | Any information relating to the proceedings | Engagement in processes internal to Cafcass or CAFCASS Cymru which relate to the maintenance of necessary records concerning the proceedings, or to ensuring that Cafcass or CAFCASS Cymru functions are carried out to a satisfactory standard |

**Communication to and by Ministers of the Crown and Welsh Ministers**

4.1 A person specified in the first column of the following table may communicate to a person listed in the second column such information as is specified in the third column for the purpose or purposes specified in the fourth column –

| | | | |
|---|---|---|---|
| A party or any person lawfully in receipt of information relating to the proceedings | A Minister of the Crown with responsibility for a government department engaged, or potentially engaged, in an application before the European Court of Human Rights relating to the proceedings | Any information relating to the proceedings of which he or she is in lawful possession | To provide the department with information relevant, or potentially relevant, to the proceedings before the European Court of Human Rights |

| | | |
|---|---|---|
| A Minister of the Crown | The European Court of Human Rights | For the purpose of engagement in an application before the European Court of Human Rights relating to the proceedings |
| A Minister of the Crown | Lawyers advising or representing the United Kingdom in an application before the European Court of Human Rights relating to the proceedings | For the purpose of receiving advice or for effective representation in relation to the application before the European Court of Human Rights |
| A Minister of the crown or a Welsh Minister | Another Minister, or Ministers, of the Crown or a Welsh Minister | For the purpose of notification, discussion and the giving or receiving of advice regarding issues raised by the information in which the relevant departments have, or may have, an interest |

5.1 This paragraph applies to communications made in accordance with paragraphs 2.1, 3.1 and 4.1 and the reference in this paragraph to 'the table' means the table in the relevant paragraph.

5.2 A person in the second column of the table may only communicate information relating to the proceedings received from a person in the first column for the purpose or purposes –

(a) for which he or she received that information; or
(b) of professional development or training, providing that any communication does not, or is not likely to, identify any person involved in the proceedings without that person's consent.

6.1 In this Practice Direction –

'accreditation body' means –
- (a) The Law Society,
- (b) Resolution, or
- (c) the Lord Chancellor in exercise of the Lord Chancellor's functions in relation to legal aid;

'adoption panel' means a panel established in accordance with regulation 3 of the Adoption Agencies Regulations 2005 or regulation 3 of the Adoption Agencies (Wales) Regulations 2005;

'approved research project' means a project of research –
- (a) approved in writing by a Secretary of State after consultation with the President of the Family Division,
- (b) approved in writing by the President of the Family Division, or
- (c) conducted under section 83 of the Act of 1989 or section 13 of the Criminal Justice and Court Services Act 2000;

'body assessing quality assurance systems' includes –
- (a) The Law Society,
- (b) the Lord Chancellor in exercise of the Lord Chancellor's functions in relation to legal aid, or
- (c) The General Council of the Bar;

'body or person responsible for investigating or determining complaints in relation to legal representatives or professional legal advisers' means –
- (a) The Law Society,
- (b) The General Council of the Bar,
- (c) The Institute of Legal Executives,
- (d) The Legal Services Ombudsman; or
- (e) The Office of Legal Complaints.

'Cafcass' has the meaning assigned to it by section 11 of the Criminal Justice and Courts Services Act 2000;

'CAFCASS Cymru' means the part of the Welsh Assembly Government exercising the functions of Welsh Ministers under Part 4 of the Children Act 2004;

'criminal investigation' means an investigation conducted by police officers with a view to it being ascertained –
- (a) whether a person should be charged with an offence, or
- (b) whether a person charged with an offence is guilty of it;

'health care professional' means –
- (a) a registered medical practitioner,
- (b) a registered nurse or midwife,
- (c) a clinical psychologist, or
- (d) a child psychotherapist;

'lay adviser' means a non-professional person who gives lay advice on behalf of an organisation in the lay advice sector;

'McKenzie Friend' means any person permitted by the court to sit beside an unrepresented litigant in court to assist that litigant by prompting, taking notes and giving him advice; and

'social worker' has the meaning assigned to it by section 55 of the Care Standards Act 2000.

## PRACTICE DIRECTION 12K –
## CHILDREN ACT 1989: EXCLUSION REQUIREMENT

This Practice Direction supplements FPR Part 12

Under s 38A(5) and s 44A(5) of the Children Act 1989 the court may attach a power of arrest to an exclusion requirement included in an interim care order or an emergency protection order. In cases where an order is made which includes an exclusion requirement, the following shall apply:

(1) If a power of arrest is attached to the order then unless the person to whom the exclusion requirement refers was given notice of the hearing and attended the hearing, the name of that person and that an order has been made including an exclusion requirement to which a power of arrest has been attached shall be announced in open court at the earliest opportunity. This may be either on the same day when the court proceeds to hear cases in open court or where there is no further business in open court on that day at the next listed sitting of the court.

(2) When a person arrested under a power of arrest cannot conveniently be brought before the relevant judicial authority sitting in a place normally used as a courtroom within 24 hours after the arrest, he may be brought before the relevant judicial authority at any convenient place but, as the liberty of the subject is involved, the press and the public should be permitted to be present, unless security needs make this impracticable.

(3) Any order of committal made otherwise than in public or in a courtroom open to the public, shall be announced in open court at the earliest opportunity. This may be either on the same day when the court proceeds to hear cases in open court or where there is no further business in open court on that day at the next listed sitting of the court. The announcement shall state –

(a) the name of the person committed,
(b) in general terms the nature of the contempt of the court in respect of which the order of committal has been made, and
(c) the length of the period of committal.

## PRACTICE DIRECTION 12M –
## FAMILY ASSISTANCE ORDERS: CONSULTATION

This Practice Direction supplements FPR Part 12

1 This Practice Direction applies to any family proceedings in the High Court or the family court in which the court is considering whether to make a family

assistance order under section 16 of the Children Act 1989, as amended ('the 1989 Act'). It has effect from 1 October 2007.

2 Before making a family assistance order the court must have obtained the opinion of the appropriate officer about whether it would be in the best interests of the child in question for a family assistance order to be made and, if so, how the family assistance order could operate and for what period.

3 The appropriate officer will be an officer of the Service, a Welsh family proceedings officer or an officer of a local authority, depending on the category of officer the court proposes to require to be made available under the family assistance order.

4 The opinion of the appropriate officer may be given orally or in writing (for example, it may form part of a report under section 7 of the 1989 Act).

5 Before making a family assistance order the court must give any person whom it proposes be named in the order an opportunity to comment upon any opinion given by the appropriate officer.

6 Issued by the President of the Family Division, as the nominee of the Lord Chief Justice, with the agreement of the Lord Chancellor.

# APPENDIX 4

# FAMILY PROCEDURE RULES 2010, SI 2010/2955, PART 14

PROCEDURE FOR APPLICATIONS IN ADOPTION, PLACEMENT AND RELATED PROCEEDINGS

**14.1 Application of this Part and interpretation**

(1) The rules in this Part apply to the following proceedings –

- (a) adoption proceedings;
- (b) placement proceedings; and
- (c) proceedings for –
    - (i) the making of a an order under section 26 or an order under section 51A(2)(a) of the 2002 Act;
    - (iaa) the making of an order under section 51A(2)(b) of the 2002 Act;
    - (ii) the variation or revocation of –
        - (aa) an order under section 27 of the 2002 Act; or
        - (bb) an order under section 51A(2) of the 2002 Act in accordance with section 51B(1)(c);
    - (iii) an order giving permission to change a child's surname or remove a child from the United Kingdom under section 28(2) and (3) of the 2002 Act;
    - (iv) a section 84 order;
    - (v) a section 88 direction;
    - (vi) a section 89 order; or
    - (vii) any other order that may be referred to in a practice direction.

(2) In this Part –

'Central Authority' means –
- (a) in relation to England, the Secretary of State; and
- (b) in relation to Wales, the Welsh Ministers;

'Convention adoption order' means an adoption order under the 2002 Act which, by virtue of regulations under section 1 of the Adoption (Intercountry Aspects) Act 1999 (regulations giving effect to the Convention on Protection of Children and Co-operation in Respect of Intercountry Adoption, concluded at the Hague on 29 May 1993), is made as a Convention adoption order;

'guardian' means –
- (a) a guardian (other than the guardian of the estate of a child) appointed in accordance with section 5 of the 1989 Act; and

(b) a special guardian within the meaning of section 14A of the 1989 Act;

'provision for contact' has the meaning given to it in rule 13.1(2);

'section 88 direction' means a direction given by the High Court under section 88 of the 2002 Act that section 67(3) of that Act (status conferred by adoption) does not apply or does not apply to any extent specified in the direction.

Amendments—SI 2014/843.

## 14.2 Assignment of a serial number

(1) This rule applies where –

(a) any application in proceedings is made by a person who intends to adopt a child; or
(b) an adoption order in respect of the child has been made and an application is made for –
  (i) a contact order under section 51A(2)(a) of the 2002 Act;
  (ii) an order prohibiting contact with the child under section 51A(2)(b) of the 2002 Act; or
  (iii) the variation or revocation of an order under section 51A(2) of the 2002 Act in accordance with section 51B(1)(c).

(2) In a case under paragraph (1)(a), a serial number must be assigned to identify the person intending to adopt the child in connection with the proceedings in order for the person's identity to be kept confidential in those proceedings.

(3) In a case under paragraph (1)(b), a serial number must be assigned to the person in whose favour the adoption order has been made to keep the identity of the person confidential in proceedings referred to in paragraph (1)(b).

(4) The court may at any time direct that a serial number assigned to a person under paragraph (2) or (3) must be removed.

(5) When a serial number has been assigned to a person under paragraph (2) or (3) –

(a) the court officer will ensure that any notice sent in accordance with these rules does not contain information which discloses, or is likely to disclose, the identity of that person to any other party to that application who is not already aware of that person's identity; and
(b) the proceedings on the application will be conducted with a view to securing that the person is not seen by or made known to any party who is not already aware of the person's identity except with the person's consent.

Amendments—Substituted by SI 2014/843. Amended by SI 2016/1013.

### 14.3 Who the parties are

(1) In relation to the proceedings set out in column 1 of the following table, column 2 sets out who the application may be made by and column 3 sets out who the respondents to those proceedings will be.

| Proceedings for | Applicants | Respondents |
|---|---|---|
| An adoption order (section 46 of the 2002 Act). | The prospective adopters (sections 50 and 51 of the 2002 Act). | Each parent who has parental responsibility for the child unless that parent has given notice under section 20(4)(a) of the 2002 Act (statement of wish not to be informed of any application for an adoption order) which has effect; any guardian of the child unless that guardian has given notice under section 20(4)(a) of the 2002 Act (statement of wish not to be informed of any application for an adoption order) which has effect; any person in whose favour there is provision for contact; any adoption agency having parental responsibility for the child under section 25 of the 2002 Act; any adoption agency which has taken part at any stage in the arrangements for adoption of the child; |

| Proceedings for | Applicants | Respondents |
| --- | --- | --- |
| | | any local authority to whom notice under section 44 of the 2002 Act (notice of intention to adopt or apply for a section 84 order) has been given; |
| | | any local authority or voluntary organisation which has parental responsibility for, is looking after or is caring for, the child; and |
| | | the child where – |
| | | - permission has been granted to a parent or guardian to oppose the making of the adoption order (section 47(3) or 47(5) of the 2002 Act); |
| | | - the child opposes the making of an adoption order; |
| | | - a children and family reporter recommends that it is in the best interests of the child to be a party to the proceedings and that recommendation is accepted by the court; |
| | | - the child is already an adopted child; |

| Proceedings for | Applicants | Respondents |
| --- | --- | --- |
|  |  | - any party to the proceedings or the child is opposed to the arrangements for allowing any person contact with the child, or a person not being allowed contact with the child after the making of the adoption order;<br>- the application is for a Convention adoption order or a section 84 order;<br>- the child has been brought into the United Kingdom in the circumstances where section 83(1) of the 2002 Act applies (restriction on bringing children in);<br>- the application is for an adoption order other than a Convention adoption order and the prospective adopters intend the child to live in a country or territory outside the British Islands after the making of the adoption order; or<br>- the prospective adopters are relatives of the child. |
| A section 84 order. | The prospective adopters asking for parental responsibility prior to adoption abroad. | As for an adoption order. |

| Proceedings for | Applicants | Respondents |
|---|---|---|
| A placement order (section 21 of the 2002 Act). | A local authority (section 22 of the 2002 Act). | Each parent who has parental responsibility for the child: any guardian of the child; any person in whose favour an order under the 1989 Act is in force in relation to the child; any adoption agency or voluntary organisation which has parental responsibility for, is looking after, or is caring for, the child; the child; and the parties or any persons who are or have been parties to proceedings for a care order in respect of the child where those proceedings have led to the application for the placement order. |
| An order varying a placement order (section 23 of the 2002 Act). | The joint application of the local authority authorised by the placement order to place the child for adoption and the local authority which is to be substituted for that authority (section 23 of the 2002 Act). | The parties to the proceedings leading to the placement order which it is sought to have varied except the child who was the subject of those proceedings; and any person in whose favour there is provision for contact. |
| An order revoking a placement order (section 24 of the 2002 Act). | The child; the local authority authorised to place the child for adoption; or | The parties to the proceedings leading to the placement order which it is sought to have revoked; and |

| Proceedings for | Applicants | Respondents |
|---|---|---|
| | where the child is not placed for adoption by the authority, any other person who has the permission of the court to apply (section 24 of the 2002 Act). | any person in whose favour there is provision for contact. |
| An order under section 26 of the 2002 Act. | The child; the adoption agency; any parent, guardian or relative; | The adoption agency authorised to place the child for adoption or which has placed the child for adoption; |

| Proceedings for | Applicants | Respondents |
|---|---|---|
| | any person in whose favour there was provision for contact under the 1989 Act which ceased to have effect on an adoption agency being authorised to place a child for adoption, or placing a child for adoption who is less than six weeks old (section 26(1) of the 2002 Act); if a child arrangements order was in force immediately before the adoption agency was authorised to place the child for adoption or (as the case may be) placed the child for adoption at a time when he or she was less than six weeks old, any person named in the order as a person with whom the child was to live; | the person with whom the child lives or is to live; each parent with parental responsibility for the child; any guardian of the child; and the child where – <br>- the adoption agency authorised to place the child for adoption or which has placed the child for adoption or a parent with parental responsibility for the child opposes the making of the order under section 26 of the 2002 Act; <br>- the child opposes the making of the order under section 26 of the 2002 Act; |

| Proceedings for | Applicants | Respondents |
|---|---|---|
| | a person who by virtue of an order made in the exercise of the High Court's inherent jurisdiction with respect to children had care of the child immediately before that time; or any person who has the permission of the court to make the application (section 26 of the 2002 Act). | - existing provision for contact is to be revoked;<br>- relatives of the child do not agree to the arrangements for allowing any person contact with the child, or a person not being allowed contact with the child; or<br>- the child is suffering or is at risk of suffering harm within the meaning of the 1989 Act. |
| An order varying or revoking an order under section 26 of the 2002 Act (section 27 of the 2002 Act). | The child; the adoption agency; or any person named in the order (section 27(1) of the 2002 Act). | The parties to the proceedings leading to the order which it is sought to have varied or revoked; and any person named in the order. |
| An order permitting the child's name to be changed or the removal of the child from the United Kingdom (section 28(2) and (3) of the 2002 Act). | Any person including the adoption agency or the local authority authorised to place, or which has placed, the child for adoption (section 28(2) of the 2002 Act). | The parties to proceedings leading to any placement order; the adoption agency authorised to place the child for adoption or which has placed the child for adoption; any prospective adopters with whom the child is living; each parent with parental responsibility for the child; and any guardian of the child. |

| Proceedings for | Applicants | Respondents |
|---|---|---|
| A contact order under section 51A(2)(a) of the 2002 Act. | The child; or any person who has obtained the court's leave to make the application. | A person who has applied for the adoption order or in whose favour the adoption order is or has been made; and

Any adoption agency having parental responsibility for the child under section 25 of the 2002 Act. |
| An order prohibiting the person named in the order from having contact with the child (section 51A(2)(b) of the 2002 Act). | any person who has obtained the court's leave to make the application.

the child; or

any person who has obtained the court's leave to make the application. | A person against whom an application is made who –

(but for the child's adoption) would be related to the child by blood (including half-blood), marriage or civil partnership;

is a former guardian of the child;

is a person who had parental responsibility for the child immediately before the making of the adoption order;

is a person who was entitled to make an application for an order under section 26 of the 2002 Act in respect of the child (contact with children placed or to be placed for adoption) by virtue of subsection (3)(c), (d) or (e) of that section; |

| Proceedings for | Applicants | Respondents |
| --- | --- | --- |
| | | is a person with whom the child has lived for a period of at least one year; and |
| | | any adoption agency having parental responsibility for the child under section 25 of the 2002 Act. |
| The variation or revocation of a contact order or an order prohibiting contact under section 51A(2) of the 2002 Act (section 51B(1)(c) of that Act). | The child; | The parties to the proceedings leading to the contact order or an order prohibiting contact which it is sought to have varied or revoked; and |
| | a person in whose favour the adoption order was made; or | any person named in the contact order or the order prohibiting contact. |
| A section 88 direction. | The adopted child; the adopters; any parent; or any other person. | The adopters; the parents; the adoption agency; the local authority to whom notice under section 44 of the 2002 Act (notice of intention to apply for a section 84 order) has been given; and |
| | | the Attorney-General. |
| A section 89 order. | The adopters; the adopted person; any parent; | The adopters; the parents; the adoption agency; and |

| Proceedings for | Applicants | Respondents |
|---|---|---|
| | the relevant Central Authority; the adoption agency; the local authority to whom notice under section 44 of the 2002 Act (notice of intention to adopt or apply for a section 84 order) has been given; the Secretary of State for the Home Department; or any other person. | the local authority to whom notice under section 44 of the 2002 Act (notice of intention to adopt or apply for a section 84 order) has been given. |

(2) The court may at any time direct that a child, who is not already a respondent to proceedings, be made a respondent to proceedings where –

  (a) the child –
    (i) wishes to make an application; or
    (ii) has evidence to give to the court or a legal submission to make which has not been given or made by any other party; or
  (b) there are other special circumstances.

(3) The court may at any time direct that –

  (a) any other person or body be made a respondent to proceedings; or
  (b) a party be removed.

(4) If the court makes a direction for the addition or removal of a party, it may give consequential directions about –

  (a) serving a copy of the application form on any new respondent;
  (b) serving relevant documents on the new party; and
  (c) the management of the proceedings.

Amendments—SI 2014/843.

## 14.4 Notice of proceedings to person with foreign parental responsibility

(1) This rule applies where a child is subject to proceedings to which this Part applies and –

  (a) a parent of the child holds or is believed to hold parental responsibility for the child under the law of another State which subsists in

accordance with Article 16 of the 1996 Hague Convention following the child becoming habitually resident in a territorial unit of the United Kingdom; and
(b) that parent is not otherwise required to be joined as a respondent under rule 14.3.

(2) The applicant shall give notice of the proceedings to any parent to whom the applicant believes paragraph (1) applies in any case in which a person who was a parent with parental responsibility under the 1989 Act would be a respondent to the proceedings in accordance with rule 14.3.

(3) The applicant and every respondent to the proceedings shall provide such details as they possess as to the identity and whereabouts of any parent they believe to hold parental responsibility for the child in accordance with paragraph (1) to the court officer, upon making, or responding to the application as appropriate.

(4) Where the existence of such a parent only becomes apparent to a party at a later date during the proceedings, that party must notify the court officer of those details at the earliest opportunity.

(5) Where a parent to whom paragraph (1) applies receives notice of proceedings, that parent may apply to the court to be joined as a party using the Part 18 procedure.

## 14.5 Who is to serve

(1) The general rules about service in Part 6 are subject to this rule.

(2) In proceedings to which this Part applies, a document which has been issued or prepared by a court officer will be served by the court officer except where –
   (a) a practice direction provides otherwise; or
   (b) the court directs otherwise.

(3) Where a court officer is to serve a document, it is for the court to decide which of the methods of service specified in rule 6.23 is to be used.

## 14.6 What the court or a court officer will do when the application has been issued

(1) As soon as practicable after the application has been issued in proceedings –
   (a) the court will –
      (i) if section 48(1) of the 2002 Act (restrictions on making adoption orders) applies, consider whether it is proper to hear the application;
      (ii) subject to paragraph (4), set a date for the first directions hearing;
      (iii) appoint a children's guardian in accordance with rule 16.3(1);
      (iv) appoint a reporting officer in accordance with rule 16.30;
      (v) consider whether a report relating to the welfare of the child is required, and if so, request such a report in accordance with rule 16.33;

(vi) set a date for the hearing of the application; and
(vii) do anything else that may be set out in a practice direction; and
(b) a court officer will –
   (i) subject to receiving confirmation in accordance with paragraph (2)(b)(ii), give notice of any directions hearing set by the court to the parties and to any children's guardian, reporting officer or children and family reporter;
   (ii) serve a copy of the application form (but, subject to sub-paragraphs (iii) and (iv), not the documents attached to it) on the persons referred to in Practice Direction 14A;
   (iii) send a copy of the certified copy of the entry in the register of live-births or Adopted Children Register and any health report attached to an application for an adoption order to –
      (aa) any children's guardian, reporting officer or children and family reporter; and
      (bb) the local authority to whom notice under section 44 of the 2002 Act (notice of intention to adopt or apply for a section 84 order) has been given;
   (iv) if notice under rule 14.9(2) has been given (request to dispense with consent of parent or guardian), in accordance with that rule inform the parent or guardian of the request and send a copy of the statement of facts to –
      (aa) the parent or guardian;
      (bb) any children's guardian, reporting officer or children and family reporter;
      (cc) any local authority to whom notice under section 44 of the 2002 Act (notice of intention to adopt or apply for a section 84 order) has been given; and
      (dd) any adoption agency which has placed the child for adoption; and
   (v) do anything else that may be set out in a practice direction.

(2) In addition to the matters referred to in paragraph (1), as soon as practicable after an application for an adoption order or a section 84 order has been issued the court or the court officer will –

(a) where the child is not placed for adoption by an adoption agency –
   (i) ask either the Service or the Assembly to file any relevant form of consent to an adoption order or a section 84 order; and
   (ii) ask the local authority to prepare a report on the suitability of the prospective adopters if one has not already been prepared; and
(b) where the child is placed for adoption by an adoption agency, ask the adoption agency to –
   (i) file any relevant form of consent to –
      (aa) the child being placed for adoption;
      (bb) an adoption order;
      (cc) a future adoption order under section 20 of the 2002 Act; or
      (dd) a section 84 order;

(ii) confirm whether a statement has been made under section 20(4)(a) of the 2002 Act (statement of wish not to be informed of any application for an adoption order) and if so, to file that statement;
(iii) file any statement made under section 20(4)(b) of the 2002 Act (withdrawal of wish not to be informed of any application for an adoption order) as soon as it is received by the adoption agency; and
(iv) prepare a report on the suitability of the prospective adopters if one has not already been prepared.

(3) In addition to the matters referred to in paragraph (1), as soon as practicable after an application for a placement order has been issued –

(a) the court will consider whether a report giving the local authority's reasons for placing the child for adoption is required, and if so, will direct the local authority to prepare such a report; and
(b) the court or the court officer will ask either the Service or the Assembly to file any form of consent to the child being placed for adoption.

(4) Where it considers it appropriate the court may, instead of setting a date for a first directions hearing, give the directions provided for by rule 14.8.

## 14.7 Date for first directions hearing

Unless the court directs otherwise, the first directions hearing must be within 4 weeks beginning with the date on which the application is issued.

## 14.8 The first directions hearing

(1) At the first directions hearing in the proceedings the court will –

(a) fix a timetable for the proceedings including a timetable for the filing of –
　i) any report relating to the suitability of the applicants to adopt a child;
　(ii) any report from the local authority;
　(iii) any report from a children's guardian, reporting officer or children and family reporter;
　(iv) if a statement of facts has been filed, any amended statement of facts;
　(v) any other evidence, and
　(vi) give directions relating to the reports and other evidence;
(b) consider whether the child or any other person should be a party to the proceedings and, if so, give directions in accordance with rule 14.3(2) or (3) joining that child or person as a party;
(c) give directions relating to the appointment of a litigation friend for any protected party or child who is a party to, but not the subject of, proceedings unless a litigation friend has already been appointed;

(d) consider in accordance with rule 29.17 whether the case needs to be transferred to another court and, if so, give directions to transfer the proceedings to another court;
(e) give directions about –
  (i) tracing parents or any other person the court considers to be relevant to the proceedings;
  (ii) service of documents;
  (iii) subject to paragraph (2), disclosure as soon as possible of information and evidence to the parties; and
  (iv) the final hearing.

(Under Part 3 the court may also direct that the case be adjourned if it considers that non-court dispute resolution is appropriate.)

(2) Rule 14.13(2) applies to any direction given under paragraph (1)(e)(iii) as it applies to a direction given under rule 14.13(1).

(3) In addition to the matters referred to in paragraph (1), the court will give any of the directions listed in Practice Direction 14B in proceedings for –

(a) a Convention adoption order;
(b) a section 84 order;
(c) a section 88 direction;
(d) a section 89 order; or
(e) an adoption order where section 83(1) of the 2002 Act applies (restriction on bringing children in).

(4) The parties or their legal representatives must attend the first directions hearing unless the court directs otherwise.

(5) Directions may also be given at any stage in the proceedings –

(a) of the court's own initiative; or
(b) on the application of a party or any children's guardian or, where the direction concerns a report by a reporting officer or children and family reporter, the reporting officer or children and family reporter.

(6) For the purposes of giving directions or for such purposes as the court directs –

(a) the court may set a date for a further directions hearing or other hearing; and
(b) the court officer will give notice of any date so fixed to the parties and to any children's guardian, reporting officer or children and family reporter.

(7) After the first directions hearing the court will monitor compliance by the parties with the court's timetable and directions.

Amendments—SI 2013/3204; SI 2014/843.

### 14.9 Requesting the court to dispense with the consent of any parent or guardian

(1) This rule applies where the applicant wants to ask the court to dispense with the consent of any parent or guardian of a child to –

- (a) the child being placed for adoption;
- (b) the making of an adoption order except a Convention adoption order; or
- (c) the making of a section 84 order.

(2) The applicant requesting the court to dispense with the consent must –

- (a) give notice of the request in the application form or at any later stage by filing a written request setting out the reasons for the request; and
- (b) file a statement of facts setting out a summary of the history of the case and any other facts to satisfy the court that –
  - (i) the parent or guardian cannot be found or is incapable of giving consent; or
  - (ii) the welfare of the child requires the consent to be dispensed with.

(3) If a serial number has been assigned to the applicant under rule 14.2, the statement of facts supplied under paragraph (2)(b) must be framed so that it does not disclose the identity of the applicant.

(4) On receipt of the notice of the request –

- (a) a court officer will –
  - (i) inform the parent or guardian of the request unless the parent or guardian cannot be found; and
  - (ii) send a copy of the statement of facts filed in accordance with paragraph (2)(b) to –
    - (aa) the parent or guardian unless the parent or guardian cannot be found;
    - (bb) any children's guardian, reporting officer or children and family reporter;
    - (cc) any local authority to whom notice under section 44 of the 2002 Act (notice of intention to adopt or apply for a section 84 order) has been given; and
    - (dd) any adoption agency which has placed the child for adoption; and
- (b) if the applicant considers that the parent or guardian is incapable of giving consent, the court will consider whether to –
  - (i) appoint a litigation friend for the parent or guardian under rule 15.6(1); or
  - (ii) give directions for an application to be made under rule 15.6(3);
  - (iii) unless a litigation friend is already appointed for that parent or guardian.

### 14.10 Consent

(1) Consent of any parent or guardian of a child –

(a) under section 19 of the 2002 Act, to the child being placed for adoption; and
(b) under section 20 of the 2002 Act, to the making of a future adoption order,

must be given in the form referred to in Practice Direction 5A or a form to the like effect.

(2) Subject to paragraph (3), consent –

(a) to the making of an adoption order; or
(b) to the making of a section 84 order,

may be given in the form referred to in Practice Direction 5A or a form to the like effect or otherwise as the court directs.

(3) Any consent to a Convention adoption order must be in a form which complies with the internal law relating to adoption of the Convention country of which the child is habitually resident.

(4) Any form of consent executed in Scotland must be witnessed by a Justice of the Peace or a Sheriff.

(5) Any form of consent executed in Northern Ireland must be witnessed by a Justice of the Peace.

(6) Any form of consent executed outside the United Kingdom must be witnessed by –

(a) any person for the time being authorised by law in the place where the document is executed to administer an oath for any judicial or other legal purpose;
(b) a British Consular officer;
(c) a notary public; or
(d) if the person executing the document is serving in any of the regular armed forces of the Crown, an officer holding a commission in any of those forces.

## 14.11 Reports by the adoption agency or local authority

(1) The adoption agency or local authority must file the report on the suitability of the applicant to adopt a child within the timetable fixed by the court.

(2) A local authority that is directed to prepare a report on the placement of the child for adoption must file that report within the timetable fixed by the court.

(3) The reports must cover the matters specified in Practice Direction 14C.

(4) The court may at any stage request a further report or ask the adoption agency or local authority to assist the court in any other manner.

(5) A court officer will send a copy of any report referred to in this rule to any children's guardian, reporting officer or children and family reporter.

(6) A report to the court under this rule is confidential.

### 14.12 Health reports

(1) Reports by a registered medical practitioner ('health reports') made not more than 3 months earlier on the health of the child and of each applicant must be attached to an application for an adoption order or a section 84 order except where –

    (a)    the child was placed for adoption with the applicant by an adoption agency;
    (b)    the applicant or one of the applicants is a parent of the child; or
    (c)    the applicant is the partner of a parent of the child.

(2) Health reports must contain the matters set out in Practice Direction 14D.

(3) A health report is confidential.

### 14.13 Confidential reports to the court and disclosure to the parties

(1) The court will consider whether to give a direction that a confidential report be disclosed to each party to the proceedings.

(2) Before giving such a direction the court will consider whether any information should be deleted including information which –

    (a)    discloses, or is likely to disclose, the identity of a person who has been assigned a serial number under rule 14.2(2) or (3); or
    (b)    discloses the particulars referred to in rule 29.1(1) where a party has given notice under rule 29.1(2) (disclosure of personal details).

(3) The court may direct that the report will not be disclosed to a party.

Amendments—SI 2014/843.

### 14.14 Communication of information relating to proceedings

For the purposes of the law relating to contempt of court, information (whether or not it is recorded in any form) relating to proceedings held in private may be communicated –

    (a)    where the court gives permission;
    (b)    unless the court directs otherwise, in accordance with Practice Direction 14E; or
    (c)    where the communication is to –
        (i)    a party;
        (ii)    the legal representative of a party;
        (iii)    a professional legal adviser;
        (iv)    an officer of the service or a Welsh family proceedings officer;
        (v)    a welfare officer;
        (vi)    the Director of Legal Aid Casework (within the meaning of section 4 of the Legal Aid, Sentencing and Punishment of Offenders Act 2012);
        (vii)    an expert whose instruction by a party has been authorised by the court for the purposes of the proceedings; or
        (viii)    a professional acting in furtherance of the protection of children.

**Amendments**—SI 2013/534, subject to savings.

## 14.15 Notice of final hearing

A court officer will give notice to the parties, any children's guardian, reporting officer or children and family reporter and to any other person to whom a practice direction may require such notice to be given –

      (a)   of the date and place where the application will be heard; and
      (b)   of the fact that, unless the person wishes or the court requires, the person need not attend.

## 14.16 The final hearing

(1) Any person who has been given notice in accordance with rule 14.15 may attend the final hearing and, subject to paragraph (2), be heard on the question of whether an order should be made.

(2) A person whose application for the permission of the court to oppose the making of an adoption order under section 47(3) or (5) of the 2002 Act has been refused is not entitled to be heard on the question of whether an order should be made.

(3) Any member or employee of a party which is a local authority, adoption agency or other body may address the court at the final hearing if authorised to do so.

(4) The court may direct that any person must attend a final hearing.

(5) Paragraphs (6) and (7) apply to –

    (a)   an adoption order;
    (b)   a section 84 order; or
    (c)   a section 89 order.

(6) Subject to paragraphs (7) and (8), the court cannot make an order unless the applicant and the child personally attend the final hearing.

(7) The court may direct that the applicant or the child need not attend the final hearing.

(8) In a case of adoption by a couple under section 50 of the 2002 Act, the court may make an adoption order after personal attendance of one only of the applicants if there are special circumstances.

(9) The court cannot make a placement order unless a legal representative of the applicant attends the final hearing.

## 14.17 Proof of identity of the child

(1) Unless the contrary is shown, the child referred to in the application will be deemed to be the child referred to in the form of consent –

    (a)   to the child being placed for adoption;
    (b)   to the making of an adoption order; or
    (c)   to the making of a section 84 order,

where the conditions in paragraph (2) apply.

(2) The conditions are –

(a) the application identifies the child by reference to a full certified copy of an entry in the registers of live-births;
(b) the form of consent identifies the child by reference to a full certified copy of an entry in the registers of live-births attached to the form; and
(c) the copy of the entry in the registers of live-births referred to in sub-paragraph (a) is the same or relates to the same entry in the registers of live-births as the copy of the entry in the registers of live-births attached to the form of consent.

(3) Where the child is already an adopted child paragraph (2) will have effect as if for the references to the registers of live-births there were substituted references to the Adopted Children Register.

(4) Subject to paragraph (7), where the precise date of the child's birth is not proved to the satisfaction of the court, the court will determine the probable date of birth.

(5) The probable date of the child's birth may be specified in the placement order, adoption order or section 84 order as the date of the child's birth.

(6) Subject to paragraph (7), where the child's place of birth cannot be proved to the satisfaction of the court –

(a) the child may be treated as having been born in the registration district and sub-district in which the court sits where it is probable that the child may have been born in –
 (i) the United Kingdom;
 (ii) the Channel Islands; or
 (iii) the Isle of Man; or
(b) in any other case, the particulars of the country of birth may be omitted from the placement order, adoption order or section 84 order.

(7) A placement order identifying the probable date and place of birth of the child will be sufficient proof of the date and place of birth of the child in adoption proceedings and proceedings for a section 84 order.

Amendments—SI 2013/3204.

## 14.18 Disclosing information to an adopted adult

(1) The adopted person has the right, on request, to receive from the court which made the adoption order a copy of the following –

(a) the application form for an adoption order (but not the documents attached to that form);
(b) the adoption order and any other orders relating to the adoption proceedings;
(c) orders containing any provision for contact with the child after the adoption order was made; and
(d) any other document or order referred to in Practice Direction 14F.

(2) The court will remove any protected information from any copy of a document or order referred to in paragraph (1) before the copies are given to the adopted person.

(3) This rule does not apply to an adopted person under the age of 18 years.

(4) In this rule 'protected information' means information which would be protected information under section 57(3) of the 2002 Act if the adoption agency gave the information and not the court.

Amendments—SI 2014/843.

## 14.19 Translation of documents

(1) Where a translation of any document is required for the purposes of proceedings for a Convention adoption order the translation must –

    (a)    unless the court directs otherwise, be provided by the applicant; and
    (b)    be signed by the translator to certify that the translation is accurate.

(2) This rule does not apply where the document is to be served in accordance with the Service Regulation.

## 14.20 Application for recovery orders

(1) An application for any of the orders referred to in section 41(2) of the 2002 Act (recovery orders) may be made without notice, in which case the applicant must file the application –

    (a)    where the application is made by telephone, the next business day after the making of the application; or
    (b)    in any other case, at the time when the application is made.

(2) Where the court refuses to make an order on an application without notice it may direct that the application is made on notice in which case the application will proceed in accordance with rules 14.1 to 14.17.

(3) The respondents to an application under this rule are –

    (a)    in a case where –
        (i)    placement proceedings;
        (ii)    adoption proceedings; or
        (iii)    proceedings for a section 84 order,
        are pending, all parties to those proceedings;
    (b)    any adoption agency authorised to place the child for adoption or which has placed the child for adoption;
    (c)    any local authority to whom notice under section 44 of the 2002 Act (notice of intention to adopt or apply for a section 84 order) has been given;
    (d)    any person having parental responsibility for the child;
    (e)    any person in whose favour there is provision for contact;
    (f)    any person who was caring for the child immediately prior to the making of the application; and

(g) any person whom the applicant alleges to have effected, or to have been or to be responsible for, the taking or keeping of the child.

Amendments—SI 2013/3204.

### 14.21 Inherent jurisdiction and fathers without parental responsibility

Where no proceedings have started an adoption agency or local authority may ask the High Court for directions on the need to give a father without parental responsibility notice of the intention to place a child for adoption.

### 14.22 Timing of applications for section 89 order

An application for a section 89 order must be made within 2 years beginning with the date on which –

(a) the Convention adoption or Convention adoption order; or
(b) the overseas adoption or determination under section 91 of the 2002 Act,

to which it relates was made.

### 14.23 Custody of documents

All documents relating to proceedings under the 2002 Act must, while they are in the custody of the court, be kept in a place of special security.

### 14.24 Documents held by the court not to be inspected or copied without the court's permission

Subject to the provisions of these rules, any practice direction or any direction given by the court –

(a) no document or order held by the court in proceedings under the 2002 Act will be open to inspection by any person; and
(b) no copy of any such document or order, or of an extract from any such document or order, will be taken by or given to any person.

### 14.25 Orders

(1) An order takes effect from the date when it is made, or such later date as the court may specify.

(2) In proceedings in Wales a party may request that an order be drawn up in Welsh as well as English.

(Rule 37.9 makes provision for the court to endorse an order prohibiting contact under section 51A(2)(b) of the 2002 Act with a penal notice on the application of the person entitled to enforce the order.)

Amendments—SI 2014/843.

**14.26 Copies of orders**

(1) Within 7 days beginning with the date on which the final order was made in proceedings, or such shorter time as the court may direct, a court officer will send –

- (a) a copy of the order to the applicant;
- (b) a copy, which is sealed[GL], authenticated with the stamp of the court or certified as a true copy, of –
  - (i) an adoption order;
  - (ii) a section 89 order; or
  - (iii) an order quashing or revoking an adoption order or allowing an appeal against an adoption order,

to the Registrar General;

- (c) a copy of a Convention adoption order to the relevant Central Authority;
- (d) a copy of a section 89 order relating to a Convention adoption order or a Convention adoption to the –
  - (i) relevant Central Authority;
  - (ii) adopters;
  - (iii) adoption agency; and
  - (iv) local authority;
- (e) unless the court directs otherwise, a copy of an order under section 26 of the 2002 Act or a variation or revocation of such order under section 27 of the 2002 Act to the –
  - (i) person with whom the child is living;
  - (ii) adoption agency; and
  - (iii) local authority;
- (ee) unless the court directs otherwise, a copy of a contact order under section 51A(2)(a) of the 2002 Act, an order prohibiting contact under section 51A(2)(b) of that Act or a variation or revocation of such orders under section 51B(1)(c) of that Act to the parties to the proceedings; and
- (f) a notice of the making or refusal of –
  - (i) the final order; or
  - (ii) an order quashing or revoking an adoption order or allowing an appeal against an order in proceedings,
  to every respondent and, with the permission of the court, any other person.

(2) The court officer will also send notice of the making of an adoption order or a section 84 order to –

- (a) any court in Great Britain which appears to the court officer to have made any such order as is referred to in section 46(2) of the 2002 Act (order relating to parental responsibility for, and maintenance of, the child); and
- (b) the principal registry, if it appears to the court officer that a parental responsibility agreement has been recorded at the principal registry.

(3) A copy of any final order may be sent to any other person with the permission of the court.

(4) The court officer will send a copy of any order made during the course of the proceedings to the following persons or bodies, unless the court directs otherwise –

- (a) all the parties to those proceedings;
- (b) any children and family reporter appointed in those proceedings;
- (c) any adoption agency or local authority which has prepared a report on the suitability of an applicant to adopt a child;
- (d) any local authority which has prepared a report on placement for adoption.

(5) If an order has been drawn up in Welsh as well as English in accordance with rule 14.25(2) any reference in this rule to sending an order is to be taken as a reference to sending both the Welsh and English orders.

Amendments—SI 2014/843.

### 14.27 Amendment and revocation of orders

(1) Subject to paragraph (2), an application under –

- (a) section 55 of the 2002 Act (revocation of adoptions on legitimation); or
- (b) paragraph 4 of Schedule 1 to the 2002 Act (amendment of adoption order and revocation of direction),

may be made without serving a copy of the application notice.

(2) The court may direct that an application notice be served on such persons as it thinks fit.

(3) Where the court makes an order granting the application, a court officer will send the Registrar General a notice –
- (a) specifying the amendments; or
- (b) informing the Registrar General of the revocation,

giving sufficient particulars of the order to enable the Registrar General to identify the case.

### 14.28 (revoked)

## PRACTICE DIRECTION 14A – WHO RECEIVES A COPY OF THE APPLICATION FORM FOR ORDERS IN PROCEEDINGS

This Practice Direction supplements FPR Part 14, rule 14.6(1)(b)(ii)

### Persons who receive copy of application form

1 In relation to each type of proceedings in column 1 of the following table, column 2 sets out which persons are to receive a copy of the application form:

| Proceeding for | Who Receives a Copy of the Application Form |
|---|---|
| An adoption order (section 46 of the Act); or a section 84 order | Any appointed children's guardian, children and family reporter and reporting officer; the local authority to whom notice under section 44 (notice of intention to apply to adopt or apply for a section 84 order) has been given; the adoption agency which placed the child for adoption with the applicants; any other person directed by the court to receive a copy. |
| A placement order (section 21 of the Act); or an order varying a placement order (section 23 of the Act) | Each parent with parental responsibility for the child or guardian of the child; any appointed children's guardian, children and family reporter and reporting officer; any other person directed by the court to receive a copy. |
| An order revoking a placement order (section 24 of the Act) | Each parent with parental responsibility for the child or guardian of the child; any appointed children's guardian and children and family reporter; the local authority authorised by the placement order to place the child for adoption; any other person directed by the court to receive a copy. |

| Proceeding for | Who Receives a Copy of the Application Form |
|---|---|
| A contact order (section 26 of the Act); an order varying or revoking a contact order (section 27 of the Act); an order permitting the child's name to be changed or the removal of the child from the United Kingdom (section 28(2) of the Act); a recovery order (section 41(2) of the Act); a contact order under section 51A(2)(a) of the Act; the making of an order prohibiting contact with the child under section 51A(2)(b) of the Act; the variation or revocation of an order under section 51A(2) of the Act in accordance with section 51B(1)(c) of the Act; a section 89 order; and a section 88 direction | All the parties; any appointed children's guardian and children and family reporter; any other person directed by the court to receive a copy. |

## PRACTICE DIRECTION 14B –
## THE FIRST DIRECTIONS HEARING – ADOPTIONS WITH A FOREIGN ELEMENT

This Practice Direction supplements FPR Part 14, rule 14.8(3)

### Application

1 This Practice Direction applies to proceedings for:

- (a) a Convention adoption order;
- (b) a section 84 order;
- (c) a section 88 direction;
- (d) a section 89 order; and
- (e) an adoption order where the child has been brought into the United Kingdom in the circumstances where section 83(1) of the Act applies.

### The first directions hearing

2 At the first directions hearing the court will, in addition to any matters referred to in rule 14.8(1):

(a) consider whether the requirements of the Act and the Adoptions with a Foreign Element Regulations 2005 (S.I. 2005/392) appear to have been complied with and, if not, consider whether or not in a case in the family court, it is appropriate that the case should be considered by a puisne judge of the High Court sitting in the family court (who may in turn consider whether or not it is appropriate to transfer the case to the High Court);

(b) consider whether all relevant documents are translated into English and, if not, fix a timetable for translating any outstanding documents;

(c) consider whether the applicant needs to file an affidavit setting out the full details of the circumstances in which the child was brought to the United Kingdom, of the attitude of the parents to the application and confirming compliance with the requirements of The Adoptions with A Foreign Element Regulations 2005;

(d) give directions about:
  (i) the production of the child's passport and visa;
  (ii) the need for an officer of the Service or a Welsh family proceedings officer and a representative of the Home Office to attend future hearings; and
  (iii) personal service on the parents (via the Central Authority in the case of an application for a Convention Adoption Order) including information about the role of the officer of the Service or the Welsh family proceedings officer and availability of legal aid to be represented within the proceedings; and

(e) consider fixing a further directions appointment no later than 6 weeks after the date of the first directions appointment and timetable a date by which the officer of the Service or the Welsh family proceedings officer should file an interim report in advance of that further appointment.

## PRACTICE DIRECTION 14C –
## REPORTS BY THE ADOPTION AGENCY OR LOCAL AUTHORITY

This Practice Direction supplements FPR Part 14, rule 14.11(3)

### Matters to be contained in reports

1.1 The matters to be covered in the report on the suitability of the applicant to adopt a child are set out in Annex A to this Practice Direction.

1.2 The matters to be covered in a report on the placement of the child for adoption are set out in Annex B to this Practice Direction.

1.3 Where a matter to be covered in the reports set out in Annex A and Annex B does not apply to the circumstances of a particular case, the reasons for not covering the matter should be given.

## ANNEX A – REPORT TO THE COURT WHERE THERE HAS BEEN AN APPLICATION FOR AN ADOPTION ORDER OR AN APPLICATION FOR A SECTION 84 ORDER

Section A: The Report and Matters for the Proceedings

Section B: The Child and the Birth Family

Section C: The Prospective Adopter of the Child

Section D: The Placement

Section E: Recommendations

Section F: Further information for proceedings relating to Convention Adoption Orders, Convention adoptions, section 84 Orders or adoptions where section 83(1) of the 2002 Act applies.

### SECTION A: THE REPORT AND MATTERS FOR THE PROCEEDINGS

*Part 1 – The report*

For each of the principal author/s of the report:

- (i) name;
- (ii) role in relation to this case;
- (iii) sections completed in this report;
- (iv) qualifications and experience;
- (v) name and address of the adoption agency; and
- (vi) adoption agency case reference number.

*Part 2 – Matters for the proceedings*

- (a) Whether the adoption agency considers that any other person should be made a respondent or a party to the proceedings, including the child.
- (b) Whether any of the respondents is under the age of 18.
- (c) Whether a respondent is a person who, by reason of mental disorder within the meaning of the Mental Health Act 1983, is incapable of managing and administering his or her property and affairs. If so, medical evidence should be provided with particular regard to the effect on that person's ability to make decisions in the proceedings.

### SECTION B: THE CHILD AND THE BIRTH FAMILY

*Part 1*

*(i) Information about the child*

- (a) Name, sex, date and place of birth and address including local authority area.
- (b) Photograph and physical description.
- (c) Nationality.
- (d) Racial origin and cultural and linguistic background.

(e) Religious persuasion (including details of baptism, confirmation or equivalent ceremonies).
(f) Details of any siblings, half-siblings and step-siblings, including dates of birth.
(g) Whether the child is looked after by a local authority.
(h) Whether the child has been placed for adoption with the prospective adopter by a UK adoption agency.
(i) Whether the child was being fostered by the prospective adopter.
(j) Whether the child was brought into the UK for adoption, including date of entry and whether an adoption order was made in the child's country of origin.
(k) Personality and social development, including emotional and behavioural development and any related needs.
(l) Details of interests, likes and dislikes.
(m) A summary, written by the agency's medical adviser, of the child's health history, his current state of health and any need for health care which is anticipated, and date of the most recent medical examination.
(n) Any known learning difficulties or known general medical or mental health factors which are likely to have, or may have, genetic implications.
(o) Names, addresses and types of nurseries or schools attended, with dates.
(p) Educational attainments.
(q) Any special needs in relation to the child (whether physical, learning, behavioural or any other) and his emotional and behavioural development.
(r) Whether the child is subject to a statement under the Education Act 1996.
(s) Previous orders concerning the child:
 (i) the name of the court;
 (ii) the order made; and
 (iii) the date of the order.
(t) Inheritance rights and any claim to damages under the Fatal Accidents Act 1976 the child stands to retain or lose if adopted.
(u) Any other relevant information which might assist the court.

*(ii) Information about each parent of the child*

(a) Name, date and place of birth and address (date on which last address was confirmed current) including local authority area.
(b) Photograph, if available, and physical description.
(c) Nationality.
(d) Racial origin and cultural and linguistic background.
(e) Whether the mother and father were married to each other at the time of the child's birth or have subsequently married.
(f) Where the parent has been previously married or entered into a civil partnership, dates of those marriages or civil partnerships.
(g) Where the mother and father are not married, whether the father has parental responsibility and, if so, how it was acquired.

(h) If the identity or whereabouts of the father are not known, the information about him that has been ascertained and from whom, and the steps that have been taken to establish paternity.
(i) Past and present relationship with the other parent.
(j) Other information about the parent, where available:
 (i) health, including any known learning difficulties or known general medical or mental health factors which are likely to have, or may have, genetic implications;
 (ii) religious persuasion;
 (iii) educational history;
 (iv) employment history; and
 (v) personality and interests.
(k) Any other relevant information which might assist the court.

*Part 2*
*Relationships, contact arrangements and views.*

*The child*

(a) If the child is in the care of a local authority or voluntary organisation, or has been, details (including dates) of any placements with foster parents, or other arrangements in respect of the care of the child, including particulars of the persons with whom the child has had his home and observations on the care provided.
(b) The child's wishes and feelings (if appropriate, having regard to the child's age and understanding) about adoption, the application and its consequences, including any wishes in respect of religious and cultural upbringing.
(c) The child's wishes and feelings in relation to contact (if appropriate, having regard to the child's age and understanding).
(d) The child's wishes and feelings recorded in any other proceedings.
(e) Date when the child's views were last ascertained.

*The child's parents (or guardian) and relatives*

(a) The parents' wishes and feelings before the placement, about the placement and about adoption, the application and its consequences, including any wishes in respect of the child's religious and cultural upbringing.
(b) Each parent's (or guardian's) wishes and feelings in relation to contact.
(c) Date/s when the views of each parent or guardian were last ascertained.
(d) Arrangements concerning any siblings, including half-siblings and step-siblings, and whether any are the subject of a parallel application or have been the subject of any orders. If so, for each case give:
 (i) the name of the court;
 (ii) the order made, or (if proceedings are pending) the order applied for; and
 (iii) the date of order, or date of next hearing if proceedings are pending.

(e) Extent of contact with the child's mother and father and, in each case, the nature of the relationship enjoyed.
(f) The relationship which the child has with relatives, and with any other person considered relevant, including:
　(i) the likelihood of any such relationship continuing and the value to the child of its doing so; and
　(ii) the ability and willingness of any of the child's relatives, or of any such person, to provide the child with a secure environment in which the child can develop, and otherwise to meet the child's needs.
(g) The wishes and feelings of any of the child's relatives, or of any such person, regarding the child.
(h) Whether the parents (or members of the child's family) have met or are likely to meet the prospective adopter and, if they have met, the effect on all involved of such meeting.
(i) Dates when the views of members of the child's wider family and any other relevant person were last ascertained.

## Part 3
*A summary of the actions of the adoption agency*

(a) Brief account of the agency's actions in the case, with particulars and dates of all written information and notices given to the child and his parents and any person with parental responsibility.
(b) If consent has been given for the child to be placed for adoption, and also consent for the child to be adopted, the names of those who gave consent and the date such consents were given. If such consents were subsequently withdrawn, the dates of these withdrawals.
(c) If any statement has been made under section 20(4)(a) of the Adoption and Children Act 2002 (the '2002 Act') that a parent or guardian does not wish to be informed of any application for an adoption order, the names of those who have made such statements and the dates the statements were made. If such statements were subsequently withdrawn, the dates of these withdrawals.
(d) Whether an order has been made under section 21 of the 2002 Act, section 18 of the Adoption (Scotland) Act 1978 or Article 17(1) or 18(1) of the Northern Ireland Order 1987.
(e) Details of the support and advice given to the parents and any services offered or taken up.
(f) If the father does not have parental responsibility, details of the steps taken to inform him of the application for an adoption order.
(g) Brief details and dates of assessments of the child's needs, including expert opinions.
(h) Reasons for considering that adoption would be in the child's best interests (with date of relevant decision and reasons for any delay in implementing the decision).

## SECTION C: THE PROSPECTIVE ADOPTER OF THE CHILD

*Part 1*
*Information about the prospective adopter, including suitability to adopt*

(a) Name, date and place of birth and address (date on which last address was confirmed current) including local authority area.
(b) Photograph and physical description.
(c) Whether the prospective adopter is domiciled or habitually resident in a part of the British Islands and, if habitually resident, for how long they have been habitually resident.
(d) Racial origin and cultural and linguistic background.
(e) Marital status or civil partnership status, date and place of most recent marriage (if any) or civil partnership (if any).
(f) Details of any previous marriage, civil partnership, or relationship where the prospective adopter lived with another person as a partner in an enduring family relationship.
(g) Relationship (if any) to the child.
(h) Where adopters wish to adopt as a couple, the status of the relationship and an assessment of the stability and permanence of their relationship.
(i) If a married person or a civil partner is applying alone, the reasons for this.
(j) Description of how the prospective adopter relates to adults and children.
(k) Previous experience of caring for children (including as a step-parent, foster parent, child-minder or prospective adopter) and assessment of ability in this respect, together where appropriate with assessment of ability in bringing up the prospective adopter's own children.
(l) A summary, written by the agency's medical adviser, of the prospective adopter's health history, current state of health and any need for health care which is anticipated, and date of most recent medical examination.
(m) Assessment of ability and suitability to bring up the child throughout his childhood.
(n) Details of income and comments on the living standards of the household with particulars of the home and living conditions (and particulars of any home where the prospective adopter proposes to live with the child, if different).
(o) Details of other members of the household, including any children of the prospective adopter even if not resident in the household.
(p) Details of the parents and any siblings of the prospective adopter, with their ages or ages at death.
(q) Other information about the prospective adopter:
 (i) religious persuasion;
 (ii) educational history;
 (iii) employment history; and
 (iv) personality and interests.

(r) Confirmation that the applicants have not been convicted of, or cautioned for, a specified offence within the meaning of regulation 23(3) of the Adoption Agencies Regulations 2005 (S.I. 2005/389).
(s) Confirmation that the prospective adopter is still approved.
(t) Confirmation that any referees have been interviewed, with a report of their views and opinion of the weight to be placed thereon and whether they are still valid.
(u) Details of any previous family court proceedings in which the prospective adopter has been involved (which have not been referred to elsewhere in this report.)

Part 2
Wishes, views and contact arrangements

Prospective Adopter

(a) Whether the prospective adopter is willing to follow any wishes of the child or his parents or guardian in respect of the child's religious and cultural upbringing.
(b) The views of other members of the prospective adopter's household and wider family in relation to the proposed adoption.
(c) Reasons for the prospective adopter wishing to adopt the child and extent of understanding of the nature and effect of adoption. Whether the prospective adopter has discussed adoption with the child.
(d) Any hope and expectations the prospective adopter has for the child's future.
(e) The prospective adopter's wishes and feelings in relation to contact.

Part 3
Actions of the adoption agency

(a) Brief account of the Agency's actions in the case, with particulars and dates of all written information and notices given to the prospective adopter.
(b) The Agency's proposals for contact, including options for facilitating or achieving any indirect contact or direct contact.
(c) The Agency's opinion on the likely effect on the prospective adopter and on the security of the placement of any proposed contact.
(d) Where the prospective adopter has been approved by an agency as suitable to be an adoptive parent, the agency's reasons for considering that the prospective adopter is suitable to be an adoptive parent for this child (with dates of relevant decisions).

## SECTION D: THE PLACEMENT

(a) Where the child was placed for adoption by an adoption agency (section 18 of the 2002 Act), the date and circumstances of the child's placement with prospective adopter.

(b) Where the child is living with persons who have applied for the adoption order to be made (section 44 of the 2002 Act), the date when notice of intention to adopt was given.
(c) Where the placement is being provided with adoption support, this should be summarised and should include the plan and timescales for continuing the support beyond the making of the adoption order.
(d) Where the placement is not being provided with adoption support, the reasons why.
(e) A summary of the information obtained from the Agency's visits and reviews of the placement, including whether the child has been seen separately to the prospective adopter and whether there has been sufficient opportunity to see the family group and the child's interaction in the home environment.
(f) An assessment of the child's integration within the family of the prospective adopter and the likelihood of the child's full integration into the family and community.
(g) Any other relevant information that might assist the court.

SECTION E: RECOMMENDATIONS

(a) The relative merits of adoption and other orders with an assessment of whether the child's long term interests would be best met by an adoption order or by other orders (such as child arrangements and special guardianship orders).
(b) Recommendations as to whether or not the order sought should be made (and, if not, alternative proposals).
(c) Recommendations as to whether there should be future contact arrangements (or not).

SECTION F: FURTHER INFORMATION FOR PROCEEDINGS RELATING TO CONVENTION ADOPTION ORDERS, CONVENTION ADOPTIONS, SECTION 84 ORDERS OR AN ADOPTION WHERE SECTION 83(1) OF THE 2002 ACT APPLIES.

(a) The child's knowledge of their racial and cultural origin.
(b) The likelihood of the child's adaptation to living in the country he/she is to be placed.
(c) Where the UK is the State of origin, reasons for considering that, after possibilities for placement of the child within the UK have been given due consideration, intercountry adoption is in the child's best interests.
(d) Confirmation that the requirements of regulations made under sections 83(4), (5), (6) and (7) and 84(3) and (6) of the 2002 Act have been complied with.
(e) For a Convention adoption or a Convention Adoption Order where the United Kingdom is either the State of origin or the receiving State, confirmation that the Central Authorities of both States have agreed that the adoption may proceed.

(f) Where the State of origin is not the United Kingdom, the documents supplied by the Central Authority of the State of origin should be attached to the report, together with translation if necessary.

(g) Where a Convention adoption order is proposed, details of the arrangements which were made for the transfer of the child to the UK and that they were in accordance with the Adoptions with a Foreign Element Regulations 2005 (S.I. 2005/392).

## ANNEX B – REPORT TO THE COURT WHERE THERE HAS BEEN AN APPLICATION FOR A PLACEMENT ORDER

Section A: The Report and Matters for the Proceedings

Section B: The Child and the Birth Family

Section C: Recommendations

### SECTION A: THE REPORT AND MATTERS FOR THE PROCEEDINGS

*Part 1*
*The report*

For each of the principal author/s of the report:

(i) name;
(ii) role in relation to this case;
(iii) section completed in this report;
(iv) qualifications and experience;
(v) name and address of the adoption agency; and
(vi) adoption agency case reference number.

*Part 2*
*Matters for the proceedings*

(a) Whether the adoption agency considers that any other person should be made a respondent or a party to the proceedings.
(b) Whether any of the respondents is under the age of 18.
(c) Whether a respondent is a person who, by reason of mental disorder within the meaning of the Mental Health Act 1983, is incapable of managing and administering his or her property and affairs. If so, medical evidence should be provided with particular regard to the effect on that person's ability to make decisions in the proceedings.

### SECTION B: THE CHILD AND THE BIRTH FAMILY

*Part 1*

*(i) Information about the child*

(a) Name, sex, date and place of birth and address including local authority area.
(b) Photograph and physical description.
(c) Nationality.

(d) Racial origin and cultural and linguistic background.
(e) Religious persuasion (including details of baptism, confirmation or equivalent ceremonies).
(f) Details of any siblings, half-siblings and step-siblings, including dates of birth.
(g) Whether the child is looked after by a local authority.
(h) Personality and social development, including emotional and behavioural development and any related needs.
(i) Details of interests, likes and dislikes.
(j) A summary, written by the agency's medical adviser, of the child's health history, his current state of health and any need for health care which is anticipated, and date of the most recent medical examination.
(k) Any known learning difficulties or known general medical or mental health factors which are likely to have, or may have, genetic implications.
(l) Names, addresses and types of nurseries or schools attended, with dates.
(m) Educational attainments.
(n) Any special needs in relation to the child (whether physical, learning, behavioural or any other) and his emotional and behavioural development.
(o) Whether the child is subject to a statement under the Education Act 1996.
(p) Previous orders concerning the child:
   (i) the name of the court;
   (ii) the order made; and
   (ii) the date of the order.
(q) Inheritance rights and any claim to damages under the Fatal Accidents Act 1976 the child stands to retain or lose if adopted.
(r) Any other relevant information which might assist the court.

*(ii) Information about each parent of the child*

(a) Name, date and place of birth and address (date on which last address was confirmed current) including local authority area.
(b) Photograph, if available, and physical description.
(c) Nationality.
(d) Racial origin and cultural and linguistic background.
(e) Whether the mother and father were married to each other at the time of the child's birth, or have subsequently married.
(f) Where the parent has been previously married or entered into a civil partnership, dates of those marriages or civil partnerships.
(g) Where the mother and father are not married, whether the father has parental responsibility and, if so, how it was acquired.
(h) If the identity or whereabouts of the father are not known, the information about him that has been ascertained and from whom, and the steps that have been taken to establish paternity.
(i) Past and present relationship with the other parent.
(j) Other information about the parent, where available:

(i) health, including any known learning difficulties or known general medical or mental health factors which are likely to have, or may have, genetic implications;
(ii) religious persuasion;
(iii) educational history;
(iv) employment history; and
(v) personality and interests.
(k) Any other relevant information which might assist the court.

## Part 2
### Relationships, contact arrangements and views

#### The child

(a) If the child is in the care of a local authority or voluntary organisation, or has been, details (including dates) of any placements with foster parents, or other arrangements in respect of the care of the child, including particulars of the persons with whom the child has had his home and observations on the care provided.
(b) The child's wishes and feelings (if appropriate, having regard to the child's age and understanding) about the application, its consequences, and adoption, including any wishes in respect of religious and cultural upbringing.
(c) The child's wishes and feelings in relation to contact (if appropriate, having regard to the child's age and understanding).
(d) The child's wishes and feelings recorded in any other proceedings.
(e) Date when the child's views were last ascertained.

#### The child's parents (or guardian) and relatives

(a) The parents' wishes and feelings about the application, its consequences, and adoption, including any wishes in respect of the child's religious and cultural upbringing.
(b) Each parent's (or guardian's) wishes and feelings in relation to contact.
(c) Date/s when the views of each parent or guardian were last ascertained.
(d) Arrangements concerning any siblings, including half-siblings and step-siblings, and whether any are the subject of a parallel application or have been the subject of any orders. If so, for each case give:
  (i) the name of the court;
  (ii) the order made, or (if proceedings are pending) the order applied for; and
  (iii) the date of order, or date of next hearing if proceedings are pending.
(e) Extent of contact with the child's mother and father and in each case the nature of the relationship enjoyed.
(f) The relationship which the child has with relatives, and with any other person considered relevant, including:
  (i) the likelihood of any such relationship continuing and the value to the child of its doing so; and

(ii) the ability and willingness of any of the child's relatives, or of any such person, to provide the child with a secure environment in which the child can develop, and otherwise to meet the child's needs.
(g) The wishes and feelings of any of the child's relatives, or of any such person, regarding the child.
(h) Dates when the views of members of the child's wider family and any other relevant person were last ascertained.

*Part 3*
*Summary of the actions of the adoption agency*

(a) Brief account of the Agency's actions in the case, with particulars and dates of all written information and notices given to the child and his parents and any person with parental responsibility.
(b) If consent has been given for the child to be placed for adoption, and also consent for the child to be adopted, the names of those who gave consent and the date such consents were given. If such consents were subsequently withdrawn, the dates of these withdrawals.
(c) If any statement has been made under section 20(4)(a) of the 2002 Act that a parent or guardian does not wish to be informed of any application for an adoption order, the names of those who have made such statements and the dates the statements were made. If such statements were subsequently withdrawn, the dates of these withdrawals.
(d) Details of the support and advice given to the parents and any services offered or taken up.
(e) If the father does not have parental responsibility, details of the steps taken to inform him of the application for a placement order.
(f) Brief details and dates of assessments of the child's needs, including expert opinions.
(g) Reasons for considering that adoption would be in the child's best interests (with date of relevant decision and reasons for any delay in implementing the decision).

**SECTION C: RECOMMENDATIONS**

(a) The relative merits of a placement order and other orders (such as a child arrangements or special guardianship order) with an assessment of why the child's long term interests are likely to be best met by a placement order rather than by any other order.
(b) Recommendations as to whether there should be future contact arrangements (or not), including whether a contact order under section 26 of the 2002 Act should be made.

## PRACTICE DIRECTION 14D – REPORTS BY A REGISTERED MEDICAL PRACTITIONER ('HEALTH REPORTS')

This Practice Direction supplements FPR Part 14, rule 14.12(2)

### Matters to be contained in health reports

1.1 Rule 14.12(1) requires that health reports must be attached to an application for an adoption order or a section 84 order except where:

(a) the child was placed for adoption with the applicant by an adoption agency;
(b) the applicant or one of the applicants is a parent of the child; or
(c) the applicant is the partner of a parent of the child.

1.2 The matters to be contained in the health reports are set out in the Annex to this Practice Direction.

1.3 Where a matter to be contained in the health report does not apply to the circumstances of a particular case, the reasons for not covering the matter should be given.

### ANNEX – CONTENTS OF HEALTH REPORTS

This information is required for reports on the health of children and their prospective adopter(s). Its purpose is to build up a full picture of each child's health history and current state of health, including strengths and weaknesses. This will enable local authorities' medical adviser to base their advice to the court on the fullest possible information when commenting on the health implications of the proposed adoption. The reports made by the examining doctor should cover, as far as practicable, the following matters.

### 1 The child

Name, date of birth, sex, weight and height.

A A health history of each natural parent, so far as is possible, including:

(i) name, date of birth, sex, weight and height;
(ii) a family health history, covering the parents, the brothers and sisters and the other children of the natural parent, with details of any serious physical or mental illness and inherited and congenital disease;
(iii) past health history, including details of any serious physical or mental illness, disability, accident, hospital admission or attendance at an out-patient department, and in each case any treatment given;
(iv) a full obstetric history of the mother, including any problems in the ante-natal, labour and post-natal periods, with the results of any tests carried out during or immediately after pregnancy;
(v) details of any present illness including treatment and prognosis;
(vi) any other relevant information which might assist the medical adviser; and

(vii) the name and address of any doctor(s) who might be able to provide further information about any of the above matters.

B A neo-natal report on the child, including:
   (i) details of the birth, and any complications;
   (ii) results of a physical examination and screening tests;
   (iii) details of any treatment given;
   (iv) details of any problem in management and feeding;
   (v) any other relevant information which might assist the medical adviser; and
   (vi) the name and address of any doctor(s) who might be able to provide further information about any of the above matters.

C A full health history and examination of the child, including:
   (i) details of any serious illness, disability, accident, hospital admission or attendance at an out-patient department, and in each case any treatment given;
   (ii) details and dates of immunisations;
   (iii) a physical and developmental assessment according to age, including an assessment of vision and hearing and of neurological, speech and language development and any evidence of emotional or conduct disorder;
   (iv) details, if relevant, of the impact of any addiction or substance use on the part of the natural mother before, during or following the pregnancy, and its impact or likely future impact on the child;
   (v) the impact, if any, on the child's development and likely future development of any past exposure to physical, emotional or sexual abuse or neglectful home conditions and/or any non-organic failure to thrive;
   (vi) for a child of school age, the school health history (if available);
   (vii) any other relevant information which might assist the medical adviser; and
   (viii) the name and address of any doctor(s) who might be able to provide further information about any of the above matters.

D The signature, name, address and qualifications of the registered medical practitioner who prepared the report, and the date of the report and of the examinations carried out.

## 2 The applicant

(If there is more than one applicant, a report on each applicant should be supplied covering all the matters listed below.)

A

   (i) name, date of birth, sex, weight and height;
   (ii) a family health history, covering the parents, the brothers and sisters and the children of the applicant, with details of any serious physical or mental illness and inherited and congenital disease;

(iii) marital history, including (if applicable) reasons for inability to have children, and any history of domestic violence;
(iv) past health history, including details of any serious physical or mental illness, disability, accident, hospital admission or attendance at an out-patient department, and in each case any treatment given;
(v) obstetric history (if applicable);
(vi) details of any present illness, including treatment and prognosis;
(vii) a full medical examination;
(viii) details of any consumption of alcohol, tobacco and habit-forming drugs;
(ix) any other relevant information which might assist the medical adviser; and
(x) the name and address of any doctor(s) who might be able to provide further information about any of the above matters.

B The signature, name, address and qualifications of the registered medical practitioner who prepared the report, and the date of the report and of the examinations carried out.

### PRACTICE DIRECTION 14E – COMMUNICATION OF INFORMATION RELATING TO PROCEEDINGS

This Practice Direction supplements FPR Part 14, rule 14.14(b)

#### Communication of information relating to proceedings

1.1 Rule 14.14 deals with the communication of information (whether or not it is recorded in any form) relating to proceedings.

1.2 Subject to any direction of the court, information may be communicated for the purposes of the law relating to contempt in accordance with paragraphs 1.3 or 1.4.

1.3 A person specified in the first column of the following table may communicate to a person listed in the second column such information as is specified in the third column for the purpose or purposes specified in the fourth column.

#### Communication of information without permission of the court

| Communicated by | To | Information | Purpose |
| --- | --- | --- | --- |
| A party | A lay adviser or a McKenzie Friend | Any information relating to the proceedings | To enable the party to obtain advice or assistance in relation to the proceedings. |

| | | | |
|---|---|---|---|
| A party | The party's spouse, civil partner, cohabitant or close family member | | For the purpose of confidential discussions enabling the party to receive support from his spouse, civil partner, cohabitant or close family member. |
| A party | A health care professional or a person or body providing counselling services for children or families | | To enable the party or any child of the party to obtain health care or counselling. |
| A party | The Secretary of State, a McKenzie Friend, a lay adviser or an appeal tribunal dealing with an appeal made under section 20 of the Child Support Act 1991 | | For the purposes of making or responding to an appeal under section 20 of the Child Support Act 1991 or the determination of such an appeal. |

| | | | |
|---|---|---|---|
| A party or other person lawfully in receipt of information | The Secretary of State, a McKenzie Friend, a lay adviser or the Upper Tier Tribunal dealing with an appeal under section 24 of the Child Support Act 1991 in respect of a decision of the First-tier Tribunal that was made under section 20 of that Act | | For a purpose connected with an appeal under section 24 of the Child Support Act 1991 in respect of a decision of the First-tier Tribunal that was made under section 20 of that Act |
| A party | An adoption panel | | To enable the adoption panel to discharge its functions as appropriate. |
| A party | A local authority's medical adviser appointed under the Adoption Agencies Regulations 2005 or the Adoption Agencies (Wales) Regulations 2005 | | To enable the medical adviser to discharge his or her functions as appropriate |
| A party or any person lawfully in receipt of information | The Children's Commissioner or the Children's Commissioner for Wales | | To refer an issue affecting the interests of children to the Children's Commissioner or the Children's Commissioner for Wales. |

| | | | |
|---|---|---|---|
| A party or a legal representative | A mediator | | For the purpose of mediation in relation to the proceedings. |
| A party, any person lawfully in receipt of information or a proper officer | A person or body conducting an approved research project | | For the purpose of an approved research project. |
| A party, a legal representative or a professional legal adviser | A person or body responsible for investigating or determining complaints in relation to legal representatives or professional legal advisers | | For the purposes of making a complaint or the investigation or determination of a complaint in relation to a legal representative or a professional legal adviser. |
| A legal representative or a professional legal adviser | A professional indemnity insurer | | To enable the professional indemnity insurer to be notified of a claim or complaint, or potential claim or complaint, in relation to the legal representative or a professional legal adviser, and the legal representative or professional legal adviser to obtain advice in respect of that claim or complaint |
| A legal representative or a professional legal adviser | A person or body assessing quality assurance systems | | To enable the legal representative or professional legal adviser to obtain a quality assurance assessment. |

| A legal representative or a professional legal adviser | An accreditation body | Any information relating to the proceedings providing that it does not, or is not likely to, identify any person involved in the proceedings | To enable the legal representative or professional legal adviser to obtain accreditation. |
|---|---|---|---|
| A party | An elected representative or peer | The text or summary of the whole or part of a judgment given in the proceedings | To enable the elected representative or peer to give advice, investigate any complaint or raise any question of policy or procedure. |
| A party | The General Medical Council | | For the purpose of making a complaint to the General Medical Council. |
| A party | A police officer | | For the purpose of a criminal investigation. |
| A party or any person lawfully in receipt of information | A member of the Crown Prosecution Service | | To enable the Crown Prosecution Service to discharge its functions under any enactment. |

1.4 A person in the second column of the table in paragraph 1.3 may only communicate information relating to the proceedings received from a person in the first column for the purpose or purposes:

(a) for which he received that information, or
(b) of professional development or training, providing that any communication does not, or is not likely to, identify any person involved in the proceedings without that person's consent.

1.5 In this Practice Direction:

(1) 'accreditation body' means:

(a) The Law Society,
(b) Resolution, or
(c) the Lord Chancellor in exercise of the Lord Chancellor's functions in relation to legal aid;
(1A) 'adoption panel' means a panel established in accordance with regulation 3 of the Adoption Agencies Regulations 2005 or regulation 3 of the Adoption Agencies (Wales) Regulations 2005;
(2) 'approved research project' means a project of research:
(a) approved in writing by a Secretary of State after consultation with the President of the Family Division,
(b) approved in writing by the President of the Family Division, or
(c) conducted under section 83 of the Act of 1989 or section 13 of the Criminal Justice and Court Services Act 2000;
(3) 'body assessing quality assurance systems' includes:
(a) The Law Society,
(b) the Lord Chancellor in exercise of the Lord Chancellor's functions in relation to legal aid, or
(c) The General Council of the Bar;
(4) 'body or person responsible for investigating or determining complaints in relation to legal representatives or professional legal advisers' means:
(a) The Law Society,
(b) The General Council of the Bar,
(c) The Institute of Legal Executives, or
(d) The Legal Services Ombudsman;
(5) 'cohabitant' means one of two persons who are neither married to each other nor civil partners of each other but are living together as husband and wife or as if they were civil partners;
(6) 'criminal investigation' means an investigation conducted by police officers with a view to it being ascertained:
(a) whether a person should be charged with an offence, or
(b) whether a person charged with an offence is guilty of it;
(7) 'elected representative' means:
(a) a member of the House of Commons,
(b) a member of the National Assembly for Wales, or
(c) a member of the European Parliament elected in England and Wales;
(8) 'health care professional' means:
(a) a registered medical practitioner,
(b) a registered nurse or midwife,
(c) a clinical psychologist, or
(d) a child psychotherapist;
(9) 'lay adviser' means a non-professional person who gives lay advice on behalf of an organisation in the lay advice sector;
(10) 'McKenzie Friend' means any person permitted by the court to sit beside an unrepresented litigant in court to assist that litigant by prompting, taking notes and giving him advice;
(11) 'mediator' means a family mediator who is:

(a) undertaking, or has successfully completed, a family mediation training course approved by the United Kingdom College of Family Mediators, or
(b) a member of the Law Society's Family Mediation Panel;
(12) 'peer' means a member of the House of Lords as defined by the House of Lords Act 1999.

## PRACTICE DIRECTION 14F –
## DISCLOSING INFORMATION TO AN ADOPTED ADULT

This Practice Direction supplements FPR Part 14, rule 14.18(1)(d)

### How to request for information

1.1 Rule 14.18 states that an adopted person who is over the age of 18 has the right to receive from the court which made the adoption order a copy of:
(a) the application form for an adoption order (but not the documents attached to that form);
(b) the adoption order and any other orders relating to the adoption proceedings; and
(c) orders allowing any person contact with the child after the adoption order was made.

1.2 An application under rule 14.18 must be made in form A64 which is contained in the practice direction supplementing rule 5 and must have attached to it a full certified copy of the entry in the Adopted Children Register relating to the applicant.

1.3 The completed application form must be taken to the court which made the adoption order along with evidence of the applicant's identity showing a photograph and signature, such as a passport or driving licence.

### Additional documents that the adopted person is also entitled to receive from the court

2 The adopted adult is also entitled to receive the following documents:
(a) any transcript or written reasons of the court's decision; and
(b) a report made to the court by:
(i) a children's guardian, reporting officer or children and family reporter;
(ii) a local authority; or
(iii) an adoption agency.

### Before the documents are sent to the adopted adult

3 The court will remove protected information from documents before they are sent to the adopted adult.

# APPENDIX 5

# CARE PLANNING, PLACEMENT AND CASE REVIEW (ENGLAND) REGULATIONS 2010, SI 2010/959

## PART 1
### GENERAL

**1 Citation and commencement**

(1) These Regulations may be cited as the Care Planning, Placement and Case Review (England) Regulations 2010 and come into force on 1 April 2011.

(2) These Regulations apply in relation to England only.

**2 Interpretation**

(1) In these Regulations –

'the 1989 Act' means the Children Act 1989;
'the 2012 Act' means the Legal Aid, Sentencing and Punishment of Offenders Act 2012;
'the Fostering Services Regulations' means the Fostering Services (England) Regulations 2011;
'appropriate person' means –
    (a) P, where C is to live, or lives, with P;
    (b) F, where C is to be placed, or is placed, with F;
    (c) where C is to be placed, or is placed, in a children's home, the person who is registered under Part 2 of the Care Standards Act 2000 in respect of that home; or
    (d) where C is to be placed, or is placed, in accordance with other arrangements under section 22C(6)(d), the person who will be responsible for C at the accommodation;
'area authority' means the local authority for the area in which C is placed, or is to be placed, where this is different from the responsible authority;
'C' means a child who is looked after by the responsible authority;
'care plan' means the plan for the future care of C prepared in accordance with Part 2;
'case record' has the meaning given in regulation 49;
'connected person' has the meaning given in regulation 24;
'detention placement plan' has the meaning given in regulation 47C;
'director' means the person in charge of a secure training centre;

'director of children's services' means the officer of the responsible authority appointed for the purposes of section 18 of the Children Act 2004;

'F' means a person who is approved as a local authority foster parent and with whom it is proposed to place C or, as the case may be, with whom C is placed;

'fostering service provider' has the meaning given in regulation 2(1) of the Fostering Services Regulations;

'full assessment process' has the meaning given in regulation 24(2)(c);

'governor' means the person in charge of a young offender institution;

'health plan' has the meaning given in regulation 5(b)(i);

'independent visitor' means the independent person appointed to be C's visitor under section 23ZB;

'IRO' means the independent reviewing officer appointed for C's case under section 25A(1);

'long term foster placement' means an arrangement made by the responsible authority for C to be placed with F where –
- (a) C's plan for permanence is foster care,
- (b) F has agreed to act as C's foster parent until C ceases to be looked after, and
- (c) the responsible authority has confirmed the nature of the arrangement to F, P and C,

and any reference to the responsible authority placing C in such a placement includes, where C is already placed with F, leaving C with F in a long term foster placement;

'nominated officer' means a senior officer of the responsible authority nominated in writing by the director of children's services for the purposes of these Regulations;

'P' means –
- (a) a person who is C's parent;
- (b) a person who is not C's parent but who has parental responsibility for C; or
- (c) where C is in the care of the responsible authority and there was a child arrangements order which regulated C's living arrangements in force immediately before the care order was made, a person named in the child arrangements order as a person with whom C was to live;

'pathway plan' has the meaning given in section 23E(1)(a);

'personal adviser' means the personal adviser arranged for C under paragraph 19C of Schedule 2 to the 1989 Act;

'personal education plan' has the meaning given in regulation 5(b)(ii);

'placement' means –
- (i) arrangements made by the responsible authority for C to live with P in accordance with section 22C(2), where C is in the care of the responsible authority, or
- (ii) arrangements made by the responsible authority to provide for C's accommodation and maintenance by any of the means specified in section 22C(6);

'placement plan' has the meaning given in regulation 9(1)(a);
'plan for permanence' has the meaning given in regulation 5(1)(a);
'R' means the representative of the responsible authority who is appointed to visit C in accordance with arrangements made by them under section 23ZA;
'registered manager' means the person who is registered under Part 2 of the Care Standards Act 2000 as a manager of a secure children's home;
'remand to local authority accommodation' has the meaning given in section 91(3) of the 2012 Act;
'remand to youth detention accommodation' has the meaning given in section 91(4) of the 2012 Act;
'responsible authority' means the local authority that looks after C;
'secure children's home' has the meaning given in section 102(11) of the 2012 Act;
'secure training centre' has the meaning given in section 43(1)(d) of the Prison Act 1952;
'special educational needs' and 'special educational provision' have the meanings given in section 579 of the Education Act 1996;
'temporary approval' has the meaning given in regulation 24(1); and
'working day' means any day other than –

    (a)   a Saturday or a Sunday,
    (b)   Christmas day or Good Friday, or
    (c)   a bank holiday in England and Wales under the Banking and Financial Dealings Act 1971.

'young offender institution' has the meaning given in section 43(1)(aa) of the Prison Act 1952.

(2) In these Regulations any reference to any document or other record includes any such document or record that is kept or provided in a readily accessible form and includes copies of original documents and electronic methods of recording information.

(3) Save as otherwise appears –

    (a)   any reference in these Regulations to a numbered section is a reference to that section in the 1989 Act; and
    (b)   any reference in these Regulations to a numbered regulation, Part or Schedule is a reference to that regulation, Part or Schedule in these Regulations.

Amendments—SI 2011/581; SI 2013/706; SI 2014/852; SI 2014/2103; SI 2015/495.

## 3

These Regulations do not apply in relation to any child who is looked after by a local authority and who has been placed for adoption under the Adoption and Children Act 2002 unless the child falls within regulation 47A.

Amendments—SI 2013/706.

## PART 2
## ARRANGEMENTS FOR LOOKING AFTER A CHILD

### 4 Care planning

(1) Where C is not in the care of the responsible authority and a care plan for C has not already been prepared, the responsible authority must assess C's needs for services to achieve or maintain a reasonable standard of health or development, and prepare such a plan.

(2) Except in the case of a child to whom section 31A (care orders: care plans) applies, or where paragraph (6) applies, the care plan must be prepared before C is first placed by the responsible authority or, if it is not practicable to do so, within ten working days of the start of the first placement.

(3) When assessing C's needs under paragraph (1), the responsible authority must consider whether C's placement meets the requirements of Part 3 of the 1989 Act.

(4) Unless paragraph (5) applies, the care plan should, so far as is reasonably practicable, be agreed by the responsible authority with –

(a) any parent of C's and any person who is not C's parent but who has parental responsibility for C, or
(b) if there is no such person, the person who was caring for C immediately before the responsible authority arranged a placement for C.

(5) Where C is aged 16 or over and agrees to be provided with accommodation under section 20, the care plan should be agreed with C by the responsible authority.

(6) Where C was first placed by the responsible authority before 1 April 2011, the care plan must be prepared as soon as reasonably practicable.

### 5 Preparation and content of the care plan

(1) The care plan must include a record of the following information –

(a) the long term plan for C's upbringing ('the plan for permanence'),
(b) the arrangements made by the responsible authority to meet C's needs in relation to –
 (i) health, including the information set out in paragraph 1 of Schedule 1 ('the health plan'),
 (ii) education and training, including, so far as reasonably practicable, the information set out in paragraph 2 of Schedule 1 ('the personal education plan'),
 (iii) emotional and behavioural development,
 (iv) identity, with particular regard to C's religious persuasion, racial origin and cultural and linguistic background,
 (v) family and social relationships and in particular the information set out in paragraph 3 of Schedule 1,
 (vi) social presentation, and

(vii) self-care skills,
(c) except in a case where C is in the care of the responsible authority but is not provided with accommodation by them by any of the means specified in section 22C, the placement plan,
(d) the name of the IRO, and
(e) details of the wishes and feelings of the persons listed in section 22(4) about the arrangements referred to in sub-paragraph (b) and the placement plan that have been ascertained and considered in accordance with section 22(4) and (5) and the wishes and feelings of those persons in relation to any change, or proposed change, to the care plan.
(f) where C is –
  (i) a victim, or there is reason to believe C may be a victim, of trafficking in human beings within the meaning of the Council of Europe Convention on Action against Trafficking in Human Beings,
  (ii) an unaccompanied asylum seeking child within the meaning of the Immigration Rules and has applied, or has indicated to the responsible authority an intention to apply, for asylum and has not been granted indefinite leave to remain,
that fact.

(2) In this regulation 'Immigration Rules' means the rules for the time being laid down by the Secretary of State as mentioned in section 3(2) of the Immigration Act 1971.

Amendments—SI 2014/1917.

## 6

(1) The responsible authority must keep C's care plan under review in accordance with Part 6 and, if they are of the opinion some change is required, they must revise the care plan or prepare a new care plan accordingly.

(2) Save as otherwise provided in these Regulations, the responsible authority must not make any significant change to the care plan unless the proposed change has first been considered at a review of C's case.

(3) Subject to paragraph (4), the responsible authority must give a copy of the care plan –

(a) to C, unless it would not be appropriate to do so having regard to C's age and understanding,
(b) to P,
(c) to the IRO,
(d) where C is to be placed, or is placed, with F, to the fostering service provider that approved F in accordance with the Fostering Services Regulations,
(e) where C is to be placed, or is placed, in a children's home, to the person who is registered under Part 2 of the Care Standards Act 2000 in respect of that home, and

(f) where C is to be placed, or is placed, in accordance with other arrangements under section 22C(6)(d), to the person who will be responsible for C at the accommodation.

(4) The responsible authority may decide not to give a copy of the care plan, or a full copy of the care plan, to P if to do so would put C at risk of significant harm.

Amendments—SI 2011/581.

## 7 Health care

(1) Before C is first placed by them or, if that is not reasonably practicable, before the first review of C's case, the responsible authority must make arrangements for a registered medical practitioner to –

(a) carry out an assessment of C's state of health, and
(b) provide a written report of the assessment, addressing the matters specified in paragraph 1 of Schedule 1,

as soon as reasonably practicable.

(2) Paragraph (1) does not apply if, within a period of three months immediately preceding the placement, an assessment of C's state of health has been carried out and the responsible authority has obtained a written report that meets the requirements of that paragraph.

(3) The responsible authority must make arrangements for a registered medical practitioner or a registered nurse or registered midwife acting under the supervision of a registered medical practitioner to review C's state of health and provide a written report of each review, addressing the matters specified in paragraph 1 of Schedule 1 –

(a) at least once in every period of six months before C's fifth birthday, and
(b) at least once in every period of 12 months after C's fifth birthday.

(4) Paragraphs (1) and (3) do not apply if C refuses consent to the assessment, being of sufficient age and understanding to do so.

(5) The responsible authority must take all reasonable steps to ensure that C is provided with appropriate health care services, in accordance with the health plan, including –

(a) medical and dental care and treatment, and
(b) advice and guidance on health, personal care and health promotion issues.

## 8ZA Contact with a child in care

When considering whether contact between C and any of the persons mentioned in paragraphs (a) to (d) of section 34(1) of the 1989 Act is consistent with safeguarding and promoting C's welfare, the responsible authority must have regard to C's care plan.

Amendments—Inserted by SI 2014/1556.

## 8 Contact with a child in care

(1) This regulation applies if C is in the care of the responsible authority and they have decided under section 34(6) (refusal of contact as a matter of urgency) to refuse to allow contact that would otherwise be required by virtue of section 34(1) or an order under section 34 (parental contact etc. with children in care).

(2) The responsible authority must immediately give written notification to the following persons of the information specified in paragraph (3) ('the specified information') –

- (a) C, unless it would not be appropriate to do so having regard to C's age and understanding,
- (b) P,
- (c) where, immediately before the care order was made, a person had care of C by virtue of an order made in exercise of the High Court's inherent jurisdiction with respect to children, that person,
- (d) any other person whose wishes and feelings the responsible authority consider to be relevant, and
- (e) the IRO.

(3) The specified information is –

- (a) the responsible authority's decision,
- (b) the date of the decision,
- (c) the reasons for the decision,
- (d) the duration of the decision (if applicable), and
- (e) remedies available in case of dissatisfaction.

(4) The responsible authority may depart from the terms of any order made under section 34 by agreement with the person in relation to whom the order is made, provided that –

- (a) C, being of sufficient age and understanding, also agrees, and
- (b) written notification of the specified information is given within five working days to the persons listed in paragraph (2).

(5) Where the responsible authority has decided to vary or suspend any arrangements made (otherwise than under an order under section 34) with a view to affording any person contact with C, the responsible authority must immediately give written notification containing the specified information to the persons listed in paragraph (2).

(6) The responsible authority must record any decision made under this regulation in C's care plan.

## PART 3
## PLACEMENTS – GENERAL PROVISIONS

### 9 Placement plan

(1) Subject to paragraphs (2) and (4), before making arrangements in accordance with section 22C for C's placement, the responsible authority must –

    (a) prepare a plan for the placement ('the placement plan') which –
        (i) sets out how the placement will contribute to meeting C's needs, and
        (ii) includes all the matters specified in Schedule 2 as are applicable, having regard to the type of the placement, and
    (b) ensure that –
        (i) C's wishes and feelings have been ascertained and given due consideration, and
        (ii) the IRO has been informed.

(2) If it is not reasonably practicable to prepare the placement plan before making the placement, the placement plan must be prepared within five working days of the start of the placement.

(3) The placement plan must be agreed with, and signed by, the appropriate person.

(4) Where the arrangements for C's placement were made before 1 April 2011, the responsible authority must prepare the placement plan as soon as reasonably practicable.

### 10 Avoidance of disruption in education

(1) Subject to paragraphs (2) and (3), if C is a registered pupil at a school in the fourth key stage, a decision to make any change to C's placement that would have the effect of disrupting the arrangements made for C's education must not be put into effect until it has been approved by a nominated officer.

(2) Before approving a decision under paragraph (1), the nominated officer must be satisfied that –

    (a) the requirements of regulation 9(1)(b)(i) have been complied with,
    (b) the educational provision made for C at the placement will promote C's educational achievement and is consistent with C's personal education plan,
    (c) the designated teacher at the school has been consulted, and
    (d) the IRO has been consulted.

(3) Paragraph (1) does not apply in any case where –

    (a) the responsible authority terminates C's placement in accordance with regulation 14(3), or
    (b) it is necessary for any other reason to change C's placement in an emergency,

and in such a case the responsible authority must make appropriate arrangements to promote C's educational achievement as soon as reasonably practicable.

(4) In any case not falling within paragraph (1), but where the responsible authority propose making any change to C's placement that would have the effect of disrupting the arrangements made for C's education or training, the responsible authority must ensure that other arrangements are made for C's education or training that meet C's needs and are consistent with C's personal education plan.

(5) In this regulation –

(a) 'registered pupil' has the meaning given in section 20(7) of the Children and Young Persons Act 2008, and
(b) 'school' has the meaning given in section 4 of the Education Act 1996.

## Placement out of Area

### 11 Placement decision

(1) Subject to paragraphs (2) to (4), a decision to place C outside the area of the responsible authority (including a placement outside England) –

(a) must not be put into effect until it has been approved by a nominated officer, or
(b) in the case of a proposed placement which is also at a distance, must not be put into effect until it has been approved by the director of children's services.

(2) Before approving a decision under paragraph (1), the nominated officer or, as the case may be, the director of children's services must be satisfied that –

(a) the requirements of regulation 9(1)(b)(i) have been complied with,
(b) the placement is the most appropriate placement available for C and consistent with C's care plan,
(c) C's relatives have been consulted, where appropriate,
(d) in the case of a decision falling within -
   (i) paragraph (1)(a), the area authority have been notified, or
   (ii) paragraph (1)(b), the area authority have been consulted and have been provided with a copy of C's care plan, and
(e) the IRO has been consulted.

(3) In the case of a placement made in an emergency, paragraph (2) does not apply and before approving a decision under paragraph (1) the nominated officer must –

(a) be satisfied that regulation 9(1)(b)(i) and the requirements of sub-paragraph (2)(b) have been complied with, and
(b) take steps to ensure that regulation 9(1)(b)(ii) and the requirements set out in sub-paragraphs (2)(c) and (d) are complied with by the responsible authority within five working days of approval of the decision under paragraph (1).

(4) Paragraphs (1) and (2) do not apply to a decision to place C outside the area of the responsible authority with –

(a) F who is a connected person, or
(b) F who is approved as a local authority foster parent by the responsible authority.

(5) In this regulation 'at a distance' means outside the area of the responsible authority and not within the area of any adjoining local authority.

Amendments—SI 2013/3239.

## 12 Placements outside England and Wales

(1) This regulation applies if –

(a) C is in the care of the responsible authority, and
(b) the responsible authority make arrangements to place C outside England and Wales in accordance with the provisions of paragraph 19 of Schedule 2 to the 1989 Act (placement of a child in care outside England and Wales).

(2) The responsible authority must take steps to ensure that, so far as is reasonably practicable, requirements corresponding with the requirements which would have applied under these Regulations had C been placed in England, are complied with.

(3) The responsible authority must include in the care plan details of the arrangements made by the responsible authority to supervise C's placement.

## 13 Notification of placement

(1) Subject to paragraph (3), the responsible authority must give written notification to the persons listed in paragraph (2) of the arrangements for C's placement before the placement is made or, if the placement is made in an emergency, within five working days of the start of the placement, unless it is not reasonably practicable to do so.

(2) The persons referred to in paragraph (1) are –

(a) C, unless it would not be appropriate to do so having regard to C's age and understanding,
(b) P,
(c) if C is in the care of the responsible authority, any person who is allowed contact with C under section 34(1) and any person who has contact with C by virtue of an order under section 34,
(d) if C is looked after but is not in the care of the responsible authority, any person who has contact with C pursuant to an order made under section 8 (residence, contact and other orders with respect to children),
(e) any person who was caring for C immediately before the arrangements were made,
(f) the National Health Service Commissioning Board and the clinical commissioning group (or in the case of a child living or to be placed in

Wales, the local health board) for the area in which C is living and, if different, for the area in which C is to be placed,
- (g) C's registered medical practitioner and, where applicable, the registered medical practitioner with whom C is to be registered during the placement,
- (h) any educational institution attended by, or person providing education or training for, C, and
- (i) the IRO.

(3) The responsible authority may decide not to give notification to any of the persons listed in sub-paragraphs (b) to (e) if to do so would put C at risk of significant harm.

(4) In the case of a placement outside the area of the responsible authority (including a placement outside England) –

- (a) the responsible authority must give written notification to the area authority of the arrangements for C's placement before the placement is made or, if the placement is made in an emergency, within five working days of the start of the placement unless it is not reasonably practicable to do so, and
- (b) that notification must include –
    - (i) details of the responsible authority's assessment of C's needs and the reasons why the placement is the most suitable for responding to these,
    - (ii) a copy of C's care plan (where this has not already been provided to the area authority by virtue of regulation 11(2)(d)(ii)).

Amendments—SI 2013/235; SI 2013/3239.

## 14 Termination of placement by the responsible authority

(1) Subject to paragraphs (3) and (5), the responsible authority may only terminate C's placement following a review of C's case in accordance with Part 6.

(2) Subject to paragraphs (3) and (4), before terminating C's placement, the responsible authority must –

- (a) make other arrangements for C's accommodation, in accordance with section 22C,
- (b) inform the IRO,
- (c) so far as is reasonably practicable, give written notification of their intention to terminate the placement to –
    - (i) all the persons to whom notification of the placement was given under regulation 13,
    - (ii) the person with whom C is placed,
    - (iii) where C is placed in the area of another local authority, that authority.

(3) Where there is an immediate risk of significant harm to C, or to protect others from serious injury, the responsible authority must terminate C's placement, and in those circumstances –

(a) paragraph (1) does not apply, and
(b) they must comply with paragraph (2)(a) and (b) as soon as reasonably practicable.

(4) If it is not reasonably practicable to notify any person in accordance with paragraph (2)(c), then the responsible authority must give written notification to that person, within ten working days of the date on which the placement is terminated, of the fact that the placement has been terminated.

(5) This regulation does not apply where C's placement is terminated under regulation 19(c), regulation 23(2) or regulation 25(6), nor where section 22D (review of child's case before making alternative arrangements for accommodation) applies.

## PART 4
## PROVISION FOR DIFFERENT TYPES OF PLACEMENT

*Chapter 1;*
*Placement of a Child in Care with P*

### 15 Application

(1) This Chapter applies if C is in the care of the responsible authority and they, acting in accordance with section 22C(2), propose to place C with P.

(2) Nothing in this Chapter requires the responsible authority to remove C from P's care if C is living with P before a placement decision is made about C.

### 16 Effect of contact order

The responsible authority must not place C with P if to do so would be incompatible with any order made by the court under section 34.

### 17 Assessment of P's suitability to care for a child

Before deciding to place C with P, the responsible authority must –

(a) assess the suitability of P to care for C, including the suitability of –
   (i) the proposed accommodation, and
   (ii) all other persons aged 18 and over who are members of the household in which it is proposed that C will live,
(b) take into account all the matters set out in Schedule 3 in making their assessment,
(c) consider whether, in all the circumstances and taking into account the services to be provided by the responsible authority, the placement will safeguard and promote C's welfare and meet C's needs set out in the care plan, and
(d) review C's case in accordance with Part 6.

## 18 Decision to place a child with P

(1) The decision to place C with P must not be put into effect until it has been approved by a nominated officer, and the responsible authority have prepared a placement plan for C.

(2) Before approving a decision under paragraph (1), the nominated officer must be satisfied that –

- (a) the requirements of regulation 9(1)(b)(i) have been complied with,
- (b) the requirements of regulation 17 have been complied with,
- (c) the placement will safeguard and promote C's welfare, and
- (d) the IRO has been consulted.

## 19 Circumstances in which a child may be placed with P before assessment completed

Where the nominated officer considers it to be necessary and consistent with C's welfare, the responsible authority may place C with P before their assessment under regulation 17 ('the assessment') is completed provided that they –

- (a) arrange for P to be interviewed in order to obtain as much of the information specified in Schedule 3 about P and the other persons living in P's household who are aged 18 and over as can be readily ascertained at that interview,
- (b) ensure that the assessment and the review of C's case are completed in accordance with regulation 17 within ten working days of C being placed with P, and
- (c) ensure that a decision in accordance with regulation 18 is made and approved within ten working days after the assessment is completed, and –
  - (i) if the decision is to confirm the placement, review the placement plan and, if appropriate amend it, and
  - (ii) if the decision is not to confirm the placement, terminate the placement.

## 20 Support for P

Where C is placed, or is to be placed, with P, the responsible authority must provide such services and support to P as appear to them to be necessary to safeguard and promote C's welfare and must record details of such services and support in C's care plan.

*Chapter 2;*
*Placement with Local Authority Foster Parents*

## 21 Interpretation

(1) In this Chapter 'registered person' has the same meaning as in the Fostering Services Regulations.

(2) Where C is placed jointly with two persons each of whom is approved as a local authority foster parent, any reference in these Regulations to a local authority foster parent is to be interpreted as referring equally to both such persons and any requirement to be satisfied by or relating to a particular local authority foster parent must be satisfied by, or treated as relating to, both of them.

Amendments—SI 2011/581.

## 22 Conditions to be complied with before placing a child with a local authority foster parent

(1) This regulation applies where the responsible authority propose to place C with F.

(2) The responsible authority may only place C with F if –

- (a) F is approved by –
    - (i) the responsible authority, or
    - (ii) provided that the conditions specified in paragraph (3) are also satisfied, another fostering service provider,
- (b) the terms of F's approval are consistent with the proposed placement, and
- (c) F has entered into a foster care agreement either with the responsible authority or with another fostering service provider in accordance with regulation 27(5)(b) of the Fostering Services Regulations.

(3) The conditions referred to in paragraph (2)(a)(ii) are that –

- (a) the fostering service provider by whom F is approved consents to the proposed placement, and
- (b) where any other local authority currently have a child placed with F, that local authority consents to the proposed placement.

Amendments—SI 2011/581.

## 22A Placement following consideration in accordance with section 22C(9B)(c) of the Act

(1) This regulation applies where the responsible authority decides to place C in accordance with section 22C of the 1989 Act with a local authority foster parent who is also an approved prospective adopter following consideration in accordance with section 22C(9B)(c) of the 1989 Act.

(2) The decision to place C must not be put into effect until it has been approved by a nominated officer, and the responsible authority have prepared a placement plan for C.

(3) Before approving a decision under paragraph (2), the nominated officer must –

- (a) be satisfied that the placement is the most appropriate placement available for C and will safeguard and promote C's welfare;

(b) be satisfied that the requirements of regulation 9(1)(b) have been complied with; and

(c) if their whereabouts are known to the responsible authority, notify the parent or guardian of C of the proposed placement.

Amendments—Inserted by SI 2014/1556.

## 22B Conditions to be complied with before placing C in a long term foster placement

(1) This regulation applies where the responsible authority propose to place C with F in a long term foster placement.

(2) The responsible authority may only place C with F if –

(a) the responsible authority have prepared a placement plan for C,
(b) the requirements of regulation 9(1)(b)(i) have been complied with,
(c) the placement will safeguard and promote C's welfare,
(d) the IRO has been consulted,
(e) C's relatives have been consulted, where appropriate, and
(f) F intends to act as C's foster parent until C ceases to be looked after.

Amendments—Inserted by SI 2015/495.

## 23 Emergency placement with a local authority foster parent

(1) Where it is necessary to place C in an emergency, the responsible authority may place C with any local authority foster parent who has been approved in accordance with the Fostering Services Regulations, even if the terms of that approval are not consistent with the placement, provided that the placement is for no longer than six working days.

(2) When the period of six working days referred to in paragraph (1) expires, the responsible authority must terminate the placement unless the terms of that person's approval have been amended to be consistent with the placement.

Amendments—SI 2011/581.

## 24 Temporary approval of relative, friend or other person connected with C

(1) Where the responsible authority is satisfied that –

(a) the most appropriate placement for C is with a connected person, notwithstanding that the connected person is not approved as a local authority foster parent, and
(b) it is necessary for C to be placed with the connected person before the connected person's suitability to be a local authority foster parent has been assessed in accordance with the Fostering Services Regulations,

they may approve that person as a local authority foster parent for a temporary period not exceeding 16 weeks ('temporary approval') provided that they first comply with the requirements of paragraph (2).

(2) Before making a placement under paragraph (1), the responsible authority must -

(a) assess the suitability of the connected person to care for C, including the suitability of –
(i) the proposed accommodation, and
(ii) all other persons aged 18 and over who are members of the household in which it is proposed that C will live,
taking into account all the matters set out in Schedule 4,
(b) consider whether, in all the circumstances and taking into account the services to be provided by the responsible authority, the proposed arrangements will safeguard and promote C's welfare and meet C's needs set out in the care plan, and
(c) make immediate arrangements for the suitability of the connected person to be a local authority foster parent to be assessed in accordance with the Fostering Services Regulations ('the full assessment process') before the temporary approval expires.

(3) In this regulation 'connected person' means a relative, friend or other person connected with C.

Amendments—SI 2011/581.

## 25 Expiry of temporary approval

(1) Subject to paragraph (4), the responsible authority may extend the temporary approval of a connected person if –

(a) it is likely to expire before the full assessment process is completed, or
(b) the connected person, having undergone the full assessment process, is not approved and seeks a review of the decision in accordance with Regulations made under paragraph 12F(1)(b) of Schedule 2 to the 1989 Act.

(2) In a case falling within paragraph (1)(a), the responsible authority may extend the temporary approval once for a further period of up to eight weeks.

(3) In a case falling within paragraph (1)(b), the responsible authority may extend the temporary approval until the outcome of the review is known.

(4) Before deciding whether to extend the temporary approval in the circumstances set out in paragraph (1), the responsible authority must first –

(a) consider whether placement with the connected person is still the most appropriate placement available,
(b) seek the views of the fostering panel established by the fostering service provider in accordance with the Fostering Services Regulations, and
(c) inform the IRO.

(5) A decision to extend temporary approval must be approved by a nominated officer.

(6) If the period of temporary approval and of any extension to that period expires and the connected person has not been approved as a local authority

foster parent in accordance with the Fostering Services Regulations, the responsible authority must terminate the placement after first making other arrangements for C's accommodation.

Amendments—SI 2011/581.

## 25A Temporary approval of prospective adopter as foster parent

(1) Where the responsible authority is satisfied that –

(a) the most appropriate placement for C is with a person who is not approved as a local authority foster parent, but who is an approved prospective adopter, and

(b) it is in C's best interests to be placed with that person,

the responsible authority may approve that person as a local authority foster parent in relation to C for a temporary period ('temporary approval period') provided that the responsible authority first comply with the requirements of paragraph (2).

(2) Before approving an approved prospective adopter as a local authority foster parent under paragraph (1), the responsible authority must –

(a) assess the suitability of that person to care for C as a foster parent, and

(b) consider whether, in all the circumstances and taking into account the services to be provided by the responsible authority, the proposed arrangements will safeguard and promote C's welfare and meet C's needs set out in the care plan.

(3) The temporary approval period expires –

(a) on C's placement with the approved prospective adopter being terminated by the responsible authority,

(b) on the approved prospective adopter's approval as a prospective adopter being terminated,

(c) on the approved prospective adopter being approved as a foster parent in accordance with the Fostering Services Regulations,

(d) if the approved prospective adopter gives written notice to the responsible authority that they no longer wish to be temporarily approved as a foster parent in relation to C, with effect from 28 days from the date on which the notice is received by the responsible authority, or

(e) on C being placed for adoption with the approved prospective adopter in accordance with the Adoption and Children Act 2002.

(4) In this regulation 'approved prospective adopter' means a person who has been approved as suitable to adopt a child under the Adoption Agencies Regulations 2005 and whose approval has not been terminated.

Amendments—Inserted by SI 2013/984.

## 26 Independent fostering agencies – discharge of responsible authority functions

(1) A responsible authority may make arrangements in accordance with this regulation for the duties imposed on it as responsible authority by regulation 14(3) and regulation 22 to be discharged on their behalf by a registered person.

(2) No arrangements may be made under this regulation unless the responsible authority has entered into a written agreement with the registered person which includes the information set out in paragraph 1 of Schedule 5, and where the responsible authority proposes to make an arrangement under this regulation in relation to a particular child, the written agreement must also include the matters set out in paragraph 2 of Schedule 5.

(3) The responsible authority must report to the Chief Inspector of Education, Children's Services and Skills any concerns they may have about the services provided by a registered person.

## Chapter 3;
## Other Arrangements

## 27 General duties of the responsible authority when placing a child in other arrangements

Before placing C in accommodation in an unregulated setting under section 22C(6)(d), the responsible authority must –

- (a) be satisfied that the accommodation is suitable for C, having regard to the matters set out in Schedule 6,
- (b) unless it is not reasonably practicable, arrange for C to visit the accommodation, and
- (c) inform the IRO.

## PART 5
## VISITS BY THE RESPONSIBLE AUTHORITY'S REPRESENTATIVE ETC.

## 28 Frequency of visits

(1) As part of their arrangements for supervising C's welfare, the responsible authority must ensure that their representative ('R') visits C in accordance with this regulation, wherever C is living.

(2) Subject to paragraphs (3) to (6), the responsible authority must ensure that R visits C –

- (a) within one week of the start of any placement,
- (b) at intervals of not more than six weeks for the first year of any placement, and
- (c) thereafter –
    - (i) where the placement is intended to last until C is aged 18, at intervals of not more than three months,

(ii) and in any other case, at intervals of not more than six weeks.

(3) Where regulation 19 applies, the responsible authority must ensure that R visits C –

- (a) at least once a week until the first review carried out in accordance with Part 6, and
- (b) thereafter at intervals of not more than six weeks.

(3A) Where –

- (a) C is in a long term foster placement and has been in that placement for at least one year, and
- (b) C, being of sufficient age and understanding, agrees to be visited less frequently than required by paragraph (2)(c),

the responsible authority must ensure that R visits C at intervals of no more than 6 months.

(4) Where regulation 24 applies, or where an interim care order has been made in relation to C under section 38 (interim orders) and C is living with P, the responsible authority must ensure that R visits C –

- (a) at least once a week until the first review carried out in accordance with Part 6, and
- (b) thereafter at intervals of not more than four weeks.

(5) Where a care order has been made in relation to C under section 31 (care and supervision orders) and C is living with P, the responsible authority must ensure that R visits C –

- (a) within one week of the making of the care order, and
- (b) thereafter at intervals of not more than six weeks.

(6) Where C is in the care of the responsible authority but another person is responsible for the arrangements under which C is living for the time being ('C's living arrangements'), the responsible authority must ensure that R visits C –

- (a) within one week of the start of C's living arrangements and within one week of any change to C's living arrangements,
- (b) at intervals of not more than six weeks for the first year thereafter, and
- (c) at intervals of not more than three months in any subsequent year.

(7) In addition to visits in accordance with paragraphs (2) to (6), the responsible authority must ensure that R visits C –

- (a) whenever reasonably requested to do so by –
  - (i) C,
  - (ii) where paragraphs (2), (3), (3A) or (4) apply, the appropriate person, or
  - (iii) where paragraph (5) applies, the person responsible for C's living arrangements,
- (b) within one week of first receiving notification under section 30A of the Care Standards Act 2000 (notification of matters relating to persons

carrying on or managing certain establishments or agencies), where the children's home in which C is placed for the time being is referred to in that notification.

Amendments—SI 2015/495.

## 29 Conduct of visits

On each visit, R must speak to C in private unless –

(a) C, being of sufficient age and understanding to do so, refuses,
(b) R considers it inappropriate to do so, having regard to C's age and understanding, or
(c) R is unable to do so.

## 30 Consequences of visits

Where, as the result of a visit carried out in accordance with this Part, R's assessment is that C's welfare is not adequately safeguarded and promoted by the placement, the responsible authority must review C's case in accordance with Part 6.

## 31 Advice, support and assistance for the child

When making arrangements in accordance with section 23ZA(2)(b) for advice, support and assistance to be available to C between R's visits, the responsible authority must ensure that –

(a) the arrangements –
   (i) are appropriate having regard to C's age and understanding, and
   (ii) give due consideration to C's religious persuasion, racial origin, cultural and linguistic background and to any disability C may have, and
(b) so far as is reasonably practicable having regard to C's age and understanding, C knows how to seek appropriate advice, support and assistance from them.

## PART 6
## REVIEWS OF THE CHILD'S CASE

## 32 General duty of the responsible authority to review the child's case

(1) The responsible authority must review C's case in accordance with this Part.

(2) The responsible authority must not make any significant change to C's care plan unless the proposed change has first been considered at a review of C's case, unless this is not reasonably practicable.

(3) Nothing in this Part prevents any review of C's case being carried out at the same time as any other review assessment or consideration of C's case under any other provision.

## 33 Timing of reviews

(1) The responsible authority must first review C's case within 20 working days of the date on which C becomes looked after.

(2) The second review must be carried out not more than three months after the first, and subsequent reviews must be carried out at intervals of not more than six months.

(3) The responsible authority must carry out a review before the time specified in paragraph (1) or (2) if –

- (aa) the responsible authority considers that C is, or has been, persistently absent from a placement,
- (ab) the responsible authority is notified that the appropriate person, P, or the area authority is concerned that C is at risk of harm,
- (ac) subject to paragraph (4), C so requests,
- (a) the IRO so requests,
- (b) regulation 30 applies,
- (c) C is provided with accommodation under section 21(2)(b) or (c) and a review would not otherwise occur before C ceases to be so provided with accommodation,
- (d) C is in the care of the responsible authority and is detained in a secure training centre or a young offenders institution, and a review would not otherwise occur before C ceases to be so detained, or
- (e) C is looked after but is not in the care of the responsible authority and
  - (i) the responsible authority propose to cease to provide accommodation for C, and
  - (ii) accommodation will not subsequently be provided for C by C's parents (or one of them) or any person who is not C's parent but who has parental responsibility for C.

(4) The responsible authority is not required to carry out a review pursuant to sub-paragraph (3)(ac) if the IRO considers that a review before the time specified in paragraph (1) or (2) is not justified.

Amendments—SI 2013/3239.

## 34 Conduct of reviews

*Local authority's policy on reviews*

(1) The responsible authority must prepare and implement a written policy regarding the manner in which they will review cases in accordance with this Part.

(2) The responsible authority must provide a copy of their policy to –

- (a) C, unless it would not be appropriate to do so having regard to C's age and understanding,
- (b) C's parents, or any person who is not C's parent but who has parental responsibility for C, and

(c) any other person whose views the responsible authority consider to be relevant.

## 35 Considerations to which the responsible authority must have regard

The considerations to which the responsible authority must have regard in reviewing each case are set out in Schedule 7.

## 36 The role of the IRO

(1) The IRO must –

- (a) so far as reasonably practicable, attend any meeting held as part of the review ('the review meeting') and, if attending the review meeting, chair it,
- (b) speak to C in private about the matters to be considered at the review unless C, being of sufficient understanding to do so, refuses or the IRO considers it inappropriate having regard to C's age and understanding,
- (c) ensure that, so far as reasonably practicable, the wishes and feelings of C's parents, or any person who is not C's parent but who has parental responsibility for C, and the views of the appropriate person, have been ascertained and taken into account, and
- (d) ensure that the review is conducted in accordance with this Part and in particular –
  - (i) that the persons responsible for implementing any decision taken in consequence of the review are identified, and
  - (ii) that any failure to review the case in accordance with this Part or to take proper steps to implement decisions taken in consequence of the review are brought to the attention of an officer at an appropriate level of seniority within the responsible authority.

(2) The IRO may, if not satisfied that sufficient information has been provided by the responsible authority to enable proper consideration of any of the matters in Schedule 7, adjourn the review meeting once for not more than 20 working days, and no proposal considered in the course of the review may be implemented until the review has been completed.

Amendments—SI 2015/495.

## 37 Arrangements for implementing decisions arising out of reviews

The responsible authority must –

- (a) make arrangements to implement decisions made in the course, or as a result, of the review, and
- (b) inform the IRO of any significant failure to make such arrangements, or any significant change of circumstances occurring after the review that affects those arrangements.

### 38 Records of reviews

The responsible authority must ensure that a written record of the review is prepared, and that the information obtained in the course of the review, details of proceedings at the review meeting, and any decisions made in the course, or as a result, of the review are included in C's case record.

## PART 7
## ARRANGEMENTS MADE BY THE RESPONSIBLE AUTHORITY FOR CEASING TO LOOK AFTER A CHILD

### 39 Arrangements to be made when the responsible authority is considering ceasing to look after C

(1) This regulation applies where the responsible authority are considering ceasing to look after C.

(2) Before deciding to cease to look after C the responsible authority must –

- (a) carry out an assessment of the suitability of the proposed arrangements for C's accommodation and maintenance when C ceases to be looked after by them,
- (b) carry out an assessment of the services and support that C and, where applicable P, might need when the responsible authority ceases to look after C,
- (c) ensure that C's wishes and feelings have been ascertained and given due consideration, and
- (d) consider whether, in all the circumstances and taking into account any services or support the responsible authority intend to provide, that ceasing to look after C will safeguard and promote C's welfare.

(3) The responsible authority must include in C's care plan (or where regulation 47B(4) applies, the detention placement plan) details of the advice, assistance and support that the responsible authority intend to provide for C when C ceases to be looked after by them.

(4) Subject to paragraph (5), where C has been a looked after child for at least 20 working days, any decision to cease to look after C must not be put into effect until it has been approved by a nominated officer.

(5) In any case where C is aged 16 or 17 and is not in the care of the local authority, the decision to cease to look after C must not be put into effect until it has been approved by the responsible authority's director of children's services.

(6) Before approving a decision under paragraph (4) or (5), the nominated officer or director of children's services must be satisfied that –

- (a) the requirements of regulation 9(1)(b)(i) have been complied with,
- (b) ceasing to look after C will safeguard and promote C's welfare,
- (c) the support the responsible authority intend to provide will safeguard and promote C's welfare,
- (d) C's relatives have been consulted, where appropriate,

(e) the IRO has been consulted, and
(f) where appropriate, regulations 40 to 43 have been complied with.

**Amendments**—Last substituted by SI 2015/495.

## 40 Eligible children

*Meaning of eligible child*

(1) For the purposes of paragraph 19B(2)(b) of Schedule 2 to the 1989 Act (meaning of eligible child), the prescribed period is 13 weeks and the prescribed age is 14.

(2) For the purposes of paragraph 19B(3)(b) of that Schedule, if C is a child to whom regulation 48 applies, C is not an eligible child despite falling within paragraph 19B(2) of that Schedule.

## 41 General duties

If C is an eligible child, the responsible authority must –

(a) assess C's needs in accordance with regulation 42, and
(b) prepare C's pathway plan, in accordance with regulation 43.

## 42 Assessment of needs

(1) The responsible authority must complete the assessment of C's needs in accordance with paragraph 19B(4) of Schedule 2 to the 1989 Act not more than three months after the date on which C reaches the age of 16 or becomes an eligible child after that age.

(2) In carrying out their assessment of C's likely needs when C ceases to be looked after, the responsible authority must take account of the following considerations –

(a) C's state of health (including physical, emotional and mental health) and development,
(b) C's continuing need for education, training or employment,
(ba) where C falls within regulation 5(1)(f), any needs C has as a result of that status,
(c) the support that will be available to C from C's parents and other connected persons,
(d) C's actual and anticipated financial resources and capacity to manage personal finances independently,
(e) the extent to which C possesses the practical and other skills necessary for independent living,
(f) C's need for continuing care, support and accommodation,
(g) the wishes and feelings of –
(i) C,
(ii) any parent of C's and any person who is not C's parent but who has parental responsibility for C,
(iii) the appropriate person,

(h) the views of –
   (i) any person or educational institution that provides C with education or training and, if C has a statement of special educational needs, the local authority who maintain the statement (if different),
   (ii) the IRO,
   (iii) any person providing health (whether physical, emotional or mental health) or dental care or treatment to C,
   (iv) the personal adviser appointed for C, and
   (v) any other person whose views the responsible authority, or C, consider may be relevant.

Amendments—SI 2014/1917.

## 43 The pathway plan

(1) The pathway plan must be prepared as soon as possible after the assessment of C's needs and must include, in particular –

(a) C's care plan, and
(b) the information referred to in Schedule 8.

(2) The pathway plan must, in relation to each of the matters referred to in paragraphs 2 to 10 of Schedule 8, set out –

(a) the manner in which the responsible authority propose to meet C's needs, and
(b) the date by which, and by whom, any action required to implement any aspect of the plan will be carried out.

## 44 Functions of the personal adviser

The personal adviser's functions in relation to C are to –

(a) provide advice (including practical advice) and support,
(b) participate in reviews of C's case carried out under Part 6,
(c) liaise with the responsible authority in the implementation of the pathway plan,
(d) co-ordinate the provision of services and take reasonable steps to ensure C makes use of such services,
(e) remain informed about C's progress and wellbeing, and
(f) maintain a written record of their contacts with C.

## PART 8
## INDEPENDENT REVIEWING OFFICERS AND INDEPENDENT VISITORS

## 45 Additional functions of independent reviewing officers

(1) The IRO must ensure that, having regard to C's age and understanding, C has been informed by the responsible authority of the steps C may take under the 1989 Act and in particular, where appropriate, of –

(a) C's rights to apply, with leave, for a section 8 order (residence, contact and other orders with respect to children) and, where C is in the care of the responsible authority, to apply for the discharge of the care order, and

(b) the availability of the procedure established by them under section 26(3) for considering any representations (including complaints) C may wish to make about the discharge by the responsible authority of their functions, including the availability of assistance to make such representations under section 26A (advocacy services).

(2) If C wishes to take legal proceedings under the 1989 Act, the IRO must –

(a) establish whether an appropriate adult is able and willing to assist C to obtain legal advice or bring proceedings on C's behalf, and

(b) if there is no such person, assist C to obtain such advice.

(3) In the following circumstances the IRO must consider whether it would be appropriate to refer C's case to an officer of the Children and Family Court Advisory and Support Service -

(a) in the opinion of the IRO, the responsible authority have failed in any significant respect to –
  (i) prepare C's care plan in accordance with these Regulations,
  (ii) review C's case in accordance with these Regulations, or effectively implement any decision taken in consequence of a review,

or are otherwise in breach of their duties to C in any material respect, and

(b) having drawn the failure or breach to the attention of persons at an appropriate level of seniority within the responsible authority, it has not been addressed to the satisfaction of the IRO within a reasonable period of time.

(4) When consulted by the responsible authority about any matter concerning C, or when informed of any matter relating to C in accordance with these Regulations, the IRO must –

(a) ensure that the responsible authority have ascertained and, subject to C's age and understanding, given due consideration to, C's wishes and feelings concerning the matter in question, and

(b) consider whether to request a review of C's case.

## 46 Qualifications and experience of independent reviewing officers

(1) The IRO must be registered as a social worker in Part 16 of the register maintained by the Health and Care Professions Council under article 5 of the Health and Social Work Professions Order 2001, in the register maintained by Social Care Wales under section 80 of the Regulation and Inspection of Social Care (Wales) Act 2016, or in a corresponding register maintained under the law of Scotland or Northern Ireland.

(2) The IRO must have sufficient relevant social work experience with children and families to perform the functions of an independent reviewing officer set out in section 25B(1) and under these Regulations in an independent manner and having regard to C's best interests.

(3) The responsible authority must not appoint any of the following as the IRO –

(a) a person involved in preparing C's care plan or the management of C's case,
(b) R,
(c) C's personal adviser,
(d) a person with management responsibilities in relation to a person mentioned in sub-paragraphs (a) to (c), or
(e) a person with control over the resources allocated to the case.

Amendments—SI 2012/1479; SI 2017/52.

### 47 Independent visitors

A person appointed by the responsible authority as an independent visitor under section 23ZB(1) is to be regarded as independent of that authority where the person appointed is not connected with the responsible authority by virtue of being –

(a) a member of the responsible authority or any of their committees or sub-committees, whether elected or co-opted,
(b) an officer of the responsible authority employed in relation to the exercise of the functions referred to in section 18(2) of the Children Act 2004, or
(c) a spouse, civil partner or other person (whether of different sex or the same sex) living in the same household as the partner of a person falling within sub-paragraph (a) or (b).

## PART 8A
## APPLICATION OF THESE REGULATIONS WITH MODIFICATIONS TO CHILDREN ON REMAND

### 47A Application of these Regulations with modifications to children on remand

(1) These Regulations apply with the modifications set out in this Part while C is –

(a) remanded to local authority accommodation, or
(b) remanded to youth detention accommodation ('YDA').

(2) In these Regulations –

(a) where C is remanded to local authority accommodation, or to YDA, references to 'the responsible authority' are to be read as if they were references to the local authority designated by the court under section 92(2) or section 102(6), as the case may be, of the 2012 Act,

(b) where C is remanded to YDA, references to C being 'placed' are to be read as if they were references to C being so remanded,

(c) where C is remanded to YDA, references to the 'placement plan' (and where C is a looked after child only by reason of being so remanded, references to the 'care plan') are to be read as if they were references to the 'detention placement plan'.

**Amendments**—Inserted by SI 2013/706.

### 47B

(1) Part 2 (arrangements for looking after a child) applies with the following modifications.

(2) Where C is a looked after child only by reason of being remanded to local authority accommodation –

(a) in regulation 4(2), the care plan must be prepared within five working days of C being so remanded, and

(b) regulation 5(a) does not apply.

(3) Where C is remanded to YDA and was a looked after child immediately before being so remanded –

(a) regulation 5(c) does not apply, and instead the care plan must include a detention placement plan,

(b) in regulation 6(3), the responsible authority must also give a copy of the care plan to the director, governor or registered manager (as the case may be) of the YDA,

(c) regulation 7(1) to (4) does not apply.

(4) Where C is a looked after child only by reason of being remanded to YDA –

(a) regulation 5 does not apply, and instead the responsible authority must prepare a detention placement plan, which also includes details of the wishes and feelings of the persons listed in section 22(4) about the detention placement plan that have been ascertained and considered in accordance with section 22(4) and (5), and the wishes and feelings of those persons in relation to any change, or proposed change, to the detention placement plan,

(b) regulation 7(1) to (4) does not apply, and regulation 7(5) applies with the modification that for 'health plan' there is substituted 'detention placement plan'.

**Amendments**—Inserted by SI 2013/706.

### 47C

(1) Part 3 (placements) applies with the following modifications.

(2) Where C is remanded to YDA, regulations 9, 10, 11 and 14 do not apply, and instead –

(a) the responsible authority must prepare a plan for the remand ('the detention placement plan') within ten working days of C's remand to YDA which –
  (i) sets out how the YDA will meet C's needs, and
  (ii) includes the address of the YDA and all the matters specified in Schedule 2A,
(b) the responsible authority must ensure –
  (i) that C's wishes and feelings have been ascertained and given due consideration,
  (ii) where C was looked after immediately before being so remanded, that the IRO has been informed of the remand,
(c) the detention placement plan must be agreed with, and signed by, the director, governor or registered manager (as the case may be) of the YDA.

(3) Where C is remanded to local authority accommodation, regulation 9(1) applies with the modification that the placement plan must be prepared within five working days of C being so remanded.

**47D**

Part 4 (provision for different types of placement) does not apply where C is remanded to YDA.

**Amendments**—Inserted by SI 2013/706.

**47E**

Part 5 (visits by the responsible authority's representative etc.) applies with the modification that in regulation 28(7)(a), the responsible authority must also ensure that R visits C, where C is remanded to YDA, whenever reasonably requested to do so by the director, governor or registered manager (as the case may be) of the YDA.

**Amendments**—Inserted by SI 2013/706.

**47F**

Part 6 (reviews) applies with the modification that in regulation 35, the considerations to which the responsible authority must have regard in reviewing C's case where C is remanded to YDA, are set out in paragraphs 1, 4, and 6 to 13, of Schedule 7 (considerations to which the responsible authority must have regard when reviewing C's case).

**Amendments**—Inserted by SI 2013/706.

## PART 9
## MISCELLANEOUS

### 48 Application of these Regulations with modifications to short breaks

(1) In the circumstances set out in paragraph (2) these Regulations apply with the modifications set out in paragraph (3).

(2) The circumstances are that –

- (a) C is not in the care of the responsible authority,
- (b) the responsible authority have arranged to place C in a series of short-term placements with the same person or in the same accommodation ('short breaks'), and
- (c) the arrangement is such that –
  - (i) no single placement is intended to last for longer than 17 days,
  - (ii) at the end of each such placement, C returns to the care of C's parent or a person who is not C's parent but who has parental responsibility for C, and
  - (iii) the short breaks do not exceed 75 days in total in any period of 12 months.

(3) The modifications are that –

- (a) regulations 5 and 9 do not apply, but instead the care plan must set out the arrangements made to meet C's needs with particular regard to -
  - (i) C's health and emotional and behavioural development, in particular in relation to any disability C may have,
  - (ii) promoting contact between C and C's parents and any other person who is not C's parent but who has parental responsibility for C, during any period when C is placed,
  - (iii) C's leisure interests, and
  - (iv) promoting C's educational achievement,
  
  and must include the name and address of C's registered medical practitioner, and the information set out in paragraph 3 of Schedule 2, where appropriate,
- (b) regulations 7, 13 and 49(2)(b) do not apply,
- (c) regulation 28(2) does not apply, but instead the responsible authority must ensure that R visits C on days when C is in fact placed, at regular intervals to be agreed with the IRO and C's parents (or any person who is not C's parent but who has parental responsibility for C) and recorded in the care plan before the start of the first placement, and in any event –
  - (i) the first visit must take place within three months of the start of the first placement, or as soon as practicable thereafter, and
  - (ii) subsequent visits must take place at intervals of not more than six months, for as long as the short breaks continue,
- (d) regulation 33 does not apply, but instead –
  - (i) the responsible authority must first review C's case within three months of the start of the first placement, and

(ii) the second and subsequent reviews must be carried out at intervals of not more than six months.

## 49 Records

*Establishment of records*

(1) The responsible authority must establish and maintain a written case record for C ('C's case record'), if one is not already in existence.

(2) The case record must include –

- (a) C's care plan, including any changes made to the care plan and any subsequent plans,
- (b) reports obtained under regulation 7,
- (c) any other document created or considered as part of any assessment of C's needs, or of any review of C's case,
- (d) any court order relating to C,
- (e) details of any arrangements that have been made by the responsible authority with any other local authority or with an independent fostering agency under regulation 26 and Schedule 5, or with a provider of social work services, under which any of the responsible authority's functions in relation to C are discharged by that local authority or independent fostering agency or provider of social work services.

## 50 Retention and confidentiality of records

(1) The responsible authority must retain C's case record either –

- (a) until the seventy-fifth anniversary of C's birth, or
- (b) if C dies before attaining the age of 18, for fifteen years beginning with the date of C's death.

(2) The responsible authority must secure the safe keeping of C's case record and take any necessary steps to ensure that information contained in it is treated as confidential subject only to –

- (a) any provision of, or made under or by virtue of, a statute under which access to such a record or information may be obtained or given,
- (b) any court order under which access to such a record or information may be obtained or given.

\* \* \* \*

## SCHEDULE 1
## CARE PLANS

**1 Information to be included in the health plan**

(1) C's state of health including C's physical, emotional and mental health.

(2) C's health history including, so far as practicable, C's family's health history.

(3) The effect of C's health and health history on C's development.

(4) Existing arrangements for C's medical and dental care including –

   (a)   routine checks of C's general state of health, including dental health,
   (b)   treatment for, and monitoring of, identified health (including physical, emotional and mental health) or dental care needs,
   (c)   preventive measures such as vaccination and immunisation,
   (d)   screening for defects of vision or hearing, and
   (e)   advice and guidance on promoting health and effective personal care.

(5) Any planned changes to existing arrangements.

(6) The role of the appropriate person, and of any other person who cares for C, in promoting C's health.

## 2 Information to be included in the personal education plan

(1) C's educational and training history, including information about educational institutions attended and C's attendance and conduct record, C's academic and other achievements, and C's special educational needs, if any.

(2) Existing arrangements for C's education and training, including details of any special educational provision and any other provision made to meet C's particular educational or training needs, and to promote C's educational achievement, and including the name and contact details of the person appointed under section 22(3B) of the 1989 Act for the purpose of discharging the responsible authority's duty under section 22(3A) (duty to promote the educational achievement of children looked after by the authority).

(3) Any planned changes to existing arrangements for C's education or training and, where any changes to the arrangements are necessary, provision made to minimise disruption to that education or training.

(4) C's leisure interests.

(5) The role of the appropriate person, and of any other person who cares for C, in promoting C's educational achievements and leisure interests.

Amendments—SI 2013/706; SI 2014/1556.

## 3 Family and social relationships

(1) If C has a sibling for whom the responsible authority or another authority are providing accommodation, and the children have not been placed together, the arrangements made to promote contact between them, so far as is consistent with C's welfare.

(2) If C is looked after by, but is not in the care of, the responsible authority, details of any order relating to C made under section 8.

(3) If C is in the care of the responsible authority, details of any order relating to C made under section 34 (parental contact etc with children in care).

(4) Any other arrangements made to promote and maintain contact in accordance with paragraph 15 of Schedule 2 of the 1989 Act, so far as is reasonably practicable and consistent with C's welfare, between C and –

(a) any parent of C's and any person who is not C's parent but who has parental responsibility for C, and
(b) any other connected person.

(5) Where section 23ZB(1) applies, the arrangements made to appoint an independent visitor for C or, if section 23ZB(6) applies (appointment of independent visitor not made where child objects), that fact.

## SCHEDULE 2
## MATTERS TO BE DEALT WITH IN THE PLACEMENT PLAN

**1 Information to be included in C's placement plan**

(1) How on a day to day basis C will be cared for and C's welfare will be safeguarded and promoted by the appropriate person.

(2) Any arrangements made for contact between C and any parent of C's and any person who is not C's parent but who has parental responsibility for C, and between C and any other connected person including, if appropriate –

(a) the reasons why contact with any such person would not be reasonably practicable or would not be consistent with C's welfare,
(b) if C is not in the care of the responsible authority, details of any order made under section 8,
(c) if C is in the care of the responsible authority, details of any order relating to C made under section 34,
(d) the arrangements for notifying any changes in the arrangements for contact.

(3) The arrangements made for C's health (including physical, emotional and mental health) and dental care including –

(a) the name and address of C's registered medical and dental practitioners and, where applicable, any registered medical or dental practitioner with whom C is to be registered following the placement,
(b) any arrangements for the giving or withholding of consent to medical or dental examination or treatment for C.

(4) The arrangements made for C's education and training including –

(a) the name and address of any school at which C is a registered pupil,
(b) the name of the designated teacher at the school (if applicable),
(c) the name and address of any other educational institution that C attends, or of any other person who provides C with education or training,
(d) where C has a statement of special educational needs, details of the local authority that maintains the statement.

(5) The arrangements made for R to visit C in accordance with Part 5, the frequency of visits and the arrangements made for advice, support and assistance to be available to C between visits in accordance with regulation 31.

(6) If an independent visitor is appointed, the arrangements made for them to visit C.

(7) The circumstances in which the placement may be terminated and C removed from the appropriate person's care in accordance with regulation 14.

(8) The name and contact details of –

    (a) the IRO,
    (b) C's independent visitor (if one is appointed),
    (c) R, and
    (d) if C is an eligible child, the personal adviser appointed for C.

## 2 Additional information to be included where C is placed with P

(1) Details of support and services to be provided to P during the placement.

(2) The obligation on P to notify the responsible authority of any relevant change in circumstances, including any intention to change address, any changes in the household in which C lives, and of any serious incident involving C.

(3) The obligation on P to ensure that any information relating to C or C's family or any other person given in confidence to P in connection with the placement is kept confidential, and that such information is not disclosed to any person without the consent of the responsible authority.

(4) The circumstances in which it is necessary to obtain the prior approval of the responsible authority for C to live in a household other than P's household.

(5) The arrangements for requesting a change to the placement plan.

(6) The circumstances in which the placement will be terminated in accordance with regulation 19(c)(ii).

## 3 Additional information to be included where C is placed with F, in a children's home or in other arrangements

(1) The type of accommodation to be provided, the address and, where C is placed under section 22C(6)(d), the name of the person who will be responsible for C at that accommodation on behalf of the responsible authority (if any).

(1ZA) Where C is placed with F in a long term foster placement, that fact.

(1A) Where –

    (a) the responsible authority has, or is notified of, child protection concerns relating to C, or
    (b) C has gone missing from the placement or from any previous placement,

the day to day arrangements put in place by the appropriate person to keep C safe.

(2) C's personal history, religious persuasion, cultural and linguistic background, and racial origin.

(3) Where C is not in the care of the responsible authority –

(a), (b) *(revoked)*
(c) the expected duration of the arrangements and the steps which should be taken to bring the arrangements to an end, including arrangements for C to return to live with C's parents, or any person who is not C's parent but who has parental responsibility for C, and
(d) where C is aged 16 or over and agrees to being provided with accommodation under section 20, that fact.

(4) The respective responsibilities of the responsible authority, C's parents, and any person who is not C's parent but who has parental responsibility for C.

(4A) Any delegation of authority to make decisions about C's care and upbringing by the persons mentioned in paragraph (4) (as appropriate) to –

(a) the responsible authority,
(b) F, and
(c) where C is placed in a children's home, the appropriate person,

in relation to the matters set out in paragraph (4B), and identifying any matters about which the persons mentioned in paragraph (4) consider that C may make a decision.

(4B) The matters referred to in paragraph (4A) are –

(a) medical and dental treatment,
(b) education,
(c) leisure and home life,
(d) faith and religious observance,
(e) use of social media,
(f) any other matters which the persons mentioned in paragraph (4) consider appropriate.

(5) The responsible authority's arrangements for the financial support of C during the placement.

(6) Where C is placed with F, the obligation on F to comply with the terms of the foster care agreement made under regulation 27(5)(b) of the Fostering Services Regulations.

**Amendments**—SI 2011/581; SI 2013/984; SI 2013/3239; SI 2015/495.

## SCHEDULE 2A
## MATTERS TO BE DEALT WITH IN THE DETENTION PLACEMENT PLAN

**1**

How on a day to day basis C will be cared for and C's welfare will be safeguarded and promoted by the staff of the

**2**

Any arrangements made for contact between C and any parent of C's and any person who is not C's parent but who has parental responsibility for C, and between C and any other connected person including, if appropriate –

(a) the reasons why contact with any such person would not be reasonably practicable or would not be consistent with C's welfare,
(b) if C is not in the care of the responsible authority, details of any order made under section 8,
(c) if C is in the care of the responsible authority, details of any order relating to C made under section 34,
(d) the arrangements for notifying any changes in the arrangements for contact.

**3**

The arrangements made for R to visit C in accordance with Part 5, the frequency of visits and the arrangements made for advice, support and assistance to be available to C between visits in accordance with regulation 31.

**4**

If an independent visitor is appointed, the arrangements made for them to visit C.

**5**

The arrangements made by the staff of the YDA for C's health (including physical, emotional and mental health) and dental care.

**6**

The arrangements made by staff of the YDA for C's education and training including –

(a) the name and address of any educational or training institution C was attending, or any other person providing C with education or training, immediately before his detention,
(b) where C has a statement of special educational needs, details of the local authority that maintains the statement.

**7**

C's personal history, religious persuasion, cultural and linguistic background, and racial origin, and the arrangement put in place by the staff of the YDA for meeting C's religious, cultural or linguistic needs.

**8**

The arrangements put in place by the staff of the YDA for supporting C to develop self-care skills.

**9**

The name and contact details of –

(a) the IRO,
(b) C's independent visitor (if one is appointed),
(c) R,
(d) if C is an eligible child, the personal adviser appointed for C,
(e) the person appointed under section 22(3B) of the 1989 Act for the purpose of discharging the responsible authority's duty under section 22(3A) (duty to promote the educational achievement of children looked after by the authority).

Amendments—SI 2014/1556.

**10**

Details of how C's welfare should be adequately safeguarded and promoted when C ceases to be remanded to YDA, in particular –

(a) whether C will be provided with accommodation by the responsible authority or another local authority, and
(b) whether any other services should be provided by the responsible authority or another local authority in the exercise of their duties under the 1989 Act.

Amendments—Inserted by SI 2013/706.

## SCHEDULE 3
## MATTERS TO BE TAKEN INTO ACCOUNT WHEN ASSESSING THE SUITABILITY OF P TO CARE FOR C

**1**

In respect of P –

(a) P's capacity to care for children and in particular in relation to C to –
   (i) provide for C's physical needs and appropriate medical and dental care,
   (ii) protect C adequately from harm or danger, including from any person who presents a risk of harm to C,
   (iii) ensure that the home environment is safe for C,

- (iv) ensure that C's emotional needs are met and C is provided with a positive sense of self, including any particular needs arising from C's religious persuasion, racial origin and cultural and linguistic background, and any disability C may have,
- (v) promote C's learning and intellectual development through encouragement, cognitive stimulation and the promotion of educational success and social opportunities,
- (vi) enable C to regulate C's emotions and behaviour, including by modelling appropriate behaviour and interactions with others, and
- (vii) provide a stable family environment to enable C to develop and maintain secure attachments to P and other persons who provide care for C,

(b) P's state of health including P's physical, emotional and mental health and medical history including any current or past issues of domestic violence, substance misuse or mental health problems,

(c) P's family relationships and the composition of P's household, including particulars of –
- (i) the identity of all other members of the household, including their age and the nature of their relationship with P and with each other, including any sexual relationship,
- (ii) any relationship with any person who is a parent of C,
- (iii) other adults not being members of the household who are likely to have regular contact with C, and
- (iv) any current or previous domestic violence between members of the household, including P,

(d) P's family history, including –
- (i) particulars of P's childhood and upbringing including the strengths and difficulties of P's parents or other persons who cared for P,
- (ii) P's relationships with P's parents and siblings, and their relationships with each other,
- (iii) P's educational achievement and any specific learning difficulty or disability,
- (iv) a chronology of significant life events, and
- (v) particulars of other relatives and their relationships with C and P,

(e) particulars of any criminal offences of which P has been convicted or in respect of which P has been cautioned,

(f) P's past and present employment and other sources of income, and

(g) the nature of the neighbourhood in which P's home is situated and resources available in the community to support C and P.

2

In respect of members of P's household aged 18 and over, so far as is practicable, all the particulars specified in paragraph 1 except sub-paragraphs (d), (f) and (g).

## SCHEDULE 4
## MATTERS TO BE TAKEN INTO ACCOUNT WHEN ASSESSING THE SUITABILITY OF A CONNECTED PERSON TO CARE FOR C

1

In respect of the connected person –
- (a) the nature and quality of any existing relationship with C,
- (b) their capacity to care for children and in particular in relation to C to –
  - (i) provide for C's physical needs and appropriate medical and dental care,
  - (ii) protect C adequately from harm or danger including from any person who presents a risk of harm to C,
  - (iii) ensure that the accommodation and home environment is suitable with regard to the age and developmental stage of C,
  - (iv) promote C's learning and development, and
  - (v) provide a stable family environment which will promote secure attachments for C, including promoting positive contact with P and other connected persons, unless to do this is not consistent with the duty to safeguard and promote C's welfare,
- (c) their state of health including their physical, emotional and mental health and medical history including any current or past issues of domestic violence, substance misuse or mental health problems,
- (d) their family relationships and the composition of their household, including particulars of –
  - (i) the identity of all other members of the household, including their age and the nature of their relationship with the connected person and with each other, including any sexual relationship,
  - (ii) any relationship with any person who is a parent of C,
  - (iii) any relationship between C and other members of the household
  - (iv) other adults not being members of the household who are likely to have regular contact with C, and
  - (v) any current or previous domestic violence between members of the household, including the connected person,
- (e) their family history, including –
  - (i) particulars of their childhood and upbringing including the strengths and difficulties of their parents or other persons who cared for them,
  - (ii) their relationships with their parents and siblings, and their relationships with each other,
  - (iii) their educational achievement and any specific learning difficulty or disability,
  - (iv) a chronology of significant life events, and
  - (v) particulars of other relatives and their relationships with C and the connected person,
- (f) particulars of any criminal offences of which they have been convicted or in respect of which they have been cautioned,
- (g) their past and present employment and other sources of income, and

(h) the nature of the neighbourhood in which their home is situated and resources available in the community to support C and the connected person.

## SCHEDULE 5
## AGREEMENT WITH AN INDEPENDENT FOSTERING AGENCY RELATING TO THE DISCHARGE OF THE RESPONSIBLE AUTHORITY'S FUNCTIONS

**1**

The agreement must contain the following information –

(1) the services to be provided to the responsible authority by the registered person,
(2) the arrangements for the selection by the responsible authority of F from those approved by the registered person,
(3) a requirement for the registered person to submit reports to the responsible authority on any placements as may be required by the responsible authority, and
(4) the arrangements for the termination of the agreement.

**2**

Where the agreement relates to a particular child, it must also contain the following information –

(1) F's details,
(2) details of any services that C is to receive and whether the services are to be provided by the responsible authority or by the registered person,
(3) the terms (including as to payment) of the proposed placement agreement,
(4) the arrangements for record keeping about C and for the return of records at the end of the placement,
(5) a requirement for the registered person to notify the responsible authority immediately in the event of any concerns about the placement, and
(6) whether, and on what basis, other children may be placed with F.

## SCHEDULE 6
## MATTERS TO BE CONSIDERED BEFORE PLACING C IN ACCOMMODATION IN AN UNREGULATED SETTING UNDER SECTION 22(6)(D)

**1**

In respect of the accommodation, the –

(a) facilities and services provided,
(b) state of repair,
(c) safety,

(d) location,
(e) support,
(f) tenancy status, and
(g) the financial commitments involved for C and their affordability.

**2**

In respect of C, C's –

(a) views about the accommodation,
(b) understanding of their rights and responsibilities in relation to the accommodation, and
(c) understanding of funding arrangements.

## SCHEDULE 7
## CONSIDERATIONS TO WHICH THE RESPONSIBLE AUTHORITY MUST HAVE REGARD WHEN REVIEWING C'S CASE

**1**

The effect of any change in C's circumstances since the last review, in particular of any change made by the responsible authority to C's care plan, whether decisions taken at the last review have been successfully implemented, and if not, the reasons for that.

**2**

Whether the responsible authority should seek any change in C's legal status.

**3**

Whether there is a plan for permanence for C.

**4**

The arrangements for contact and whether there is any need for changes to the arrangements in order to promote contact between C and P, or between C and other connected persons.

**5**

Whether C's placement continues to be the most appropriate available, and whether any change to the placement plan or any other aspects of the arrangements made to provide C with accommodation is, or is likely to become, necessary or desirable before the next review of C's case.

**5A**

Whether C's placement safeguards and promotes C's welfare, and whether any safeguarding concerns have been raised.

Amendments—Inserted by SI 2013/3239.

**6**

C's educational needs, progress and development and whether any change to the arrangements for C's education or training is, or is likely to become, necessary or desirable to meet C's particular needs and to promote C's educational achievement before the next review of C's case, having regard to the advice of any person who provides C with education or training, in particular the designated teacher of any school at which C is a registered pupil.

**7**

C's leisure interests.

**8**

The report of the most recent assessment of C's state of health obtained in accordance with regulation 8 and whether any change to the arrangements for C's health care is, or is likely to become, necessary or desirable before the next review of C's case, having regard to the advice of any health care professional received since the date of that report, in particular C's registered medical practitioner.

**9**

Whether C's needs related to C's identity are being met and whether any particular change is required, having regard to C's religious persuasion, racial origin and cultural background.

**10**

Whether the arrangements made in accordance with regulation 31 continue to be appropriate and understood by C.

**11**

Whether any arrangements need to be made for the time when C will no longer be looked after by the responsible authority.

**12**

C's wishes and feelings, and the views of the IRO, about any aspect of the case and in particular about any changes the responsible authority has made since the last review or proposes to make to the C's care plan.

**13**

Where regulation 28(3) applies, the frequency of R's visits.

Amendments—SI 2011/581.

**14**

Where C falls within regulation 5(1)(f), whether C's needs as a result of that status are being met.

Amendments—Inserted by SI 2014/1917.

**15**

Whether the delegation of authority to make decisions about C's care and upbringing, if any, recorded in C's care plan by virtue of paragraph 3(4A) of Schedule 2, continues to be appropriate and in C's best interests.

Amendments—Inserted by SI 2015/495.

# SCHEDULE 8
# MATTERS TO BE DEALT WITH IN THE PATHWAY PLAN

**1**

The name of C's personal adviser.

**2**

The nature and level of contact and personal support to be provided to C, and by whom.

**3**

Details of the accommodation C is to occupy when C ceases to be looked after.

**4**

The plan for C's continuing education or training when C ceases to be looked after.

**5**

How the responsible authority will assist C in obtaining employment or other purposeful activity or occupation.

**6**

The support to be provided to enable C to develop and sustain appropriate family and social relationships.

**7**

A programme to develop the practical and other skills C needs to live independently.

**8**

The financial support to be provided to enable C to meet accommodation and maintenance costs.

**9**

C's health care needs, including any physical, emotional or mental health needs and how they are to be met when C ceases to be looked after.

**10**

The responsible authority's contingency plans for action to be taken in the event that the pathway plan ceases to be effective for any reason.

\*\*\*\*

# APPENDIX 6

# SPECIAL GUARDIANSHIP REGULATIONS 2005, SI 2005/1109

### PART 1
### INTRODUCTORY

**1 Citation, commencement and application**

(1) These Regulations may be cited as the Special Guardianship Regulations 2005 and shall come into force on 30th December 2005.

(2) These Regulations apply to England only.

**2 Interpretation**

(1) In these Regulations –

'the Act' means the Children Act 1989;
'couple' has the same meaning as in section 144(4) of the Adoption and Children Act 2002;
'Local Health Board' means a Local Health Board established by the National Assembly for Wales under section 16BA of the National Health Service Act 1977;
'prospective special guardian' means a person –
    (a) who has given notice to a local authority under section 14A(7) of the Act of his intention to make an application for a special guardianship order in accordance with section 14A(3) of the Act; or
    (b) in respect of whom a court has requested that a local authority conduct an investigation and prepare a report pursuant to section 14A(9) of the Act;

'relevant child' means a child in respect of whom –
    (a) a special guardianship order is in force;
    (b) a person has given notice to a local authority under section 14A(7) of the Act of his intention to make an application for a special guardianship order in accordance with section 14A(3) of the Act; or
    (c) a court is considering whether a special guardianship order should be made and has asked a local authority to conduct an investigation and prepare a report pursuant to section 14A(9) of the Act;

'universal credit' means universal credit under Part 1 of the Welfare Reform Act 2012].

(2) In any case where –

(a) a person aged 18 or over is in full-time education or training; and
(b) immediately before he reached the age of 18, financial support was payable in relation to him under Chapter 2 of Part 2 of these Regulations,

then, for the purposes of the continued provision of financial support and any review of financial support, these Regulations shall have effect in relation to him as if he were still a child.

Amendments—SI 2013/630.

## PART 2
## SPECIAL GUARDIANSHIP SUPPORT SERVICES

*Chapter 1*
*Provision of Services*

### 3 Prescribed services

(1) For the purposes of section 14F(1)(b) of the Act the following services are prescribed as special guardianship support services (in addition to counselling, advice and information) –

(a) financial support payable under Chapter 2;
(b) services to enable groups of –
   (i) relevant children;
   (ii) special guardians;
   (iii) prospective special guardians; and
   (iv) parents of relevant children,
   to discuss matters relating to special guardianship;
(c) assistance, including mediation services, in relation to arrangements for contact between a relevant child and –
   (i) his parent or a relative of his; or
   (ii) any other person with whom such a child has a relationship which appears to the local authority to be beneficial to the welfare of the child having regard to the factors specified in section 1(3) of the Act;
(d) services in relation to the therapeutic needs of a relevant child;
(e) assistance for the purpose of ensuring the continuance of the relationship between a relevant child and a special guardian or prospective special guardian, including –
   (i) training for that person to meet any special needs of that child;
   (ii) subject to paragraph (3), respite care;
   (iii) mediation in relation to matters relating to special guardianship orders.

(2) The services prescribed in paragraph (1)(b) to (e) may include giving assistance in cash.

(3) For the purposes of paragraph (1)(e)(ii) respite care that consists of the provision of accommodation must be accommodation provided by or on behalf of a local authority under section 23 of the Act (accommodation of looked after children) or by a voluntary organisation under section 59 of the Act.

**4 Arrangements for securing provision of services**

(1) The following are prescribed for the purposes of section 14F(9)(b) of the Act (persons who may provide special guardianship support services) –

- (a) a registered adoption society;
- (b) a registered adoption support agency;
- (c) a registered fostering agency;
- (d) a Local Health Board[, a clinical commissioning group and the National Health Service Commissioning Board];
- (e) (*revoked*)

(2) In paragraph (1) –

- (a) 'registered adoption society' has the same meaning as in the Adoption and Children Act 2002;
- (b) 'adoption support agency' has the same meaning as in the Adoption and Children Act 2002 and 'fostering agency' has the same meaning as in the Care Standards Act 2000 and 'registered' in relation to any such agency means that a person is registered in respect of it under Part 2 of the Care Standards Act 2000.

Amendments—SI 2010/1172, SI 2013/235.

**5 Services for persons outside the area**

(1) Section 14F of the Act (special guardianship support services) applies to a local authority in respect of the following persons who are outside the authority's area –

- (a) a relevant child who is looked after by the local authority or was looked after by the local authority immediately before the making of a special guardianship order;
- (b) a special guardian or prospective special guardian of such a child;
- (c) a child of a special guardian or prospective special guardian mentioned in sub-paragraph (b).

(2) But section 14F ceases to apply at the end of the period of three years from the date of the special guardianship order except in a case where the local authority are providing financial support under Chapter 2 and the decision to provide that support was made before the making of the order.

(3) Nothing in this regulation prevents a local authority from providing special guardianship support services to persons outside their area where they consider it appropriate to do so.

*Chapter 2*
*Provision of Financial Support*

**6 Circumstances in which financial support is payable**

(1) Financial support is payable under this Chapter to a special guardian or prospective special guardian –

- (a) to facilitate arrangements for a person to become the special guardian of a child where the local authority consider such arrangements to be beneficial to the child's welfare; or
- (b) to support the continuation of such arrangements after a special guardianship order is made.

(2) Such support is payable only in the following circumstances –

- (a) where the local authority consider that it is necessary to ensure that the special guardian or prospective special guardian can look after the child;
- (b) where the local authority consider that the child needs special care which requires a greater expenditure of resources than would otherwise be the case because of his illness, disability, emotional or behavioural difficulties or the consequences of his past abuse or neglect;
- (c) where the local authority consider that it is appropriate to contribute to any legal costs, including court fees, of a special guardian or prospective special guardian, as the case may be, associated with –
  - (i) the making of a special guardianship order or any application to vary or discharge such an order;
  - (ii) an application for an order under section 8 of the Act;
  - (iii) an order for financial provision to be made to or for the benefit of the child; or
- (d) where the local authority consider that it is appropriate to contribute to the expenditure necessary for the purposes of accommodating and maintaining the child, including the provision of furniture and domestic equipment, alterations to and adaptations of the home, provision of means of transport and provision of clothing, toys and other items necessary for the purpose of looking after the child.

**7 Remuneration for former foster parents**

(1) Financial support under this Chapter may include an element of remuneration but only where the decision to include it is taken before the special guardianship order is made and the local authority consider it to be necessary in order to facilitate arrangements for a person to become a special guardian in a case where –

- (a) the special guardian or prospective special guardian has been a local authority foster parent in respect of the child; and
- (b) an element of remuneration was included in the payments made by the local authority to that person in relation to his fostering the child.

(2) But that element of remuneration ceases to be payable after the expiry of the period of two years from the making of the special guardianship order unless the local authority consider its continuation to be necessary having regard to the exceptional needs of the child or any other exceptional circumstances.

## 8 Payment of financial support

Financial support under this Chapter may be paid –

- (a) periodically, if it is provided to meet a need which is likely to give rise to recurring expenditure; or
- (b) in any other case by a single payment or, if the local authority and the special guardian or prospective special guardian agree, by instalments.

## 9 Cessation of financial support

Financial support ceases to be payable to a special guardian or prospective special guardian if –

- (a) the child ceases to have a home with him;
- (b) the child ceases full-time education or training and commences employment;
- (c) the child qualifies for [universal credit,] income support[, jobseeker's allowance or employment and support allowance] in his own right; or
- (d) the child attains the age of 18 unless he continues in full-time education or training, when it may continue until the end of the course or training he is then undertaking.

Amendments—SI 2008/1879, SI 2013/630.

## 10 Conditions

(1) Where financial support is to be paid periodically it is not payable until the special guardian or prospective special guardian agrees to the following conditions –

- (a) that he will inform the local authority immediately if –
  - (i) he changes his address;
  - (ii) the child dies;
  - (iii) any of the changes mentioned in regulation 9 (cessation of financial support) occurs; or
  - (iv) there is a change in his financial circumstances or the financial needs or resources of the child which may affect the amount of financial support payable to him,
  
  and, where the information is given orally, to confirm it in writing within seven days;
- (b) that he will complete and supply the local authority with an annual statement as to the following matters –
  - (i) his financial circumstances;
  - (ii) the financial needs and resources of the child;
  - (iii) his address and whether the child still has a home with him.

(2) The local authority may provide financial support subject to any other conditions they consider appropriate, including the timescale within which, and purposes for which, any payment of financial support should be utilised.

(3) Subject to paragraph (4), where any condition imposed in accordance with this regulation is not complied with, the local authority may –

(a) suspend or terminate payment of financial support; and
(b) seek to recover all or part of the financial support they have paid.

(4) Where the condition not complied with is a failure to provide an annual statement in accordance with an agreement referred to in paragraph (1), the local authority shall not take any steps under paragraph (3) until –

(a) they have sent to the person who entered into the agreement a written reminder of the need to provide an annual statement; and
(b) 28 days have expired since the date on which that reminder was sent.

## Chapter 3
## Assessment and Plans

**11 Request for assessment**

(1) The following persons are prescribed for the purposes of section 14F(3) of the Act (persons at whose request an assessment must be carried out) –

(a) a relevant child who is looked after by the local authority or was looked after by the local authority immediately before the making of a special guardianship order;
(b) a special guardian or prospective special guardian of such a child;
(c) a parent of such a child.

(2) Paragraph (3) applies if the local authority receive a written request from or, in the case of a child, on behalf of any of the following persons (not being a person falling within paragraph (1)) for an assessment of his needs for special guardianship support services –

(a) a person mentioned in section 14F(3)(a) to (c) of the Act;
(b) a child of a special guardian;
(c) any person whom the local authority consider to have a significant and ongoing relationship with a relevant child.

(3) The local authority must, if they are minded not to carry out an assessment, give the person notice of the proposed decision (including the reasons for it) and must allow him a reasonable opportunity to make representations in relation to that decision.

(4) Where the request of a person for an assessment relates to a particular special guardianship support service, or it appears to the local authority that a person's needs for special guardianship support services may be adequately assessed by reference to a particular special guardianship support service, the local authority may carry out the assessment by reference to that service only.

## 12 Procedure for assessment

(1) Where the local authority carry out an assessment of a person's needs for special guardianship support services they must have regard to such of the following considerations as are relevant to the assessment –

- (a) the developmental needs of the child;
- (b) the parenting capacity of the special guardian or prospective special guardian, as the case may be;
- (c) the family and environmental factors that have shaped the life of the child;
- (d) what the life of the child might be like with the person falling within sub-paragraph (b);
- (e) any previous assessments undertaken in relation to the child or a person falling within sub-paragraph (b);
- (f) the needs of a person falling within sub-paragraph (b) and of that person's family;
- (g) where it appears to the local authority that there is a pre-existing relationship between a person falling within sub-paragraph (b) and the parent of the child, the likely impact of the special guardianship order on the relationships between that person, that child and that parent.

(2) The local authority must, where they consider it appropriate to do so –

- (a) interview the person whose needs for special guardianship support services are being assessed;
- (b) where the person falling within sub-paragraph (a) is a child, interview –
  - (i) any special guardian or prospective special guardian, as the case may be, of the child; or
  - (ii) any adult the local authority consider it appropriate to interview.

(3) Where it appears to the local authority that the person may have a need for services from [a Local Health Board, a clinical commissioning group, the National Health Service Commissioning Board] or [another local authority], they must, as part of the assessment, consult [that board, group or authority].

(4) After undertaking an assessment, the local authority must prepare a written report of the assessment.

Amendments—SI 2010/1172, SI 2013/235.

## 13 Assessment of need for financial support

(1) This regulation applies where the local authority carry out an assessment of a person's need for financial support.

(2) In determining the amount of financial support, the local authority must take account of any other grant, benefit, allowance or resource which is available to the person in respect of his needs as a result of becoming a special guardian of the child.

(3) Subject to paragraphs (4) and (5) the local authority must also take account of the following considerations –

(a) the person's financial resources, including any tax credit or benefit, which would be available to him if the child lived with him;
(b) the amount required by the person in respect of his reasonable outgoings and commitments (excluding outgoings in respect of the child);
(c) the financial needs and resources of the child.

(4) The local authority must disregard the considerations in paragraph (3) where they are considering providing financial support in respect of legal costs, including court fees, in a case where a special guardianship order is applied for in respect of a child who is looked after by the local authority and the authority support the making of the order or an application is made to vary or discharge a special guardianship order in respect of such a child.

(5) The local authority may disregard any of the considerations in paragraph (3) –

(a) where they are considering providing financial support in respect of –
  (i) initial costs of accommodating a child who has been looked after by the local authority;
  (ii) recurring costs in respect of travel for the purpose of visits between the child and a related person; or
  (iii) any special care referred to in regulation 6(2)(b) in relation to a child who has been looked after by the local authority; or
(b) where they are considering including an element of remuneration under regulation 7.

(6) In paragraph (5)(a)(ii) 'related person' means a relative of the child or any other person with whom the child has a relationship which appears to the local authority to be beneficial to the welfare of the child having regard to the factors specified in section 1(3) of the Act.

## 14 Plan

(1) This regulation applies in relation to the requirement in section 14F(6) of the Act for the local authority to prepare a plan in accordance with which special guardianship support services are to be provided.

(2) The local authority must prepare a plan if –

(a) they propose to provide special guardianship support services to a person on more than one occasion; and
(b) the services are not limited to the provision of advice or information.

(3) Where it appears to the local authority that the person may have a need for services from [a Local Health Board, a clinical commissioning group, the National Health Service Commissioning Board] or [another local authority], they must consult [that board, group or authority] before preparing the plan.

(4) The local authority must nominate a person to monitor the provision of the services in accordance with the plan.

Amendments—SI 2010/1172, SI 2013/235.

## 15 Notice of proposal as to special guardianship support services

(1) Before making any decision under section 14F(5) of the Act as to a person's needs for special guardianship support services, the local authority must allow the person an opportunity to make representations in accordance with this regulation.

(2) The local authority must first give the person notice of the proposed decision and the time allowed for making representations.

(3) The notice must contain the following information –

- (a) a statement as to the person's needs for special guardianship support services;
- (b) where the assessment relates to his need for financial support, the basis upon which financial support is determined;
- (c) whether the local authority propose to provide him with special guardianship support services;
- (d) the services (if any) that are proposed to be provided to him;
- (e) if financial support is to be paid to him, the proposed amount that would be payable; and
- (f) any proposed conditions under regulation 10(2).

(4) In a case where the local authority propose to provide special guardianship support services and are required to prepare a plan under section 14F(6) of the Act, the notice must be accompanied by a draft of that plan.

(5) The local authority shall not make a decision until –

- (a) the person has made representations to the local authority or notified the local authority that he is satisfied with the proposed decision and, where applicable, the draft plan; or
- (b) the period of time for making representations has expired.

## 16 Notification of decision as to special guardianship support services

(1) After making their decision under section 14F(5) of the Act as to whether to provide special guardianship support services to a person, the local authority must give the person notice of that decision, including the reasons for it.

(2) Where the local authority are required to prepare a plan under section 14F(6) of the Act, the notice must include details of that plan and the person nominated under regulation 14(4).

(3) If the local authority decide that financial support is to be provided, the notice given under paragraph (1) must include the following information –

- (a) the method of the determination of the amount of financial support;
- (b) where financial support is to be paid in instalments or periodically –
  - (i) the amount of financial support;
  - (ii) the frequency with which the payment will be made;
  - (iii) the period for which financial support is to be paid;
  - (iv) when payment will commence;

(c) where financial support is to be paid as a single payment, when the payment is to be made;
(d) where financial support is to be paid subject to any conditions imposed in accordance with regulation 10(2), those conditions, the date (if any) by which the conditions are to be met and the consequences of failing to meet the conditions;
(e) the arrangements and procedure for review, variation and termination of financial support;
(f) the responsibilities of –
   (i) the local authority under regulations 17 and 18 (reviews); and
   (ii) the special guardian or prospective special guardian pursuant to any agreement mentioned in regulation 10.

## Chapter 4
## Reviews

### 17 Reviews: general procedure

(1) This regulation applies where the local authority provide special guardianship support services for a person other than financial support payable periodically.

(2) The local authority must review the provision of such services –

(a) if any change in the person's circumstances which may affect the provision of special guardianship support services comes to their notice;
(b) at such stage in the implementation of the plan as they consider appropriate; and
(c) in any event, at least annually.

(3) Regulations 12 and 13 apply in relation to a review under this regulation as they apply in relation to an assessment under Chapter 3 of this Part.

(4) If the local authority propose to vary or terminate the provision of special guardianship support services to any person, before making any decision as a result of the review they must give the person an opportunity to make representations and for that purpose they must give him notice of the proposed decision and the time allowed for making representations.

(5) The notice must contain the information mentioned in regulation 15(3) and, if the local authority propose to revise the plan, a draft of the revised plan.

(6) The local authority must, having regard to the review and after considering any representations received within the period specified in the notice –

(a) decide whether to vary or terminate the provision of special guardianship support services for the person; and
(b) where appropriate, revise the plan.

(7) The local authority must give the person notice of their decision (including the reasons for it) and, if applicable, details of the revised plan.

## 18 Review of financial support payable periodically

(1) This regulation applies where the local authority provide financial support for a person payable periodically.

(2) The local authority must review the financial support –

- (a) on receipt of the annual statement mentioned in regulation 10;
- (b) if any relevant change of circumstances or any breach of a condition mentioned in regulation 10 comes to their notice; and
- (c) at any stage in the implementation of the plan that they consider appropriate.

(3) In paragraph (2) a relevant change of circumstances is any of the changes that the person has agreed to notify under regulation 10.

(4) Regulations 12 and 13 apply in relation to a review under this regulation as they apply in relation to an assessment under Chapter 3 of this Part.

(5) If the local authority propose, as a result of the review, to reduce or terminate financial support or revise the plan, before making that decision, the local authority must give the person an opportunity to make representations and for that purpose they must give the person notice of the proposed decision and the time allowed for making representations.

(6) But paragraph (5) does not prevent the local authority from suspending payment of financial support pending that decision.

(7) The notice must contain the information mentioned in regulation 15(3) and, if applicable, a draft of the revised plan.

(8) The local authority must, having regard to the review, and after considering any representations received within the period specified in the notice –

- (a) decide whether to vary or terminate payment of the financial support or whether to seek to recover all or part of any financial support that has been paid; and
- (b) where appropriate, revise the plan.

(9) The local authority must give the person notice of their decision, including the reasons for it, and, if applicable, the revised plan.

## Chapter 5
## Urgent Cases and Notices

### 19 Urgent cases

Where any requirement applicable to the local authority in this Part in relation to carrying out an assessment, preparing a plan or giving notice would delay the provision of a service in a case of urgency, that requirement does not apply.

**20 Notices**

(1) Any notice required to be given under this Part must be given in writing.

(2) If the person to whom notice is to be given is a child and –

- (a) it appears to the local authority that the child is not of sufficient age and understanding for it to be appropriate to give him such notice; or
- (b) in all the circumstances it is not appropriate to give him such notice,

the notice must be given to his special guardian or prospective special guardian (where applicable) or otherwise to the adult the local authority consider most appropriate.

### PART 3
### MISCELLANEOUS PROVISIONS IN RELATION TO SPECIAL GUARDIANSHIP

**21 Court report**

The matters specified in the Schedule are the matters prescribed for the purposes of section 14A(8)(b) of the Act (matters to be dealt with in report for the court).

**22 Relevant authority for the purposes of section 24(5)(za) of the Act**

For the purposes of section 24(5)(za) of the Act (persons qualifying for advice and assistance) the relevant authority shall be the local authority which last looked after the person.

### SCHEDULE
### MATTERS TO BE DEALT WITH IN REPORT FOR THE COURT

Regulation 21

The following matters are prescribed for the purposes of section 14A(8)(b) of the Act.

**1**

In respect of the child –

- (a) name, sex, date and place of birth and address including local authority area;
- (b) a photograph and physical description;
- (c) nationality (and immigration status where appropriate);
- (d) racial origin and cultural and linguistic background;
- (e) religious persuasion (including details of baptism, confirmation or equivalent ceremonies);
- (f) details of any siblings including their dates of birth;
- (g) the extent of the child's contact with his relatives and any other person the local authority consider relevant;
- [(ga) any harm which the child has suffered;

(gb) any risk of future harm to the child posed by the child's parents, relatives or any other person the local authority consider relevant;]
(h) whether the child is or has been looked after by a local authority or is or has been provided with accommodation by a voluntary organisation and details (including dates) of placements by the authority or organisation;
(i) whether the prospective special guardian is a local authority foster parent of the child;
(j) a description of the child's personality, his social development and his emotional and behavioural development and any related [current needs or likely future] needs;
(k) details of the child's interests, likes and dislikes;
(l) a health history and a description of the state of the child's health which shall include any treatment the child is receiving;
(m) names, addresses and types of nurseries or schools attended with dates;
(n) the child's educational attainments;
(o) whether the child is subject to a statement of special educational needs under the [Children and Families Act 2014]; and
(p) details of any order made by a court with respect to the child under the Act including –
 (i) the name of the court;
 (ii) the order made; and
 (iii) the date on which the order was made.

## 2

In respect of the child's family –

(a) name, date and place of birth and address (and the date on which their last address was confirmed) including local authority area of each parent of the child and his siblings under the age of 18;
(b) a photograph, if available, and physical description of each parent;
(c) nationality (and immigration status where appropriate) of each parent;
(d) racial origin and cultural and linguistic background of each parent;
(e) whether the child's parents were married to each other at the time of the child's birth or have subsequently married and whether they are divorced or separated;
(f) where the child's parents have been previously married or formed a civil partnership, the date of the marriage or civil partnership;
(g) where the child's parents are not married, whether the father has parental responsibility and, if so, how it was acquired;
(h) if the identity or whereabouts of the father are not known, the information about him that has been ascertained and from whom, and the steps that have been taken to establish paternity;
(i) the past and present relationship of the child's parents;
(j) where available, the following information in respect of each parent –
 (i) health history, including details of any serious physical or mental illness, any hereditary disease or disorder or disability;
 (ii) religious persuasion;

        (iii) educational history;
        (iv) employment history;
        (v) personality and interests;
    (k) in respect of the child's siblings under the age of 18 –
        (i) the person with whom the sibling is living;
        (ii) whether the sibling is looked after by a local authority or provided with accommodation by a voluntary organisation; and
        (iii) details of any court order made with respect to the sibling under the Act, including the name of the court, the order made and the date on which the order was made.

3

In respect of the wishes and feelings of the child and others –

   (a) an assessment of the child's wishes and feelings (considered in light of his age and understanding) regarding –
       (i) special guardianship;
       (ii) his religious and cultural upbringing; and
       (iii) contact with his relatives and any other person the local authority consider relevant,
       and the date on which the child's wishes and feelings were last ascertained.
   (b) the wishes and feelings of each parent regarding –
       (i) special guardianship;
       (ii) the child's religious and cultural upbringing; and
       (iii) contact with the child,
       and the date on which the wishes and feelings of each parent were last ascertained; and
   (c) the wishes and feelings of any of the child's relatives, or any other person the local authority consider relevant regarding the child and the dates on which those wishes and feelings were last ascertained.

4

In respect of the prospective special guardian or, where two or more persons are jointly prospective special guardians, each of them –

   (a) name, date and place of birth and address including local authority area;
   (b) a photograph and physical description;
   (c) nationality (and immigration status where appropriate);
   (d) racial origin and cultural and linguistic background;
   (e) if the prospective special guardian is –
       (i) married, the date and place of marriage;
       (ii) has formed a civil partnership, the date and place of registration of the civil partnership; or
       (iii) has a partner, details of that relationship;
   (f) details of any previous marriage, civil partnership, or relationship;

(g) where the prospective special guardians wish to apply jointly, the nature of their relationship and an assessment of the stability of that relationship;
(h) if the prospective special guardian is a member of a couple and is applying alone for a special guardianship order, the reasons for this;
(i) whether the prospective special guardian is a relative of the child;
[(j) an assessment of the nature of the prospective special guardian's current and past relationship with the child;]
(k) a health history of the prospective special guardian including details of any serious physical or mental illness, any hereditary disease or disorder or disability;
(l) a description of how the prospective special guardian relates to adults and children;
(m) previous experience of caring for children;
[(n) an assessment of the prospective special guardian's parenting capacity, including:
  (i) their understanding of, and ability to meet the child's current and likely future needs, particularly, any needs the child may have arising from harm that the child has suffered;
  (ii) their understanding of, and ability to protect the child from any current or future risk of harm posed by the child's parents, relatives or any other person the local authority consider relevant, particularly in relation to contact between any such person and the child;
  (iii) their ability and suitability to bring up the child until the child reaches the age of eighteen;]
(o) where there have been any past assessments as a prospective adopter, foster parent or special guardian, relevant details as appropriate;
(p) details of income and expenditure;
(q) information about the prospective special guardian's home and the neighbourhood in which he lives;
(r) details of other members of the household and details of any children of the prospective special guardian even if not resident in the household;
(s) details of the parents and any siblings of the prospective special guardian, with their ages or ages at death;
(t) the following information –
  (i) religious persuasion;
  (ii) educational history;
  (iii) employment history; and
  (iv) personality and interests;
(u) details of any previous family court proceedings in which the prospective special guardian has been involved (which have not been referred to elsewhere in this report);
(v) a report of each of the interviews with the three persons nominated by the prospective special guardian to provide personal references for him;

- (w) whether the prospective special guardian is willing to follow any wishes of the child or his parents in respect of the child's religious and cultural upbringing;
- (x) the views of other members of the prospective special guardian's household and wider family in relation to the proposed special guardianship order;
- (y) an assessment of the child's current and future relationship with the family of the prospective special guardian;
- (z) reasons for applying for a special guardianship order and extent of understanding of the nature and effect of special guardianship and whether the prospective special guardian has discussed special guardianship with the child;
  - (aa) any hopes and expectations the prospective special guardian has for the child's future; and
  - (bb) the prospective special guardian's wishes and feelings in relation to contact between the child and his relatives or any other person the local authority considers relevant.

5

In respect of the local authority which completed the report –

- (a) name and address;
- (b) details of any past involvement of the local authority with the prospective special guardian, including any past preparation for that person to be a local authority foster parent or adoptive parent or special guardian;
- (c) where section 14A(7)(a) of the Act applies and the prospective special guardian lives in the area of another local authority, details of the local authority's enquiries of that other local authority about the prospective special guardian;
- (d) a summary of any special guardianship support services provided by the authority for the prospective special guardian, the child or the child's parent and the period for which those services are to be provided; and
- (e) where the local authority has decided not to provide special guardianship support services, the reasons why.

6

A summary prepared by the medical professional who provided the information referred to in paragraphs 1(l) and 4(k).

7

The implications of the making of a special guardianship order for –

- (a) the child;
- (b) the child's parent;
- (c) the prospective special guardian and his family; and
- (d) any other person the local authority considers relevant.

**8**

The relative merits of special guardianship and other orders which may be made under the Act or the Adoption and Children Act 2002 with an assessment of whether the child's long term interests would be best met by a special guardianship order.

**9**

A recommendation as to whether or not the special guardianship order sought should be made in respect of the child and, if not, any alternative proposal in respect of the child.

**10**

A recommendation as to what arrangements there should be for contact between the child and his relatives or any person the local authority consider relevant.

Amendments—SI 2014/2103, SI 2016/111.

# APPENDIX 7

# EMERGENCY PROTECTION ORDER: THE *X COUNCIL* GUIDANCE

(See **Judgment of Munby J** in *X Council v B (Emergency Protection Orders)* [2005] 1 FLR 341, paragraph 57).

(i) An EPO, summarily removing a child from his parents, is a 'draconian' and 'extremely harsh' measure, requiring 'exceptional justification' and 'extraordinarily compelling reasons'. Such an order should not be made unless the FPC is satisfied that it is both necessary and proportionate and that no other less radical form of order will achieve the essential end of promoting the welfare of the child. Separation is only to be contemplated if immediate separation is essential to secure the child's safety: 'imminent danger' must be 'actually established'.

(ii) Both the local authority which seeks and the FPC which makes an EPO assume a heavy burden of responsibility. It is important that both the local authority and the FPC approach every application for an EPO with an anxious awareness of the extreme gravity of the relief being sought and a scrupulous regard for the European Convention rights of both the child and the parents.

(iii) Any order must provide for the least interventionist solution consistent with the preservation of the child's immediate safety.

(iv) If the real purpose of the local authority's application is to enable it to have the child assessed then consideration should be given to whether that objective cannot equally effectively, and more proportionately, be achieved by an application for, or by the making of, a CAO under s 43 of the Children Act 1989.

(v) No EPO should be made for any longer than is absolutely necessary to protect the child. Where the EPO is made on an ex parte (without notice) application very careful consideration should be given to the need to ensure that the initial order is made for the shortest possible period commensurate with the preservation of the child's immediate safety.

(vi) The evidence in support of the application for an EPO must be full, detailed, precise and compelling. Unparticularised generalities will not suffice. The sources of hearsay evidence must be identified. Expressions of opinion must be supported by detailed evidence and properly articulated reasoning.

(vii) Save in wholly exceptional cases, parents must be given adequate prior notice of the date, time and place of any application by a local authority for an EPO. They must also be given proper notice of the evidence the local authority is relying upon.

(viii) Where the application for an EPO is made ex parte the local authority must make out a compelling case for applying without first giving the parents notice. An ex parte application will normally be appropriate only if the case is genuinely one of emergency or other great urgency – and even then it should normally be possible to give some kind of albeit informal notice to the parents – or if there are compelling reasons to believe that the child's welfare will be compromised if the parents are alerted in advance to what is going on.

(ix) The evidential burden on the local authority is even heavier if the application is made ex parte. Those who seek relief ex parte are under a duty to make the fullest and most candid and frank disclosure of all the relevant circumstances known to them. This duty is not confined to the material facts: it extends to all relevant matters, whether of fact or of law.

(x) Section 45(7)(b) of the Children Act 1989 permits the FPC to hear oral evidence. But it is important that those who are not present should nonetheless be able to know what oral evidence and other materials have been put before the FPC. It is, therefore, particularly important that the FPC complies meticulously with the mandatory requirements of rr 20, 21(5) and 21(6) of the Family Proceedings Courts (Children Act 1989) Rules 1991. The FPC must 'keep a note of the substance of the oral evidence' and must also record in writing not merely its reasons but also any findings of fact.

(xi) The mere fact that the FPC is under the obligations imposed by rr 21(5), 21(6) and 21(8), is no reason why the local authority should not immediately, on request, inform the parents of exactly what has gone on in their absence. Parents against whom an EPO is made ex parte are entitled to be given, if they ask, proper information as to what happened at the hearing and to be told, if they ask: (i) exactly what documents, bundles or other evidential materials were lodged with the FPC either before or during the course of the hearing; and (ii) what legal authorities were cited to the FPC. The local authority's legal representatives should respond forthwith to any reasonable request from the parents or their legal representatives either for copies of the materials read by the FPC or for information about what took place at the hearing. It will, therefore, be prudent for those acting for the local authority in such a case to keep a proper note of the proceedings, lest they otherwise find themselves embarrassed by a proper request for information which they are unable to provide.

(xii) Section 44(5)(b) of the Children Act 1989 provides that the local authority may exercise its parental responsibility only in such manner 'as is reasonably required to safeguard or promote the welfare of the child'. Section 44(5)(a) provides that the local authority shall exercise its power of removal under s 44(4)(b)(i) 'only … in order to safeguard the welfare of the child'. The local authority must apply its mind very carefully to whether removal is essential in order to secure the child's immediate safety. The mere fact that the local authority has obtained an EPO is not of itself enough. The FPC decides whether to make an EPO. But the local authority decides whether to remove. The local authority, even after it has obtained an EPO, is under an obligation to consider less drastic alternatives to emergency removal. Section 44(5) requires a process within the local authority whereby there is a further consideration of the action to be taken after the EPO has been obtained. Though no procedure is specified, it will obviously be prudent for local authorities to have in place procedures to ensure both that the required decision-making actually takes place and that it is appropriately documented.

(xiii) Consistently with the local authority's positive obligation under Art 8 to take appropriate action to reunite parent and child, s 44(10)(a) and s 44(11)(a) impose on the local authority a mandatory obligation to return a child who it has removed under s 44(4)(b)(i) to the parent from whom the child was removed if 'it appears to [the local authority] that it is safe for the child to be returned'. This imposes on the local authority a continuing duty to keep the case under review day by day so as to ensure that parent and child are separated for no longer than is necessary to secure the child's safety. In this, as in other respects, the local authority is under a duty to exercise exceptional diligence.

(xiv) Section 44(13) of the Children Act 1989 requires the local authority, subject only to any direction given by the FPC under s 44(6), to allow a child who is subject to an EPO 'reasonable contact' with his parents. Arrangements for contact must be driven by the needs of the family, not stunted by lack of resources.

# INDEX

References are to paragraph numbers.

Abuse *see also* Harm; Neglect
  child in need, due to     1.18, 1.19
Adoption *see also* Placement order
  care plan for     21.33–21.50, 22.44, 22.45
  human rights     28.4
  international element, with     28.6
  legislative background     28.7–28.19
  no delay principle     28.10
  order
    contact with child     28.36–28.44
    s 8, under     28.42
    opposition to     28.24–28.35
    requirements for making     28.20–28.23
  parental responsibility, and     28.3
  process for     28.1–28.5
  service, LA duty to provide     1.31
  welfare checklist     28.8, 28.9, 28.13–28.19
Adoption agency
  local authority, as     1.31
Adoption order
  care order, effect on     23.63
  statistics     1.22
  welfare of child     2.3
Age
  child
    17 years or over, no care order     2.48
    assessment of child's needs     2.20, 2.21, 28.13, 29.14
    party to proceedings     12.71, 12.74–12.76
    section 8 order, and     26.28–26.32
    views of, contact for     16.45
    variation of order     18.49
Appeals
  appellant's notice     30.27–30.40
    skeleton argument, with application     30.36–30.40
    grounds for     30.24–30.26
  orders pending appeal     30.52–30.56
  permission to appeal     30.3, 30.4, 30.12–30.16
  procedure     30.1, 30.2, 30.6–30.11
  respondent's notice     30.41–30.51
    documents supporting     30.50, 30.51
    skeleton argument, with     30.44–30.49
  stay     30.7
  time limits     30.17–30.23
    application for extension     30.22, 30.23
  transfer of proceedings     30.5

Assistance
  family assistance order, under     2.69
  supervisor, by     25.6
Assisted reproduction
  parental responsibility, and     2.38, 2.39

Befriending
  family assistance order, under     2.69
  supervisor, by     25.6
Best interests of child *see also* No delay principle; No order principle; Welfare of child
  adoption, and     19.43, 28.14, 28.37, 28.43
  BIIR, and     3.41, 3.43–3.46, 3.48–3.50, 3.52–3.55
  Cafcass officer to protect     12.66
  care order, discharge of     24.14
  care plan     20.3
  compulsory intervention, and     7.7
  contact, and     8.24, 18.10, 28.43, 29.25
  determination of order, for     2.43
  evaluation     2.15
  family plan, for     6.16
  interim care plan     16.25
  no delay principle, and     2.30
  placement order     29.15
  representation in proceedings     12.67–12.76
  safeguarding     8.22
  state interference, and     1.7
  timetable for proceedings     10.33
  transfer of jurisdiction     3.18, 3.43–3.46, 3.48–3.50, 3.52, 3.53, 3.55
Birth mother *see also* Parent; Parental responsibility
  parental responsibility     2.34, 12.25
    assisted reproduction     2.38, 2.39
  party to care proceedings     12.3
Brussels II Revised
  central authority     3.10
  contracting states     3.3, 3.4
Bundle
  arrangement of     19.55
  contents     19.53–19.57
  lodging     19.59
  size     19.58

Cafcass
  emergency protection order, and     9.14

## Cafcass—continued
family assistance orders, and    2.69, 2.70
officer
    role in proceedings    12.66
welfare reports    2.73

## Care order *see also* Care proceedings; Supervision order
application    2.48–2.51
discharge of    23.33–23.38, 24.1–24.16, 24.18–24.33
    child applicant    24.27–24.29
    local authority applicant    24.10–24.13
    parent applicant    24.14–24.16, 24.18–24.26
    procedure    24.4–24.9
    third party, applicant as    24.30–24.33
    welfare of child    24.2
duration    2.55, 23.29–23.32
effect of    23.1–23.11
evidence    19.26–19.52
existing orders, effect on    23.62
final care plan    21.25, 21.26
    adoption    21.33–21.50
grounds    2.57
harm, child at risk    13.1–13.4
inherent jurisdiction    23.65–23.73
interim *see* Interim order
jurisdiction to make    26.4–26.8
lawful removal
    Guernsey, to    23.64
    Isle of Man, to    23.64
    Northern Ireland, to    23.64
local authority
    designation    23.15–23.20
    duties    2.51, 23.12–23.14
        provision of accommodation    23.21–23.28
no order made    21.27–21.32
parental responsibility, effect on    2.52–2.54, 22.9–22.12, 23.42–23.60
    human rights    23.57–23.60
plan for    23.4–23.11
procedure    10.1–10.9
    26 weeks rule    10.10–10.20
    case management hearing    10.34–10.41
    documents from previous proceedings    10.59–10.63
    evidence    10.45–10.58
    expert    10.67–10.72
    guardian report    10.73–10.77
    issue and allocation    10.30–10.33
    issues resolution hearing    10.42–10.44
    key stages    10.24
    parenting assessment    10.64–10.66
    pre-proceedings checklist    10.25–10.29
    timetable for child    10.21–10.23
    withdrawal of application    10.78, 10.79
statistics    1.22
subsequent orders, effect of    23.63

## Care order —continued
substitution, supervision order, for    24.34, 24.35
threshold criteria    7.1–7.8
welfare of child, test for
    making    21.1–21.8
    checklist    21.13–21.18
    proportionality    21.51–21.54
    standard for    21.9–21.12
    wishes of child    21.19–21.22
    role of judge    21.23, 21.24

## Care proceedings *see also* Care order; Public Law Outline; Supervision order
26 weeks rule    2.28–2.31
appeals *see* Appeals
applications under HRA 1998    4.81–4.87
court, role of    1.29–1.37
duty to avoid delay *see* No delay principle
fact finding hearing    19.1, 19.2
fair trial in *see* Fair trial, right to
family involvement in    1.24–1.28
final hearing    20.1
    bundles    19.53–19.59
    case management    19.19–19.25
    evidence    19.26–19.52, 20.26–20.46, 20.65, 20.66
        guardian, from    19.49–19.52
        local authority, from    19.40–19.48
    experts    20.62–20.64
    judgment    20.72–20.74
    jurisdiction    20.18–20.21
    submissions, legal representatives, by    20.67–20.71
    threshold criteria    20.2–20.8
        burden of proof    20.9, 20.10, 20.12–20.17
    welfare of child    20.2–20.8
    witnesses    20.22–20.25, 20.47–20.61
intervention, leave for    12.21–12.23
issues resolutions hearing    19.20–19.24
joinder, application for    12.10–12.20
    best interests principle    12.16
    father without PR    12.13–12.15
    form for    12.10
    grandparent    12.17–12.20
    human rights    12.14
    no delay principle    12.15
    welfare of child    12.15
jurisdiction, international *see* International jurisdiction
litigation capacity    12.37–12.64
    ability to give evidence    12.59–12.61
    assessment of    12.43–12.50
    certificate of    12.48, 12.49
    intermediary assessment    12.62–12.64
    litigation friend    12.53–12.58
    party contesting lack of    12.51, 12.52
local authority, role of    1.29–1.37
no order principle    2.44–2.47
orders available    2.43–2.78

## Index

Care proceedings —*continued*
  parties to 12.1–12.9
    biological father 12.4
    birth mother 12.3
    child arrangements order, and 12.7
    disputed parentage of child 12.5
    special guardianship order, and 12.8
    step-parent 12.6
    unmarried father 12.3
  pre-proceedings process 6.1–6.37
    commencement of
      proceedings 6.29–6.32
    family group conference 6.13–6.16
    letter before proceedings 6.20–6.28
    meeting 6.17–6.19
    parents, mental health issues,
      with 6.6–6.9
    preparation 6.33–6.35
    proceedings involving new-borns 6.36, 6.37
    records 6.35
    wider family members,
      identification 6.10–6.12
  private law orders in *see* Section 8
    orders 26.1, 26.2, 27.1
  representation 12.24–12.36
    carers/family members without
      PR 12.34, 12.35
    child 12.65–12.73
      solicitor for 12.66, 12.74–12.76
    father without PR 12.27, 12.28
    intervenors 12.36
    parents with PR 12.25, 12.26
    PR by child arrangements
      order 12.29–12.31
    PR by special guardianship
      order 12.32, 12.33
  split hearing
    decision to undertake 19.3–19.12
    parties to 19.16–19.18
    preparation for 19.13–19.15
  statistics for 1.22, 1.23
  threshold hearing 19.1, 19.2

Case management
  final hearing 19.19–19.25
  issues resolutions hearing 19.20–19.24
  placement orders 29.37–29.39
  special guardianship order, making
    of 27.31–27.39

Child
  at risk *see* Harm; Child in need
  best interests of *see* Best interests of
    child
  circumstances
    change in, effect, consideration
      for court 2.20, 2.21, 28.13, 29.14
  contact with *see* Contact with child
  emergency intervention *see*
    Emergency protection order;
    Police

Child—*continued*
  local authority accommodation *see*
    Section 20 accommodation
  protection of 1.1–1.23
    court, role of 1.29–1.37
    family involvement in 1.24–1.28
    judicial view of 1.7–1.10
    local authority, role of 1.29–1.37
    need for, court process 1.10
    public perception of 1.11, 1.12
    'social engineering' 1.7
    statistics for 1.13–1.21
  welfare of *see* Welfare of child

Child arrangements order *see also*
  Prohibited steps order; Section 8
  orders; Special guardianship
  order; Specific issues order
  alternative to care order, as 17.43–17.47
  application
    child subject to special
      guardianship order 27.21, 27.22
  care order, effect on 23.63
  discharge
    care order, by 23.62
  local authority, role of 2.76
  making of 2.74, 2.75
  meaning 26.20
  parental responsibility, and 2.41, 2.42, 2.77
  purpose 26.21
  s 37 report 2.76
  terms, in 26.25
  when used 2.77

Child assessment order
  application for 5.31–5.38

Child in need
  abuse, due to 1.18, 1.19
  determination 1.14, 5.9
  'development' 5.7
  disabled child 5.8
  factors to consider 1.19
  meaning 5.6, 5.7
  neglect, due to 1.18, 1.19
  promotion of upbringing 5.10
  services for 5.5–5.12
    wishes and feelings of child 5.11
  statistics for 1.15–1.21

Child leaving care
  local authority duties 23.39–23.41

Child protection conference 5.42–5.50
  attendance 5.43
  core group meeting 5.47, 5.48
  further action 5.51
  minutes 5.50
  procedure 5.46–5.50
  purpose 5.42
  removal of parents 5.45
  reports 5.44–5.46
  representatives 5.49

Child protection plan
  categories 5.40
  registration 5.41

Children's guardian
  appointment                     12.65
  powers and duties        12.67–12.73
  role                            12.66
Contact with child
  adoption order, subject to   28.36–28.44
  conditions imposed           18.18–18.20
  court, role of               18.14–18.25
  emergency protection order, subject
    to                          9.51–9.56
  forms of                           18.6
  importance of                 18.1–18.3
  interim order, following    16.43–16.53
    child's views                   16.45
    no contact                16.54–16.57
    supervised                16.49–16.53
  leave to apply for          18.41–18.48
  local authority duty         18.4–18.13,
                              22.28–22.37
    child's views                   22.36
    discretion                18.11–18.13
    supervised                22.33–22.35
    no contact                22.38–22.41
  no order principle                28.43
  orders
    circumstances for
      making                  18.30–18.40
    decision to make          18.26–18.29
      welfare of child        18.26–18.29
    types of                  18.18–18.20
    variation or discharge          18.36
  placement order, child subject
    to                        29.25–29.31
  police protection in               8.24
  refusal of                  18.21–18.25
  variation, child's consent, with  18.49,
                                    18.50
  welfare checklist                 28.43
Convention of the Rights of the Child
  family
    role of                           1.3
Court
  appeals see Appeals
  role in proceedings see also No
    delay principle; No order
    principle; Welfare of child     1.34,
                                     1.35
  transfer of proceedings       3.37–3.58

Education
  child's needs                      2.20
Emergency protection order
  alternative to
    exclusion undertakings      9.37–9.42
    family assessment orders    9.34–9.36
    voluntary arrangements      9.30–9.33
  application for               9.12–9.15
    out of hours                      8.9
    police, by                   8.29, 8.30
    without notice              9.16–9.20
  care order, effect on             23.63
  contact with child            9.51–9.56

Emergency protection order—continued
  discharge                     9.64–9.66
  duration                      9.57–9.63
  effect of                    9.1, 9.9–9.11
  evidence in support of        9.21–9.24
  expiry, consequences of        9.67, 9.68
  extension                      9.62, 9.63
  grounds for                   9.25–9.29
  nature of                      9.1–9.8
  no right of appeal                  9.2
  notice for                          9.2
  parental responsibility, and   9.1, 9.43,
                                      9.44
  removal of child         9.45, 9.47–9.50
    safeguards                        9.46
  statistics                         1.22
  welfare of child, and          9.28, 9.56
European Convention for the
  Protection of Human Rights and
  Fundamental Freedoms
  family
    role of                      1.4–1.6
Evidence see also Expert
  child, from                 20.32–20.46
    ABE interview             20.44–20.46
    assessment of capability  20.37–20.41
    decision, court by         20.42, 20.43
  contested                         20.23
  final hearing, at           19.26–19.52
    evidence
      guardian, from          19.49–19.52
      local authority, from   19.40–19.48
  general rule for, FPR        19.37, 20.22
  hearsay                      20.26, 20.27
  interim order hearings      15.19–15.27
  live submissions            15.34–15.42
  oral                         20.65, 20.66
  parents, from               20.28–20.31
  power of court to control         19.36
Expert
  cross-examination of        20.62–20.64
  reports by                  15.49–15.53

Fair trial, right to see also Human
    rights                      4.20–4.50
  communication of information      4.26
  impartiality of court         4.40–4.50
  judgments                      4.29, 4.30
  no delay principle            4.31–4.39
  press, admission of               4.28
  public hearing                4.23–4.30
Family
  autonomy, importance of       1.2–1.6
  rights of see Private and family life,
    right to
  state intervention, in        1.1–1.12
    judicial view of            1.7–1.10
    process to assess need for      1.10
    public perception of        1.11, 1.12
Family assistance order
  application for               2.69–2.73
  consent for                         2.72
  duration                            2.73

## Index

Family assistance order—*continued*
  requirements under    2.70
Family court
  appeals to    30.4
Family life, right to *see* Private and family life, right to
Final care plan
  adoption for    22.44, 22.45
  content    22.1
  no jurisdiction of court    22.2
  placement of child    22.13–22.27
  purpose    22.3
  requirements    22.4–22.8
Foster carer
  placement with    16.28–16.33
  special guardianship order applicant    27.6

Grandparent
  contact
    child subject to adoption order    28.40
    joinder, care proceedings    12.17–12.20

Hague Convention on Parental Responsibility
  central authority    3.10
  contracting states    3.3, 3.4
Harm
  child at risk
    'attributable to the care provided'    7.25–7.28, 13.1–13.4, 25.40, 26.4
    court to have regard to    2.20, 2.21, 28.13, 29.14
    investigation by local authority    5.14–5.18
    police intervention
      reasonable cause    8.10, 8.11
    'significant'    7.9–7.19, 8.11, 13.1–13.4, 25.40, 26.4
    'suffering or likely to suffer'    7.20–7.24, 8.10, 8.11, 13.1–13.4, 25.40, 26.4
    threshold criteria    7.1–7.8
    care by 'reasonable parent'    7.29–7.32
    interim/final    7.38, 7.39
    risk beyond parental control    7.33–7.37
Human rights
  acts incompatible with    4.5
  adoption    28.4
  applicable law    4.1–4.7
  care proceedings
    no order principle    2.45
    deprivation of child's liberty    4.8–4.10, 4.12–4.19
    local authority duty    4.11
  family, role of    1.2–1.6
  infringement, public authority by    4.6, 4.64–4.72
    declaration of incompatibility    4.64

Human rights—*continued*
  infringement, public authority by—*continued*
    remedies    4.67–4.72
  parental responsibility, and    23.57–23.60
  police removal of child    8.13
  section 20 accommodation applications    4.35–4.39, 4.73–4.80

Independent reviewing officer
  appointment    22.42
  functions    22.43
Interim care plan
  best interests of child    16.25
  contents    16.24, 16.25
  duty to provide    16.21, 16.22
  review and revision    16.23
Interim order
  alternative options    17.1, 17.2
  care plan, changes to    17.10–17.17
    court, referral to    17.11–17.17
  case management    15.1–15.53
    directions    15.11–15.14
  child arrangements order    17.43–17.47
  circumstances for making    13.11–13.15, 13.17–13.30
  contact with child    16.43–16.53
    child's views    16.45
    supervised    16.49, 16.51–16.53
  court power to make    2.56, 2.61
  documents lodged    15.29–15.33
  evidence    15.19–15.27
    live submissions    15.34–15.42
  exclusion requirement    16.11–16.17
    power of arrest    16.15
  expert reports    15.49–15.53
  grounds    2.57, 2.62
  hearing    15.28
  interim supervision orders    17.38–17.42
  jurisdiction    15.15–15.18
  local authority duties    16.18–16.20
  medical/psychiatric assessment    15.43–15.48, 16.58–16.64
  nature of    14.12–14.16
  no contact with child    16.54–16.57
  no removal of child    17.3–17.6
    court, role of    17.3, 17.4
    local authority, role of    17.3, 17.4
  parental responsibility under    16.6–16.10
  placement of child    16.26–16.42
    'connected person', with    17.8, 17.9
    family/friends    16.34–16.36
    local authority foster carers    16.28–16.33
    'parent and child' foster care    17.7
    parents    16.37–16.42
  purpose    16.1–16.5
  removal of child    14.17–14.20
    challenging decision    17.18–17.25
    injunctions under HRA 1998    17.26–17.28
    judicial review    17.29–17.34

**Interim order**—*continued*
  removal of child—*continued*
    s 20 accommodation    17.35–17.37
  threshold criteria    13.31–13.68
  timescale of proceedings    13.5–13.10
  welfare decisions    14.1–14.48
    burden of proof    14.36–14.38
    child's psychological
      welfare    14.32–14.35
    neglect    14.28–14.31
    removal of child    14.39–14.48
    siblings    14.21
**International jurisdiction**    3.1–3.58
  applicable law    3.2
  Brussels II Revised    3.3–3.6
    scope    3.6
  central authority    3.10
  child absent from jurisdiction    3.33–3.36
  cooperation    3.9
  determination    3.16
  final hearing    20.18–20.21
  habitual residence    3.17–3.32
  Hague Convention on Parental
    Responsibility    3.3–3.6
    scope    3.6
  practical issues    3.7–3.15
    information sharing    3.9–3.11
  transfer
    best interests of child    3.18
    transfer of proceedings    3.37–3.58
    child's connection to member
      state    3.47

**Jurisdiction**
  abroad *see* International jurisdiction
  private law orders    26.4–26.8
  public law orders    26.4–26.8
  welfare principle, and    26.4–26.7

**Liberty and security, right to**    4.8–4.19
**Local authority**
  accommodation, voluntary *see*
    Section 20 accommodation
  adoption agency, as    1.31
  duties
    child leaving care    23.39–23.41
    contact arrangements    18.4–18.10
  duty to provide
    accommodation    23.21–23.28
  investigation by    5.13–5.18
    child suffering harm    5.14–5.18
  parental responsibility, acquisition
    of    2.52–2.54
  receiving child into care    23.12–23.20
  s 37 direction    5.19–5.30
  safeguarding welfare of child    5.39–5.51
  s 20 accommodation    5.52–5.79
  social services functions    1.30–1.33
  supervisor, designation of    25.7
  support, duty to provide    5.1–5.12
  welfare reports from    2.73, 5.25, 10.25

**Needs of child**
  court to have regard to    2.20, 2.21, 28.13, 29.14
  parent's capability to meet    2.20, 2.21
**Neglect** *see also* Abuse; Harm
  child in need, due to    1.18, 1.19
**No delay principle**    2.1
  26 weeks rule    2.28–2.31
  adoption, and    28.10
  fair trial right, and    4.31–4.39
  placement order, and    29.31
  section 20 accommodation
    applications    4.35–4.39
  welfare of child, and    2.26, 2.27
**No order principle**    2.44
  contact with child    28.43
  human rights    2.45
  parental responsibility, and    2.45–2.47
  supervision order, and    25.50–25.64

**Oral evidence** *see also* Evidence; Expert
  court directions    20.65, 20.66
  when used    19.37, 20.22

**Parent** *see also* Birth mother;
    Unmarried father
  capability to meet child's needs    2.20, 2.21
  child protection conference
    attendance    5.43
  consent to adoption    29.47
    dispensing with    29.48–29.51
  party to proceedings    12.24–12.28
    conflict of interest    12.26
  placement with    16.37–16.42
  s 20 accommodation
    consent to    5.52, 5.58–5.60
      capacity to provide    5.61–5.63
      dispensing with    5.52
      duress    5.70
      freely given    5.64–5.67
      right to legal advice    5.68
      withdrawal of    5.69, 5.71, 5.72
  witness, as    20.27–20.31
**Parental responsibility**    2.32–2.42
  acquisition    2.36, 2.37, 2.41
    child arrangements order, by    2.41, 2.42
    special guardianship order, by    2.41, 2.42
  adoption, and    28.3
  assisted reproduction, effect on    2.38, 2.39
  birth mother    2.34, 2.38, 2.39
  care order, effect on    22.9–22.12, 23.42–23.60
    human rights    23.57–23.60
  child arrangements order, and    2.77
  child in police protection, and    8.21, 8.22
  definition    2.34, 2.35
  emergency protection order, and    9.1, 9.43, 9.44
  interim order, and    16.6–16.10
  local authority, acquisition of    2.52–2.54

**Parental responsibility**—*continued*
  loss of                                     2.37, 2.42
  married couple                                    2.34
  meaning                                     2.32, 2.33
  no surrender or transfer                          2.36
  person who has                              2.35, 2.36
  placement order, and                       29.23, 29.24
  prohibited steps order, and                       2.78
  same sex couple                                   2.40
  second female parent                              2.39
  section 8 orders, and                      26.26, 26.27
  special guardianship order, and                   2.64,
                                   2.68, 12.8, 27.13–27.16
  state interference, and                            1.7
  supervision order, and                 2.59, 25.3, 25.4
  welfare checklist, and                            2.40
**Placement of child**                              22.13
  first directions hearing                          29.38
  friends/family, with                      22.19–22.21
  local authority foster care               22.14–22.18
  parents, with                             22.22–22.27
**Placement order** *see also* Adoption
  application for                           29.33–29.36
    local authority by                              29.35
  care order, effect on                             23.63
  case management                           29.37–29.39
  contact with child                         29.25–29.31
  effect of                         29.21, 29.22, 29.32
  making of                                  29.1–29.12
  no delay principle                                29.31
  parental consent                                  29.47
    dispensing with                         29.48–29.51
  parental responsibility, and               29.23, 29.24
  special guardianship order,
    alternative to                           27.47–27.50
  welfare checklist                         29.13–29.20,
                                               29.40–29.46
  welfare of child                                    2.3
**Police**
  child in protection of
    application for EPO                       8.29, 8.30
    contact with parents                      8.23, 8.24
    discharge from                                   8.20
    duration                                  8.18, 8.19
    involvement of local
      authority                                8.25–8.28
    parental responsibility, and              8.21, 8.22
    police role/duty                            8.1, 8.2
    power to remove                             8.3–8.24
      grounds for                             8.10–8.15
      human rights                                   8.13
      reasonable cause                        8.10, 8.11
      s 20 accommodation                         8.7–8.9
    records                                    8.31, 8.32
    suitable accommodation                    8.16, 8.17
    welfare of child                                  8.2
  child protection conference
    attendance                                       5.43
  investigation of offenders                          8.2
  power to remove                             8.25–8.32
**Private and family life, right to** *see also*
  Human rights

**Private and family life, right to**          4.51–4.61
  no order principle                               2.45
  police removal of child                          8.13
  state interference, protection
    from                                       1.4–1.6
**Private law proceedings** *see also* Child
  arrangements order; Prohibited
  steps order; Section 8 orders;
  Special guardianship; Specific
  issues order
**Prohibited steps order** *see also* Child
  arrangements order; Section 8
  orders; Special guardianship;
  Specific issues order
  application
    child subject to special
      guardianship order                            27.23
  making of                                          2.75
  meaning                                           26.20
  parental responsibility, and                       2.78
  when used                                          2.78
**Public Law Outline** *see also* Care
  proceedings
  26 weeks rule                             10.10–10.20
  applicable law                               10.8, 10.9
  case management hearing                   10.34–10.41
  issue and allocation                      10.30–10.33
  issues resolution hearing                 10.42–10.44
  pre-proceedings checklist                 10.25–10.29
  purpose                                     10.1–10.4
  revised                                     10.5–10.7
  timetable for child                       10.21–10.23
**Public law proceedings** *see* Care
  proceedings

**Relative**
  contact
    child subject to adoption order            28.40
    placement with                          16.34–16.36
    special guardianship order applicant        27.6
**Section 8 orders** *see also* Child
  arrangements order; Prohibited
  steps order; Special
  guardianship; Specific issues
  order                                              26.3
  applicants                                 26.14, 26.15
  application
    child subject to special
      guardianship order                            27.23
  court's power to make                      26.11–26.13
  directions/conditions attached to                 26.23
  discharge of                      26.22, 26.33–26.35
  duration                          26.24, 26.28–26.32
  effect of                                   26.9, 26.10
  jurisdiction to make                         26.4–26.8
  leave to apply                             26.16–26.19
  orders available                           26.20–26.25
  parental responsibility, and               26.26, 26.27
  restrictions on making                     26.16–26.18,
                                                26.29–26.32

Section 8 orders —*continued*
   threshold criteria   26.4–26.8
   variation of   26.22, 26.33–26.35
Section 20 accommodation
   alternative to care order, as   17.35–17.37
   circumstances for use   5.73–5.79
   human rights   4.35–4.39, 4.73–4.80, 5.59
   jurisdiction   3.15
   no delay principle   4.35–4.39
   parental consent   5.58–5.60
      capacity to provide   5.61–5.63
      dispensing with   5.52
      freely given   5.64–5.67
      information about rights   5.68–5.70
      withdrawal of   5.71, 5.72
   police protection, and   8.7–8.9
   provision of, duty   5.52–5.79
Significant harm *see* Harm
   risk of   1.10
Special guardian
   parental responsibility, and   12.8
   party to care proceedings   12.8
Special guardianship
   parental responsibility, and   27.13–27.16
Special guardianship order *see also*
   Child arrangements order;
   Prohibited steps order; Section 8
   orders; Specific issues order
   ancillary matters, consideration
      of   27.40–27.43
   assessment for   2.65
   care order, effect on   23.63
   case management   27.31–27.39
   child subject to
      further applications   27.21–27.23
   court's power to make   27.7, 27.8, 27.28–27.30
   discharge of   27.9, 27.24–27.27
   duration   2.67, 27.9
   effect of   2.66, 26.9, 26.10, 27.13–27.27
      birth parents, position of   27.17–27.20
      last resort, presumption   27.51–27.53
   leave to apply   2.63
   legal background   27.1–27.5
   local authority
      notice to   2.65
      support services, provided by   2.66
   meaning   27.6
   parental responsibility, and   2.41, 2.42, 2.64, 2.68
   public law proceedings in   27.11, 27.12
   statistics   1.22
   variation of   27.10, 27.24–27.27
   welfare principle   27.7, 27.8, 27.44–27.50
Specific issue order *see also* Child
   arrangements order; Prohibited
   steps order; Section 8 orders;
   Special guardianship order
   application
      child subject to special
         guardianship order   27.23
   making of   2.75

Specific issue order —*continued*
   meaning   26.20
Step-parent
   party to care proceedings   12.6
Supervision order *see also* Care order;
   Care proceedings
   application   2.48–2.50
   court's power   25.31–25.39
   decision to make   25.44–25.49
   directions under   25.66–25.71
   discharge
      supervisor's duty to consider   25.6
   discharge of   24.36–24.40, 25.85, 25.86
   duration   2.60, 25.75–25.89
   duties under   25.6
   effect of   2.58
   evidence   19.26–19.52
   extension   2.60, 25.84
   failure to co-operate with   25.16–25.23
   grounds   2.62
   interim *see* Interim order
   jurisdiction to make   26.4–26.8
   making of   25.1, 25.2
      circumstances   25.24–25.30
      medical/psychiatric
         assessment   25.72–25.74
   nature of   25.6–25.15
   no order principle   25.50–25.64
   no parental responsibility   2.59
   parental responsibility, and   25.3, 25.4
   proportionality rule   25.5
   statistics   1.22
   supervisor, duties of   25.65, 25.66
   terms of   25.65–25.74
   threshold criteria   7.1–7.8, 25.40
   variation of   24.36–24.40, 25.85, 25.86
   welfare decision,
      paramountcy   25.41–25.43

Universal Declaration of Human
   Rights
   family
      role of   1.2
Unmarried father *see also* Parent;
   Parental responsibility
   parental responsibility acquired   2.35
      loss of   2.42
   party to care proceedings   12.3

Voluntary accommodation *see* Section
   20 accommodation

Welfare of child *see also* Best interests
   of child; No delay principle; No
   order principle
   adoption, and   2.3, 28.8, 28.9, 28.13–28.19
   care order
      discharge of   24.2
      test for making   21.1–21.8
      checklist   21.13–21.18

**Welfare of child** —*continued*
  care order—*continued*
    test for making—*continued*
      proportionality       21.51–21.54
      standard for         21.9–21.12
      wishes of child      21.19–21.24
  care plan                     20.3–20.8
  contact with child           28.43
  delay, and                  2.26, 2.27
  emergency protection order, and    9.28, 9.56
  interim orders          14.10, 14.11
  orders for contact, and         18.23, 18.26–18.29
  paramountcy   2.1–2.8, 2.22, 3.45, 21.3, 21.4, 24.2, 25.41–25.43, 28.43, 29.17, 29.31
  parental responsibility, and      2.40
  parent's involvement, in       2.6–2.8
  placement order, and    2.3, 29.13–29.20, 29.40–29.46
  protection by police            8.2
  safeguarding, local authority duty   5.3, 5.5, 5.39–5.51
  s 20 accommodation       5.52–5.79
  special guardianship order, and   27.44–27.50
  special guardianship, and     27.7, 27.8

**Welfare of child** —*continued*
  state intervention, and          1.10
  supervision order, and      25.41–25.43
  welfare checklist           2.18–2.25
  yardstick for                2.9–2.13
    assessment of            2.14–2.17
**Welfare of child paramountcy**       2.26
**Welfare report**
  court's power to call for    2.73, 5.25, 10.25

**Wishes of child** *see also* Best interests of child; Welfare of child
  care order, test for making    21.19–21.24
  contact, and             16.45, 18.49
  court to have regard to   2.20, 2.21, 26.8, 28.13, 29.14

**Witness**
  cross examination             19.39
  evidence
    oral                     19.37, 20.22
    written               19.37, 20.22
  expert *see* Expert
  final hearing
    attendance            20.22–20.25
    statements            19.39, 20.24
  vulnerable             20.47–20.61
    ground rules hearing   20.57–20.61